Caring and Doing for Others

*The John D. and Catherine T. MacArthur Foundation Series on
Mental Health and Development*

STUDIES ON SUCCESSFUL MIDLIFE DEVELOPMENT

Also in the series

Sexuality across the Life Course
Edited by Alice S. Rossi

The Parental Experience in Midlife
Edited by Carol D. Ryff and Marsha Mailick Seltzer

Multiple Paths of Midlife Development
Edited by Margie E. Lachman and Jacquelyn Boone James

Welcome to Middle Age!
(And Other Cultural Fictions)
Edited by Richard A. Shweder

CARING AND DOING FOR OTHERS

Social Responsibility in the Domains of Family, Work, and Community

Edited by

Alice S. Rossi

The University of Chicago Press
Chicago and London

THE UNIVERSITY OF CHICAGO PRESS, CHICAGO 60637
THE UNIVERSITY OF CHICAGO PRESS, LTD., LONDON

© 2001 by The University of Chicago
All rights reserved. Published 2001
Printed in the United States of America

10 09 08 07 06 05 04 03 02 01   1 2 3 4 5
ISBN: 0-226-72872-2

The University of Chicago Press gratefully acknowledges a subvention from the
John D. and Catherine T. MacArthur Foundation in partial support
of the costs of production of this volume.

Library of Congress Cataloging-in-Publication Data

Caring and doing for others : social responsibility in the domains of family, work,
and community / edited by Alice S. Rossi.
     p. cm. — (John D. and Catherine T. MacArthur Foundation series on
   mental health and development. Studies on successful midlife development)
   Includes bibliographical references and indexes.
   ISBN 0-226-72872-2 (cloth : alk. paper)
   1. Social ethics. 2. Social justice. 3. Social contract.   I. Rossi, Alice S.,
   1922–   II. Series.
HM665 .C37 2001
303.3′72—dc21

00-048011

To the John D. and Catherine T. MacArthur Foundation,
institutional exemplar of social responsibility

CONTENTS

This volume is one of several collaborative publications of the John D. and Catherine T. MacArthur Foundation Research Network on Successful Midlife Development, known by the acronym "MIDMAC." The network was established in 1989 and funded by the foundation in three, three-year grants. Chaired by Orville G. Brim, the network consisted of a core group of thirteen members, supplemented over the years by upwards of thirty-five junior research associates who worked under the direction of one or more members of the core group.

Network members acquired their initial training in a number of fields: psychology (Paul Baltes, Carol Ryff, Margie Lachman, Hazel Markus); sociology (Alice Rossi, David Featherman); demography (Larry Bumpass); medical sociology (Paul Cleary, Ron Kessler); anthropology (Richard Shweder); and medicine (Michael Marmot, William Hazzard). Our first three years together were largely devoted to developing a shared perspective on midlife development, inviting specialist speakers from relevant fields not represented in our midst, and preparing for the benefit of other network members lectures and reports on our own individual research that was relevant to the conceptualization of midlife development. It is doubtful that any of the network members have been converted to a totally different social science perspective as a result of our decade-long collaboration, but there has clearly been a blurring of the boundaries between our disciplines and a pooling of our ideas and methods in the research we undertook. We have emerged from this experience deeply committed to the importance of interdisciplinary research, in particular to a biopsychosocial perspective on adult development. In all our studies, we have given attention to physical and mental health, psychological well-being, and social location in terms of social class, all in the context of a life-course trajectory.

Network members live and work in widely separated locations: Michael Marmot in London; Paul Baltes in Berlin; Paul Cleary, Ron

Kessler, Margie Lachman, and Alice Rossi in Massachusetts; Carol Ryff and Larry Bumpass in Wisconsin; Richard Shweder in Illinois; David Featherman in Michigan; William Hazzard in North Carolina followed by Washington; and Hazel Markus in Michigan followed by California. We collaborated by meeting four or five times a year for two to five days at a time, with numerous letters, memos, and shared research findings circulating between each of these meetings.

During the first years of our network history, many of the network members conducted small pilot studies, largely to develop new measures of key concepts and to test their utility in data analysis. Once we made the decision to launch a large-scale survey of the adult American population, the pace of our work picked up, work groups were established for the major topics to be covered in the national survey, and six large pilot surveys were undertaken. These pilot surveys typically contained a thousand respondents, randomly chosen and interviewed by phone. The work groups analyzed the results and reported their findings at network meetings.

The most fundamental decision affecting the design of the national survey concerned the key criteria for assessing midlife development. Drawing on our special interests and skills, it is hardly surprising that the three criteria embraced physical and mental health (drawing on the medical expertise of Marmot, Kessler, Cleary, and Hazzard); psychological well-being (Ryff, Lachman, Baltes, Brim, and Markus); and social responsibility (Rossi, Bumpass, and Featherman). The chief focus of this volume is on the third of our outcome criteria—social responsibility.

The contributing authors in this volume are indebted to many people. The health program staff of the MacArthur Foundation provided not only financial support, but enthusiastic intellectual support, urging patience as we worked through the early, halting stages of our collaboration. At the design stage, every aspect of the national survey benefited from input by almost all the members of the research network and many of the research associates. Of the utmost importance has been the role of the network chair, Orville "Bert" Brim. Bert has a most unusual array of talents, which we all drew upon: he is a superb administrator, an outstanding intellectual mentor, a charming companion, and a good friend. Quick to appreciate and reward good ideas as well as to provide good food and drink, he facilitated our work at every stage of its development.

Nadine Marks and Larry Bumpass were of particular help in the design of the module on social responsibility, as they were in two of the pilot surveys that preceded the launching of the national survey. Margie Lachman and Carol Ryff provided important help in the construction of our variables on marriage, parenthood, personality, and psychological well-being. The measures of mental health were contributed by Ronald Kessler, and those of physical health, by Paul Cleary, William Hazzard, and Michael Marmot.

As editor and author, I am deeply grateful for the help of a number of people who facilitated work on this volume: My assistants Dee Weber and Karen Mason were invaluable aides with computer work and library searches. Drafts of many chapters were carefully reviewed and commented on by Carol Ryff, Larry Bumpass, and Bert Brim. Sections of chapter 7 on the developmental roots of adult social responsibility that summarized relevant work in behavioral genetics were graciously read and commented on by an external reviewer, Dr. David Rowe.

A very special acknowledgment of gratitude is due my husband and colleague, Peter H. Rossi. For more than forty years, he has been my major sounding board for discussion of ideas and methods of survey data analysis. For this volume, Peter played a major role, from an early memorandum summarizing sociological approaches to the study of social norms, to frequent help on the proper and innovative use of STATA statistical software, to critical reviews of every draft of the chapters I wrote, on down to the production of camera-ready figures for my chapters. As in all domains of our life together, Peter has been a steadying source of patience, wisdom, and encouragement.

I have had a long, pleasurable, and productive relationship with the University of Chicago Press. Executive editor David Brent was an enthusiastic supporter throughout the production of this volume, as he was when I edited the first volume in this special series on midlife, *Sexuality across the Life Course* (1994). Manuscript preparation was greatly facilitated by the editorial assistance of K. Nadine Kavanaugh. Jenni L. Fry is the very best manuscript editor I have ever worked with. To all those at the Press whose skills enhanced this volume, my deep appreciation and gratitude.

One last note must be made. Regrettably, one of the finest and most relevant books on community, Robert D. Putnam's *Bowling Alone: The Collapse and Revival of American Community* (2000), was published during the copyediting stage of this book's production, too late for the authors of this volume to take into consideration and to refer to at the numerous points in our analyses where Putnam's data and insights are most germane. See note 1 to chapter 1 for a brief description of the complementary emphases of this volume compared to Putnam's.

Alice S. Rossi

I INTRODUCTION

ONE

Contemporary Dialogue on Civil Society and Social Responsibility[1]

Alice S. Rossi

INTRODUCTION

The following are some examples of changes noted in a volume on "recent social trends" in American society:

1. Parenting is far more difficult today than in the past because of the enormous increase in the number and variety of influences affecting children.

2. Increasing numbers of workers are being displaced, and studies show only a fifth of them are able to find work in their former occupations.

3. Due to technological changes, increasing numbers of employers are letting middle-aged and older workers go and replacing them with younger, cheaper workers.

4. There's been a sharp decline in the percentage of eligible voters who vote in presidential elections.

5. Protestant churches are giving much greater attention to social issues and activism on such matters as social justice, racial problems, international affairs, and working conditions.

6. There has been a decline in religious sanctions for sexual conduct as public approval of sexual freedom increases.

7. Recent changes in religious beliefs within many Protestant churches led one commentator to make the following caustic observation: "Nothing holds the liberals and fundamentalists together except the billions of dollars invested in church property."

Do these trends sound familiar? If I tell you the time frame used in this study covered thirty years, which thirty years in American history would you take them to be? 1950s to 1980s? 1960s to mid-1990s? 1930s to 1960s? None of these apply: the trends concern the time period 1900 to 1930 and come from the final report of the President's Research Committee on Social Trends in the United States, *Recent Social Trends,* edited by sociologist William Ogburn (1934). Lawrence Frank, who wrote the chapter on children from which comment 1 above was drawn, is referring to the fact that in 1900 compared to 1930 there were no "movies," no radio programs, few magazines, no tabloids, and only a limited number of organized playgrounds, camps, and programs for leisure time for children. Today one hears comparable complaints concerning the influence of TV, Internet chat rooms, video games, and peer culture that further undermine parental influence over children, and unique to our time but absent in Lawrence Frank's chapter, worry that full-time employed moms with very young children are not providing even "good-enough" child care and rearing.

In comments 2 and 3, Leo Wolmon and Gustav Peck, authors of the chapter on labor in the Ogburn report, are describing the effect of increased mechanization of industry that involved replacing skilled workers with semi- and unskilled workers, and noting that in tight competitive markets employers showed strong preference for young, nimble, and cheaper workers to man the assembly lines. Today when the 1990s are compared to the 1960s, one hears similar complaints about recent downsizing and outsourcing that leaves many middle-aged employees out of work for long periods and then rehired at far lower salaries in different occupations than those they spent most of their working lives in (Mishel, Bernstein, and Schmitt 1999). Concern today also applies to those who lack the education or skills to be employed in the first place, particularly young black males.

Comment 4 is by Charles Merriam, the political scientist who wrote the chapter on government and society, reporting the decline from 80 % of eligible voters actually voting in the 1900 presidential election to 61% in the 1928 election. Similar points have been made in recent years noting a continuing trend toward lower rates of voting in national elections, particularly among young voters (Verba, Schlozman, and Brady 1995).

Comments 5 and 6, by C. Luther Fry, concern changes in religious organizations during the first three decades of the century. Fry notes that the modern use of the term "fundamentalist" dates back to 1910, when contributions by two wealthy laymen made it possible to circulate millions of copies of a booklet entitled *The Fundamentals: A Testimony to the Truth.* The doctrines held to be fundamental include belief in the virgin birth of Jesus, the physical resurrection of Christ, the inerrancy of the scriptures, and the physical Second Coming of Christ— doctrines held by fundamentalists in the 1990s as in 1910 (Strozier 1994). The ferment in Protestant churches in the 1920s reflected the pressure to accommodate religious belief with scientific knowledge, es-

4

pecially evolutionary theory (heightened by the Scopes trial in 1925), as well as the competition for the time and interests of parishioners as Sabbath observance and service attendance had to compete with Sunday drives in the family car, movies, and active or spectator sports.

Much the same problem besets mainline churches in the 1990s, although secular activities may be easier to combine with religious observance on the Sabbath, thanks to the hundreds of Christian radio stations and TV channels with numerous early morning services that free the remainder of the day for more secular pursuits (Miller 1999). There are, for example, some sixteen hundred evangelical Christian radio stations in the United States. In 1999, a group of wealthy Roman Catholic entrepreneurs became convinced that the nation's religious radio programming was dominated by the evangelical Protestants and funded a radio network intended to broadcast conservative Catholic programs (Goodstein 1999). Mainline Protestant churches are now heightening efforts through marketing strategies adapted from business practices to bring their people back into the pews (Considine 1995; Kotler, Wrenn, and Rath 1992; Willmer and Schmidt 1998).

The last, caustic comment, on the liberal versus fundamentalist cleavage within Protestant churches held together by investment in church property, is by the prominent political and social critic Walter Lippmann (1929), as quoted by Fry. Fry ends his interesting chapter on religious congregations by noting that except in small towns and rural counties, church buildings by 1930 appeared "trivial and unimportant in contrast to the enormous skyscrapers of commerce and finance" (Fry 1934, 1019). He would no doubt look on with disbelief had he lived to see the megachurches in cities like Dallas or Houston that can seat thousands, much less the extensive childcare facilities, cafeterias, tennis courts, and gyms that fill out such churches' properties.

I have begun this introductory chapter with comments from Ogburn's 1934 report as a reminder that social change is an ongoing, often cyclic process in American history. There have been numerous times in our history when contemporary critics claimed the social fabric was being frayed irrevocably, that people were losing trust in social institutions, that alienation was on the increase, crime rampant, behavior in public crude. In other words, any array of disturbing social indicators is not unique to the last few decades of the twentieth century, nor to the first few decades for that matter. Even those who look back with nostalgia from the 1990s to the 1950s forget the very great changes taking place at that time: the advent of nuclear war capabilities, the explosion of world population, the massive migration to the suburbs, the on-set of the baby-boom birth cohort (which no one predicted), the prosperity we hardly knew what to do with and the materialism that followed, and the possibility after the war that America would plunge back into another depression. As Alan Ehrenhalt reminds us, "there is a pendulum at work in the manners and values of a society, and . . . it can swing when no one expects it to" (Ehrenhalt 1995, 279).

Similar cycles of change occurred in the nineteenth century as well. The serious crime rate rose steadily from the beginning of the nine-teenth century, peaked in the 1840s, and gradually declined by the end of the nineteenth century, only to surge again in the 1970s and '80s. Drunkenness was far more prevalent in the nineteenth century than it is today. Francis Fukuyama (1999) reports, for example, that early in the nineteenth century annual alcohol consumption was six gallons for every person over the age of fifteen. The figure dropped to two gallons by century's end and climbed in our time to three gallons per person. Taverns in the United States and pubs in England were more frequently sites of social gathering and interaction than were churches throughout the nineteenth century and well into the twentieth century, for men if not for women.

Aspects of the "roaring twenties" echo on the American scene today: explosive speculation in the financial markets, ethnic and racial prob-lems, sexual behavior flaunted in more public ways, to cite but a few. The current phenomenon of high-risk-taking speculative behavior is particularly familiar. The odds seem high that today's day traders are as persuaded that they are "investing" in the market rather than "playing" the market as stock investors were before the crash of 1929 (Wysocki 1999). Day traders are just as much gamblers as lottery ticket buyers and casino players are. It is not clear whether today's market gamblers worry about the bursting of the market bubble any more than their twenties counterparts did before the crash in 1929 (Lee and McKenzie 1999; Malkiel 1999).

A more fundamental similarity between the historic period covered by Ogburn and his colleagues and the last decades of the twentieth cen-tury concerns basic changes in the nature of the national economy. The first decades of the twentieth century were a tumultuous period. Mil-lions of immigrants and native-born farm workers were being absorbed into expanding industries in rapidly growing cities. For the last three decades of the twentieth century the American economy has been un-dergoing comparable changes. In the Rust Belt, industries retooled to become more efficient and less costly competitors to foreign firms. This involved letting go thousands of high-pay union workers in the Midwest in favor of lower-pay non-union workers in other parts of the country. In the 1990s, the transition to an information and service economy affected workers in all parts of the country, in small towns as in large cities, during the same time period that manufacturing firms were downsizing or outsourcing to other countries with cheap labor. Today, negotiations between the United Automobile Workers and automobile manufacturers focus more on job security and health benefits than on wage increases. Firms competing to retain their best skilled employees are resorting to such tangible things as lawn service, monthly housecleaning, or vacation bonus checks in their efforts to create loyalty in their employees. These perks are less costly than high turnover and the recruitment and training of new hires (Garrigan 1999). Ahead of us in the coming decade may be yet another significant economic change as e-commerce replaces many middlemen between producers and consumers, and between firms.

Each of the most fundamental shifts in production throughout human history—from hunting and gathering to settled agriculture to industrialization to information and service economies—have been associated with numerous changes in human lives. Where and with whom people lived; what they ate; how mobile they were; how much time and energy was expended in productive labor; how many children were born; how healthy they were; and how long they lived—all were determined in part by the methods and resources used to produce life-sustaining goods. This implies that whenever social, political, or civic problems are cause for public concern, one should pay close attention to the associated changes taking place in the economic domain. Further, any assessment of the cohesiveness of the larger social fabric ought to focus on how well people are performing in their work roles as well as in their family, political, and social roles.

But concern for the quality of the work people perform to earn their way or the effects of rapid change in economic organization is sadly lacking in contemporary discussions of morality, civic virtue and participation, and overall personal responsibility. Alarmists of the past decade are to be found in any number of social circles—academe, politics, the media. Within academe, a wide spectrum of disciplines (sociology, political science, and moral philosophy, in particular) have written much about the presumed breakdown of the family, the alienation of the public from the political process, the decline in civic partic-

ipation in voluntary associations, and the loss of civility in public encounters with each other. A wide array of reasons for such social and
moral breakdown has been argued: excessive individualism with its at-
tendant overemphasis on individual rights and downplaying of individual responsibilities; the residue of counterculture lifestyles from the
1960s; the loss of religious faith; overdependence on a bloated federal
government; the excessive focus on sex and violence on TV; the fragility
of families as a consequence of premarital cohabitation, births outside
marriage, and the high divorce rate. But little is said about economic
change and job performance.

Indeed, one would be hard pressed to cite any indicator of social or
psychological well-being that suggests life is good in America or that
Americans are good people. If we were to take personally all the bad
news and faults one hears and reads about, we should all be in a state
of deep depression. Americans are berated in almost every aspect of
their lives: of being too individualistic and neglectful of their civic and
family responsibilities; of spending too much and saving too little; of
either neglecting or overindulging their children; of not taking their
marriage vows seriously enough or bypassing marriage altogether in
preference for cohabiting; of eating too much of the wrong foods
(sugar, fat, salt) and of being overweight, if not obese. Indeed, hardly
a week goes by without some media warning of yet another potential
carcinogenic factor in our food, in the air we breathe, or in the water
we drink. But notice: rarely are American workers criticized, nor are
the characteristics of their jobs analyzed as potential sources of the
faults Americans are accused of.

For those like myself and my MIDMAC colleagues, who have spent
the past four years looking closely at the lives of over three thousand
American adults in a broad framework that provided data on their
work, their family life, and their roles in the community, it is difficult
to understand the alarmist criticisms leveled against Americans. As will
be shown in the chapters to follow, there are many reasons for qualify-
ing the alarmist charges against adults in our society. It is not clear what
proportion of the population is guilty of the faults the alarmists cite.
Are the same or different people being criticized in these various ways?
Are full-time employed women less likely to be involved in community
organizations or to serve as volunteers? Do divorced adults report more
problems in their children's lives than married adults do? Is the American family so fragmented that ties between the generations are loose or
nonexistent? What proportion of married adults engage in extramarital

sex? And what of adults' own assessments of their lives? Are any significant proportion deeply unhappy? What areas of life are they most satisfied with, what areas least? Have they run away from obligations to family members? Do they feel overburdened by caregiving—or by the hours they have to put in on their jobs and the pace at which they feel compelled to work? These are among the questions we pursue in this volume on social responsibility.

The majority of the chapters (2, 3, 7, 8, 10, and 11) are based on data from a national survey, Midlife Development in the United States (MIDUS), which we conducted in 1995. To achieve the necessary comparative framework for a study of the middle years, we screened for relatively settled young adults, well past the transition to adulthood; adults in the middle years; and largely healthy elderly adults on the young side of old age, which provided a life-course trajectory from twenty-five to seventy-four years of age. Other chapters are based on smaller, spin-off samples from the MIDUS survey: an eight-day time budget study (chapter 4); a small sample re-interviewed by Anne Colby and her associates, focusing on in-depth explorations of social responsibility (chapter 12); and yet another qualitative set of interviews on the self, part of which explores the range of meanings adults have in mind when they rate themselves in terms of "responsibility" (chapter 9). One unique feature links all these special studies to the major national survey: the subjects interviewed were drawn from the sample of MIDUS respondents, which means the small samples can be compared on key sociodemographic variables with the larger representative national sample.

The New York City studies were not spin-off samples from MIDUS, but special studies conducted in New York neighborhoods varying in their concentration of black, Puerto Rican, and Dominican residents: The survey instrument included many abbreviated versions of variables in MIDUS (chapter 6). Chapter 5 is based on in-depth interviews with poor black and Latino adults in New York.

Structural and Demographic Characteristics of Contemporary American Society

In this chapter I will discuss the structural and demographic characteristics that provide the broad societal context within which our research subjects are living. This involves attention to major characteristics of family structure, the economy, and the polity of contemporary American society, and what "community" means in our time compared to in the past. I roam widely in my discussion of the contemporary dialogue about civil society and social responsibility, organized by the same three dimensions that underlie the design of the modules on social responsibility in the MIDUS survey: family, work, and community. In the course of this broad overview I will refer at numerous points to the specific chapters and findings that are relevant to the topics under review.

Family Structure

It has long been a truism in the social sciences that all societies are organized to facilitate and perpetuate two primary behavioral modes imperative for human and societal survival: the *production* of goods and services necessary for sheer physical survival, and the *reproduction* of their kind. Human labor in an economy, and procreation and child-rearing in the family are the two most basic societal necessities. Both the economy and the family are fundamental social institutions that require cooperation among their participants. The requirement of cooperation implies a critical characteristic of individuals in all human societies: we are innately *social* creatures, not self-sufficient individuals standing alone in the world. However fundamental and simplistic this conception may seem, it nonetheless has *not* been a premise of much philosophy since the Enlightenment or even of the social sciences in this century. Increasingly, however, moral philosophy has been confronting and integrating with evolutionary biology and psychology, an occurrence premised on the importance of our biological predisposition to sociality and generosity (Midgley 1978; Ridley 1996; Ruse 1986; Wilson 1998). To even imagine as an intellectual exercise a totally autonomous individual apart from society as rational choice theorists have done (e.g., Rawls 1971) is, bluntly put, bizarre. The majority of the characteristics that are included in standard personality scales assume social relationships and interaction; it is not an inanimate world but a social world that is implied in rating the extent to which individuals are friendly, outgoing, sympathetic, dominant, talkative, caring, hardworking, outspoken, and so forth.

Any human and most animal family systems are organized around the twin axes of age and sex; hence the critical human social relationships in the family are between men and women, and between the generations. When critics point to family "breakdown" as a primary source of contemporary social problems, they are speaking far more often of the male-female relationship than of the parent-child relationship and tend to give only slight attention to the fact that family relationships embrace more than two generations. It is misleading to focus just on the nuclear family, which is itself embedded in a larger, multigenerational kindred. In our age, as never before, the construct of "family" should not be construed in terms of household composition alone: ease and rapidity of transportation and communication permit more frequent contact between close kin who reside many miles apart—by phone, "snail mail," FAX, e-mail, weekend and holiday visits. In the MIDUS survey, respondents report contact with one or more close relatives several times a week, and close kin are ever on the alert to drop their own daily activities to cope with emergencies in the lives of parents, siblings, and grown children. Studies repeatedly show that family members provide 70 to 80% of long-term care to the elderly (Stone, Cafferata, and Sangl 1987), and two-thirds of severely mentally handicapped children live with their parents (Gilbert 1983; Seltzer et al. 1996). As hospital stays have been severely reduced and outpatient surgery has become more common as part of cost-cutting efforts in the healthcare system—the care of still seriously ill patients has shifted increasingly to family and home. It has become common practice for home care by family members to include the administration of parenteral nutrition, chemotherapy, and narcotics. Wives, mothers, and daughters are typically in charge of such procedures that call for more knowledge and use of equipment than even licensed practical nurses are permitted to manage in hospitals (Abel and Nelson 1990; Fisher and Tronto 1990; Koren 1986).

Academic scholars and media personnel may live hundreds if not thousands of miles away from their place of birth, but the lower the social class, the more it is the case that only short distances exist between the residences of parents and adult children (Rossi and Rossi 1990). Most single moms, for example, are not alone in the world, but live in close proximity to their own siblings, parents, and grandparents. Precisely because of the elongation of the human life span in modern times, most families today consist of three generations, often four. Even a five-generation lineage is no longer exceptional. The four- or five-generation lineages are more typical of the impoverished sectors of society, due to earlier ages of first births in each generation, and often involve more hands-on parenting by the grandparents than by the parents of young children. Diane Hughes illustrates this point in chapter 6, focusing on ethnic and racial communities in New York City. In our time the relationship between parents and adult children persists for *three* times the number of years devoted to rearing dependent young-sters (sixty years vs. twenty), assuming the parents live to age eighty and most children remain at least economically dependent on parents through late adolescence.

Much is said about the fragility of the family due to the high inci-dence of out-of-wedlock births, single parenting, divorce, and the fail-ure of divorced or unwed fathers to lend economic and social support to the rearing of their youngsters. Indeed, the Institute of American Values under David Blankenhorn's leadership has made strengthening marriage a major goal of their public education campaigns and publi-cations (Blankenhorn 1995; Blankenhorn, Bayme, and Elshtain 1990; Council on Families in America 1995; Poponoe, Elshtain, and Blan-kenhorn 1996; Poponoe and Whitehead 1999). Punishing deadbeat dads, or urging covenant marriages or marital counseling for couples in discord do not address some of the fundamental reasons for the weakness of the marital bond or avoidance of marriage altogether. Two factors call for special attention: First, we continue to be in a transi-tional stage in the social and legal status of women and in the relation-ship between cohabiting or married men and women. That the ma-jority of married women are engaged in productive labor is far from unprecedented (Davis 1984; Davis and van den Oever 1982). The aber-ration was the period from the Civil War through the 1950s, the only time in our history when the majority of married women were *not* in-volved in productive labor. Before the Civil War, women were co-producers on the farm or co-workers with their husbands in small craft enterprises or retail shops in towns and cities. Only in the last third of the nineteenth century and the first half of the twentieth were most women largely restricted to homemaking and childrearing once they married. Glass ceilings that restrict women's movement into top posi-tions in large for-profit corporations still remain (though they are be-ginning to crack), but in today's transformed economy, women's train-ing and skills are in demand in the expanding information and service sectors. In the family arena, however, there is ongoing stress and unre-solved problems regarding the division of labor between men and women—in roles as spouses, parents, and workers in domestic mainte-nance. Our analysis of MIDUS data in chapter 11 shows that even if married couples put in the same number of hours on the job and com-muting, women still spend *almost twice* the hours on domestic chores and childcare as do their husbands. Those women who consider this division of labor *unfair* show heightened marital dissatisfaction, often the precursor to marital breakdown and divorce. It will no doubt take at least another generation before greater sex equity in family roles is widespread. With increased levels of labor force participation and greater continuity to women's work histories, marriage is no longer the primary path to economic support for women, and they have fewer reasons to remain in an unsatisfactory marriage.

In addition, it is only through a rosy nostalgic lens that family relationships in the past can be considered better than what we find today, a nostalgic myth Stephanie Coontz (1992, 1997) puts to rest. As Arthur Miller's play *Broken Glass* dramatically illustrates, couples with highly stressed marriages in an era when divorce was stigmatized remained together, but marital discord had insidious negative effects on both partners and on their children. With divorce and out-of-wedlock births so prevalent as to be commonplace, contemporary children whose parents divorced are not subject to social stigma among their peers. (A friend of mine who lives in Berkeley, California, once told me that her son felt deprived because he was the only kid on the block who had "only one dad"!) Consistent with this point, Nicholas Wolfinger (1996) has shown a significant reduction in the tendency of children of divorce to also divorce: in early cohorts, children of divorce were *two and a half* times more likely to divorce than children from intact families, whereas in more recent cohorts, children of divorced parents are only *one and a half* times more likely to divorce than those from intact families. Twenty years from now, it is quite possible that a researcher will find no cross-generational divorce proneness at all. If, at the same time, there are significant changes that make life easier for solo parents to function well (e.g., greater flextime options and more family leave from work, higher pay in female-dominant occupations, increased availability of affordable high-quality child care, close and stable relationships between children and adult males other than their biological fathers), any residual negative effect of single-parent households would become minimal if not nonexistent.

A second, equally important factor to consider when passing judgments on the nature of contemporary family life is the impact of the economy upon life choices of young adults, particularly young poor adults. Mating strategies differ by sex: both men and women seek mates who are stable, companionable, trustworthy, and dependable, but men also seek youth and beauty, whereas women seek some evidence of an ability to provide resources to a potential family, should they desire or have to depend on husbands for economic support. (See Rossi 1994 for an extended review of research on this topic.) The postponement of marriage until the mid-twenties for women and late twenties for most men is a consequence of the need for more education and job experience and the high probability that men will hold down several jobs before settling into one that will provide a steady income. Poor adolescent girls have little reason to be hopeful about finding and marrying a male with adequate resources to support her; if she is black, the odds are she has higher educational attainment than her black brothers, many of whom have spent or are spending time in prison or as homeless persons. Frank Levy and Richard Michel have shown that the mean annual earnings of young, high school-educated men declined by 16% among those working full time between the early 1970s and 1990; among young males who had dropped out of high school the decline was almost twice as great (Levy and Michel 1991). Robert Mare and Christopher Winship (1991) and William J. Wilson (1991) report even greater declines in employment and wages of young black males, which produces an increasingly smaller marriage pool of desirable mates for black females.

Note, too, that in the past a large proportion of brides were pregnant when they married, but such marriages were less stable with a high probability of marital discord and separation. In even earlier times, male mortality often left young widows to rear their children on their own. It is not clear which circumstance (having an unmarried or a divorced or a widowed mother) is better for a child's growth and development. In conservative circles in our day, the assumption is that fatherless children fare very poorly, but the evidence in support of this claim is far from firm (Dunlop and Burns 1995; Furstenberg and Cherlin 1991; Garfinkel and McLanahan 1986; McLanahan and Sandefur 1994; Wallerstein and Blakeless 1989). Some policy analysts who wish to reduce the number of children in poverty support efforts that encourage young people to marry on the grounds that it now takes two parents to support a family. This is an interesting but in a way sad recommendation. For one, it illustrates how socially acceptable dual-earning couples have become; in the past it was maternal employment that was considered undesirable to children's growth and development, an assumption underlying Aid to Families with Dependent Children at its inception. Second, it would not require two parents to prevent child poverty if a single mother's earnings were adequate to support herself and her children at a reasonable level of comfort and amenities. It is not having a single mother or being fatherless that produces problematic circumstances for children, but living in run-down, drug-ridden, anonymous neighborhoods, the low wages and the lack of benefits available in occupations that are socially devalued when they are over-whelmingly held by women, and the lack of quality child care (Hayes, Palmer, and Zaslow 1990). It is doubtful that professional or manage-rial women rearing children on their own have less well adjusted, less healthy children than comparable professional two-parent families do. Public attitudes on these matters have undergone significant change in recent years: the majority of respondents in the MIDUS sample *rejects* the view that to grow up emotionally healthy children need to be raised by both parents, and the majority *endorses* the view that single parents can rear children just as well as married adults can.

Although the full story is not yet in, there have been increasing press reports at this writing (August 1999) indicating a significant increase in the proportion of children living in poverty among those whose moth-ers moved off the welfare rolls and into low paying, often temporary jobs without benefits. The political rhetoric of recent presidential ad-ministrations and many members of Congress to the effect that our economy continues to produce hundreds of thousands of new jobs and a low unemployment rate masks the fact that the jobs that are opening up at such a high rate are far more largely temporary jobs with no bene-fits than they are high-skill jobs with adequate benefits. Manpower, Inc., in Chicago, a major enterprise supplying temporary workers, is to-day the largest business in the nation. The temporary help industry has grown enormously since the 1960s: Mack Moore identified between six hundred and eight hundred temporary help firms in the 1960s (Moore 1963). By the mid-1990s there were more than four thousand such firms with twenty-four thousand offices in the United States, with an annual payroll of approximately $42 billion (Ofstead 1999; Parker 1994).

There is also a quite different factor that is important to bear in mind in any analysis of the fragility of marriage and the high incidence of out-of-wedlock births: the consequences attending the long-term drop in the age of sexual maturation. Today girls experience their first menstrual period at an average age of 12.6 years. Although considerable variance exists around this average age at menarche, many girls are early maturers at nine or ten years of age. The earlier the age of sexual maturation, the earlier the age of sexual initiation, and the higher the probability of dropping out of school and of experiencing an unwanted pregnancy. In a peer world inundated with sexually explicit, alluring

15

messages in movies, the press, and television, appeals to abstinence ring hollow. In addition, unprotected sex for a fifteen-year-old girl today is far more likely to result in a pregnancy than in the past because she has not had the protection of postmenarcheal irregularity of ovulation that girls her age used to have. Hence unprotected sex among teenagers today is far more likely to occur and far more likely to lead to a pregnancy. This is a particular problem for young girls growing up in poor households. Menarcheal timing is 30% genetically determined, therefore many very early maturing women have early maturing sons and daughters (Garn 1980; Goldman and Schneider 1987; Rossi 1994). Unwed mothers tend to be early maturers from poor family backgrounds, often growing up in homes that were fatherless as well, and increasing evidence suggests that the absence of the biological father in the home *lowers* the menarcheal age of daughters. (See Rossi 1998 for a review of this literature.) If social and economic considerations press for later ages at marriage—mid- to late twenties—this leaves more than a decade spent as sexually mature adolescents and young adults. Is abstinence a reasonable expectation under such changed circumstances? This decade-long period of sexual maturity combined with prolonged years of education and an insecure hold on stable employment in early adulthood have clearly been significant factors in the rising incidence of premarital sex and cohabitation in Western societies.

Nor is the birth control pill a panacea assuring no unwanted births outside marriage, any more than its use is the *cause* of increased sexual activity outside marriage since the 1960s, as many claim. Effective pill usage requires advance intention and consistency of use. Adolescent girls are often "caught" unprepared because the initiator of intercourse is more often the male partner. There is also typically a period of time following the ending of one relationship and the beginning of another when adolescent girls feel there is no reason for using the pill (Laumann et al. 1994; Thompson 1994, 1995; Udry 1979; Udry and Campbell 1994). In addition, it is often forgotten that unwanted births were controlled reasonably well for decades before the pill became available in the 1960s: condom and diaphragm use or reliance on the rhythm method, and if need be, resort to an illegal abortion, were responsible for the drop in the fertility rate during the Depression years of the 1930s when many couples who wished to have large families found it necessary to restrict family size simply because they could not afford to have another child. Note as well that in these earlier decades young couples' parents had no social security or any significant amount of savings to see them through their retirement years, much less to have the financial wherewithal to help their adult children and grandchildren with the financial assistance and gifts that today's elderly are able to provide. As will be shown in chapter 3, money now flows at a significant rate from the elderly to young adult children; in chapter 8, we report that financial difficulties are among the main problems in the lives of our respondents' adult children; and in chapter 11 we report that at all educational levels, among both married and unmarried adults, the oldest respondents (sixty to seventy-four years of age) are the *least* likely to tell us they do not have enough money to meet their needs. (The subgroup in our survey *most* likely to report income inadequacy are the youngest adults in the sample, particularly young unmarried women.)

Intellectuals and social commentators on the state of the American family make numerous rhetorical claims that the family is the incubator of civic values and democratic skills, an irreplaceable cornerstone of a healthy civic society, because the family is society's chief buffer against excessive individualism. But the recommendations that flow from this assessment are largely confined to one major point: restore in every way possible the two-parent family. As Don Eberly puts it: "A society that denies so many of its children the basic birthright of a stable, two-parent family can only expect more angry, socially dysfunctional, and distrustful citizens" (Eberly 1998, 159). The implication of such a recommendation is that the sheer presence of a father will assure that children grow up in a climate of love and affection tempered by an equal emphasis on parental modeling of high ethical standards and training of the children in morals and general competencies as social creatures. I find no evidence in family research to support such a reliance on the simple fact of a one-parent versus two-parent family as the major factor responsible for all the ills of modern society, whether one has in mind lack of trust in major institutions, excessive individualism, or a lack of civic concern for the major democratic values of equality, justice, and mutual respect. The most damaging influences on the healthy development of competent, responsible young adults are more invidious and widespread, affecting parents and children in any type of family composition. Consider the following social factors:

1. Permissive rather than authoritative childrearing. Developmental psychologists have long emphasized the importance of two dimensions of childrearing: affection and discipline (Damon 1998). Working with these two dimensions, one can differentiate among four basic styles of

17

childrearing: Rejecting (low affection, low discipline); Authoritarian (low affection, high discipline); Permissive (high affection, low discipline); and Authoritative (high affection, high discipline).

Clinicians have a long history of working with children of Rejecting parents. These children never experience the deep love and commitment of a parent to the young child, nor are they taught lessons about how to control themselves or to conform to minimum standards of ethical behavior in interpersonal relationships. Altruistic behavior has its roots in empathy, the ability to read emotions in others. In the absence of such an awareness of another's need or despair, there can be no *caring* toward others (Goleman 1995). One likely outcome of exposure to such a Rejecting parental regimen is illustrated tragically by the fourteen-year-old boy who mugged an eighty-year-old blind woman, stealing her purse and beating her. When asked if he felt sympathy for the old woman because of the pain he had caused her, he said, "Why should I? After all, she isn't me!" (Damon 1995, 78).

There is no evidence that American parents today feel less love and affection for their children during the critical formative years of infancy and early childhood compared to fifty years ago; indeed our heritage as social creatures is grounded in the intense bond between mothers and their infants, which is part of our biological nature, and any scale on parental affection shows a striking asymmetry tipped to the high end of the scale. What is problematic is not the presence of parental love, but its absence, and we are well advised to search for psychological impairment or dire environmental influences when we examine extreme lack of attachment to the young by adults.

The discipline dimension of childrearing, by contrast, is highly subject to cultural norms and changes in historical context. In the views of many child developmental psychologists and family sociologists, American parents have tended over the past thirty years to shift from an Authoritative to a Permissive style of childrearing. This is particularly the case among better-educated adults in the upper middle class, especially compared to their lesser-educated counterparts in a stable working-class community. (Duane Alwin has traced this trend in childrearing patterns; see his most recent summary, Alwin 1996). An extremely permissive childrearing style leaves young children's early self-centeredness intact, but children cannot thrive psychologically on such a foundation. They must instead learn to dedicate themselves to purposes beyond their own desires. As a society we view ourselves as "child-centered," but this has become a justification for every manner of overindulgent childrearing practice, a tendency toward which working parents are particularly prone—to compensate for the hours they are not with their children—but common as well among male-breadwinner-only families, in a cultural setting with a continual high-pitch barrage of advertising urging ever more spending on and indulgence of self and child.

In this area, family size takes on special significance: in families with three or more children, the sheer press of household management assures that even young children have experience in carrying their weight by doing various domestic chores. By contrast, in the typical one- or two-child families of today, the children are usually spared making contributions to domestic maintenance. This situation cheats them of critical learning experiences regarding meeting the needs of others, an important building block toward an enlargement of such service to wider concerns in the community at later stages in their development. The importance of family size in this regard is illustrated in the developmental profile predictive of adult social responsibility in chapter 7 of this volume. When childhood focuses on pleasure-oriented activities, it is little wonder that surveys of students show hardly *a quarter* of American youngsters place top priority on "working hard." By contrast, surveys in Japan, a society with a more authoritative rather than permissive childrearing pattern, report not *one*-quarter but *three*-quarters of student samples give priority to "working hard" (Damon 1995, 37).

It is not merely to compensate for guilty feelings that hard-working parents do a poor job of disciplining their children, teaching them skills, and insisting on routines that involve serving others than themselves. Any parent seeking advice from parenting guides in recent years would find an inordinate emphasis on the importance of building up the self-esteem of children by supporting and praising them every step of the way, allowing them to develop at their own pace by withholding judgment or criticism. It is therefore not surprising that they grow up believing that good ends can be achieved without struggling or unpleasantness. As William Damon points out, the belief that nothing can be done until a child has a high level of self-esteem is to put the cart before the horse and is a misreading of child development literature: self-esteem is best grounded when earned by demonstrating learned skills and moral values; measures of self-esteem have no correlation with measures of intelligence, achievement, or emotional maturity (Damon 1995, 75). In fact schoolyard bullies and gang members are the ones who tend to have the highest self-regard.

2. Misguided educators and psychological counselors. It is not just parents, but teachers, guidance counselors, and psychotherapists who have become convinced that building self-esteem is the answer to all childhood problems: "[W]e are to assure children, at all times and regardless of the circumstances, that they are 'terrific' in every possible way" (Damon 1995, 23). With experts standing in the wings to deal with every conceivable personal problem, something is lost from an individual's ability to feel confident enough to cope with problems on his or her own: marital discord leads to marital counseling; a child's shyness or misbehavior to a school guidance counselor or private psychiatrist, sometimes by the parent's initiative, often by that of the school administration or counseling office. As Christopher Lasch has argued in his numerous writings, most recently in the collection of essays edited by his daughter Elisabeth after his death (Lasch 1997), the army of therapeutic experts undercuts both personal responsibility and giving or seeking help from loved ones who care most deeply about our welfare in favor of reliance on the "caring" professions. As Bruce Charlton puts it, we have come to believe that "people who care about us . . . are disqualified from being helpful because they are too 'involved,' 'too judgmental,' too 'directive,' and because they have not mastered the theory and skills of one or another of the schools of psychotherapy" (Charlton 1998, 33). Bruce Cooper and Dennis O'Keefe contend that in both America and Britain, education has "set aside discipline and obedience, and replaced them with false love and slackness" (Cooper and O'Keefe 1998, 61).

As a result of permissiveness combined with an excessive emphasis on self-esteem, busy parents often take the easy way out by doing things children could master on their own, but that would take time. Parents also often assume many things are beyond children's capacities and therefore better done *for* them: they dress the children quickly in order to catch a nursery school bus; drive them short distances that the children could walk or bike alone; hold them back in school for fear they would be too challenged if they moved ahead; and so forth. Low expectations lead to low results (Damon 1995, 104).

3. Cultural emphasis on money. There are, as well, any number of forces at work in today's society that suggest hard work may not pay off as it once did: corruption in high places, misuse of political campaign funds, and scandalous behavior on the part of people presumed to be of high moral character abound. The rapid increase in gambling over the past decade must surely add to the belief not only that money

matters most, but that there are easy ways to acquire it. The sale of state lottery tickets, the vast expansion of the gambling casinos in Las Vegas and on Indian reservations, and the mounting proportion of adults playing the stock market are surely indicative of the complex combina-tion of high cultural emphasis on money and the pleasures it can bring, along with the belief that gambling is a reliable route to acquiring such money. This pattern clearly is not unique to our time. It had its coun-terpart in the first two decades of the twentieth century. Terence Da-vies, a director of a play based on Edith Wharton's novel *House of Mirth,* commented recently, "We live in an age of surfaces. They did then [in the high society Wharton portrays acerbically at the turn of the century], and we do today. What's true today is that how you look and how much money you have is what matters. Being a good person doesn't matter, and it applies now as it did in 1905" (Lyall 1999, 19).

4. Unintended consequences of concern for child safety. One issue for which parents have a limited capacity to deal concerns child safety. Many urban, and not-so-urban, communities are not safe territory for children to traverse on their own. As a compromise, parents warn their children to be cautious when approached by anyone not known to them: do not talk to strangers; do not take anything they offer you; do not let anyone strange touch your body. The unintended consequence of such parental warnings is a restriction of children's exploration of the social world around them. Even children from healthy loving fami-lies that instill in them trust in others and a desire to be helpful to oth-ers are prevented from moving on to the next developmental stage of extending that circle of others to encompass persons outside the family. Instead they learn that the world is a fearful scary place and that it is best to stay safely within a narrowly defined, cautious world of known adults and peer friends. These are hardly fruitful grounds for the devel-opment of social responsibility and civic morality.

5. School curricula. Added to the view that the world out there is a dangerous place is the impact of a politically correct curriculum: an unrelentingly negative view of American history, with its emphasis on the "white man" giving smallpox-infected blankets to Native American populations; a narrow view of Jefferson as a slaveholder; and American wars that oppressed Cubans, Philippinos, and Vietnamese—all with-out proper balanced attention to great democratic documents and na-tional heroes. There is little wonder that children may acquire a view of our history as largely one of oppression and aggression. Schools also dim children's visions of even festive highlights of the year, when

Thanksgiving becomes a secular apology to the Indians rather than a joyous celebration of our land's plenty, for example. Michael and Diane Medved cite a letter the public schools in Pasadena, California, sent home with the children, which included the following message: "To many Native American peoples today, Thanksgiving is a day of mourning because it is a reminder that in return for their help, knowledge, and tolerance of original European settlers, they were 'repaid' with the rape of their land and the genocide of their people" (Medved and Medved 1998, 114). The Anti-Bias Curriculum, issued by the National Association for the Education of Young Children, officially suggests that teachers blend December holidays into one nonreligious celebration or ignore Christmas altogether. With a curriculum like this, it is hardly surprising that children bring to their more mature years a pervasive pessimism about the state of American institutions.

6. Ambivalent cultural attitudes toward religion. As a political liberal and religious skeptic I confess to having special difficulty in dealing with a major finding from the MIDUS analysis on the roots of adult social responsibility: respondents who grew up in families in which religion was very important were predisposed from youth to develop concern for the well-being of others—not just family, but those in need in the community at large. I found it perfectly reasonable that respondents who reported their parents were models of generativity (meaning their parents were very generous and helpful to others *outside the family*) would have internalized such values and as adults believe and act in accord with the same values by participating in volunteer work and giving money to charitable causes. But why did a religious background have an independent effect on social responsibility in adulthood beyond generativity?

To pose such a question may evoke a smile from readers who hold deeply felt religious beliefs, but this has not been a topic that has attracted very many traditionally trained psychologists or sociologists. What David Tracy put very well more than twenty years ago applies as well today: "Religion is the single subject about which many intellectuals can feel free to be ignorant" (Tracy 1981, 13). Indeed, there is hardly any attention given in the whole of child development literature to spiritual or religious needs, despite the common view that healthy psychological development involves learning to dedicate oneself to purposes beyond our own narrow desires. That dedication is what religious traditions have called *transcendence*, faith in concerns larger than oneself. One sees this in the lives of the saints, in people like Gandhi, Mandela, or Mother Teresa. Within a more normal human population range, Anne Colby and Bill Damon identify the values that motivated unusual adults who performed extraordinary acts of service to others in their study of *moral exemplars* (Colby and Damon 1992). Kristen Monroe provides intensive life histories of altruists who, at great personal cost, rescued Jews during World War II (Monroe 1996). High on the list of the major qualities of moral exemplars are: a high level of spirituality; an intense belief in the transcendent goodness of people, combined with a high sense of civic obligations; the special type of personality that predisposes to an *openness to experience,* prompting a search for enriching experiences in life even if they carry a high risk element; and *agency,* the ability to be forceful actors in the social worlds they move in or seek out.

Perhaps a critical factor contributing to the neglect of religion and spirituality in research on child development can be traced to the antipathy to religion of many early psychological theorists, for example, Freud and Piaget. In Freud's theory, the emphasis was on a seething cauldron of repressed motivational forces (the id), with the ego being a beleaguered center of rationality that his therapeutic practice attempted to free from the impact of the repressed id. In later generations of Freud's successors, the ego gained the upper hand in being linked to conscious choices through rational self-analysis (Karen Horney) or in close articulation between psychosexual and cognitive development (Harry Stack Sullivan). With the advent of these modern developments in psychotherapeutic theory, Kenneth Gergen suggests "the torso was essentially severed at the waist" and "ego psychology" and "object relations" theories took hold (Gergen 1991, 40).

In Piaget's work, he dismissed children's statements about God as animistic beliefs they would outgrow in the course of normal development. But children are intensely curious about the mysteries of life, and we underestimate their capacity to cope with discussions of the beliefs people have held in the past, and those they hold today, to explain why we exist at all or how life and the universe began and where it is going in the future. There is no reason to think that children who can imaginatively relate to Mickey Mouse, Barney, a robot, or an alien would not be equally enthralled with Greek gods, the lives of saints, a cargo cult, a Homeric or Celtic legend, or the miracles imputed to Christ in biblical narratives. Children are not fragile innocents easily traumatized, but sturdy and resilient. As James Fowler suggests, religious stories help children sort out the meaning of their own relationship to the universe (Fowler 1989).

A culture that prizes "tolerance" above all else leaves parents as rudderless as their children: by being fearful of being "judgmental" or taking firm stands on anything important like the fundamentals of right and wrong, parents fail to offer their children even a "fortune cookie's worth of wisdom," as Diane West puts it in a book review (West 1998).

A more extended discussion of the role of religious belief in contemporary society can be found in the concluding section of chapter 7.

Work

A persistent factor throughout the discussion of the contemporary family is the close relationship between work and family life. The sharp increase in female employment over the past quarter-century reflects three basic influences: the feminist movement, with its impact on women's aspirations and its political pressure on government and employers, which has opened doors in many occupations previously closed to women; changes in the economy itself that have made women's skills more relevant—the rising demand for workers in human service and information occupations, simultaneous with a decreasing demand for men's skills, as manufacturing has become increasingly mechanized and jobs have been sent overseas; and the fact that working- and middle-class workers have lost ground financially to such an extent that it now takes two workers per family to sustain a standard of living possible in the past with one wage earner (Danziger and Gottschalk 1993, 1995). Men in nonsupervisory jobs, for example, experienced a 15% drop in real wages between 1979 and 1997, in large measure because high-paying manufacturing jobs have been replaced by low-paying service jobs (Mishel, Bernstein, and Schmitt 1999).

The commodity in shortest supply for adults rearing children is *time:* Americans work harder, put in longer hours on the job, and have shorter vacations than adults in any other Western society (Schor 1992). For example, the average annual number of paid vacation days for employed adults in the United States is twelve, compared to twenty-eight in Britain, thirty-five in Germany, and forty-two in Italy (Shapiro 1999). Overall, a new study by the International Labor Organization found the number of hours Americans work each year has climbed sharply, while working hours in most industrial countries are falling; Americans work 350 more hours a year (equivalent to almost nine work weeks) than Europeans do (Greenhouse 1999, 1). Eben Shapiro claims part of the reason for this contrast is that European unions favor more time off and shorter work weeks, whereas unions in the United States focus on pay increases in exchange for less time off. Americans also spend more time commuting between home and the workplace, reflecting not only increased miles as a result of urban sprawl, but also traffic jams on overused roads. In our pilot survey on work and family, the majority of employed adults said they would prefer to work far fewer hours per week than they do, even if that meant a reduction of their wages. (Only well-educated women who were working part time said they would prefer to work longer hours.) Juliet Schor, author of the 1992 book *The Overworked American,* recently said evidence now suggests that roughly a third of the labor force in the United States is working more hours than they want to (Greenhouse 1999, 4).

If anything, pressures on employed adults have increased in recent years and for a variety of reasons: fear of job loss in an era of corporate downsizing, increasing need for more income in light of rising costs of housing and of higher education for their children; worry on the part of middle-aged and younger workers that social security may not be secure when they face retirement; higher material desire, stimulated by the advertising industry, for more and improved products—cars, houses, appliances, clothing, all manner of gadgetry (Schor 1998); and finally, the decline in unionization that could lend pressure on employers to improve wages and working conditions, especially in the service and professional sectors of the economy where unionization has barely obtained a foothold, and where workers are less apt to watch the clock than those in routinized manufacturing jobs are. On the employer side, there has been far less willingness, since the end of the Cold War, to be receptive to demands from employees, because employers no longer need worry that workers harbor any vision of alternatives to a capitalist economy. In a curious way, Big Government has replaced Big Business in our time, compared to earlier in the twentieth century, as a domestic enemy to be curbed.

From considerations such as these, we predicted and confirmed the hypothesis that MIDUS respondents would report more negative spillover effects of their jobs on their home life than the reverse, negative effects of home life upon jobs. These results are reported in chapter 11. The profile of the subgroup in the sample reporting the highest ratings on negative effects of jobs on home life are men whose jobs involve a great deal of stress, who report negative effects of their jobs on their mental or physical health, or both, who spend long hours at work and commuting each day (particularly if they often work outside regular weekday hours), and who have children under age thirteen at home. A hint that upcoming cohorts of young adults wish for a more balanced life than the contemporary workplace allows is suggested by our finding that it is *young, better-educated men* who show the *lowest* average score on a scale of work obligation. I would like to believe that many such young men have taken to heart the message of the late Massachusetts senator Paul Tsongas, something to the effect of "nobody on his deathbed has ever said, 'I wish I'd spent more time in the office.'"

Americans are rarely faulted for falling down on their jobs (in a figurative sense). Despite their long hours under pressure on the job, and despite what they so often feel are negative effects on their families, absenteeism is not a widespread problem. In chapter 10 Ron Kessler and his associates report their analysis of the impact of physical and mental health problems on job productivity, the latter measured by the number of days of sick leave respondents report they have taken, and the number of days on which some physical or mental/emotional problem kept them from doing all they normally do at work. Work cutback of either sort is not very high and from Kessler's analysis seems to be largely limited to actual physical and mental health status. They found no evidence of numerous no-shows in order to indulge in a golf game or a shopping spree or just lazing around. Few critics, then, would charge Americans with falling short in terms of the values and informal rules they follow in the workplace. They are largely cooperative, dependable, and meet their obligations. In other words, Americans demonstrate no shortage of *social capital* in this domain of life. Indeed, they seem willing to take on more responsibility than many jobs have traditionally allowed them, something increasingly possible as private corporations have favored decentralized or flattened, rather than hierarchical, organizational structures (see Fukuyama 1999, especially chapter 15). Daniel Goleman has made this point colorfully: "[T]he jungle fighter symbolizes where the corporation has been; the virtuoso in interpersonal skills is the corporate future" (Goleman 1995, 149). Here, too, is another reason why today women seek and are sought for jobs in corporate America: the restructuring has made their skills and predispositions highly appropriate.

Americans are remarkable in another sense as well: they can scarcely be accused of being miserly as taxpayers. Despite the ongoing political discourse and debate on tax reform in the Congress over the past several years, citizen response on poll after poll ranks reduction of taxes low on their sense of political priorities; more important than lowering their own federal income tax, in the public's view, are lowering the deficit, reducing government spending, protecting social security and Medicare, assuring public health and safety, and working toward a cleaner environment. This is all the more remarkable when one realizes that a family earning a median income of $38,000 in 1993 had to pay $8,000 more, in 1993 dollars, in taxes of all kinds than their counter parts earning a median income in 1953 would have had to pay (Barlett and Steele 1994). Political leaders, the interest groups that support them, and the wealthy are the miserly ones, not the majority of taxpayers (Shlaes 1999).

Changes in the Demography of the Life Course

Among the most fundamental indicators for depicting macro-level characteristics of a society and changes in those characteristics are demographic trends. The human life course has undergone major changes in its shape and duration over this past century with significant implications for understanding family structure, the economy, the polity, and their combined influences upon civic participation. In my earlier discussion of family structure, I pointed to several of these demographic changes: earlier sexual maturation, prolonged schooling, later marriage, smaller families, higher divorce rates, longer lives. Improved nutrition and health care have contributed to both the early maturation and the increased longevity we now enjoy. Changes in the economy—moving from a farming to a manufacturing to a service and telecommunications era—have made higher education and job training a necessity for most young people, and marketplace competition, domestically and internationally, with its downsizing and outsourcing, demands residential relocation of employed workers. There is no assurance of job security for middle-aged employees at any workplace, whether federal or state civil service, nonprofit organizations, or for-profit corporations and small businesses. Fewer adults can look forward to settling down for a lifetime in jobs with a single agency or firm; the likelihood is that adults will work in six to eight jobs, including many shifts in occupation, over the course of their work histories.

Individual expectations often lag behind government policy in anticipating the impact of the changed shape of the life course. When the Social Security Act was passed in the 1930s, life expectancy was for survival of only five or six years beyond the age of sixty-five; many workers were expected to die before they received *any* social security checks. It seems likely that today's retired elderly, as their grandparents before them, did not expect to live as long as they are doing. I have a keen memory of my own grandmother attending my graduation from elementary school, saying how glad she was to still be alive to see me graduate; she had no expectation that she would live another thirty-five years! A similar sense of a shorter than probable life ahead of them may explain why three in four retirees today retired before the age of sixty-five. But there is no evidence that the baby-boom cohort expects to retire at an older age, despite the fact that early retirees in the future will receive only 75% of the full amount they would receive if they retire at age sixty-five, rather than the current 80% (Social Security Administration 1995).

More surprising still, a *Wall Street Journal*/NBC News poll conducted in March 1999 reports that a full 46% of Generation X-ers (eighteen to thirty-four years of age) say they expect to retire under the age of sixty. This does not mean they anticipate relying on the federal social security system for their elderly years: 36% of the same younger age group said they expect to receive "nothing at all" in terms of social security benefits when they reach retirement age (*Wall Street Journal Special Quarterly* 1999).

How is it possible that so many young adults expect little or nothing from social security yet expect to retire so young? For one, Generation X-ers are the first cohort to be able to take advantage of 401(k) pension plans enacted in 1982. For another, business pension benefits have become more common and may become a larger proportion of income for retired persons in the period after 2010 (Reno 1993). But as investors, the younger generation has never known a bear market, lives beyond its income by overuse of credit cards, and perceives personal bankruptcy as far less of a social stigma than earlier generations have. One analyst suggests the youngest generation has less emotional attachment to social security than their parents and grandparents have had, and that they are increasingly convinced they can get a better return from investment in stocks than what the federal government gives on social security. Another pollster said, "Young people trust the market more than they trust the government" (*Wall Street Journal Special Quarterly* 1999, A12).

The aging of the population in Western societies is almost invariably viewed in a somber, negative light (e.g., Peterson 1999): because people live so much longer, they get more out of their pension plans than they put in; they overwhelm the healthcare system, particularly in the last year of their lives; they are indulgent, self-centered, and leisure-oriented, if not quite "greedy geezers"; they place the burdens of caregiving on their adult children, who are often overwhelmed with their own children's needs; they are represented by the powerful lobbyists for the American Association of Retired Persons (AARP)—a roadblock to funding for the young, whose needs are far greater but who lack powerful lobbies of their own. As economist Sylvia Hewitt puts it, the United States over the past few decades has "socialized the cost of growing old and privatized the cost of childhood" (quoted in Coontz 1992, 86). Peter Peterson reports correspondence with Andrew Hacker that points to the "slowing down of the pace of social life" as a consequence of so many elderly in the population: it takes more time to board buses because the elderly move slowly; or to get service at a bank or post office because the elderly require more help in such transactions; or even to drive around town because so many seventy- and eighty-something drivers are slow and pokey on the road (Peterson 1999, 259).

But is there not also a positive side to an aging population? Might it not provide a brake on the frenzied pace of urban life and technological change that would redound to the health of young and old alike? A source of knowledge about work, politics, peace, and war in earlier decades? Kinkeepers who can inform the young about their parents and their other relations when they were children, providing for them a sense of past family continuity and an understanding of their roles in future family history? Today's cohort of elderly adults are an important source of financial assistance to their adult children, helping with down payments on first homes, establishing trust funds for grandchildren, often providing backup childcare service for grandchildren when the usual arrangements break down or the grandchildren are ill. The elderly are not only recipients of caregiving, but donors as well, as will be reported in chapter 3. Persons sixty-five to seventy-four years of age are also the most generous givers to charitable causes, donating almost 4% of their incomes, compared to a national average of 1.9% (Schembari 1998). It is estimated that baby boomers will inherit $5.6 trillion from their parents over the next several decades (Kuczynski 1998). Note too that as the proportion of the population over eighty-five years of age increases in coming years, those most likely to be providing assistance in daily living will not be middle-aged children rearing their own children, but rather, old children who, because of early retirement, have time to meet their parents' needs.

Retired adults are also a potent source of volunteers as charitable support shifts away from the federal to state and local levels, and over the coming few decades they will be better educated and more computer savvy than today's elderly. They already participate in elections at a greater rate than younger adults do (a pattern that has been in place for decades) and will no doubt continue to do so. Chances are also great that the lifestyles of the elderly are more frugal, less polluting, and less wasteful of natural resources.

Finally, some caution is called for where self-appointed lobbyists for the elderly are concerned. Most members of the AARP joined the organization to obtain discounts of various sorts, especially those on medicines, not as politically motivated supporters of the organization's efforts in Washington. The efforts during the 1998 and 1999 sessions of Congress to fashion legislation ensuring "quality care" in HMOs assumes that, just as the lobbyists proclaim, HMO patients are deeply dissatisfied with their care compared to traditional plan patients. In fact opinion polls at the time showed an insignificant 4% difference in the proportion claiming they are "satisfied with quality" of their medical care—88% of HMO patients versus 92% of traditional care patients. On the issue of healthcare *costs,* patients in HMOs are actually *more* satisfied than traditional care patients—79% versus 65% (Peterson 1999, 258).

Yet another demographic trend worth noting is the increasing tendency for adults to be living alone: single-person occupancy in housing has been increasing in all Western societies, reflecting the longer number of early adult years prior to marriage; the interim between marriages among divorced adults and the lower rate of remarriage among divorced women; and the considerable gap in longevity by sex, with far more widows than widowers in the ranks of the elderly. As of 1997, one in four of all households in the United States contained individuals living alone. This is higher than earlier in the twentieth century, but still very much lower than in many European countries: the percentage of all households with single occupancy is 46% in Norway and 50% in Denmark (Fukuyama 1999, 114), and Lionel Tiger reports the astonishing rate of 75% in the city of Oslo (Tiger 1999).

For our gregarious species, being alone is often an unpleasant, depressing experience. For example, when subjects of a 1997 survey were beeped, they recorded where they were and with whom; those alone were unhappier than those with friends or family members (Csikszentmihalyi 1997). There is even evidence of a physiological pathway involved in the effects shown: an increase in the hormone oxytocin (OT) is associated with a rush of warm feelings in situations of social stimulation and interaction. Being with others stimulates a *rise* in OT secretion; being alone triggers a *drop* (Insel 1992). Communication by means of phone, fax, or e-mail, vicarious identification with others on TV or radio, or interacting with someone in an Internet chat room is no substitute for the sensory, social, and hormonal stimulation of face-to-face interaction.

One last point on demographic trends: it is highly unlikely that historical events special to the United States are relevant in any explanation of changes in civic participation over time. All the family and economic trends summarized above hold for all other major developed societies over the past thirty-five years, as Francis Fukuyama has demonstrated in fine detail in his most recent book, *The Great Disruption:* higher crime rates, illegitimacy, late marriage, higher divorce rates, and increased female participation in the labor force are found in Britain, Sweden, France, Germany, Italy, Canada, New Zealand, Australia, and Japan as well. Rates may vary across countries in a particular year, but the trend across time is very similar from one to another of these developed societies.

Community

Unlike the domains of family and work, "community" is a nebulous concept holding many meanings (Rossi 1972). In common parlance, one understands the term in a very general sense: for example, when we ask someone new in town, "How do you like the community?" or when someone bemoans the loss of "community spirit." In these cases, the reference is clearly to a *residential locality.* But "community" is increasingly used in a quite different sense, referring to a social group that shares some common characteristics and whose members are conscious of belonging to that group, with no necessary assumption that the group in question is limited to a particular locality or that its members are personally known to each other. It is this sense which encompasses frequently heard references such as "academic community," the "black community," even the "sado-masochistic community." Some contemporary authors link the two meanings of community. For example, Digby Anderson and Peter Mullen claim the word "community" is displayed on more buildings in bigger letters once a place has ceased to be a genuine community. In their view, the term is among those sentimental, superficial forms of reference that "like ghosts, persist long after the reality has disappeared" (Anderson and Mullen 1998, 5). There is a trace of nostalgia to their view that the idea of community has become debased, closer to the idea of a "sect" than any traditional conception of community.

The point is that sociologists have been reporting the loss of a "sense of community" for decades. Maurice Stein's 1960 review of major sociological and anthropological community studies concludes with the central finding of a disappearance of the sense of community among residents of the towns studied (Stein 1960). Even earlier, when Robert and Helen Lynd revisited in the mid-1930s the community of Muncie, Indiana, which they first studied in the late 1920s, they too traced the loss of a "sense of community" residents felt over the course of their lives there (Lynd and Lynd 1929, 1937). In all such cases, one suspects that invoking the "loss of community" is a disguised reference to the changing composition and size of the resident population that makes old-time residents uncomfortable in any number of ways. At the same time, putting this in terms of "loss of community spirit" obscures the point that, for better or worse, the life of either individuals or communities never *are* "what they used to be."

Repeated reports about the "loss" of a sense of community may be putting negatively what, from another perspective, is in fact a positive development: an expansion of the social worlds that carry meaning for us, extending far from the particular neighborhood, town, or city we happen to bed down in. Fewer of us are tightly bound to any given locale. Many people work in one city but live in another, even crossing state boundaries in commuting between home and job—for example, those who work in Manhattan and commute to homes in New Jersey or Connecticut. Many adults who belong to no local associations and do not participate in any local charitable drives or political campaigns have numerous affiliations with an array of organizations and social movements on the national level. In becoming less local, we have become more cosmopolitan, not only moving out into the world by travel, job relocation, or organizational memberships, but inviting the world into our personal lives via television, movies, books, and the Internet.

A very new, loose use of the concept of community is also apparent in contemporary society: in 1998, through a Yahoo search engine, you could enter a cyberspace "community" and find ninety-six hundred Web sites to visit; through the Lycos search engine, twenty thousand, and through Web Crawler, eighty-seven thousand (Freie 1998). Such "virtual communities" reduce the concept of community to the barest essential of simple communication between individuals or within groups. Participants are usually not even known to each other by name; anonymity or the use of a pseudonym is typical. Close observers of cyberspace report that the millions of people who log on to the Internet each day are not merely seeking information, but trying to satisfy their desire for connectedness (Bennahum 1999; Freie 1998; Rheingold 1993; Seabrook 1997; Turkle 1995). For the growing proportion of adults who live alone and put in long, stressful hours on the job, an evening in an Internet chat room may be psychologically irresistible.

What we mean by "community" in this volume is the rich array of associational affiliations that mediate between individuals and the larger society beyond the primary ties of family, co-workers, and friends—what sociologists from the earliest days of the discipline have called "secondary groups." Émile Durkheim thought the major secondary groups in modern societies would be occupations and professions. In his classic work *Division of Labor in Society* he argued that a nation can be maintained only if, between the state and the individual, there is a whole series of secondary groups near enough to the individual to attract them strongly and draw them into the general torrent of social life. Durkheim believed it was the destiny of occupational groups to fill this role (Durkheim 1964).

The American experience of secondary groups is much richer than just occupational affiliations. Among the earliest theorists who first noted and analyzed the significance of the broad, cross-cutting networks of associations in American life was Alexis de Tocqueville, whose book *Democracy in America,* based on his travels in the United States during the early 1830s, has long been a classic in all studies of civil society and democracy. De Tocqueville claims that Americans, compared to his own countrymen, show a unique and rich "art of association." He saw a country where the most ordinary citizens come together in voluntary associations dealing with a wide array of issues for both civic and political purposes, learning in the process cooperative habits that permit democracy to thrive. Robert Putnam has provided a dramatic empirical study based on this theory to explain why vitality and progressivism characterized the north of Italy, whereas the Sicilian south has been hierarchic and corruption ridden. Only in the north has there been a wide range of mediating associations between the individual and the state, including numerous church groups, sports clubs, and social and political organizations that facilitate the development of social,

economic, and political competencies and cooperative habits conducive to economic progress in a politically democratic climate. By contrast there has been little connection between strong clans and government in the South, and the Mafia hold has been, as a consequence,
strong and corrupting (Putnam 1993a).

In more recent years the case for the rich proliferation of voluntary
associations has taken on more specifically political overtones. Peter
Berger and Richard Neuhaus published an important paper in 1977, *To
Empower People*—a paper republished together with commentaries by
the American Enterprise Institute under Michael Novak's editorship
(1996). Berger and Neuhaus's original thesis concerned the importance
of "mediating structures," the institutions that stand between the private world of individuals and the large, impersonal structures of modern society. By "mediating," they were referring to the structures' role
in protecting the individual against the alienation and anomie of modern life, while assuring that the state would gain democratic legitimacy
by being related to the values that governed the actual lives of ordinary
people (Novak 1996, 148–49). From the vantage point of their 1996 re-
assessment, their focus has changed significantly in a political sense to
concern for how to protect mediating structures from the fatal embrace
of government regulation. The thesis now emphasizes the threat that
government programs have posed in weakening the mediating structures of family, church, neighborhood, and voluntary associations: at
a minimum the government should not undercut these intermediary
bodies, at best, strengthen and support them. The Berger-Neuhaus thesis has provided significant theoretical backing to political conservatives' case against the welfare state.

But as E. J. Dionne (1998) points out, the Berger-Neuhaus thesis
overemphasized the federal government side of the equation, to the neglect of the effect of the economic market on neighborhood and family
life. Both Alan Wolfe, in his book *Whose Keeper?* and Alan Ehrenhalt,
in articles and in his book *The Lost City,* argue that while liberals did
not give sufficient attention to the negative impact that *government*
could have on the mediating structures in a civil society, conservatives
did not give sufficient attention to how the *market* has disrupted neighborhoods and family life. (Ehrenhalt 1995, 1998; Wolfe 1989). A society
premised on ever greater production of material goods requires an advertising industry to persuade consumers they need to purchase such
goods in ever greater quantities and to replace still serviceable goods
with the latest fashion in a second or third car, a second house, a reno-

vated kitchen with new appliances. These consumer desires drive the trends noted in the section on work: long hours of work by dual-earning couples, overuse of credit cards, and job insecurity in an era of downsizing and automation. Very few economists or policy-makers support the concept of a "no-growth" or "steady-state" economy. Herman Daly, a former World Bank senior economist, is among the minority who advocate sustainable development through a no-growth economy on the grounds that there cannot be *infinite* economic growth within a *finite* ecological system. Daly believes his colleagues in economics and policy-makers in government are largely insensitive and unknowledgeable about the extent to which social systems are dependent on natural systems (Daly 1996).

The most devastating results that can develop when there are no functioning mediating structures in place in a society have occurred in Eastern Europe in recent years. In the decade since the end of the Cold War, we have witnessed the turmoil that followed the collapse of communist control in the Soviet Union and Yugoslavia. The Soviet regime controlled every institution in society—education, the government, the economy, religion, and the arts. Party members in schools, neighborhoods, and workplaces urged people to inform on each other, inserting a troubling wedge into relationships between parents and children, siblings, neighbors, and co-workers. By encouraging such actions, the tightly controlling state destroyed a rich and diverse range of extensive, interlocking social ties among the citizenry. Complicating the circumstances even further, the Soviets sent hundreds of thousands of educated Russians into the far-flung republics to occupy the top positions in government, factories, and the professions. By so doing, they set the stage for struggles for independence on the part of the subjugated republics once the Soviet government collapsed. After seven decades of tight communist control and the destruction of relationships of trust between individuals and social groups, people were left distrustful of everything and everybody. Voluntary associations and the cooperative habits they encourage were simply absent, leaving the republics without cushion or anchor to ease the implementation of reforms.

It clearly did not help matters that the American penchant for quick fixes in order to make quick political points paved the way for reforms that could not work under such circumstances. Just as when American politicians urge elections as soon as possible after the collapse of dictatorial governments, without sufficient time for political groups with democratic values to develop, the stage was set for failure, not success, in the reform of the Russian economy. Western advisors advocated a shock therapy to jumpstart the Russian economy by price liberalization (which quickly triggered inflation, exhausting the meager savings of the public); budget stabilization; and a slashing of subsidies on the belief that privatization of state assets could be done first, and market and legal infrastructural change would follow in its wake. The result has been economic and political disaster, as former state enterprise managers became owners, joining forces with banking and government officials out for their own personal gains, sending from $200 to $500 billion abroad as fast as the World Bank and the International Monetary Fund poured money into the country (O'Brien 1999). In the absence of proper banking and legal accounting systems, and with only a meager portion of the social capital that accrues to a rich and independent civil society, the capitalism that was artificially fostered in Russia simply became capital flight (Lloyd 1999). The average citizens in Russia, seeing their government as both inefficient and criminally corrupt, having their own lives marked by job insecurity or lack of pay for work done, and lacking both the trust in others and the social skills that flourish in more democratic societies, have become easy prey to xenophobia, hence stoking renewed anti-Semitism and deepening their distrust of the intentions of Western nations.

It is not inconceivable that a similar fate awaits China in the twenty-first century. The Communist Party, dominated by one nationality, the Han, followed the Soviet pattern in sending hundreds of thousands of Han party members to the distant provinces, where they occupy top positions of control over the major institutions of the communities they dominate. Unlike the Soviet Union, Chinese economic policy has followed a program of very gradual change from state-owned enterprises to a state-approved expansion of private investments and private firms. To date, the rumblings for political reform have been limited to Beijing and major east coast cities. In contrast to the Soviet pattern that undermined the family and attempted to abolish religion, family relations in China have remained strong, reinforced by the rapid development of family businesses in both rural and urban areas. Western suspicion and some degree of latent hostility toward the Far East may protect China from the intrusion of hasty Western policy recommendations affecting both politics and the economy in a postcommunist era in China's future.

In decided contrast to the Soviet experience is the comparable process of decentralization of authority in Great Britain. With a rich tradition of democratic rule, respect for human rights, and a vibrant civil society, Great Britain is undergoing a significant process of decentralization: Scotland has elected an Independent parliament; Wales is in favor of electing its own assembly; and a commission established by Tony Blair's administration is developing a plan to restructure a new Chamber to replace the hereditary Peers in the House of Lords. Andrew Sullivan suggests that the contraction to a far smaller, more representative entity may eventually make "United Kingdom" seem as anachronistic as "Soviet Union" (Sullivan 1999, 78–79).

For the past fifty years we have seen the number of nation-states in the United Nations increase from the 74 members who signed the original charter in 1946 to 188 members today. The newly independent Baltic countries and former Soviet republics, plus the still evolving smaller independent units emerging from the collapse of Yugoslavia may eventually add to the number but decrease the average size of the nation-states in the world. Among the three most recent nations to join the UN is the incredibly small island of Nauru, with only eleven thousand people and 8.1 square miles. Smaller states may prosper more readily in the twenty-first century than they ever could before, as a consequence of the increased interdependence of all nation-states. Indeed, a cosmopolitan visionary like Vaclav Havel foresees the eventual abandonment of any extensive role for nation-states as a major development of the twenty-first century. In an address to the Canadian Senate and House of Commons in April 1999, he developed this point as follows: "The idol of state sovereignty must inevitably dissolve in a world that connects people, regardless of borders, through millions of links of integration ranging from trade, finance, and property, up to information links that impart a variety of universal notions and cultural patterns. In such a world blind love for one's own state inevitably turns into a dangerous anachronism" (Havel 1999, 26–27). Havel does not mean the nation-state will be abandoned, but rather that many of its functions will be taken away: *downward* from the national level by gradually transferring many of its tasks to the organs and structures of civil society, and *outward* to various regional, transnational, or global markets and organizations.

A small but interesting indicator of the future direction of global social organization is suggested by a meeting in November 1998 in Cambridge, Massachusetts. The meeting brought together one hundred young people, ten to sixteen years of age, from many countries to attend a global forum at the Media Laboratory at the Massachusetts Institute of Technology. These youngsters had access to the almost unlimited computer power at MIT and were funded by a Japanese magnate, Isao Okawa (chairman of a firm making business software and of another making video games). Okawa had agreed to contribute $27 million, one of the largest donations MIT had ever received, to build a "Center for Future Children" next door to the Media Lab. What did the children set about doing at such a forum? They were planning to create an on-line country, to be known as Nation1, where anyone, anywhere on the globe, could automatically become a citizen, so long as they were under nineteen years of age! High on their list of goals for such a new nation were: reduction of child labor worldwide; improvement of the environment across the globe; simplification of computer technology; and assurance that children learn real skills by engaging in actual real-time work—for example, by organizing and planning a global Earth Day on which children all over the world would plant trees (Goldberg 1998). Nation1 seemed a fanciful notion to the diplomats, World Bank officials, and corporate sponsors who attended the forum at which the young people presented their plans, but the entire occasion is symbolic of the trend Vaclav Havel foresees in the twenty-first century: the declining significance of identification with nation-states. These particular teenagers are, to be sure, hardly representative of their birth cohort, but they do suggest a tendency among those whose entire adult lives will be lived out in the twenty-first century. To them, as the *New York Times* reporter Carey Goldberg put it, even the Model of the United Nations "seemed so pallid, so retro, so . . . 20th century" (Goldberg 1998).

While not representative, the young people forming Nation1 may be what Vern Bengtson has called "forerunner pioneers" of their birth cohort, a minority whose values will be more widely shared in subsequent birth cohorts (Bengtson, Rosenthal, and Burton 1990), and consistent with Vaclav Havel's prediction concerning developments in the twenty-first century. It is highly likely that a significant proportion of corporate executives already share such a perspective, though few are as blunt as Alfred Zeien, CEO of Gillette Corporation, who says thinking in terms of national boundaries is old-fashioned: "[W]e treat the world as a single nation" (Zakaria 1998).

The urge to seek ties across national borders may reflect the vast expansion of knowledge of other countries and cultures that attends higher education, modern telecommunications, and the increasing globalization of the world's economies. There is another important factor at work as well. With the end of the Cold War, international friction has lessened and cooperation has increased between the United States and the former Soviet republics. Jean Elshtain (1987) has argued that patriotism and social cohesion is high when international tensions exist, but once international peace is attained, internal disharmony within a nation often follows. We can see a reflection of this process in social trends over recent years in Americans' trust and confidence in our major national institutions. Figure 1.1 provides data from the National Opinion Research Center's General Social Survey (GSS) on social trends in public confidence in a variety of major social institutions in the United States over a quarter-century, from 1972 to 1996. Three salient points are illustrated: first, the overall decline in the proportion of adults who feel a "great deal of confidence" in the six institutions represented in the graph; second, the press and the federal government (as represented by the executive branch and the Congress) are the institutions for which respondents hold the very lowest levels of confidence. Even in the 1970s and early '80s, fewer than one in four adults had high confidence in government or the press; by 1996, confidence had dropped to less than one in ten adults where Congress was concerned. Third, note the effect of the Gulf War in 1991, which heightened public confidence, dramatically where the military was concerned, but also concerning the federal government. But notice how short-lived this surge in public confidence was: within two years the downward trend reasserted itself. Change in the political party in control of either Congress or the White House had no effect on the trends shown, perhaps reflecting the great increase in the proportion of Americans who consider themselves political "independents," not partisans of one or the other major political party, and who are apt to crossover vote or simply stay away from the polls. Some political commentators suggest an even stronger point, as Katha Pollitt did in April 1996: "[H]ow much faith can a rational and disinterested person have in the set-up that produced our current crop of leaders? . . . Love your neighbor if you can, but forget civic trust. What we need is more civic skepticism" (Pollitt 1996, 9).

The GSS trend shown in figure 1.1 is consistent with other survey results gathered by the Gallup Organization and the University of Michigan National Election Studies. For example, the Michigan survey asked the question, "How much of the time do you trust the government in Washington to do the right thing: just about always, most of

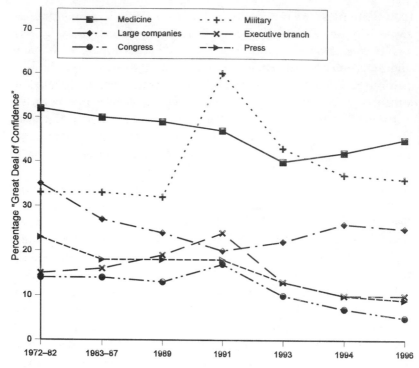

FIGURE 1.1. Trends in public confidence in selected American institutions, 1972–96. The data are from the NORC General Social Survey. The question reads, "I am going to name some institutions in this country. As far as the people running these institutions are concerned, would you say that you have a *great deal* of confidence, *only some* confidence, or *hardly any* confidence in them at all?" Base *N*s vary slightly from one survey to another but average 1,052 cases for individual years 1989, 1991, and 1993; 1,920 cases for 1994 and 1996. The data were aggregated across all surveys between 1972 and 1982, and between 1983 and 1987.

the time, only some of the time, or none of the time?" The percentage saying "all" or "most" of the time declined from 61% in 1968 to 33% in 1998, a remarkable shift when one remembers the degree to which the late 1960s was characterized by urban riots, counterculture movements, and the rise in antiwar sentiment. The Gallup Organization asked which of three institutions—Big Business, Big Labor, or Big Government—the public considered the "biggest threat to the country in the future." The number who responded "Big Government" increased from 35% in 1965 to 59% in 1998, a sharper increase than for Big Business—17% to 25%. For Big Labor, there was an actual decline—29% to 11% (Broder and Morin 1998).

Scholars and commentators on the condition of civil society in America have bemoaned this increasing distrust of and dissociation from government, particularly when discussing political participation by the citizenry, stressing the low turnout of eligible voters in national elections (e.g., only 39% in 1994). Sidney Verba and his associates (1995) report an average rate of decline in voting from the mid-1940s to the mid-1970s, so this trend is not just a recent phenomenon. Comparing their earlier study in 1967 with the GSS in 1987, Verba reports similar declines in voting in both presidential and local elections. Furthermore, the voting rate is lower in the United States than it is in Austria, the Netherlands, or the United Kingdom. The low turnout is particularly true of young Americans. Richard Thau, executive director of Third Millennium, a nonpartisan Generation-X advocacy group, suggests this generation's sentiments are well illustrated by bumper stickers he saw on New York City streets: "If I don't vote, will they go away?" (*Wall Street Journal Special Quarterly* 1999).

On the other hand, Verba and his political science associates point out that voting decline can be very misleading; it does not necessarily mean declines in *other* forms of political activity. Political participation can involve *time* (e.g., attending political meetings, marching in a protest parade), *money* (e.g., sending a check to a particular candidate, party, or a specific political advocacy group), or *skills* (e.g., contacting officials about a specific issue or working in a campaign with a politically active organization). When the United States is compared with other West European countries on these indicators of political participation, the United States shows *higher* rates: for example, 27% of the people in the United States have contacted public officials, versus an average of 11% in the four West European countries. Similar differences were found for campaign work and political meeting attendance. In yet another trend analysis of American data, Verba reports an increase between 1967 and 1987 in the percentage who gave money to a political candidate or cause (13% to 23%), and in the percentage who contacted a public official regarding a specific issue (11% doubling to 22%). When nonparticipants in any form of political activity were asked *why* they did not participate, the major reason they gave was "lack of time" (Verba, Schlozman, and Brady 1995, 129). As noted earlier in the discussion of work in America, time is a commodity in short supply, far more limited than money: one has to expend time on a daily basis, it cannot be "saved up" for later use as money can, and as Benjamin Hunnicutt points out, the trend toward a shorter work week ended by World War II in the United States (Hunnicutt 1988). Besides time pressures, a commonly offered explanation for not voting was "the important things in my life have nothing to do with politics."

A dim view of American politics is not something that is apt to disappear any time soon, if one notes the views of young college students in surveys over time—for example, annual surveys of college freshmen (300,000 students at more than 600 colleges) conducted by the UCLA Higher Education Research Institute. Their 1998 survey of the class of 2002 shows a very low proportion of freshmen think it important to "keep up with politics"—26%, compared to 58% in the survey conducted in 1966 (as reported in the *Wall Street Journal*, February 2, 1999). So too, Elinor Birkett's qualitative interviews with young conservative women in various regions of the United States shows highly negative views of national politics. Birkett describes these women in the following strong terms: "What defines their generation is less what they believe in than what they don't believe in: government. In their world, the federal government doesn't foment positive change: it foments problems. In post–Cold War America, the federal government has replaced the Soviet Union as the enemy" (Birkett 1998, 31).

Americans' negative view of politics and suspicion concerning the integrity of political leaders may be part of a more generalized perspective of growing distrust toward other people in general, a trend shown not only in surveys of adults in recent years, but also in surveys of young people just graduating from high school: for example, data from the Monitoring the Future Survey of High School Students shows a decline in such generalized "trust toward other people," from 35% in 1976 to a mere 19% in 1992 (Smith 1997), a reflection perhaps of the unintended consequences of parental concern for safety discussed in a previous section of this chapter.

Voluntary Association Membership

Within the domain of community, membership in voluntary associations is an indicator of the vitality of civil society. Many scholars and social commentators have claimed that membership in all manner of voluntary associations has declined over the past several decades: fewer adults belong to the Jaycees, the Elks, Kiwanis Clubs, Boy Scouts, the League of Women Voters, Lions Clubs, Parent-Teacher Associations

(PTAs), and numerous other formal organizations (Council on Civil Society 1998; Dionne 1998; Eberly 1998; Ehrenhalt 1995; Etzioni 1993; Fukuyama 1995, 1999; Glendon and Blankenhorn 1995; Hodgkinson and Weitzman 1993; Independent Sector 1996; National Council on Civic Renewal 1998; Poponoe 1995; Putnam 1993b, 1995a,1995b; Wilson 1993; Wolfe 1998; Wright 1994; Wuthnow 1991, 1994, 1998; Wuthnow et al. 1990). However, the actual empirical evidence is often either at variance with the claims of some of these scholars, or subject to an interpretation that differs from theirs. Let me cite some examples and suggest some reasons the evidence can be misleading:

1. Parental involvement in schools. The PTA is often cited as a prime example of declining membership over the past thirty years. The organization's Chicago headquarters reports that membership peaked in 1962, with 12.1 million members, falling off to a low of 5.3 million members by 1981. Since these were precisely the years during which the birth rate was falling, one interpretation of the decline is simply that young adults had fewer children to draw them into involvement with a PTA. On the other hand, by the mid-1990s less than one in four public and private kindergarten through twelfth grade schools had affiliates of the national PTA. It turns out, however, that many parent groups across the country simply de-affiliated from the traditional PTA and formed independent, locally focused PTOs—Parent-Teacher Organizations. Everett Ladd did a special survey of a sample of public and private schools in Connecticut and Kansas and found virtually *all* the schools had active parent-teacher associations, the majority of which had no affiliation with the national, Chicago-based PTA (Ladd 1999a, 1999b). Other surveys by the Gallup Organization and also the Princeton Survey Research Associates poll show similar evidence of high parental involvement in their children's schools.

2. Youth organizations. The evidence is strong that membership in the Boy Scouts has declined dramatically over recent decades, but the reason is that there are now more competitors to the Boy Scouts for youth involvement. For example, the U.S. Youth Soccer Association, by the mid-1990s, boasted over 2.5 million players and half a million adult volunteers (Ladd 1999a). Girl Scouts and athletic teams for girls, rarely mentioned by those claiming a rapid decline in voluntary association membership, have actually experienced an expanding membership, with more girls and more adult volunteers in the 1990s than in the 1950s. With increased funding for athletic programs for girls in schools and colleges, women's sports has greatly expanded, as witness

the development of and enthusiastic public response to the Women's National Basketball Association (WNBA) and women's soccer competitions in the 1998 and 1999 seasons.

3. Bowling and other adult sports. Bowling merits special mention because of the widespread discussion of Robert Putnam's essay "Bowling Alone" (Putnam 1995a; see Skocpol 1996 and Stengel 1996 for critiques in addition to Ladd's referred to above). Putnam is correct that there has been a decline in bowling *leagues,* but the reason is that many such leagues were sponsored by local industries and unions in an effort to stimulate firm and union loyalty, a pattern now largely defunct. What Putnam does *not* mention is that a typical bowling night in the past was a "boys' night out," when men joked and drank while bowling with male friends or co-workers. By the mid-1990s, bowling was not done "alone" or just with male friends, but increasingly with spouses, teenage children, and other families. Katha Pollitt suggests the change can be described as one of "happy progress," from a "drink-sodden night of spouse avoidance . . . to temperate and spontaneous fun with one's intimate friends and relations" (Pollitt 1996, 9). Note too that in John Robinson and Geoffrey Godbey's time budget survey (1997), only 4% of the respondents reported that they had bowled in the previous two weeks. The sport does not have a high priority in leisure-time practice of many adults. Tennis and golf remain strong favorites, no longer restricted to private clubs for upper- and middle-class adults; less well off players now flock to the increased number of public courts. Local Little League and adult baseball and football teams continue strong in communities all across the United States.

4. Fitness regimens. Also to be reckoned with as competitors to associational membership are fitness regimens. This "no pain, no gain" lifestyle was a major theme in the 1980s and typically involved individuals or pairs engaging in jogging, running, weightlifting, or swimming, keeping track of distance and time to chart increased fitness. For a while it seemed that medical studies confirmed the benefits of a vigorously active lifestyle, but Robinson and Godfrey report that the love affair Americans have with fitness may be on the decline, as the public gets mixed signals regarding the risks of injury from sporting activities, such as joint strain in the knees and feet from jogging, and muscle damage from weightlifting. As a result, more Americans by the late 1990s were moving away from very vigorous exercise in favor of milder forms on a less frequent schedule. College-educated adults had been the heaviest participants in vigorous regular exercise, but by the mid-1990s they

were clearly departing from the "no pain, no gain" philosophy of fitness (Robinson and Godbey 1997, 183–84). Interestingly, our analysis of time devoted to volunteer work in chapter 3 found that those in "excellent" health were *less* likely to devote time to volunteer work than those with lower ratings in health, perhaps because the former were more dedicated to active sports, while the latter took to the more sedentary nature of most volunteer service.

5. Decentralized organizations. Within traditional voluntary associations, there has been a decline of complex organizational structures. Groups such as the League of Women Voters, the American Legion, or the Kiwanis Clubs typically had tiers at the city, state, and national levels. In earlier periods of our history, these three-tier federated organizations served useful purposes: providing hierarchic ladders that members could work their way up systematically, as they gained increasing experience and commitment to the organization; and disseminating information from a national headquarters so that local chapters could gain advice and knowledge of what other chapters around the country were doing and how, thus sharing experiences widely (Skocpol 1992, Skocpol and Fiorina 1999). Theda Skocpol argues that participation in these federated associations provided men and women in the past with dual involvement as local citizens and as participants on the national stage. Strikingly, many of these federations not only tailored their efforts to particular local conditions, but coordinated their campaigns at higher levels, an effort designed to have an impact on society as a whole. Nor did they see any gap between Christian morality and local voluntarism with public commitments and in cooperation with state and national governments. This profile held for the abolition and suffrage movements in the nineteenth and early twentieth centuries, and for the Women's Christian Temperance Union, the General Federation of Women's Clubs, and the National Congress of Mothers. As Skocpol put it, "people could be part of something immediate—with fellow locals they knew every day—and part of grander endeavors at the same time" (Skocpol 1999). In an interesting sense, the "flattening" of voluntary associations, from the three-tier organizational structures to more flexible horizontal organizations, mirrors the flattening that has occurred in corporate organizations, and also the efforts of the federal government in recent years to decentralize by sending funds to the states for the implementation of social services. William Whyte's *Organization Man* (1956) and David Riesman's "outer-directed conformists" in his book *The Lonely Crowd* (1950) capture the ethos of the

1950s; they are clearly no longer appropriate metaphors for contemporary life.

So too, as Robert Wuthnow reminds us (1998), the equivalent of the 1950s Organization Man was the Club Woman: in the 1950s there were an estimated 100,000 such clubs in the United States. In the decades since the 1950s women have been far more attracted to activist organizations than to what many view as stodgy, old-line women's clubs; Women's Equity Action League, the National Organization for Women, a variety of environmental watchdog groups, Mothers against Drunk Driving, pro-life or pro-choice organizations, and so forth have far greater appeal than a local women's club or the League of Women Voters (Sheard 1995).

There are two important points to be made here. First, it is misleading to focus too narrowly on formal voluntary associations when one's concern is for civic involvement and political participation. Millions of people become activists in social and political movements that exist without any formal voluntary association membership. Many such movements began and grew at an astonishing rate during the 1960s and 1970s—the civil rights movement, the women's rights movement, the consumer movement, the environmental movement, and the anti–Vietnam War movement, to cite the major ones. Participation in such social movements does not require membership in a voluntary association. Rallies and parades, for example, are occasional events that attract large audiences with no necessary affiliation with the organizations that planned and ran the events. In the movement I know best, the feminist movement in the late 1960s and the 1970s, countless numbers of women were in small consciousness-raising groups or caucuses within professional associations, with no necessary ties to major national organizations like the National Organization for Women; abortion rallies were organized by leaders in pro-choice or pro-life organizations, but those in attendance often had no formal affiliation with those associations. If asked only about what voluntary associations they belonged to, such participants might have reported nothing of their most important civic and political actions. In my panel study of the delegates to the first-ever national women's conference in Houston in 1977, it was already clear that a marked contrast in the nature of political involvement differentiated younger from older delegates: the older delegates had an extensive array of organizational memberships (an astonishing average of twelve!). The younger delegates, by contrast, were not "joiners" and belonged to relatively few formal clubs or organizations. Instead, they reported a great number of direct political actions on issues of concern to them and a preference for informal peer groups (Rossi 1982).

Second, the entire "third sector" of nonprofit organizations, including foundations and nonprofit firms, are as important as any number of community voluntary associations of the type studied by those concerned for civil society. There are hundreds of thousands of Americans who take jobs in the nonprofit sector at lower rates of pay than they could earn in the for-profit sector precisely because their priorities are to be of service to others in need (Goddeeris and Weisbrod 1997). In the same panel study of delegates to the national women's conference cited above, I found that over 70% of the delegates claimed they contributed a great deal "on their jobs" to improving the status of women (Rossi 1982). Many of the delegates worked for nonprofit organizations or in civil service jobs, and many in professional occupations had largely female clients, patients, or students. We will report below that employees in nonprofit organizations and civil servants are also more likely to do volunteer work apart from their jobs than are employees of for-profit firms.

Lester Salamon has studied intensively the entire nonprofit sector in American society and described its sharp expansion, largely since 1960. For example, from a survey of nonprofit human service organizations in sixteen American communities he studied in 1982, he found that 65% had been created since 1960, a phenomenon not unique to the United States but found in all the major Western democracies; Salamon reports that the number of private associations also skyrocketed in France, Italy, and Germany during these years. The Green Movement in particular experienced a phenomenal growth on the continent, sufficient for the German Green Party to become a major national force and the Swedish Green Party in 1988 to become the first new party to enter the Swedish Parliament in seventy years. In that same decade, Italian environmental groups became powerful enough by the election campaign of November 1987 to end the Italian nuclear energy program (Salamon 1995, 244–49, and the European references he cites). In a telling generalization, Salamon also suggests that in the United States for much of the past fifty years or more, both the political Right and the political Left have tended to downplay nonprofit institutions, "the Left to justify the expansion of state involvement in the social welfare field and the Right to justify attacks on the state as destroyers of such 'intermediary institutions'" (Salamon 1995, 245).

This is not the place for any extended discussion of the importance of this third sector in American society (the most useful references on the topic are Clotfelter 1992; Goddeeris and Weisbrod 1997; Lenkowsky 1996; Salamon 1995; Sealander 1997; Smith and Lipsky 1993; Smucker 1998; Wolpert 1993), but those concerned for social and civic responsibility in our society should note a few important points relevant to the broad issues addressed in this introductory chapter:

1. There has never been a time in American history when government and nonprofit institutions were not closely interconnected. Even before the American Revolution, colonial governments gave financial assistance to private educational institutions, a pattern that persisted well into the nineteenth century: the state of Massachusetts used a special tax to help support Harvard College, as did the state of Connecticut for Yale; significant income to major private hospitals in the nineteenth century came from the government; and in the early history of private social service agencies, government support played an even more significant role. For example, in New York City, private benevolent institutions handled the care of prisoners and paupers, but increasingly with city funds—a pattern characteristic of the District of Columbia as well, where about *half* of the public funds allocated for assistance to the poor went to private charitable institutions (see Salamon 1995, 84–86, and his references for greater detail on this history). We will be learning a great deal about the history of close connections between nonprofit organizations and the state as the research from the Harvard Civic Engagement Project becomes published. As Theda Skocpol pithily puts it, pundits and scholars are wrong to "presume that our country's civic past was *aseptically local*" (Skocpol 1999). So too are political conservatives in error when advocating local voluntarism as something new, apart from or in opposition to government; what they advocate is not a return to the past, but a break with it.

2. There are some 400,000 nonprofit organizations in the United States, with a total annual revenue of $600 billion, employing 6% of the labor force engaged in support of educational, welfare, health, cultural, and other services. Only $125 billion of this total comes from private donations; $475 billion comes from fees for services and from government grants and contracts (Wolpert 1993, 17).

3. Nonprofit organizations are, to an important extent, part of a "shadow" federal government. Much has been said and written by President Clinton and Vice President Gore about the reduction in the size of the federal government. In 1996, the most recent year for which

there are reasonably good statistics, the federal government was in fact some ten times as large as the head count President Clinton used when he announced "the end of big government": full-time federal civil servants totaled 1.8 million, uniformed military personnel, 1.5 million, plus there were .85 million postal workers. But beyond that is the shadow federal workforce: 2.4 million federal grant–created employees, 4.7 million state and local mandate–encumbered employees, and 5.6 million contract-created workers (Light 1999). Nonprofit organizations figure large in the latter two categories because state and local governments contract with nonprofit agencies to provide the services mandated by funds the states get from the federal government (Smith and Lipsky 1993). Under the modern welfare state, the federal government *finances,* the state and local governments *administer,* and the nonprofit organizations actually *deliver* the *majority* of the services involved. Drawing on data from IRS and Census Bureau files, Lester Salamon calculates that only 23% of the revenues of nonprofit organizations came from private charitable giving by individuals, corporations, and foundations; the remainder came from public government funds.

4. The increasing dependence of nonprofit organizations on government funds has some serious consequences for the nonprofits: Stephen Smith and Michael Lipsky point out that under pressures to secure and maintain funding and in response to the oversight demands of government agencies, the nonprofits are professionalizing and becoming more businesslike, but often at the expense of diminished capability for being adequately responsive to their clients or for fostering unique community values. "All too often the rise of contract income has transformed nonprofit organizations, literally, into agents of the state" (Smith and Lipsky 1993, 72). Many faith-based community agencies have had to drop staff and volunteers and hire others to comply with the nondiscrimination policies of the government (Olasky 1996a, 1996b). The required professional social work orientation often contradicts the values of community organizations like battered women's shelters or programs for the poor or homeless that were founded on philosophies of self-help, political action, and lay control of services. Smith and Lipsky conclude that "critics who would see the private nonprofit sector as representing an important alternate to state action must recognize that the sector is significantly compromised in its ability to offer clear alternatives" (Smith and Lipsky 1993, 206–7).

5. One last point concerning nonprofit organizations: there has been

an increasing trend toward conversion to for-profit status. This is particularly the case for HMOs, but also a trend for prisons, "privatized" through management contracts, and public schools in places like Minneapolis and Hartford, put under private sector management by firms like the Edison Project or the Apollo Group, Inc. Several factors contribute to this conversion trend: for one, though nonprofits generally possess tax advantages, they are legally restricted from distributing any profits to managers connected with the organization. Managers with greater concern for finances are replacing those whose visions were of public service. Second, nonprofit status is desirable only when assets are low; as assets mount, managers and boards face increasing temptation to distribute some of the market value to themselves—something they cannot do as a nonprofit organization. Federal and state laws require assets of a nonprofit to be directed toward charitable activities. Third, managers in a converted nonprofit can purchase ownership shares at a low rate before the organization is valued in the stock market, thereby profiting greatly when the organization goes public. John Goddeeris and Burton Weisbrod (1997, 26) point out that this occurred in California in the early 1980s, when directors and managers of converted HMOs quickly became millionaires as a result of the capital gains on stock in the new companies. The greatest criticism concerning these conversions is that they so often serve little or no worthwhile social goal: "[T]ransferring control to a private enterprise organization presumptively shifts resources from an organization with some degree of social mission to one with a mission of profit" (Goddeeris and Weisbrod 1997, 32).

Cutting across the various political and civic domains of social life is a more general process of change toward more informality in associational life all told. Just as casual dress is now prevalent in workplaces and when traveling, so too institutional structures have more fluid boundaries. These changes are ably traced in Robert Wuthnow's most recent book, *Loose Connections* (1998). Wuthnow argues that the increasing porousness of American society makes it harder for established civic organizations to function effectively. Wuthnow links the concept of "loose connections" to the blurring of the boundaries of family and work and political action. Less stable marriages, having children outside wedlock, and increased cohabitation blur the lines between who are kin and who are not kin; the increase in opportunities to work at home or at networked suburban satellite offices invites the blurring of the boundaries between family and job. Work often overlaps with leisure as more people wear beepers at social events, carry cell phones to ball games, and use laptop computers in airport terminals and hotels. Political activity has also changed: telephone trees and group e-mail lists permit political activists to quickly inform a thousand others to write, phone, or e-mail a congressional representative on some issue.

All such trends and opportunities combine to permit people, goods, information, and other resources to flow across the boundaries of family, work, and politics. Together these forces press for the decline of formal civic organizations in favor of new, innovative forms of groups, networks, and organizations, often established on a short-term basis to deal with one specific issue. This model also makes recruitment easier for a time-pressed public; busy adults find it far easier to fit a short term of service into their routines than to join a longstanding organization and then submit to social influence to take on one responsibility after another over a long stretch of time.

Despite these new patterns of civic participation, Verba and his associates (1995) report that United States remains the leader among Western nations in the degree of formal organizational membership: 76%, compared to 50% in West Germany and only 26% in Italy. Francis Fukuyama (1999) reviews comparable trends in Europe in the World Values Survey, directed by Ronald Inglehart of the University of Michigan, and makes the interesting observation that compared to European countries, the United States is unique in one respect: it shows the highest level of distrust toward institutions while also having the highest rates of membership in voluntary associations. Whether one views this as surprising or not may depend on an understanding of the changes in the types of associations contemporary Americans belong to. Macro-institutional labels—Big Business, the executive branch of government, Big Labor—are highly nonspecific and very distant from an ordinary citizen. One could well feel distrustful toward such distant abstract entities in preference for pouring one's energy and time into known, small, local groups. To cite Francis Fukuyama's useful construct, the "radius of trust" for many people remains in the relatively narrow social world of a local community; others have a very extended radius of trust that embraces far-flung national or even international organizations and causes. In our time, perhaps those with the widest radius of trust, embracing all humankind, are motivated by deeply felt religious beliefs (Leege and Kellstedt 1993; Thiemann 1996). As discussed above, MIDUS data analysis in chapter 7 shows that growing up in a religious home is a strong predictor of adult generativity and social responsibility to others beyond the circle of family and friends. ▸

In his study of middle-class adults, Alan Wolfe (1998) reports what at first seems a contradictory profile: his informants say people have less and less time for voluntary activity but then proceed to describe all kinds of social activities and association memberships in their own lives, more in civic and religious organizations than in social and fraternal types of organizations. Commenting on Wolfe's finding, Fukuyama seems to find it strange (1999, 55) that so few of Wolfe's subjects were members of social and fraternal organizations since they report high levels of social activities. I suspect Wolfe's subjects may have no need to belong to social and fraternal organizations because they already have a rich informal network of people they share social activities with; hence their associational membership is greater in civic and religious groups.

Studies of community involvement and participation tend to be one of two types: either rich, in-depth, qualitative studies that provide interesting profiles of individual lives, such as Alan Wolfe's study and many of Robert Wuthnow's books, or they report the distribution of responses to single items across several points in time to chart social trends, such as Fukuyama's recent work comparing trends across several developed societies (1999). Occasionally, as in the Verba, Schlozman, and Brady study of political behavior, one finds bivariate analyses that report variance by age, sex, or income. One of the strengths of the MIDUS analysis in the community domain is the fact that we developed multi-item scores and scales on several dimensions of community involvement and subjected them to multivariate analyses. By so doing one can demonstrate the *array* of factors associated with one or another dimension of community involvement, as well as the relative, independent strength of each of the significant explanatory factors.

Volunteer Work

Among the best sources of information on the giving and volunteering patterns of Americans are the surveys the Independent Sector, working in conjunction with the Gallup Organization, has conducted every two years since 1988. The following results, from their 1995 survey of adults eighteen or older and from their 1996 survey of youngsters twelve to seventeen years of age (Hodgkinson and Weitzman 1996; Independent Sector 1996), provide a profile of the extent of volunteer work reported:

1. In 1995, 93 million adults served as volunteers, representing 49%

of the adult population. The teenage sample surveyed in 1996 included 13.3 million teenagers who volunteered, representing 59% of their age group, a higher rate of volunteering than among adults.

2. Adult volunteers said they served an average of 4.2 hours a week. Teenagers volunteered for a slightly shorter period of time, 3.5 hours per week. Retired older-American volunteers exceed this time commitment by a good deal, one in four doing volunteer work for ten or more hours a week.

3. The amount of adult volunteer time in 1995 totaled 20.3 billion hours, with a dollar value of $202 billion. Teens volunteered for 2.4 billion hours, for a total worth of $7.7 billion. David Smith (1997) estimates that volunteer workers contribute 28 million full-time equivalents to the U.S. domestic economy each year.

4. Recruitment is a critical inducement to volunteering. Of teenagers who were asked to volunteer, 93% actually did so, compared to 29% of the teens who were not asked. Similarly high proportions of adults volunteer if asked; those asked to volunteer were four times more likely to do so than those who were not asked.

On a question that reads, "Do you, yourself, happen to be involved in any charity or social service activities, such as helping the poor, the sick, or the elderly?" the Gallup Organization surveys over the years since 1977 show a steady increase in the proportion of adults who say yes, they have done so: from 26% in the 1977 survey, to 39% a decade later in 1987, to a high of 46% in 1991 (Wuthnow 1998, 253). ABC/*Washington Post* polls have shown a similar increase over time in the proportion of the public reporting having done some kind of volunteer work, from 44% in 1984 to 55% in 1997 (Ladd 1999b). As will be reported in chapter 3, these levels of volunteer work are of roughly the same magnitude in the 1995 MIDUS survey, despite slight differences in the questions used and the restriction of the MIDUS sample to adults twenty-five to seventy-four years of age (thus excluding young adults eighteen to twenty-four or older adults over seventy-four, who are included in the Gallup surveys).

Wuthnow's Economic Values Survey shows the correlation between type of employment and involvement in volunteer service. Using the same Gallup question cited in the previous paragraph, Wuthnow found that 20% of those working in for-profit firms report having done some volunteer work, 36% of those in civil service jobs, and a full half, 50%, of employees of nonprofit organizations (Wuthnow 1994). Note, too, that three-fourths of *all* volunteering is performed in conjunction with nonprofit organizations (Hodgkinson and Weitzman 1996). From a 1989 survey that forms the basis of the analysis in Wuthnow's book *Acts of Compassion* (1991), we learn further that adults draw on a different constellation of values for their volunteer activity than for the work they do for a living: Volunteer activity is strongly associated with a general commitment to being helpful to others, valuing religious commitments, and high levels of family involvement. For most adults, except for those in occupations like the clergy or counselors in nonprofit social service agencies, these factors play a minimal role in their job commitments.

One of the interesting findings reported in chapter 11 is that a significant predictor of volunteer service among adult women is a *low* rate of job satisfaction. With volunteers in high demand for tasks of a very varied nature, and with most women working in routinized clerical, retail, or factory jobs, it is understandable why many such women would find volunteer work more gratifying than the work they do to support themselves and their families. On a related point, Anne Colby reports in chapter 12 many examples of how individuals concentrate on selected aspects of quite ordinary jobs in order to help themselves feel that they are assisting others and contributing to the general welfare.

One of the more telling examples of the changes taking place in community involvement in the United States is reported by Robert Wuthnow: a *decline* in organizational membership but an *increase* in volunteer service. Between 1974 and 1991, membership in at least one organization declined from 74% to 56%, whereas individual volunteering increased from 26% to 46% between 1977 and 1991 (Wuthnow 1998, 76–77). One contributing factor to this profile may be the resistance to change on the part of traditional organizations. If in the past they tended to hold group meetings during the day, it may be an institutional lag on their part to not think in terms of evening and weekend meetings to accommodate the increased employment rate of women and the prevalence of dual-earning couples with complex domestic agendas. Penny Becker reports a recent survey of pastors of congregations in four upstate New York communities showing that close to *half* of them had experimented with the timing of worship services and fellowship meetings (Becker 1998). Both the increase in competing choices for the use of nonwork time and the rigidity of adhering to old organizational customs may be greater deterrents to individual volunteering than sheer time pressure per se. Penny Becker and Heather Hofmeister, in other analyses from the same NYS survey ($N = 1,006$), report that they found no evidence to support the theory that dual-earning couples, even those working unusually long hours, cut back on community membership and civic participation. In sum, they found no support for the "time bind" thesis in their data on local community involvement (Becker and Hofmeister 1999).

Adults currently engaged in volunteer work show a continuity with their activity levels as youths, as measured by youth group membership, participation in religious organizations or in student government, or other adolescent volunteer work (Hodgkinson and Weitzman 1996). With more detail on the quality of life in MIDUS respondents' families of origin available for analysis, chapter 7 shows a range of early factors that predispose for adult involvement in volunteer service.

Most of the data on volunteer service reported above charts volunteer service over time, but the increases noted are subject to varied interpretations. To a degree the increases may be explained by the aging of the population and the increase in educational attainment of Americans, because both age and education are positively correlated with volunteer service. It requires more fine-grained micro-level data analysis to ferret out more specific factors that affect the level of volunteer work or the factors that explain individual participation over time.

John Wilson and Marc Musick provide a new perspective on such issues. For one, they propose a theory of volunteer work that embraces the *resources* people bring to volunteer work, the *rewards* they derive from it, and the *context* in which the service is performed (Wilson and Musick 1997). Second, they report a first effort to explain what characteristics determine continued attachment to volunteer work (Wilson and Musick 1999). To this end, they use data from the Americans' Changing Lives panel study to test the significance of the three dimensions specified in their theory of volunteering by exploring change in or continuity of volunteer work in 1989 (the second wave of the panel study) compared to the volunteer work reported in 1986 (the first wave).

The *resources* part of their theory as applied to attachment to volunteering is supported by the data: the likelihood of remaining in the volunteer workforce is greater for those with more education; those with greater formal and informal social interaction with family, friends, and neighbors; and those with children in the household (the more children, the greater the attachment to volunteer service, particularly among women). Interestingly, worsening health between the two waves did *not* predict withdrawal from volunteer service, which the authors interpret on the grounds that volunteer work typically does not involve heavily taxing labor, so declining health does not affect participation in volunteer work as it might labor force participation. Those who reported putting in more hours on the job in the second wave compared to the first showed a reduction of the hours contributed to volunteer service, if not a total withdrawal.

Analysis of the *context* of the volunteer service showed one firm result: more than any other context, *church-related* work shows persistence of involvement across the two waves of the study. It is not the intensity of religious belief that matters in volunteer attachment, however, but regularity of church attendance, which may reinforce the commitment to volunteer service through at least weekly association with others engaged in similar efforts.

The results of the panel study provided only weak support for the *rewards* component of Wilson and Musick's theory. Whether volunteer tasks had been completed or not was judged not to affect any change in volunteer service. The number of hours volunteered, as a measure of commitment, did predict greater continued attachment: the more hours respondents were contributing at wave one, the greater the likelihood they were still volunteering at wave two. Enjoying the work had no effect on attachment, and being satisfied with the work done somehow *decreased* attachment.

As others have done, Wilson and Musick emphasize the point that a great deal of productive work performed in the United States goes unrecognized and uncounted by conventional measures of regular employment: labor in the home or in nonprofit community organizations is ignored while market work is recognized and honored (Herzog and Morgan 1992; Tilly and Tilly 1994). Furthermore, the consolidation of private firms through mergers, and the geographic distance that often separates corporate headquarters from working plants, must carry some responsibility for the changed character of civic involvement. As Wuthnow points out, these developments have made it hard for nonprofit organizations to collaborate with corporations in local community projects; hence his judgement is that "the corporate sector is deeply implicated in the changing nature of civic involvement. The unraveling of communities, families, and commitment to service organizations is as much attributable to markets as it is to morals" (Wuthnow 1998, 214).

Since the 1980s there have been several efforts to stimulate more community service, particularly among young people. Advocates of such movements claim that community service can infuse a self-centered generation with a civic ethos, thus decreasing the generation's civic disengagement. It is questionable, however, if *requiring* community service is the route to go: Detroit high school students are now required to put in two hundred hours of community service before graduation; Atlanta students have a seventy-five-hour minimum requirement (Boyte and Kari 1996). To *require* such a service may pave the way to future service for some students, but build resistance and resentment for other students simply because the service is not voluntarily offered. Harry Boyte and Nancy Kari point out that the kinds of service these students engage in are individual voluntary efforts: working in food banks or homeless shelters, helping in nursing homes or hospitals, tutoring projects, and so forth. They argue for more cooperative projects for young people that involve hands-on creative activities, not doing for others as individuals but actual creative labor through public work. The reasoning here is to counter the American excessive focus on *individual* contributions with pooled efforts in collaborative *communal* endeavors. An example is a team of AmeriCorps young people in Bozeman, Montana, that set up a program of public work for themselves under the guidance of adults with the appropriate skills. In the course of a year the Bozeman young people retrieved 110 miles of wilderness trails, built 8 disability accessible playgrounds, planted 1,500 trees, repaired 15 senior citizen homes, restored streams, and repaired cavern tunnels built by the Civilian Conservation Corps in the 1930s (Boyte and Kari 1996, 198). There is little question that young people who participate in programs like AmeriCorps, particularly if they are as active and creative in the projects they undertake as the Bozeman group was, are highly likely to remain active in community volunteer service during their adulthood, as the Independent Sector survey of adult volunteers' youthful profile suggested.

But AmeriCorps is a small program that has involved only tens of thousands of the millions of young people of their age cohort. For many of the rest of their age group, nonschool hours are more likely to be spent on part-time jobs in retail stores and restaurants in the malls all over the country, earning money as a means to the end of personal consumption. Peering into the future at the new look for malls that developers are now working on is not encouraging. For example, the SONY Corporation is currently building a new complex in San Francisco, Metreon, that will combine shops, theaters, restaurants, hi-tech video games, and two stadium-size exhibit halls—The Ways Things Work, and Where the Wild Things Are. The aim of the developers is a bid for "the leisure time of the shopping class!" as New York Times reporter Leslie Kaufman put it (1999). The teenagers and adults who frequent such mega-malls may get some physical exercise, but they will be as much passive onlookers as they are at home watching TV, a video movie, or surfing the Web.

Financial Contributions

The literature on civic participation in terms of contributing time in the form of volunteer service to community organizations is rich, as illustrated by the numerous examples from many surveys reported in the previous section. By comparison, the literature on individual contributions of money is sparse. I have found no published empirical study based on a representative sample of the population that informs us about the extent to which individuals contribute financial assistance to others, apart from family members. We know a great deal about the level of voting, what differentiates a voter from a nonvoter, and for whom people vote. Similarly, we can profile volunteers' individual characteristics, something of their motivation, and how they are distributed by type of organization. By comparison, any overview of the state of financial contributions to community organizations and charitable causes must rely on aggregate statistics rather than individual data from national surveys. This is one of the merits of the MIDUS survey, for we asked respondents to estimate how much money they gave in an average month to particular family members (children or grandchildren, parents, in-laws, other kin, and close friends) and to a variety of community organizations and causes (religious groups, political organizations or causes, or "any other" organizations, causes, or charities, including donations made through monthly payroll deductions). Analyses of such financial contributions are reported in chapters 3 and 11, using data from the MIDUS survey, and in chapter 4, using data from the eight-day time budget study.

THE DESIGN OF MIDUS ON SOCIAL RESPONSIBILITY
AND THE ORGANIZATION OF THIS VOLUME
Design of MIDUS

This volume's focus, social responsibility, is one of the three primary dimensions the MacArthur research network considered critical to an assessment of adult development with particular attention to the middle years of the life course. The two other primary dimensions are physical and mental health, and psychological well-being. This triad of concerns reflects the interdisciplinary approach we considered essential to understanding human behavior, consistent with our underlying bio-psychosocial theoretical perspective. Many professional journal articles and books have been published by members of the research network, and still others are in the process of being written. Some have a primary focus on physical and mental health, others on psychological well-being, others on specific aspects of social responsibility. Our major goal, however, was not to produce separate analyses on each of the three outcome criteria, but wherever possible and relevant, to pull together into the same analysis framework measures of health, well-being, and social responsibility. The various aspects of human behavior are intricately interrelated, not discrete in the way the social behavioral disciplines historically have presented them. The state of one's health affects one's psychological well-being, and both together may set limits on one's ability to contribute to the welfare of others. But so too, social involvement in caring and doing for others affects psychological well-being, which in turn may improve physical and mental health. Consequently, although the formal title and major focus in this volume is on social responsibility, we draw upon measures of health and well-being in the analyses in many chapters.

The MacArthur research network had a primary interest in adult development during the middle years of the life course, a phase of life defined in various ways, but at a minimum, the years from forty to sixty. In order to chart not merely changes during these two decades of life, but to compare them with young and old adults, the sample consists of respondents between twenty-five and seventy-four years of age. We excluded those under twenty-five in order to concentrate on young adults who are relatively well established in work and family status, and we excluded adults older than seventy-four to concentrate on the elderly who were as a group still healthy and active. Age takes on very special significance in this volume on social responsibility because almost all the literature reviewed in this introductory chapter gave either *no* or *very little* attention to adult development. Even those who charted social trends over time rarely mentioned, much less controlled for, changes in age distribution in the aging populations surveyed in Western nations. As will be seen in numerous chapters in this volume, there is no uniformity of behavior or of subjective ratings of self or of contribution to others across the life course: age matters greatly on all the topics analyzed in this volume.

A similar point holds on sex and gender issues. One rarely encounters serious theoretical or empirical attention to whether men and women are similar or different in their participation in community life, with the exception of some attention to the increased participation of women in the labor force over the past several decades. This omission is less prevalent in the literature on civil society than is the neglect of age, but it is nonetheless widespread. So too, except for studies of voting behavior, the effect of social class or educational attainment is given little focused attention. As the reader will be made keenly aware, all the empirical analyses reported in this volume give major attention to the three significant demographic variables of age, sex, and educational attainment.

A conventional approach to the design of a study on social responsibility could well have been restricted to community participation: membership in voluntary associations, time devoted to volunteer work, how obligated adults felt to civic duties, how much of a financial contribution they made to charitable causes, church, and political organizations, or some combination of these dimensions of social responsibility. To so limit the study, however, would predictably have provided a very limited view of social responsibility in American society, and one that would in addition have been class-biased, because we already know that both money and time given to community organizations is greatest among those with sufficient income, reputation, and educational attainment to be either recruited or voluntarily contribute in these ways. We assumed that even more important as indicators of social responsibility was doing well in one's family and work roles. Hence the design of MIDUS included comparable measures in the domains of family and work to those developed for the domain of community. Also important is that our conception of family is not limited to co-residents in a household, but enlarged to embrace adult grown children, grandchildren, parents, or in-laws as well.

Within these three domains of life—family, work, and community—we measured various dimensions: (1) the underlying normative obligations adults express; (2) their involvement in providing care to others through listening, comforting, or giving advice and social support, or through hands-on caregiving to family members or close friends; and (3) in the domains of family and community, how much financial assistance adults gave to family members or to community organizations. Table 3.1 provides descriptions of the domains and dimensions, and details the items, scores, and scales developed for the analysis of social responsibility. Details on the sample and the response rate of the study appear in the appendix.

A survey designed by twelve major researchers from diverse fields necessarily involves a good deal of negotiation and compromise. Had all the network members gotten all the measures they wished, it would have taken a respondent a full day to provide the data we sought! We conducted six pilot surveys in advance of the design of MIDUS, testing many candidate items to measure new constructs or to revise old ones. Factor analysis of such items in the pilot surveys often permitted us to forward only certain items for inclusion in MIDUS, items that explained 90% or more of the variance resulting from the longer battery. This was the case, for example, for our scale on generativity: from thirteen items in a pilot survey, six emerged that explained 93% of the variance on the thirteen-item scale. The same procedure applied to Carol Ryff's six scales on psychological well-being; only shortened versions of them were included in the MIDUS instrument.

Despite the compromises made, the MIDUS instrument was nonetheless a lengthy one: a half-hour telephone interview, supplemented by two self-administered questionnaires mailed to respondents, which took anywhere from one to two hours or more for respondents to fill out. In addition, funds were made available for several spin-off follow-up studies to provide more depth to constructs measured in MIDUS itself. These results appear in three chapters in this volume: chapter 4 charts temporal patterns in social responsibility based on data from the eight-day time study designed by Ron Kessler and Don Almeida; chapter 9 uses data from a study designed by Hazel Markus and Carol Ryff to explore in depth what respondents meant by "responsibility" and how it was reflected in their lives, an aspect of Markus and Ryff's interests in self-schemas; and chapter 12, by Anne Colby and her associates, scrutinizes qualitative interviews on the domains of life in which respondents showed responsibility toward others, focusing, in this particular analysis of the data set, on the work domain. In order to explore in depth what determining factors might be special to the social and economic position of racial and ethnic minorities in the United States, a special task force within the research network designed surveys for administration in New York City and Chicago that included an abbreviated version of MIDUS along with numerous topics of special relevance to those living in poor and disadvantaged minority communities. In this volume, two studies explore data from the New York survey:

chapter 6, by Diane Hughes, is based on data from the Latino and black respondents; and chapter 5, by Katherine Newman, draws on data from her ethnographic in-depth interviews with blacks, Puerto Ricans, and Dominicans.

Organization of the Volume

The empirical chapters of the volume begin with a broad stroke: in chapter 2, William Fleeson analyzes our most general single-item rating of social responsibility, using the same rating scheme with which respondents rated numerous other domains of life, so that one can see how respondents' ratings on contributing to others' welfare compare with their self-ratings on marriage, relations to children, finances, health, job, and sex life. Part II also contains chapter 3, which provides the most detailed sociodemographic analysis of the domains and dimensions of social responsibility; chapter 4, on temporal patterns in social responsibility; and chapters 5 and 6, based on the racial/minority samples. Part III contains three chapters on developmental issues: the first, chapter 7, analyzes characteristics of respondents' family of origin as they bear upon personality and current profile of social responsibility to family and community; chapter 8 analyzes the extent to which spouses, parents, and adult children have problems in their lives and relates them to respondents' own characteristics; and chapter 9 provides the qualitative analysis by Markus and Ryff mentioned above. Part IV focuses on various aspects of work: how chronic medical problems impair work (chapter 10); the combined impact of family and work characteristics upon service in the broader context of the community (chapter 11), and once again a close-up analysis from qualitative data on the extent and the ways in which respondents consider aspects of their jobs to be their contributions to the larger society (chapter 12). The concluding chapter emphasizes the implications of our findings for the direction of future research on the broad issues of civic participation and social responsibility.

NOTE

1. As noted in the preface, Robert D. Putnam's most recent book, *Bowling Alone: The Collapse and Renewal of American Community* (2000) was published during the copyediting phase of this book's production. This is most unfortunate because Putnam's data analysis and insights are extremely relevant to many topics in this chapter, as they are to numerous other chapters in this volume. At the heart of Putnam's work is his re-analysis of three national surveys containing numerous questions that were repeated in survey after survey over the years from the 1970s to the mid-1990s.

This permitted Putnam to empirically demonstrate cohort change that supports his thesis of long-term decline in social trust and in fundamental social-political values during the last quarter of the twentieth century: that is, compared to young adults surveyed in the 1970s, young adults in the 1990s are less trustful of major social institutions or individuals encountered during their daily rounds, less civically engaged, and more highly focused on their own private pursuits in life rather than on the common good.

Putnam points to numerous factors to explain this long-term social trend, but high on his list is the turning away from social engagement in favor of private indulgence in excessive amounts of time devoted to television viewing and Internet scanning. Consistent with what sociologists and social psychologists have been reporting for many years, Putnam links the high rates of withdrawal from social connectedness to the psychological impact of such "thin" social networks, as illustrated by the rising rates of suicide and depression among young people today compared to young adults twenty-five years ago.

The major data pool utilized in our book is limited to cross-sectional surveys rather than a series of surveys over long stretches of time. This precludes any empirical evidence of social change on successive cohorts of adults. The strength of our major data set lies in the great deal of information we gathered about individuals, covering all the major domains of their lives as spouses, parents, workers, neighbors, and community members. Retrospective data concerning respondents' mothers and fathers, family structure, childrearing values held by their parents, among many other variables, permitted us to demonstrate, rather than to just suggest, the importance of families as the socialization settings in which fundamental values are transmitted across the generations. By contrast, Putnam's emphasis is on broad societal factors as they impinge on one generation at one point in time compared to generations in earlier decades. If the major strength of Putnam's book is cohort analysis, our strength is maturational and intergenerational analysis. He gives little attention to change in childrearing values during the last quarter of the twentieth century, in particular the decrease in parental discipline and supervision of children in favor of greater permissiveness. Parental practices have changed in the past and could well change again if the upcoming cohorts of parents focus more on encouraging skill acquisition by their children rather than on giving them unearned praise; if they make more room in their daily lives for interaction with their children; and if they exercise moderation in warnings to their children about contact with strangers. While parents have reason to urge caution in an era marked by numerous media reports of child molestation and sexual abuse, they should not give such dire warnings that children overreact and withdraw into a tiny world of close intimates rather than outward in a developmentally appropriate enlarged social network.

Putnam's book fulfills its title's promise of demonstrating the *collapse* of community, but it does less well in demonstrating *renewal* of community in America. Apart from some hopeful suggestions of *possible* reversals in the decades-long collapse, one of the only empirical indicators of renewal that he cites is an increase in recent years in the proportion of high school graduates who have done volunteer service during their previous two years at school. What he does not note, however, is that there has been an increase in the number of schools that now *require* some amount of volunteer service to qualify for graduation. It is an open question whether such mandatory volunteer service has any spillover effect on voluntary service following high school graduation.

The MIDUS analyses project a more hopeful image of future trends because we report higher levels of volunteer service in the United States than in any other Western society, and in an aging society, the finding that volunteer service increases with age augurs well for a retention of, if not an actual increase in, the proportion of adults who contribute to the welfare of others. Even more important is the high level of intergenerational ties of affection, strong feelings of obligation, and actual contributions of time and financial assistance to kin and friends that are reported by MIDUS respondents. In our judgement, these intergenerational ties are the most fundamental indices of societal cohesion, of far greater importance than political participation, or hours of television viewing by adults exhausted at day's end that Putnam makes so much of.

But we urge readers of this volume to enjoy the complementary pleasures and insights that Putnam's important new book will provide them with.

References

Abel, E. M., and M. K. Nelson. 1990. Circles of care: An introductory essay. In *Circles of care: Work and identity in women's lives,* ed. E. M. Abel and M. K. Nelson, 1–34. Albany: State University of New York Press.

Alwin, D. 1996. Parental socialization in historical perspective. In *The parental imperative in midlife,* ed. C. Ryff and M. Seltzer, 105–67. Chicago: University of Chicago Press.

Anderson, D., and P. K. Mullen. 1998. *Faking it: The sentimentalisation of modern society.* London: Social Affairs Unit.

Barlett, D. L., and J. B. Steele. 1994. *America: Who really pays the taxes?* New York: Simon and Schuster.

Becker, P. E. 1998. Religion and family: A preliminary report on a comparative case study of four communities. Paper presented at the Society for the Scientific Study of Religion annual meeting, Montreal, Canada.

Becker, P. E., and H. Hofmeister. April 1999. Is there a time bind? Work and community involvement in Upstate New York. Cornell Careers Institute, Ithaca, NY. Mimeographed.

Bengtson, V. L., C. J. Rosenthal, and L. M. Burton. 1990. Families and aging: Diversity and heterogeneity. In *Handbook on aging and the social sciences,* ed. R. H. Binstock and L. George, 263–87. New York: Academic Press.

Bennahum, D. S. 1999. *Extra life: Coming of age in cyberspace.* New York: Basic Books.

Birkett, E. 1998. *The right women: A journey through the heart of conservative America.* New York: Scribner.

Blankenhorn, D. 1995. *Fatherless America: Confronting our most urgent social problem.* Westport, CT: Basic Books.

Blankenhorn, D., S. Bayme, and J. B. Elshtain, eds. 1990. *Rebuilding the nest.* Milwaukee, WI: Family Service of America.

Boyte, H. C., and N. N. Kari. 1996. *Building America: The democratic promise of work.* Philadelphia: Temple University Press.

Broder, D. S., and R. Morin. 1998. American values: 1968–1998. *Washington Post,* 27 December.

Charlton, B. 1998. Life before health. In *Faking it: The sentimentalisation of modern society,* ed. D. Anderson and P. Mullen, 19–38. London: Social Affairs Unit.

Clotfelter, C. T., ed. 1992. *Who benefits from the nonprofit sector?* Chicago: University of Chicago Press.

Colby, A., and W. Damon. 1992. *Some do care: Contemporary lives of moral commitment.* New York: Free Press.

Considine, J. J. 1995. *Marketing your church: Concepts and strategies.* Kansas City: Sheed and Ward.

Coontz, S. 1992. *The way we never were: American families and the nostalgia trap.* New York: Basic Books.

———. 1997. *The way we really are: Coming to terms with America's changing families.* New York: Basic Books.

Cooper, B. S., and D. O'Keefe. 1998. Sweetness and light in schools: The sentimentalisation of children. In *Faking it: The sentimentalisation of modern society,* ed. D. Anderson and P. Mullen, 54–80. London: Social Affairs Unit.

Council on Civil Society. 1998. *A call to civil society: Why democracy needs moral truths.* New York: Institute for American Values.

Council on Families in America. 1995. Marriage in America: A report to the nation. In *Promises to keep,* ed. D. Poponoe, J. B. Elshtain, and D. Blankenhorn, 293–318. Lanham, MD: Rowman and Littlefield.

Csikszentmihalyi, M. 1997. *Finding flow: The psychology of engagement in everyday life.* NY: Basic Books.

Daly, H. 1996. Sustainable growth? No thank you. In *The case against the global economy and for a turn toward the local,* ed. J. Mander and E. Goldsmith, 192–96. San Francisco, CA: Sierra Club Press.

Damon, W. 1995. *Greater expectations: Overcoming the culture of indulgence in America's homes and schools.* New York: Free Press.

———, ed. 1998. *Handbook of child psychology.* 4 vols. New York: John Wiley and Sons.

Danziger, S., and P. Gottschalk. 1995. *America unequal.* Cambridge: Harvard University Press.

———, eds. 1993. *Uneven tides: Rising inequality in America.* New York: Russell Sage Foundation.

Davis, K. 1984. Wives and work: Consequences of the sex role revolution. *Population and Development Review* 10:397–418.

Davis, K., and P. van den Oever. 1982. Demographic foundations of new sex roles. *Population and Development Review* 8:495–511.

Dionne, E. J., ed. 1998. *Community works: The revival of civil society in America.* Washington, DC: Brookings Institution Press.

Dunlop, R., and A. Burns. 1995. The sleeper effect—myth or reality? *Journal of Marriage and the Family* 58:375–81.

Durkheim, É. 1964. *Division of labor in society.* 1933. Reprint, New York: Free Press.

Eberly, D. E. 1998. *America's promise: Civil society and the renewal of American culture.* New York: Rowman and Littlefield.

Ehrenhalt, A. 1995. *The lost city: The forgotten virtue of community in America.* New York: Basic Books.

———. 1998. Where have all the followers gone? In *Community works: The revival of civil society in America,* ed. E. J. Dionne Jr., 93–100. Washington, DC: Brookings Institution Press.

Elshtain, J. B. 1987. *Women and war.* New York: Basic Books.

Etzioni, A. 1993. *The spirit of community: Rights, responsibilities, and the communitarian agenda.* New York: Crown.

Fisher, B., and J. Tronto. 1990. Toward a feminine theory of caring. In *Circles of care: Work and identity in women's lives,* ed. E. K. Abel and M. K. Nelson, 35–62. Albany: State University of New York Press.

Fowler, J. 1989. Strength for the journey: Early childhood and the development of selfhood and faith. In *Faith development and early childhood,* ed. D. Blazer. Kansas City, MO: Sheed and Ward.

Freie, J. F. 1998. *Counterfeit community: The exploitation of our longings for connectedness.* Lanham, MD: Rowman and Littlefield.

Fry, C. L. 1934. Changes in religious organizations. In *Recent social trends in the United States,* ed. W. Ogburn, 1009–60. New York: Whittlesey House.

Fukuyama, F. 1995. *Trust: The social virtues and prosperity.* London: Hamish Hamilton.

Fukuyama, F. 1999. *The great disruption: Human nature and the reconstitution of social order.* New York: Free Press.

Furstenberg Jr., F., and A. Cherlin. 1991. *Divided families: What happens to children when parents part.* Cambridge: Harvard University Press.

Garfinkel, I., and S. McLanahan. 1986. *Single mothers and their children: A new American dilemma.* Washington, DC: Urban Institute Press.

Garn, S. M., 1980. Continuities and changes in maturational timing. In *Constancy and change in human development,* ed. O. G. Brim Jr. and J. Kagan, 113–62. Cambridge: Harvard University Press.

Garrigan, L. M. 1999. Work hard. You might win a prize. Big or small, perks help build loyalty. *New York Times,* 8 August. Business section.

Gergen, K. J. 1991. *The saturated self: Dilemmas of identity in contemporary life.* New York: Basic Books.

Gilbert, N. 1983. *Capitalism and the welfare state: Dilemmas of social benevolence.* New Haven, CT: Yale University Press.

Glendon, M. A., and D. Blankenhorn, eds. 1995. *Seedbeds of virtue; Sources of competence, character, and citizenship in American Society .* Landam, MD: Madison Books.

Goddeeris, J. H., and B. A. Weisbrod. 1997. *Conversion from nonprofit to for-profit legal status: Why does it happen and should we care?* Working Paper WP-97-14. Evanston, IL: Northwestern University Institute for Policy Research.

Goldberg, C. 1998. For youngsters, new world is on line. *New York Times,* 22 November, sec. A.

Goldman, C. A., and Schneider, H. G. 1987. Menstrual synchrony: Social and personality factors. *Journal of Social Behavior and Personality* 2:243–50.

Goleman, D. 1995. *Emotional intelligence.* New York: Bantam Books.

Goodstein, L. 1999. Catholics contest evangelicals' radio dominance. *New York Times,* 15 August.

Greenhouse, S. 1999. Running on empty: So much work, so little time. News of the Week. *New York Times,* 5 September.

Havel, V. 1999. Beyond the nation-state. *The Responsive Community* 9:26–33.

Hayes, C. D., J. L. Palmer, and M. J. Zaslow, eds. 1990. *Who cares for America's children? Child care policy for the 1990s.* Washington, DC: National Academy Press.

Herzog, A. R., and J. Morgan. 1992. Age and gender differences in the value of productive activities. *Research on Aging* 14:169–98.

Hodgkinson, V. A., and M. S. Weitzman. 1993. *From belief to commitment: The community service activities and finances of religious congregations in the United States.* Washington, DC: Independent Sector.

Hodgkinson, V. A., and M. S. Weitzman. 1996. *Giving and volunteering in the United States.* Washington, DC: Independent Sector.

Hunnicutt, B. K. 1988. *Work without end: Abandoning shorter hours for the right to work.* Philadelphia: Temple University Press.

Independent Sector. 1996. *Giving and volunteering in the United States.* Washington, DC: Independent Sector.

Insel, T. R. 1992. Oxytocin—a neuropeptide for affiliation: Evidence from behavioral receptor, autoradiographic, and comparative studies *Psychoneuroendocrinology* 17:3–35.

Kaufman, L. 1999. SONY builds a mall but don't call it that. *New York Times,* 25 July, sec. 3.

Koren, M. J. 1986. Home care—who cares? *New England Journal of Medicine* 314: 917–20.

Kotler, P., B. Wrenn, and G. Rath. 1992. *Marketing for congregations: Choosing to serve people more effectively.* Nashville, TN: Abingdon Press.

Kuczynski, A. 1998. The very rich pay to learn how to give money away. *New York Times,* 3 May.

Ladd, E. C. 1999a. Bowling with Tocqueville: Civic engagement and social capital. *The responsive community: Rights and responsibilities* 9:11–21.

———. 1999b. *The Ladd report.* New York: Free Press.

Lasch, C. 1997. *Women and the Common Life.* Edited by E. Q. Lasch. New York: Norton.

Laumann, E.O., J. H. Gagnon, R. T. Michael, and S. Michaels. 1994. *The social organization of sexuality: Sexual practices in the United States.* Chicago: University of Chicago Press.

Lee, D. R., and R. B. McKenzie. 1999. *Getting rich in America.* New York: Harper Business.

Leege, D. C., and L. A. Kellstedt. 1993. *Rediscovering the religious factor in American politics.* Armonk, NY: M.E. Sharpe.

Lenkowsky, L. 1996. Philanthropy and the welfare state. In *To empower people: From state to civil society,* ed. M. Novak, 85–93. Washington, DC: AEI Press.

Levy, F., and R. Michel. 1991. *The economic future of American families: Income and wealth trends.* Washington, DC: Urban Institute Press.

Light, P. C. 1999. Big government is bigger than you think. *Wall Street Journal,* 13 January, sec. A.

Lippmann, W. 1929. *A preface to morals.* New York: MacMillan.

Lloyd, J. 1999. The Russian devolution. *New York Times Magazine* 15 August, 34–41, 52, 61, 64.

Lyall, S. 1999. In a grim house far from her usual haunts. *New York Times,* 5 September, Arts and Leisure section.

Lynd, R. S., and H. M. Lynd. 1929. *Middletown.* New York: Harcourt Brace.

———. 1937. *Middletown in transition.* New York: Harcourt Brace.

Malkiel, B. G., 1999. Day trading and its dangers. *Wall Street Journal,* 3 August, sec. A.

Mare, R., and C. Winship. 1991. Socioeconomic change and the decline of marriage for blacks and whites. In *The Urban Underclass,* ed. C. Jencks and P. E. Peterson. Washington, DC: Brookings Institution Press.

McLanahan, S., and G. Sandefur. 1994. *Growing up with a single parent: What hurts, what helps.* Cambridge: Harvard University Press.

Medved, M., and D. Medved. 1998. *Saving childhood: Protecting our children from the national assaults on innocence.* New York: Harper Collins.

Midgley, M. 1978. *Beast and man: The roots of human nature.* Ithaca, NY: Cornell University Press.

Miller, L. 1999. God goes online. *Wall Street Journal,* 25 March, sec. W.

Mishel, L., J. Bernstein, and J. Schmitt. 1999. *The state of working America.* Ithaca, NY: Cornell University Press.

Monroe, K. R. 1996. *The heart of altruism: Perceptions of a common humanity.* Princeton, NJ: Princeton University Press.

Moore, M. A. 1963. The role of temporary help services in the clerical labor market. Ph.D. diss., University of Wisconsin-Madison. Quoted in C. M. Ofstead, Temporary help firms as entrepreneurial actors, *Sociological Forum* 14:274.

National Council on Civic Renewal. 1998. *A nation of spectators: How civic disengagement weakens America and what we can do about it.* College Park, MD: National Commission on Civic Renewal.

Novak, M., ed. 1996. *To empower people: From state to civil society.* 2d ed. Washington, DC: AEI Press.

O'Brien, T.L. 1998. *Bad bet.* New York: Times Business.

Ofstead, C. M. 1999. Temporary help firms as entrepreneurial actors. *Sociological Forum* 14:273–94.

Ogburn, W., ed. 1934. *Recent social trends in the United States.* New York: Whittlesey House.

Olasky, M. 1996a. *Renewing American compassion.* New York: Free Press.

———. 1996b. The corruption of religious societies. In *To empower people: From state to civil society,* ed. M. Novak, 94–104. Washington, DC: AEI Press.

Parker, R. E. 1994. *Flesh peddlers and warm bodies: The temporary help industry and its workers.* New Brunswick, NJ: Rutgers University Press.

Peterson, P.G. 1999. *Gray dawn: How the coming age wave will transform America—and the world.* New York: Random House/Times Books.

Pollitt, K. 1996. For whom the ball rolls. *The Nation,* 15 April, 9.

Poponoe, D. 1995. The roots of declining social virtue: Family, community, and the need for a "Natural communities" policy. In *Seedbeds of virtue,* ed. M. A. Glendon and D. Blankenhorn, 71–104. Lanham, MD: Madison Books.

Poponoe, D., J. B. Elshtain, and D. Blankenhorn, eds. 1996. *Promises to keep: Decline and renewal of marriage in America*. Lanham, MD: Rowman and Littlefield.

Poponoe. D., and B. D. Whitehead. 1999. *The state of our unions*. Rutgers, NJ: National Marriage Project.

Putnam, R. D. 1993a. *Making democracy work: Civic traditions in modern Italy*. Princeton, NJ: Princeton University Press.

———. 1993b. The prosperous community: Social capital and public life. *The American Prospect* 13:35–42.

———. 1995a. Bowling alone: America's declining social capital. *Journal of Democracy* 6:65–78.

———. 1995b. Tuning in, tuning out: The strange disappearance of social capital in America. *PS: Political Science and Politics* 28:664–83.

———. 2000. *Bowling alone: The collapse and renewal of American Community*. New York: Simon and Schuster.

Rawls, J. 1971. *A theory of justice*. Cambridge: Harvard University Press.

Reno, V. P. 1993. The role of pensions in retirement income. In *Pensions in a changing economy*, ed. R. V. Burkhauser and D. L. Salisbury, 19–32. Washington, DC: Employee Benefit Research Institute.

Ridley, M. 1996. *The origins of virtue: Human instincts and the evolution of cooperation*. New York: Viking.

Riesman, D. 1950. *The lonely crowd*. New Haven, CT: Yale University Press.

Rheingold, H. 1993. *The virtual community: Homesteading on the electronic frontier*. Reading, MA: Addison-Wesley.

Robinson, J. P., and G. Godbey. 1997. *Time for life: The surprising ways Americans use their time*. University Park, PA: Pennsylvania State University Press.

Rossi, A. S. 1982. *Feminists in politics: A panel analysis of the first National Women's Conference*. New York: Academic Press.

———. 1994. Eros and caritas: A biopsychosocial approach to human sexuality and reproduction. In *Sexuality across the life course*, ed. A.S. Rossi, 3–38. Chicago: University of Chicago Press.

———. 1998. The impact of family structure and social change on adolescent sexual behavior. *Children and Youth Review* 19:369–400.

Rossi, A. S., and P. H. Rossi. 1990. *Of human bonding: The parent-child relationship across the life course*. New York: Aldine de Gruyter.

Rossi, P. H. 1972. Community social indicators. In *The human meaning of social change*, ed. A. Campbell and P. E. Converse, 87–126. New York: Russell Sage Foundation.

Ruse, M. 1986. *Taking Darwin seriously: A naturalistic approach to philosophy*. Cambridge, MA: Blackwell.

Salamon, L. M. 1995. *Partners in public service: Government-nonprofit relations in the modern welfare state*. Baltimore, MD: Johns Hopkins University Press.

Schembari, J. 1998. Can a generation learn to share? *New York Times*, 27 September.

Schor, J. B. 1992. *The overworked American: The unexpected decline in leisure*. New York: Basic Books.

———. 1998. *The overspent American: Upscaling, downshifting, and the new consumer*. New York: Basic Books.

Seabrook, J. 1997. *Deeper: My two-year odyssey in cyberspace.* New York: Simon and Schuster.

Sealander, J. 1997. *Private wealth and public life.* Baltimore, MD: Johns Hopkins University Press.

Seltzer, M. M., M. W. Krauss, S. C. Choi, and J. Hong. 1996. Midlife and later-life parenting of adult children with mental retardation. In *The Parental experience in midlife,* ed. C. D. Ryff and M. M. Seltzer, 459–92. Chicago: University of Chicago Press.

Shapiro, E. 1999. The life of leisure. *Wall Street Journal,* 11 January, Millennium section, R38.

Sheard, J. 1995. From lady bountiful to active citizen: Volunteering and the voluntary sector. In *An introduction to the voluntary sector,* ed. J. Smith, C. Rochester, and R. Hedley, 114–27. New York: Routledge.

Shlaes, A. 1999. *The greedy hand: How taxes drive Americans crazy and what they can do about it.* New York: Random House.

Skocpol, T. 1992. *Protecting soldiers and mothers: The political origins of social policy in the United States.* Cambridge: Belknap Press/Harvard University Press.

———. 1996. The Tocqueville problem: Civic engagement in American democracy. *Social Science History* 21:455–79.

———. 1999. How Americans became civic. In *Civic engagement in American democracy,* ed. T. Skocpol and M. P. Fiorina. Washington, DC: Brookings Institution Press and the Russell Sage Foundation.

Skocpol, T., and M. P. Fiorina. 1999. Making sense of the civic engagement debate. In *Civic engagement in American democracy,* ed. T. Skocpol and M. Fiorina. Washington, DC: Brookings Institution Press.

Smith, D. H. 1997. The rest of the nonprofit sector: Grassroots associations as the dark matter ignored in the prevailing "flat earth" map of the sector. *Nonprofit and Voluntary Sector Quarterly* 16:114–31.

Smith, S. R., and M. Lipsky. 1993. *Nonprofits for hire: The welfare state in the age of contracting.* Cambridge: Harvard University Press.

Smucker, B. 1998. *The nonprofit lobbying guide: Advocating your cause—and getting results.* Washington, DC: Independent Sector.

Social Security Administration. 1995. *Annual statistical supplement.* Washington, DC: Government Printing Office.

Stein, M. 1960. *The eclipse of community.* Princeton, NJ: Princeton University Press.

Stengel, R. 1996. Bowling together: Civic engagement in America isn't disappearing but reinventing itself. *Time,* 22 July, 35–36.

Stone, R., G. L. Cafferata, and J. Sangl. 1987. Caregivers of the frail elderly: A national profile. *The Gerontologist* 27:616–26.

Strozier, C. B. 1994. *Apocalypse: On the psychology of fundamentalism in America.* Boston: Beacon Press.

Sullivan, A. 1999. There will always be an England. *New York Times Magazine,* 12 February, 39–45, 54, 72–73, 78, 79.

Thiemann, R. F. 1996. *Religion in public life: A dilemma for democracy.* Washington, DC: Georgetown University Press.

Thompson, S. 1994. Changing lives, changing genres: Teenage girls' narratives

70

about sex and romance. In *Sexuality across the life course,* ed. A. S. Rossi, 209–32. Chicago: University of Chicago Press.

———. 1995. *Going all the way: Teenage girls' tales of sex, romance, and pregnancy.* New York: Hill and Wang.

Tiger, L. 1999. *The decline of males.* New York: Golden Books. Quoted in F. Fukuyama, *Trust: The social virtues and prosperity* (London: Hamish Hamilton, 1999), 314.

Tilly, C., and C. Tilly. 1994. Capitalist work and labor markets. In *Handbook on economic sociology,* ed. N. Smelser and R. Swedberg, 283–313. Princeton, NJ: Princeton University Press.

Tocqueville, A. de. 1945. *Democracy in America.* 1835. Reprint, New York: Vintage.

Tracy, D. 1981. *Analogical imagination.* New York: Crossroads.

Turkle, S. 1995. *Life on the screen: Identity in the age of the Internet.* New York: Simon and Schuster.

Udry, J. 1979. Age at menarche, at first intercourse, and at first pregnancy. *Journal of Biosocial Science* 11:433–41.

Udry, J., and B. C. Campbell. 1994. Getting started on sexual behavior. In *Sexuality across the life course,* ed. A. S. Rossi, 187–207. Chicago: University of Chicago Press.

Verba, S., K. L. Schlozman, and H. E. Brady. 1995. *Voices and equality: Civic voluntarism in American politics.* Cambridge: Harvard University Press.

Wall Street Journal Special Quarterly: American Opinion. 1999. Gray power comes of age. 11 March.

Wallerstein, J., and S. Blakeless.1989. *Second chances: Men, women, and children a decade after divorce.* New York: Tichnor and Fields.

West, D. 1998. Treat your children well. Review of *A tribe apart: A journey into the heart of adolescence,* by P. Hersch. *Wall Street Journal,* 22 April.

Whyte, W. H. 1956. *Organization man.* New York: Simon and Schuster.

Willmer, W. K., and J. D. Schmidt, with M. Smith. 1998. *The prospering parachurch: Enlarging the boundaries of God's kingdom.* San Francisco: Jossey-Bass.

Wilson, J., and M. A. Musick. 1997. Who cares? Toward an integrated theory of volunteering. *American Sociological Review* 62:694–713.

———. 1999. Attachment to volunteering. *Sociological Forum* 14:243–72.

Wilson, E. O. 1998. *Consilience: The unity of knowledge.* New York: Knopf.

Wilson, J. Q. 1993. *The moral sense.* New York: Free Press.

Wilson, W. J. 1991. Public policy research and the truly disadvantaged. In *The Urban Underclass,* ed. C. Jencks and P. E. Peterson. Washington, DC: Brookings Institution Press.

Wolfe, A. 1989. *Whose keeper? Social science and moral obligation.* Berkeley, CA: University of California Press.

———. 1998. *One nation, after all.* New York: Viking.

Wolfinger, N. H. 1996. Time trends in the intergenerational transmission of divorce. Paper presented at the Society for the Study of Social Problems annual meeting, New York City.

Wolpert, J. 1993. *Patterns of generosity in America: Who's holding the safety net?* New York: Twentieth Century Fund Press.

Wright, R. 1994. *The moral animal: The new science of evolutionary psychology.* New York: Pantheon Books.

Wuthnow, R. 1991. *Acts of compassion: Caring for others and helping ourselves.* Princeton, NJ: Princeton University Press.

———. 1994. *Sharing the journey: Support groups and America's new quest for community.* New York: Free Press.

———. 1998. *Loose Connections: Joining together in America's fragmented communities.* Cambridge: Harvard University Press.

Wuthnow, R., V. A. Hodgkinson, and associates. 1990. *Faith and philanthropy in America.* Washington, DC: Independent Sector.

Wysocki, B. 1999. High rollers: How life on the edge became mainstream in today's America. *Wall Street Journal,* 3 August, sec. A.

Zakaria, F. 1998. Our hollow hegemony: Why foreign policy can't be left to the market. *New York Times Magazine,* 1 November, 44–45.

II Life Course and Social and Structural Variation in Social Responsibility

Judgments of One's Own Overall Contribution to the Welfare of Others

Life-Course Trajectories and Predictors

William Fleeson

The purpose of this chapter is to describe the general parameters of social responsibility in adulthood, taking advantage of MIDUS, a large and semi-representative sample of adult Americans, to provide answers to perennial and broad questions about social responsibility: First, what is the overall level of social responsibility among adult Americans? That is, to what extent do Americans see themselves as contributing to the well-being of others? Second, do men and women contribute different amounts to the well-being of others? Some theory suggests that women are disproportionately burdened with responsibilities for others or that women have greater interest in and greater ability to care for others (e.g., Antonucci and Akiyama 1997; Heimer 1996; MacDermid, Heilbrun, and DeHaan 1997); both of these notions would suggest that American women contribute more than American men. Third, how does social responsibility vary across the life span? Both theorists of midlife and theorists of social responsibility have separately argued that social responsibility peaks in the middle years of adulthood (Erikson 1963; Levinson 1978). Nonetheless, data testing this idea have been rare or have produced mixed findings (McAdams, de St. Aubin, and Logan 1993). The MIDUS survey offers two particular advantages on this point: it is a probability sample of all Americans (allowing generalizability and a near-definitive answer); and it is large, granting the power to test several possible age trajectories. The results will show that men and women have different age trajectories, with women showing the predicted midlife peak and men not, and a substantial portion of this chapter will be devoted to trying to explain this difference. Finally, the last question concerns whether there is reward to virtue: Specifically, what is the relationship of social responsibility to the well-being of the socially responsible actor?

This chapter acts somewhat as a table setting for the remaining, more analytic chapters in this volume. Whereas I treat social responsibility as a whole, other chapters focus on more specific aspects. Whereas I analyze the entire sample, other chapters analyze specific subsamples. Whereas I focus on gross demographic associates of social responsibility, other chapters focus on specific predictors and consequences. In this way, I hope to provide a framework within which to locate the more precise and analytic findings from the following chapters.

THEORETICAL ISSUES IN CONCEPTUALIZING AND MEASURING OVERALL SOCIAL RESPONSIBILITY

Existing theory and measurement of social responsibility is diverse, doing justice to its complex nature (Bradley 1997; Erikson 1963; McAdams and de St. Aubin 1992; Ryff and Heincke 1983). Here, I take one particular approach to conceptualizing social responsibility, and this is reflected in the measurement of social responsibility. Specifically, the conception of social responsibility used here is inclusive and subjective. In the following, I discuss the implications, advantages, and disadvantages of this conceptualization and measurement of social responsibility. Such issues are important qualifiers for interpretations of the answers to this chapter's central questions.

Inclusivity

My focus is on overall, or global, social responsibility, in an explicit attempt to be inclusive of all forms of contribution to others and of diverse theoretical conceptions of social responsibility. Consequently, respondents were instructed to take into account all that they do as a result of their concern for others and to consider all possible recipients of their contributions. In the section of the MIDUS survey concerning community involvement, each respondent answered the following question: "Using a scale from 0 to 10 where 0 means 'the worst possible contribution to the welfare and well-being of other people' and 10 means 'the best possible contribution to the welfare and well-being of other people,' how would you rate your contribution to the welfare and well-being of other people these days? Take into account all that you do, in terms of time, money, or concern, on your job, and for your family, friends, and the community." Thus, the item is a summary statement of the respondent's overall contribution to others.

As is clear from the above question, the survey defines social responsibility in a way that includes all of what people do, think, and feel that they consider to be a contribution to others. The definition is not limited to volunteering, donating money, parenting, mentoring, or career-related contributions, but includes them all. It is not limited to voluntary contributions, but rather includes both obligatory and chosen contribution. Excluded are other meanings of "responsibility": this conceptualization does not include "being responsible" in the sense of being dependable and conscientious, nor in the sense of controlling and making decisions, nor in the sense of originating or being in power.

The advantage of such a definition is that it provides the big picture: It allows answering questions about Americans' total, overall contribution to others' well-being. As a corollary advantage, the definition is evaluatively neutral and counts different forms of social responsibility equivalently. Different individuals can be socially responsible in different manners, and such a definition does not exclude those who do not fit into more narrow categories of social responsibility. For example, an individual who donates little time or money because his or her work is consuming and socially responsible (e.g., a consumer advocate) is not counted as socially irresponsible when using an inclusive definition. (See chapter 12 for more on how work can be a means to express social responsibility.) On the other hand, inclusivity here entails a lack of specificity. It is not clear from this measure exactly what socially responsible individuals are doing or feeling, and it is not clear which aspects of social responsibility account for the findings discussed below.

This definition of social responsibility overlaps with but is not identical to other conceptions of socially responsible behavior. One conception that has received considerable attention in the psychological literature recently is *generativity*. Generativity, as the name implies, focuses more on one particular type of social responsibility: caring for the next generation, including generating it, maintaining it, and benefiting it (Bradley 1997; Erikson 1963; Kotre 1984; McAdams and de St. Aubin 1992; Peterson and Stewart 1993). Although different writers have proposed different versions of generativity, all versions share an emphasis on caring for the next generation. Many such writers also agree that caring for the next generation often includes caring for the current generation, as a way of maintaining and improving social institutions for the benefit of the next generation. The current chapter, in contrast, does not specify which generation is the recipient of the contribution, and so includes caring for the current generation as much as caring for the next or even the previous generation (see Brody 1985 for a discussion of the considerable obligation caring for the previous generation can entail). Thus, the present conception is broader and more inclusive than generativity; on the flip side, this measure thereby loses some of generativity's unique features.

Other overlapping concepts include ethical behavior and virtuous behavior. Although social responsibility and these two concepts all overlap, none of them includes the entirety of any other. Socially responsible behavior is likely but not necessarily ethical or virtuous. For example, caring for one group of people may be at the expense of hurting another group or even oneself. Likewise, ethical or virtuous behavior does not always involve contributing to the well-being of others (though some Utilitarian theorists would argue that it does). This discussion is obviously too large for this chapter; the point here is that social responsibility is not synonymous with ethical or virtuous behavior.

In sum, this measure is inclusive of several conceptions of social responsibility (e.g., generativity); the downside is that it loses the richness of more specific conceptions. It is inclusive of many actions involved in social responsibility (i.e., "all that you do"); the downside is that this chapter provides no information on the different aspects of social responsibility. It is inclusive of concern as well as action; the downside is that we don't know whether an individual's response comes from action or from thought. (See chapter 3 for discussion of narrower definitions of social responsibility, such as found in Putnam 1995 and Seligman 1992.) This chapter's purpose is only to consider American individuals' overall level of social responsibility, and the measure's inclusiveness is primarily an advantage for that purpose.

Subjectivity

Committing to a truly comprehensive definition of social responsibility suggests using a subjective definition. That is, in order to include all forms of contribution to others, it may be best to allow the individual respondent to evaluate his or her actions as socially responsible or not. There are at least two reasons for this. First, humans can be very creative in the ways they contribute to the welfare of others (Colby and Damon 1992; chapter 9, this volume). Any definition based on a specific set of criteria or on a specific set of actions must be limited to those specific criteria and actions, thereby leaving out some of the more creative ways of being socially responsible. For example, defining social responsibility as the number of hours volunteered leaves out those individuals who are socially responsible through work or family. A subjective measure allows each individual to include his or her unique forms of social responsibility.

Second, social responsibility is itself a largely subjective concept. Evaluating whether an action is socially responsible (whether it contributes to the welfare of others) requires personal judgment. It requires deciding at least whether the consequences of the action are beneficial for the others or not, and whether the motivation was to help others or not (though the extent to which motivation is relevant is arguable). For example, a career in the human services may be socially responsible, or it simply may be a convenient career choice. Objective measures of social responsibility necessarily smooth over such variations across individuals and leave the judgment up to the researchers. This is not to imply that the individual is the best judge of whether his or her actions are socially responsible, but to the extent that motivation is part of the judgment, the actor is at least a relatively informed judge.

On the other hand, such a definition has the normal problems with self-report (e.g., response bias, social desirability), which may be exacerbated in this case because of the measure's inclusiveness and obvious social desirability. That is, the evaluation and judgment concerns a much greater amount of behavior than a typical self-report item (it asks about all that respondents do for others vs., for example, asking how often they donate money to organizations). This wide latitude in judgment potentially opens the door to self-enhancing bias, such as selective recall, and to the use of different comparison standards by different individuals (Kobrynowicz and Biernat 1997). The main consequence for the present chapter, assuming that such biases are reasonably randomly distributed throughout the population, is an increase in error variance, making results harder to find (i.e., a reduction in power). It is also possible that these problems lead to biases in the results (e.g., men use different standards than women), but this is less likely.

The measure follows from this definition, asking each respondent to evaluate his or her own actions. The measure does refer to actual behavior ("take into account all that you do"), but both the definition and evaluation of what the respondent does is left up to the respondent. Such a measure is inappropriate for some purposes; the proposal here is that such a measure is useful for obtaining a comprehensive summary of each individual's total contribution to the well-being of others.

Using a Single Item

A third issue concerns the operational definition of social responsibility: I used a single item to measure social responsibility. Single-item measures suffer from reliability problems more than do multiple-item measures. That is, a larger percentage of the variance in this measure will be error variance than is typical for multiple-item scales. Of course, this is a quantitative and not a qualitative difference between single-item and multiple-item scales: it means only that there is more error variance in this measure, not that there is only or mostly error variance in this measure. The primary consequence is that it works against finding results (it reduces the power of the analyses).

Again, however, this may be acceptable given the conceptual focus: investigating a global and subjective measure of total contribution to others. It would be difficult to construct additional items without becoming specific (sacrificing generality) or without becoming objective (sacrificing the advantages of a subjective measure). In any event, the potentially large component of error in this measure must be kept in mind when interpreting the results.[1]

It should also be noted that most of the other chapters in this volume deal with more specific, more objective, and multiple-item measures of social responsibility. This chapter's inclusivity may provide a context within which to locate the other chapters, and a comprehensive conceptualization of social responsibility may be best for providing such a context.

ARE AMERICANS SOCIALLY RESPONSIBLE?

The first question is a simple one: In general, how much do Americans contribute to the welfare of others? The answer includes not only what the average amount of contribution to others is, but also the diversity of levels of contributions across adult Americans. That is, the answer speaks also to the issue of whether social responsibility is evenly distributed among Americans or whether the burden is shouldered by only a few, while the rest avoid responsibility. This question is interesting in its own right, simply as one way of gauging the overall social responsibility of Americans in the 1990s. This question also has interest for developmental-theoretical reasons. By describing the extent to which Americans develop into socially responsible adults naturally, and assuming that social responsibility is a valued developmental aim, the answer to this question describes how far Americans get toward this goal. Finally, this question may also be useful in forming public policy. For example, the current state of social responsibility to others may be informative to efforts to increase or even to rely on social responsibility to solve our social problems (see Putnam 1995; chapters 1 and 3, this volume).

This study provides a unique opportunity to answer this question. The size of the sample (over 3,500 respondents) allows for a relatively precise and accurate estimate of the level of social responsibility in the population of Americans as a whole. The sampling method (random-digit dialing) provides a quality representation of all Americans (see the appendix for a full description of the sample and method for this study, as well as for a description of the representativeness of the sample).

The average response to the single item cited previously was 6.58 ± .07, and the standard deviation was 2.24, on the 0–10 rating scale. Given that a response of "0" means the "worst possible contribution" and a response of "10" means the "best possible contribution," an average response of about six and a half is only somewhat encouraging. It is indeed closer to the best possible contribution (the midpoint of the scale is 5) than to the worst possible, but not by much. As noted, the sample size makes this a fairly accurate representation of the average American. As the standard error is only .037, the 95% confidence interval on the population mean ranges from 6.51 to 6.65; the social responsibility of the average American is just over 6.5.

The large standard deviation (2.24) also provides valuable information. Primarily it shows the considerable variation in the extent to which Americans take on social responsibility. As shown in figure 2.1,

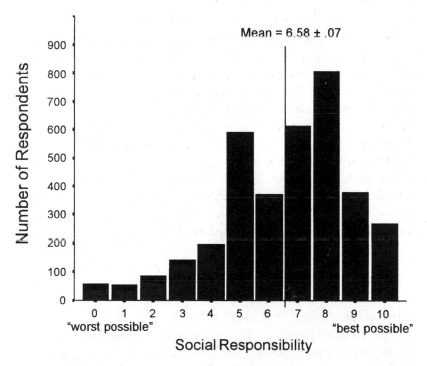

FIGURE 2.1. Distribution of responses to "How would you rate your contribution to the welfare and well-being of other people?"

many individuals reported the best possible or close to the best possible contribution to others (18% responded with a 9 or a 10), whereas many others consider themselves to be making close to the worst contribution to the well-being of others possible (10% responded with a 3 or lower, and over 30% responded below the midpoint of the scale).

A useful comparison standard is the respondents' responses to several similar questions in other parts of the survey. Using the same "worst possible" (0) to "best possible" (10) scale, respondents rated the quality of other domains in their life: work, marriage (or close relationship), relationship to children, finances, sexual life, health, and life as a whole. Thus, the quality of respondents' contributions to others can be compared with the quality of other aspects of their lives. The means for each of these eight life domains is shown in figure 2.2. The most striking result is that all but two of the domains were rated as higher quality than was contribution to the well-being of others. An ANOVA revealed that the means differ from each other, $F(7, 14539) = 521.57$, $p < .001$, and follow-up Scheffé tests revealed that each mean differed significantly from each other mean, all F's > 15. That is, Americans report that their health, work, relationship with children, marriage, and overall life are all better than their contributions to others. Only their financial situation and their sex life are seen as worse than their contribution to others. Whether the cause of this is priorities, effort, or

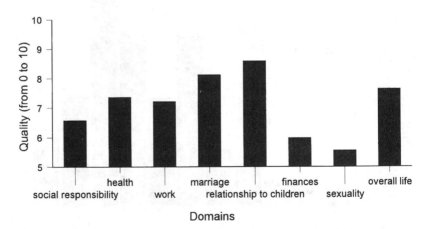

FIGURE 2.2. Quality of social responsibility in comparison to quality of other life domains. *N*s vary from 2,561 to 3,762, primarily reflecting variations in marital status, having children, and employment status.

something else, Americans are doing better at getting their own lives in order than they are at contributing to the well-being of others. By this standard, Americans' average level of social responsibility is low.

AGE- AND GENDER-RELATED DIFFERENCES IN SOCIAL RESPONSIBILITY

From the beginning, researchers have closely related social responsibility to adult-developmental theory and to adulthood. Some theorists have pinpointed it as an issue for the middle years of adulthood. Simply put, they argue that the confluence of maximal resources (the power to be socially responsible), maximal societal demand (the societal expectation that midlife adults will be the contributors), and maximal desire to help (the desire to contribute, aroused by developmental milestones) leads to a midlife peak in social responsibility (e.g., Erikson 1963). McAdams and de St. Aubin (1992), for example, hypothesized that there are two sources of generativity, and that these are strongest in adulthood. First, there is cultural demand, encoded in the work-related, lifestyle-related, and ideological opportunities and obligations that society puts on individuals. Second is inner desire. As adults age they often become more aware of their own mortality, which leads to twin desires to contribute to others: a need to feel needed by others, and a need to leave a lasting legacy (Kotre 1984). This inner desire may also be fueled by reminders of others' needs for receiving contributions (e.g., children prominently need contribution and care), and these reminders may become more insistent and salient in the middle adult years. These and similar ideas have sometimes led to an association of midlife with social responsibility.

Similarly, gender is often integral to theorizing about social responsibility. One main form of this theorizing concerns strong gender differences in the forms and amounts of socially responsible behavior. Some theorists have maintained that women are burdened with greater social responsibility than are men. Partly because men more often take the role of financial provider, women are theorized to more often take generative roles within the family and volunteering roles outside the family. Thus, such theories predict that women contribute more to the well-being of others than do men. Other theorists agree that there are gender-segregated types of social responsibility but argue that they balance out, so that men and women end up contributing equally to the well-being of others (Rossi and Rossi 1990). For example, men may be socially responsible at work (by mentoring, donating money, working pro bono, or through the work itself). These theorists predict equal levels of social responsibility for men and women. The present chapter will test for gender differences in overall amount of social responsibility but, because of the generalized nature of the measure, will not test for gender differences in specific types of social responsibility (see chapter 3 for more detail on gender differences in the various domains and dimensions of responsibility).

In the following I test these theories about age- and gender-related differences in social responsibility. First, I test whether men and women, ignoring age, differ in average level of social responsibility. Second, I test for age differences or age trajectories in overall social responsibility, ignoring gender. The minimum age in the sample is twenty-five, disallowing comparison of adults to pre-adults (McAdams and de St. Aubin [1992] did find a difference), but adults of different ages can be compared on their contribution to the well-being of others. In particular, I test whether there exists a midlife peak. Finally, I will combine age and gender to test whether women and men have differing age trajectories.

As mentioned previously, the size and representativeness of the sample allows for fairly precise and accurate answers to these questions. The few previous tests of the midlife-peak hypothesis have received some mixed support (McAdams, de St. Aubin, and Logan 1993; Peterson and Stewart 1990; Ryff and Heincke 1983; Ryff and Migdal 1984). That is, there is currently sufficient evidence to keep looking, but not enough to answer the question. Thus, this chapter may provide one of the first definitive answers to these basic questions about social responsibility. One additional advantage of this sample is that it affords high statistical power: If a relationship between age and social responsibility exists, this sample will reveal it. Furthermore, this sample has the power to reveal exactly what the shape of that relationship is. That is, I have the opportunity to accurately test several shapes of the relationship between age and social responsibility: linear (e.g., a steady increase with age); quadratic (e.g., a peak in midlife); cubic (e.g., a peak in the late thirties and a nadir in the late sixties); and several other smooth curves. At the same time, this study is no more likely than any other to make a type I error: if no relationship between age and social responsibility exists, this study is no more likely than any other study to reveal one. In sum, the power of this sample allows finding the precise shape of the age and social responsibility relationship.

Of course, the disadvantages of the present sample are also apparent, such as the slight positive sampling (e.g., only Americans possessing telephones were contacted) and the over-representation of white Americans. An additional limitation for the analyses in this chapter is the cross-sectional nature of the study. Comparisons across ages in levels of current social responsibility are comparisons across different individuals, preventing certainty about what happens as any given individual ages. Rather, different cohorts of the differently aged individuals may be responsible for the trajectories. (However, as will be seen shortly, each individual did supply ratings on past and future social responsibility, providing a version of within-person age trajectories.)

Gender-Related Differences in Social Responsibility

First investigating gender, a *t*-test revealed that women were more socially responsible than men, $t(3574) = 8.76$, $p < .001$ (for women, $M = 6.90$; for men, $M = 6.25$). This difference is about two-thirds of a point on the original scale (about one-third of a standard deviation). Thus, this sample provides support for the notion that women contributed more to the well-being of others than did men in America in the mid-1990s.

Age-Related Differences in Social Responsibility

Age-related curves were investigated with regression analyses predicting social responsibility from age. In a regression on the whole sample, no linear relationship between age and social responsibility was evident, $b = .005$, $p = .10$.[2] However, a quadratic relationship was revealed, $b_{age} = .094$, $b_{age-squared} = -.0009$, $p < .001$, and no higher power relationship was significant. As shown in figure 2.3, this curve is precisely the shape and location predicted by the midlife-peak hypothesis: social responsibility is lowest, $M = 6.12$, at age 25, climbs to a peak of 6.75 at age 51, and steadily declines again to almost 6.12 at age 75, for a total change of about one-half scale point in each direction. This effect is small, accounting for only half a percent of variance in social responsibility, but it is real, and the hypothesis is supported.

The interpretation of this curve, however, is qualified by an interaction with gender. As described earlier, I performed regressions to test for different age trajectories for men and women. A significant interaction between the quadratic age term and gender, $b_{interaction} = -.0014$, $p = .001$, allowed investigating age trajectories separately for men and for women. The most striking finding is that only women show the quadratic relationship (and no higher power relationship). For men,

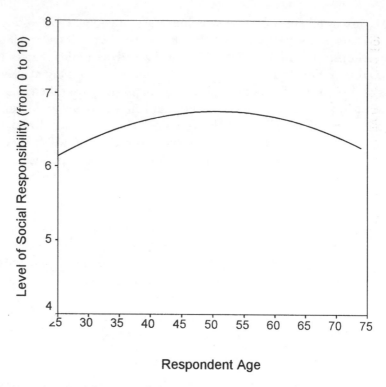

FIGURE 2.3. Social responsibility across ages. Shown are respondents' own estimates of their level of contribution to the well-being of others. All respondents are included in this significant curvilinear relationship.

age was linearly related to social responsibility (no higher power of age added a significant amount of variance to the prediction of men's social responsibility). The linear trend was positive and slight, $b_{age} = .011$, $p < .01$, such that every decade was associated with a tenth of a point increase in social responsibility—over fifty years of adulthood, this accumulates to a half-point increase.

For women, the midlife peak was evident and stronger than for the sample as a whole, $b_{age} = .16$, $b_{age\text{-}squared} = -.0016$, $p < .001$. Figure 2.4 shows the two age gradients. Women go from a low of 6 at age 25 to a peak of 7.2 at age 47.5, and back down to approximately 6.4 at age 75. Thus the effect for women is over 1 point (about one-half standard deviation) and accounts for almost 2% of the variance. Still a small effect, but now of worthwhile magnitude.

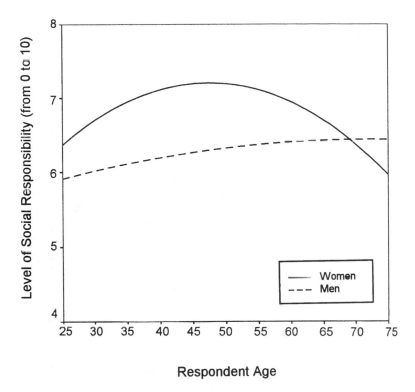

FIGURE 2.4. Social responsibility across ages, separately by gender. Shown are respondents' own estimates of their level of contribution to the well-being of others. The interactions between age and gender and between age-squared and gender were both significant. The curvilinear age-related trend was significant for women only.

Additional support for this finding comes from two related items in the survey. Respondents indicated also how good they expected their contribution to be ten years in the future, and how good they remembered it to have been ten years in the past. These two items were otherwise identical to ratings of current social responsibility. Analyses were repeated for these items. Panel A of figure 2.5 shows the results for women. All three questions showed quadratic relations to age (and no higher power relationships), and they all converged on the same conclusion: social responsibility among women is highest in the late forties, with smooth increases to that peak and smooth decreases from that peak. What is remarkable about this convergence is that the answers are from different women. That is, the women who remembered their

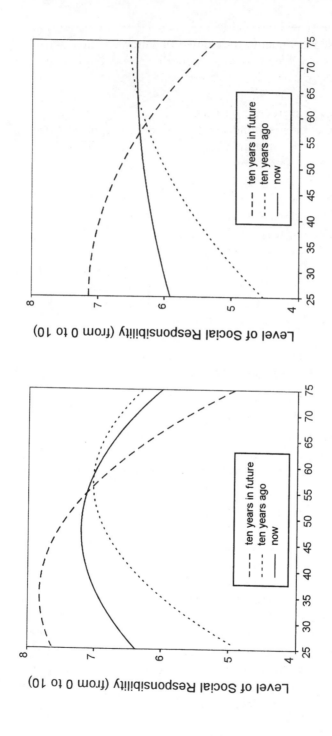

FIGURE 2.5. Social responsibility across respondents' ages. Shown are respondents' own estimates of their level of contribution to the well-being of others now, ten years in the past, and ten years in the future. Curvilinear age-related trends were significant for all but the men responding about their current contributions.

level of social responsibility as being the highest ten years previous were the sixty-year-old respondents; the women who most anticipated being more socially responsible in ten years were the forty-year-old women; and the women who reported the highest level of current social responsibility were the fifty-year-old women.

The results for men are less consistent, as shown in panel B of figure 2.5. The older the male respondents, the more they reported current social responsibility, the more they remembered having been highly socially responsible in the past, but the less they expected to be socially responsible in the future. That is, the younger men anticipated grand contributions to the well-being of others, and the older men remembered grand contributions to the well-being of others; the line for present contributions shows that neither holds true.[3]

In summary, there is strong support for the midlife-peak hypothesis of social responsibility, but only for women. In contrast, men show a nearly flat line across age, with a steady but slow increase that first gets them to the level of women at about age seventy. When it comes to women, those theorists of social responsibility who emphasized a midlife peak appear to be correct: American women in their late forties are contributing more to the well-being of others than are women of any other age, and than are men of any age at all. These findings may also clarify the previously mixed picture. Many previous studies have either included both men and women or defined midlife in a way that excludes the late forties. Only studies that focus on women in their late forties or early fifties would provide clear evidence for the midlife peak. The following section describes some attempts to explain this peak for women.[4]

Why the Midlife Peak for Women?

Women showed a midlife peak in social responsibility, as expected. This expectation was based on the presumed confluence of cultural demands and individual development (e.g., McAdams and de St. Aubin 1992).That is, midlife is a unique time when (1) younger individuals may not yet have acquired the resources to be socially responsible and older adults may witness the waning of resources; and (2) immediate contextual factors such as responsibility at work or parenting may similarly reach maximum demand in midlife and then decline thereafter. The purpose of most of the remainder of this chapter is to address the age-trajectory of social responsibility for women. It is beyond the chapter's scope to fully explain the midlife peak; nonetheless, a brief exploration of some of the more obvious explanations for why women in midlife are more socially responsible than women in young or older adulthood is possible.

Candidate explanations hinge upon features of women's midlife that (1) are not present in young or older adulthood; and (2) increase social responsibility. Similarly, they may also involve features of young or older adult women's lives that are (1) not present in midlife; and (2) decrease social responsibility. (Note that such features may be different for younger and older women.) It is also possible that a feature has greater influence on social responsibility in one period of life (more positive in midlife or more negative at other ages). For example, having children may be more strongly associated with increased social responsibility in midlife than in older adulthood. I will explore four such features: two cultural demands (career and parenthood), and two developmentally influenced resources (health and income) (Peterson and Klohnen 1995).

Cultural Demands: Career and Parenthood

Career is certainly an open venue for social responsibility. On the one hand, it is possible that more women work in midlife than at other ages, and that this is responsible for the peak. On the other hand, it is possible that only in midlife does career increase social responsibility. That is, younger adults may not have the power or responsibilities to make social contributions through work, and older adults may scale back their work-related activities. Such possibilities suggest that the midlife peak exists for employed women but not for non-employed women. Conversely, quite the opposite is also possible. Women and men who work may be consumed with work responsibilities, leaving only non-employed women to demonstrate social responsibility. This possibility predicts that the midlife peak in social responsibility may be evident only among non-employed women.

Three identical regression analyses, one for full-time employed women, one for part-time employed women, and one for non-employed women, showed the same quadratic curve for each group of women, with a peak in midlife. Thus, women working full-time experience the midlife peak the same as women who do not work or women who work part-time. Employment status does not explain the midlife peak.

However, not all full-time employment produces power and responsibility, and perhaps only women in responsibility-enhancing careers experience this peak. It is beyond this chapter to test such an idea fully, but a rough test is possible. As described previously, respondents indicated the overall quality of their work situation (as shown in figure 2.2). I repeated regressions holding this measure of work quality constant to see whether it accounts for the peak. That is, if the peak is due to women in midlife holding the highest quality careers, then holding quality of work constant should remove the age effect. The results for this regression were very similar to those presented earlier: controlling for quality of work did not affect the curvilinear relationship between age and social responsibility in women. I performed a second analysis to test for interaction effects. That is, it may be possible that only women in high-quality work situations show the midlife peak. A regression with an age-by-work-quality interaction term added no significant variance, suggesting that the midlife peak occurs equally among women in all qualities of work situation. Note that the statistical power afforded by this study makes type II errors unlikely: if this interaction were present, this analysis would have detected it.

In sum, career does not seem to account for this peak. Given that men do not show a midlife peak in social responsibility, it may not be too surprising that employment is not the explanation for this finding. However, not being employed (or being under-employed) is also not the explanation, as working and non-working women both showed the midlife peak. Of course it may require studies designed specifically to explore the reasons for the midlife peak to obtain a more definitive answer.

A second possibility is childbearing. Having children certainly increases demands to contribute to the well-being of others (i.e., the children) (Snarey et al. 1987). In addition, children may arouse a desire to care for others that is translated into a general increase in social responsibility. This increase in social responsibility may begin with the birth of the child in the twenties and rise steadily throughout childhood (until the late forties); after the children leave the home, these demands may slowly trail off. Such a theory would suggest that the midlife peak would exist for women with children but not for women without children. However, regressions showed the same quadratic curve for both groups of women, with a peak in midlife. Thus, women without children experience the same midlife peak as do women with children.

Although it is beyond this chapter to test fully, it is possible that the quality of relationship to the children accounts for the midlife peak. However, neither regressions holding quality of relationship to children constant, nor regressions with age-quality interaction terms showed any change in the quadratic relationships: the midlife peak occurs equally among women with all qualities of relationship to their children.

Neither work nor parenting seems to account for the midlife peak, at least according to the results of these admittedly limited tests. One final possibility is that the relationships above did not change because the peak is a result of work for some women but a result of parenthood for other women (MacDermid, Heilbrun, and DeHaan 1997; Peterson and Stewart 1996). I performed one last test. Due to the large sample size, there were 34 women in the sample who did not work and who did not have children. I completed regressions for these 34 women, and found the same quadratic midlife peak of social responsibility, $b_{age} = .48$, $b_{age-squared} = -.005$, $p < .05$, although these results should be interpreted with caution due to the small sample size.

Development of Resources: Health and Income

I also explored the resource side—development in resources to provide for others may explain why younger and older women show lower levels of social responsibility. First, health may be a limiting factor in being socially responsible. In particular, older women may find that poorer health interferes with their available time and energy. However, controlling for health quality (the self-report item depicted in figure 2.2) did not eliminate the midlife peak. That is, older women are not less socially responsible because of worsened health. Health status also did not interact with age-squared in predicting social responsibility. That is, even those with the best possible health also decline in social responsibility in later adulthood; thus, that decline can not be attributed to poor health. Interestingly, health quality did interact with the age term in the full quadratic equation, meaning that the age of the peak in social responsibility varied significantly with health status. Specifically, good health pushes the peak back such that the better one's health, the later in life one can maintain high levels of social responsibility.

A second resource is total household income. Income may provide a means to be socially responsible and may do so most strongly in midlife. Younger women may not yet have acquired sufficient income to give to others, and older adult women may find household income again becoming restricted. Controlling for income did not eliminate the midlife peak in social responsibility. However, household income did in fact interact with age squared in predicting social responsibility. Specifically, those with higher levels of income did not decline in social responsibility with age, but rather showed a steady linear increase across the life span. Those with middle or lower levels of household income showed the midlife peak. Thus, income provides a partial explanation. Part of the decline in social responsibility in later adulthood is associated with a decline in the resource of income. However, these results leave open some questions and raise others. These results do not explain the lowered levels of social responsibility in young adulthood (even the wealthiest were low in social responsibility in young adulthood); they do not explain why the midlife peak exists for those with middle to low income; nor do the results explain why social responsibility increases steadily with age among those with higher income levels.

This question—why does social responsibility peak for women in midlife—will have to remain unanswered in this chapter. Additional possible explanations include having different standards of social responsibility at different ages; achieving peak social status (women may experience a general social status peak in midlife); reaching peak emotional expressivity (there is some evidence that emotional expressivity leads to social responsibility, see Rossi and Rossi 1990 for evidence of this relationship); acquiring a broader understanding of political activity (Stewart and Gold-Steinberg 1990); or belonging to a particular cohort (perhaps women born in the early 1940s were socialized more to be socially responsible than were women born before or after that period, although this would not explain the peaks for the other two questions as shown in figure 2.5). It is well beyond the scope of this chapter to investigate all of these possibilities; the central purpose of this chapter is to answer the long-standing questions about levels of social responsibility cited at its start. This study clearly shows the hypothesized midlife peak in social responsibility, but only among women. It remains for future research to investigate the many possible explanations for this peak.

RELATIONSHIP OF WELL-BEING TO SOCIAL RESPONSIBILITY

A final goal of this chapter is to investigate the relationship between overall social responsibility and well-being. There are at least two reasons to expect a positive association between social responsibility and well-being. On the one hand, it is likely that having a good life leads to trying to improve others' lives. It is more difficult to give when one has very little, whereas those who have much should be able to part with it more easily. In addition, having more than others may lead to a sympathetic interest in sharing some of that wealth. In the complementary direction, giving may increase well-being. A sense of satisfaction with oneself and happiness upon receiving gratitude may result in increased well-being (Fisher 1995; MacDermid, Heilbrun, and DeHaan 1997; de St. Aubin and McAdams 1995). Given that both causal directions are likely, the association between social responsibility and well-being ought to be rather strong. That is, since the association is the sum of both causal directions, the two added together should be of considerable magnitude.

Although results may differ with more affective measures of well-being, I tested this possibility with a cognitive definition of well-being: the item asking respondents to indicate the overall quality of their lives from 0 (worst possible) to 10 (best possible). The result of a regression predicting life quality from level of social responsibility was significant, $b = .17$, $R^2 = .05$, $p < .001$. This relationship did not depend on gender, age, or on the gender-by-age interaction. Thus, there was a positive relationship between social responsibility and quality of life.

The magnitude of this relationship was nonetheless much smaller than expected (although consistent with other research, e.g., Fleeson and Baltes 1998). Both suggestions received support, but at a weaker level than anticipated. Thus, if "having" increases giving at all, it is only to a slight degree; if giving increases well-being at all, it is also only to a slight degree.

Conclusion

The purpose of this chapter was to explore the overall level of contributions to others among adult Americans of a wide age range, using an inclusive and subjective definition of social responsibility. I was able to show that Americans are only moderately socially responsible, and levels of social responsibility vary widely. I found that a small part of this variance is associated with well-being, suggesting that having a good life is only a small part of the explanation for differential levels of contributing. Second, women were more likely than men to contribute to the well-being of others. The central finding of this chapter, however, refers to the age trajectories. The large size and near-representativeness of this sample allowed for a clear affirmation of Erikson's original thesis that social responsibility peaks in midlife. However, this peak is not large, occurs only among women, and does not reach its zenith until the late forties or early fifties. It was beyond this chapter's scope to fully explore possible explanations for this peak, but I did find that part of the decline in older women's social responsibility is associated with lowered income. The full explanation will have to wait for future research.

NOTES

1. Alice Rossi, in chapter 3 of this volume, shows that this measure correlates moderately and positively with all more precise indicators of social responsibility included in this survey (with the exception of number of hours worked), suggesting some convergent validity as well as comprehensiveness to this measure.

2. All presented betas are unstandardized.

3. There were slight quadratic trends for men for both the retrospective and anticipative items, both p's < .02. Thus, the quadratic trends for all three items are depicted, although figure 2.4 shows clearly the predominance of the linear trend.

4. Alice Rossi, in chapter 3 of this volume, reports a slight midlife peak in generativity for men and a stronger midlife peak for women. The generativity scale was limited to six items; those showing the midlife peak for men concerned teaching others, giving advice, and passing on skills; these items may represent a specific work-related form of generativity.

REFERENCES

Antonucci, T., and H. Akiyama. 1997. Concern with others at midlife: Care, comfort, or compromise? In *Multiple paths of midlife development,* ed. M. E. Lachman and J. B. James, 145–69. Chicago, IL: University of Chicago Press.

Bradley, C. L. 1997. Generativity-stagnation: Development of a status model. *Developmental Review* 17:262–90.

Brody, E. M. 1985. Parent care as a normative family stress. *Gerontologist* 25:19–29.

Colby, A., and W. Damon. 1992. *Some do care: Contemporary lives of moral commitment.* New York: Free Press.

de St. Aubin, E., and D. P. McAdams. 1995. The relations of generative concern and generative action to personality traits, satisfaction/happiness with life, and ego development. *Journal of Adult Development* 2:99–112.

Erikson, E. 1963. *Childhood and society.* New York: Norton.

Fisher, B. J. 1995. Successful aging, life satisfaction, and generativity in later life. *International Journal of Aging and Human Development* 41:239–50.

Fleeson, W., and P. B. Baltes. 1998. Beyond present-day personality assessment: An encouraging exploration of the measurement properties and predictive power of subjective lifetime personality. *Journal of Research in Personality* 32:411–30.

Heimer, C. A. 1996. Gender inequalities in the distribution of responsibility. In *Social differentiation and social inequality,* ed. J. N. Baron, D. B. Grusky, and D. J. Treiman, 241–73. Boulder, CO: Westview Press.

Kobrynowicz, D., and M. Biernat. 1997. Decoding subjective evaluations: How stereotypes provide shifting standards. *Journal of Experimental Social Psychology* 33: 579–601.

Kotre, J. 1984. *Outliving the self: Generativity and the interpretation of lives.* Baltimore, MD: Johns Hopkins University Press.

Levinson, D. J. 1978. *Seasons of a man's life.* New York: Ballantine Books.

MacDermid, S. M., G. Heilbrun, and L. G. DeHaan. 1997. The generativity of employed mothers in multiple roles: 1979 and 1991. In *Multiple paths of midlife development,* ed. M. E. Lachman and J. B. James, 207–40. Chicago, IL: University of Chicago Press.

McAdams, D. P., and E. de St. Aubin. 1992. A theory of generativity and its assessment through self-report, behavioral acts, and narrative themes in autobiography. *Journal of Personality and Social Psychology* 62:1003–15.

McAdams, D. P., E. de St. Aubin, and R. L. Logan. 1993. Generativity among young, midlife, and older adults. *Psychology and Aging* 8:221–30.

Peterson, B. E., and E. C. Klohnen. 1995. Realization of generativity in two samples of women and midlife. *Psychology and Aging* 10:20–29.

Peterson, B. E., and A. J. Stewart. 1990. Using personal and fictional documents to assess psychosocial development: A case study of Vera Brittain's generativity. *Psychology and Aging* 5:400–411.

———. 1993. Generativity and social motives in young adults. *Journal of Personality and Social Psychology* 65:186–98.

———. 1996. Antecedents and contexts of generativity motivation at midlife. *Psychology and Aging,* 11:21–33.

Putnam, R. D. 1995. Bowling alone: America's declining social capital. *Journal of Democracy* 6:65–78.

Rossi, A. S., and P. H. Rossi. 1990. *Of human bonding: Parent-child relations across the life course.* New York: Aldine de Gruyter.

Ryff, C. D., and S. G. Heincke. 1983. Subjective organization of personality in adulthood and aging. *Journal of Personality and Social Psychology* 44:807–16.

Ryff, C. D., and S. Migdal. 1984. Intimacy and generativity: Self-perceived transitions. *Signs* 9:470–81.

Seligman, A. B. 1992. *The idea of civil society.* Princeton, NJ: Princeton University Press.

Snarey, J., L. Son, V. S. Kuehne, S. Hauser, and G. Vaillant. 1987. The role of parenting in men's psychosocial development: A longitidunal study of early adulthood infertility and midlife generativity. *Developmental Psychology* 23:593–603.

Stewart, A. J., and S. Gold-Steinberg. 1990. Midlife women's political consciousness: Case studies of psychosocial development and political commitment. *Psychology of Women Quarterly* 14:543–66.

THREE

Domains and Dimensions of Social Responsibility
A Sociodemographic Profile
Alice S. Rossi

INTRODUCTION

This chapter provides a sociodemographic profile of three dimensions of social responsibility—normative obligations, time commitments, and financial contributions—in two of the three major domains, family and community. The domain of work is incorporated into the analysis in only two respects: in a comparison of the level of obligation to work with the levels of obligation toward family and community as they vary by age, sex, and education, and as a control variable in the analysis of time and money contributions to either family or community. The hours spent on the job are a fundamental characteristic of daily life around which other activities are organized, and hence are a necessary consideration for the analytic focus of this chapter. The impact of job characteristics on family and community participation is dealt with explicitly in chapter 11.

Social responsibility in both the family and the community domains has been a focus of attention in recent years by politicians and policymakers, media pundits, and social scientists in a variety of disciplines. We hear endlessly about family breakdown, the decline of civic virtue, and loss of community cohesion. But political and media discourse about either family breakdown or the decline of civic virtue is skimpy or misleading in terms of empirical facts. I reviewed much of this literature in chapter 1, but it is important in setting the context for the analysis to follow to emphasize several assumptions underpinning the design of the MIDMAC national survey. Below, I briefly summarize my reading of the evidence in each of the two domains.

Family Structure

The social statistics used to defend the view that American families are breaking down focus on the following trends: earlier sexual initiation, high rates of teenage pregnancy and births out of wedlock, a continuing high divorce rate, deadbeat dads who neglect child support payments, and welfare dependency that undermines individual responsibility and weakens the work ethic. A more careful inspection of the historic trends suggests numerous qualifications. For one, there is no evidence that teenage pregnancies are unique to our era: historically, young women under twenty years of age have produced children at about the same rate for most of this century (Luker 1996), and the vast majority of these teenage mothers are not thirteen- to fifteen-year-old girls, but eighteen- and nineteen-year-old women. What *has* changed over time is the proportion of births to never-married women: at the turn of the century only 1 in 100 births involved never-married women; in more recent years, from 1970 to 1995, the proportion of births to never-married women more than doubled. But out-of-wedlock births are not restricted to teenagers: such births have gone up at every age, and the majority are births to white women, not black women in urban ghettos. Furthermore, although such women are not married, many are cohabiting with the infant's father (Bumpass 1994), and many noncohabiting fathers remain in close contact with the child.[1]

The most significant change supportive of the family breakdown thesis is the change in attitudes toward marriage as an institution. The majority of both women and men now acquire sexual experience prior to marriage, but how could this be otherwise in an era when the age at sexual maturation has dropped to an average of twelve, schooling has been extended by many years, and the prospects for stable marriages are brighter when the marriages are contracted after schooling is completed and economic independence assured? Under such circumstances, there is little likelihood that young men and women will live a celibate life for a decade or more before marriage. What flows from such circumstances is increasing acceptance of cohabitation, which itself is an index of the erosion of marriage norms, as Larry Bumpass and Minya Choe (1996) have pointed out in their comparison of attitudes toward marriage in the United States, Japan, and Korea. The belief has become widespread across all Western societies that it is not necessary to marry or to have children in order to enjoy a happy fulfilled life, a finding confirmed by the majority of both men and women in our MIDUS survey of 1995. Last, the increasing rate and persistence of even young mothers in the labor force adds further to weakened marriage norms, because there is less pressure on women to enter or remain in marriages out of sheer economic dependence on men.

If one's conception of "family" is restricted to a couple with dependent children, then it is indeed the case that from that perspective, the family has undergone major and perhaps irreversible change. But if one's conception of family is of a three-generational lineage, the prospects are quite different. With adults living longer, and with no need for either child labor or economic support of the elderly, there has been an intensification of the bonds between parents and grown children. The less family members must depend on each other for material benefits, the more they can enjoy the potential for emotional and social rewards. As Mihaly Csikszentmihalyi put it, "the modern family, with all its problems, opens up new possibilities for optimal experiences that were much more difficult to come by in previous times" (Csikszentmihalyi 1997, 85). The strengthened bond between the generations is particularly striking between women and their children, and between women and their parents and other kin (Rossi and Rossi 1990). Our MIDUS survey found two-thirds of our respondents reported contact (by phone, visit, letter, or e-mail) with relatives (parents, grown children, siblings) at least several times a week, a mere 7% only once a month or less, a level of contact even higher than that with friends.

The lesson we drew from these considerations was the need to empirically define family obligations, caregiving support, and financial assistance not merely with reference to spouses and children, but to the broader array of kin and close friends, including cohabiting partners, parents, in-laws, grandchildren, and other relatives.

The Community Domain

On the issue of declining civic virtue and communal participation, about which so much has been written in recent years, the evidence is mixed. There is firm evidence that voting has declined among registered voters; and increasing numbers of adults have no party affiliation, instead defining themselves as politically independent. As reported in chapter 1, trust in the executive and legislative branches of government has undergone a continuous decline over the past thirty years. The ranks of volunteers are reported to have thinned. Indeed Robert Putnam's essays (1995a, 1995b, 1996) have focused on what he views as the "strange disappearance of civil America." Perhaps best known is Putnam's metaphor to the effect that Americans are now "bowling alone" rather than bowling in leagues (1995b).[2]

Numerous explanations have been offered for the presumed decline of civic participation. As early as 1985, Robert Bellah and his associates attributed such decline to excessive individualism encouraged by political alienation, increased consumerism, the decline in formal religious affiliations, occupational advances contingent on geographic relocation, and the anonymity of living in declining city centers or suburban sprawls. Women's continuing transition from homemakers to paid employees has been offered as an explanation for the assumed decline in volunteerism. Passive entertainment at home, now increasingly possible thanks to the expanding number of TV channels and rental movies and the widespread availability of the Internet, has been cited by Putnam and others as responsible for withdrawal into private pleasures rather than responsible citizenship and social involvement in community affairs.

In light of the fact that the majority of couples who have preschool- or school-age children are now dual-earners, it is a reasonable expectation that time management is a critical issue for them. Time may be the "ultimate scarce resource," as Csikscentmihalyi claims (1997, 8). As Juliet Schor states in her book, aptly titled *The Overworked American* (1992), Americans work longer hours with less vacation time or family leave than workers in any other Western society. But is it the case that dual-earning couples therefore provide less social-emotional support to close kin and friends and engage less frequently in community service? We took this to be a question eminently worthy of special attention in the design of our survey.

There were also other bits of evidence to support some degree of skepticism toward the claim of declining civic participation. There is reason to believe that there has been a subtle change in the kinds of institutions adults form or affiliate with. Rather than belonging to formal organizations, clubs, or teams as often as former generations did, contemporary adults are innovating a set of smaller institutions of a more flexible nature: small groups sharing similar tastes, problems, or lifestyles. Such small groups are less socially visible because they carry no identifiable labels, occupy no permanent sites, and engage in little self-promoting publicity, but they *do* represent vital connecting threads in the social fabric. Robert Wuthnow's *Sharing the Journey* (1994) is an excellent account of such small groups and their quest for a new sense of community. Churches and synagogues actively sponsor and house many of these groups, which often involve youth and adults who are not even members of the congregation: 6 in 10 congregations report such usage (Hodgkinson and Weitzman 1993a, 1993b). In fact in 1991 congregations offered as many programs in human services as they did religious services and religious education programs. Participation in such groups associated with a religious congregation paves the way to volunteer service and participation in community activities, which explains the title of the Independent Sector's report—*From Belief to Commitment* (Hodgkinson and Weitzman 1993b).

Another quiet development less often noted is the great expansion that has taken place over the past few decades in the services provided by private charities, often with religious affiliations, such as Catholic Charities, the Jewish Federation, the Lutheran Social Services, and the Salvation Army, an expansion largely attributable to the fact that more states and municipalities are now contracting with such private agencies to provide, more cheaply and with less inefficiency than public agencies, such services as job training, foster care, homeless shelters, day care, and drug rehabilitation. The changes taking place under recent welfare reform add to this growth of private charities, blurring still further the line between the private and public spheres, as public funds are directed to private agencies for program implementation. Such religiously affiliated charities draw on volunteers to provide some part of such services.

What adults take to be their "community" may also have undergone very great change. When we were a rural society, community clearly referred to a defined physical locale. Limited to the slow pace of a horse and wagon, early nineteenth-century Americans had little social contact beyond their closest neighbors, with at most a weekly trek to town to attend church services or to purchase needed supplies.[3] A shuttle flight between Boston and Washington now takes less than an hour; early in the nineteenth century, it would take more than a week by stagecoach; only a few decades ago, it took a good part of a day by railroad or bus. Through phone calls, letters, and e-mail, we can and do remain in contact with close kin and friends on a very frequent basis, and thanks to air travel, sharing holidays and special family events is possible even for a short weekend visit between kin separated by a continent, at least for the relatively affluent members of society.

But "community" has still other new meanings. As Émile Durkheim predicted long ago in his *The Division of Labor in Society* (1964), belonging to a national union or professional association may hold more meaning for many adults than residence in a particular neighborhood or town. So too, membership in organizations may link individuals not to their local residential communities, but to national communities, whether or not such organizations have city or state chapters. A growing source even of political funding comes not from local constituents, but from like-minded citizens in other states. Many of us contribute more money to congressional campaigns in other states than to campaigns in our own state. Increasingly, the pool of contributors to many social and political causes, for example, numerous organizations and special interest groups concerned with environmental issues, abortion, health, drug addiction, the disabled, and so forth, span the nation. A contemporary equivalent to Alexis de Tocqueville would clearly have to be concerned not merely with *local* voluntary associations, but the infinitely more complex and far-ranging organizations and causes to which Americans now contribute time and money.

The conclusion we drew from such trends in the design of the MI-DUS module on social responsibility was that we should *not* limit questions to those measuring participation in the local residential community through meeting attendance or volunteer service, both of which imply geographic proximity, but that we should include questions on financial contributions to organizations, causes, or charities that may not be local at all. So too, in the family domain, we asked not only about direct caregiving that requires local access, such as help with household chores or child care, but social-emotional support in the form of advice, providing comfort to another person, or sheer listening, all of which can be done by phone or letter. We also asked about financial as well as time contributions to family members because close relatives in need of help may live miles away. Telephone wires and letter carriers are now crucial though invisible links that bind us to close kin and to distant like-minded fellow citizens.

One last consideration in our formulation of social responsibility bears special emphasis. A longstanding tradition in both sociology and political science has been to define social responsibility very narrowly, in terms of voluntary associations in local politics (e.g, Putnam 1995a, 1995b, 1996; Seligman 1992). That we have broadened the conception of social responsibility to include the domains of family and work stems from our assumption that role competence in these domains is as vital a social and personal measure of a successful life as involvement in community organizations, however extensively defined. To think of social responsibility otherwise is to do particular disservice to those of limited social status and financial means whose productive labor and heavy home responsibilities take so great a toll that there is neither time, nor energy, nor the financial means to involve themselves directly in community affairs. Most people in most societies today, as in the past, contribute to their communities and nations through their pri-

1

mary ties to children, parents, siblings, and friends, through the work they do to earn their way in life, and though involuntary, through the taxes they pay, which provide needed services to the poor, the sick and disabled, and the elderly. From this perspective, men and women who hold down jobs, actively rear their children, and spend leisure time only with close friends and kin are no less responsible citizens than those who attend a dozen meetings of community organizations or contribute thirty hours of volunteer service to a hospital or youth group each month.

DATA AND METHODOLOGY

The analysis to follow is restricted to the 3,032 respondents in the 1995 MIDUS survey, aged twenty-five to seventy-four, who participated in the initial telephone interview and returned the two self-administered booklets questionnaires sent to them following the interview. This sample was stratified by age and sex, with oversampling of males between sixty-five and seventy-four, and undersampling of young adults twenty-five to thirty-nine. Compared to the proportions of adults in numerous social demographic categories shown in the October 1995 Current Population Survey, the unweighted MIDUS sample has *fewer* less well educated, young, and married adults, and *fewer* racial and ethnic minority members. (For more detail on the sample and response rate, see the appendix.) All components of the weighting variables (age, sex, education) are major independent variables in the analysis to follow. As a result multivariate analyses based on the unweighted sample are largely unbiased and efficient (Winship and Radbill 1994). The multivariate regression analyses we report did not differ when weights were used; hence we report analyses of the unweighted sample.

Table 3.1 provides descriptions of our major measures of social responsibility, organized in terms of the domains and dimensions of the empirical scales, scores, and ratings, with illustrative items from the survey instruments where appropriate. Time and money measures are estimates of hours per month or dollar contributions per month, summated across specific categories of persons or organizations. Normative obligation scales (family, work, and civic obligation, and altruism) consist of self-assessments of the degree of obligation respondents feel in a variety of situations depicted in the items (or *would* feel were they confronted by such a situation). As noted in the descriptive detail column, the scales have good to excellent reliability (alphas from .68 to

2">103

TABLE 3.1 Domains and Dimensions Tapped by Major
Social Responsibility Measures

Domain	Dimension	Measure	Descriptive Detail
Family	Norms	Family obligation	Eight-item scale of eleven-point ratings of degree of obligation felt toward children, parents, spouse, friends, from 0 = no obligation to 10 = very great obligation (0–80 scale range, alpha = .82, mean = 60, SD = 13.2).
	Time	Social-emotional support	Summated score of hours per month providing emotional and social support, e.g., comforting, listening to, advising) to five types of recipients: spouse, parents, in-laws, children/grandchildren, other family or close friends.
		Hands-on caregiving	Summated score of hours per month providing unpaid assistance, e.g., help around the house, transportation, child care, to four types of recipients: parents, in-laws, children/grandchildren, other family or close friends.
	Money	Financial contribution	Summated score of dollars per month respondents or family living with them contribute (including dollar value of food, clothing, or other goods) to four types of recipients: parents, in-laws, grandchildren/grown children, other family members or close friends.
Work	Norms	Work obligation	Three-item scale of eleven-point ratings of degree of obligation felt toward job, from 0 = no obligation to 10 = very great obligation, e.g., "to do more than most people would do on your kind of job" (0–30 scale range, alpha = .68, mean = 22.9, SD = 5.2).
Community	Norms	Civic obligation	Four-item scale of eleven-point ratings of degree of obligation felt toward civic participation, e.g., "to serve on a jury if called" or "to vote in local or national elections" (0–40 scale range, alpha = .78, mean = 30.7, SD = 7.8).
		Altruism	Four-item scale of eleven-point ratings of degree of obligation felt in situations involving helping others at expense to self, e.g., "to pay more for your health care so that everyone had access to health care" (0–40 scale range, alpha = .80, mean = 23.4, SD = 8.9).
	Time	Volunteer service	Summated score of hours per month doing volunteer work to four types of organizations/causes/charities: hospital/health-related, school/youth-related, political, and other.
		Meeting attendance	Summated score of number of meetings attended involving four types of organizations/causes/charities: religious, sports or social, union or other professional, and other.
	Money	Financial contribution	Summated score of dollars per month contributed to three types of organizations/causes/charities: religious, political, and other.
Overall Self-Rating		Contribution to others	Single-item rating of contribution to welfare and well-being of others, eleven-point rating from 0 = worst to 10 = best.

.82) and considerable variation in range. The last measure shown in table 3.1 is an overall self-rating of the extent to which respondents feel they contribute to the welfare and well-being of "others" (not specified in terms of life domain). This is the general self-rating analyzed by William Fleeson in chapter 2.

Table 3.2 shows the matrix of correlation coefficients between all pairs of fifteen measures of social responsibility, organized to distinguish between the four family variables (shown in the upper left triangle), and the five community variables (shown in the lower right triangle). Also included in the matrix are measures on work and home life. The job pride and home pride scales are based on the extent to which respondents take *pride* from the work they do on their jobs (or in their homes), and the *respect* others show for the work they do on their jobs or at home. Time devoted to household chores is included as well (domestic care) because time is one of the major dimensions of the measures of social responsibility in both the family and community domains

Of the 105 coefficients in the matrix, 21 (italic in the table) do not reach statistical significance and 40 show significant but low correlations (under .10); only 14 coefficients are .20 or higher, and 7 of them are above .30. Closer inspection suggests several points of substantive interest:

1. The highest correlation in the matrix, .48, is between hands-on caregiving and social-emotional support given in the family domain— hardly surprising in light of the fact that any caregiving activity almost invariably entails listening to and comforting the recipient of care, though it is not necessarily the case that those to whom we provide social-emotional support require hands-on care as well.

2. The four scales on normative obligations (items 1, 7, 10, and 11 in the matrix) are highly correlated with each other, with six correlations ranging between .26 and .46, as shown in boldface in table 3.2. The common latent factor illustrated here is a general predisposition for helpfulness toward others. The highest correlation in the matrix (.48, also shown in boldface) is between social-emotional support and hands-on caregiving, hardly surprising because time spent giving hands-on care is itself a measure of giving social support; that the correlation is not higher reflects the fact that giving social support does not necessarily involve any hands-on care but may consist merely of such things as listening to a relative's problems on the phone or during a visit. Modest correlations (.24, .26, .28, and .33) hold between the four

TABLE 3.2 Correlation Coefficients between Social Responsibility Measures

Domain	Dimension	1	2	3	4	5	6	7	8	9	10	11	12	13	14	15
Family	1. Family obligation	—														
	2. Social-emotional support	.14	—													
	3. Hands-on caregiving	.08	.48	—												
	4. Financial contribution	.08	.05	.13	—											
Home	5. Home pride	.13	.05	.05	.02	—										
	6. Domestic care	.14	.22	.15	-.01	.01	—									
Work	7. Work obligation	**.42**	.07	.04	.07	.17	.06	—								
	8. Job pride	.09	.02	.02	.04	.27	-.01	.24	—							
	9. Hours	-.02	.00	-.02	.07	.03	-.24	.09	-.04	—						
Community	10. Civic obligation	**.36**	-.01	-.02	.05	.16	.07	**.46**	.17	.00	—					
	11. Altruism	**.46**	.04	.04	.07	.12	.06	**.40**	.11	.00	**.45**	—				
	12. Volunteer service	.08	.07	.02	.08	.06	.07	.09	.06	-.02	.13	.19	—			
	13. Meeting attendance	.05	.04	0.2	.08	.05	.01	.04	.06	.03	.11	.12	.35	—		
	14. Financial contribution	.05	-.02	-.03	.18	.04	.00	.07	.09	.04	.14	.09	.24	.21	—	
Overall Self-Rating	15. Contribution to others	.28	.10	.09	.11	.15	.07	.26	.16	-.05	.24	.33	.22	.11	.14	—

Note: Italic coefficients are not statistically significant; all others are significant at $p < .05$ to $p < .001$. Boldface coefficients indicate normative obligation scales across the three major domains of family, work, and community.

obligation scales and the overall self-rating on contribution to the welfare of others.[4]

3. Normative obligations and social behavior are only modestly correlated, and only *within domains,* with correlations ranging from .08 to .14 in the family domain and somewhat higher in the community domain, .09 to .19. Norms indicate predispositions to help or participate, but clearly existential circumstances in the lives of donors and recipients dictate whether such norms are acted upon or not.

4. Among the behavioral measures themselves, only one coefficient is above .10: those who contribute financial aid to family members are also somewhat predisposed to contribute money to community organizations and charities ($r = .18$). As shown below, money contributions are far more dependent on educational attainment and household financial resources than are caregiving or providing informal social support.

The overall profile projected by the correlation matrix implies that our major construct—social responsibility—is highly differentiated by both domain of life and dimension of expression. We infer that general normative obligations may be rooted in early socialization and parental modeling, whereas behavioral manifestations of social responsibility are more affected by the existential circumstances in the individual lives of our subjects and of their kin and friends. We begin our analysis by detailing the extent of variation by age, sex, and education in the several behavioral indicators of social responsibility in the family and community domains.

SOCIAL DEMOGRAPHY OF SOCIALLY RESPONSIBLE BEHAVIOR

Tables 3.3 through 3.6 provide the full detail on all the major behavioral dimensions of social responsibility: table 3.3 pertains to the three dimensions in the family domain (social-emotional support, hands-on caregiving, and financial contribution), and table 3.4, the two dimensions in the community domain (volunteer service and financial contribution). In both tables, we show two major measures: the *percentage* of each age-sex-education subgroup that contributes *any* time or money; and the *average amount* of time or money per month given to family members or to community organizations or causes among those who give *some* support or money. For those interested only in the major findings shown in these detailed tables, table 3.5 summarizes the statistically significant differences by age, sex, and education, and

TABLE 3.3 Contributions to the Dimensions of Social Responsibility in the Family Domain, by Age, Sex, and Education

	Men			Women		
Dimension and Education	25–39	40–59	60–74	25–39	40–59	60–74
A. Social-emotional support						
Percentage giving any						
Low education	96.2	91.7	84.0	95.7	96.5	87.7
High education	96.1	97.5	95.6	99.8	99.5	96.8
Average amount given per month (hours)[a]						
Low education	73.4	56.8	48.4	117.6	69.6	52.3
High education	60.2	44.9	37.9	84.0	66.6	42.1
B. Hands-on caregiving						
Percentage giving any						
Low education	79.0	74.3	67.9	78.5	80.7	63.1
High education	74.4	74.3	72.2	74.3	75.7	78.2
Average amount given per month (hours)[a]						
Low education	28.3	28.5	24.2	48.3	38.9	29.6
High education	27.6	22.9	24.5	34.9	31.5	26.9
C. Financial contribution						
Percentage giving any						
Low education	40.1	55.2	49.6	43.6	55.1	45.8
High education	37.1	54.1	67.1	38.7	58.3	55.1
Average amount given per month ($)[a]						
Low education	144	147	206	137	142	85
High education	143	227	215	125	205	173
Percentage of total household income given						
Low education	2.5	3.0	3.9	4.1	5.7	8.9
High education	1.8	2.4	2.8	3.4	2.8	2.7

Note: See table 3.5 for a summary of the statistical significance (and its direction) of age, sex, and educational differences on the dimensions of social responsibility shown in this table.

[a] Among those who gave some.

table 3.6 specifies the particular sex-age-education subgroups with the *highest* and *lowest* degree of help provided in the family or community domains.

We recognize three major points of interest from the presented data:

1. Age differences. Age is *negatively* related to providing social-emotional support and caregiving, but *positively* related to providing fi-

TABLE 3.4 Contributions to the Dimensions of Social Responsibility in the Community Domain, by Age, Sex, and Education

Dimension and Education	Men			Women		
	25–39	40–59	60–74	25–39	40–59	60–74
A. Volunteer service						
Percentage doing any						
Low education	26.8	29.5	35.1	38.2	36.8	31.3
High education	39.8	49.1	51.9	46.8	57.4	54.5
Average amount done per month (hours) [a]						
Low education	14.1	9.8	14.8	13.3	10.1	11.8
High education	12.3	10.7	12.3	12.6	12.5	15.7
B. Financial contribution						
Percentage giving any						
Low education	54.8	63.1	74.1	57.5	59.7	60.3
High education	68.1	82.5	82.9	71.5	81.9	80.1
Average amount given per month ($) [a]						
Low education	88	83	110	61	91	68
High education	97	145	190	86	118	146
Percentage of total household income given						
Low education	1.8	1.7	2.8	1.5	2.0	4.7
High education	1.9	2.0	3.1	2.2	2.5	4.3

Note: See table 3.5 for a summary of the statistical significance (and its direction) of age, sex, and educational differences on dimensions of social responsibility shown in this table.

[a] Among those who gave some.

nancial assistance and volunteers service in the community: young adults are most heavily invested in the primary world of family, while older adults show expanded horizons involving the larger world of the community and have the financial wherewithal to provide financial assistance in both the family and community domains. One cannot help but wonder to what extent the greatly improved financial condition of the middle-aged and elderly in our time is a major explanation of this latter finding. Compared to their parents and grandparents, younger adults at the end of the twentieth century are less secure financially, experience greater financial strain, show higher levels of debt and bankruptcy, higher rates of employment for married women with very young children, and lesser ability to purchase a home than their parents or grandparents at comparable ages. These days, young adults are sub-

TABLE 3.5 Summary of Statistically Significant Differences, by Dimensions
of Social Responsibility in Family and Community Domains, by Age, Sex,
and Education (*F* statistics on ANOVA)

Domain	Dimension	Age	Sex	Education
Family	Social-emotional support	46.8*** (yg > mid > old)	50.1*** (women > men)	17.2*** (low > high)
	Hands-on caregiving	2.9* (yg > mid > old)	16.5*** (women > men)	7.6** (low > high)
	Financial assistance	6.9** (mid > old > yg)	7.3** (men > women)	15.5*** (high > low)
	Percentage of income	—	6.7** (women > men)	9.5** (low > high)
Community	Volunteer service	4.0* (old > yg > mid)	—	—
	Financial contribution	11.1*** (old > mid > yg)	10.9*** (men > women)	27.6*** (high > low)
	Percentage of income	16.2*** (old > mid > yg)	4.8* (women > men)	—

*$p < .05$.   **$p < .01$.   ***$p < .001$.

jected to very conflicting messages: they are criticized for not saving
enough but tempted by advertisers to buy and consume more products, torn between the choice of accepting more credit cards than they
need (and thus more debt) or gambling on high returns on stock market investments. It is an open question whether today's young adults
and their parents will enjoy the level of financial security in their old
age that the elderly of the last two decades have enjoyed.

    2. Sex differences. In the family domain, the data show a distinct dif-
ference between women and men, similar to that shown in previous
studies (e.g., Rossi and Rossi 1990): women exceed men in the time
committed to providing social-emotional support and hands-on caregiving, and men exceed women in financial contributions in both the
family and the community domains. Although the measure used is total household income, the fact that, among dual-earning couples, the
men have considerably higher earnings than the women may provide
the rationale for the men to handle budget matters and hence to give
more financially than the women do to both family members and community organizations. Note, however, that an important qualification
is called for when attention is given not to the total *amount* of money
contributed, but to the *proportion* of total income. On this measure the
pattern reverses: women give a larger proportion of their income than
do men. This is most dramatically shown among older, lesser-educated

TABLE 3.6 Summary of Lowest and Highest Contributions to Social Responsibility Dimensions in Family and Community Domains, by Age, Sex, and Education

	Young (25–39)	Middle-Aged (40–59)	Old (60–74)
A. Men			
Low education	Lowest percentage doing any volunteer service (26.8) Lowest percentage giving any money to the community (55)	Lowest number of hours per month of volunteer service (10)	Lowest percentage giving any social-emotional support (84)
High education	Lowest percentage giving any money to family (37) Lowest percentage of income given to family (1.8)	Lowest number of hours per month of hands-on caregiving (23) Highest amount per month given to family ($227)	Highest percentage giving some money to the community (83) Highest percentage giving some money to family (67) Highest amount per month given to the community (190)
B. Women			
Low education	Highest number of hours per month giving social-emotional support (118) Highest number of hours per month of hands-on caregiving (48)	Highest percentage doing some hands-on caregiving (81)	Lowest percentage doing some hands-on caregiving (63) Lowest amount per month given to family ($85) Lowest amount per month given to the community ($68) Highest percentage of income given to family (8.9) and the community (4.7)
High education		Highest percentage doing some volunteer service (54.7) Highest percentage giving some social-emotional support (99.5)	Highest number of hours per month of volunteer service (16) Lowest number of hours per month giving social-emotional support (42)

adults: as seen in table 3.3, older, lesser-educated women give 8.9% of their income to family members, whereas men in the same category give only half that proportion—3.9%. Table 3.4 shows a similar sex difference in the community domain: older, lesser-educated women give 4.7% of their income to community organizations or charities, compared to only 2.8% among men in this category.

3. Educational differences. A major distinction between lesser- and well-educated adults is the difference between time and money contributions, similar to the sex differences noted above: lesser-educated adults exceed well-educated adults in the *time* contributed to both family members and community organizations, whereas *money* contributions are greater from well-educated adults than from lesser-educated adults. Note, however, that here too the proportion of income contributed to family members reverses on education, at least in the family domain: as seen in table 3.3 compared to table 3.4, lesser-educated adults contribute a larger proportion of their income to family members than do the well educated (e.g., among older women, those less well educated contribute 8.9%, but well-educated older women only give 2.7% of their income to family members). No comparable education differences are found in proportion of income contributed to organizations.[5]

Our next step in analysis is to include additional sociodemographic variables relevant to the level of time and money contributions, and to test whether age, sex, or educational attainment have direct or indirect effects on the behavioral indicators of social responsibility. The results are shown in table 3.7, which consists of six regression analyses, three measures each for the family and community domains. The new variables round out the *resources* of adults (income and employment hours in addition to education), and *family status* (married or not, and the number of children). Marriage and childrearing enlarge the kinship network and heighten both personal desire for and social pressure toward greater involvement with both kin and local organizations in the community (O'Donnell 1983; Rossi and Rossi 1990).[6] Long hours of employment were expected to place restraints on the time adults have available for community participation as volunteers, and perhaps on the time available for caregiving and social-emotional support of family members as well.

Table 3.7 shows several significant differences in the pattern of predictors by both domain and dimension of social responsibility, as follows:

TABLE 3.7 Regressions of Behavioral Dimensions of Social Responsibility in the Family and Community Domains on Social-Demographic Characteristics (beta coefficients)

Predictor variable	Family[a]			Community[b]		
	Hands-on caregiving	Social-emotional support	Financial contribution	Frequent meeting attendance	Volunteer service	Financial contribution
Resources						
Education	-.086***	-.090***	.042*	.159***	.158***	.162***
Total household income	-.012	-.024	.211***	.021	.014	.210***
Hours of work per week	-.027	-.004	.063	.010	-.070**	-.035
Family status						
Marital status[c]	.008	.168***	-.063***	.011	.051**	.068***
Number of children	.111***	-.114**	.115***	.018	.073***	.037***
Age	-.117***	-.250***	.064***	.020	-.008	.092***
Sex[d]	.058**	.149***	-.017	.018	.047*	-.020
R^2	.032***	.113***	.063***	.030***	.036***	.117***
N	2,966	2,966	2,966	2,966	2,966	2,966

[a]Includes family members and close friends.
[b]Includes organizations, causes, and charities.
[c]Married = 1; not married = 0.
[d]Men = 1; women = 2.
* $p < .05$. ** $p < .01$. *** $p < .001$.

1. Time versus money contributions. The results of the multivariate analysis show that in the family domain, all three core sociodemographic characteristics—age, sex, and education—have direct net effects on the three measures in the family domain. Being young, less well educated, and female are all conducive to providing social-emotional support and caregiving; in addition, being married and having several children predicts more social-emotional support to family members. On financial assistance to family members, income counts for more than education, and it is unmarried adults who give more money than do married adults. Time spent in paid employment shows no significant direct effect on any behavioral measure in the family domain, though the *direction* of effect is for fewer hours at work to be associated with more rather than less caregiving.

Major predictors of time and money contributions are less sharply differentiated in the community domain: the major contributors of both time and money are well-educated, married adults with a number of children. Unique to volunteer service are both sex and hours at work: women and those who are either not employed or put in fewer hours on the job are more likely to contribute time to volunteer service.

2. Age as a predictor of social responsibility. The largest single standardized coefficient in table 3.7 is the negative relationship of age and giving social support to family members (−.250, significant at the .001 level): young adults are very much more active in this regard than older adults. An important qualification must be noted: young adults not only *provide* more caregiving and social-emotional support than older adults, they also *get* more help from family members and close friends. The beta coefficient of age in identical equations predicting *getting* social support is −.172 (significant at the .01 level; data not shown). Thus in personal support involving time contributions in the family domain, reciprocity rules: those who *give* help to others also *get* support from others. This is not the case when comparing *giving* with *getting* financial help: table 3.7 shows older adults report giving more money than young adults (.064, significant at the .001 level), but analysis of the amount of money received from family members shows a negative sign on age (−.172, significant at the .001 level). Older adults *give* financial support, young adults *get* financial help.

From the perspective of social structure, note how different the interpretation of social responsibility would be if we were only analyzing community level participation as the exclusive domain of social responsibility, which would suggest that well-educated, higher income, married adults are the most socially responsible members of society. Such an interpretation is clearly qualified by the different profile shown for socially responsible behavior in the family domain, in which it is the less well educated, lower income, young adults who show a greater degree of personal caregiving and social support than do well-educated, higher income adults.

It is important to note that lower income families, particularly in urban areas, have a far more difficult task as parents than higher income families have. They often must combat dangerous, disorganized neighborhoods and poor schools rife with danger and temptations for young children and adolescents. Working-poor parents also have less job security and work long hours at tedious and often physically exhausting jobs. Money management is difficult, child care often unreliable, child supervision more necessary to protect youngsters from harm and social deviance. To find higher levels of social support and caregiving to elderly parents, siblings, and grown children after an early adulthood of more complex childrearing is a tribute to their endurance and stamina. In sum, it takes far greater parental investment for the working-poor adult than for the upper-middle-class adult to achieve the same outcomes in child health, character, and competence. As my colleague Larry Bumpass notes, "taking care of one's own" may also be the most cost-effective involvement from which the society at large benefits. When such involvement and investment in families are *not* made by the working poor, the consequences for society are very great indeed. In chapter 5, Kathy Newman reports that the working poor she interviewed in New York City consider the care and supervision of their children to be their major contribution to the *community*.

Enriching the Scope of Predictor Variables of Social Responsibility

The sociodemographic variables in the analysis to this point provide only a bare-bones profile of what prompts socially responsible behavior. Human motivation draws upon more than existential pressures and resources; we act out of many longstanding values and personality predispositions not captured by factors such as income, age, or sex. Sociodemographic variables are often proxies for deeper qualities motivating human action. So too, to define family status simply in terms of marital status and family size is to neglect the larger kindred from which and within which family life develops. To enrich and expand the analysis, we add a variety of additional variables to the multivariate analysis. First, we draw on the normative obligation scales described in table 3.1. As will be shown in chapter 7, such normative obligations have roots in earlier phases of the life course and are therefore assumed to be predictors of the time and money contributions measured here.

In addition, we add a measure of generativity, a modified version of the Loyola Generativity Scale (McAdams and de St. Aubin 1992). This scale measures the extent to which adults feel that they are sought out for advice, that other people need them, that they have made unique contributions to society, and that they have had a good influence on the lives of many people. We further round out family measures with the frequency of contact with *relatives* in the family domain equations (and frequency of contact with *friends* in the community domain equations), and a scale measuring the extent to which relatives react to our respondents in a positive or critical way. Frequency of religious service attendance is added both as a reflection of religious values predisposing to helpfulness to others and as an index of involvement in the larger social context of neighborhood or parish. Self-ratings of physical health are included to test whether poor health constitutes a constraint on helpful behavior. To simplify this expanded step of analysis, we confine attention to one measure each of time and money contributions in the two domains of family and community: social-emotional support and financial contribution in the family domain, volunteer service and financial contribution in the community domain. Table 3.8 shows the results of this expanded regression analysis in the family domain, table 3.9, in the community domain. Table 3.10 summarizes the significant results from both tables viewed simultaneously, to pinpoint the variables that significantly predict one or both *domains* of social responsiblity, and one or both *dimensions* of social responsibility (i.e., time, money, or both).

With the additional predictor variables added to the array of sociodemographic variables, the amount of explained variance is increased (as indexed by the larger R^2s in all four equations in tables 3.8 and 3.9, compared to those in table 3.7), and there is no significant change in the direction of effect or statistical significance of the sociodemographic predictors. Hence we restrict discussion of these tables to the effect of the new variables, as follows:

1. The most striking finding is that the generativity scale is a significant predictor of all four dependent variables: the higher the score on generativity, the greater the likelihood that respondents provide time

TABLE 3.8 Regressions of Time and Money Contributions
in the Family Domain (beta coefficients)

Predictor variable	Time Contribution[a]	Financial Contribution[b]
Normative predisposition		
Generativity	.088***	.067***
Family obligation	.061***	.089***
Social embeddedness		
Marital status[c]	.174***	−.059***
Number of children	.093***	.091***
Frequent contact with relatives	.086***	.125***
Positive regard of ego by kin	.032	−.074***
Frequent religious service attendance	−.041*	−.023
Resources		
Education	−.094***	.038*
Total household income	−.030	.209***
Constraints		
Hours of work per week	−.015	.028
Health self-rating[d]	−.016	−.022
Age	−.231***	.091***
Sex[e]	.124***	.052**
R^2	.133***	.099***
N	2,845	2,845

[a] Hours per month giving social-emotional support.
[b] Amount of money per month given to family members and close friends.
[c] Married = 1; not married = 0.
[d] Poor to excellent.
[e] men = 1; women = 2.
$*p < .05.$ $**p < .01.$ $***p < .001.$

and money to both the family and community. As highlighted in table 3.10, generativity stands alone in this regard.

2. Normative obligation scales are tailored to one or the other of the two domains: table 3.8 shows that the family obligation scale predicts time and money contributions to family members; similarly, high scores on the altruism scale are stimulants for volunteer service, though not significantly so to financial contributions in the community domain. By contrast, the civic obligation scale contributes nothing independent of the more general altruism measure, perhaps because the items in the civic obligation scale refer to such things as voting and jury service rather than to volunteer service in youth- or health-related organizations, which are the major types of service in the four-item score on volunteer service.

TABLE 3.9 Regressions of Time and Money Contributions
in the Community Domain (beta coefficients)

Predictor Variable	Time Contribution[a]	Financial Contribution[b]
Normative predisposition		
Generativity	.124***	.040*
Civic obligation	.001	.020
Altruism	.126***	.026
Social embeddedness		
Marital status[c]	.054**	.040*
Number of children	.058**	.020
Frequent contact with friends	.094***	.049***
Frequent religious service		
attendance	.140***	.323***
Resources		
Education	.113***	.114***
Total household income	.014	.226***
Constraints		
Hours of work per week	−.081***	−.032
Hours caregiving	.008	−.003
Health self-rating	−.010	−.001
Age	−.038	.047*
Sex[d]	.002	−.062***
R^2	.118***	.235***
N	2,866	2,866

[a] Hours per month of volunteer service.
[b] Amount of money per month given to organizations, causes, and charities.
[c] Married = 1; not married = 0.
[d] Men = 1; women = 2.
*$p < .05$. **$p < .01$. ***$p < .001$.

3. Physical health has no significant effect as a constraint against time or money contributions in either domain, although the sign is negative in all four equations. In other analyses we have conducted, health self-rating was consistently *negatively* associated with volunteer service. This does not mean sick people are high volunteers; rather, it is likely that those in truly excellent health may prefer to spend their leisure hours in more active pursuits (e.g., jogging, tennis) than in the more sedentary activities that characterize most volunteer work in hospitals, schools, or political groups. Here is a potentially important factor that works against engaging in volunteer work, reflecting the increasing attention paid to active lifestyles in recent decades: a preference to spend one's leisure hours working out in a gym or running for a couple of miles before or after work, rather than contributing time on a hospital volunteer staff or as a political clerk at election time.

TABLE 3.10 Significant Predictors of Social Responsibility, by Domain
and Dimension of Contribution

	Dimension		
Domain	Time	Time and Money	Money
Family	Low education Female Infrequent religious service attendance	High family obligation Large number of children High contact with kin	High education Not married Kin critical of ego
Family and community	Married Large number of children	HIGH GENERATIVITY	Old High income Male
Community	High altruism Low work hours	Married High contact with friends Frequent religious service attendance High education	

Note: Significant predictors in regression analyses as shown in tables 3.8 and 3.9.

4. Religious service attendance shows a strong effect, but only in the community domain: the more frequent such attendance, the greater the extent of volunteer service, and even more so, the greater the financial contribution to organizations and charities. Indeed, religious service attendance has the *largest* net effect on the latter (beta coefficient of .323, significant at the .001 level) of all the predictors in this regard. This is not the case in the family domain, where infrequent religious service attendance is associated with providing *more* social-emotional support to family members. It may be that families that lack affiliation with a religious institution necessarily rely more on each other than on the social and spiritual support from clergymen or fellow parishioners. The scale on religiosity (based on ratings of the extent to which respondents consider religion important to them, prefer to be with people who share their religious affiliation, and consider it important to marry within their religious preference group) contributes only modestly to community service (data not shown), suggesting it is actual social participation at services and social interaction with fellow parishioners that stimulate adults to contribute time and money to organizations and charities, rather than religious values per se.

5. Frequency of contact with friends may operate in much the way religious service attendance does: the greater the frequency of such contact, the greater are both volunteer service and dollar contributions.

It is likely that friendships are formed in the course of volunteer work as well as friendship networks providing access to and motivation for volunteer service in sports or social clubs, parish, school, or health-related organizations.

6. Worth noting because it was *not* expected is the finding that respondents who report family members have a high regard for them (e.g., who care for and understand them, and with whom they can "open up" about personal problems) contribute not *more* but *less* money to family members. On a parallel scale measuring *negative* feelings toward them (e.g., kin making too many demands or being critical), a comparable pattern was found: respondents reporting high criticism by their family give *more* money than those with low scores on the negative kin affect scale (data not shown). These findings may reflect reliance on money to soothe troubled kin relations or involve kin with troubled personalities with whom it is difficult to get along but toward whom one feels an obligation to provide financial assistance when they are in need, for example, a depressed or ill elderly parent, or a grown child who cannot hold down a steady job or sustain an intimate relationship with a significant other. (Chapter 8 explores the impact of family problems on social responsibility.)

Table 3.10 helps to distill the findings from tables 3.8 and 3.9, permitting one to identify the cluster of characteristics associated with one or both domains simultaneously with one or both time and money dimensions of contributions to others. For example, the upper left cell of table 3.10 contains adults who contribute only time and only in the family domain: they tend to be less educated, young females who rarely if ever attend religious services. By contrast, the middle cell at the bottom of the figure contains adults who contribute both time and money, but only to community organizations, not family: they tend to be highly educated, married adults who are in frequent contact with friends and frequently attend religious services. As noted above, generativity is the one major predictor variable that is strongly associated with both time and money contributions in both domains.

Close inspection of these profiles of net predictors of adult responsibility suggests a differentiation by both *social structure* and *phase of the life course*. Adults of low social status (indexed here by education and income) are heavy providers of social-emotional support to family members and close friends, and also of hands-on caregiving, as seen in table 3.5. If they are also married women with a number of children, they contribute time to both family and community. Their social world is densely peopled by family and kin; they make infrequent excursions into the larger world of neighborhood, church, and community organizations. By contrast, it is high income, well-educated adults who are more apt to limit their contribution in the family domain to financial assistance, but provide both time and money in the community domain. Their social world extends away from the family to more involvement with friends, parish, and community organizations.

Phase of the life course is a second axis of differentiation in social responsibility: the family domain preoccupies young people, whereas older adults show greater involvement in community affairs. This finding is consistent with the age profile of scores on the four normative obligation scales. This life course trajectory is shown with a finer classification of age, and separately for men and women in figure 3.1. For both men and women, obligation felt toward family and close friends shows a significant *decline* with age; by contrast, mean scores on both the civic obligation and altruism scales show highly significant *increases* with age. The implication is that as childrearing is completed by midlife, and fewer adults have older living parents, family obligations subside whereas commitments deepen and expand to encompass the larger world of community and to the welfare of others in need.

Special note must also be made of the trajectory of the work obligation scale, which shows a linear increase in felt obligation across the life course, except for the downward dip among older women over seventy, few of whom were ever stable members of the workforce and may as a result feel less obligation even in imagining themselves in such an employed status. That young adults show the *lowest* level of work obligation is surprising. After all, these respondents are not all that young; they are between twenty-five and thirty-nine years of age, hardly newcomers to the labor force. We have reason to believe these young adults, especially the well-educated men among them, are less firmly attached to their work roles than older men are (or were in the past), but we postpone discussion of the possible cohort change to chapter 11.

The interpretation of age differences in cross-sectional data must be approached with caution, because it is difficult to disentangle cohort from maturational factors. Were we to find that scores on all four normative obligation scales *increased* uniformly with age, we might be tempted to explain the results as a cohort change reflecting the alien-

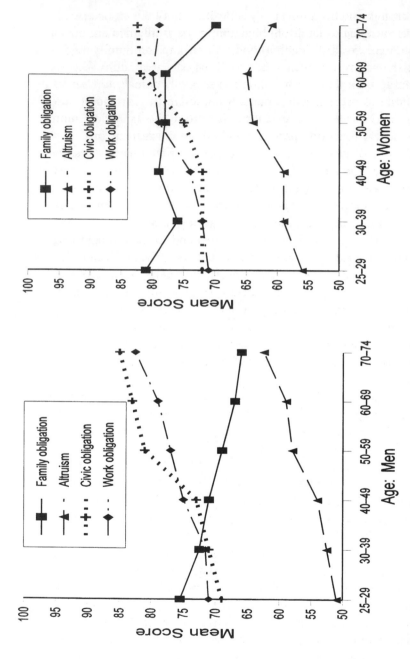

FIGURE 3.1. Normative obligations, by domain, age, and sex. The means are converted to a 0–100 range to permit comparisons across scales. Differences across age groups are significant at $p \leq .01$ or $p \leq .001$. Overall, women score significantly higher than men on the family obligation scale ($p \leq .001$) and the altruism scale ($p \leq .001$), but there are no significant sex differences on the civic and work obligation scales.

ation of the young from major social institutions. The fact that young adults espouse *higher* levels of obligation in the family domain puts a cohort interpretation in question, since it is precisely the family domain that has shown significant demographic change in recent decades, as indexed by lower marriage and fertility rates, more cohabitation, more births outside marriage, and a continuing high divorce rate (Bumpass 1990, 1994; Rossi 1993; Thornton 1989). Indeed, our younger MIDUS respondents themselves show much higher endorsement than do older respondents of the view that neither marriage nor having children is important to living a full happy life.[7]

Nonetheless, it is our younger respondents in their late twenties and thirties, whether married or not, or whether they have children or not, who report higher levels of obligation to family and kin than do older respondents. The age profile on family norms mirrors actual behavior, as reported above; that is, young adults both give and get more help from family and friends than do older adults. Note too that the indicators of family breakdown in the demographic literature concern nuclear family formation, stability, and childbearing, whereas our empirical findings refer to the more stable three-generational lineage linking individuals and nuclear families to their larger kindred.

In most of the analysis we have conducted, a maturational interpretation of age differences has had greater credibility and relevance than a cohort interpretation. We illustrate this assessment in the section to follow, in which we analyze two of the major predictors of adult social responsibility: religiosity and generativity.

INTERPRETING AGE DIFFERENCES: MATURATION VERSUS COHORT

Figure 3.2 displays the age profile of mean scores on the religiosity and generativity scales, shown separately for men and women. For both sexes, religiosity shows a highly significant increase over the life course. By contrast, the age profile on generativity shows a peak in the middle years, followed by a decline. The increases in generativity from early adulthood to the peak years of midlife is consistent with Erikson's life stage developmental task theory; that is, that generativity is to a great extent developed with maturity, as knowledge and skills are acquired and honed through practice. The channels for generativity are particularly intense in childbearing and childrearing, but not exclusively so. There are other channels for the expression of generative impulses, for example, through special devotion to nieces and nephews by childless

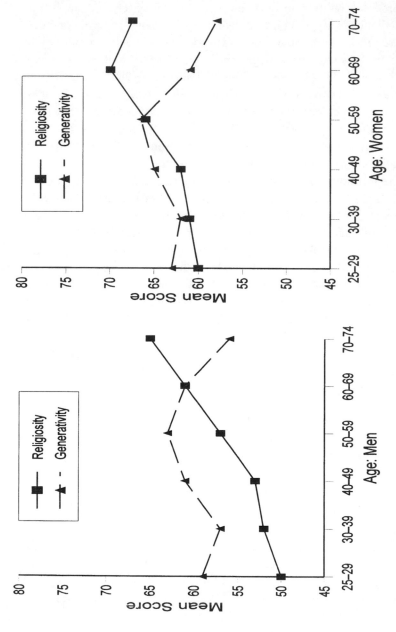

FIGURE 3.2. Age and sex differences in religiosity and generativity. The means are converted to a 0–100 range. Age differences in religiosity are statistically significant at $p \leq .001$.

adults, through many occupations such as teaching or social work, or through volunteer work to improve the quality of life for future generations (de St. Aubin and McAdams 1995; Erikson 1963, 1964). But why generativity shows a downturn in the elderly years is an open question. It would be interesting to have cross-cultural data on the life course profiles of generativity. The decline in generativity scores among MIDUS adults in their sixties and seventies may reflect loss of status or relevant skills compared to younger adults in a fast-changing developed society. In nonmodern societies where the elderly are considered stores of wisdom and are recipients of high levels of respect, generativity may show no decline in the years following midlife, but rather a linear positive increase with age.

Many scholars claim that the lower level of religiosity of young adults compared with older adults reflects a historic move away from religious values (a cohort interpretation) rather than people becoming more religious as they age (a maturational interpretation). Andrew Greeley (1995) has provided evidence in favor of a maturational interpretation by following age cohorts across the life span who were measured for church attendance and prayer frequency. He found that whether surveyed in the 1980s or the 1930s, older adults were more apt to attend church and to pray frequently than young adults. In fact, the surveys show that frequency of praying has actually increased in the 1980s compared with the 1930s. In the European Study of Values surveys, Greeley reports that "belief in life after death" increased between the 1930s and the 1980s and is most frequently espoused by Americans (78%), much less so in Britain (56%) and Germany (54%). He concludes that "the massive deterioration of religion in the modern Western world, so dearly beloved by rationalist critics of religion and 'viewers with alarm' in the religious institutions, may reveal more about those who think they are observing deterioration than about the actual religious situation" (Greeley 1995, 87).

Indirect but powerful support for a maturational interpretation can be gleaned from an additional step using MIDUS data. We asked respondents how important religion was in their families while they were growing up, and how sociable, helpful, and generous their parents were to people *outside the family*. This latter measure we view as proxies for parental generativity. In figure 3.3 we show the age profile of respondents' current religiosity by the three levels of early family religious importance, and their current generativity by the three levels of parents as generativity models. Note, first of all, the high degree to which there is

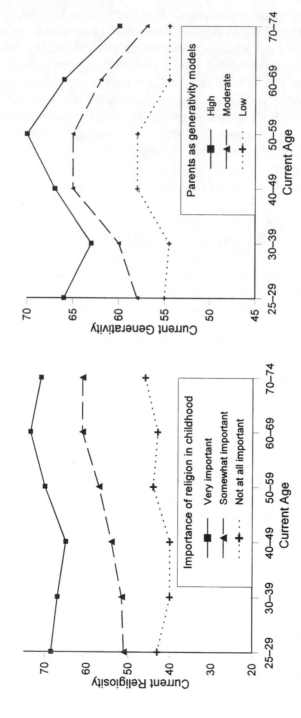

FIGURE 3.3. Age differences in current religiosity (left panel) and generativity (right panel), by comparable characteristics of parents and family of origin during respondents' childhood and adolescence. The means converted to a 0–100 range. All age differences are significant at $p \leq .05$.

cross-generational continuity on both measures: at any age, respondents from highly religious family backgrounds or whose parents were rated as very high in generativity are themselves more religious and more generative than those from families in which religion was not at all important or whose parents were low in generativity. Second, note that the same age profile is found *within* each of the three levels of early family religiosity or parental generativity: religiosity increases significantly with age, whereas generativity peaks in the middle years. An interesting example of the emergence of generativity in midlife was offered by Nancy Moses, who explained her career shift from managing partner of a marketing communications company to director of a Philadelphia museum: "When I was hit by a *midlife urge to give something back to the community,* I sold my interest in the firm and dusted off my master's degree in historic museum management" (Moses 1997, A18; emphasis added).

A maturational interpretation of age differences in religiosity is further supported by our finding that women are currently much more religious than men ($\chi^2 = 99.9$, significant at the .001 level), but that the sexes do not differ in the importance of religion in their families of origin ($\chi^2 = 8.6$, not statistically significant), suggesting a greater upturn in religiosity among women during their lifetimes than among men. Also of interest are the correlations between the importance of religion in the family of origin and current religiosity and generativity across the life course: on religiosity, the intergenerational correlation declines from .48 among those in their twenties and thirties to .36 among those in old age. By contrast, early family religiosity has no significant correlation with generativity for those under forty years of age, but turns increasingly significant from early midlife on. The latter pattern implies a "sleeper effect" of early exposure to religious values, activated during the middle years by increased concern for the welfare of others, a midlife transition consistent with the shift from higher endorsement of family than civic obligations in early adulthood to greater emphasis on civic than family obligations during mid- and late adulthood, as shown in figure 3.2.

Conclusion

In concluding this chapter, I cover two topics: first, a brief summary of the major findings on the social demography of social responsibility; and second, a discussion of these findings with special attention to the question of what, if anything, is unique to midlife.

Major Findings

1. Social responsibility is a multidimensional construct and social phenomenon, highly differentiated by life domain (family, work, or community) and by the domain's major dimensions (normative obligations, time and energy, and financial contributions). This alerts us to the caution necessary in interpreting whether or not adults are socially responsible, because such an assessment depends on whether we rely on a wide or narrow range of empirical indicators of social responsibility. With a narrow range, one researcher may characterize a nonvoter as low in social responsibility, yet such a person may be a heavy provider of care to elderly parents; those who devote a great deal of time to local politics may be viewed as highly responsible, despite the fact that they hardly ever lend a helping hand or an ear to friends or kin. A pluralist society seems best served by great diversity in the arenas that define social responsibility.

2. Empirical measures on each of the three domains and their major dimensions contribute independently to an adult's self-perception as someone who contributes a great deal or very little to the welfare of others. The high endorsement of normative obligations to family, work, and community that our respondents show provides the foundation for actual behavior that contributes to the well-being of others. Such norms are in part grounded in religious beliefs, and as will be shown in chapter 7, in early family life when basic personality and values are laid down. Whether adults act in conformity to their sense of obligation depends on a variety of factors, either the press of job and family responsibilities that limit the time and energy available to do well by others outside their immediate family, or the needs of potential recipients of their support and caregiving.

3. The extent of social responsibility is strongly influenced by social structure and phase of the life course: the lower social strata of society (as indexed by education and income) have higher commitments to hands-on caregiving and social-emotional support to primary group family members and close friends, whereas the higher social strata predominate in the contribution of both time and money to the larger community, through a heightened sense of civic obligations, more volunteer work, and financial contributions to organizations and charities. Younger adults report higher obligation to family, older adults, to broader civic participation. Note too that higher status, well-educated members of society are more likely to be approached by representatives

of community organizations to serve in some capacity in community affairs, whether personally inclined to do so or not. A poorly educated plumber in the same community is far less likely to be recruited to service in a community organization, on a fund drive, or as a lay deacon of a church. Hence social class differentials play a role in recruitment into service both in time as volunteers and as financial contributors. (See chapter 9 for interesting detail on this point.)

4. Sex differences remain pervasive and significant in the patterning of social responsibility: women exceed men in caregiving and social-emotional support to family and friends and in volunteer work in youth- and health-related community institutions. Men exceed women in financial contributions to both family and community. There are echoes here of the distinctions drawn by Joan Tronto (1993) between caregiving as fate versus caregiving as opportunity (i.e., that women's roles as wives, mothers, and daughters predispose them to hands-on caregiving not merely out of personal desire but of social expectations by others). Men drawn to caregiving may find opportunities for social recognition in the public domain by "taking care of" others' needs in indirect ways, a role differentiation seen in numerous other social domains: doctors "take care of" patients while nurses "give care"; fated direct caregiving links women in this view to other lower status direct providers of care—janitors, servants, slaves. In a less serious vein, as some comedians have noted, men tend to the important matters like tax policy or foreign affairs, while women attend to the needs of others in direct personal relationships.

What is Unique to Midlife?

The terrain covered in this chapter, as well as research reported elsewhere, suggest an interesting cluster of findings concerning several important characteristics unique to the middle years:

1. In the family domain, with childrearing largely completed by midlife, parents undergo a significant transition in their relations with grown children, renegotiating the relationship toward one of a more peer-like quality, which is facilitated by the child's own experience of childbearing and a new appreciation for what trials their own parents underwent in rearing them (Nydegger and Mitteness 1996). Particularly striking is the high degree of reciprocity between the generations, as indexed by the strong relationship between giving and getting social support among family members, undoubtedly facilitated by the high frequency of social contact between members of the kindred. We have

yet to learn whether extreme upward mobility from one's parents' social-economic status imposes a barrier to close social contact between the generations, but it is clearly the case that high earning adults in their middle and later years are providing financial assistance to relatives in need, largely children and grandchildren. Whatever romantic hopes parents hold for their children's future is clearly tempered by reality as the adult children's abilities are tested in the job and marriage markets. Most parents are no less concerned for their children's problems when they are grown and living independently than they were when the children were young and members of the household. We will explore this further in chapter 8, which examines the impact of children's problems on the lives of their parents.

2. Another analysis of MIDUS data suggests that the experience of midlife is strongly influenced by the experience of aging: the menopausal transition for women and the onset of serious illnesses for men and their male friends involves coming to grip with mortality and searching for the meaning of life, which may be why we noted the increase in religiosity among those in the middle years. For those not disposed to involvement in institutionally grounded religion, other avenues may be pursued: finding meaning in spirituality of a more diffuse nature, showing greater concern for protecting the environment, even resorting to astrology and magic, as Greeley (1995) noted among self-defined atheists in the European Values Study. In the data reported in this chapter, it is relevant to remember that early family religiosity has a sleeper effect on adult generativity, because the importance of religion in the family of origin has no correlation with generativity in adults' twenties and thirties, but becomes increasingly significant from forty to sixty years of age.

3. Time pressures are acute for families rearing young children, particularly now that the modal pattern is for dual-earning parents. Social contact with and social-emotional support of relatives is possible evenings and weekends, but there is little time for scheduled work as volunteers in the larger community, unless one is strongly motivated to seek improvement in schools and other youth-related programs. From our analysis of changes in both norms and behavior, the middle years loom as a watershed phase of life during which family obligations decline and open the way for the acquisition of new interests and concerns, as indexed by the rise in civic obligations and altruism and the peaking of generativity in midlife.

At the same time, however, it is not the case that there is any one narrow point in the long stretch of years from thirty-five to sixty that constitutes *the* critical years of transition, for the simple reason that there is great individual variation in the timing of major life events like marriage or the first and last births of children, in the timing of biological transitions such as menopause, the age at which adults first experience a serious debilitating illness, or the age at which they reach a plateau in their careers. If this is true of most individual lives, by the same token it is true of other members of the three-generational lineage. For example, some midlifers at forty-five have already lost both parents yet have children still in school, while other midlifers at forty-five are already grandparents and are providing care for a widowed mother. Yet at some point during the middle years, most adults wish to turn back the clock, to be younger than they are, while their children want to push the clock ahead, to be older and more independent than they are, not understanding parental admonitions about life being too short to rush through too quickly. Like survey analysts with cross-sectional data, adults can only know what troubles and pleasures lie behind them, not whether there are calm waters or a sea of troubles ahead.

NOTES

1. In a Baltimore sample of birth registrations in 1983, Hardy (1989) studied all men who fathered children by mothers under the age of eighteen. Almost none of the fathers of children born to black mothers were married to the mothers (2% vs. 32% among white teenage mothers), but most of the noncohabiting, nonmarried fathers had frequent contact with the child during its first three months of life: 92% of black mothers, 83% of white mothers reported the father spent time with the child. Over half of the noncohabiting fathers visited the child *daily,* 27% *weekly,* during the first three months; by the time the child was fifteen to eighteen months of age, only 16% of the fathers had no contact with the child whatsoever.

2. After a flurry of press coverage and uncritical acceptance of Putnam's thesis in 1995 (e.g., Sam Roberts's article in the *New York Times* entitled "Alone in the Vast Wasteland"), skepticism set in. Nicholas Lemann (1996) suggests that the really interesting question is *why* Putnam's notion that the bonds of civic association are dissolving was so widely and uncritically accepted. As discussed in chapter 1, the significant point where bowling is concerned is that leagues have indeed declined, but largely because business firms no longer sponsor them as they did in the past; in place of being the men's "night out with the boys," bowling has become more prevalent among dating and married couples and their teenage children.

Putnam's more elaborate recent analysis (2000) of civic participation and public trust is far more persuasive. At the heart of his empirical analysis of trends shown in three national surveys conducted over three decades is the overall finding that today's young adults are less engaged in civic affairs, feel less positive toward public institutions, and have less trust in other citizens than young adults did thirty years ago.

3. It should also be noted that settlement occurred in a very different manner in the United States than in many European countries. Our Homestead Act required settlers to live on and work the land for five years before it became their own. In Italy, by contrast, it was more typical for peasants to reside in small towns and travel each day to the land they tilled. Perhaps American value emphasis on autonomy and independence contributed to the nature of the legislative requirements governing settlement of the West, but there is evidence that the same focus on autonomy and independence characterizes even planned communities in our day. Residents are attracted to such planned communities not out of a desire for close association with their neighbors but for privacy and security, a pattern Blakely and Snyder (1997) found especially in the gated communities in the Sunbelt, replete with guardhouse, electronic surveillance systems, and physical barriers. A contributing factor to the strong desire for security may be that such residents are often on the move, traveling for pleasure, business, or both, hence leaving unattended houses full of very expensive furniture and equipment.

4. In a regression analysis of the overall self-rating on contribution to others, all but one of the major normative and behavioral variables on social responsibility make independent contributions to these self-ratings (data not shown). Interestingly, the single exception is frequency of meeting attendance, perhaps because motivation for such participation is grounded as much in self-interest as in concern for the welfare of others, exemplified by those ambitious to hold public office who find participation in local voluntary associations imperative to advance their political goals.

5. Married adults give a significantly larger proportion of income to both family and community than unmarried adults, with the single exception of young and middle-aged women, among whom the *unmarried* give a much larger proportion than *married* women of comparable ages (7% vs. 1.8%, respectively). This is perhaps a reflection of the fact that unmarried daughters are often in a better position than their married sisters to provide both care and money to elderly or ill parents, because they are not rearing young children or seeing adolescent children through years of higher education. Unmarried women with children may be an emerging category of such providers, perhaps helping to support grown children who have little education and are in need of financial help continuing beyond their adolescence.

6. We emphasize social pressure, not merely personal desire, because there may well be a sizable element of what Alan Walker (1993) calls "compulsory altruism" in the increased involvement of young parents with neighbors, relatives, and youth-oriented activities in the community.

7. In the total sample, fully 69.4% agree that "women can have full and happy lives without having any children"; only 17% disagree; and 13% are ambivalent and express no opinion. It can be noted, however, that our survey data on overall life satisfaction do not lend much support to this view: in all age groups, respondents who are married or who have at least one child report higher scores on overall life satisfaction than unmarried or childless adults do.

REFERENCES

Bellah, R. N., R. Madsen, W. M. Sullivan, A. Swidler, and S. M. Tipler. 1985. *Habits of the heart: Individualism and commitment in American life.* Berkeley, CA: University of California Press.

Blakely, E. J., and M. G. Snyder. 1997. *Fortress America: Gated communities in the United States.* Washington, DC: Brookings Institution Press.

Bumpass, L. L. 1990. What is happening to the family? Interaction between demographic and institutional change. *Demography* 27:483–98.

———. 1994. The declining significance of marriage: Changing family life in the United States. NSFH Working Paper No. 66. Madison, WI: Center for Demography and Ecology.

Bumpass, L. L., and M. K. Choe. 1996. Attitudes toward marriage and family life in Korea, Japan, and the United States. Paper presented at the Population Association of America annual meeting, May 9–11. New Orleans.

Csikszentmihalyi, M. 1997. *Finding flow: The psychology of engagement with everyday life.* New York: Basic Books.

de St. Aubin, E., and D. P. McAdams. 1995. The relation of generative concern and generative action to personality traits, satisfaction/happiness with life, and ego development. *Journal of Adult Development* 2:99–112.

Durkheim, É. 1964. *The division of labor in society.* 1933. Reprint, Glencoe, IL: Free Press.

Erikson, E. H. 1963. *Childhood and society.* 2d ed. New York: Norton.

———. 1964. *Insight and responsibility.* New York: Norton.

Greeley, A. 1995. *Religion as poetry.* New Brunswick, NJ: Transaction Publishers.

Hardy, J. E., A. K. Duggan, K. Masnyk, and C. Pearson. 1989. Fathers of children born to young urban mothers. *Family Planning Perspectives* 21:159–63, 187.

Hodgkinson, V. A., and M. S. Weitzman. 1993a. Giving and volunteering in the United States. Washington, DC: Independent Sector.

———. 1993b. *From belief to commitment: The community service activities and finances of religious congregations in the United States.* Washington, DC: Independent Sector.

Lemann, N. 1996. Kicking in groups. *Atlantic Monthly,* April, 22–26.

Luker, K. 1996. *Dubious conceptions: The politics of teenage pregnancies.* Cambridge: Harvard University Press.

McAdams, D. P., and de St. Aubin, E. 1992. A theory of generativity and its assessment through self-report, behavioral acts, and narrative themes in autobiography. *Journal of Personality and Social Psychology* 62:1003–15.

Moses, N. 1997. The nonprofit motive. *Wall Street Journal,* 17 March, A18.

Nydegger, C. N., and L. S. Mitteness. 1996. Midlife: The prime of fathers. In *The parental experience in midlife,* ed. C. D. Ryff and M. M. Seltzer, 533–60. Chicago: University of Chicago Press.

O'Donnell, L. 1983. The social world of parents. *Marriage and Family Review* 5:9–36.

Putnam, R. D. 1995a. Tuning in, tuning out: The strange disappearance of social capital in America. *PS: Political Science and Politics* 28:664–83.

———. 1995b. Bowling alone: America's declining social capital. *Journal of Democracy* 6:65–78.

———. 1996. The strange disappearance of civil America. *American Prospect* 24:34–49.

———. 2000. *Bowling alone: The decline and renewal of American community.* New York: Simon and Schuster.

Roberts, S. 1995. Alone in the vast wasteland. *New York Times,* 24 December, sec. 4.

Rossi, A. S. 1993. The future in the making: Recent trends in the work-family interface. *American Journal of Orthopsychiatry* 63:166–76.

Rossi, A. S., and P. H. Rossi. 1990. *Of human bonding: Parent-child relations across the life course.* New York: Aldine de Gruyter.

Schor, J. B. 1992. *The overworked American: The unexpected decline of leisure.* New York: Basic Books.

Seligman, A. B. 1992. *The idea of civil society.* Princeton, NJ: Princeton University Press.

Thornton, A. 1989. Changing attitudes toward family issues in the United States. *Journal of Marriage and the Family* 51:873–93.

Tronto, J. C. 1993. *Moral boundaries: A political argument for an ethic of care.* New York: Routledge.

Walker, A. 1993. Intergenerational relations and welfare restructuring: The social construction of an intergenerational problem. In *The changing contract across generations,* ed. V. Bengtson and W. A. Achenbaum, 139–65. New York: Aldine de Gruyter.

Winship, C., and L. Radbill. 1994. Sampling weights and regression analysis. *Sociological Methods and Research* 23:230–57.

Wuthnow, R. 1994. *Sharing the journey: Support groups and America's new quest for community.* New York: Free Press.

FOUR

Temporal Patterns in Social Responsibility

David M. Almeida, Daniel A. McDonald, John J. Havens,

and Paul G. Schervish

In this chapter we discuss the temporal aspects of social responsibility by examining patterns of giving behaviors within the domains of family and community and at different stages of the adult life course. We believe that the experiences of individuals fluctuate on a day-to-day and seasonal basis. John Nesselroade (1991, 94) calls this intra-individual variation the "hum" of life. Intraindividual *variation* refers to short-term reversible changes from occasion to occasion in a given phenomenon, such as fluctuating moods and emotions. Intraindivid-ual covariation occurs when two or more phenomena fluctuate in sync from occasion to occasion (Almeida and McDonald 1998). Such intra-individual variation and covariation should not be identified as nuisance or error variance but rather as a "coherent interpretable steady state hum that describes the condition of the individual" (Nesselroade and Featherman 1991, 61). When this hum is patterned over time, it becomes a rhythm. The question we pose is: To what extent is the hum of varied giving behaviors patterned across the days of the week and the seasons of the year?

Although episodes of life are often treated as discrete and unique in time and space, they are rather frequently part of a continually fluctu-ating systematic structure, a rhythm (Zerubavel 1979). Rhythm is the measured repetition of recurring events happening in a regular, se-quential, and predictive pattern over time (Fraenkel 1994). In music, rhythm is the organizing and energizing structure through which tone and pitch find expression. Notes in measured time and space, but-tressed by beat and tempo, and arranged within an infrastructure of measures, phrases, and movements result in music. Likewise, temporal

Portions of this paper were presented at the meetings of the International Soci-ety of Behavioural Development, Bern, Switzerland, July 1998. This project was sup-ported by the MacArthur Foundation Research Network on Successful Midlife De-velopment, the W. K. Kellogg Foundation, and the National Institute of Mental Health.

rhythms of days, weeks, months, seasons, and years provide the score for the performance of daily life.

While the concepts of months and seasons were derived from the patterned movements of the sun and moon, the notion of the weekly cycle appears to be a creation of humankind having no association with the natural world (Zerubavel 1985). Nearly all cultures throughout history have grouped varying numbers of days into segments for religious, economic, or philosophical reasons. For instance, the Romans had an eight-day week, with each day named for a planetary deity (Sorokin and Merton 1937). In West Africa a four-day market week still exists concurrently with the ubiquitous seven-day week (Zerubavel 1985). Although socially constructed temporal rhythm is quantifiable in its calendrical regularity, it is the qualitative character of its periodicity, derived through the collective activities and customs of groups, that lends meaning to the otherwise arbitrary divisions of days, weeks, and months (James 1890; Sorokin and Merton 1937). Conceptualizing time as circular with recurring patterns provides us the cognitive convenience to organize our lives in a way that is somewhat predictable (Zerubavel 1985), and thereby, temporal rhythms may play the reciprocal role of determining when activities and customs are carried out. John Havens and Paul Schervish (1996) show that individual giving habits are often entrained by the cycle of social seasons, such that volunteering and contributing money to organizations follows a pattern consistent with religious holidays and traditional periods of family vacations. In this chapter we examine how the temporal rhythms of the week and the calendar seasons play vital roles in how often and how much people give both time and money to their family and their community.

One's own life calendar may also play an important role in giving behavior. Theoretical formulations as well as empirical research suggest that during midlife people more often engage in socially responsible behavior than at any other time in life. That it is "better to give than to receive" is engrained in our social being through prayers, poems, and platitudes and is expressed through our daily interactions with others (Havens and Schervish 1996). Erik Erikson (1959) proposes that this virtue is the major theme of psychosocial development during middle adulthood, that one of the developmental goals of this stage of the adult life cycle is to achieve a balance between generativity and stagnation. The desire to assure one's own destiny by providing for the welfare of others, especially future generations, evolves over time and apparently peaks at midlife (see chapter 3, this volume). An outward focus characterizes this generative behavior, which may be demonstrated through socially responsible actions such as making monetary contributions to organizations or individuals, providing practical help or assistance to others, or giving emotional support to family, friends, co-workers, or neighbors. Examining the temporal rhythms of such giving enables us to view the fluctuating nature of our philanthropic behaviors at different points across adulthood.

DATA AND METHODOLOGY
Sample and Procedure

Data for the analyses are from the National Study of Daily Experiences (NSDE), one of the in-depth studies conducted under the auspices of the Midlife research network. The NSDE sample consists of two groups of adults: 1,031 randomly selected respondents from the MIDUS survey and 452 twins from a special survey of twins. Respondents in the two subsamples had completed both the telephone interview and the self-administered questionnaires of the MIDUS instruments. The 452 twins we selected had a high self-reported certainty of zygosity, including 116 identical twin pairs and 110 fraternal twin pairs.

Respondents in the NSDE completed short telephone interviews about their daily experiences on each of eight consecutive evenings. On the final evening of interviewing, respondents also answered several questions about their previous week. Data collection spanned an entire year (March 1996 to March 1997) and consisted of forty separate "flights" of interviews, with each flight representing the eight-day sequence of interviews for approximately 38 respondents. Of the 1,843 MIDUS respondents we attempted to contact, 1,483 agreed to participate, yielding a response rate of 81%. Respondents completed an average of 7 of the 8 interviews, resulting in a total of 10,389 daily interviews.

The analyses we report in this chapter used the 571 respondents (244 men, 327 women) in the random digit dialed MIDUS subsample who completed interviews on at least 7 consecutive days. If the respondents completed all 8 days, we averaged their first and last interview day (which would always be the same day of the week). Thus our analyses involved 3,997 days (571 respondents over 7 days). For many of the analyses discussed here, we used the week as the unit of aggregation by summing variables across the 7 days.

Table 4.1 compares characteristics of the total and restricted NSDE

TABLE 4.1 Demographic Comparison of the MIDUS Sample
and the NSDE Subsamples

Demographic Variable	Breakdown	MIDUS[a] (%)	NSDE[b] (%)	Restricted NSDE[c] (%)
Age	Young adults, 25–39	33.2	33.5	26.7
	Midlife adults, 40–59	46.0	45.0	44.6
	Older adults, 60–74	20.8	21.5	28.7
Sex	Male	48.5	45.5	42.8
	Female	51.5	54.5	57.2
Education	12 years or less	39.2	37.7	35.8
	13 years or more	60.8	62.3	64.2
Marital status	Married	64.1	65.4	68.6
	All others	35.9	34.6	31.4
Children in household[d]	Yes	39.0	37.8	32.0
	No	61.0	62.2	68.0
Race	Caucasian	87.8	90.3	93.5
	African American	6.8	5.9	3.6
	All other races	4.4	3.8	2.9

[a] Respondents in the MIDUS survey who participated in the initial telephone interview and returned the two self-administered questionnaire booklets following the interview ($N = 3,032$).

[b] Respondents in the NSDE study, all of whom had previously participated in the MIDUS initial telephone interview and returned the two self-administered questionnaire booklets following the interview ($N = 1,031$).

[c] Respondents in the NSDE study who completed at least seven days of interviews in a row ($N = 571$).

[d] At least one child, age eighteen or younger, living in the house.

subsamples with the MIDUS sample from which they were drawn. The three samples have very similar distributions for age, marital status, and parenting status. The NSDE has slightly more women, as well as better educated and fewer minority respondents than the MIDUS sample. These differences are greater for the restricted sample we used for the analyses reported here. At the time of the study, respondents were on average forty-seven years old. Seventy-seven percent of the women and 85% of the men were married. Forty-seven percent of the respondents reported having at least one child in the household. The average family income was between $50,000 and $55,000. Men were slightly older than women and had similar levels of education.

Measures

The daily telephone interview included questions about experiences within the previous twenty-four hours concerning time use, daily giving (i.e., financial and time contributions), mood, physical symptoms,

TABLE 4.2 Domains and Dimensions Tapped
by Daily Giving Measures

Domain	Dimension	Descriptive Detail
Family/individual	Emotional support	Summated score of days per week and hours per week providing emotional support such as comforting, listening to, or advising family members, friends, neighbors, and co-workers.
	Informal assistance	Summated score of days per week and hours per week providing unpaid assistance such as free babysitting or help with shopping for family members, friends, neighbors, and co-workers.
	Financial assistance	Summated score of days per week and dollars per week of money or goods donated to family members, friends, neighbors, and co-workers.
Community	Volunteer service	Summated score of days per week and hours per week doing formal volunteer work at a church, hospital, senior center, or any other organization.
	Financial contribution	Summated score of days per week and dollars per week of money or goods donated to charities, religious organizations, or political groups.

productivity, cutbacks, and daily stressors. Table 4.2 describes the measures of daily giving behaviors. We tried to match the dimensions as much as possible to those determined for the family and community domains in the MIDUS analyses (see table 3.1). Our focus on daily giving allowed us to extend the MIDUS analyses by not only measuring how much people gave but also assessing how often people gave. For each dimension of daily giving, we estimated the weekly *frequency* of giving and the weekly *quantity* of giving. The frequency of giving was assessed by summing the number of days per week respondents gave any money or time in each of the dimensions. The actual quantity of giving was estimated by summing the total amount of either time or money each respondent gave each day across the entire week.

The correlations among the daily giving variables are shown in table 4.3. The upper triangle shows the correlations for the quantity mea-

TABLE 4.3 Correlation of Coefficients among Daily Giving Measures

Domain	Dimension	1	2	3	4	5
Family/individual	1. Emotional support	.53**	.06	.09*	−.01	.04
	2. Informal assistance	.15**	.62**	.09*	.02	.02
	3. Financial contribution	.18**	.16**	.36**	.07	.12**
Community	4. Volunteer service	.06	.01	.02	.84**	.18**
	5. Financial contribution	.20**	.06	.08	.17**	.45**

Note: The upper triangle provides the correlations among the quantity of daily giving variables. The lower triangle provides the correlations among the frequency of daily giving variables. The diagonal elements (in bold) are the correlations between the frequency and quantity for each dimension of daily giving. $N = 571$.

$*p < .05.$ $**p < .01.$

sures of daily giving. Quantity of financial contributions to family members and friends is associated with quantity of time spent giving emotional support and informal assistance to family members and friends as well as quantity of financial contributions to community. Respondents who spent more time in volunteer service also gave more money to the community. The lower triangle shows the correlations between the frequency measures of daily giving. Measures of frequency of giving are slightly associated within each domain. Although the pattern of correlations suggests some overlap across the variables, particularly within each of the domains, the size of the correlations are quite small (e.g., the largest $r = .20$). Thus, as was the case in the MIDUS analysis (see chapter 3), these correlations provide evidence for separate dimensions for quantity of daily giving as well as frequency of daily giving.

Not surprisingly, the degree of association is much greater between the frequency and quantity measures for each dimension of daily giving. These correlations are shown in bold along the diagonal of table 4.3. Respondents who gave more frequently tended to give more in absolute terms. For example, individuals who more often contributed financially to their community also gave more money across the week, compared to those who contributed less frequently. Frequency and quantity of *giving time* are more related than frequency and quantity of *giving money.*

Age and Sex Differences

In chapter 3, Alice Rossi shows that many dimensions of social responsibility, particularly socially responsible *behavior,* vary according to age and sex. Older adults are more inclined to provide financial support and volunteer time than are younger adults. Men contribute more in absolute terms to family and community than do women, yet the proportion of income contributed is higher for women than for men. Rossi based her findings on respondent recall of giving for the previous month. We extended this research by examining daily reports of giving behaviors aggregated over the week.

Table 4.4 describes daily giving of time in the family domain (emotional support and informal assistance) and in the community domain (volunteer service). In this table we show differences in age and sex, including: (1) the percentage of participants who made any contribution of time during the week; (2) the average number of days per week participants gave time; and (3) the average number of hours per week given to family or community organizations. Over 80% of the total sample gave emotional support to a family member, friend, or co-worker at some point during the week. The average frequency of providing this emotional care was slightly over two days per week, with an average time spent of two hours and twenty minutes. Forty-three percent of the sample provided informal assistance to friends or family at least once a week, with an average duration of three hours per week. Approximately one-quarter of the respondents in this sample volun-

TABLE 4.4 Time Given in the Family and Community Domains, by Age and Sex

	Total	Men			Women		
Dimensions	Sample	25–39	40–59	60–74	25–39	40–59	60–74
Family domain							
Emotional support							
Percentage giving any	83.4	83.6	73.9	72.1	85.7	87.9	89.5
Average days per week	2.21	1.85	1.93	1.76	2.17	2.69	2.47
Average hours per week	2.38	1.31	1.86	1.69	3.40	3.09	2.36
Informal assistance							
Percentage giving any	43.8	38.2	33.0	47.1	48.8	42.1	57.9
Average days per week	0.80	0.53	0.49	0.96	0.88	0.95	1.03
Average hours per week	3.00	1.42	1.02	2.81	5.73	3.48	3.79
Community domain							
Volunteer work service							
Percentage giving any	26.8	30.1	24.4	35.3	21.4	21.8	32.6
Average days per week	0.49	0.58	0.32	0.71	0.34	0.46	0.66
Average hours per week	1.02	1.33	0.50	1.33	0.55	1.06	1.59

Note: Calculations for days and hours per week are based on the total sample rather than just those who gave or volunteered. $N = 571$.

teered an average of one hour per week, with a likelihood of recurrence once every two weeks.

Table 4.5 presents information regarding financial contributions in the family and community domains made by anyone in the respondent's household. For questions concerning monetary contributions, respondents were asked if they or *anyone in their household* contributed to an individual or organization. For this reason we first divided our sample into categories of married or single and then subdivided the single group by sex. Almost one-quarter of the sample donated money or goods within the family domain, averaging approximately $20 per week with a likelihood of occurring about one day out of each month. Approximately half of the respondents made financial contributions within the community domain, for an average contribution of $37.40 per week. Contributions of this type occurred less than once per week. Table 4.6 provides a summary of results from a set of 3 × 2 ANOVAs that tested the differences among age and sex categories by domain and dimension of social responsibility.

Age Differences

Age is positively related to the frequency of providing informal assistance to family members and financial contributions to community organizations. Older adults are more apt to provide assistance to family and friends or donate money to organizations than middle and young adults, but do not differ significantly from those groups in regard to the total quantity given. Age is also positively related to the number of hours per week participants reported serving as volunteers in the community. Older adults show a greater propensity to participate in volunteer activities than do younger age groups, perhaps because they are no longer constrained by the demands of raising children or full-time employment. Whereas Rossi (see chapter 3) found a negative association between caregiving hours and age, we found that the frequency of informal assistance increases with age. Older adults lend a hand more often, but not necessarily for a longer duration of time. Interestingly, our results do not support the theoretical formulations predicting a peak in generativity at midlife. On the contrary, we found that in all of the significant age effects, the older adult age group exceeds the young and middle age groups. One possible explanation for this is the age limitation of our sample. Had our sample included participants beyond age seventy-four, we may have observed a fall-off in the frequency and quantity of giving.

TABLE 4.5 Financial Contributions in the Family and Community Domains, by Marital Status and Age

Dimensions	Total Sample	Married			Single Male			Single Female		
		25–39	40–59	60–74	25–39	40–59	50–74	25–39	40–59	60–74
Family domain										
Financial contribution										
Percentage giving any	23.8	14.7	22.4	26.1	11.8	19.2	33.3	32.0	37.7	34.9
Average days per week	.28	.17	.25	.36	.15	.23	.25	.50	.38	.40
Average dollars per week	20.3	17.2	13.6	38.6	4.7	4.5	8.8	26.3	29.8	13.3
Community domain										
Financial contribution										
Percentage giving any	45.7	47.7	42.5	52.3	41.2	34.6	33.3	28.0	51.0	53.5
Average days per week	.62	.58	.57	.82	.47	.48	.67	.30	.63	.73
Average dollars per week	37.4	28.2	49.3	55.9	12.4	26.2	21.8	9.3	24.8	20.4

Note: Calculations for days and dollars per week are based on the total sample rather than just those who contributed. $N = 571$.

TABLE 4.6 Age and Sex Differences in the Frequency
and Quantity of Daily Giving

Dimension	Age	Sex
Family/individual domain		
Emotional support		
Frequency	—	15.5**
		(women > men)
Hours	—	8.9**
		(women > men)
Informal assistance		
Frequency	4.3*	8.7**
	(older > young and middle)	(women > men)
Hours	—	9.0**
		(women > men)
Financial contribution		
Frequency	—	3.25**
		(SF > married and SM)
Dollars	—	—
Community domain		
Volunteer service		
Frequency	4.2*	—
	(older > young and middle)	
Hours	3.7*	—
	(older > young and middle)	
Financial contribution		
Frequency	4.8**	—
	(older > middle > young)	
Dollars	—	2.9*
		(married > SM and SF)

Note: SM = single male. SF = single female.
$*p < .05.$ $**p < .01.$

Sex Differences

Consistent with Rossi's findings (chapter 3) that women provide more hours of social support and caregiving than do men, we found a distinguishable difference between men and women concerning the frequency and duration of giving in the family domain. Women comfort, advise, or otherwise instrumentally help family and friends more often and for longer periods of time than do men. In terms of financial contributions, single women provide goods and money to family, friends, neighbors, and co-workers more frequently than do married couples or single men. On the other hand, the quantity contributed to community organizations is higher for married couples than for either single males or single females. This finding reflects the higher total household income of married couples. More disposable income may enable dual wage–earning couples to contribute more in quantity than their single counterparts.

Temporal Factors of Giving

Daily Variation

In the next series of analyses we examined temporal factors associated with giving. First we investigated if the day of the week plays any role in whether and how much individuals give of their time and money to family, friends, and community. The day of the week can powerfully influence how we structure our time and activities. According to Randy Larsen and Margaret Kasimatis, "[t]he day of the week tells us much about what will happen in our immediate future. The week thus serves as a temporal map and tells us what to expect" (1990, 165). These authors show how college students' moods are entrained by a seven-day cycle. The day of the week is also associated with the amount of discretionary time available. John Robinson and Geoffrey Godbey's national studies of time use (1997) show that Americans report marked increases in their free time on weekend days compared to weekdays. Although weekends are associated with more housework and shopping, they also are associated with fewer hours of child care (e.g., helping with homework). The largest increase in the way time is spent on the weekend involves religious activities, which occur eight times more often on Sunday than on any other day of the week. Giving behaviors may also be linked to the weekly calendar when giving involves family, work, school, or religious activities.

The goal of the next analysis was to compare frequency and quantity of giving on weekdays with that on weekend days. In addition we tested whether daily patterns of giving differ according to age and sex. The results of a series of $2 \times 3 \times 2$ (day of week $\times$ age category $\times$ sex) mixed-model ANOVAs appear in table 4.7, and show evidence for day-of-week effects on time spent giving emotional support to family and friends, volunteering, and contributing money to community organizations.

Figure 4.1 shows the average amount of time per day that respondents gave emotional support to friends and family on weekdays and weekend days for each of the age categories. Overall, our respondents spent more time giving emotional support on weekdays. This result is concentrated among the young adults in the sample, who spent an average of nine minutes more on weekdays than weekend days listening

TABLE 4.7 Day of Week Differences in the Frequency
and Quantity of Daily Giving

Dimension	Day of Week	Age × Day of Week	Sex × Day of Week
Family/individual domain			
Emotional support			
Frequency	27.2*	2.9*	—
	(weekday > weekend)	(young and weekday)	
Hours	11.8*	2.8*	—
	(weekday > weekend)	(young and weekday)	
Informal assistance			
Frequency	—	—	—
Hours	—	—	—
Financial contribution			
Frequency	—	—	—
Dollars	—	—	—
Community domain			
Volunteer service			
Frequency	—	3.6*	6.4
		(young and weekend)	(men and weekday)
Hours	—	4.9**	—
		(young and weekend)	
Financial contribution			
Frequency	34.9**	—	—
	(weekend > weekday)		
Dollars	3.83*	3.0*	—
	(weekend > weekday)	(older and weekend)	

Note: $N = 571$.
*$p < .05$. **$p < .01$.

to and giving advice to others. An examination of who is getting the support provides some clues for this difference. Respondents in each age category most often give emotional support to their children (27% of the total time they gave support) and friends (30% of the total time they gave support). Younger adults were more likely to give support to spouses and co-workers and less likely to give support to neighbors than were older adults. To the extent that spouses and co-workers are seeking support for problems experienced at work, younger adults' support-giving may be more often tied to work schedules than is support given by older adults.

The day-of-week pattern for engaging in volunteer work is shown in figure 4.2. Although there was no overall main effect for day of week across the entire sample, there was a significant day of week × age interaction. Older adults are more likely to volunteer on the weekdays

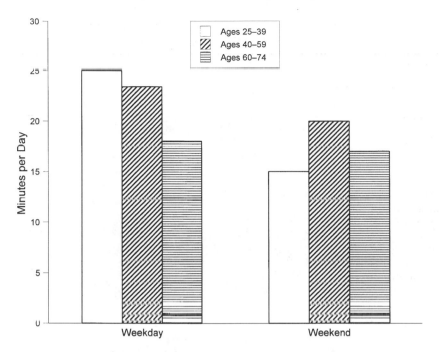

FIGURE 4.1. Time spent giving emotional support to family and friends, by day of week and age.

while younger adults are more likely to volunteer on the weekend. Again the influence of paid work schedules may be playing an important role as to when individuals have time to give. Seventy percent of respondents in the older age category reported spending no time in paid employment activities, compared to only 20% of the younger age group.

The other type of giving related to day of week is financial contribution to the community, as shown in figure 4.3. Respondents in each age category gave more on the weekend days than on weekdays. Although there is no age-related pattern in the *frequency* of giving on the weekend, there is a difference in the *quantity* of giving (see table 4.7). This daily pattern is magnified for the older adults, who gave an average of $7.71 more on weekend days. The age-related difference on weekends is primarily due to increased contributions to religious organizations on the part of older individuals. Older adults contributed an average of $11.50 to religious organizations, compared to $5.75 and $5.44 for middle and younger adults, respectively. Thus it appears that older

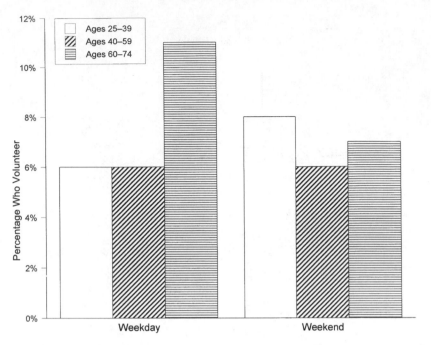

Figure 4.2. Percentage of respondents who engaged in volunteer service, by day of week and age.

adults do not contribute more frequently on the weekend, but they do contribute more.

Evidence demonstrating weekly rhythms has been shown in previous research on mood (Larsen and Kasimatis 1990), leisure-time activities and household chores (Robinson and Godbey 1997), and work-family linkages (Almeida and McDonald 1998). Our findings show that day of week, in conjunction with sex and age, plays an important role in the manifestation of socially responsible actions as well. Older adults have a greater tendency to give informal assistance to friends and family, make larger contributions on weekends, and are more likely to volunteer during weekdays than are younger adults. Not surprisingly, women spend more time providing social support and caregiving than do men, while those in married households make larger financial contributions to community organizations. Interestingly, our sample provided more emotional support on weekdays than weekends, which seems contrary to what the long distance telephone service marketing slogan "five-cents-a-minute Sundays" might suggest. Perhaps the epi-

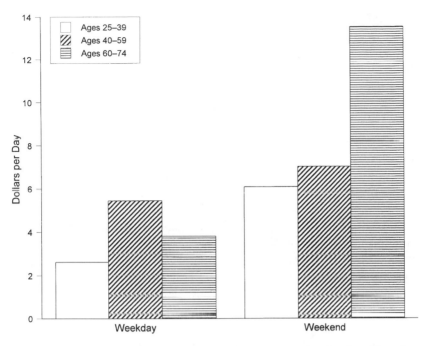

FIGURE 4.3. Financial contribution to the community, by day of week and age.

sodes of providing emotional support are tied more closely to the work and school schedules of spouses and children than to weekend socializing and connecting with family.

Seasonal Variation

The frequency and quantity of giving are also likely to fluctuate across the calendar year. Evidence for this contention is apparent in the Boston Area Diary Study (BADS), which charted the giving and caring behavior of participants from a sample of fifty households in the Boston area on a weekly basis during 1995 (Havens and Schervish 1996). The temporal patterns of giving behavior for families and individuals in the BADS exhibit specific cycles and rhythms throughout the year, guided by factors idiosyncratic to each family or individual as well as by factors common to most or all participants in the study. At times families drew inward, impelled by family needs such as injuries and illnesses. Families also joined with others to solve common problems (e.g., carpooling to drive kids to and from school and after-school activities) or to support local social networks (e.g., volunteering to assist with church-sponsored activities). At a number of times during the year, family members would assist others who were not part of their own social network. These activities were concentrated during the year-end holiday season, when the families' outreach activities focused on the needy through financial contributions, volunteer efforts, and informal assistance.

In this section we explore and identify patterns in giving behavior associated with temporal cycles during the twelve-month NSDE data-collection period. As for the analyses reported above, we examined five areas of giving behavior: emotional support, informal assistance, volunteer service, financial contribution to individuals, and financial contribution to community and national organizations. The NSDE permits us a weekly glimpse of the giving behavior of a group of respondents mixed by geographic location, economic condition, and social circumstance. We averaged the daily reports of respondents who were interviewed during the same month and pieced the monthly averages together to explore and identify national seasonal patterns in giving.

This methodology necessarily reduces the influence of factors other than seasonal ones, which affect our groups relatively uniformly, such as holidays, school calendar, and weather patterns. The end of the year (the end of the federal tax period) prompts giving among those seeking tax deductions for charitable contributions. Many charitable organizations launch fund drives in late spring and again in late fall. One would expect peaks of contributions during these times as well. Organizations also seek volunteer help to prepare for these drives several weeks before they launch them. One might expect, therefore, to discover mini-peaks in volunteering activity at these times.

Figure 4.4 presents the seasonal patterns for the prevalence of giving behavior as measured by the percentage of respondents engaged in each realm of giving. Emotional support and financial contributions to individuals are the only measures that evidence statistically significant seasonal patterns [$F(11,561) = 2.09, p < .01; F(11,561) = 2.10, p < .01$, respectively]. Nevertheless, the seasonal patterns for all five areas of giving behavior are roughly similar. During middle and late winter, especially the month of February, respondents reported little giving behavior on any of our measures. Whether this was because of dank and dreary weather, lack of personal reserves of energy, lack of financial resources after the holiday season and post-holiday bills, or just lack of

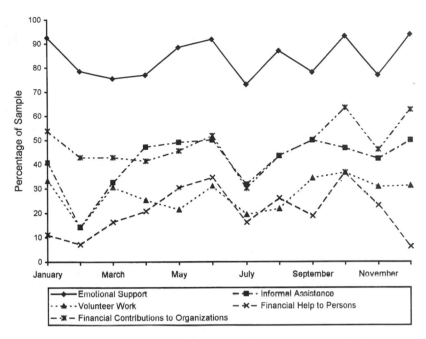

FIGURE 4.4. Percentage of sample engaged in giving activities, by month.

opportunities is a matter of speculation. However, there is no mistaking this low point in giving. On the other hand, the advent of summer in May/June, coinciding with the end of the school year, prompted high levels of giving. While not consistent for all measures of giving, the fall generally showed some resurgence in giving behavior, with October as the season's high point. Finally, as previously mentioned, the year-end holiday season produced another spike in giving.

We note that for all seasons of the year, the prevalence of emotional support exceeded informal assistance to others as well as contributions to charitable organizations. These giving behaviors, in turn, surpassed the prevalence of volunteering and financial help extended directly to individuals and families. Thus there was a rough hierarchy in the proportion of the sample involved in each of these types of giving activity, and this hierarchy was maintained throughout the calendar year.

We measured the quantity of giving by calculating the average number of hours per week devoted to emotional support, informal assistance, and volunteering (figure 4.5). The peak levels of informal assistance occur in May and in August. It is interesting to note that these

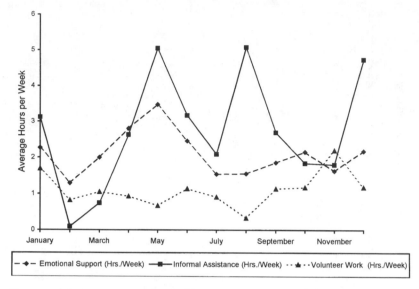

FIGURE 4.5. Average number of hours spent per week helping others.

months coincide with periods during which many individuals and families reorganize their activities in accord with the school calendar. Just as with prevalence of giving, February and July are months of relatively low amounts of time spent giving emotional support and informal assistance, though August rather than July is the summer nadir for time volunteered.

The seasonal variations in the quantity of financial contributions to charitable organizations and, less formally, directly to individuals are different from the general pattern apparent in the other realms of social responsibility and from each other (see figure 4.6). During February, when other forms of giving are at their nadir, the average amount of contributions are at a very high level. In May, when other forms of giving are relatively high, the amount of contributions to charitable organizations is low. Moreover, the quantity contributed to charitable organizations exhibited changes that are almost the reverse of those for family contributions to persons for many months of the year. This suggests a type of compensatory model of how people express their support for other individuals and for social organizations. When giving is unable to be expressed in one dimension, it is expressed in another. A model that combines seasonal variation with compensatory modes of giving may be an appropriate theoretical construct allowing us to un-

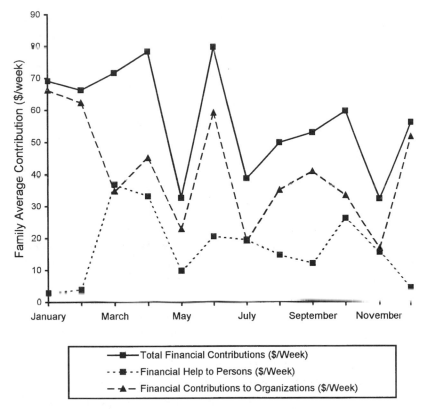

FIGURE 4.6. Family average financial contribution per week.

derstand and analyze how longer cycles affect an individual's giving behavior.

CONCLUSION

The exploration of temporal cycles of socially responsible activity is a relatively neglected area of research. In this chapter we have begun to explore and identify short cycle and long cycle rhythms in this behavior. For the sample as a whole, the evidence in support of the existence of such cycles is statistically weak, except for the relationship between weekday/weekend cycles and the amount of family financial resources given to charitable (including religious) organizations. From this we conclude that time itself and the societal rhythms entailed in the passage of time generally do not affect all persons and individuals in the same way. In this exploratory research we have indeed shown that age and gender are two such factors affecting weekday/weekend cycles. As for seasonal variation, only the very largest societal rhythms affect people in a fairly uniform way. The shift from spring to summer, the December/January holiday season, and the post-holiday period in February are the only major periods that were linked to all five areas of socially responsible behavior examined in this chapter.

The findings presented in this chapter are mostly descriptive in nature. They set the stage for more detailed exploration of how the passage of time interacts with daily experiences to facilitate or inhibit socially responsible behavior. We believe it is necessary to chart daily intersections of individuals' multiple giving behaviors with other aspects of their day-to-day lives in order to understand the rhythmic nature of these synchronous experiences.

To appreciate how social responsibility is embedded in daily life, it is useful to examine the descriptions of giving experiences provided by NSDE participants. Through the Daily Inventory of Stressful Events (Almeida 1998), we acquired short narratives of particular stressful events that occurred during the day. Often these events either coincided with or were about giving or providing care to others. By examining these qualitative data in conjunction with the reports of giving behaviors, we develop a clearer picture of the interconnecting rhythms of the dimensions of social responsibility.

One illustration comes from a fifty-six-year-old woman who described a stressful incident occurring midweek in the month of August, which involved her adult stepson: "[I needed] to help him out with his electric bill. I was concerned because he said they cut the electricity off." This participant reported that assisting her stepson interrupted her volunteer work at her church. In addition to volunteering and providing financial assistance to her stepson, she also provided unpaid assistance to a friend and emotional support to her stepson and to a friend within the same twenty-four-hour period.

Other examples of intersecting giving behaviors include a thirty-seven-year-old man who provided emotional support to his father: "I felt I needed to give my father support. . . . He was emotionally, well, he wasn't really sad, but he had a hard time speaking. . . . I felt I had to give him a hand and support him." On that Sunday in May, this participant also volunteered at a community organization and donated money to a local charity. A forty-seven-year-old mother described providing emotional support and financial assistance to her adult daughter on a weekend day in the summer after her daughter had a miscarriage: "We went over there for emotional support. They're both pretty devastated about it. [We're trying] to be emotionally supportive. We help pay for some of the bills." On that day she also reported volunteering her services at a local organization. On a weekday in April, a fifty-three-year-old man provided informal assistance to a friend within the same twenty-four-hour period in which his aunt had died. He described his response to the needs of his family in the following excerpt: "A death in the family is somewhat stressful, an aunt . . . There are problems in the family, and I'm kind of the in-between man. I had to make phone calls, and I volunteered to be of any help."

These descriptions illustrate the multiple ways in which people give and care that are part of their daily lives. The findings in this chapter suggest that such activities are structured and accentuated partly by the metered ebb and flow of social temporal rhythms. However it is important to mention that individuals often need to improvise when others are in need or when they themselves require help, regardless of temporal constraints. Our challenge and that of other researchers is to place giving and caring activities in the context of individuals' everyday lives. In the next step of our analysis we will begin to meet this challenge by examining how day-to-day giving and receiving are related to other daily experiences such as work stressors, family demands, and physical health problems.

REFERENCES

Almeida, D. M. 1998. Daily inventory of stressful events: Interview and coding manual. Typescript.

Almeida, D. M., and D. A. McDonald. 1998. Weekly rhythms of parents' work stress, home stress, and parent-adolescent tension. In *Rhythms in adolescent development: New directions in child development*, ed. R. Larson and A. Crouter, 53–67. San Francisco: Jossey-Bass.

Erikson, E. H. 1980. *Identity and the life cycle.* New York: W. W. Norton.

Fraenkel, P. 1994. Time and rhythm in couples. *Family Process* 33:37–51.

Havens, J. J., and P. G. Schervish. 1996. *Daily bread: Findings from the first diary study on giving and volunteering.* Boston: Social Welfare Research Institute.

James, W. J. [1890] 1950. *The principles of psychology.* Reprint, New York: Dover.

Larsen, R. J., and M. Kasimatis. 1990. Individual differences in entrainment of mood to the weekly calendar. *Journal of Personality and Social Psychology* 58: 164–71.

Nesselroade, J. R. 1991. Interindividual differences in intraindividual change. In *Best methods for the analysis of change: Recent advances, unanswered questions, future directions,* ed. L. M. Collins and J. L. Horn, 92–105. Washington, DC: American Psychological Association.

Nesselroade, J. R., and D. L. Featherman. 1991. Intraindividual variability in older adults' depression scores: Some implications for developmental theory and longitudinal research. In *Problems and methods in longitudinal research: Stability and change,* ed. D. Magnusson, L. Bergman, and B. Torestad, 46–66. London: Cambridge University Press.

Robinson, J. P., and G. Godbey, eds. 1997. *Time for life: The surprising ways Americans use their time.* University Park: Pennsylvania State University Press.

Sorokin, P. A., and R. K. Merton. 1937. Social time: A methodological and functional analysis. *American Journal of Sociology* 42:615–29.

Zerubavel, E. 1979. *Patterns of time in hospital life.* Chicago: University of Chicago Press.

———. 1985. *The seven-day cycle.* New York: Free Press.

FIVE

Local Caring
Social Capital and Social Responsibility in New York's Minority Neighborhoods
Katherine S. Newman

Robert Putnam's much discussed article, "Bowling Alone" (1995), has prompted a burst of concern over the diminishing involvement of Americans in community groups that build social capital, including voluntary organizations, churches, parent-teacher associations, and the like. Erosion of the participatory spirit has been blamed upon working mothers no longer available to staff the PTA, working fathers running to stay one step ahead of the downsizing ax and therefore unable to coach the soccer league, and the excessive materialism of an American middle class more concerned about the models of their cars than the health of their community institutions. Even the lowly television has been blamed for privatizing recreation, making couch potatoes of those who would otherwise be drawn to neighborhood activities. Diminished social ties, we are told, produce weak forms of solidarity and even weaker levels of trust or engagement in public institutions (e.g., government).

Nowhere has the worry over declining social capital been keener than in studies of American ghettos. Beginning with James Coleman's seminal article, "Social Capital in the Creation of Human Capital" (1988), and continuing with William Julius Wilson's arresting portraits of neighborhood disintegration (1987, 1996), researchers have suggested that poor minorities are suffering the consequences of a withdrawal from public life. Coleman argues that declining parental participation in schooling reduces a child's human capital (individual skills or formal credentials) because parents lack the resources that derive from the social ties with others (especially fellow parents and teachers) that are necessary to monitor and influence a child's educational performance. Wilson points to the erosion of economic opportunity in inner-city communities, which opens up avenues for the dangerous trades (drugs, guns) and the violent behavior that goes with them) and forces families to remain in the privacy of their homes for safety's sake. The more law-abiding families withdraw, the more the institutions they once bolstered (from churches to stores) depart the scene. An empty "commons" is the death knell for social capital in the inner city, and all its residents pay the price.

For both Coleman and Wilson—to name only two sociologists who have written on this topic—social capital is a two-sided medium. It is one part participation in formal or informal organizations and one part personal, social ties with family, friends, and neighbors. Indeed, the two aspects of social capital are thought to go hand in hand: folks who are active in the first domain tend to be equally engaged in the second. Social responsibility, the theme of this volume, might be thought of as the moral force that drives individuals to engage in the participatory activities essential for the creation and sustenance of social capital. If individuals feel morally compelled to give of themselves to causes, organizations, or institutions that stand outside their own narrow interests, then, if Coleman and Wilson are right, they will also flourish in the more private sphere of personal relations. But the driving force here remains connecting to others in organizations and the push factor is a sense that social responsibility is morally worthy (however much it may also be instrumentally valuable for the health of one's community).

In this chapter, I argue that for inner-city communities, participation in formal organizations and financial donations may not constitute the best barometers of social responsibility. Measures that rely upon participation in formal institutions—giving money, volunteering in some official capacity—define a form of social responsibility which may well predominate among middle-class families. Among the comparatively well heeled, the financial resources to support philanthropic generosity are available, and participation in voluntary organizations is expected as a culturally approved signal of public engagement. For urban minorities, particularly the poor among them, social responsibility is expressed in a different form, one that is paradoxically privatized and directed not at the general social good, but at those defined as "one's own." Men and women living in problematic neighborhoods regard the daunting task of raising their children, or tending to the safety of the streets, as both a personal obligation *and* a contribution to the well-being of society as a whole.

The borders of community are narrowly circumscribed by urban minorities. Drawing boundaries around the people to whom one owes selfless acts is a complex process, moving out from the immediate family, to the surrounding neighborhood, to groups of people who occupy similar positions in the racial or economic hierarchy. Formal organizations, particularly the church, can become a vehicle for urban minorities to express commitment to others, but more often than not, private behavior and informal practices fulfill the responsibility which ethno-racially or economically defined groups feel for their members.

The emphasis in this chapter lies only partly on socially responsible *behavior.* I focus equally on the *subjective* dimension of obligation and belonging, on the ways urban minority families define their position in a stratified society. Any complete understanding of social responsibility involves this deeper sense of to whom that responsibility is owed. I explore these issues drawing upon a set of qualitative interviews conducted in New York City in 1995–96 as an offshoot of a special survey of African Americans, Puerto Ricans, and Dominicans sponsored by the MacArthur Foundation's Network on Successful Midlife Development. Nine hundred respondents, one-third from each of these ethnic groups, completed a face-to-face survey, which overlapped on many items with the nationwide MIDUS sample. A representative subset of this New York population, totaling one hundred in all, were then recontacted for lengthy life history interviews, conducted in Spanish or English in the respondents' homes.[1] Selected demographic characteristics of this qualitative sample compared to the entire New York sample are provided in table 5.1.[2]

This chapter draws primarily upon the portion of the qualitative interview that focused on social responsibility, but is informed by the perspectives of these African American, Puerto Rican and Dominican midlife adults on the problems they encounter raising families in poor neighborhoods and the complexities of living in a racially stratified society. Only when we situate these families in their community context can we fully appreciate how they define the character of their responsibilities toward others and the motives that move them to live up to these commitments.

Mapping the contours of social responsibility is most easily and parsimoniously done by radiating out from the most private sphere of the family, to the neighborhood, to social groups defined by race and ethnicity. This is both a logical arrangement and, as it happens, the map that most accurately describes the social spheres of participation and self-definition that make the most sense out of the data we gathered. Within each concentric circle, beginning with the family and ending with groups defined by national origin or race, we must ask how the respondent relates cultural position to social obligation.

TABLE 5.1 Comparative Characteristics of the New York City Sample
and the Qualitative Sample

	New York City Sample ($N = 900$)	Qualitative Sample ($N = 100$)
Average age	44.2	43.6
Gender (%male)	50.6	41.8
Ethnicity (%)		
Black	37.6	34.7
Dominican	31.1	33.7
Puerto Rican	31.3	31.6
Employment status (%)		
Employed	45.9	52.1
Unemployed	11.9	8.2
Immigrant status (%)		
U.S. born	53.2	53.1
Immigrated < 18 years old	10.4	9.2
Immigrated 18+ years old	28.7	27.5
Neighborhood type (%)		
30% or more white	10.5	9.2
51% or more own ethnic group	35.0	36.7
Mixed	54.3	54.1
Mean neighborhood income	$27,306	$27,016
Public aid (%)		
AFDC		
African Americans	—	15
Puerto Ricans	—	27
Dominicans	—	22
SSI		
African Americans	—	15
Puerto Ricans	—	24
Dominicans	—	22

FAMILY VALUES: SOCIALLY RESPONSIBLE CHILDREARING

Elsewhere in this volume, Alice Rossi has suggested that attending to family obligations, particularly those that bind the three living generations of child-parent-grandparent, is an important facet of social responsibility. These are fairly universal definitions of intergenerational obligation, though they may be met by financial outlays among middle-class families (for elder care or child care) and by time outlays by those less affluent (see chapter 3). But it would probably be fair to say that most middle-class, midlife Americans define these responsibilities as private, primarily oriented toward the quality of family life and the personal obligations generations owe to one another.

Among the black and Latino New Yorkers studied for this chapter, however, childrearing is understood both as a personal responsibility and as a *public* obligation. For them, bringing up the kids is a contribution to the well-being of a community, particularly when one can point to a host of families who have not followed through, leaving neighbors and strangers to contend with the consequences of their parental failures. This is more than a subtle difference. Although middle-class families consider parental "work" as a serious moral obligation, its social character is not as well developed. Parents raise their children because their private lives are circumscribed by these responsibilities. In poorer communities, taking care of one's children is almost as much an obligation to the peace, security, and well-being of neighbors and fellow community members as it is to the success and comfort of the next generation in the family.

Rosa Picante is a thirty-eight-year-old Dominican immigrant living in a poor neighborhood on Manhattan's upper west side. She does not have the time for volunteer work, nor does she have the resources or the inclination to donate money to charity, apart from an occasional contribution to her parish. If Rosa were to complete the MIDUS questionnaire, she would score low on many indices of social responsibility. Yet she sees herself as a good citizen of her community because she has taken care of her private responsibilities and in so doing, contributes in positive ways to the quality of life of her neighbors and friends. "Bring your children up with an education, yes, you are helping the community. Helping the society, so that the area that you live in is not so bad. Because if everyone contributes his part to do something good on their own, they are doing something for the community." Jason Norwald, a thirty-two-year-old African American who works as an assistant teacher, would agree that taking responsibility for family members is key for both personal integrity and public order: "If something were to happen to my brother and his wife, there would be no question as to where their children would go. . . . The children would be my responsibility. I don't have a problem with that. My parents would be largely my responsibility. . . . My brother and I would probably share the responsibility for my parents, for our parents. My aunt—there was never a question. . . . I think that's how we have to look at it. They took care of me when I was young, so, I should take care of them now that they're old." Here Jason expresses a social contract between generations that, at one level, has nothing to do with the world outside close kin. But he defines his obligations in contrast to the way he perceives more affluent families shuffling their older relatives off to nursing homes where they have no family ties. He rejects this path as an abrogation of a contract between generations. In accepting his personal responsibilities to care for his own, he feels that he also makes good on a commitment to keep his family business out of the "burden column" for the rest of society. In short, for urban minorities, private acts—caring for the elderly, raising children, monitoring public behavior on the streets around their homes, visiting with a child's teacher—take on a larger resonance as examples of commitment to the community.

How does private conduct come to be defined as socially responsible behavior? Families who do not do their part, who let their children run wild, sow the seeds of neighborhood decline. In communities facing a daily onslaught of petty crime, disorderly or belligerent conduct, graffiti, and broken windows, the stable, law-abiding, respectable families who dominate the local culture recognize that the environmental problems they face are "homegrown." [3] Little credence is given to the liberal position that society has failed urban youth (through poor schools, cutbacks in social policy, and the like). Instead, the view that childrearing is a family's moral responsibility takes center stage.

Adults like Rosa and Jason believe that young troublemakers are the end product of neglectful parents who let the community down when they let their children run wild. The consequences of private irresponsibility spill out into public spaces. For this reason the community has an immediate interest in domains that would be considered no one else's business in most suburban settings. As Mason Bradley, an African American resident of Brooklyn put it: "You can be responsible for the community just by taking care of things at home. This way the community is not bothered with some of your own home problems, things that can be stopped at home such as dealing with the children, curbing their attitudes, things such as that. So this way, if you trained your child correctly at home, when he comes out into the community someone else will not have to . . . curb your child."

The reverse argument also holds in ghetto life. Families bound by social norms, who raise their children to "do right," express a commitment to the social good, to the protection of their communities from behavior that would—absent their vigilance—degrade the quality of life in inner-city neighborhoods. The private *becomes* public in this very special sense, and the task of raising children becomes an expression of commitment to the well-being of the neighborhood as well to the family. The well-behaved child is subtracted from the ledger of potential problem cases that residents of poor blocks must contend with. Since that ledger can be long, the source of much daily grief for families struggling to live in peace in the midst of run-down conditions, the kudos that accrues to the responsible parent is significant.

Middle-class families also hold themselves accountable for their children's behavior. But since they are blessed, on the whole, with orderly neighborhoods and stable social institutions, they are less likely to create a public problem if they neglect private family obligations. A child who grows up a stain on his family's honor in suburban America is a matter of personal shame. He is less likely to be a threat to his neighbors.[4]

Credit for successful childrearing is given where it is due in part because inner-city parents understand that the obstacles in the way of producing children who behave themselves are many and very serious.[5] Suburban parents can expect their children to develop in acceptable ways until they confront the temptations of casual drug use or driving under the influence, which usually do not present themselves until the latter years of high school. Even there, the normative framework of expectations (for academic achievement, conventional behavior) and the affluence that permits a consumerist life shield most suburban teens from serious involvement with crime or delinquency.

The vast majority of inner-city teenagers are equally conventional in their behavior, portraits of a deviant underclass notwithstanding. Yet the potholes in the road to adulthood they confront are certainly larger than those facing suburban youth (Brooks-Gunn et al. 1993). Reaching a positive end does not come about so easily, despite the fact that the overwhelming majority of inner-city teens arrive at that destination. Drug dealers with a lot of spare cash to flash around are not in short supply, yet neither are church-going families. Presented with both destructive role models and positive ones, poor youth in segregated enclaves face pressures to choose between alternatives that most middle-class teenagers never encounter.

Because the obstacles to a conventional adulthood are considerable, families that navigate these waters successfully are looked upon as success stories, people who have surmounted the odds. Their efforts to leap those hurdles—to raise their children without them succumbing to negative influences—are therefore culturally defined as an expression of social responsibility toward the surrounding community as well as a personal achievement.

Expanding the Circle

The term "community" has been invoked in myriad ways to refer to groups that feel a degree of mutual obligation and trust. Among the African Americans, Dominicans, and Puerto Ricans we interviewed, the boundaries of social solidarity are complex and shifting. To understand what social responsibility means to these urban dwellers, we must explore the range of communities with which they identify and toward whom they feel a sense of obligation.

At the most intimate level, "community" refers to the families and friends who live nearby. These are the people to whom one owes primary allegiance, for whom members should express social responsibility. Lucia Noventa was brought to New York from Puerto Rico when she was six months old. As a married woman with four children, ages three to nineteen, Lucia draws clear boundaries around her obligations. They stretch only as far as her own family: "The only obligation that I have is to my kids and to my husband. That's it, and of course, God forbid, to my mamma. My mother, first God, then my mother. My obligation is to my kids. They didn't ask me to bring them into this world. I brought them in. So, as long as I am physically able, I am obligated to give [to] them, to provide for them, so that they can grow up and provide for themselves." Lucia sees her first task as insuring her children's survival, making sure they have a roof over their heads. Her independence reflects the experience of the working poor who know all too well that securing the well-being of the next generation is not an easy task. It cannot be taken for granted that they will be safe; it is a duty that requires constant vigilance.

But her desire for independence extends beyond her obligation to take care of her children. It expands to encompass the responsibility she has for making sure that she will not become a burden to them in her old age: "I am not asking for them, when I grow older, 'Oh, you gotta give me something from your paychecks.' 'If you want to help me out, you help me out. If you don't want to, power to you.'" Lucia's comments reflect the darker side of the immigration experience. Puerto Ricans and Dominicans who come from cultures that emphasize familial solidarity, the obligations that bind generations together, confront an American code that values autonomy, that subtracts from the social contract between generations the duty to provide financially.[6] Affection and respect are meant to be unhinged from economic responsibility.

These are truly foreign ideas in the eyes of other cultures, and they come hard to those who arrive on American shores.

Carol Stack's classic work, *All Our Kin* (1974), explores much the same tension among African Americans in the neighborhood she calls the "Flats," a segregated and poor community in southern Illinois. Descendants of the generation that migrated out of the rural towns of Mississippi and Alabama on their way to the northern metropolis of Chicago, the residents of the Flats confront poverty with extended and fictive kin ties that provide a private safety net. Goods and money circulate from one household to another, insuring some protection against fluctuating resources (aid checks cut off, jobs lost). "What goes around, comes around," Stack's informants explain: givers become receivers, building up mutual obligations over time which insure a modicum of security. But the cost of such an arrangement is serious: it puts a brake on the upward mobility of individuals enmeshed in the web of dense ties, for they cannot hoard resources against the claims of "partners" if they expect to be able to ask for help in the future.

Social responsibility in the Flats extends outward from the natal household to encompass extended family and close friends, but it is always cross-cut by the thoroughly American desire to break free and prosper independently. The tension is ever-present when good fortune shines on one individual and he or she must decide whether to break from the leveling power of the social network or rest within, an insurance policy against future need.

For many of the immigrant and native-born poor in New York, a similar drama plays itself out as families contend with the shifting social norms that define the relations among their members. For Lucia Noventa, the tide has shifted in favor of independence, of grooming her children to make it on their own, with the hope that they will not forget who made their good fortune possible: "I want to instill in them a sense of family, the sense of self-confidence in themselves. Otherwise, who am I going to be obligated to? I am looking for my best work if I can [get it]. I will give it my best effort, but I am not going to be obligated [to the workplace]. My obligation is to my kids, and once they grow up then they are obligated to make sure that they can take care of themselves."

This volume emphasizes the importance of caregiving and nurturing across the generations as a form of social responsibility. For low income families, these obligations take on additional weight. Not only are these moral imperatives, they are often the only source of support that aging parents can expect to receive. Men and women who have spent a lifetime in irregular employment or the nontaxed economy (e.g., black and Latina women who work as domestics) often lack pensions, access to social security, and medical care. Moreover, because poverty leaves its traces in poor health, the minority elderly are frequently not so old. Illnesses that more affluent Americans expect to see develop in their sixties and seventies surface among inner-city adults in their fifties (Geronimus 1995). Demands for their care fall on the shoulders of their family members both in accordance with custom and because there are few other alternatives. The resources that permit middle-class and wealthy families to buy services—home aids, nursing care, assisted living—are not available.

I suggest we should understand caregiving within families somewhat differently at the low income end of the spectrum. To the extent that we believe society bears some obligation toward the support of the elderly (expressed through social security, Medicare, pensions, and other benefits), it should be clear that the substitutional character of family care among the poor is more than a private act. It is a form of social responsibility.

Neighbors

Poor neighborhoods in New York have no shortage of problems. Almost everyone in our study complained of robberies, drug users and drug pushers, unemployment, and families that do too little to control their children's behavior. The literature on the urban underclass suggests that under these circumstances, the natural response is to withdraw into private spaces, ceding the public domain to the negative elements (Anderson 1999). In some of the nation's tougher housing projects, this isolation strategy may predominate (Venkatesh 1997)—hardly a recipe for social responsibility.

Yet in the barrios and black ghettos of Harlem, the South Bronx, and Bedford-Stuyvesant, communal efforts have developed that reflect an outward-turning commitment to the stability and safety of the neighborhood. Housing projects have established tenant patrols, self-imposed curfews, and escort services for the elderly in an effort to reduce the burdens of crime. These informal activities take time, energy, and an underlying social solidarity that transcends the privacy of households.

Missy Darden, a black woman in her late fifties, has been mugged a time or two. The experience motivated her to do something to help herself and others: "I tried to start a civilian patrol and a buddy system within the neighborhood or the complex I live in. People [who have to come home from work] late at night get together and have a telephone chain of people who are coming in at the same hours so people come in together. A person wouldn't have to walk down the street by themselves." Neighborhood watch groups, informal escort services, and the like provide a vehicle to educate residents about the best way to avoid victimization. As Missy explains: "You can wear certain items or walk a certain way. Having been a victim of muggings more than once, I've noticed that on those occasions [I was saying], 'Here I am.' I had to learn to walk like I was nuts, talking to myself and waving, and that sort of deterred people from bothering me. I really try to warn people or make them aware that certain things they do, certain things they can avoid, like walking in dark places or places that happen to be deserted, being aware of who's around you. That doesn't always work, but it's a start." Missy is confident this will make her neighbors less vulnerable and sees it as her obligation to educate them in protective strategies. But she also sees the local patrols as a vehicle for rallying the troops. Missy realizes that the only way she will see more cops on the beat in her neighborhood is to amass public support and pressure that will be hard for officials to ignore.

Missy has also organized a yearly fair in her housing complex, which brings the neighbors together in an effort to raise some money: "Every year I have this [event] on the plaza where we sell table space. I even include the young people. . . . Once people pay for their table space, whatever they earn after that belongs to them. I have culture groups come in dancing. . . . It's not a big money-making thing, but it's something to have people doing something together within the complex and the neighborhood." Missy follows up by taking groups of young people to local African festivals. "Last year," she remembers, "I had about fifteen of them with me, teenagers, young people that are hanging around." Missy prefers to have them involved in things around their community, "cultural things," she says, "rather than just hanging out."

Missy is not alone in her efforts. Juana Herrera, a Dominican immigrant in her early sixties, has many of the same concerns and has moved toward the same neighborhood-based solutions: "[What we have to do is] unite and have reunions with the community and the police. Now we are doing that because [robberies] were occurring here. The Mexicans were being assaulted when they came from work late at night. The poor things, with all the working hard they have to do, so that others try to take it away from them!" In studies of Chicago neighborhoods, Robert Sampson and his colleagues have found that, controlling for median income and ethnic composition, neighborhoods that exhibit high levels of social capital—dense networks and frequent interaction—suffer considerably lower levels of crime and disorder than those where residents are more anomic (*New York Times* 1997).

Social responsibility, expressed in the form of neighborhood-based solidarity, works. This lesson has not been lost on Jason Norwald, who has observed the idea in practice: "There are floors that have break-ins, and there are floors that don't—simply because the neighbors watch out for each other. Not an organized—not necessarily organized kind of thing, but, 'Hey, that doesn't sound like Rose at the door. So let me see who's out there.' With, of course, you being aware of the possibility of putting yourself in danger, but still looking out for the neighbor." There are types of social responsibility at the neighborhood level that are not expressed in organized form. Sentiments of solidarity surface as personal practices of reciprocity, as Henry Montez, a native New Yorker of Puerto Rican descent, reports: "I think neighbors should look out for one another, for the elderly. My neighbors love me. Whenever they ask me for something, I will try to help them out. [Some people] will try to take advantage of me. But if you are nice people and I see you need help, well, . . . what goes around comes around. Today you have money and tomorrow you have nothing. Today you are healthy and tomorrow you are sick. [So you have to help others.]" Henry's work brings him into contact with many of his neighbors. While he always hopes to be paid for his work, he also provides "pro bono" services to elderly Puerto Ricans in his Brooklyn neighborhood who cannot afford to pay for the plumbing help they need. Henry knows that the good he does will be rewarded in the future and considers this kind of reciprocity both a cultural obligation and a good investment.

Donna Thornton, a seventy-one-year-old African American who was born and raised in New York, sees the same advantages in being considerate and outgoing toward people she knows mainly by sight: "You can be friendly to people as you see them. When I go to school, I see these people every morning, and I try to say hello and good morning to them, because they're taking the kids. I don't know them but they're going the same way taking the kids to school. This way you get to know people. . . . And it's good to know people in the neighborhood because when you're walking down and something [bad] is happening,

168

someone will say, that's Miss so-and-so, the lady I know who lives on this block. And they'll sort of help you and protect you." This kind of reciprocal giving is a form of personal insurance, expressed in the form of ongoing ties between neighbors. The instrumental and strategic aspects of local ties are mixed in with sentiments of solidarity and time-honored forms of self-help. It "takes a village" to insure the viability of a neighborhood in these inner-city communities and the investment in building social capital is time consuming.

RACE AND ETHNICITY

I have characterized neighborhoods as arenas within which social responsibility is expressed by poor minorities who recognize the redeeming, protective consequences of reciprocity and engagement. Yet these same enclaves can be divided by race and ethnicity. The poor are forced into areas with low housing costs and poor job opportunities, pitting groups against one another in the scramble for scarce resources. Where these conditions produce deep cleavages, solidarity develops inside ethnic and racial boundaries rather than across them.

Indeed, the MIDUS survey shows that, even after controlling for total household income, educational attainment, and home ownership, African Americans report lower ratings of safety and social cohesion in their neighborhoods than all other racial groups do. This undoubtedly reflects the toll that racial segregation is taking on neighborhoods and the relative lack of trust that characterizes poorer neighborhoods where even middle-income blacks are likely to live (Massey and Denton 1990). MIDUS also shows, however, that African Americans have more frequent social contact with their neighbors than other ethnic groups, even when controlling for levels of neighborhood safety, income, home ownership, and family size.[7] This suggests a level of in-group interaction in the national sample that is consistent with the New York area findings.

There is, of course, a long-standing tradition of self-help and inward-turning social responsibility in the African American community. Beginning with Booker T. Washington and Marcus Garvey and extending to Malcolm X and beyond, the notion that helping one's own—through a racially bounded church, a program of "buying black," or an organization like the Black Panthers—is a primary obligation. It contrasts with a more universal definition of civic commitment.

Similarly, immigrants are known for their propensity to foster the well-being of co-ethnics, beginning with the chain migration patterns that bring relatives or former neighbors from their nations of origin to the receiving communities in the United States (Mahler 1994; Kasinitz 1992). Suspicion of outsiders, especially when the market (for housing, jobs, etc.) thrusts particular immigrant groups into competition with one another or with the native born, enhances group solidarity and complementary wariness toward nonmembers.

These forces surface in the form of strong and abiding sentiments that one's primary social responsibility lies in addressing the needs of one's own ethno-racial group. This definition of social responsibility must be distinguished from that which fosters engagement in the neighborhood, even though co-residents may also be defined by their common racial or ethnic heritage. Here I refer to the ways in which individuals identify themselves as members of a racial group that transcends neighborhood, city, or even personal acquaintance. Obligations flow between people who share a skin color, a national origin, or a common heritage of discrimination on account of language or appearance, whether or not they are personally known to each other.

Social responsibility toward one's race/ethnicity can be expressed as a hierarchy, leaving room for more universal commitments as well: first I serve my own, and then I can turn my attention toward outsiders. For others, the attitude is more exclusionary: I owe a great deal to my own and little to others. Either way, racial and ethnic groups turn inward toward the protection, sustenance, and promotion of the life chance of their members.

Irene Mandel, a forty-six-year-old assistant principal, has been an educator all her professional life. She is frankly nationalistic in her commitments, noting that she feels "responsible to African Americans." Her racially defined sense of social responsibility led her to change jobs so that she could act on this bounded commitment: "I left the school district that I taught in—Sheep's Head Bay. I was sent there when they were balancing racially. And I felt like I had a responsibility to come back to my neighborhood or a neighborhood similar to mine and share my expertise for the children and my attitude toward children's learning and the possibilities for [black] children." Irene does feel a general commitment to children as a whole; this is her motivation for being a teacher. But she sees the world in terms of racial groups and conceives of her responsibilities as flowing first to African American children.

Aida Gonzalez, a forty-six-year-old Dominican, shares Irene's feelings: "I feel responsible to my own group. Like for instance, if I can open a day care [home care] on a corner in a little apartment, I would try to get my own people to employ and to take care of. Even though I have Chinese and Indians and white. I would try to get more of [my own]."

The primacy of self-help is often driven by the view that ethnic communities, particularly inner-city black neighborhoods, are uniquely plagued by (or even targeted for) social pathologies like drug abuse and violence. It does not escape the notice of ghetto dwellers that drug dealers ply their trade in the ghettos and not on Park Avenue. They resent the fact that police corruption and abusive treatment is more often found in their communities than in middle-class enclaves. Hence, while a "race-conscious" nationalism can produce an inward-turning sense of social responsibility, so too can a feeling of victimization—indeed the two sentiments are not unrelated.

As Mason Bradley put the matter: "We [speak] to kids—underprivileged kids, that is—white, black, everybody under the rainbow. But I want to especially reach out my hand to people of color, those children, and let them know, 'Listen, you can do better.' . . . We have to stop promoting a lot of [bad] things that go on. This guy sells drugs, but [the kids think] it's okay. No, it is not okay. That is wrong. And we will not tolerate that in this neighborhood. . . . You take those drugs somewhere else! I love my people. I am a black man; I am going to stand up for the black woman and the black man. How can I truly call myself a black man, and you are out here poisoning my people, poisoning my children." Immigrants share the preoccupation of African Americans with self-help and racial solidarity. When asked to whom he feels obligated, Fred Moreno, a twenty-six-year-old Dominican college student, was quick to answer: "My Dominicans. I want us to have a power. I want us to have a say. I want us to be better than we are. That is something that motivates me, that drives me. Yeah." Fred moved to New York from the Republic when he was eight years old and has lived inside the barrio of Washington Heights ever since. His closest ties, from the family to peers, are contained within this ethnic enclave. Washington Heights is surrounded by other ethnic groups who are competitors for housing, jobs, and most other forms of opportunity. Fernando has learned from this ethnically segregated milieu that he should define himself in terms of his own people, rather than a pan-ethnic or American identity.

Cleaving to one's own is a natural response in neighborhoods that are divided by race or national origin. Even when residents face common problems and locate themselves (sociologically) by neighborhood, these divisions can be hard to surmount. Edna Carson, a black woman whose parents migrated from North Carolina to Brooklyn, is raising a family of her own in a mixed community. Solidarity based on common location has proven elusive in her neighborhood: "You got to think where you're living in the neighborhood when people are from different places. A lot of them don't have their green cards, a lot of them don't have immigration cards, so you don't have a real lot of unity. You're just American Black and you've got your papers because you ain't never went nowhere, so you don't have that kind of unity with them because they're scared. You have Mexicans, you got Hispanics, and a lot of Dominicans—they don't have their papers. So they're not going to help you protect anything because they just want to stay by themselves and they don't want immigration bothering them. So, you lost it, you lost that bridge to come together because there's so many gaps in between."

The Missing Poor

Most of the people who were interviewed for this study live in households with incomes that exceed the poverty line, but not always by much. There are teachers, accountants, and professionals among them, but the majority have spent their working lives as blue-collar operatives, or in hospitals where they wore white but earned a modest salary. Over half of the qualitative sample had household incomes below $25,000, even with multiple earners in the family. They do not think of themselves as impoverished, though they live in low income neighborhoods from which the more affluent have fled. Indeed, their modest earnings do not permit them to run from the problems of poor communities: crime, violence, and drugs surround them.

In their world, as in most middle-class communities, race is the most visible marker of social position. Class, by contrast, is a missing category. That is not because they do not recognize that they live in a poor community, beset with problems that make daily life problematic. It is because if they attribute this fate to any cause, it will almost always be race or ethnicity that trumps class as the force behind their social and geographic location.

Perhaps for this reason, it is striking how questions about social responsibility fail to elicit much commentary on the needs of "the poor." One hears lengthy discussion about the obligations individuals have to their families, to their communities, and to their groups, but not to those who are poor. Part of the explanation for this gap may lie in the commitments some have made to "the church," an institution that provides services to the poor in New York's barrio neighborhoods. Indeed, more than a third of this sample said that they felt obligated to give to the church, though they complained a good deal about their churches as well.

It may also be that, living so close to the poverty line themselves, the working (or retired) poor tend not to feel as much sympathy toward those less fortunate as do others who are socially distant and looking for a target for their charitable impulses.[8] So much publicity has been given to AFDC and its problems that my informants often equate "the poor" with "welfare mothers," (as do middle-class supporters of time limits and the end of "welfare as we know it.") The working poor see finer gradations of status at the bottom of the social hierarchy and do not confuse themselves with the homeless, the hopeless, or the welfare dependent. Indeed, the welfare dependent come in for a great deal of criticism amongst them (see Newman 1999).

At the same time, our interviews contain consistent references to the "truly needy": young children, the indigent beggar on the corner, young mothers over their heads with family responsibilities, and the like. Hence while the category of "the poor" is little discussed, particular poor people are the objects of sympathy and charity. In this, our respondents mirror the attitudes discussed in Herbert Gans's powerful book, *The War against the Poor* (1995). Gans explains that while sympathy is shown toward specific individuals, the poor are demonized as a social category. Indeed, this negative view of the category of the poor is a powerful source of antipathy toward welfare and other programs that ameliorate poverty. To the extent that social responsibility is politically defined, our sample seems to embrace a fairly mainstream view that distinguishes the deserving poor from the rest.

The Missing Nation

Equally absent from my informants' understandings of social responsibility is an abstract conception of the nation, the society as a whole, as an entity toward which commitment must be expressed. The absence of citizenship as a moral obligation is partly explained by the immigration status of the Dominican respondents in our study. Puerto Ricans, in turn, draw upon a mixed and wary view of the United States as a place which has incorporated them, but not on their own terms. The Puerto Rican community is the poorest of New York's Latino populations. Factory jobs that absorbed the mass migration of Puerto Ricans in the 1940s have long since disappeared, leaving succeeding generations of migrants fewer opportunities to earn a living wage. Puerto Ricans and Dominicans face mobility barriers based on language, and many with dark skin experience the same prejudices leveled at the African Americans with whom they are often confused (especially by employers).

Earlier waves of immigrants who entered the country when the economy was on an upswing achieved their economic mobility over time. Waves of Americanization, molded by World War II and consolidated by postwar affluence, generated attachment to "the best country in the world." Rapid suburbanization fostered a break from the ethnic enclaves of the cities and sped the process of cultural assimilation. The nation became an identity and a source of solidarity among American-born descendants of Italian and Irish immigrants. Civic or community-wide conceptions of social responsibility developed only over time, as relative newcomers gradually became privileged members of the middle class.

Few of these conditions held fast by the mid-1970s, as waves of Puerto Rican and Dominican migrants settled into cities like New York. Like the African Americans who preceded them in the Great Migration out of the rural south to the industrial north, the "new" immigrants had to find their way into the urban economy at a time when high paying industrial jobs were rapidly disappearing. The service jobs that replaced unionized, blue-collar jobs were distinguished by low pay and dead-end job ladders.

Upward mobility has become far more problematic for the new generations of immigrants in our time. Under current economic circumstances, identification with the nation has been more tenuous, and abstract ideas of social responsibility are equally strained. Solidarity with "one's own" has greater appeal when barriers to mobility are firm and persistent, precluding the development of subjective and moral commitments to the larger community. Ironically, the greatest attachment to common institutions is probably found among sports enthusiasts, who cross ethnic lines to a greater degree than those engaged in any other form of civic participation.

CONCLUSION

When we investigate the contours of social responsibility, we are asking powerful questions not only about what people do to "make good" on their conceptions of obligation, but about the boundaries they draw around their identities. How do they situate themselves in a moral sense? What are the forms of community that exert a powerful enough influence to produce a moral claim on their time, their resources, and their sense of social location? Which of these claims are trivial—satisfied by the writing of a check—and which really command attention and devotion?

Inner-city minorities are often described as socially disengaged isolates who have pulled back from wider social obligations in response to safety problems in the neighborhoods where they live. Yet in this study, we see that the migration experience, urban segregation, and limited economic mobility have all conspired to create a strong sense of belonging. The same forces have bound minority groups into enclaves that breed both solidarity and division. Loyalty is owed to those who are within the boundaries, though the lines are themselves fluid and shifting according to time and circumstance. Neighbors may see themselves as locked together in a struggle for survival or protection against fellow residents who do not share their values. Co-ethnics confronting racial barriers may divide themselves off from fellow residents of their neighborhoods who belong to another racial group or nationality.

The lived reality of these boundaries, however, is created in part by the social responsibilities insiders feel toward one another. Parents who raise their children "right" do so not only out of a sense of family values, but out of the conviction that they owe this effort to others in their community. They fault irresponsible parents not only for what they have done to destroy their children's futures, but for what they have wrought upon the neighborhood in the form of antisocial behavior. Neighbors band together to watch over one another, organizing block watch groups, youth parties, and other forms of support against a social decay that threatens their peace of mind and the safety of their children. Dominicans and Puerto Ricans think about what they should do to foster the well-being of their own people, putting them ahead of the demands of others who may be equally needy, but who must be someone else's responsibility. The ethnic "mosaic" expresses a racially fractured understanding of the community to which they belong. Yet within the boundaries these divisions create, a sense of social responsibility is clearly expressed and acted out in their daily lives.

REFERENCES

Anderson, E. 1990. *Streetwise*. Chicago: University of Chicago Press.
Brooks-Gunn, J., G. Duncan, P. K. Klebanov, and N. Sealand. 1993. Do neighborhoods influence child and adolescent development? *American Journal of Sociology* 99:353–94.

Coleman, J. 1988. Social capital in the creation of human capital. *American Journal of Sociology Supplement* 94:S95–S120.

Gans, H. 1995. *The war against the poor: The underclass and antipoverty policy*. New York: Free Press.

Geronimus, A. 1995. The translation of social inequality into reproductive inequality: A population-based test of the weathering hypothesis. *University of Michigan Population Studies Center Research Report* no. 95-323 (January).

Hannerz, U. 1969. *Soulside: Inquiries into ghetto culture and community*. New York: Columbia University Press.

Kasinitz, P. 1992. *Caribbean New York*. Ithaca: Cornell University Press.

Lewin, T. 1998. The disturbing trend: More victims and much less sense in the string of shootings at schools. *New York Times,* 22 May, sec. A.

Mahler, S. 1994. *American dreaming*. Princeton: Princeton University Press.

Massey, D., and N. Denton. 1990. *American apartheid*. Cambridge: Harvard University Press.

New York Times. 1997. Study links violence rate to cohesion of community. 17 August, sec. A.

Newman, K. 1998. Place and race. In *Welcome to Middle Age!* ed. R. Shweder, 259–93. Chicago: University of Chicago Press.

———. 1999. *No shame in my game: The working poor in the inner city*. New York: Knopf/Russell Sage.

Putnam, R. D. 1995. Bowling alone: America's declining social capital. *Journal of Democracy* 6:65–78.

———. 1996. The strange disappearance of civic America. *American Prospect* 24 (winter):34–48.

Stack, C. 1974. *All our kin: Strategies for survival in a black community*. New York: Harper and Row.

Venkatesh, S. 1997. An invisible community: Inside Chicago's public housing. *American Prospect* 34 (September–October):35–40.

Wilson, W. J. 1987. *The truly disadvantaged*. Chicago: University of Chicago Press.

———. 1996. *When work disappears*. New York: Knopf.

NOTES

1. Our life history interviews took an average of three hours to tape record, since they covered everything from the respondents' migration histories, employment experiences, and perceptions of race relations to their cultural definitions of social obligations.

2. The life history sample is generally representative of the New York survey. There were fewer women in the qualitative study and fewer married couples. Moreover, the life history group is somewhat better educated than the sample as a whole, with a larger proportion of high school graduates. But these variations are modest and none were statistically significant.

3. Elijah Anderson (1990) argues that ghetto communities distinguish between respectable families and deviant ones. Ulf Hannerz (1969) makes the same distinction.

4. The recent rash of mass shootings in rural and suburban schools may force a change in this view. In most of these cases, a troubled child who was known to family members and acquaintances as having expressed threatening intentions acted on those sentiments to devastating result. Retrospective accounts suggest that most of these individuals were known for their aberrant attitudes but either were not taken seriously or were regarded as a private, personal problem for their families to tend to. As the consequences of that privatized approach more frequently become painful for the community as a whole, we may see a more intrusive or communal definition of childrearing responsibilities. In these tragic episodes, middle-class communities take on some of the more unfortunate characteristics of the inner-city neighborhoods from which my interviews emerge: enclaves where the private matters become public concern in a hurry. See Lewin 1998.

5. Elsewhere (Newman 1998) I define success as the absence of failure for poor families in run-down neighborhoods. Pride accrues to those who have managed to see their children to adulthood without teen pregnancy, involvement in the illegal trades, or major problems with the law.

6. Middle-class white families who experience downward mobility often confront the discord that attends this conception of generational autonomy. Parents who have fallen on hard times or adult children who have lost their jobs and find that they need to borrow money feel intensely uncomfortable about this dependency. It violates a cultural code which separates love from money, demanding a continuous expression of the former and only the most time-limited offering of the latter. Parents are responsible for supporting children—with funds flowing in this direction only—until they reach maturity. Economic dependency thereafter is a source of shame.

7. Alice Rossi, personal communication, 25 March 1998.

8. Fifty-two percent of the qualitative sample were working. Only 8.2% were unemployed. Across all three ethnic groups, approximately 18% reported AFDC receipt in their households.

Cultural and Contextual Correlates of Obligation to Family and Community among Urban Black and Latino Adults

Diane Hughes

This chapter examines social responsibility as it is manifested in a sense of obligation to and participation in two primary domains—family and community—among Puerto Rican, Dominican, and Black men and women living in New York City. The data are drawn from a study of midlife experiences among urban ethnic minority adults in New York conducted as a companion study to the national MIDUS study. One objective of the chapter is to describe normative obligation to family and community, and associated behaviors, within this New York sample. The availability of comparable items in the national MIDUS study and the New York study provides an important opportunity to examine diversity across cultures and contexts in experiences of and attitudes toward caring and giving during the midlife period. An additional objective of the chapter is to examine the extent to which phenomena associated with living in urban neighborhoods diminish participants' feelings of obligation and their ability to participate in family and community life. In this regard, an important feature of the New York study is its emphasis on elucidating ways in which the social context of adults' lives shapes life patterns and well-being during the midlife period. As described below, the sample consists of ethnic minority adults of high and low socioeconomic status living in ethnically and socioeconomically diverse communities. The availability of both individual and neighborhood-level socio-structural indicators permits an examination of hypotheses concerning constraints on giving and caring associated with residency in economically marginal neighborhoods.

An examination of social responsibility as it emerges in the lives of urban ethnic minority adults in differing community contexts may be informative for many reasons. For one, scholars studying social responsibility and related concepts, such as generativity, have suggested that these are both culturally conditioned and deeply connected to external experiences, particularly as these experiences are defined by one's position in the social structure. In the work of McAdams and colleagues (McAdams and de St. Aubin 1992; McAdams, de St. Aubin, and Logan 1993; McAdams, Hart, and Maruna 1998) for instance, cultural demand occupies a prominent position, alongside inner desire, in the nomological network of constructs defining generativity: cultural demand is encoded in age-graded norms and expectations regarding the timing of particular role contributions throughout the life cycle and about the domains most important for generative expression (McAdams, Hart, and Maruna 1998). Thus, what is expected as socially responsible behavior, the age-related trajectories of such expectations, and the domains in which social responsibility is displayed vary across groups.

Family and community are two domains of social responsibility that may be particularly susceptible to the sorts of cultural norms and socio-structural influences that scholars have described. For instance, in middle-class America, young adults are expected to devote their energies to childrearing and career building. Contributions to social institutions and causes are expected later, when one's childrearing demands have diminished and one's career trajectory has peaked (Cohler, Hostetler, and Boxer 1998; MacDermid, Franz, and De Reus 1998; Rossi, this volume). However, Stack and Burton (1993) describe an operative timetable among African Americans living in rural communities that differs dramatically from that which previous scholars have described. Women expect to bear children during their mid-teen years, but their primary caregiving responsibilities are to their grandmothers who had reared them rather than to their own offspring. In turn, young women's birth mothers expect to have primary caregiving responsibilities for their grandchildren, as their own grandmothers had for them. Other studies, too, suggest that social and economic demands within African American families are managed by extended and nuclear family members (Jayakody, Chatters, and Taylor 1993; Tolson and Wilson 1990). Reliance on extended kin throughout the life cycle has been described in scholarly work on Dominican (Grasmuck and Pessar 1996) and Puerto Rican (Carrasquillo and Sanchez-Korrol 1996) families as well. Thus, in some cultural contexts, family obligations are not limited to one's own offspring or to particular periods of adult life. Moreover, phenomena such as the "empty nest syndrome" that mark phases of midlife are notably absent, with implications for adults' availability to involve themselves in community as well. To understand social responsibility as a critical component of success in midlife, the domains of inquiry need to be extended to include the manifold ways in which it is experienced and expressed across groups.

In addition to variation in the meaning and correlates of social responsibility across cultural groups, scholars have suggested variation across social status categories, due to differences in constraints against and opportunities for generative behavior. Again, such variation may be especially likely to manifest itself in the family and community domains. For instance, Keyes and Ryff (1998) argue that socio-structural factors such as low income and education create alienation and decrease personal agency, thus diminishing generativity, other forms of social responsibility, and general well-being. Using data from two national probability samples, Keyes (1998) found that more highly educated adults' mean values on five indicators of social well-being, including social integration and social contribution, were higher than those of their less well educated counterparts. Again, however, the socio-economic correlates of social responsibility may differ across groups as a function of variation both in normative practices and in the incremental psychological resources (agency, self-efficacy) that socio-economic status may yield.

Finally, implicit in theoretical frameworks put forth in Keyes and Ryff 1998, Keyes 1998, and elsewhere is the notion that ecological and contextual factors may constrain the definition and enactment of socially responsible behaviors, due to feelings of alienation and dislocation that stressful environments promote. Katherine Newman (chapter 5, this volume), in particular, suggests that the expression of social responsibility may be uniquely tailored to the demands and stressors inherent in urban communities. When environments are risky, threatening, or treacherous to navigate, one's sense of obligation may be unlikely to extend far beyond one's own family and, possibly, one's narrowly defined ethnic group. In Newman's life history interviews with a subsample of respondents who participated in the New York study, references to volunteerism or donations to organizations and institutions were notably absent from participants' narratives regarding social responsibility. Thus, an empirical examination of family and community participation and obligation among adults living in different neighborhood contexts may provide important insight into socio-structural and psychological processes that promote or inhibit social responsibility.

FOCUS OF THE PRESENT CHAPTER

In focusing on family and community participation and obligation among urban ethnic minority adults, the present chapter attempts to address three major questions. First, to what extent do Puerto Rican, Dominican, and Black adults in the present sample report obligation to and participation in family and community domains? In this regard, the goal of the chapter is a simple one: to present pertinent descriptive data for each of the three ethnic groups. Although many studies of minority adults' involvement in kin networks have been conducted (Hatchett and Jackson 1993; McAdoo 1980, 1981; Stack 1974; Wilson 1986, 1989), as have a few studies of minority adults' political participation and community involvement (Brown 1991; Cole and Stewart 1996; Milburn and Bowman 1991), studies of psychological constructs such as normative obligation and generativity have relied upon data from ethnically homogenous White samples (see Cole and Stewart 1996; McAdams and Azarow 1996; and McAdams, Hart, and Maruna 1998 for exceptions). Thus, little empirical information is available regarding ethnic minority adults' psychological sense of obligation or generativity, leaving room for theoretical speculation about the erosion of family and community values in inner-city minority neighborhoods.

Second, the chapter examines the extent to which patterns of relationships between social responsibility in family and community domains and socio-structural variables such as age and education in the present sample mirror patterns reported in the national MIDUS sample (Keyes and Ryff 1998; Rossi, chapter 3, this volume) and in other studies of generativity (McAdams, de St. Aubin, and Logan 1993). To the extent that the meaning and significance of socio-structural indicators vary across groups and social contexts, it is important to examine the extent to which linkages between these indicators and obligation and participation vary across groups as well. Age, gender, and socioeconomic status receive particular attention in this regard because previous studies have highlighted their importance in shaping profiles of social responsibility and generativity. As a proxy for adult development, age has been of considerable interest because it is thought to provide information about shifts in psychological processes during midlife, particularly in terms of culturally mediated conceptions of time and mortality. Education and gender have been of interest as markers of power and social location that, directly or indirectly, promote social responsibility.

A third and final question concerns the extent to which family and community obligation and participation vary across different ethnic, immigrant status, and religious preference groups, as well as across different economic and cultural contexts. The focus on ethnic markers (e.g., ethnicity, immigrant status) is embedded in the recognition that different minority groups in the United States have different histories and experiences and occupy different social spaces. American-born Blacks, for instance, constitute what Ogbu (1985) terms a "caste-like" minority, having been enslaved and transported to the United States involuntarily and encountering present-day racial bias and structural disadvantage relative to Whites in occupational, educational, and political arenas (Essed 1990; Feagin and Sikes 1994). Unlike Blacks, Dominicans and Puerto Ricans immigrated voluntarily to the United States, most often seeking economic opportunity and fleeing oppressive economic conditions in their home country. Dominicans and Puerto Ricans also encounter negative attitudes toward their group and blocked opportunity in educational and occupational domains; second-generation Dominican and Puerto Rican adults typically fare worse in this regard than do more recent immigrants (Grasmuck and Pessar 1996; Pessar 1995). In other ways, however, the two groups differ dramatically from one another. Historically, Puerto Ricans have been the largest Hispanic group in New York City and have developed a presence and degree of political clout that Dominicans have not yet developed (Grasmuck and Pessar 1996). Puerto Ricans' right to U.S. citizenship is accompanied by access to certain federal benefits, the right to vote, and transcontinental mobility. Compared with Puerto Ricans, Dominicans are a more recent, but rapidly growing segment of the population. In New York City, they are, on average, among the youngest, the poorest, and the least well educated of immigrant groups. The observation that Dominican New Yorkers have little political presence has been attributed to their commitment to native politics, their deep ties to the Dominican Republic, and a "transient mentality" focused primarily on their eventual return to their homeland (Grasmuck and Pessar 1996; Torres-Saillant 1989). Thus, differences in the history and circumstances of these minority groups may manifest themselves in differences in the origins and expressions of family and community participation and obligation. Puerto Ricans, African Americans, and Dominicans also differ from one another in terms of their religious affiliation and the strength of their ties to their religious beliefs and values. Because religion plays a central role in people's ideas about morality and responsibility (see

Rossi, chapters 3 and 7, this volume), it seems critical to untangle the influences of ethnicity, per se, from the influences of religiosity—to the extent that such disentanglement is possible.

The focus of the present chapter on neighborhood context is embedded in the view that ecological settings promote norms and behaviors that vary according to their social and economic attributes. For instance, Wilson's (1987) elaboration of the concept of social isolation emphasizes the importance of structural factors and neighborhood social networks, which link residents to opportunity structures and mainstream values, in shaping normative values and patterns of behavior. Mayer and Jencks (1989) have also argued that neighborhood characteristics influence individuals' behaviors by way of multiple mechanisms including contagion mechanisms (wherein individuals imitate normative behaviors of others in their neighborhood) and socialization mechanisms (wherein individuals internalize community norms). Social psychological theories concerning ambient environmental stress (Aldwin and Stokols 1988) suggest that low community resources or high community problems may promote disengagement from social life and an inward focus, resulting in low normative obligation and low participation in family and community. A neighborhood's ethnic makeup has also been hypothesized to influence neighborhood cohesion and the development of community-based norms. For instance, a high degree of ethnic heterogeneity is thought to erode the development of neighborhood-based social networks (Sampson 1992; Sampson and Morenoff 1997), which may, in turn, influence the nature of community-level transactions and residents' involvement in community social structures. Taylor, Gottfredson, and Brower (1985) report less neighborhood attachment in heterogenous as compared with homogeneous settings, suggesting that ethnic heterogeneity increases interpersonal conflict and inhibits the development of shared community norms. Accordingly, in focusing on the possibility that neighborhood contexts promote or constrain family and community participation and obligation, this chapter gives particular attention to neighborhood socioeconomic status, neighborhood problems, and neighborhood ethnic composition. An examination of aggregate-level ecological data in relation to family and community involvement and participation may promote increased theoretical understanding of processes underlying social responsibility and of ecological theories regarding contextual influences on values and behaviors.

Overview of the Study

The data presented in this chapter are drawn from Ethnic and Racial Minorities in Urban Areas, a study of midlife experiences among ethnic minority adults living in New York City and Chicago. The study was conducted by an interdisciplinary group of scholars as a companion study to the national MIDUS effort. It was designed to investigate a range of factors as they influenced midlife adults' experiences, including neighborhood context, discrimination, stressful life events, social network factors, and a range of intrapersonal constructs that overlap with constructs central to the national MIDUS survey. The sample was drawn from selected neighborhoods, or census block groups, in New York City and Chicago. For purposes of parsimony, I focus in this chapter on findings from participants in the New York study—Puerto Rican, Dominican, and Black adults aged twenty-five years and older.[1]

Eligible respondents were identified using a two-stage sampling procedure that combined identification of census block groups within preselected strata and quota sampling of qualified respondents. Thus, within a selected census block group, trained interviewers identified eligible participants by screening residents door to door. These adults participated in 1.5- to 2-hour structured interviews, conducted in English or Spanish (according to the respondent's language preference) by interviewers who had received more than twenty hours of training. Standard back-translation procedures were used to ensure the comparability of the English and Spanish protocols. The final New York sample consisted of 906 Puerto Rican, Dominican, and Black participants who lived in sixty-four census block groups throughout New York City. With quota selection of respondents, the samples were not intended to make generalizations about a particular population but rather to test theoretical propositions regarding ethnicity, social context, and experiences during midlife.

Demographic characteristics of each ethnic group of participants in the study are presented in table 6.1. As the table shows, there was substantial inter- and intragroup variation on these demographic variables. The Puerto Rican subsample of respondents was quite diverse. Just over 40% of them were married; about 27% were married with children under eighteen in the home; an additional 23% were single parents with children under eighteen in the home. Most Puerto Rican respondents were young (twenty-one to thirty-nine years old) or

Table 6.1 Sample Demographic Characteristics

	Puerto Rican ($N = 284$)	Dominican ($N = 283$)	Black ($N = 339$)
Family structure (%)			
Married with children under 18 in home	26.8	24.4	16.5
Married with no children under 18 in home	14.8	12.0	12.1
Not married with children under 18 in home	22.9	33.9	22.4
Not married with no children under 18 in home	35.6	29.7	49.0
Age (%)			
21–39	41.8	47.0	46.6
40–59	42.5	42.8	31.6
60+	15.8	8.5	16.2
Gender (% male)	51.8	46.3	50.7
Education (%)			
No high school diploma	41.9	46.3	19.5
High school diploma	29.2	25.8	31.3
Courses beyond high school	21.1	18.7	35.1
Immigrant status (%)			
U.S. born	50.7	9.9	91.7
Foreign born	49.3	90.1	8.3
Age at immigration			
0–17	53.9	31.03	2.2
18–25	27.0	24.7	21.4
26+1	9.14	4.3	46.4
Years in the U.S.			
Mean	33.7	19.1	25.8
SD	13.2	11.5	15.2
English language fluency (%)	62.3	24.3	100.0
Mean[a]	2.79	1.77	4.93
SD	1.29	1.0	1.34
Catholic (%)	72.2	84.8	14.5
Religiosity[b]	00.0	−.02	.03
Standardized values	.76	.75	.78
Median family income	$22,000.00	$14,200.00	$27,000.00
Neighborhood context			
Median neighborhood income	$25,351.00	$21,595.78	$31,250.00
Perceived neighborhood problems			
Mean[c]	1.71	1.90	1.67
SD	.66	.67	.62
Neighborhood ethnic density (%)			
High density (>30%) own ethnicity	60.9	56.2	61.7
Low density (<30%) own ethnicity	39.1	43.8	38.3
High density Dominican	28.8	—	13.1
High density Puerto Rican	—	77.4	39.2
High density Black	42.3	16.1	—
Ethnically mixed[d]	28.8	5.6	47.4

[a] 1 = low; 5 = high.

[b] Religiosity is the mean of four standardized items, each with a mean of 0 and standard deviation of 1.

[c] 1 = low; 3 = high.

[d] Ethnically mixed neighborhoods were defined as those less than 30% Puerto Rican, Dominican, or Black. On average, ethnically mixed neighborhoods were 14.0% Puerto Rican (range = 4–24%), .8% Dominican (range = 0–4%), 17.6% African American (range = 10–29%), and 29.6% non-Hispanic White (range = 11–62%).

middle-aged (forty to fifty-nine years old) adults. Half the Puerto Ricans had completed high school or the equivalent, a figure that is comparable to the high school completion rate for Puerto Ricans in New York City in 1990. The Puerto Rican sample was equally divided between those born in the mainland United States and those born in Puerto Rico. Among the latter group, almost 54% had immigrated to the mainland United States before the age of eighteen; on average, they had been in the United States for more than thirty years. Accordingly, almost two-thirds of the Puerto Rican respondents reported that they were equally fluent in English and Spanish. The majority of them were Catholic. Annual family income among Puerto Rican respondents was higher than that among Dominican respondents, but it was lower than that among Black respondents. Sixty-one percent of Puerto Rican respondents were living in high density Puerto Rican neighborhoods, defined as census block groups in which more than 30% of residents were Puerto Rican. These respondents were drawn primarily from Sunset Park in Brooklyn and various neighborhoods in the Bronx such as University/Kingsbrook Heights, Castle Hill, and Bruckner. Puerto Rican respondents living in low density neighborhoods (<30% Puerto Rican) were drawn from other ethnic minority neighborhoods in New York. Among them were Washington Heights (a high density Dominican neighborhood in northern Manhattan), Eastchester (a high density Black neighborhood in the Bronx), and Fort Greene and Cobble Hill (ethnically mixed neighborhoods north of Prospect Park in Brooklyn). Thus, notably absent from the sample were second- or third-generation Puerto Rican adults living in middle- to upper-income White neighborhoods throughout the city.

Dominican respondents in the sample were also mostly young or middle-aged men and women, but they were less likely to be married and more likely to be single parents than were their Puerto Rican counterparts. Dominican respondents were less well educated than were Puerto Rican or Black respondents, consistent with the overall low levels of education among Dominicans in New York City (Grasmuck and Pessar 1996). More than 90% of the Dominican respondents were foreign born, and of these, most (69%) had immigrated to the United States during adulthood. On average, Dominican immigrants had been in the United States for about nineteen years, although many of them (27.5%) had immigrated within the past ten years. The majority of Dominican respondents reported that Spanish was their dominant language: only 24% of them reported at least equal competence in English and Spanish. More than 80% of Dominican respondents were Catholic. The annual family income among Dominican participants was comparable to that for the average Dominican family in New York City as of the 1990 U.S. census, but it was significantly lower than that for Puerto Rican or Black respondents in the present study. Approximately 56% of the Dominican respondents lived in high density Dominican neighborhoods, the majority of them in Washington Heights. It is important to note, for purposes of a later discussion, that Washington Heights is among the poorest neighborhoods in New York City. In the present sample, respondents living in Washington Heights reported significantly more problems in their neighborhoods than did respondents living elsewhere (mean number of major problems = 3.56 in Washington Heights vs. 2.33 elsewhere; $t(904) = -4.22$, $p < .05$). Dominican respondents living in low density neighborhoods resided in Puerto Rican neighborhoods in Brooklyn and the Bronx (e.g., Sunset Park, Borum Hill). Very few of them lived in high density Black neighborhoods or in neighborhoods that were ethnically mixed.

The Black subsample of respondents consisted primarily of U.S.-born African Americans; fewer than 10% of them were foreign born. Black respondents were much less likely than their Puerto Rican or Dominican counterparts to be married with children. They were much more likely than either Hispanic group to be unmarried with no children younger than eighteen years of age in the home. Blacks had more years of schooling than their Dominican and Puerto Rican counterparts. Sixteen percent of Black and Puerto Rican respondents were aged sixty or older, compared with 9% of Dominican respondents. Only one in five of the Black respondents had not obtained a high school diploma or its equivalent, compared with 42% and 46% of Puerto Ricans and Dominicans, respectively. Black respondents were much less likely to be Catholic (15%) than were other respondents; the largest percentage identified themselves as Baptist (39%). More than 60% of Black respondents were drawn from high density (>30%) Black neighborhoods, which were primarily in Brooklyn surrounding Prospect Park (e.g., Fort Greene, Clinton Hill, Prospect Heights) or in the Bronx bordering Westchester. Unlike high density Puerto Rican or Dominican neighborhoods, these were primarily middle-income neighborhoods in which residents were professionals, students, and artists. Notably absent from the sample were Blacks living in high poverty, high density Black neighborhoods throughout New York, such as central Harlem, East New York, or the central Bronx. Thus, the sample of Black respondents consisted of middle- to upper-income Black New Yorkers living in relatively stable areas throughout the city.

Assessing Family and Community Obligation and Participation

Indicators of family and community participation and obligation used in the study are listed in table 6.2. The measures vary considerably in terms of their similarity to measures used in the national MIDUS study and in terms of the texture and detail provided. In both the family and community domains, measures of normative obligation (e.g., normative family obligation, civic obligation, and altruism) were parallel to measures used in the national MIDUS study, a primary advantage being the opportunity to locate ethnic minority adults on these measures relative to the national sample. Principal axes factor analysis (available from the author) of the full set of items tapping normative role obligations yielded a factor structure that was comparable to that identified in the national MIDUS sample, reducing concerns about the equivalence of these measures across groups. As described in greater detail later, mean values on measures tapping normative role obligations in the present sample were also comparable to those reported for the national MIDUS sample (see chapter 3).

Measures of family contributions and community contributions used in the New York study were more global and less nuanced than were measures of similar constructs in the national MIDUS study. In the family domain, respondents were asked about contributions of money or material goods to family and friends but not about contributions of social support or caregiving. Moreover, respondents were not asked to distinguish the type of contribution (e.g., money vs. food) or the recipient of the contribution (e.g., parents vs. adult children vs. grandchildren). Nor were they asked about nonfinancial contributions of time or services to family or friends. Likewise, in the community domain, respondents were asked about contributions of money or material goods to religious or other organizations but were not asked to specify the type of contribution (e.g., money vs. goods) or the type of organization (e.g., local vs. national; ethnic vs. non-ethnic). Nor were they asked about contributions of time or services to organizations. Thus, in focusing exclusively on financial and material exchanges, measures of contribution in both the family and the community domains may underestimate respondents' participation, especially among less financially advantaged respondents in the sample for whom obligation and participation may be expressed in other ways. In addition to limi-

189

TABLE 6.2 Description of Measures Assessing Family
and Community Obligation and Participation

Domain	Dimension	Measure	Measure Description
Family	Obligation	Family obligation	Eight-item scale identical to that used in MIDUS. Respondents utilized an eleven-point (0–10) rating scale to indicate the degree of obligation felt toward children, parents, spouse, and friends, e.g., "to be in touch with your parents on a regular basis" or "to take a friend into your home who could not afford to live alone" (scale range = 0–80; alpha = .83; mean for the full sample = 63.74; SD = 13.37).
	Participation	Family contributions	Respondents were asked whether or not they currently contribute money, food, clothing, or other goods to a family member (including parents, in-laws, adult children, or grandchildren) or friends (0 = no contributions, 1 = contributes to family *or* friends, 2 = contributes to family *and* friends; mean = .96; SD = .94).
		Frequency of contact	Respondents were asked, "How often are you in contact with any members of your family—that is, any of your brothers, sisters, parents, or children who do not live with you—including visits, phone calls, letters, or electronic mail messages?" Respondents answered on a eight-point interval level scale (1 = never/hardly ever, 2 = less than once a month, 3 = about once a month, 4 = 2–3 times a month, 5 = about once a week, 6 = several times a week, 7 = about once a day, 8 = several times a day; mean = 6.44; SD = 1.70).
Community	Obligation	Civic obligation	Four-item scale identical to that used in MIDUS. Respondents used an eleven-point (0–10) rating scale to indicate the degree of obligation felt toward participation in civic affairs, e.g., "to vote in national or local elections" (scale range = 0–40; alpha = .91; mean for the full sample = 29.20; SD = 9.00).
		Altruism	Four-item scale identical to that used in MIDUS. Respondents used an eleven-point (0–10) rating scale to indicate the degree of obligation felt toward helping others at one's own expense, e.g., "to collect contributions for heart or cancer research if asked to do so" (scale range = 0–40; alpha = .89; mean for the full sample = 26.49; SD = 10.83).
	Participation	Community contributions	Respondents were asked whether they contributed money, food, clothing, or other goods to a religious group or to any other organization (0 = does not contribute, 1 = contributes to religious *or* nonreligious organizations, 2 = contributes to religious *and* nonreligious organizations; mean = .71; SD = .86).
		Community attachment	Four-item scale utilizing the top-loading items from Buckner's (1989) measure of neighborhood cohesion. Respondents indicated the extent to which they felt embedded in and loyal to their neighborhood, e.g., "Living in this neighborhood gives me a sense of community" (range = 0–4; alpha = .93; mean for the full sample = 3.31; SD= .88).

tations due to narrowness of coverage, any single-item measure is subject to greater error variance than are multi-item indicators. Nevertheless, respondents' reports about *whether or not* they have given to any family member, religious group, or organization may be more accurate than their reports about the actual amount of money or value of goods given.

Frequency of family contact and community attachment were also assessed as indicators of family and community participation. As with measures of contribution, the single-item question concerning frequency of family contact provides little detail regarding specific nonresident family members with whom respondents maintain contact or regarding the vehicle for such contact. Because contact with any nonresident family member through any medium is included, the high level of contact suggested by the mean values in table 6.2 is not surprising. Indeed, most of the variance in the measure distinguished respondents who reported daily (59.7%) vs. weekly (24.2%) contact with nonresident family members. Thus, the measure may not be as sensitive as other measures we included to the sorts of predictor variables examined here. As a multi-item indicator, the measure of community attachment is more comprehensive and less subject to error variance than is the measure of frequency of contact. However, it focuses exclusively on respondents' subjective sense of community, although other aspects of attachment, such as intention to remain in the neighborhood, may be important indicators of community attachment as well.

Additional variables examined in the chapter (not shown in table 6.2) were measured and coded as follows: In all multivariate analyses, family structure variables were statistically controlled, although such variables receive little substantive attention. Respondents were coded according to marital status (0 = not married; 1 = married) and parental status (0 = no children under eighteen living in the home; 1 = at least one child under eighteen living in the home). Age was measured in years as of the respondent's most recent birthday. Respondents were categorized according to three age groups: young (ages twenty-one to thirty-nine); middle-aged (ages forty to fifty-nine) and older (ages sixty and older) adults. Education was assessed using a twelve-point interval level scale (1 = some grade school; 12 = Ph.D., ED.D., M.D.). As with the indicator of age, respondents were grouped according to three categories: no high school diploma; high school diploma or GED; and courses beyond high school. Annual household income was assessed as an interval level variable in increments of $5,000 to $10,000. Respondents were asked to choose the category that best represented their total annual household income from all sources before taxes. The midpoint of each interval was used to estimate a continuous variable representing annual income in U.S. dollars. Respondents' ethnicity was represented in all multivariate analyses with two dummy variables representing Puerto Ricans (0 = no; 1 = yes) and Dominicans (0 = no; 1 = yes). In all analyses, Blacks served as the reference group. Immigrant status was a binary variable (0 = U.S. born; 1 = foreign born). English language fluency was determined by a single-item question in which respondents indicated on a five-point interval scale the language they usually think in (1 = Spanish only; 5 = English only). To represent differences in religious affiliation across ethnic groups, a dummy variable was included to distinguish respondents who were Catholic from those who were not (0 = not Catholic; 1 = Catholic). To assess religiosity, respondents were asked four questions concerning their commitment to religion (1 = not at all religious; 4 = very religious), frequency of church attendance (1 = never; 5 = more than once a week), reliance on religion to make decisions (1 = never; 4 = often), and reliance on religion to cope with difficulties (1 = never; 4 = often). Due to the different response formats for these questions, the mean of the standardized items was used as an indicator of religiosity ($\alpha = .79$, $M = 0$, $SD = 1$). Census block group data from the 1990 U.S. census was used to assess median neighborhood income. Neighborhood ethnic density was assessed using census block group data on neighborhood ethnic composition. Respondents were coded as living in high (>30% own ethnicity) or low (<30% own ethnicity) density neighborhoods based on the proportion of residents within the census block group who were of the same ethnicity (e.g., non-Hispanic Black, Dominican, Puerto Rican) as the respondent. Although there are limitations to using block group data to represent neighborhood-level phenomena (e.g., block group geographic boundaries may not correspond to neighborhood boundaries as perceived by residents), such aggregate-level data does provide some insight into the characteristics of residential areas. To assess neighborhood problems, respondents were asked to indicate on a three-point scale the extent to which eleven conditions (e.g., youth who have little respect for property; poor schools; violent arguments) were problems in their current neighborhood (1 = not a problem; 3 = a big problem). Respondents' ratings across these eleven potential problems were averaged.

Results

In this section, results of analyses concerning participation and obligation are presented separately for indicators in the family and community domains. For each domain, descriptive data concerning participation and involvement are presented first. Then, findings regarding the extent to which participation and obligation vary as a function of individual-level socio-structural variables, ethnic markers, and neighborhood contextual variables are presented in turn.

Family Obligation and Participation

Table 6.3 presents means and zero-order correlations for indicators of family participation and normative obligation. The table shows extensive engagement with and obligation to family within the sample. Over one-half of the respondents reported contributions of money or material goods to family members or friends; more than 40% of them reported contributions to both. Contact with nonresident family members was also extensive. Additional analyses (not shown) showed that 55% of respondents within each ethnic group reported contact with nonresident family members on a daily basis. An additional 28% reported contact at least once a week. Consistent with their participation in family networks, respondents also reported relatively high normative family obligation, with scores on the 0–80 scale that were quite comparable to those reported by respondents in the national MIDUS sample (65.3, 63.9, and 62.3 for Puerto Rican, Dominican, and Black respondents, respectively, vs. 60.0 for respondents in the national MIDUS sample [see chapter 3]).

Zero-order correlations presented in table 6.3 show that indicators

TABLE 6.3 Means, Standard Deviations, and Zero-Order Correlation Coefficients for Indicators of Family Participation and Obligation

	Mean	SD	1	2	3
1. Family contributions[a]	.96	.94			
2. Frequency of contact[b]	6.43	1.71	−.07*		
3. Normative family obligation[c]	63.74	13.37	.07*	.04	

[a] 0 = no contributions; 1 = contributes to family or friends; 2 = contributes to family and friends.
[b] 1 = less than once a year; 8 = several times a day
[c] Range = 0–80.
*$p < .05$.

of family obligation and participation were only weakly associated with one another, with all coefficients below .10. Family contribution was negatively correlated with frequency of contact, indicating that respondents with less frequent contact with family were more likely to report financial/material contributions to them than were respondents with more frequent contact. To explore this relationship further, I examined whether foreign-born respondents with family living in the United States were less likely to make contributions to family and more likely to maintain frequent contact with them than respondents whose family members are largely living abroad. However, not only were respondents with and without family in the United States equally likely to contribute to family ($M_{\text{family contributions}}$ = 1.00 and .95, respectively), but the negative correlation between family contribution and frequency of contact was significant in both groups. Thus, a more plausible explanation is that giving financial assistance to family diminishes contact (perhaps because such contact heightens demands for assistance), or that material contributions substitute for time given to family. Frequency of contact was positively correlated with normative family obligation, not surprising since both are expressions of commitment to family. Indeed, one might expect this correlation to be larger, since a general pattern of engagement with family is likely to include both frequent family contact and high family obligation. Thus, the relatively small correlation may be a function of the concentration of respondents at the upper tail of the distribution for both normative family obligation and frequency of contact.

To examine the extent to which socio-structural variables, ethnic markers, and neighborhood contextual variables were significant in predicting the three indicators of family participation and obligation, I estimated a series of ordinary least squares regression equations. Again, the primary goals here were: (1) to examine the extent to which relationships between socio-structural variables and indicators of obligation and participation mirror those reported for the national MIDUS sample; and (2) to assess whether family obligation and participation varied as a function of ethnic markers and neighborhood context variables once socio-structural variables were controlled. In the equations, I regressed each of the three criterion variables onto sets of conceptually linked predictor variables, in turn. I entered family structure variables (marital and parental status) as demographic controls at step one. Then, I entered sets of socio-structural variables (age, education, annual income, gender), racial and ethnic markers (ethnicity, immigrant status, English language fluency, Catholicism, religiosity) and neighborhood context variables (median neighborhood household income, perceived neighborhood problems, neighborhood ethnic density) into each equation in three sequential steps. At the final step (step 5) of each equation, I entered two multiplicative interaction terms (Dominican ×￼ >30% own ethnicity; Puerto Rican × >30% own ethnicity). The interaction terms tested whether the slopes of the coefficient for neighborhood ethnic density among Puerto Rican and Dominican respondents, respectively, was equivalent to that among the reference group of Black respondents. I centered each of the interaction terms, and the main effects involved in them, around the sample mean to reduce multicollinearity between components of the equations.

Results of the regression equations are presented in table 6.4. In the table, ΔR^2 and F refer to the increment in explained variance at each step upon entry of the set of predictor variables. These coefficients provide information about whether or not the variables within each set contribute jointly to explained variance in the criterion. The standardized regression coefficients are from the final equations with all variables entered. Thus, they indicate whether each predictor variable in the model contributes to explained variance in the criterion, controlling for all other variables in the model including those contained within the set.

I begin by examining relationships between socio-structural variables and each of the three indicators of family participation and obligation. Recall that in previous studies, social responsibility and generativity in the family domain have been found to diminish with age, due to diminishing family responsibilities, and to increase with income and education, due to the incremental resources these provide. As table 6.4 shows, entry of the set of socio-structural variables was not significant in the equation for family contributions but resulted in a significant, albeit small, increment in explained variance in equations for frequency of contact and normative family obligation. Correspondingly, few of the socio-structural variables were significant in the final equations. Beginning with age, table 6.4 shows that only one of the six coefficients representing age (two dummy variables × three equations) was significant in the final model: older (but not middle-aged) adults reported lower normative family obligation than did young adults. Gender was significant in the equations for frequency of contact and normative family obligation: women reported more frequent contact with family and greater obligation to assist them than did men. Respondents with higher annual household incomes reported more frequent contact

TABLE 6.4 OLS Regressions of Indicators of Family Participation and Obligation on Family Structure, Socio-structural Variables, Ethnic Markers, and Neighborhood Context Variables (beta coefficients)

	Family Contribution	Frequency of Contact	Normative Family Obligation
Family structure			
Marital status[a]	.05	−.03	.01
Parental status[b]	.00	−.02	.02
ΔR^2	.01**	.00	.01*
$F(2,888)$	5.02	1.10	3.75
Socio-structural variables			
Age[c]			
40–59	.02	−.04	−.06
60+	.03	−.03	−.13**
Gender[d]	−.05	.11**	.09**
Education[e]			
High school diploma	−.01	.04	.01
Courses beyond high school	.03	−.02	−.02
Annual household income	.08[+]	.08*	.06
ΔR^2	.01	.02*	.02**
$F(6,882)$	1.75	2.44	3.49
Ethnic markers			
Ethnicity[f]			
Puerto Rican	.26***	−.05	.05
Dominican	.04	.11	.01
Immigrant status[g]	.01	−.06	.01
English language fluency[h]	.04	.05	.05
Catholicism	−.14**	.03	.06
Religiosity	.06[+]	.00	−.02
ΔR^2	.04***	.02*	.01
$F(6,876)$	17.63	2.25	1.60
Neighborhood context			
Median neighborhood household income	−.02	−.04	−.15***
Perceived neighborhood problems	−.10**	−.00	−.15***
Neighborhood ethnic density[i]	−.11**	.04	−.02
ΔR^2	.03***	.00	.03***
$F(3,873)$	8.78	.69	10.56
Interaction terms[j]			
Puerto Rican × >30% neighborhood ethnic density	.12**	−.09**	.02
Dominican × >30% neighborhood ethnic density	−.09*	.00	−.04
ΔR^2	.03***	.01*	.00
$F(2,871)$	15.50	3.25	1.15
Total adjusted R^2	.19**	.09	.07**

[a] 0 = not married; 1 = married.
[b] 0 = no child <18 lives in home; 1 = child <18 lives in home.
[c] Age reference group = 21–39.
[d] 0 = male; 1 = female.
[e] Reference group = no high school diploma.
[f] Reference group = Black.
[g] 0 = U.S. born; 1 = foreign born.
[h] 1 = Spanish only; 5 = English only.
[i] 0 = <30% own ethnicity; 1 = >30% own ethnicity.
[j] Reference group = Black.
[+] $p < .10$. * $p < .05$. ** $p < .01$. *** $p < .001$.

with family than did their less financially advantaged counterparts. Here, it is notable that educational attainment was not significantly associated with any of the three indicators of family participation and obligation in the final equations. In the national MIDUS study, both education and income were associated with financial contributions, time, and emotional support given to family (see chapter 3). To ensure that the nonsignificant relationship was not due to the shared variance between educational attainment and annual household income, I conducted supplementary analyses omitting annual household income from the model. Still, neither of the dummy variables representing educational attainment was statistically significant in any of the three equations.[2] As discussed in more detail later, the lack of a significant relationship between educational attainment and family obligation and participation in the present study may be a function of a high level of involvement and participation, even among respondents in the lowest education categories.

At step three of each regression equation, we can examine relationships between ethnic markers and indicators of family participation and obligation. As suggested earlier, family participation and obligation may vary across groups because of differences in cultural norms and in the social spaces groups occupy. As table 6.4 shows, entry of the set of ethnic markers resulted in a significant increment in explained variance in equations for family contributions and frequency of contact. Such ethnic markers were especially important in the equation for family contributions, explaining an incremental 4% of the variance in scores. In the final equation, coefficients for ethnicity and Catholicism were each statistically significant. Thus, controlling for all other variables in the model, Puerto Rican and Dominican respondents were each more likely than was the reference group of Blacks to report family contributions. It is not immediately apparent why ethnic group differences in giving should exist here, unless respondents of differing ethnic backgrounds also differ in their subjective construction of their own and others' financial situations. For instance, Blacks would be more likely than Dominican or Puerto Rican respondents with similar financial resources to feel financially squeezed if they maintain as a reference group better-off Black middle-class neighbors or Whites who live in the Park Slope or Westchester neighborhoods that border Black communities from which we drew the sample. Alternatively, it may also be that because Black respondents were more financially advantaged than were Puerto Rican or Dominican respondents, their families may have been less likely than were families of Puerto Rican or Dominican respondents to need financial assistance. Respondents who were Catholic were less likely than the reference group of non-Catholics to report family contributions. Post hoc analyses showed that this difference was significant across each of the three ethnic groups. Again, the mechanisms underlying such a difference is not readily apparent. Perhaps Catholic respondents are embedded in families that are larger than those of non-Catholic respondents, such that at any given income level there are fewer resources to distribute. It may also be that Catholic respondents' families are less likely than other families to need financial assistance.

In the equation for frequency of contact, although the 2% increment in explained variance upon entry of the set of ethnic markers was statistically significant, none of the individual predictors within the set were significant—either upon entry or in the final equation. This is due, in part, to the shared variance between predictors within the set: zero-order correlation coefficients showed that Puerto Rican respondents reported less frequent contact with family than did others $r = -.10$, $p < .05$), whereas Dominican respondents reported more frequent contact with family than did others $r = .07$, $p = .08$). The final equation, however, suggested that such ethnic differences were not significant when other ethnic markers in the model were held constant.

Next, I turn to an examination of the main effects of neighborhood context variables, entered at step four of each equation. Examination of these neighborhood context variables permits one to evaluate hypotheses regarding the influence of ambient stressors and ethnic heterogeneity on giving and caring behaviors. Table 6.4 shows that neighborhood context variables were especially important in predicting family contributions and normative family obligation. In both equations, the set of neighborhood context variables accounted for a 3% increment in explained variance, after socio-structural variables and ethnic markers had been statistically controlled. Respondents who perceived more neighborhood problems were less likely to report family contributions and reported lower normative family obligation than did their counterparts who perceived fewer neighborhood problems. Respondents in neighborhoods with lower median household incomes also reported less normative family obligation than did their counterparts in more economically advantaged neighborhoods. Overall, respondents in high density neighborhoods were less likely to report family contributions than were their counterparts in low density neighborhoods.

However, as described below, significant interaction terms in the final equations indicated that the nature of mean differences between respondents living in high and low ethnic density neighborhoods varied across ethnic groups.

At step five of each equation, I entered the set of ethnicity × neighborhood ethnic density interaction terms. Significant ethnicity × neighborhood ethnic density interaction terms indicate that differences in predicted means for those living in high and low ethnic density neighborhoods were not uniform across groups. When significant interaction terms emerged, I estimated and plotted predicted means. These means are presented in figures 6.1 and 6.2. As shown in figure 6.1, Puerto Rican respondents in high density Puerto Rican neighborhoods were more likely than were their counterparts in low density

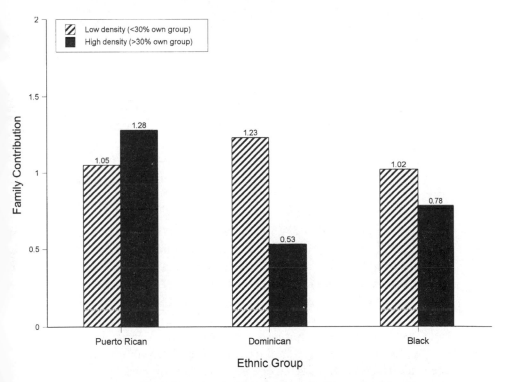

FIGURE 6.1. Predicted means for family contributions, by ethnic group and neighborhood ethnic density. Predicted means estimated with all variables in the full model held constant. For family contributions, 0 = gives to no one; 1 = gives to family or friends; 2 = gives to family and friends.

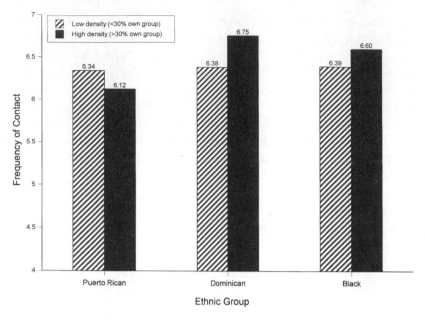

FIGURE 6.2. Predicted means for frequency of contact, by ethnic group and neighborhood ethnic density. Predicted means estimated with all variables in the full model held constant. For frequency of contact, 1 = never or hardly ever; 2 = less than once a month; 3 = about once a month; 4 = two or three times a month; 5 = about once a week; 6 = several times a week; 7 = about once a day; 8 = several times a day.

Puerto Rican neighborhoods to report family contributions. Dominican respondents in high density Dominican neighborhoods were significantly less likely to report family contributions than were their counterparts in low density Dominican neighborhoods. Black respondents in high ethnic density neighborhoods did not differ from Black respondents in low density Black neighborhoods in reported family contributions. Post hoc exploration of this finding suggested that the contrast between findings for Puerto Rican and Dominican respondents is due largely to a low incidence of family contributions among Hispanic respondents living in Dominican neighborhoods, whether Puerto Rican or Dominican. Notably, almost one-third of Puerto Rican respondents in low density neighborhoods lived in high density Dominican neighborhoods. Thirty-two percent of Puerto Rican respondents in high density Dominican neighborhoods reported any giving to family or friends compared with 70% of Puerto Rican respondents in other types of neighborhoods. Only 34% of Dominican respondents in high density Dominican neighborhoods reported any giving to family or friends compared with 70% of Dominicans in other types of neighborhoods. The few Black respondents ($n = 23$) who lived in high density Dominican neighborhoods were slightly more likely to give to family than were other Blacks, perhaps because their families were less financially advantaged than were the families of other Blacks in the sample.

In the equation for frequency of contact, only the product term comparing Puerto Rican respondents in low and high density neighborhoods with Black respondents in low and high density neighborhoods was significant. As shown in figure 6.2, Puerto Rican respondents living in high density Puerto Rican neighborhoods reported less frequent contact with family than did Puerto Rican respondents living in low density neighborhoods. Black respondents living in high density Black neighborhoods and Dominican respondents living in high density Dominican neighborhoods reported more frequent contact with family than did their counterparts in low density neighborhoods. Again, post hoc examination of means across different neighborhood types showed that extensive (daily) contact with family was more prevalent in Dominican neighborhoods than in other types of neighborhoods among both Puerto Rican and Dominican respondents. For instance, 89% of Puerto Rican respondents in high density Dominican neighborhoods reported daily contact with family, whereas only 49% of their counterparts in other neighborhoods reported such daily contact ($\chi^2 = 15.69$, $p < .01$). Sixty-seven percent of Dominican respondents in Dominican neighborhoods reported daily contact with family, whereas 56% of their counterparts in other neighborhoods reported daily contact ($\chi^2 = 3.66$, $p < .06$).

To summarize briefly, analyses so far have suggested a high level of participation in and obligation toward family in the present sample. Indeed, the majority of respondents reported giving money or material goods to family, most had contact with family on a daily or weekly basis, and most reported high obligation to help family. In contrast to patterns identified in previous studies, indicators of participation and obligation did not vary greatly as a function of socio-structural variables. Age and educational attainment were not highly related to any of the three indicators of family participation and obligation: the only significant relationship to emerge was that older adults reported lower normative family obligation than did the reference group of young adults. A higher annual household income was associated with more frequent contact with family, but it was only marginally associated with contributions to family and was unrelated to normative family obligation. Consistent with other studies, however, gender was associated with family obligation and participation: women reported more frequent contact with family and higher obligation to assist than men did. After controlling for these sorts of socio-structural variables, the set of ethnic markers was quite important in explaining family contributions but relatively unimportant in explaining the other indicators. Blacks were less likely to report family contributions than were Dominican or Puerto Rican respondents. This may be because at any given income level they feel more disadvantaged than do Puerto Ricans and Dominicans. Alternatively, it may be that financial need was greater among Dominican and Puerto Rican families than among the families of their better-off Black counterparts. Catholics were also less likely to report family contributions than were non-Catholics, reflecting the high likelihood that Catholic respondents have larger families (and more financial obligations to meet) than do their non-Catholic counterparts. Contributions to family, and expressed obligation to assist them, also appeared to vary considerably as a function of neighborhood context variables, especially perceived neighborhood problems and neighborhood ethnic composition. Respondents living in neighborhoods where resources were low or problems were high (or both) were less likely to report family contributions and reported lower obligation to assist family. Moreover, family obligation and participation were expressed differently in different ethnic neighborhoods. Puerto Rican and Dominican respondents in high density Dominican neighborhoods were especially unlikely to report financial or material contributions to family. In contrast, contact with family was especially high in such neighborhoods. In Puerto Rican neighborhoods, the incidence of giving was higher and the frequency of contact with family was lower than in Dominican neighborhoods. Later, I will discuss these sorts of findings from both a structural and a cultural perspective, both of which seem plausible. I turn now to an examination of community obligation and participation.

Civic Participation and Altruism

Only a few studies in the psychological literature have examined community participation among ethnic minority adults (e.g., Brown 1991; Cole and Stewart 1996; Milburn and Bowman 1991; Saegart

1990; Serrano-Garcia 1984). Saegart's ethnographic description of Black women's involvement in community housing efforts (1990) and Serrano-Garcia's description of women involved in empowerment movements in Puerto Rico (1984) suggest ethnic minority adults' involvement in local efforts. However, obligation toward the larger social good is likely to be quite distinct from participation in or obligation to one's family or local community. For groups who have historically been marginalized and, indeed, discriminated against, responsibility in service of a social system that has shunned them probably ranks bottom among entities to which they are likely to feel obligated. As noted previously, Newman (chapter 5, this volume) observed that few respondents mentioned obligation to community institutions or to larger social structures in their narratives regarding social responsibility.

Table 6.5 presents descriptive information on the distribution of community obligation and participation variables in the present sample and on the correlations between them. About 44% of respondents reported contributing money or material goods to religious or other organizations—significantly fewer than the 60% of respondents who reported contributing money or material goods to family members or friends. Respondents were more likely to report contributing to religious than to other types of organizations (39% vs. 30.9%, respectively). Only about one-quarter of the respondents reported contributions of money or material goods to *both* religious and nonreligious organizations. However, respondents reported a relatively high sense of community attachment, with mean values of 3.3 on a four-point scale. As in the national MIDUS sample, respondents' obligation to community was lower than was their obligation to family. Mean values for both civic participation and altruism were significantly lower than those for family obligation, a pattern that was consistent across each of the ethnic groups.[3] Notably, respondents' mean values on measures of civic obligation and altruism were also similar to those reported for the national MIDUS sample: for civic obligation, $M = 29.9$, 28.8, and 28.9 for Puerto Ricans, Dominicans and Blacks, respectively, vs. 30.7 for the national MIDUS sample; for altruism, $M = 27.8$, 27.9, and 24.3 for Puerto Ricans, Dominicans and Blacks, respectively, vs. 23.4 for the national MIDUS sample.

Table 6.5 also shows that indicators of community participation and obligation were moderately to highly correlated with one another. All zero-order correlation coefficients were significant at $p < .01$. The weakest correlation was between community contribution and com-

TABLE 6.5 Means, Standard Deviations and Zero-Order Correlation
Coefficients for Indicators of Community
Participation and Obligation

	Mean	SD	1	2	3	4
1. Community contributions[a]	.31	.46		.09**	.20**	.27**
2. Community attachment[b]	3.31	.88			.19**	.26**
3. Civic obligation[c]	29.20	9.0				.52**
4. Altruism[d]	26.49	10.83				

[a] 0 = no contributions; 1 = contributes to religious or nonreligious; 2 = contributes
to religious and nonreligious organizations.
[b] 1 = low; 4= high.
[c] Range = 0–40.
[d] Range = 0–40.
** $p < .01$.

munity attachment, $r = .09$); the largest was between civic obligation
and altruism, $r = .52$). Thus, respondents who reported participation
in community life in the form of financial contributions and high loyalty to their neighborhoods were also more likely to express obligation
to participate in civic affairs and to help others, probably because
norms regarding community contributions are likely to result in behaviors that are consistent with them.

As with indicators of family obligation and participation, an important objective of the analyses was to examine the extent to which socio-
structural variables, ethnic markers, and neighborhood contextual
variables were significant in predicting community participation and
obligation. As in equations for family obligation and participation, I
entered conceptually linked sets of predictor variables into each equation in five sequential steps. At step one, I entered marital and parental
status, followed by socio-structural variables (age, education, gender,
annual household income) at step two, racial and ethnic markers (ethnic background, immigrant status, English language fluency, Catholicism, religiosity) at step three, and neighborhood context variables
(median neighborhood household income, perceived neighborhood
problems, neighborhood ethnic density) at step four. I entered two
multiplicative interaction terms (Dominican $\times$ >30% own ethnicity;
Puerto Rican $\times$ >30% own ethnicity) at step five of each equation to
evaluate the extent to which mean differences in obligation and participation for those living in high and low ethnic density neighborhoods
differed across ethnic groups. I centered each of the interaction terms,

and the main effects involved in them, around the sample mean to re-duce multicollinearity between components of the equations.

Results of the equations examining the four indicators of commu-nity participation and obligation are presented in table 6.6. In the table, the ΔR^2 and F shown for each set represent the increment in the propor-tion of variance explained at the step at which the set was entered. The standardized regression coefficients are from the final equations with all variables entered. Thus, they represent the unique contribution of each predictor variable when all other variables in the model were held constant.

I begin, again, with an examination of relationships between socio-structural variables and indicators of community participation and ob-ligation. Recall that in previous writings, researchers have viewed age, education, and income as important contours of social responsibility and generativity in the community domain. Community obligation is thought to increase with age, due to the increased freedom from child-rearing responsibility that age carries, and with income and education, due to the increased feelings of agency that income and education pro-vide. Table 6.6 shows that these sorts of socio-structural variables ac-counted for a significant increment in explained variance in equations for three of the four indicators of community participation and obliga-tion, including community contributions, community attachment, and altruism. Older and middle-aged adults reported greater community attachment than did the reference group of young adults. Women re-ported less community attachment, and marginally higher altruism, than men did. Moreover, as in the national MIDUS study, education and income were generally associated with indicators of community obligation and participation. In the final equation, those with a high school diploma were more likely to report community contributions and reported higher community attachment and higher altruism than did the reference group of respondents with no high school diploma. Those with a higher annual household income were more likely to re-port community contributions than were those with a lower annual household income. As in the analysis of family obligation and partici-pation, I conducted supplementary analyses in which income and edu-cation were examined separately because of the correlation between them. In these analyses, educational attainment was significant in each equation; annual household income was significant in all equations ex-cept that for community attachment.

Step 3 of each regression equation examines the extent to which in-

TABLE 6.6 OLS Regressions of Indicators of Community Participation and Obligation on Family Structure, Socio-structural Variables, Ethnic Markers, and Neighborhood Context Variables (beta coefficients)

	Family Contribution	Community Attachment	Civic Obligation	Altruism
Family structure				
Marital status[a]	.01	.01	.03	.02
Parental status[b]	.04	−.02	−.01	.00
ΔR^2	.02***	.01*	.01$^+$	.01$^+$
$F(2,888)$	9.12	4.36	2.77	2.56
Socio-structural variables				
Age[c]				
40–59	.04	.08*	−.03	.03
60+	.07$^+$	.14**	−.01	.02
Gender[d]	−.04	−.08**	.03	.06$^+$
Education[e]				
High school diploma	.06$^+$	.08	.06	.08**
Courses beyond high school	.04	−.01	.08$^+$	.07$^+$
Annual household income	.12**	.00	.06	.07$^+$
ΔR^2	.04***	.04***	.01	.02**
$F(6,882)$	5.74	5.92	1.70	3.17
Ethnic markers				
Ethnicity[f]				
Puerto Rican	.14**	−.03	.06	−.03
Dominican	−.03	.02	.00−	.13$^+$
Immigrant status[g]	.08*	.14**	.17**	.18**
English language fluency[h]	−.02	−.00	.11$^+$	−.09
Catholicism	−.08*	.04	−.00	.12**
Religiosity	.27**	.17**	.11**	.19**
ΔR^2	.10***	.05***	.03***	.10***
$F(6,876)$	17.63	8.39	5.00	16.25
Neighborhood context				
Median neighborhood household income	.07$^+$	.04−	.02−	.01
Perceived neighborhood problems	−.06$^+$	.00−	.08**	.10**
Neighborhood ethnic density[i]	−.05	.00	−.05	.00
ΔR^2	.01**	.00	.01**	.01*
$F(3,873)$	4.17	.82	3.95	2.75
Interaction terms[j]				
Puerto Rican × >30% neighborhood ethnic density	.16**	−.09**	.09**	.06$^+$
Dominican × >30% neighborhood ethnic density	−.06	−.02	−.08**	−.08*
ΔR^2	.04***	.01*	.02***	.02
$F(2,871)$	19.70	3.27	10.75	7.53
Total adjusted R^2	.19**	.09	.07**	.13**

[a] 0 = not married; 1 = married.
[b] 0 = no child <18 lives in home; 1 = child <18 lives in home.
[c] Age reference group = 21–39.
[d] 0 = male; 1 = female.
[e] Reference group = no high school diploma.
[f] Reference group = Black.
[g] 0 = U.S. born; 1 = foreign born.
[h] 1 = Spanish only; 5 = English only.
[i] 0 = <30% own ethnicity; 1 = >30% own ethnicity.
[j] Reference group = Black.

$^+ p < .10.$ $^* p < .05.$ $^{**} p < .01.$ $^{***} p < .001.$

dicators of community obligation and participation vary as a function of the sorts of ethnic markers included in this study. As table 6.6 shows, the set of ethnic markers accounted for a significant increment in explained variance in all four equations, but most notably in the equations for community contributions and altruism. In this regard, immigrant status and religiosity emerged as especially important and robust predictors; both were significant in each of the four final equations. Foreign-born respondents and those reporting greater religiosity reported more community contributions, greater community attachment, greater civic obligation, and greater altruism than did their U.S.-born and less religious counterparts. Ethnicity, per se, was not highly related to these criterion variables: only one of the eight (four equations × two dummy variables) coefficients were significant in the final equations. Puerto Ricans were more likely to report community contributions than was the reference group of Blacks. Catholicism remained significant in the equations for community contributions and altruism. Catholics were less likely to report community contributions than were non-Catholics, but they also reported higher altruism.

Turning to the set of neighborhood context variables, table 6.6 shows a significant increment in explained variance in the equations for community contributions, civic obligation, and altruism. Respondents who perceived more neighborhood problems were less likely to report community contributions and reported lower civic obligation than did respondents who perceived fewer neighborhood problems, supporting the proposition that ambient environmental stressors may promote an inward focus and disengagement from community life. Perceived neighborhood problems was positively associated with altruism, a finding that is paradoxical in the context of the ambient environmental stress framework. However, exposure to the sorts of neighborhood problems we probed (drugs, violence, crime) may heighten concern about issues that affect one's local community (e.g., health care, poverty) while diminishing one's obligation to participate in broader civic affairs.

Turning next to findings concerning neighborhood ethnic density, table 6.6 shows that living among one's own ethnic group was not significant in any of the four equations. However, entry of the set of ethnicity × neighborhood ethnic density interaction terms resulted in a significant increment in explained variance in each of the four equations, indicating that relationships between neighborhood ethnic density and criterion variables were not uniform across ethnic groups. As in the equation for family obligation and participation, when signifi-

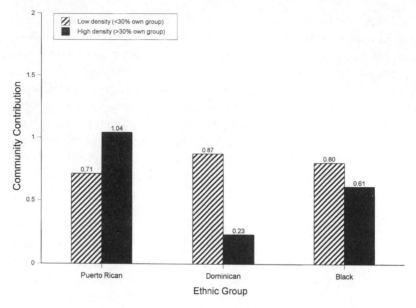

FIGURE 6.3. Predicted means for community contributions, by ethnic group and neighborhood ethnic density. Predicted means estimated with all variables in the full model held constant. For community contributions, 0 = gives to no organization; 1 = gives to religious or nonreligious organization; 2 = gives to religious and nonreligious organizations.

cant interaction terms emerged, I estimated and plotted predicted means, shown in figures 6.3–6.6. In figure 6.3, we see that Puerto Rican respondents in high density Puerto Rican neighborhoods were more likely to report community contributions than were their counterparts in other types of neighborhoods. In contrast, Dominican respondents in high density Dominican neighborhoods and Black respondents in high density Black neighborhoods were less likely than were their counterparts in low density neighborhoods to report community contributions. As in analyses for family contributions, post hoc analyses suggested that the neighborhood differential largely resulted from an especially low incidence of giving among respondents living in high density Dominican neighborhoods. For instance, 11% of Puerto Rican respondents in high density Dominican neighborhoods gave to an organization, compared with 59% of Puerto Rican respondents in other types of neighborhoods ($\chi^2 = 24.11$, $p < .001$). Seventeen percent of

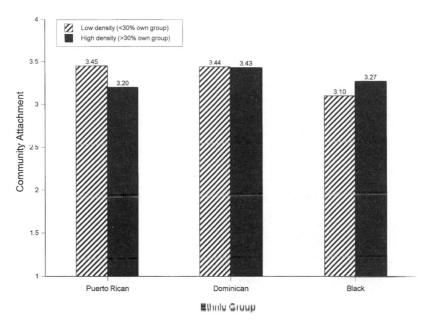

FIGURE 6.4. Predicted means for community attachment, by ethnic group and neighborhood ethnic density. Predicted means estimated with all variables in the full model held constant. For community attachment, 1 = low; 4 = high.

Dominican respondents in high density Dominican neighborhoods gave to an organization, compared with 51% of their counterparts in other types of neighborhoods ($\chi^2 = 36.75$, $p < .001$). Thirteen percent of Black respondents in high density Dominican neighborhoods gave to an organization, compared with 47% of Black respondents in all other types of neighborhoods combined ($\chi^2 = 9.74$, $p < .01$), but the incidence of giving among Blacks in high density Black neighborhoods was also low (39%) relative to the incidence of giving among Blacks in Puerto Rican or ethnically mixed neighborhoods (65% and 57%, respectively).

Figure 6.4 presents mean levels of community attachment among respondents living in high and low density neighborhoods. In the equation for community attachment only the interaction term comparing Puerto Ricans with Blacks was statistically significant. As indicated by the predicted means, shown in figure 6.4, Puerto Rican respondents living in high density Puerto Rican neighborhoods reported *less* attachment to their communities than did Puerto Rican respondents living in

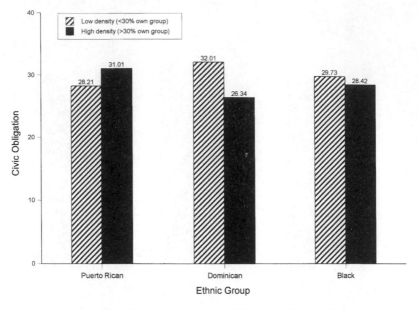

FIGURE 6.5. Predicted means for civic obligation, by ethnic group and neighborhood ethnic density. Predicted means estimated with all variables in the full model held constant. For civic obligation, 0 = lowest; 40 = highest.

low density neighborhoods. However, Dominican respondents in high density Dominican neighborhoods and Black respondents in high density Black neighborhoods did not differ significantly from one another in community attachment. Note that the low community attachment among Puerto Rican respondents in high density neighborhoods mirrors the less frequent contact with family among Puerto Rican respondents in high density neighborhoods that I reported earlier.

In the equations for civic obligation and altruism, the neighborhood ethnic density × ethnicity product terms for both Puerto Ricans and Dominicans were significant, although in opposite directions. Figures 6.5 and 6.6 show that Puerto Rican respondents in high density Puerto Rican neighborhoods reported *greater* civic obligation and greater altruism than did Puerto Rican respondents in low density neighborhoods. By contrast, Dominican respondents in high density Dominican neighborhoods reported significantly *less* civic obligation and altruism than did Dominican respondents in low density neighborhoods. Among Blacks, neighborhood ethnic density was unrelated to civic obligation or altruism. Post hoc analyses, conducted to explore such dif-

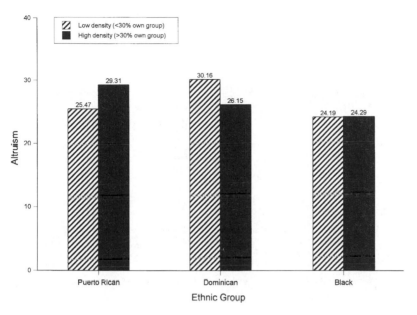

FIGURE 6.6. Predicted means for altruism, by ethnic group and neighborhood ethnic density. Predicted means estimated with all variables in the full model held constant. For altruism, 0 = lowest; 40 = highest.

ference further, indicated that (in concert with findings reported thus far) the patterns observed in figures 6.5 and 6.6 were largely a function of differences across neighborhood types in altruism and civic obligation, regardless of the respondent's own ethnic background. Specifically, respondents in high density Dominican neighborhoods reported *lower* civic obligation than did respondents in other types of neighborhoods.[4] Respondents in high density Puerto Rican neighborhoods reported *higher* civic obligation than did respondents in other types of neighborhoods.[5] A similar pattern of relationships was identified when altruism was the criterion.[6]

In sum, participation in and obligation to community in the present sample was lower than obligation to and participation in family, as it was in the national MIDUS sample. However, such obligation and participation was by no means absent. A notable minority of respondents reported contributions to organizations, and most reported high attachment to their communities. Expressions of civic obligation and altruism were moderate, however. As in the national MIDUS sample, indicators of community participation and obligation varied according to a range of socio-structural predictors. Community attachment was the only indicator of community participation and obligation to vary according to respondents' age category: older and middle-aged adults reported greater community attachment than did their younger counterparts. In general, more highly educated adults and those with greater financial resources reported more community obligation and participation than did their less educated and less financially advantaged counterparts. Although in the final regression equations, many of the coefficients representing socioeconomic indicators were not significant at $p < .05$, this was largely due to the shared variance between education and annual family income. The set of ethnic markers was important in explaining each of the indicators of community obligation and participation. Of particular note was the finding that foreign-born respondents and those reporting greater religiosity reported greater obligation and participation than did their U.S.-born and less religious counterparts in equations for each of the four criteria. Puerto Rican respondents were more likely to report community contributions than were Dominican or Black respondents. Catholic respondents were also less likely to report family contributions than were non-Catholics, which (as in the equation for family contributions) may result from a larger family size. Community participation and obligation also varied as a function of neighborhood context variables. Again, perceived neighborhood problems was an especially important predictor, with those in high problem neighborhoods reporting fewer contributions to organizations and lower civic obligation. However, those in high problem neighborhoods reported higher altruism than did their counterparts, controlling for other socio-structural and neighborhood indicators. Notably, community obligation and participation appeared to be expressed differently in different ethnic neighborhoods. Respondents in high density Puerto Rican neighborhoods were characterized by high community contributions, high civic obligation, high altruism, and low community attachment. Those in Dominican neighborhoods were characterized by low community contribution, low civic obligation, low altruism and high community attachment. I turn now to a discussion of these findings in the context of the larger goals of the chapter.

Overall Summary and Discussion

Social responsibility has been conceived as an integral component of well-being during the midlife years, reflecting close and positive ties to family and community, commitment to working for others rather than simply for personal gain, and concern for social and moral issues. Although the concept has received growing attention from researchers, little is known about the expression of social responsibility among ethnic minority adults or among adults living in neighborhoods where normative family patterns are distinct and the exigencies that must be navigated loom large. If theories about social responsibility are to be useful, researchers need to elaborate its form and expression, and the processes that underlie it, across many cultural groups and ecological settings.

As a baby step toward this objective, the present chapter focused on examining social responsibility among urban ethnic minority adults. Data were presented to provide a portrait of family and community caring and giving and their correlates *within* a socioeconomically diverse sample of Puerto Rican, Dominican, and Black respondents. The chapter was structured according to several overarching goals, as follows:

First, it sought to describe family and community participation and obligation within the sample, simply because so little research has been conducted on social responsibility among ethnic minority adults. In this regard, findings suggested extensive participation and obligation in the family domain and moderate participation and obligation in the community domain—much the same as findings from the national MIDUS sample. For instance, the majority of respondents reported that they contributed money or material goods to family, although the measure of family contribution provided no information regarding the value of the contribution or to whom it was given. Contact with non-resident family members was also quite extensive, with the overwhelming majority of respondents reporting daily or weekly contact. Although no information was available regarding with whom contact was maintained or the medium for such contact, it is not clear that differentiating these recipients or mediums would provide additional insight into the *extent* of family ties. Consistent with findings from the behavioral measures, respondents also expressed high obligation to help family, with almost two-thirds of the sample expressing very high levels of normative family obligation (mean values of 9 or above on a 0–10 scale). The overall pattern of high family engagement is consistent with a wealth of previous ethnographic and qualitative studies, which have documented extensive networks of family exchange within ethnic minority communities (McAdoo 1981, 1983; Malson 1983; Stack 1974) and extensive transnational and transcontinental family ties among immigrant families (Rumbaut 1998).

Respondents' obligation to and participation in community life was modest relative to their obligation to and participation in family life. Respondents were less likely to contribute money or material goods to organizations than they were to contribute to family, but a substantial minority of respondents reported at least some such contributions. Although respondents did not live in upscale or fancy neighborhoods, most of them nevertheless reported feelings of attachment to their communities. And, although normative obligation in the form of civic obligation and altruism was significantly lower than was obligation to family, it was far from absent. In fact, close to one-third of the sample expressed extremely high civic obligation (average values of 9 or above on a 0–10 scale) and about one-quarter expressed similarly high altruism. Although these descriptive findings are not generalizable to ethnic minority adults in New York City, due to the sampling strategy we used, their importance lies in addressing a significant omission in a broader research literature that provides little information regarding social responsibility among ethnic minority adults.

In addition to providing descriptive data, the chapter sought to examine the extent to which socio-structural markers that have commonly been viewed as important determinants of social responsibility and generativity during midlife were associated with family and community participation and obligation in the present sample. This inquiry was embedded in the notion that the definition and determinants of social responsibility may vary across groups, due to variation in normative family patterns and in the historical and present-day patterns of contact between these groups and the broader social world of which they are a part. Thus, whereas studies have consistently shown a downward trend with age in normative obligation to family (Keyes and Ryff 1998; Rossi, chapter 3, this volume), such trends were relatively weak in the present sample, with only one of three family-relevant criterion variables (normative family obligation) showing significant age effects. Even here, only the coefficient comparing adults sixty years of age and older with adults under age thirty-nine was statistically significant. The overall absence of relationships between age and family participation and obligation probably reflects respondents' ongoing involvement in the provision of social and economic support to extended kin throughout the life cycle. As noted earlier, in many ethnic/racial communities, extended kin obligations continue throughout the life cycle, operating both within and across generations to ensure family survival. Attenuation of family obligation—an important marker of midlife among middle-class White Americans—is likely to be less pronounced among ethnic minority adults.

Age-related patterns in the community domain also differed from those found in the national sample (Keyes and Ryff 1998; Rossi, chapter 3, this volume) and in other studies of generativity (McAdams and de St. Aubin 1992; McAdams, de St. Aubin, and Logan 1993; McAdams, Hart, and Maruna 1998). For instance, whereas Rossi (chapter 3, this volume) and Keyes and Ryff (1998) found that altruism and civic obligation generally increased over the life course, especially among men, neither civic obligation nor altruism were significantly associated with age in the present sample. Although this finding may be a function of continuing family obligation, civic obligation and altruism among ethnic minority adults may also be constrained by disengagement from mainstream social institutions (e.g., the court or jury system) that do not serve their group's interests. Thus, even when the constraints of childrearing have diminished, such disengagement may suppress the expression of civic obligation and altruism. Older and middle-aged adults reported greater attachment to community than did their younger counterparts. Thus, the findings support the view that civic obligation and altruism may be depressed by a general disengagement from mainstream institutions, since community attachment, which increased with age, may be indicative of the sorts of "local caring" that Newman (chapter 5, this volume) described.

Relationships between socioeconomic indicators and family participation and obligation also diverged from patterns found in the broader literature. Whereas scholars have suggested that increasing education is associated with greater generativity, due to increased agency and other psychological resources that education provides, education was not associated with indicators of family obligation and participation in the present sample. Those with no high school diploma were as likely as their counterparts with more schooling to report high family participation and obligation. Annual household income was associated with frequency of contact only. Historically, reliance on extended kin has been an integral component of survival among ethnic minority families. The fact that low educational attainment and low income did not constrain family contributions or normative family obligation among adults who participated in the present study may be a function of the importance of extended family support to the social and economic functioning of ethnic minority families. It is important to note, however, that the socioeconomic range within the present sample was somewhat limited. A relatively small proportion of respondents were college educated, and even those with relatively high incomes were not especially well off. The annual household income for those in the top income tertile was $42,000 per year. Thus, we cannot rule out the possibility that a broader socioeconomic distribution would yield findings similar to those in existing studies.

In the community domain, relationships between socioeconomic indicators and civic obligation and altruism were similar to those reported in the national MIDUS sample. In general, more highly educated adults and those with greater financial resources reported more community obligation and participation than did their less educated and less financially advantaged counterparts.

In addition to examining variation in social responsibility as a function of age and education, the present study examined social responsibility as a function of gender. Previous studies have suggested that gender is critically linked to caregiving, emotional maintenance tasks, and concern for others, with women bearing the lion's share of these responsibilities. In the present study, no predictions were made regarding differential patterns of relationships between gender and indicators of obligation and participation in the present sample as compared with the national MIDUS sample. Indeed, women reported more frequent contact with family and expressed a greater obligation to assist them than men did, although they were not more likely than men to contribute money or other material resources to family. In the community domain, women reported greater altruism than did their male counterparts, but men reported greater attachment to community. The greater family obligation and altruism among women as compared to men is consistent with previous studies, which indicate that women are more oriented than are men to ensuring the welfare of others (e.g., Heimer 1996). The finding regarding men's greater attachment to community is more difficult to explain. One possibility is that women express less loyalty and less communion with others than men because the discrepancy between their standards for neighborhood quality and their actual neighborhood experiences may be greater. Alternatively, as Rossi (personal communication) suggested, women may simply be less involved with community than are men, either because their time is absorbed by family work and obligations or because, in dangerous neighborhoods, they feel more threatened, less mobile, and less able to cope with neighborhood problems than do comparable men.

A final objective of the present chapter was to examine the extent to which family and community participation and obligation varied according to ethnic markers and neighborhood contextual variables. Earlier, I noted that different ethnic groups have different histories and experiences in the United States, which may result in differing orientations toward family and community. However, in the family domain, the only indicator of family obligation and participation to vary as a function of ethnic markers was family contributions. In this regard, Blacks were less likely than were Puerto Ricans or Dominicans to report family contributions, although findings did not generally point to a larger coherent pattern that was consistent with prior research concerning cultural patterns within these groups. Moreover, Blacks in the sample were of a higher socioeconomic status than Puerto Ricans and Dominicans, which may mean that their families were less in need of financial assistance. Overall, the similarity across groups in family obligation and participation is more pronounced than these differences and is likely to reflect similarities in normative family patterns and in experiences of economic marginality that are commonly accompanied by high extended family involvement (Wilson 1986, 1989).

In the community domain, immigrant status and religiosity differentiated respondents' reports about community participation and involvement more so than did ethnicity per se. Foreign-born respondents reported greater community attachment, more civic obligation, and more altruism than did U.S.-born respondents. It is important to note that the significant coefficient for immigrant status represented incremental explained variance not accounted for by ethnicity per se. Thus, within each ethnic group, immigrant respondents generally reported more favorable orientations toward their local communities and larger social structures than did their U.S.-born counterparts. Several underlying phenomena may account for such differences. For instance, the more favorable community orientations among immigrant respondents may reflect the sort of "immigrant ethos" described by scholars studying Blacks (Waters 1997), Dominicans (Rumbaut 1998; Grasmuck and Pessar 1996; Pessar 1995), and Puerto Ricans (Morales 1986). This ethos is characterized by strong family ties, high aspirations among children, a strong work ethic, and identification with the "American dream." However, scholars have also documented that the ethos erodes over time as immigrants and their families encounter the realities of blocked opportunity, of life in impoverished neighbor-hoods, of working long hours at low-wage jobs with little opportunity for advancement, and of discrepancies between the dream in which they invested and the actualities of their daily lives (Rumbaut 1998; Waters 1997). The higher community attachment, civic obligation, and altruism expressed by immigrant as compared with U.S.-born adults in the present sample, then, may be a function of immigrant adults' initial optimism regarding "American" ideals. It may also be that newly ar-rived immigrants maintain as a reference point the extreme poverty, hostile political conditions, and social disorganization they left behind in their homeland, compared to which their American neighborhoods may seem an improvement. Thus, they may still be in a position to dream—they are far better off than their reference group and expect to be better off in the future than they are in the present. Thus, they may not yet experience the disengagement, hopelessness, and disillusion-ment that is likely to characterize their U.S.-born Hispanic or Black counterparts.

Regarding neighborhood conditions, I suggested that particular ecological characteristics, such as the level of problems residents per-ceive and the ethnic composition of the neighborhood, influence com-munity norms regarding family and community participation and involvement and, in turn, individuals' internalized values. For instance, high problem neighborhoods or those with deteriorated and dilapi-dated structures (as one might find in low income neighborhoods) may result in apathy among residents and an inward focus, resulting in low family and community participation and involvement. Although few significant *main* effects of median neighborhood income or neighbor-hood ethnic density were identified in the present study, respondents' perceptions of neighborhood problems were associated with lower ob-ligation and participation in both family and community domains. The exception was that altruism increased as a function of perceived neigh-borhood problems. The importance of perceived neighborhood prob-lems relative to other neighborhood-level variables supports the hy-pothesis that harsh environments depress giving and caring behaviors, possibly by promoting a narrow focus on oneself and one's family and by increasing the complexity of phenomena that must be navigated during the course of daily living. In the present study, there was little evidence that neighborhood heterogeneity per se was associated with low engagement in community. Thus, there was little support for the notion put forth by Taylor and colleagues (Taylor, Gottfredson, and

Brower 1995) and Sampson (Sampson 1992; Sampson and Morenoff 1997) that ethnic mixing increases conflict among neighbors and inhibits the development of neighborhood social networks.

Perhaps the strongest evidence that community characteristics influence norms regarding caring and giving behaviors is found in the interaction between neighborhood ethnic density and respondents' own ethnicity. These results, which were robust across family and community indicators, suggested that neighborhood ethnic composition influenced caring and giving behaviors regardless of respondents' own ethnicity. These relationships remained after controlling for other factors that were associated with neighborhood ethnic composition such as annual household income, education, immigrant status, neighborhood income, and neighborhood problems. Regardless of whether respondents themselves were Puerto Rican, Dominican, or Black, those living in high density Dominican neighborhoods (primarily in Washington Heights) were far less likely to report family or community contributions and expressed less obligation to assist family, to participate in civic affairs, or to help others than did respondents living in other types of neighborhoods. In contrast, respondents living in Puerto Rican neighborhoods were generally more likely to contribute to family and community and to express high civic obligation and altruism. However, residency in a high density Puerto Rican neighborhood was also associated with less frequent contact with family and less attachment to community.

Both structural and cultural explanations seem plausible in relation to such findings. As indicated earlier, high density Dominican neighborhoods were among the poorest and most problem-ridden neighborhoods in the sample. Washington Heights, in particular, is plagued by high crime rates, dilapidated housing, and drug trading. Although structural indicators, such as median neighborhood income and perceived neighborhood problems were controlled in the equations in which significant neighborhood differences emerged, these sorts of indicators are unlikely to capture all of the differences that exist between these Dominican and other types of neighborhoods. For instance, equations do not control for factors such as source of household income or family size, and aggregate block group-level data do not always correspond to perceived neighborhood boundaries.

A cultural/contextual explanation for neighborhood-level differences is also plausible, however. In previous writings, scholars have described both the strengths and the risk factors associated with living in

New York City's Dominican communities. For instance, Torres-Saillant (1996) describes them as socially isolated havens, due in part to spatial segregation and to the emergence of enclaves where learning the social codes of mainstream North American society is not vital to survival. According to her, Dominican New Yorkers see themselves as transient visitors who will return to the island permanently once enough money has been saved. This transient mentality, she argues, contributes to political aloofness, lack of investment in learning English or pursuing citizenship status, and notable indifference toward the immediate environment. Although these sorts of descriptions reference Dominicans as individuals, findings of the present study suggest that the norms and orientations that scholars have described may be extant in Dominican communities as well. As with most studies of neighborhood influences, teasing apart neighborhood influences and selection effects in the present study is not possible. Thus, it may be that individuals who, by choice or by circumstance, are living in particular neighborhoods chose them because they were compatible with their preexisting values and orientations.

In closing, it is important to emphasize that the present chapter was an attempt to take a first look at indicators of social responsibility among ethnic minority adults. To understand the process more fully as an important component of well-being among ethnic minority adults, measures and methods that are both broader, more comprehensive, and more textured will be needed. In addition, more complete specification of the rhythms of daily life among different ethnic groups in different neighborhood contexts are needed to delineate the mechanisms through which cultures and contexts may influence midlife well-being, in particular, and social responsibility more generally.

NOTES

1. The sampling procedure included (1) prestratification of 1990 census block groups according to racial/ethnic and economic characteristics; (2) random selection of census block groups within strata predefined by ethnic density and economic criteria (e.g., low density/high socioeconomic status Puerto Ricans); (3) random numbering of residential blocks within the selected census block groups for identification of respondents; and (4) quota sampling of qualified respondents. In this regard, the New York sample was designed to achieve sixty-six complete interviews with adults in each of twelve strata defined in a 3 (Dominican, Puerto Rican, Black) × 2 (high vs. low socioeconomic status) × 2 (high vs. low same-ethnicity neighborhood density) design. A thirteenth stratum, with a target sample of sixty-six adults, was added to examine Blacks residing in hypersegregated (>70% Black) neighbor-

hoods. For each race/ethnic group, further quotas were applied so that the age distribution of male respondents and the employment distribution of female respondents within a census block group were equivalent to those of the census block group as a whole, according to 1990 census data. Respondents who self-identified as being of a particular target ethnic group were included as cases for that group. Interviewers were allowed to complete thirteen to fifteen interviews in each high concentration census block group and up to five interviews in each low concentration census block group.

2. I conducted a range of analyses to ensure that the absence of a relationship between educational attainment and the three indicators of family obligation and participation was not a statistical artifact. First, I examined unadjusted means on each of the three indicators by education category and income tertile. There were no significant differences on any of the three indicators by educational attainment or income tertile. In addition, because education and income are typically correlated, I also estimated the same equations presented in the chapter with each of these variables entered separately. Still, education was not associated with any of the three indicators of family participation and obligation, and income was associated only with frequency of contact.

3. In the present chapter, analyses of indicators of normative role obligations were based on the sum of respondents' answers to items tapping each domain in order to compare average values to those of the national MIDUS sample, which were reported as the sum of respondents' answers across relevant items. However, in order to examine the relative importance of normative family obligation, civic obligation, and altruism, the mean values (rather than the sum) on a 0–10 scale were computed ($M = 8.63$, 6.63, and 7.30 for measures of normative family obligation, civic obligation, and altruism, respectively. Comparison of means using independent samples t-tests indicated that the mean for the measure of normative family obligation was significantly higher than the mean for civic obligation [$t(901) = -19.77$, $p < .001$]. The mean for the measure of normative family obligation was also significantly higher than the mean for altruism [$t(901) = -22.52$, $p < .001$]. The mean for the measure of civic obligation was also significantly lower than the mean for the measure of altruism [$t(901) = 8.18$, $p < .001$].

4. The pattern was evident within the subsample of Puerto Rican [$M_{\text{civic obligation}} = 30.23$ and 26.79 in low and high density Dominican neighborhoods, respectively, $t(281) = 2.15$, $p < .05$], Dominican [$M_{\text{civic obligation}} = 32.01$ and 26.34 in low and high density Dominican neighborhoods, respectively, $t(278) = 5.71$, $p < .001$] and Black [$M_{\text{civic obligation}} = 29.32$ and 23.61 in low and high density Dominican neighborhoods, respectively, $t(336) = 3.15$, $p < .01$] respondents.

5. The pattern was evident within the subsample of Puerto Rican [$M_{\text{civic obligation}} = 28.21$ and 31.00 in low and high density Puerto Rican neighborhoods, respectively, $t(281) = -2.69$, $p < .01$] and Dominican [$M_{\text{civic obligation}} = 27.50$ and 31.40 in low and high density Puerto Rican neighborhoods, respectively, $t(278) = -3.63$, $p < .001$] respondents but not within the subsample of Black respondents [$M_{\text{civic obligation}} = 28.84$ and 29.43 in low and high density Puerto Rican neighborhoods, respectively, n.s.].

6. The pattern of lower altruism among respondents living in high density Dominican neighborhoods was evident within the subsample of Puerto Rican

[M_{altruism} = 28.44 and 21.96 in low and high density Dominican neighborhoods, respectively, $t(281)$ = 2.75, $p < .01$], Dominican [M_{altruism} = 30.12 and 26.13 in low and high density Dominican neighborhoods, respectively, $t(278)$ = 3.451, $p < .001$], and Black [M_{altruism} = 24.59 and 19.61 in low and high density Dominican neighborhoods, respectively, $t(336)$ = 2.25, $p < .05$] respondents. The pattern of higher altruism among respondents living in high density Puerto Rican neighborhoods was evident within the subsample of Puerto Rican [M_{altruism} = 25.43 and 29.31 in low and high density Puerto Rican neighborhoods, respectively, $t(281)$ = -2.69, $p < .01$], Dominican [$M{\text{altruism}}$ = 26.80 and 29.98 in low and high density Puerto Rican neighborhoods, respectively, $t(278)$ = -2.59, $p < .01$], and Black [M_{altruism} = 23.75 and 27.10 in low and high density Puerto Rican neighborhoods, respectively, $t(336)$ = -2.15, $p < .05$] respondents.

References

Aldwin, C., and D. Stokols. 1988. The effects of environmental change on individuals and groups: Some neglected issues in stress research. *Journal of Environmental Psychology* 8:57–75.

Brown, R. E. 1991. Political action. In *Life in Black America,* ed. J. S. Jackson, 254–63. Newbury Park, CA: Sage.

Buckner, J. C. 1989. The development of an instrument to measure neighborhood cohesion. *American Journal of Community Psychology* 17, no. 3:397–410.

Carrasquillo, H. A., and V. Sanchez-Korrol. 1996. Migration, community, and culture: The United States-Puerto Rican experience. In *Origins and destinies: Immigration, race, and ethnicity in America,* ed. S. Pedraza and R. Rumbaut, 98–109. Belmont, CA: Wadsworth.

Cohler, B. L., A. J. Hostetler, and A. M. Boxer. 1998. Generativity, social context, and lived experience: Narratives of gay men in middle adulthood. In *Generativity and adult development,* ed. D. P. McAdams and E. de St. Aubin, 265–310. Washington, DC: American Psychological Association.

Cole, E. R., and A. J. Stewart. 1996. Meanings of political participation among Black and White women: Political identity and social responsibility. *Journal of Social and Personality Psychology* 71:130–40.

Essed, P. 1990. *Everyday racism: Reports from women in two cultures.* Claremont, CA: Hunter House.

Feagin, J. R., and M. P. Sikes. 1994. *Living with racism: The Black middle class experience.* Boston: Beacon Press.

Grasmuck, S., and P. Pessar. 1996. Dominicans in the United States: First and second generation settlement. In *Origins and destinies: Immigration, race, and ethnicity in America,* ed. S. Pedraza and R. Rumbaut, 280–92. Belmont, CA: Wadsworth.

Hatchett, S. J., and J. S. Jackson. 1993. African American extended kin systems: An assessment. In *Family ethnicity: Strength in diversity,* ed. H. P. McAdoo, 81–90. Newbury Park, CA: Sage.

Heimer, C. A. 1996. Gender inequalities in the distribution of responsibility. In *Social differentiation and social inequality,* ed. J. N. Baron, D. B. Grusky, and D. J. Treiman, 241–73. Boulder, CO: Westview Press.

Jayakody, R., R. M. Chatters, and R. J. Taylor. 1993. Family support to single and married African American mothers: The provision of financial, emotional, and child care assistance. *Journal of Marriage and the Family* 55:261–76.

Keyes, C. L. M. 1998. Social well-being. *Social Psychology Quarterly* 61, no. 2:121–40.

Keyes, C. L. M., and C. D. Ryff. 1998. Generativity in adult lives: Social structural contours and quality of life consequences. In *Generativity and adult development*, ed. D. P. McAdams and E. de St. Aubin, 227–64. Washington, DC: American Psychological Association.

MacDermid, S. M., C. E. Franz, and L. A. De Reus. 1998. Generativity: At the crossroads of social roles and personality. In *Generativity and adult development*, ed. D. P. McAdams and E. de St. Aubin, 181–226. Washington, DC: American Psychological Association.

Malson, M. R. 1983. The social support systems of Black families. In *Ties that bind: Men's and women's social networks*, ed. L. Lein and M. B. Sussman, 37–57. Binghamton, NY: Haworth Press.

Mayer, S. E., and C. Jencks. 1989. Growing up in poor neighborhoods: How much does it matter? *Science* 243 (4897):1441–45.

McAdams, D. P., and J. Azarow.1996. Generativity in black and white: relations among generativity, race, and well-being. Paper presented at the convention of the American Psychological Association, Toronto, Canada.

McAdams, D. P., and E. de St. Aubin. 1992. A theory of generativity and its assessment through self-report, behavioral acts, and narrative themes in autobiography. *Journal of Personality and Social Psychology* 62:1003–15.

McAdams, D. P., E. de St. Aubin, and R. L. Logan. 1993. Generativity among young, mid-life, and older adults. *Psychology and Aging* 8:221–30.

McAdams, D. P., H. M. Hart, and S. Maruna. 1998. The anatomy of generativity. In *Generativity and adult development*, ed. D. P. McAdams and E. de St. Aubin, 7–44. Washington, DC: American Psychological Association.

McAdoo, H. P. 1980. Black mothers and the extended family support network. In *The Black woman*, ed. L. Rodgers-Rose, 125–44. Beverly Hills, CA: Sage.

———. 1981. Patterns of upward mobility in Black families. In *Black families*, ed. H. P. McAdoo, 155–70. Beverly Hills: Sage.

Milburn, N. G., and P. J. Bowman. 1991. Neighborhood life. In *Life in Black America*, ed. J. S. Jackson, 31–45. Newbury Park, CA: Sage.

Morales, J. 1986. *Puerto Rican poverty and migration: We just had to try elsewhere.* New York: Praeger.

Ogbu, J. 1985. A cultural ecology of competence among inner-city Blacks. In *Beginnings: The social and affective development of Black children*, ed. M. Spencer, G. Brookins, and W. Allen, 45–66. Hillsdale, NJ: Lawrence Erlbaum.

Pessar, P. 1995. A visa for a dream: Dominicans in the United States. Boston: Allyn and Bacon.

Rumbaut, R. G. 1998. Ties that bind: Immigration and immigrant families in the United States. In *Immigration and the family: Research and policy on U.S. immigrants*, ed. A. Booth, A. C. Crouter, and N. Landale, 3–46. Mahwah, NJ: Lawrence Erlbaum Associates.

Saegart, S. 1990. Unlikely leaders, extreme circumstances: Older Black women building community households. *American Journal of Community Psychology* 17, no. 3:295–316.

Sampson, R. J. 1992. Family management and child development: Insights from social disorganization theory. In *Advances in criminology theory,* ed. J. McCord, 3: 63–93. New Brunswick, NJ: Transition.

Sampson, R. J., and J. D. Morenoff. 1997. Ecological perspectives on the neighborhood context of urban poverty: Past and present. In *Neighborhood poverty: Policy implications in studying neighborhoods,* ed. J. Brooks-Gunn, G. J. Duncan, and J. L. Aber, 2:1–22. New York: Russell Sage Foundation.

Serrano-Garcia, I. 1984. The illusion of empowerment: Community development within a colonial context. In *Studies in empowerment: Steps toward understanding the psychological mechanisms in preventive interventions,* ed. J. Rappaport, C. Swift, and R. Hess, 75–96. New York: Haworth.

Stack, C. 1974. *All our kin: Strategies for survival in a Black community.* New York: Harper and Row.

Stack, C. B., and L. M. Burton. 1993. Kinscripts. *Journal of Comparative Family Studies* 24, no. 2:157–70.

Taylor, R. B., S. D. Gottfredson, and S. Brower. 1985. Attachment to place: Discriminant validity and impacts of disorder and diversity. *American Journal of Community Psychology* 13, no. 5:525–43.

Tolson, T. F., and M. N. Wilson. 1990. The impact of two- and three-generational Black family structure on perceived family climate. *Child Development* 61, no. 2: 416–28.

Torres-Saillant, S. 1989. Dominicans as a New York community: A social appraisal. *Punto 7 Review* 2:7–25.

Waters, M. C. 1997. Immigrant families at risk: Factors that undermine chances for success. In *Immigration and the family: Research and policy on U.S. immigrants,* ed. A. Booth, A. C. Crouter, and N. Landale, 79–91. Hillsdale, NJ: Lawrence Erlbaum.

Wilson, M. A. 1986. The Black extended family: An analytical consideration. *Developmental Psychology* 22, no. 2:246–58.

———. 1989. Child development in the context of the Black extended family. *American Psychologist* 44, no. 2:380–85.

Wilson, W. J. 1987. *The truly disadvantaged.* Chicago: University of Chicago Press.

III SOCIAL RESPONSIBILITY AND HUMAN DEVELOPMENT

SEVEN

Developmental Roots of Adult Social Responsibility
Alice S. Rossi

[L]ife must be understood backward. But . . . it must be lived
forward.

Søren Kierkegaard

INTRODUCTION

In our overview of the social demographics of social responsibility
in chapter 3, we note numerous differences across domains and dimensions as to which demographic variables—age, sex, education—are
predictors of social responsibility. For example, women and lesser-
educated adults take the lead in providing social-emotional support or
advice and hands-on caregiving to others, whereas men and the better
educated are the major providers of financial contributions to family
members and community organizations and causes. We also show that
religious beliefs and generativity contribute to high levels on all our indicators of adult social responsibility, and we hypothesize that both religious beliefs and generativity are rooted in early life experiences. To
test this hypothesis, we now probe more deeply and explicitly into the
characteristics of families of origin and trace their effects on the personalities and values of the respondents, and on the extent to which respondents show varying levels of social responsibility in adulthood in
the domains of family and community.

Before we can begin a discussion of our findings, we must address
two key issues. The first is theoretical and concerns the rationale underlying a developmental trajectory model of adult social responsibility,
which in turn hinges on two questions: first, what characteristics of
early family life are most critical in paving the way for children to grow
into responsible adults; and second, what is the most probable developmental sequence that intervenes between early family characteristics
and our outcome measures of adult responsibility. The second issue is
methodological and concerns our necessary reliance on retrospective
data.

THE DEVELOPMENTAL TRAJECTORY MODEL
Family of Origin Characteristics

Human development does not begin de novo with an individual's birth; it is well underway even before conception, in the genes, personality, and values parents bring to their marriages, which set the stage for their childbearing and childrearing styles. A parent experiencing a first birth is no more a tabula rasa than an infant is. For most adults, educational attainment, personality, and values are in place prior to marriage and typically play a role in mate selection itself. This is illustrated by the significant correlation between characteristics of mothers and fathers of our respondents: .57 in educational attainment, .38 in the personal qualities of generosity and sociability. The latter ratings, based on how "generous and helpful" and how "friendly and sociable" each parent was toward people *outside the family,* are deemed to be of special significance as predictors of personality and generativity among our respondents. We assume these generative qualities are characteristics the parents had prior to their marriage, tapping as they do relatively stable personality traits that are in place by early adulthood and that change only modestly at later stages of the life course.

The second cluster of family of origin characteristics we identify taps the two major axes of all childrearing, the degree to which each parent showed *affection* and imposed *discipline* when the respondents were growing up. (All questions were posed in such a way as to refer to the man or woman who raised the respondent, whether a biological parent or someone else, e.g., a stepparent or grandparent). The significance of parental affection for the healthy development of the child is attested to by countless novels and biographies, child developmental psychology, and clinical practice. Concern for others springs from the seedbed of family affection laid down during the years of dependency in infancy and childhood. We are literally *loved into loving.* Also, the intense attachment parents have to children is deeply rooted in human nature: like other mammalian species, we are innately social animals, necessarily so because we are totally dependent on parental care and supervision for years after birth before we can survive by our own resources. Hence, human sociality is itself grounded in the intense attachment between parent and child (unless the parent is impaired, by addiction, a crippling disease, or psychopathology, for example).

Theories concerning interpersonal attachments have varied over the past century, of course: Freud rooted human sociality and the need for interpersonal contact in the sex drive and the relationship to the mother (Freud 1930); Bowlby's attachment theory followed in Freud's footsteps, labeling adults' quests for attachment as efforts to recapture the intimate contact they had as infants with their mothers (Bowlby 1969, 1973). In more recent years, psychologists have drawn upon animal research and genetics and are more accepting of the view that humans, like other mammals, are genetically predisposed not only to bond with their infants, but to have a *need to belong* throughout life, to seek persistent caring and frequent social interaction (Baumeister and Leary 1995). It is striking to note, in fact, how thoroughly saturated with sociality at least three of the big five personality scales are. All the items that go into scales on agreeableness and extroversion have implicit reference to social relationships: outgoing, friendly, talkative, sympathetic, helpful, caring. Agency also assumes social interaction: outspoken, dominant, forceful, does not refer to inanimate objects but to interaction with other people. It follows that sociality as a species characteristic is an innate predisposition shown in the intense attachments parents show toward their infants and the immediate attachment of newborns to their parents. This in turn leads to an expectation that any empirical measure we devise for the affection component of childrearing will be highly skewed in a positive direction, an expectation borne out in our findings.

But affection, though critical to healthy development, is not sufficient. Parents are also charged with socializing their children in the ways of their society, with encouraging the acquisition of skills and values necessary for adequate functioning in adult social life. The most significant contribution to a child's success in school is the head start provided by early parental training. If affection is critical for the acquisition of *character*, discipline is critical to the acquisition of *competence* (see, e.g., Damon 1995). Loving oneself in the absence of disciplined self-control can lead to narcissism and self-indulgence, hardly a prescription for socially responsible behavior. Researchers have argued that parents' and teachers' overemphasis on children's self-esteem and underemphasis on discipline and skill acquisition can lead children to underperform academically, to wrongfully blame others, and if extended to the extreme of grandiose narcissism, to respond with aggression when confronted with criticism or when denied wishes (Bushman and Baumeister 1998; Damon 1995).

Researchers less often recognize that emphasizing a child's self-esteem rather than his or her skill acquisition and performance is a convenient parental cop-out: giving in to a child's wishes rather than investing the time and energy necessary to teach skills and to insist on consistent adherence to rules spares the parent both time and irritation. A good example of this is Alan Wolfe's finding that the middle-class parents he interviewed complained a great deal about the time their children spent watching TV and about sex and violence being so prominent on the screen (Wolfe 1998). Wolfe's informants wanted buttons or computer chips to control the channels and programs their children could watch; in other words, they favored censorship above taking responsibility for supervising the amount of time and the kinds of programs their children watch.

As suggested by this example, the content of parental discipline reflects societal and cultural norms about childrearing far more than parental affection does. Expert advice on childrearing has varied enormously over the course of the twentieth century. Behaviorists have recommended everything from strictly regulated infant feeding (e.g., Skinner 1953; Watson 1930) to permissive feeding on infant demand (e.g., Spock's numerous baby and childcare books), from insistence on obedience and conformity to permissive indulgence and encouragement of self-reliance and independence (Alwin 1990, 1996), from giving praise only for hard-earned skills to lavishing praise for mediocre performance. *Loving* a child may be enhanced by innate predispositions for attraction to and attachment to human infants; *disciplining* a child is less dependent on innate predisposition, instead reflecting childrearing norms and practices, which vary across historic time, class, and culture. Hence, a discipline scale should show a lack of consensus that produces not a skewed distribution but a more normal one, with greater variation than an affection scale has.

The third and last cluster of family of origin characteristics we identify takes into account family structure and the family economic situations and health issues that impact on children and adolescents. We give special attention to family composition, of particular importance because of the fragility of marriages in the latter half of the twentieth century. The MIDUS sample includes respondents who were reared by their mothers alone, others who were reared by a stepparent and a biological parent, and a small group of respondents who were reared by adults other than even one biological parent, presumably grandparents. In addition, we give special attention to respondents' family sizes and birth-order positions, both of which have relevance to the quality of relations with parents, the level of affection and discipline experienced in youth, and potentially, status attainment in adulthood. Measures of the socioeconomic status of the family of origin include the educational attainment of each parent, whether the family was ever on welfare (for six months or more), and the family's relative financial situation compared to an "average" family at the time. Last, we have ratings of parents' health when respondents were about sixteen years of age, which have potential relevance to both the quality of relationships between family members and the family's socioeconomic status.

Sequential Ordering of Respondent Characteristics in the Developmental Model

In his account of the history of European morals, William Lecky ([1886] 1955) describes the broad sweep of what Europeans understood by "moral unity" from the time of Augustine through Charlemagne's reign in terms of a circle of affections expanding outward from the confines of the family to encompass clan and class, then a nation, then a coalition of nations, then the whole of humanity, and finally (though not yet manifest in the 1880s when Lecky was writing), to humankind's relationship with the animal world. By the 1990s, one might easily have added our species' place in the biosphere to Lecky's account of moral concerns in Western history, as indexed by the environmental protection movement. Peter Singer, an Australian-born moral philosopher, built on Lecky's metaphor in entitling his own book *The Expanding Circle* (Singer 1981). In this book Singer deals with the implications of sociobiology for philosophers' treatment of ethics and morality. He argues that sociality and altruism are not unique to humans but shared with others in the mammalian species going far back in evolutionary time. Through the exercise of human intelligence, however, humans have gradually expanded their circle of ethical concern beyond individual selves and close kin to include fellow creatures in distant lands.

The metaphor of an expanding circle is also an apt description of human development and provides the underpinning for ordering the factors brought into play when young adults move out from their families of origin and establish independent lives. A preschool child necessarily lives within a small circle of intimates—parents, siblings, other kin, neighborhood playmates; the circle expands when the child enters school to include congenial friendships and relationships with a sequence of teachers and friends' parents. In early adulthood, job experiences, courtship, marriage, travel, and social mobility further widen the circle. With the birth of children, the circle may narrow for many, as the demands of early childcare and the economic pressures to increase income take hold. For many other young adults, however, becoming a parent opens the way to increased societal concern: even social isolates become involved with their neighbors as their children acquire neighborhood playmates; still other parents become involved with school and safety issues as their children move out and away from the protected world of family and immediate neighborhood. John Snarey and Peter Clark give a moving description of this increase in societal generativity in a case study of a father and son as the son entered puberty and early adolescence (Snarey and Clark 1998). By middle age, as family responsibilities lessen and incomes become higher and more stable, many midlifers seek opportunities to contribute to others through volunteer work and financial contributions to political causes and charities.

There is of course an idealistic vision in such a depiction. Many adults never move beyond the smaller circles of close family and friends; others remain compulsively dedicated to their personal search for wealth, power, or fame with little concern for the common good; still others are emotionally or physically incapacitated such that their horizons extend no further than their own selves.

As reviewed in chapter 1, numerous social trends have been cited to explain what is widely perceived as a decline in civility and civic virtue in American society. Prominent trends often pointed to as being responsible for such decline are the sexual revolution and the changes in gender roles stimulated by the feminist movement. Both trends have instigated changes in family life: sexual promiscuity before and during marriage, declining marriage rates, high divorce rates, births outside marriage, and parental failure to provide adequate supervision and training of children under the misguided notion that permissiveness will encourage self-reliance. Most of the essays in Mary Ann Glendon and David Blankenhorn's book, *Seedbeds of Virtue* (1995), are prominent examples of this interpretive argument. The authors consider the family to be *the* most important seedbed for the development of competence, character, and citizenship in American society (cf. especially Browning 1995 and Wilson 1995). Our measures on family of origin composition and childrearing styles provide an opportunity to test several of their assumptions. The analysis begins with what we know about our respondents' parents: their educational attainment; their level of helpfulness to and sociability with other people outside the family;

whether they are biological parents, stepparents, or some other adults; and their financial status, including whether or not the family was ever on welfare for six months or more while respondents were growing up. We relate these structural and qualitative characteristics of families of origin to the affection and discipline shown in the parents' childrearing practices as experienced and remembered by our respondents, as well as to the respondents' own educational attainment and marital and procreative history.

Along the way we also analyze parental and early family characteristics as they relate to respondents' personality traits. Because the youngest respondents in our sample are twenty-five years of age, it is not feasible to explore earlier individual psychological characteristics such as temperament, but we recognize that from an ontogenetic perspective, temperament can be considered the first "inter-individual difference indicator of personality, making individuals distinct even in the womb" (Baltes, Lindenberger, and Staudinger 1998, 1086). There is some consensus among child psychologists that activity, reactivity, emotionality, and sociability are among the major components of temperament (see Strelau and Angleitner 1991 and an overview summary in Baltes, Lindenberger, and Staudinger 1998, 1086–87), and there are echoes of these traits in several of the standard personality scales. A good example of the continuity of childhood temperament into adulthood is the finding reported by Caspi, Elder, and Bem (1987) from the Berkeley Growth and Oakland Guidance Studies that ill-tempered boys become ill-tempered men. Other researchers suggest there is a "heterotypic continuity" between childhood temperament and later phenotypically different but related personality traits, for example, the shy little girl turned introverted adult, or the highly impulsive, sensation-seeking child who as an adult scores very low on the conscientiousness scale (Zuckerman 1994).

Thus a child's early temperament characteristics may be transformed into personality traits by early adulthood and remain relatively stable at least through early old age. Studies of the very old (adults over eighty years of age) suggest some onset of age-related personality changes (Baltes, Lindenberger, and Staudinger 1998, 1088), but this need not concern us because our oldest respondents are seventy-four years of age.

Of the numerous components of personality, personality traits were deemed to be most appropriate for the purposes of our analysis. In the design of MIDUS, we measured six personality traits, adapted from standard scales (Bem 1981; Goldberg 1993; John 1990; Trapnell and Wiggins 1990): agency, agreeableness (or, as we shall refer to this scale, communion), extroversion, conscientiousness, openness to experience, and neuroticism. We chose these scales first because they are easily incorporated into a self-administered instrument, and second, because a long tradition of longitudinal research on these particular personality scales has shown high stability coefficients. Across some two dozen studies with measurement intervals from six to thirty years, Costa and McCrae (1994) estimate that *three-fifths* of the variance in true scores for these personality traits is stable across the full life course from thirty to eighty years of age (see Baltes, Lindenberger, and Staudinger 1998, 1096, for a good summary table on such results). While this finding of three-fifths stability is impressive, the residual of two-fifths allows considerable room for change over time for a significant proportion of adults.

In light of the subtle connection between early childhood temperament and relatively stable adult personality traits, it is appropriate to place personality traits *first* in the sequential order of variables that intervene between early family and subsequent adult development. A second reason for such placement is that behavioral genetic research has found that almost all of these personality traits have a large component of heritability, in a range from 40 to 60% (Scarr 1992, 3), only slightly smaller than the genetic component in intelligence. As shown below, our MIDUS data on twins are consistent with data from other twin samples. Awareness of the genetic component in personality also alerts us to the limitations of demonstrating the effects of parental childrearing style on our respondents. We have no direct behavioral measures of genetic characteristics, but we must keep in mind that genetics, along with socialization practices, will be involved in any cross-generational transmission effects we report.

In our analysis of the contribution of personality traits to adult social responsibility, we concentrate primarily on two of the aforementioned scales: agency and communion, two traits considered of primary significance as predictors of generativity in the work of Dan McAdams and his research associates, most recently in the lead chapter of an American Psychological Association publication on generativity (McAdams, Hart, and Maruna 1998). The traits tapped by the communion scale (e.g., helpful, warm, caring, sympathetic) are clearly linked to personal predispositions to empathic identification with and concern for others, which are critical to responsible behavior in both private and public life. The traits included in the agency scale (e.g., forceful, assertive, outspoken) provide a measure of predispositions to *action* on behalf of others' welfare as well as one's own. Theoretically, high scores on the communion personality scale should result from earlier exposure to high parental affection, and high scores on the agency scale should result from early exposure to high levels of parental discipline. Alternatively, it may take the combination of both high affection and high discipline (a childrearing style often labeled Authoritative) to produce high adult levels of communion and agency. In the analysis below, we first explore the contribution of family composition and parental affection and discipline as *precursors* to respondents' personality profiles, and later in the analysis sequence, the *sequelae* of personality traits as contributors to generative concern and socially responsible behavior in adulthood. As McAdams and de St. Aubin note in the epilogue to their edited volume on generativity, only one of their fourteen chapters gives attention to the developmental *antecedents* of generativity (McAdams and de St. Aubin 1998, 488). Though they caution that only longitudinal studies can tease out what early factors predict generativity in adulthood, the prospects strike us as very dim that any such longitudinal study is likely to occur within the foreseeable future. Despite the limitations of reliance on retrospective accounts, we hope to provide depth to the understanding of the predictors for and the role of generativity in adult lives.

We placed religious beliefs in a position similar to that of generativity in the sequential ordering of our developmental analysis: as shown in chapter 3, the salience of religion in the early years in families of origin is significantly related to the level of religiosity in adulthood. Such cross-generational transmission of values is supplemented by linear increases in religiosity over the course of the adult years, which we take to reflect maturational effects as adults cope with their own mortality and seek larger, transcendent meanings for their lives.

Thus far we have specified the following sequence of our proposed developmental trajectory: from the qualities and characteristics parents had prior to the births of our respondents (education, generative characteristics, religious beliefs), to the events and characteristics affecting respondents while they were growing up (family composition and size, childrearing style of parents, parental physical and mental health, and economic resources), to the personality traits of respondents by early adulthood (especially agency, communion, and conscientiousness), to their adult beliefs and concerns (religiosity, generativity). The "outcome" end of our developmental sequence consists of variables measuring normative obligations and actual behavioral indicators of social responsibility, that is, the domains and dimensions of social responsibility analyzed in chapter 3. We give priority in the sequential ordering of these outcome measures to *normative obligations* for three reasons: First, social norms, like ethical precepts, are grounded in early socialization, hence family of origin characteristics are highly likely to be more strongly related to adult normative obligations than to actual adult behaviors such as providing advice or support to others or engaging in volunteer service in the community. Second, caregiving and financial aid to family members not only reflect willingness to be of help, but also depend on existential and changing life situations: the time and financial circumstances of donors as well as the needs of recipients for such help.

Third, consistent with our developmental assumptions about the expanding circle, we have found in earlier research that there is a systematic ordering of obligations to a wide array of others in the private sphere of family, kin, friends, and neighbors (Rossi and Rossi 1990). On a rating scale from least to highest felt obligation (0 to 10) we found that obligation to parents and children rank at the top of the obligation hierarchy, followed in descending order by obligations to siblings, grandchildren, grandparents, nieces and nephews, aunts and uncles, and cousins. Greater obligations are felt to descendant kin (e.g., a niece, a grandchild) than to ascendant kin (e.g., an aunt, a grandmother). At each generational level, lower obligations are felt toward affinal kin (e.g., son-in-law, mother-in-law) than to blood kin (e.g., son, mother), in much the same way as obligations are typically stronger to a biological parent than to a stepparent. Obligations toward friends tend to be at a level similar to that toward nieces and nephews or aunts and uncles; obligations to close neighbors are at a level similar to those felt toward cousins (Rossi and Rossi 1990, 175).

Interestingly, where family and kin are concerned, the obligation hierarchy matches perfectly the ranking in degrees of genetic relatedness, although few of us could explicate the reasons for differentiating obligation level to, for example, a sister compared to an aunt. In more ways than illustrated briefly here, we found a beautiful symmetry to kinship norms, yet no one learns genealogy in school, and parents do not consciously teach their youngsters the rules of kinship or exactly how Aunt Sue (mother's sister) is related to them as compared to Aunt Alice (mother's brother's wife). Like the acquisition of language long before the rules of grammar are understood (if they ever are!), the rules of kinship may be intuited in our youth through countless discrete instances of observation and experiences of interaction with family members of varying degrees of relatedness to us and our parents. There are no doubt deeper affective vibrations that young children pick up from their parents' interactions with various kin, and from the widening circle of relatives they become acquainted with, that contribute to the symmetry of obligations. Here too, the concept of the expanding circle holds, this time within the sphere of family and kinship. It is sad to note that for young children in recent years, barriers to such an expanding circle have been so often imposed through fear-driven parental warnings to be cautious about "strangers," including adults encountered in the proximate arena of the neighborhood, a childcare center, or a school playground. Indeed, we believe this parent- and educator-encouraged barrier to forming relationships beyond the intimate circle of family and friends represents a significant new hurdle to the expanding circle of relationships that are important to human development and concern for the common good.

The very last step in the sequential order of our developmental trajectory is the relationship between time and aid given to family versus community organizations or causes. Just as the early family is a seedbed in which values and personality are formed or directed, so too it is the environment where children learn that obligations to family have priority over obligations to serve the public good as citizen, volunteer worker, or contributor to a charitable organization. Here too the expanding circle metaphor is relevant. Higher educational attainment, especially, broadens horizons and encourages responsible citizenship. However, the pressures of job, home maintenance, and childrearing may be so great that participation in the larger community is necessarily curbed during the early adult years and becomes feasible only in the middle years as family responsibilities diminish and incomes become higher and more stable, hence the prediction that for most adults, civic obligations and service in the larger community increase in the later decades of life.

This completes the descriptions of and the explanations underlying the sequential order of the variables we enter into a developmental trajectory model that extends from early childhood to the mature years of our oldest respondents. While we considered it necessary to plan such a sequential trajectory for analysis purposes, we do not imply any one-way causal direction. Human development is a complex process, with many possibilities for two-way interactions. For example, childrearing patterns themselves are no simple reflection of parental characteristics; they may be, as well, responses to the characteristics of one child compared to another. A calm healthy baby is easier to comfort than an irritable colicky baby, a compliant adolescent far easier to deal with than an adolescent engaging in socially deviant activities, and parents' rearing tactics may accommodate to such differences in the children. We necessarily focus on broad developmental patterns that disallow such subtle variations.

It should also be noted that the sequence in development we have posited to this point does not imply any mechanistic or unidimensional conception of human development. Contemporary theories of human development have moved a considerable distance from earlier theories in several important respects. The old polarities of nature-nurture, biology-culture, or individual-society have been replaced by a more dynamic systems approach that seeks to understand the interaction and mutual influences between such polarities: for example, how genes and environment constrain and influence each other, with constraints and influences that are flexible, not absolute. Genetic activity does not itself produce finished traits (Gottlieb 1991), but depends on societal and historic influences well above the cellular level. For example, while it is true that a girl's age at menarche is partially dependent on the genes she shares with her mother, it is also the case that menarcheal age has varied over historic time by social class and race as a function of progressive improvements in nutrition and health. In Western societies there has been an average decrease in menarcheal age of about four months per decade from 1840 to 1950 (Tanner 1962). In Japan over the years from World War II to 1975, an even more spectacular change has occurred, not four but eleven months per decade (Marshall and Tanner 1986), reflecting the rapid rate of improvement in nutrition and health in postwar Japan. As Richard Lerner puts it, "biological structure and function and societal structure and function are linked systematically across history" (Lerner 1998, 11). For psychologists, this perspective supports their current emphasis on a high degree of *plasticity* as a major characteristic of human development. For sociologists and social psychologists, the more complex models of human development also allow for much greater leeway for individual decision making and purposive action. Jochen Brandtstädter puts this point well: "Individuals choose and create their environments according to preferences and competencies that, as phenotypic dispositions, are linked to genotypic factors. . . . [T]hrough their actions, individuals form, and continually transform, their phenotype and extend it into their personal culture and developmental history" (Brandtstädter 1998, 810)

The new emphasis on the dynamic interaction between individuals and their social context within the historic time and place in which they live out their lives encourages the recognition that attention must be paid, and if possible incorporated into research designs, to the multi-level integrations involved in human development. Multilevel integration implies attention to the physical and psychological self (person), the social context in which individuals are embedded (family, work-place, and friendship networks), and the larger world of community and society at a given time in history. Few of us could point to very many studies that achieve so full a multilevel integration. Ideally it would call for longitudinal studies conducted with representative samples that capture the diversity of class, race, and ethnicity of at least two, preferably more, purposely selected societies with different cultures and replicated in different historic eras. Clearly there is little prospect of mounting so complex, longterm, and costly a research program, and we are necessarily limited to achieving only approximations to such an ideal. The three greatest achievements the behavioral sciences can claim to date are (1) representative large samples drawn from two or more different societies to permit macrolevel comparisons of the influence of culture on human behavior, (2) short spans of time in multiwave panel studies to permit microlevel analyses that can control for causal directions, and (3) sequential cohort studies to permit teasing out historic, period, and maturational effects in the phenomena under study.

From the perspective of the ideal, the MIDUS studies fall short in numerous respects and are outstanding in others. We attempted a multilevel set of variables, including measures of physical and mental health, psychological well-being, detailed social demographics, and key measures on work, marriage, kin relations, social networks, personality, ratings on six life domains, a special module on menstruation and menopause for the women in the sample, to say nothing of the dimensions and domains of social responsibility that are the focus of this volume. We even obtained mouth swabs from hundreds of respondents for DNA testing, which may be linked to health, social, and psychological variables in the MIDUS instrument by researchers in the future. We relied on a large representative national sample of the population and have numerous spin-off studies that go into considerable detail on any number of topics, many of them represented in various chapters in this volume. In one special recruitment effort, we gained access to a large sample of twins who were then subjected to the full battery of telephone and self-administered instruments. In this chapter, we shall incorporate some data from this twin sample in an analysis of the heritability component of personality traits. We more sparingly included a module on the family of origin in the design of MIDUS for the analysis reported in this chapter.

What we do not have are longitudinal follow-up data or an empirical way to test for cross-national differences or to change analyses reflecting the influence of historic events, although the potential is there for researchers to build on our efforts through replication in other societal settings or with follow-up studies of MIDUS respondents that could potentially span significant historic events that intervene between 1995 and other studies early in the twenty-first century.

One last point on the sequential ordering we imposed on the analysis reported in this chapter: faced with cross-sectional data, one must necessarily follow some rationale for an analysis that aims to contribute to an understanding of human development. It was our best judgment that it was better to rely on retrospective data on the families of origin for the light they could shed on the adults we studied than to merely provide a static picture of them at the specific time in their lives at which they shared so much about themselves. In the following section, we give some focused attention to the retrospective nature of many of the variables used in our analysis.

Reliance on Retrospective Data: Methodological and Analytical Issues

The perceived relevance of early life for understanding current behavior and affect differs across the social science disciplines and the professions of medicine and psychiatry. It seems likely that no field has been more concerned for understanding early life than psychiatry, dominated as it has long been by the search for clues to mental illness in the conditions of the early home environment. Psychologists have also based many of their theories on the assumption that "what was past is prologue" (Henry et al. 1995, 92) and accordingly have sought data about the prior stages of life of the children or adults they have studied. By contrast, for most of its early history sociological theory was based on an assumption that one only needed social facts to explain social facts in a concurrent time frame, a position congenial to a newly emerging field trying to carve out its own special place at the turn of the century in the academic firmament without infringing on other disciplines. In more recent decades, as sociologists became concerned with the policy implications of their research, a new factor has been at work in the avoidance of retrospective data on early life experiences: to the extent such early factors are found to be significant explanations of current behavior, any "quick fix" short-term policy recommendations would have a small probability of success, hence the preference for viewing human action as purposive and volitional and therefore more appealing to funding agencies and more amenable to policy recommendations that assume rapid changes in behavior are possible.

Developmental psychology has a long history of theory-driven concern for establishing links among variables across time. Child development research in the past often relied on mothers' recall about early stages of their children's development and their parenting practices. One example is Sears, Maccoby, and Levin's study of childrearing (1957) that was launched in 1951 with a sample of 379 mothers of kindergarten age children in the Boston area who were interviewed about their parenting practices up to and including current practices with their five-year-old children. After hundreds of similar studies, concern grew about the reliability and validity of such retrospective data (Yarrow, Campbell, and Burton 1970). A major impetus behind early longitudinal studies of children was to avoid dependence on parental recall in favor of studying changes over time as they actually unfolded in the lives of children. Longitudinal studies, however, do not completely bypass dependence on recall; in addition to repeat measures at two or more points in time, they often seek information about what happened in the intervening periods.

Very long term longitudinal studies have their own problems of respondent and researcher attrition and of often dramatic changes in the developmental issues of concern to later generations of social scientists. For example, the Wisconsin Longitudinal Study (WLS) began in 1957 with a sample of high school seniors and focused narrowly on educational and occupational aspirations. The WLS was quickly transformed into a longitudinal study of occupational status attainment (Sewell, Hauser, and Featherman 1976). In more recent years, WLS researchers expanded the topic coverage to embrace issues of health and family life as they impact on occupational careers. Thus hindsight is often better than foresight, particularly when theory and methods undergo rapid change as has occurred in the social sciences since the late 1950s. As a result, even in longitudinal studies, researchers often incorporate retrospective measures for earlier events, measures no one anticipated would be necessary, in order to test new constructs suggested by advances in theory.

The growth of longitudinal studies has facilitated special research on the reliability and validity of retrospective data by asking long-studied subjects questions about their past and comparing their recall with the data obtained from them when they were younger. A good example is the Dunedin Health and Development Study in New Zealand, which assessed agreement between retrospective recall and actual measures taken in the past for seven domains, including reading ability, residence changes, and behavior problems (Henry et al. 1995). The findings on reading ability are of special interest. The researchers found what they call a "Lake Wobegon effect" (i.e., all the children are above average): retrospective self-reports of reading ability at age thirteen showed 39% of the subjects claimed they had been *above average* readers, 48% *average,* and only 13% *below average.* Since the respondents had taken a standardized reading test at age thirteen, the group's actual scores reflected a normal distribution. Henry and his colleagues report, however, that their results did not reflect an optimistic erosion of memory over the years. When the subjects were thirteen, both they and their parents estimated their reading abilities. Similarly low proportions reported below average reading ability, suggesting that "bias toward perceptions of average or better reading ability may represent a more general source of reporting error, not a unique retrospective bias" (Henry et al. 1995, 96).

There is a message in this finding that applies to all research on social behavioral topics, whether measures are concurrent or retrospective. As David Featherman, among others, has reminded us, the difference is one of degree, not of kind, between concurrent and retrospective measures (Featherman 1980; see also Bradburn, Rips, and Shevell 1987; Robbins 1963; Wolkind and Coleman 1983). In both cases, informants are providing information through a subjective lens that may distort not only past but present reality as well, and they do so for any number of reasons: respondents' purposeful distortion of answers to project a favorable impression of self (the "social desirability" factor); respondents' misunderstanding of what is asked; respondents' faulty memory; questions that seek more precision than it is reasonable to expect; and as we have learned, the sad fact that reported memories may involve events that never actually occurred, as witness the many trials in recent years of presumed child molesters whose supposed victims were reporting memories invidiously suggested to them by police or social workers, if not the parents themselves.

A larger issue goes beyond the point that differences in reporting errors are only a matter of degree, not kind, in retrospective versus concurrent measures: the past is in fact very much present when we report on our current selves. As we move through our daily routines, there is what Winifred Gallagher felicitously described as a constant "background hum of the past" (Gallagher 1996, 79): how we interact with a grandchild, for example, evokes and is partially affected by how we related to our children at a comparable age, or even how we were treated as children by our parents and grandparents. At a deeper level, an organism's phenotype reflects past environmental influences on our genotype, so that our individual histories are encoded in the very wiring of our nervous and immune systems, as they are in responses to a researcher about our lives today. Quite apart, then, from questions of validity and reliability, retrospective measures have a *utility of their own.* As Bill Henry puts this point, "even if retrospective measures do not constitute valid indicators of features of interest to social scientists . . . they may constitute valid indicators of the individual's current perception of those features, and as such, may be useful in understanding psychological development or adjustment" (Henry et al. 1995, 93).

The major caution to observe in relying on retrospective measures is to be fully aware that their proper use is to provide *the relative standing of individuals in a distribution,* not to test hypotheses that require precise reports of event frequencies or the specific dates of their occurrence.

This general caution dictated the selection of constructs and the items used to measure them in the design of the module on the family of origin in the MIDUS survey. Some examples of the criteria used in choosing measurements are the following:

1. Time reference. We made no effort to measure changes during or specific stages of the childhood and adolescence of respondents. All questions were pegged loosely to these early years by using phrases such as "most of your childhood," "up until you were sixteen," "during most of your childhood years," "the years you were growing up." It may well be that respondents had varying ages in mind when answering such questions. Some may have focused on early childhood, others on when they were adolescents, still others may have considered the more global overview intended by the question format. In a multipurpose lengthy instrument, space limitations do not permit any attempt to capture

changes between, say, relationships to parents in childhood versus mid-adolescence. For our purposes, the broad sweep of the formative years was deemed preferable to any attempt to link questions to a specific age. The exceptions to this design rule were questions on the health status of respondents and each of their parents when respondents were sixteen, a decision dictated by our desire to measure respondents' health at an age when most were still living at home and their parents were middle-aged, a life stage when many parents (especially fathers) confront problems associated with incipient chronic diseases.

2. Ratings and response categories. For the most part, we avoided numerical frequencies, as recommended by researchers who have compared recalled events with archival records. Henry (1995) and Robins (Robins et al. 1985) report that subjects can accurately inform researchers whether or not something happened but not the number of times it occurred. Instead we used short response categories: a little, some, a lot; never, rarely, sometimes, often; or poor, fair, good, very good, excellent. We made no effort to obtain income data for families of origin; rather, we asked for a comparative judgment on how much better off or worse off financially respondents' families were as compared to the average family at the time (a lot, somewhat, a little better/ worse off or the same as an average family) and simply whether or not the family had ever been on welfare "for six months or more." Regarding fathers' employment histories, we asked merely for how much of their childhood (all, most, some, a little, or not at all) their fathers worked for pay. We restricted specific numerical information to questions regarding demographics such as the number of older and young siblings respondents had. Many (especially older) respondents did not know how much education each of their parents had. Because this is an important variable, the missing values were imputed by assigning the appropriate mean years of schooling according to our six-category age classification for respondents, a necessarily rough approximation, since we did not ask about parental age (or birth date). Allowing for sex differences in the educational attainment of the parents, we assigned the missing values on parents' education by the mean educational attainment in terms of both age and sex. For example, missing values on mothers' education were assigned by the mean educational attainment of women respondents in each of six age categories. (Respondents' age is a reasonable substitute for parents' age, in the absence of a direct question on age of parent, thus allowing for historic trends toward more education during the past several decades.)

3. Multiple-item measures. The major constructs on the family of origin are the two dimensions of affection and discipline, and parents as generativity models. A variety of items, including a global rating on the quality of the relationship to each parent (poor to excellent), were part of the instrument, mixing item candidates for the affection and discipline scales. Factor analysis clearly distinguished the predicted items for each of these two major scales. Illustrative items and psychometric characteristics of the affection and discipline scales can be found in table 7.1. The generativity model measure for each parent is based on ratings of the extent (not at all to a lot) the parent was "generous and helpful" or "sociable and friendly" to people *outside the family,* as mentioned earlier. The discipline scale items were supplemented by two additional questions on how many "regular chores" and how many "rules about how to spend your time" respondents reported (none to a lot). These items were asked generally, not specifically for each parent, and therefore they form a separate scale from the discipline scale—the chores/time use rules scale.

4. Family composition. We took great care to obtain highly specific information about the adults who were the primary parenting figures for our respondents' early years. The lead question was "Did you live with both of your biological parents up until you were sixteen?" For those who reported they did *not* grow up in intact biological families, we asked detailed follow-up questions to identify those who experienced the death of one or both parents, those whose parents were divorced or never lived together, and those who were adopted. We also asked whether the male (or female) head of the household was biological, adoptive, step, or other. All subsequent questions about parents referred to possible parent surrogates as well as the biological parents, for example, "your mother, or the woman who raised you."

With the benefit of hindsight, we would prefer to have more detailed information about the religious involvement and beliefs in the family of origin than what we obtained, but we did not anticipate that religiosity and generativity would be such major predictors of adult responsibility. At the design stage, we opted against seeking any detail on religious attendance or beliefs in youth, limiting ourselves to a general question on how important religion was in respondents' early family life (not at all to very important). We take comfort, however, from knowing that often in social research, global subjective ratings have better predictive power than all manner of specific objective information. Paul Cleary, for example, has reported that general perceived

TABLE 7.1 Constructs and Measures Used in Analysis of Developmental Roots of Adult Social Responsibility

Dimension	Measure	Descriptive Detail
Parents' premarital characteristics	Educational attainment	Years of schooling of mother and father.
	Religiosity	Single-item four-point rating of importance of religion in family of origin ("not at all" to "very" important).
	Generativity	Two-item scales of four-point ratings on extent to which mother and father were generous/helpful and friendly/sociable to people outside the family (mother: 2–8 scale range, alpha = .81, mean = 6.8, SD = 1.4; father: 2–8 scale range, alpha = .87, mean = 6.5, SD = 1.6).
Family of origin's child-rearing	Affection	Seven-item scales of four-point ratings ("not at all" to "a lot") of maternal and paternal affection, e.g., understood respondent, respondent could confide in her/him, gave time and attention to respondent when needed (maternal affection: 7–29 scale range, alpha = .91, mean = 22.9, SD = 5.0; paternal affection: 7–29 scale range, alpha = .93, mean = 20.3, SD = 5.7).
	Discipline	Four-item scales of four-point ratings on extent to which each parent exerted discipline and supervision, e.g., was strict and consistent about rules, harsh in punishment (maternal discipline: 4–16 scale range, alpha = .77, mean = 11.8, SD = 2.5; paternal discipline: 4–16 scale range, alpha = .83, mean = 11.6, SD = 3.0).
	Chores/time-use rules	Two-item scale of four-point ratings on number of regular chores and number of rules re use of time (2–8 scale range, alpha = .65, mean = 5.9, SD = 1.4).
Family of origin's existential circumstances	Relative financial status	Single-item seven-point rating of family's financial status compared to the average family when respondent was growing up, from "a lot worse off" to "a lot better off."
	Welfare dependence	Single-item (yes = 1, no = 0) on family welfare dependency for six months or more during respondent's childhood and adolescence (7% of sample report yes).
	Parents' health	Single-item five-point rating of mother's and father's health (poor to excellent) when respondent was about sixteen.

Respondent's personality traits	Communion (agreeableness)	Five-item scale of four-point ratings on helpful, warm, caring, sympathetic, softhearted (5–20 scale range, alpha = .80, mean = 17.4, SD = 2.4).
	Agency	Five-item scale of four-point ratings on forceful, self-confident, assertive, outspoken, and dominant (5–20 scale range, alpha = .79, mean = 13.7, SD = 3.3).
	Conscientiousness	Four-item scale of four-point ratings on organized, responsible, hardworking, (not) careless (4–16 scale range, alpha = .57, mean = 13.6, SD = 1.8).
	Openness to experience	Seven-item scale of four-point ratings on creative, imaginative, intelligent, curious, broad-minded, adventurous, and sophisticated (7–28 scale range, alpha = .77, mean = 21.3, SD = 3.7).
	Neuroticism	Four-item scale of four-point ratings on worrying, nervous, moody, and (not) calm (4–16 scale range, alpha = .74, mean = 9.0, SD = 2.6).
	Extroversion	Five-item scale of four-point ratings on outgoing, lively, friendly, active, talkative (5–20 scale range, alpha = .78, mean = 16.0, SD = 2.8).
Respondent's values	Generativity	Six-item scale, adapted from Loyola Generativity Scale (McAdams and de St. Aubin 1992) of self-ratings, e.g., like to teach others, feel people need you, have important skills to pass along to others (6–24 scale range, alpha = .84, mean = 17, SD = 3.7).
	Religiosity	Six-item scale of four-point ratings on religiosity, e.g., how important religion is in respondent's life, in sending children for religious instruction, in preference for socializing with those of same religion (6–24 scale range, alpha = .88, mean = 16.5, SD = 4.6).
Respondent's normative obligations	Family/friends obligation Civic obligation Altruism	See chapter 3, table 3.1
Respondent's responsible behavior	Emotional-social support to family/friends Volunteer work Contributions to family/friends Contributions to organizations/causes	See chapter 3, table 3.1

health by adults (on a global subjective rating from poor to excellent) "predicts subsequent morbidity and mortality, even controlling for other biological and health status variables" (Cleary 1997, 3) and self-evaluations of health accurately predict mortality even after statistically controlling for the presence of health problems, disability, and other risk factors (Kaplan and Camacho 1983; Mossey and Shapiro 1982). Cleary suggests that global subjective ratings often benefit from knowledge and experience known only to the respondent and provide a more integrated rating than is possible with numerous other data a researcher may have access to, including medical records, which are rarely standardized and are often based on subjective ratings by several healthcare professionals. In similar fashion, our single rating of the importance of religion, or our single ratings of how well respondents did ten years ago in specific life domains, may provide more significant information than far more detailed measures based on numerous specific indicators.

We present one last point about the use of retrospective data. An analyst can derive considerable confidence in the validity of such data in at least two ways: One procedure is to compare our research results with those from prospective studies that identify early markers in childhood that are significant predictors of adult behavior, markers close to those we obtained in our cross-sectional survey. Carol Franz, David McClelland, and Joel Weinberger provide such evidence in a thirty-six-year follow-up of the children first studied at age five by Sears, Maccoby, and Levin (1957), whom we referred to earlier. At the time of the follow-up, the subjects were forty-one years of age. Franz and her colleagues found that high measures of warmth and affection in early childhood predicted social accomplishment in midlife (as measured by long, happy marriages and good relationships with children and friends), higher levels of generativity, and engagement in more affiliative behaviors (Franz, McClelland, and Weinberger 1991).

A second procedure involves internal analysis of retrospective measures in the same cross-sectional survey. A relevant example comes from a prior study of ours that obtained retrospective ratings of how close adult respondents were to their mothers and fathers at three specified ages: ten, sixteen, and twenty-five. With respondents classified in terms of the actual historic time periods during which they were adolescents, we compared the intimacy ratings at age sixteen of two specific groups: those who were sixteen during the relatively calm social and political atmosphere of the 1950s with those who were adolescents in the late 1960s and the early 1970s, when American society was rife with social and political ferment. As predicted, the latter cohort reported significantly lower ratings of intimacy with parents than the former when they were sixteen-year-old adolescents, but there were no significant differences between the two cohorts in their ratings of intimacy when they were ten and twenty-five years of age (Rossi and Rossi 1990, 107–8). We take this to mean that memories are not necessarily just "fragmented bits of flotsam and jetsam," as psychologist Daniel Stern suggested in an interview with Winifred Gallagher (Gallagher 1996, 78). In the case of memories of our childhood and adolescence, which we have so many occasions to review and think about later in life, we may be fairly good reporters, even if our lenses are somewhat on the rosy or the dark side.

WHAT LIES AHEAD

We begin the analysis with close attention to structural and demographic characteristics of the families of origin and we trace their long-term impact on the marital and procreative histories of our respondents. Next we link family composition to the childrearing patterns of respondents' parents, following which we show how family composition and childrearing styles relate to the personality traits of respondents. Finally, bringing together the most significant early family characteristics, we test their effects upon the profile of social responsibility in the domains of family and community in adulthood.

COMPOSITION OF FAMILY OF ORIGIN AND ITS EFFECTS

Table 7.2 provides detailed descriptions of the major types of composition of our respondents' families of origin: four in five respondents grew up in intact biological or adoptive families (only thirty-three cases of adoption were reported). Note that the MIDUS survey undercounts poorly educated adults because some literacy sophistication was required to fill out the lengthy self-administered questionnaires. The extent of this selection can be seen by comparing the proportion of MIDUS respondents who grew up in intact biological families to that reported in the National Survey of Families and Households (NSFH-I) in 1987–88—83% of the former, but only 75% of the latter (Bumpass and Sweet 1989, 257). The proportion was even lower (64%) for the 1960–68 birth cohort in the NSFH survey, a drop reflecting the impact of higher divorce rates and out-of-wedlock births in the 1960s and 1970s.

The two major alternate family composition types are biological mothers alone (with or without another female, presumably the mater-

TABLE 7.2 Types of Family of Origin Composition

Type[a]	Definition	N	%
Intact	Both biological or adoptive parents[b]	2,499	82.7
Mother only	Biological mother alone, or biological mother plus other female (presumed to be respondent's maternal grandmother)	197	6.5
Mother and stepfather	Biological mother plus other male (step-father or mother's cohabiting partner)	203	6.7
Father and stepmother	Biological father alone, or biological father plus other female (stepmother or father's cohabiting partner)	67	2.2
Grandparents	Other male and female, or other female alone (presumed to be grandparents or grandmother alone)	55	1.9
Total		3,021	

Note: All questions about relationship to parents in childhood made allowance for other than the biological parent, e.g., "your mother (or the woman who raised you)."

[a] These abbreviated labels, characterizing the predominant type in these categories, will be used in subsequent tables.

[b] Sample included only thirty-three respondents who reported they were adopted.

nal grandmothers of respondents), and biological mothers plus a cohabiting partner or second husband (respondents' stepfathers). Least frequent but of special interest is the category of respondents reared by their biological fathers alone or with a cohabiting partner or second wife (respondents' stepmothers), and those reared by other men and women. (We did not ask specifically who these "other adults" were; we will assume the majority were grandparents, though there may be some cases of foster parents or older siblings in this category.)

There are predictable correlates of family composition, reflecting trends in marital stability, cohabitation, and remarriage following divorce. Table 7.3 highlights the major reflections of such trends by age and race. Age of respondents provides a linkage to the historic periods during which they grew up. Rough estimates of these time periods are shown below the three age categories. There is little variation in the percentage of intact families across white birth cohorts, but the proportion of black respondents who grew up in intact families declines sharply with each younger age group, resulting in much larger racial differences among those who grew up in the 1960s and 1970s than among those who grew up in earlier decades. The small proportion of black respondents in the MIDUS sample (6.6%) permits only a two-way age classification for the detailed family composition among non-

TABLE 7.3 Family of Origin Composition, by Age and Race

Family Composition	White				Black		
	25–39 (1960s–70s)	40–59 (1940s–50s)	60–74 (1930s–40s)		25–39 (1960s–70s)	40–59 (1940s–50s)	60–74 (1930s–40s)
Percentage intact	83.2	84.8	84.6		59.7	66.3	70.0
Percentage not intact	16.8	15.2	15.4		40.3	33.7	30.0
N	919	1,289	590		77	89	30
Mother only	31.8	38.3	42.3		41.9	41.0[a]	—
Mother and stepfather	51.9	39.2	25.7		38.7	20.5[a]	—
Father and stepmother	9.1	12.8	22.7		3.3	12.9[a]	—
Grandparent(s)	7.2	9.7	9.3		16.1	25.6[a]	—
N	154	196	97		31	39[a]	—

Note: Dates in parentheses are a rough classification of the time period during which respondents of various ages were growing up. For example, respondents who were thirty-five in 1995 were born in 1960, hence they grew up in the 1960s and 1970s, an era marked by counterculture, civil rights, and antiwar movements. By contrast, respondents fifty years of age in 1995 were born in 1945 and spent their formative years during the postwar decades of the late 1940s and early 1950s, a time of affluence and the Cold War. Respondents sixty-five years of age in 1995 were born in 1930 and grew up during the Depression in the 1930s and Word War II in the early 1940s.

[a] Includes respondents aged forty to seventy-four. The small proportion of black respondents (6.6%) in the MIDUS sample permits only a two-way age classification: under forty and forty or older.

intact families of origin, but for both races, similar trends exist: over the decades from the early 1930s through the 1970s, a *decrease* in the prevalence of growing up with a biological father and stepmother, and an *increase* in biological mothers and stepfathers (or cohabiting partners of a biological parent). These trends reflect the decline in maternal mortality, the increase in divorce, and the increase in cohabitation and remarriage of divorced women with children over these years. One additional characteristic is uniquely more prevalent among black respondents: growing up with neither biological parent, presumably with grandparents, though some may have been reared by foster parents or other kin.

Socioeconomic indicators of early family life by family structure are shown in table 7.4. Note that the historic trend toward increased amounts of education is reflected in the lower educational attainment of grandparents compared to biological parents or stepparents of respondents. (This supports our assumption that the majority of the surrogate parents are in fact grandparents, whose birth cohorts attained less education on average than that of foster parents or older siblings of

TABLE 7.4 Socioeconomic Indicators of Family of Origin Composition

Socioeconomic Indicators	Intact	Mother Only	Mother/Stepfather	Father/Stepmother	Grandparent(s)	Statistical Significant[a]
Education						
Mother/maternal figure	11.3	11.1	10.9	11.0	9.3	***
Father/paternal figure	11.0	—	11.5	9.8	9.4	***
Percentage on welfare[b]	3.6	26.4	18.2	9.0	14.6	***
Percentage "worse off" than average family[c]	24.5	58.7	39.8	28.4	30.8	***

[a] Anova f for mean educational attainment; χ^2 for percentage differences in economic indicators.

[b] "Yes" response to the question, "During your childhood and adolescence was there ever a period of *six months or more* when your family was on welfare or AFDC?"

[c] "Somewhat" or "a lot" worse off in response to the question: "When you were growing up, was your family better off or worse off financially than the average family was at that time? (If your parents lived separately and had different financial situations, answer for the family you lived with for the longest time)."

*** $p < .001$.

our respondents.) In this sample, solo mothers rearing children alone do not show significantly less education than mothers in intact families. Biological parents who divorced and remarried show slightly lower educational attainment than parents in intact families, reflecting the inverse relationship between divorce and socioeconomic status. On the other hand, stepparents are not significantly different from biological parents in educational attainment.

Far sharper contrasts exist in economic indicators by family composition type. Although solo moms are not significantly less well educated than mothers in intact families, they clearly stand out in terms of vulnerable economic circumstances during their childrearing years: respondents reared by solo mothers show the highest percentage of having been poorly off financially and of having been on welfare. Compared to all other family composition types, only 4% of intact families were on welfare at some point in the past. By contrast, solo moms and remarried moms are associated with some period of economic vulnerability: solo mothers were six times more likely and remarried mothers *four* times more likely than intact families to have depended on welfare, probably because they experienced spells of single-parent status one or more times between marital or cohabiting partners. These results mirror those reported by Sara McLanahan and Gary Sandefur (1994) regarding data from the Panel Study of Income Dynamics, that is, at each level of parental educational attainment, the poverty rate for single-parent families far exceeds that for two-parent families or stepfamilies (McLanahan and Sandefur 1994, 84).

Marital breakdown and subsequent remarriage has much less economic impact on men than on women: Only a slightly elevated percentage of remarried fathers, compared to fathers in intact parental marriages, report having been "worse off" than the average family (28.4% vs. 24.5%, respectively). Reports from remarried mothers reflect a much greater incidence of having been "worse off" than do those from mothers in intact parental marriages (39.8% vs. 24.5%, respectively), a statistic which reflects the remarried mothers' having spent some period of time in single-parent status, as previously noted.

By themselves, the differences by family composition type shown in table 7.4 provide an interesting window on the family histories of respondents in their formative years. Of far greater interest, however, is the question of whether these early experiences carry over and influence the adult characteristics of our respondents. A first profile is provided by table 7.5, which summarizes several aspects of the marital and

TABLE 7.5 Sequelae of Family of Origin Composition on Marital and Procreative History, by Sex

	Intact	Mother Only	Mother/Stepfather	Father/Stepmother	Grandparent(s)	Statistical Significance[a]
Marital history						
Current Status (%)						
Men						
Never married	12.7	19.0	13.0	3.3	9.5	
Separated/Divorced	13.0	13.9	20.6	26.7	23.8	
Married	72.2	65.8	62.0	70.0	66.7	
Widowed	2.2	1.3	4.4	—	—	
N	1,241	79	92	30	21	**
Women						
Never married	9.4	17.0	17.1	2.7	14.7	
Separated/Divorced	21.8	26.2	26.1	24.3	26.4	
Married	59.2	44.9	53.2	59.5	44.1	
Widowed	9.5	11.9	3.6	13.5	14.7	
N	1,258	118	111	37	34	**
Average age at first marriage						
Men	24.3	24.7	22.5	22.8	22.8	**
Women	21.5	21.4	21.0	21.5	19.7	n.s.

Married before age 18 (%)						
Men	1.1	1.6	4.0	3.6	0.0	***
Women	9.0	9.3	20.2	13.9	28.6	***
Number of times married (%)						
Men						
Once	76.3	68.8	58.8	57.1	52.6	
Twice	19.1	23.4	31.3	35.7	42.1	
Three or more times	4.6	7.8	9.9	7.2	5.3	*
Women						
Once	75.4	69.4	65.2	77.8	48.3	
Twice	20.4	20.4	23.9	16.7	31.0	
Three or more times	4.2	10.2	10.9	5.5	20.7	***
Procreative history						
A birth before first marriage (%)						
Men	4.8	7.1	7.9	10.7	6.7	n.s.
Women	5.5	12.9	5.1	12.9	14.8	*
Average number of children reared						
Men	2.2	2.2	2.2	2.7	3.0	n.s.
Women	2.4	2.7	2.4	2.5	3.2	n.s.

[a] Anova f for average age at first marriage and average number of children reared. All others χ^2.

$*p < .05.$ $**p < .01.$ $***p < .001.$

procreative histories of men and women from each of the family of origin types.

Respondents who grew up in intact families compared to the nontraditional families show the following characteristics: they are *more* apt to be married than single, separated, or divorced; they are *less* apt to have married before their eighteenth birthday or to have had a birth before marriage; and they are *more* likely to have been married only once. Respondents who were reared by neither biological parent present the most extreme contrast to intact families, especially women reared under such circumstances. Women in this family structure report the highest rate of very early marriages (29%, vs. 9% in intact families), represent the highest proportion with a birth before marriage (15%, vs. 5% for intact families), and suffer from the highest levels of marital instability, as indicated by the 21% who have married *three or more* times (compared to only 4% for those from intact families). Women reared by neither biological parent are particularly prone to marry at an early age (19.7%) and represent the *lowest* proportion married at the time of the survey (44%). The overall implication of these profiles is that nontraditional family structures impact on the subsequent marital and procreative experiences of women to a much greater extent than they do on men.

One other comparison worth noting is that between intact families and solo-mother families: although no more likely to marry at a young age, women reared by solo mothers are *twice* as likely to have had a first birth before marriage and *twice* as likely to have never married at all, compared to those from intact families (13% vs. 6% and 17% vs. 9%, respectively). The implication is that such women have followed a pattern similar to that of their mothers. On the other hand, neither men nor women who grew up with solo mothers have had more children than those from intact families.

There are, of course, many intervening experiences between family structure in childhood through adolescence and adult decisions to marry or not, to divorce or not, or to have a child or not. We turn now to the affective and disciplinary experiences associated with growing up in these different family structures.

Childrearing Patterns in Families of Origin

We begin with the two primary measures on childrearing, affection and discipline. The affection scale is based on seven items, ranging from an overall rating of the quality of the respondent's relationship to mother and to father while growing up, to the extent of love and affection the respondent received from each parent, to the amount of time and attention received, to the extent to which the respondent felt he or she could confide in each parent. The discipline scale is based on four items: how consistent and how strict each parent was regarding rules for the respondent's behavior, how harsh in punishment, and how restrictive in curbing the respondent's conformity to peers. (See table 7.1 for the psychometric properties of the family of origin measures.)

Figure 7.1 shows the case distribution of the affection and discipline

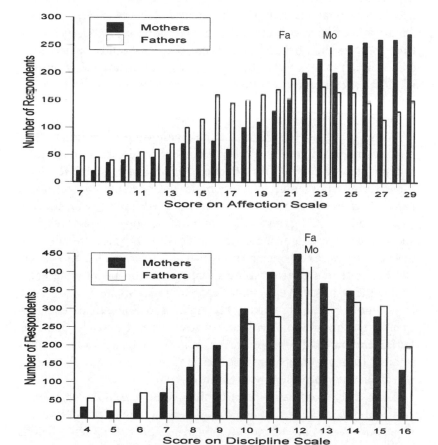

FIGURE 7.1. Case distribution and median scores on affection scale (top panel) and discipline scale (bottom panel): mothers versus fathers. Vertical lines show median scores.

scales, differentiated by maternal and paternal roles. The histogram on the affection scale is highly skewed toward the positive, whereas the discipline scale shows a more normal distribution. We believe the contrast between the two scales reflects several factors. The affection scale likely reflects a combination of social desirability reports (parents *should* show love to their children) and a biogenetic predisposition to nurturance of the young. Social norms for child discipline are far from being universal, subject as they are to changes in the recommendations of childrearing experts and pediatricians, resulting in a greater degree of variation on our scale. Comparing the distribution of cases for maternal and paternal affection, the histogram also shows more cases of *low* affection from fathers than from mothers, and an even sharper sex difference at the high end of the scale, with far more cases of *high* affection from mothers than from fathers; hence the significantly higher mean scores on the maternal affection scale than on the paternal. There are no differences between mothers and fathers in the mean discipline scores, but more fathers than mothers fall at both the low and high ends of the scale.

Table 7.6 provides evidence for the relationship between family of origin composition and seven dimensions of childrearing: in addition to reporting means from the affection and discipline scales, the table shows the effect of family structure on levels of harsh punishment and parental generativity (both dimensions reported separately for the maternal and paternal figures in the families), the importance of religion, and a scale on the chores and time use rules respondents were subjected to when they were growing up (for which data refer to the family generally rather than to each parent specifically). The major differences among the results shown in table 7.6 are as follows:

1. Unique profile of stepparents compared to biological parents. Respondents who grew up with a stepparent report *lower* levels of affection and parental generativity and a *higher* incidence of harsh punishment from the stepparent than respondents report from biological parents in any type of family structure.

2. Biological parents in intact families compared to biological parents who remarried. No differences are reported on affection or discipline, but the families formed by remarriage provided a *less* religious and *more* punitive environment.

3. Unique profile of families including neither biological parent, in particular the maternal role in such families. Grandmothers are reported to have provided *lower* affection, *higher* discipline, and a *higher*

TABLE 7.6 Dimensions of Childrearing, by Family of Origin Composition

	Intact	Mother Only	Mother/Stepfather	Father/Stepmother	Grandparent(s)	Statistical Significance[a]
Affection (mean)[b]						
Maternal	23.1	21.9	22.2	19.0	21.9	***
Paternal	20.5	—	17.3	20.3	18.6	***
Discipline (mean)[c]						
Maternal	11.8	11.3	11.5	11.6	13.0	***
Paternal	11.7	—	11.1	11.3	11.0	**
Frequency of harsh punishment (%)[d]						
Maternal	6.1	10.6	11.2	15.1	10.4	***
Paternal	7.9	—	16.3	12.8	7.1	**
Parental generativity (% high)[e]						
Maternal	62.4	61.3	55.6	40.0	57.2	***
Paternal	54.2	—	31.0	53.7	39.9	***
Religiosity (% high)[f]	81.7	75.5	71.1	63.6	87.2	***
Chores/time use rules (% high)[g]	31.7	35.1	33.5	32.8	56.3	***

[a] Significance level of anova f statistic for mean scores on scales (affection and discipline) and χ^2 significance on percentage distributions on all other measures.

[b] Scale range = 7–29.

[c] Scale range = 4–16.

[d] % report "sometimes" or "often" in response to questions regarding experiencing harsh punishment (kicked, bit, hit with fist, beat up, choked/burned/scalded) in the family when they were growing up.

[e] High = 7 or 8. Scale range = 2–8.

[f] High = "somewhat" or "very" important. The measure refers to the family generally, not to a specific parent.

[g] High = 7 or 8. Scale range = 2–8. Two items in the scale were "How many regular chores did you have during the time you were growing up?" and "How many rules did you have about how to spend your time?" The measure refers to the family generally, not to a specific parent.

** $p < .01$.   *** $p < .001$.

incidence of harsh punishment. The grandparental family type also represents the *highest* proportion with a highly religious atmosphere and the *highest* emphasis on assigning regular chores to the respondents in their youth and controlling how respondents spent their time.

4. Solo mothers compared to mothers in intact families. No major differences were reported by respondents, only a slight tendency for solo mothers to show less affection and impose less regular discipline and supervision, but to give slightly more harsh punishment and to have slightly more control over chores and time use. Solo mothers also placed less emphasis on the importance of religion compared to the profile shown for intact families. None of these differences are as sharp as those between intact families and families involving grandparents or stepparents.

Up to this point, our analysis has been largely bivariate descriptions of family composition and its correlates in childhood experiences. We turn now to a multivariate analysis of the characteristics that predict the level of affection and discipline our respondents' experienced in their childhood and adolescence. In doing so, we necessarily constrict the definition of family composition to a dummy variable that differentiates only between intact families and all other family composition types.

DETERMINANTS OF PARENTAL AFFECTION AND DISCIPLINE IN FAMILIES OF ORIGIN

In the introduction to this chapter, we differentiated between characteristics the parents of our respondents were likely to have had *prior* to their marriages and the characteristics and experiences that likely developed *after* their marriages. Most adults complete their education before they marry, and marriage per se does not change adult values and personality in any fundamental sense. Parents' religious views and their personal qualities of sociability and generosity toward other people are also largely in place before marriage and may in fact have played a role in courtship and the decision to marry. We therefore begin our analysis with the effects of these premarital characteristics—parental educational attainment, generativity, and importance of religion—upon the affection and discipline indicators of their relationships to respondents when the respondents were growing up (model 1 in tables 7.7 and 7.8), followed by a second test (model 2) that supplements the parents' premarital characteristics with an array of measures tapping what transpired during the respondents' childhood and adolescence. Model 2

TABLE 7.7 Regressions of Maternal Affection and Maternal Discipline
(beta coefficients)

Variable	Maternal Affection		Maternal Discipline	
	Model 1	Model 2	Model 1	Model 2
Mothers' premarital characteristics				
Generativity	.458***	.441***	.046**	.033
Religiosity	.126***	.103***	.200***	.189***
Educational attainment	.011	−.024	−.055**	−.045*
Sex of respondent[a]	−.129***	−.119***	.017	.024
Family of origin structure				
Family composition[b]	—	.060***	—	.018
Sibship size	—	−.045**	—	.035
Respondent oldest child[c]	—	.010	—	−.017
Respondent youngest child[d]	—	.026	—	−.078***
Family resources				
Mother's health when respondent at age 16[e]		.119***	—	.042*
Relative financial standing[f]	—	.069***	—	.001
Welfare dependency[g]	—	−.019	—	−.026
R^2	.273***	.309***	.051***	.062***
N	2,989	2,806	2,989	2,806

Note: Model 1: Premarital predictors only; Model 2: Premarital predictors plus family events/characteristics during childhood and adolescence of respondents.
[a] 1 = male; 2 = female.
[b] 1 = both biological parents; 0 = other.
[c] 1 = yes; 0 = no.
[d] 1 = yes; 0 = no.
[e] Poor to excellent.
[f] Much worse off to much better off.
[g] For a period of six months or longer. 1 = yes; 0 = no.
*$p < .05$. **$p < .01$. ***$p < .001$.

therefore tests two things: (1) how much of the variance in parental affection and discipline is explained by family of origin structure and resources; and (2) the extent to which parents' premarital characteristics retain their predictive significance when structural and resource variables are added to the equations.

Over the long stretch of years devoted to childbearing and rearing, families change as they grow in size and as they encounter economic problems and health-threatening experiences. Accordingly, the model 2 variables include family size, birth-order position, parents' health during respondents' adolescence (pegged at "sixteen" years of age, when almost all respondents were still living with their parents or parent surrogates), and two indicators of economic well-being—relative

TABLE 7.8 Regressions of Paternal Affection and Paternal Discipline
(beta coefficients)

Variable	Paternal Affection		Paternal Discipline	
	Model 1	Model 2	Model 1	Model 2
Fathers' premarital characteristics				
Generativity	.506***	.463***	.075***	.062**
Religiosity	.116***	.107***	.124***	.103***
Educational attainment	.057***	.011	−.008	.013
Sex of respondent[a]	−.030*	−.019	−.090***	−.084***
Family of origin structure				
Family composition[b]	—	.038*	—	.052**
Sibship size	—	−.049**	—	.092***
Respondent oldest child[c]	—	.008	—	−.006
Respondent youngest child[d]	—	.009	—	−.090***
Family resources				
Father's health when respondent at age 16[e]	—	.107***	—	.030
Relative financial standing[f]	—	.086***	—	−.014
Welfare dependency[g]	—	−.058***	—	−.035
R^2	.298***	.321***	.032***	.053***
N	2,807	2,519	2,807	2,519

Note: Model 1: Premarital predictors only; Model 2: Premarital predictors plus family events/characteristics during childhood and adolescence of respondents.
[a] 1 = male; 2 = female.
[b] 1 = both biological parents; 0 = other.
[c] 1 = yes; 0 = no.
[d] 1 = yes; 0 = no.
[e] Poor to excellent.
[f] Much worse off to much better off.
[g] For a period of six months or longer. 1 = yes; 0 = no.
*$p < .05$. **$p < .01$. ***$p < .001$.

financial standing and welfare dependency. Our predictions were that increasing family size would *reduce,* however modestly, the degree of affection shown to any particular child and *increase* the discipline imposed on the children, hypotheses grounded in the sociological assumptions that increases in group size typically involve diminished time with and investment in any one member and necessitate greater adherence to rules in the delegation of group tasks. On birth order, we test the common assumption that the youngest child is spared the degree of discipline and close supervision parents impose on their first-born child. Behind the image of the spoiled and indulged "baby of the family" are parents who have become more skillful and confident of themselves with each subsequent addition to the nest, with the result that they are more relaxed and less demanding in rearing the youngest child than they were in rearing a firstborn. Our findings, reported separately for mothers (table 7.7) and fathers (table 7.8), are summarized as follows:

1. Respondents' parents' premarital characteristics. Mothers and fathers who rate high in helpfulness to and sociability with others *outside the family domain* (i.e., generativity) provide the most affection. This variable retains its significance when family structure and resource variables are added to the equations, although with a slightly lower net effect as gauged by the size of the standardized beta coefficients in model 2 compared with those in model 1. Second, parents (mothers and fathers) who made religion an important feature of family life are shown to have higher levels of both affection and discipline. The religious ambience of the family remains significant in model 2 with the addition of family structure and resource characteristics. Third, better-educated fathers show higher affection than less well educated fathers, but this seems to be largely due to their ability to provide relatively good financial circumstances and to their having been in good health (as indicated by the statistical significance of father's education in model 1 but not in model 2). Mother's education is significant only on discipline: better-educated mothers impose *less* discipline than do mothers with less education and continue to do so independent of family resources or traumatic events over the years of childrearing.

2. Sex of respondent. Men report more affection from their mothers than women do, but only slightly more affection from their fathers than women do. There is no significant sex difference in maternal discipline, but sons clearly report more discipline from their fathers than daughters do. Another of our analyses (data not shown) finds that men report a much higher incidence of harsh punishment by their fathers than women do, with fathers being particularly indulgent toward daughters who are their only child. Note that such findings reflect the sex differences of the children as much as of the parents themselves; that is, as boys and adolescents, males engage in more socially deviant and disruptive behavior than females do and hence are the recipients of more paternal discipline.

3. Family structure. Respondents reared by both biological parents report higher levels of affection from both mothers and fathers than do respondents whose parents remarried or cohabited with a second partner. The multivariate analysis thus confirms the findings reported in the preceding section on family composition effects. Second, on paren-

tal discipline, the coefficient is significant only for fathers: in families with both biological parents, fathers impose more discipline than do fathers in reconstituted families including stepfathers or grandfathers. Third, our predictions are confirmed on the effects of family size and birth order: the larger the family, the lower the affection and the higher the discipline; and respondents who are the youngest children in their families report having been spared the level of discipline imposed on firstborn children.

4. Family Resources. Poor health of either mother or father *reduces* the affection shown to children and *increases* discipline only from mothers. Economic hardship takes a particular toll on fathers' affection: families who have been on welfare or worse off than the average family show reduced paternal affection. Economic hardship has no similar effect on parental discipline. These findings reflect the primary aspect of the maternal role compared to the paternal role: Women have traditionally carried the major burdens of child supervision on the homefront. If they are in poor health, they may be less affectionate and more strict in relating to their children than if they are in excellent health. Fathers' decreased affection in times of economic hardship reflects their traditional importance as the most significant breadwinners: if a father does so poorly in economic support that the family has some period of welfare dependence, he may withdraw psychologically and be seen as distant and uninvolved by his children.

5. Overall, family structure and resources have less impact on parental affection and discipline than do the qualities parents brought into their marriage in the first place, as indicated by the relatively small increment in R^2s in model 2 compared to model 1 in all four equations. Last, the battery of predictor variables explains more of the variation in parental affection than in parental discipline.

The discipline scale taps the strictness, consistency, and harshness of punishment in response to the child's wrongdoing. A rather different but related measure is provided by the chores/time use rules scale, which taps parental assignment of chores to their children and the extent to which parents controlled how their children used their time. Typically the chores children are assigned are not limited to the care of their own possessions, rooms, or clothing, but involve doing things that contribute to the larger family and home setting (e.g., laundry, household cleaning, meal preparation, or cleanup after meals). These are potentially significant means for teaching collective responsibility for others than the self, and being routinized on some regular basis may pave the way for the acquisition of good work habits, pride in the skills acquired early in life, and an internalized commitment to service by doing for others. That may seem a weighty interpretation to place on a single two-item scale, but we have found in an earlier study that domestic chore involvement as children encourages a general tendency toward greater expressivity and nurturance in adulthood (Rossi and Rossi 1990), and we shall see below a similar contribution of this aspect of childrearing to the personality traits of MIDUS respondents. Thomson, McLanahan and Curtin (1987, 104) also report (with data from NSFH-I) that a smaller proportion of solo-mom families than of two-parent families assign chores to their children and have rules about TV watching.

As previously noted, the chores/time use rules scale items are not specific to each parent, but refer to the early family generally. Hence in a multivariate analysis of this scale, we use a composite measure of parents as generativity models by adding together the maternal and paternal generativity scores. Table 7.9 shows that the most significant predictors of chores/time use rules are those in the family structure cluster: the larger the family, the higher is the parental emphasis on chore assignment and time use supervision. Not only are youngest children supervised less and given fewer chores to do, but being the oldest child increases the scores on this measure, suggesting more focused training of the firstborn child in service to others and by inference, attentiveness to a wise use of time—qualities that capture the role of oldest children as helpmeets to their parents in caring for younger children and in handling greater assignments of household chores. Families that enjoy relatively good financial circumstances place less emphasis on chores and time use than those in poor financial circumstances, a finding consistent with the greater permissiveness of better-educated parents, as well as their ability to purchase labor saving appliances or hire help. By contrast, families worse off than an average family are more dependent on the labor children can contribute to home maintenance; consequently, the children learn to value time and internalize the importance of service to others.

Family Influences on Educational Attainment

A long tradition of social science research has traced the contribution of individuals' early family life to their educational attainment (e.g., Alwin and Thornton 1984; Blake 1989; Blau and Duncan 1967; Clausen and Clausen 1973; Duncan, Featherman, and Duncan 1972;

TABLE 7.9 Regression of Chores/Time-Use Rules on Parental Characteristics, Family of Origin Structure, and Family Resources among Two-Parental Figure Families (beta coefficients)

Variable	Chores/Time-Use Rules
Parents' premarital characteristics	
Generativity	−.002
Religiosity	.172***
Averaged educational attainment[a]	−.024
Sex of respondent[b]	−.006
Family of origin structure	
Family composition[c]	−.054**
Sibship size	.117***
Respondent oldest child[d]	.050**
Respondent youngest child[e]	−.087***
Family resources	
Mother's health when respondent at age 16[f]	−.024
Father's health when respondent at age 16[g]	.022
Relative financial standing[h]	−.067**
Welfare dependency[i]	−.024
R^2	.077***
N	2,403

Note: In combining maternal and paternal childrearing scales, cases of respondents whose families of origin did not contain a male parental figure are missing values. Hence base Ns of these equations exclude respondents reared by mothers alone. Consult the text for results based on mother-alone cases.

[a] Educational attainment of mother and father are highly correlated (.58); here we use the 'average' years of schooling of the two parental figures in the family as a single predictor variable.

[b] 1 = male; 2 = female.

[c] 1 = both biological parents; 0 = other.

[d] 1 = yes; 0 = no.

[e] 1 = yes; 0 = no.

[f] Poor to excellent.

[g] Poor to excellent.

[h] Much worse off to much better off.

[i] For a period of six months or longer. 1 = yes; 0 = no.

** $p < .01$.   *** $p < .001$.

Easterlin 1980; Espenshade, Kamenske, and Turchi 1983; Heer 1985; Mare and Chen 1986; Sewell, Hauser, and Featherman 1976). It has been a sociological truism that parental social class is a major predictor of children's educational attainment, a general finding that has been interpreted largely in socialization terms: higher social classes include better-educated parents, who produce high achieving children because of their childrearing practices and because of the additional financial and intellectual resources they can put to use in enriching their children's knowledge of the world. Until recent years, when public debate has focused on the poor quality of public education, there was agreement that the different success rates among children in different schools are attributable to the qualities the children bring to these institutions, not to a variation in what the schools have to offer (Blake 1989, 297), thus highlighting the importance of what families do in rearing their children.

Since educational attainment is largely completed by early adulthood and thereafter contributes in significant ways to socioeconomic status, this is an appropriate point in the developmental trajectory to explore the contribution of numerous early family life characteristics to the educational attainment of our respondents, including socioeconomic status, family structure, and childrearing patterns, supplemented by assessments of the health of the parents and of the respondents themselves when they were adolescents. A major expectation, based on accumulated prior research (cited above), is that parents' education and family size will be the two major determinants of how far children go in the educational system. Research over the past decade and more has shown the ill effects of growing up in non-intact families. For example, children in one-parent families are far more likely than those in two-parent families to be high school drop-outs (Featherman and Hauser 1978; Furstenberg and Cherlin 1991; Garfinkel and McLanahan 1986; McLanahan and Sandefur 1994).

Note, however, that the educational attainment of parents is an index not merely of financial well-being and availability of resources to invest in providing a variety of growth-enhancing experiences for children, but also serves as an important proxy for a critical variable of which we have no direct measure: the presence of genetic predispositions to intelligence that permitted the parents to succeed educationally and which they have passed on to some extent to their children, an issue we will discuss later in this chapter. In keeping with a dynamic approach that assumes intricate linkages between genetic and environmental influences on human development, we assume that those reared in intact families have both genetic and socioeconomic advantages over children reared in nontraditional families and that they will therefore attain higher educational levels.

The results of our analysis, shown in table 7.10, support expectations grounded in prior social research. As in numerous other studies, the MIDUS data show that father's education and family size are the

TABLE 7.10 Regression of Respondents' Educational Attainment
on Parental and Family of Origin Characteristics, Total
and by Sex (beta coefficients)

Variable	Total	Men	Women
Socioeconomic status			
Father's educational attainment	.251***	.273***	.244***
Mother's educational attainment	.120***	.049	.187***
Welfare dependency[a]	−.054**	−.058*	−.060*
Family structure			
Family composition[b]	.104***	.118***	.086***
Sibship size	−.127***	−.183***	−.063**
Respondent oldest child[c]	.046*	.008	.086**
Respondent youngest child[d]	.012	−.026	.054
Childrearing patterns			
Parental affection	−.022	−.046	−.003
Parental discipline	−.054**	−.033	−.078**
Chores/time-use rules	.008	−.002	.020
Health[e]			
Father's health	.055**	.067**	.042
Respondent's health	.059**	.089***	.028
R^2	.198***	.200***	.216***
N	2,393	1,194	1,199

Note: Prior analysis showed that mother's health and the relative financial standing of the family of origin had no significant net effect on respondents' educational attainment.

[a] For a period of six months or longer. 1 = yes, 0 = no.
[b] 1 = both biological parents; 0 = other.
[c] 1 = yes; 0 = no.
[d] 1 = yes; 0 = no.
[e] When respondent at age sixteen, poor to excellent.
*$p < .05$. **$p < .01$. ***$p < .001$.

two strongest predictors of respondents' educational attainment, followed closely by growing up with both biological parents. Independent of father's education, mother's education contributes significantly to female respondents' years of schooling, but not to that of male respondents. The greater intimacy of the mother-daughter relationship, compared to the three other sex-specific parent-child dyads, may facilitate the transmission of interests and life goals of well-educated mothers to their daughters, interests and goals shaped in part by the mother's education as well as her genes.

Difficulties in early and middle adulthood that parents experienced during their childrearing years are tapped by having been on welfare for some period of time in the past and by poor health of either the fathers or the respondents themselves. Both of these factors depress the educational attainment of the children, especially sons. Regardless of a father's education, poor health or short-term dependency on welfare curbs the educational attainment of the child. Welfare dependence affects both sons and daughters, but the depressive effect of poor health on educational attainment holds only for sons: both their own and their fathers' poor health when they were adolescents have negative effects on the sons' educational success. (Unfortunately we did not gather any detail on the nature of the health problems of respondents when they were adolescents or of their parents in midlife, hence we cannot explore the possibility of some sex-linked genetic factor that may explain this pattern). Firstborn children have a slight edge in educational attainment, net of all other predictors in these equations, but in this data set, being a firstborn child provides an edge only to daughters' educational attainment.

Over and above the contributions of socioeconomic and family structural factors, our chosen childrearing measures have few direct effects: neither parental affection nor the extent to which parents emphasized chores and time use rules contribute any significant effects, and parental discipline is modestly but significantly *negative* in its impact on educational attainment. That this applies more to daughters than to sons suggests that daughters have more leeway to explore the outside world if they enjoy a more permissive atmosphere at home, with fewer restrictions and less punishment for breaking parental rules. Earlier findings to the effect that economics, family size, and family composition affect parental affection are no doubt relevant here—parental affection may be of crucial significance in early childhood—but family structural characteristics are more significant for educational attainment because they either enhance or restrict the opportunities families can provide to their adolescent children.

Our results are consistent with a decades-long tradition in the social sciences that was premised exclusively on the grounds of environmental influence. Researchers took the finding that social class differences in young people's backgrounds affect their adult achievement as evidence that differences in the family environment during the childrearing years enhance or impede the intellectual, educational, and occupational achievements of the offspring for a lifetime. From that interpretation followed the policy recommendation that educators and parents should try as much as possible to rear children the way upper-middle-class, well-educated parents do.

If working-class parents cannot or will not follow such advice, then the schools should provide compensatory experiences for these children. In recent decades, similar compensatory opportunities have been attempted for preschool children also, through Head Start programs and educational TV programs like Sesame Street. This optimistic can-do line of reasoning assumes that most of the variation in behavior—by social class, race, or sex—is environmentally produced, or "socially constructed" in the language of today's postmodernist theories. The consequence has been that social scientists and childrearing "experts" have promised more than they can deliver.

The missing variables that challenge "family socialization effects" are the genetic contributions of parents to their biological children. We transmit many primary individual characteristics to our children that have little to do with our childrearing practices, including skin color, hereditary predispositions toward numerous diseases, eventual height and weight, temperament, and personality. A fundamental error in studies of family effects is not giving due consideration to the fact that the family "environment" includes these and other genetic contributions. Genetic characteristics place limits on the extent to which childrearing practices per se can produce significant departures from the inherent predispositions of a child. As Sandra Scarr explains: "Feeding a well-nourished but short child more and more will not give him the stature of a basketball player. Feeding a below-average intellect more and more information will not make her brilliant. Exposing a shy child to socially demanding events will not make him feel less shy. The child with a below-average intellect may gain some specific skills and helpful knowledge of how to behave in specific situations, but their enduring intellectual and personality characteristics will not be fundamentally changed" (Scarr 1993).

To suggest that shared genes may play an important role in the influence of parents' educational attainment on children's educational attainment does not mean that better-educated parents' financial ability to assure high quality schooling and other cultural advantages such as books and travel are not important contributors to the intellectual curiosity and social skills of children. Studies based on the Wisconsin Longitudinal Study (WLS) have shown that even when the IQ of high school students (tested when they were still in school) is controlled in an analysis of adult occupational status attainment, parents' education and their encouragement of their children's aspirations remain important contributors to their children's success in life (Sewell, Hauser, and Featherman 1976). Our intent here is only to suggest that a desirable degree of caution is appropriate in the interpretation of family socialization effects as purely due to environmental influences; to the extent that parental genes contribute to children's characteristics, there are limitations to the effectiveness of any social or educational program to narrow social class differences or to compensate for the lesser educational performance of children born to poorly educated, less genetically endowed parents. In a later section of this chapter we will return to a discussion of the role of genes in intelligence and personality.

But for now, we turn to the next empirical step in the sequential unfolding of the developmental trajectory—the personality characteristics of our respondents.

Determinants and Correlates of Personality Traits

The MIDUS survey included thirty self-ratings of "how well each of the following describes you" (not at all, a little, some, a lot). Factor analysis yielded six scales similar to those found in personality trait literature. The descriptors for each of the six scales are as follows (see table 7.1 for the psychometric properties of the scales):

> Agency: self-confident, forceful, assertive, outspoken, dominant
> Communion (agreeableness): helpful, warm, caring, softhearted, sympathetic
> Conscientiousness: organized, responsible, hardworking, (not) careless
> Extroversion: outgoing, friendly, lively, active, talkative
> Openness to experience: creative, imaginative, intelligent, curious, broad-minded, adventurous, sophisticated
> Neuroticism: worrying, nervous, moody, (not) calm

As discussed in the introduction to this chapter, these personality traits are known to become established by early adulthood and to show little variation across the life course until very old age. In the MIDUS sample, the only significant correlation of a personality trait with age is neuroticism, which declines with age, but at a modest r of $-.16$. Preliminary analysis of the scales in our survey shows significant sex and educational differences: men score higher than women on agency and openness to experience; women score higher than men on communion, conscientiousness, and neuroticism. Better-educated adults score higher than those with less education on agency and openness to experience. In an analysis focused on predicting adult social responsibility, we have particular interest in agency, communion, and conscientiousness: communion has priority because it taps nurturant and empathic characteristics that would predispose to caring for others in both private and public life, and agency and conscientiousness tap drive and motivation to perform as responsible actors.

A long history of research on sex differences in personality traits has shown significant tendencies for men to score higher than women on agency, and for women to score higher than men on communion (or agreeableness). Several decades ago these two traits often carried the labels of masculinity and femininity rather than agency and communion (e.g., Bem 1981; Spence and Helmreich 1978). Contemporary preference is for the agency/communion labels, in part to avoid reliance on sex stereotypes, and in part to bypass any confrontation with the questions of whether or the extent to which innate biological sex differences are reflected in these personality scales. In today's political climate, charged as it is with sex and gender issues, to speak of men high on communion or women high on agency carries a less pejorative tone than to speak of men high on femininity or women high on masculinity. By the same token, to argue that social responsibility is most likely to be prevalent if adults are high on both communion and agency (nurturance combined with a drive to act upon that nurturance) may be more politically palatable than to argue in favor of androgyny defined as high femininity combined with high masculinity.

For reasons we will explore in the next section, our preference for labeling the scales agency and communion does *not* imply any assumption that sex differences on these personality scales are purely the effect of differential parental socialization of sons versus daughters or broader societal pressure for girls to be nurturant and empathic and boys to be agentic and aggressive.

But let us begin with empirical evidence from the MIDUS survey. There are clearly highly significant sex differences on the two scales, with χ^2s of 65.2 (significant at the .001 level) on the agency scale, and 229.5 (significant at the .001 level) on the communion scale. If we examine the full range of scores on these scales, separately for men and women, another point becomes very clear. As seen in the histograms in figures 7.2 and 7.3, there is far more variation *within* sex than *between*

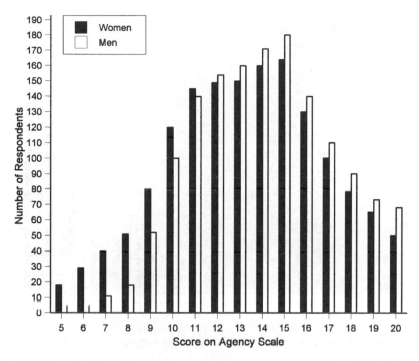

FIGURE 7.2. Case distribution of scores on agency personality scale, by sex. Sex difference is highly significant ($p \leq .001$); mean score for men is 14.0 (SD = 3.1), for women, 13.3 (SD = 3.5).

the sexes. The overwhelming majority of both men and women show a wide distribution of similar scores on both scales. It is at the tails of both distributions that sex differences are most apparent: women exceed men at a ratio of 2:1 at the *low* end of the agency scale and at the *high* end of the communion scale. Note too, that agency scores approximate a normal distribution, whereas scores on the communion scale are heavily tipped to the high end for both sexes. Like parental affection, which we earlier noted was heavily skewed to the high end of that scale (see figure 7.1), the communion scale taps the general tendency of our species toward sociality and empathic concern for others. Love and trust laid down in childhood by parental affection and care have long-term consequences for similar qualities in adulthood. We will test this empirically by positing that high parental affection in childhood and adolescence will be a significant predictor of adult personality traits, in particular communion and conscientiousness.

The fact that there is more variation within sex than between the

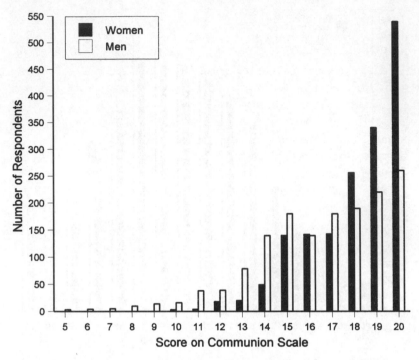

FIGURE 7.3. Case distribution of scores on communion personality scale, by sex. Sex difference is highly significant ($p \leq .001$); mean score for men is 16.7 (SD = 2.6), for women, 18.1 (SD = 2.1).

sexes does not mean small sex differences on a scale are not important in a larger social context. It is a well-known law of normally distributed traits that moderate mean differences may translate into huge differences at the extremes. At issue is a confusion between a population mean and the proportion of that population at selective cutoff points. In many life choices, the extremes are what matter. For example, if a trait is very important for a highly selected occupation, say science or engineering, the pool of potential applicants *is* at the extremes of measures such as agency, spatial rotation, or mathematical ability, with the result that far more men than women will qualify for engineering or scientific training.

The module on early family life in the MIDUS survey did not include any measures on parental differences in socializing their children along sex-stereotypic lines. That we did not include such measures was not an oversight, but was based on a review of the research on this issue. There is no solid empirical evidence that parents treat sons and daughters differently. A major meta-analysis of 172 studies of differential socialization of boys and girls (Lytton and Romney 1991) failed to show any pervasive and significant differences. In samples from North America and other parts of the world, which involved methods varying from direct observation to parent reports and child reports, and with significant variance in the year of publication (with some being unpublished), no differences were found by sex of child across a number of socialization dimensions, including parent-child interaction, encouragement of achievement, warmth, restrictiveness, discipline, or emphasis on clarity and reasoning.

The major significant difference Lytton and Romney found was in studies on the encouragement of sex-typed activities: dolls and art supplies were more frequent choices for daughters, trucks and trains for sons. However, this sex differentiation in parental choice of children's toys may be due to parental compliance with their children's requests far more than any parental imposition of sex stereotypes. An interesting cartoon in an issue of the *New Yorker* magazine a few years ago captured this point in an amusing way: in the cartoon a father observes a daughter cooing to her doll as she beds it down; he urges her to play with a new battery-operated truck he bought for her, only to find her later cooing to the truck as she tucks it into her doll's crib! The only other pattern Lytton and Romney report from a few studies is for sons to receive harsher physical punishment than daughters do. Here too, however, as we noted earlier, harsher punishment of sons than of daughters may reflect greater infraction of rules and more deviant behavior by boys than by girls.

The implication of the meta-analysis results is that personality trait differences between men and women may reflect characteristics they have had from birth, first in infancy as temperamental characteristics, later in development as personality traits. This means that some significant proportion of the personality differences between adult men and women is rooted in biology rather than parental socialization practices. To the extent this is the case, we predicted that any model of family influences on personality traits of children will explain only a small proportion of the variation on such traits, and that despite an array of family variables—parental characteristics, family structure, and child-rearing styles—the sex of respondents will remain an important and significant net predictor of personality trait variation. We will return to this issue in a section to follow on genetic and environmental effects on development.

This is *not* to say that parents have no predictable effects on children's personalities, only to say that the effects will be modest. There is every reason to expect that parents' own qualities of caring and generosity toward others will be mirrored in greater empathy and nurturance on the part of the children they rear. A review of the literature on this topic by Nancy Eisenberg (1992) reports numerous studies showing that parental modeling of altruism and generosity is mirrored in comparable qualities in children. For example, the adults who rescued Jews in Nazi Europe (Oliner and Oliner 1988)and the activists involved in the Freedom Riders movement in the South in the 1960s (Rosenham 1970)described their parents as having unusually high commitments to service and caring for others, as being parents who stood as moral exemplars for their own tendencies. One Freedom Rider activist reported that his father had carried him on his shoulders during the Sacco-Vanzetti parades, another that his father had fought on the side of the Loyalists in the Spanish Civil War, yet another that his mother "felt close to Jesus" and devoted her life to Christian education (Eisenberg 1992, 89). Similarly, the Oliners found that the rescuers of Jews in Europe reported that their parents had preached the universality of ethical standards, which they then incorporated into their own value system and acted out as rescuers of Jews (Oliner and Oliner 1988). John and Beatrice Whiting reported similar findings from cross-cultural analyses to the effect that cultures in which children are routinely assigned responsibilities for others are particularly prosocial societies (Whiting and Whiting 1973, 1975). Based on the findings of studies like these, we predicted that parental generativity and an early family life marked by the importance of religion would be significantly related to high scores on communion among our MIDUS respondents.

Table 7.11 brings together the relevant array of parental and early family characteristics as predictors of four personality traits—agency, communion, conscientiousness, and openness to experience. The major findings from these multivariate regression analyses are as follows:

1. Communion versus agency. Both personality traits are affected by the extent to which the respondents' parents were models of generosity and generativity themselves, showed high affection to their children, and placed a strong emphasis on how the children used their time and contributed to domestic chores. Beyond these shared predictors, however, a different set of factors significantly predict the two personality traits: Agency is enhanced by education, whereas communion is more typical of those with less education. Men are higher on agency, women

TABLE 7.11 Regression of Selected Personality Scales on Family of Origin Characteristics, Respondents' Sex, and Education (beta coefficients)

Variable	Agency	Communion	Conscientiousness	Openness to Experience
Premarital parental characteristics				
Generativity	.064**	.183***	−.004	.097***
Religiosity	−.016	.046*	.050*	.006
Averaged educational attainment	.018	−.025	−.036	.098***
Family structure				
Family composition[a]	−.024	−.053**	.018	−.035*
Sibship size	−.024	.026	−.019	−.019
Respondent oldest child	.015	−.010	.037*	.005
Respondent youngest child	−.063**	−.007	−.029	−.046*
Childrearing patterns				
Parental affection	.066**	.103***	.122***	.032
Parental discipline	.005	−.010	.007	.007
Chores/time-use rules	.131***	.072***	.081***	.102***
Respondent's characteristics				
Sex[b]	−.117***	.260***	.122***	.072***
Educational attainment	.108***	−.046*	.117***	.180***
R^2	.066***	.155***	.059***	.089***
N	2,610	2,614	2,614	2,607

Note: Base is two-parental figure families of origin.
[a] 1 = both biological parents; 0 = other.
[b] 1 = male; 2 = female.
* $p < .05$. ** $p < .01$. *** $p < .001$.

on communion, and judging by the size of the standardized coefficients, sex is *the* strongest predictor of communion, second only to chores/time use rules as a predictor of agency. The importance of religion in the early family predisposes to communion but has no significant relationship to agency.

Birth order has no effect on communion, but those who were the youngest children in their families are slightly less apt to be high on agency. As previously noted, youngest children are less apt to report high levels of discipline and supervision by their parents, with the possible result of less motivation to succeed than oldest children have, as indicated by the higher educational attainment of firstborns. Both John Modell (1997) and Judith Harris (1998, 365–78), among many others, have been highly critical of any claims of birth order effects on personality unless an analysis includes measures on family size and socioeconomic status. Since both measures are included in these equations, and results are consistent with previous tables including birth order, even this modest result on the effect of youngest child status is of interest. Note as well, that youngest children are significantly *less* apt to be high on openness to experience, just the reverse of Frank Sulloway's (1996) claim that lastborn children tend to have rebellious natures and often become creative pursuers of new ideas. In our data set, lastborn children are *less* curious, adventurous, and imaginative than children of other birth order positions.

2. Conscientiousness. A good childhood foundation of parental affection, exposure early on to the religious beliefs of parents, being female, and being an oldest child are the significant predictors of adult conscientiousness. Work habits acquired from carrying responsibility for domestic chores as children combined with high levels of schooling add to the profile of highly conscientious adults. To some, this profile may project an image of the Protestant work ethic, but religious affiliation does not show any relationship to scores on the conscientiousness scale in our data set (data not shown).

3. Openness to experience. Educational attainment is the most significant predictor of high scores on this personality trait, and interestingly both parental educational attainment and respondents' own attainment contribute independently to high scores on this scale. Educated parents who are generous and sociable themselves may provide children with a wider array of social contacts, more sharing of books and ideas, and encouragement of originality, all of which would predispose to the child's motivation in school work and subsequent status attainment. The fact that men score higher on this trait, coupled with the relevance of educational attainment of both parent and child, suggests some genetic predisposition is also a factor in producing high scores on openness: "intelligent" and "curious" are self-descriptors in this scale, proxies in some sense for the high heredity component in intelligence. Across numerous studies, at least *half* of the variation in IQ scores are due to inherited genes. (An excellent review of this literature is a special 1997 issue of the journal *Intelligence*. See especially essays by Plomin and Petrill and by Rowe.)

Despite the inclusion of twelve predictor variables in these equations on personality traits, the amount of explained variance is modest, with R^2s ranging only from .06 to .16. The equations contain some degree of genetic contamination because they are based on biological families only. Even assuming the effects reported are environmental, it is clear from the small amount of variance explained that more than family structure and child socialization is involved in personality development. In the section to follow, we summarize some of the major contributions behavioral genetics has made to understanding the influence of genes on intelligence and personality.

GENETIC AND SOCIALIZATION EFFECTS ON INTELLIGENCE AND PERSONALITY

It is ironic that the amount of behavioral genetics research to show environmental effects *net* of genetic effects exceeds the total of all the social science research presuming to show the great importance of family environmental effects alone (Rowe 1997). Optimal child development clearly depends on an exposure process that provides *opportunities* to learn, but children do not gain equally with each exposure because their genetic endowment affects their *capacity to learn*. What follows is a necessarily brief overview of major findings from thirty years of research in behavioral genetics that illustrates why an adequate theory of development should embrace both genes and environment. (For a useful technical primer on behavioral genetics, see Plomin 1990; for a general overview for the nonspecialist, see Gallagher 1996 and Wright 1998; for detailed overviews of findings relevant to childrearing and personality, see Eaves, Eysenck, and Martin 1989, Rowe 1994, Scarr 1992, Scarr and McCartney 1983, and Wright 1998; and for selected special studies on siblings, adopted children, and twins, see Heath et al. 1992, Hetherington, Reiss, and Plomin 1994, Plomin and Petrill 1997, and Waller et al. 1990.)

The most significant research areas that demonstrate the relative contribution of genes and family environment are twin and adoption studies. If asked whom adopted children are most like in intelligence and personality—their adoptive parents or their biological parents— most sociologists would likely claim that adopted children are "obviously" more like their adoptive parents than the biological parents they have never known. The evidence, however, is just the reverse: adopted children share more characteristics with their biological parents than with their adoptive parents. So too, identical twins reared in separate adoptive families are more like each other than they are like their genetically unrelated siblings.

It is particularly interesting to note that genetic contributions to many individual characteristics *increase* with age. For example, studies of young adoptive siblings, that is, unrelated children brought up together by the same adoptive parents, show a correlation in IQ of about .30, suggesting that almost a third of the variance in IQ is attributable to their shared family environment. But follow-up studies of the same adoptive children years later show a steady *decline* in these correlations. In one such study, the IQ correlation of unrelated children in the same family was .26 at age eight, but ten years later (at age eighteen) the correlation was −.01, suggesting that family environmental effects on IQ decline to negligible levels by late adolescence (Plomin and Petrill 1997). The reason for this decline taps a general developmental process behavioral geneticists have traced: beyond early childhood, individuals actively seek out peers and social environments more to their liking and in accord with their own personality characteristics, a process behavioral geneticists call "niche selection" (Scarr and McCartney 1983). We are all familiar with this phenomenon in a geographic sense, illustrated, for example, by the congregation of beatniks in Greenwich Village in the 1950s, hippies in San Francisco or the backwoods of Marin County in the 1960s. Since the 1960s' Age of Aquarius, thousands have been drawn each year to southwestern meccas in Sedona and Sante Fe (Gallagher 1996). In the 1990s the Northwest began to draw numerous armed survivalists to its sparsely populated mountains and canyons.

Niche selection is also dramatically illustrated in child development. As a preschooler, the young child's social circle is largely restricted to family members and neighborhood playmates, hence limiting the possibility for the child to freely choose with whom to interact and play. Upon school entry, the number of peers expands permitting the child far more ability to select congenial friends. Niche selection that is most apparent among young schoolchildren is their increasing preference for same-sex playmates and friends. Between four and six years of age, there is a sharp increase in the percent of playtime that children spend with children of their own sex, a growing apart of male and female that persists until pubertal changes stimulate a renewed interest in the other sex (Maccoby 1998; Maccoby and Jacklin 1987).

There have been numerous theories to explain this prolonged period of same-sex segregation: different metabolic rates such that boys prefer rougher, more active play; the developmental needs of boys to draw away from mother at an earlier age to acquire a male identity; possibly some genetic programming shared with other primates to prefer different types of play activity. Like other primates, the young human male engages in activity away from the core of the family or troop to engage in male play that prepares him for aggressively seeking a place in the social hierarchy, while the young female remains closer to the core of the family or troop, which prepares her through practice for her distinctive reproductive role in caring for the young. However much kindergarten teachers urge boys and girls to play together, they typically face opposition: the boys try to exclude girls from their fortress building or rough competitive play, whereas girls try to exclude boys from disrupting their dollhouse corners. It has often puzzled observers to note that males and females who grow up in intimate physical association with each other are rarely sexually attracted to each other when they enter adolescence, whether they be siblings in Western societies, unrelated children on an Israeli kibbutz, or affianced young girls in southern China, who live in close contact with their betrothed in their future parents-in-law's household for years before their marriages (Wolf 1995). In the latter example, Arthur Wolf found that this lack of sexual interest at pubescence sometimes resulted in the couple resisting consummation of the marriage and often in low rates of fertility and higher rates of extramarital sex, if not divorce. Eleanor Maccoby extrapolates from such examples to suggest that children's spontaneous avoidance of the other sex and their preference for same-sex groups up to adolescence may serve the biological function of keeping the other sex within the pool of potential mates (Maccoby 1998, 94). Gender segregation among children, like the incest taboo that averts inbreeding, may reflect genetic as well as cultural influences.

Adoption studies have been extremely useful as a corrective against narrowly defined theories of family socialization effects on children. (See Rowe 1994 for a review and critique of studies that presumed to show family socialization effects.) But it is twin studies that permit some actual calculation of genetic contributions to personality traits. In the MIDUS analysis reported above, social variables explained only a small proportion of the variance in personality, leaving room for the influence of genetic factors in some part of the unexplained residual. Estimates of the contribution of heredity in twin studies are premised on the fact that monozygotic (MZ) twins share 100% of their genes, whereas dyzygotic (DZ) twins on average share 50% of their genes. Hence, if the correlation between scores on a trait is higher for MZ twins than DZ twins, the difference is probably due to genetic effects (assuming common environmental sources are roughly the same for the two types of twins). A widely used estimate of the heredity component (h^2) in many personality and behavioral traits is calculated by doubling the difference in intraclass correlations between MZ and DZ same-sex twins (Falconer 1981).

A number of twin studies have found that 40–60% of the variance in personality is explained by heredity. (See Rowe 1994 for an overview and summary of such studies). We do not have to rely merely on other studies, however, because our research network obtained a very large sample of adult twins who completed the same instruments as all our MIDUS respondents. The sample was developed through cooperation with a national polling organization that added one question to each weekly survey they conducted: Are you or is any member of your family a twin? When a twin was located, the interviewers asked for the name and location of the other twin and permission to approach each for a special study. Over the course of only a few months, a large number of twins were identified from such surveys; a short screening questionnaire designed by a behavioral geneticist confirmed zygosity; and cases were selected to provide a balanced age and sex distribution of twins, each of whom responded to the same telephone and self-administered instruments as had all other MIDUS respondents. As a result, we can calculate the heredity component of the personality traits we have been analyzing with identical scales provided by monozygotic and dyzygotic twins. Table 7.12 shows the results of the heredity calculations for four personality traits—agency, communion, conscientiousness, and openness to experience—using the data from close to one thousand cases of twin pairs.

TABLE 7.12 Heredity Component (h^2) of Selected Personality Scales from MIDUS Twin Sample

Scale	Monozygotic	Dyzygotic Same Sex	Opposite Sex	h^2 (%)
Communion	.35***	.12*	.07 n.s.	46
Agency	.45***	.24***	.01 n.s.	42
Conscientiousness	.47***	.20***	.15*	42
Openness to experience	.41***	.24***	.18**	34
N	330–67	307–52	214–62	

h^2 = two times the difference in intraclass correlations between monozygotic and same-sex dyzygotic twins, $2x(MZr - DZr)$. Base Ns vary because correlations were computed using pairwise deletion.

*$p < .05$. **$p < .01$. ***$p < .001$.

Thus, for example, we can determine that monozygotic twins show a significant intraclass correlation on the agency scale of .45, but same-sex dyzygotic twins only .24, with a difference between them of .21. Since monozygotic twins share *all* their genes, but dyzygotic twins only *half* their genes, the heredity component estimate is two times that difference, or 42%. As shown in the last column of table 7.12, the heredity component to all four personality scales ranges from a *third* to *almost half.* Note too that the two scales with the greatest sex difference—agency and communion—are precisely the two scales on which *opposite* sex fraternal twins do not show any significant intraclass correlation.

Not shown in table 7.12 are even higher heredity components to the extroversion and neuroticism scales, with an estimated h^2 of 70% for extroversion, 56% for neuroticism. These estimates are very close to those found in other twin studies (e.g., Heath et al. 1992; Rowe 1994; Rushton et al. 1986). For example, Heath and his associates (1992) reported 73% heritability for extroversion, 63% for neuroticism, in a study of special interest because it relied not only on each twin's own self-ratings but ratings of their co-twins, with good agreement between self reports and co-twin reports on both personality measures.

Rushton and his colleagues (1986) provide particularly interesting data on the genetic component to personality traits based on analysis of adult twin pairs from the University of London Institute of Psychiatry Volunteer Twin Register. Their measures include many multi-item scales from numerous standardized personality trait inventories. Item selection was dictated by their desire to measure several dimensions of two primary constructs, altruism and aggression. Analogous to our communion scale are several of the scales they used to measure prosocial factors: for example, sixteen items on nurturance from the Jackson Personality Research Form (Jackson 1974) (e.g., a positively keyed item, "I often take young people under my wing," or a negatively keyed item, "I don't like it when friends ask to borrow my possessions"); a twenty-item altruism scale based on specific behaviors (e.g., "I have donated blood" or "I have given directions to a stranger"); and a thirty-three-item emotional empathy scale (a typical item being "I like to watch people open presents"). The two major measures selected to tap the broad construct of aggression were twenty-three items on aggressiveness from the Interpersonal Behavior Survey (Mauger and Adkinson 1980) (e.g., "some people think I have a violent temper") and a twenty-four-item assertiveness scale, also drawn from the Interpersonal Behavior Survey (a typical positively keyed item "I usually say something to a person who has been unfair" and a typical negatively keyed item "I rarely criticize other people").

The three prosocial scales are significantly *positively* correlated (e.g., $r = .43$, significant at the .001 level, for altruism and nurturance), somewhat more strongly than the two scales on aggressiveness and assertiveness ($r = .26$, significant at the .001 level). Significant *negative* correlations were reported between the aggressiveness scale and all three prosocial scales (r's of $-.23$, $-.37$, and $-.27$), but much weaker negative correlations between assertiveness and empathy ($-.10$), and actually *positive* correlations between assertiveness and nurturance (.07) and altruism (.30). The positive correlations are of particular interest because our scale on communion is most closely matched with nurturance, and agency, with assertiveness. The MIDUS scales do not tap anything close to the "violent temper" and interpersonal hostility measured by the aggressiveness scale in the British study. By contrast, the combination of assertiveness and altruism is a profile close to that of the rescuers in the Oliner study (Oliner and Oliner 1988) and to that of moral exemplars in Anne Colby and William Damon's study (1992), findings relevant to our hypothesis that individuals who are particularly outstanding in socially responsible behavior in adulthood draw on a combination of warmth and a caring disposition (the communion scale in our MIDUS study, nurturance in the British study), and forceful, purposive action (the agency scale in MIDUS, assertiveness in the British study).

At issue here, however, is the extent to which Rushton and his colleagues found significant evidence of heritability in their five measures of altruism and aggression. Comparing the intraclass correlations of MZ twins with same-sex DZ twin pairs, Rushton reports the following broad heritability estimates: 56% for altruism, 68% for empathy, 70% for nurturance, 72% for aggressiveness, and 64% for assertiveness. These are higher estimates than in the MIDUS personality scales, perhaps due to the far greater number of items in each of the British scales than in the MIDUS scales, and the inclusion of actual social behavior in the British scales (e.g, reports in the British study of actual blood donations or frequency of criticizing other people compared to the self-ratings on descriptive adjectives, e.g., assertive, helpful, outspoken, in MIDUS).

Note, too, that in research on the heritability of personality traits, the amount of variance in individual differences that is explained (40–70%) is far in excess of most published research in professional social science journals, where studies explaining less than 10% of the variance in the phenomenon under study are often considered important contributions to knowledge. To identify the extent to which intelligence, social behavior, or personality traits reflect a genetic predisposition is an important achievement, but much remains to be explored in research on the neurophysiological pathways through which genes operate. Genes only code for the production of proteins. A given genotype has no necessary one-to-one correspondence with a resulting observed phenotype; there is great variation in phenotypes depending on nongenetic influences in the course of human development. One of the tasks of genetic analysis is to explore the probabilistic *limits,* or *reaction range,* in the natural environment and to discover the specific environmental agents that affect position within a given reaction range (Scarr 1992; Scarr and McCartney 1983). Geneticists also warn us that studies of adopted children are limited by the fact that such children are carefully screened before placement, with the result that there has not been sufficient research on the low and high ends of intelligence or personality, extremes at which the environment may play a much larger role (Plomin and Petrill 1997).

The underlying paradigm in behavioral genetics is *not* biological determinism, but rather gene-environment interactions and mutual influences one on the other, a paradigm yet to be accepted by most human developmental scientists, nowhere more so than in studies of parental influence on children. Unlike most social sciences, the biological sciences take an evolutionary perspective. In seeking to understand human behavioral traits, biologists do not limit their focus to the history of just a single ontogeny. In speaking to this point, David Rowe draws a helpful analogy: "One might seek the source of the Nile at the Aswan Dam, forgetting entirely the more than 3500 miles of river upstream reaching into the African continent into what the colonial explorers named the Mountains of the Moon and Lake Victoria. The fallacy [in developmental psychology] is in believing that what forms human nature is the 14-year period of rearing, rather than a heavier weight of cultural history, and ultimately human evolutionary roots" (Rowe 1994, 163).

There is some solace to contemporary parents in this perspective, if they were to realize that evolution has not left the development of our species to the easy mercy of variations in their environments, or to any specific set of rules for human parenting. Humans are adaptive organisms who seek out "niches" congenial to their particular requirements and temperaments. We select environments that suit our predispositions (assuming there are social opportunities to do so) and avoid those that are not suited to us or are too difficult for us. Furthermore, the *upside* of high heritability is that ordinary parents probably have similar effects on their children's development as culturally defined super-parents have. While it is true that the brightest parents are more likely to have brighter children, most of the brightest children in any generation come from parents with average intelligence, for the simple reason that there are so many more average parents, and even with a high degree of assortative mating for ability, husband-wife correlations on IQ show an average correlation of only .35 (Johnson, Ahern, and Coles 1980). In fact Ronald Johnson and his colleagues claim there has been a secular *decline* in assortative mating for ability: spouse correlations on IQ averaged .47 calculated from fourteen samples in the 1928–46 period, but decreased to .29 when calculated from nineteen samples reported in the 1962–79 period. Beyond the genes parents transmit to their children, how children turn out will depend on loving them and providing them with plentiful social opportunities "in a good enough environment that supports children's development *to become themselves*" (emphasis added), as Sandra Scarr urged in her presidential address to the Society for Research in Child Development (Scarr 1992, 15). Our species, after all, would not have survived for long if children were so vulnerable that they could be led off a normal developmental track by slight variations in parenting.

As yet we know relatively little about just how genes work in terms of the neurophysiological processes through which they affect behavior. Genes, after all, do not themselves contain any blueprint for behavior. Through the production of proteins, genes lead to structures in the brain and nervous system, which in turn affect behavior; hence the focus in much recent genetic and neurological research is on hormones and neurotransmitters, neuropeptides that serve as key modulators within the genetically provided emotional operating systems of the brain that coordinate behavioral, physiological, and psychological responses to life events.

In our analysis of the determinants of personality traits, we noted the persistence of sex as a major determinant net of all family and resource characteristics, which raises the question of what it is about the genetic component of sex that produces higher scores for women on communion and for men on agency. The full answer to this question is yet to be revealed, but there are some hints in recent research. A key hormone differentiating men from women is testosterone: adult males have five times the level of free testosterone that women have: on average 99 pg/ml for men, 19 pg/ml for women (Dabbs and deLaRue 1991). In a study of 306 university students that measured aggression and prosocial nurturance and took samples of salivary testosterone, Harris and her associates (1996) report two interesting results: first, for both sexes, testosterone level is positively correlated with aggression (+.32) and negatively correlated with prosocial nurturance (−.39); second, *within each sex,* the higher the testosterone, the higher the aggression and the lower the prosocial nurturance. This in no sense means it is *only* testosterone that plays such a role in the behavior and personality of women and men, because the study could not reveal whether it is testosterone alone or some metabolite of testosterone that is important in mediating these relationships, though it is interesting that both testosterone level and aggressive behavior decline with age, particularly in men. The study more modestly suggests that a multifactorial view of aggression is more appropriate, because both aggression and nurturance are also influenced by prior learning, other developmental influences, and probably other hormones as well.

Two possible supplementary neuromodulators may be serotonin and oxytocin, which evoke positive, warm feelings of comfort and have higher secretion levels in women than in men (Panksepp 1992). Thomas Insel, a psychoneuroendocrinologist, claims that oxytocin (OT) is an important neuropeptide that predisposes to affiliative behavior. It has long been known that a key function of OT is for uterine contractions during childbirth and for milk ejection afterward. Insel extends the involvement of OT to yet another function, mediated within the central nervous system, *social affiliation.* His research evidence is largely from experiments and comparative analyses of mammals other than humans, but he points out that human sexual interactions are also associated with increased OT secretion: for example, OT increases as much as *fivefold* with male ejaculation (Carmichael et al. 1987; Murphy et al. 1987), and lactating women often experience milk ejection during coitus (Fox and Knaggs 1969; Newton 1973). From different streams of research covering behavior, receptor regulation, and comparative neuroanatomy, Insel claims such results "provide a composite picture of OT's role in a variety of mammalian processes that appear behaviorally discrete but are functionally all aspects of social affiliation" (Insel 1992, 4). Whether behavior involves two adults, as in sexual intercourse or other intimate interaction, or an infant and an adult, the end result is that individuals are brought together to form social bonds. One interesting implication is that higher levels of OT in women than in men stimulates women to be strongly motivated to seek intimate social ties with parents, friends, and children, intimate ties that in turn increase OT secretion—an interactive loop between hormones and behavior that is often found in neuroendocrinology.

Animal research has shown that when young mammals are kept in isolation, they show numerous signs of acute distress and separation anxiety which can be alleviated by injection of OT. Mihaly Csikszentmihalyi (1997) reports that being alone is a "downer" for most humans, with apathy, aversive motivation, and sadness increasing with prolonged social isolation. In studies using an Experience Sampling Method (ESM) that involves randomly beeping buzzers to which subjects respond by recording *where* and *with whom* they are and *how they feel* at that moment, people feel *best* when they are with close friends, next best with family, and *worst* when by themselves. It remains for future research to determine the role of OT in sex differences in the extent of nurturance and prosocial affiliative behavior and to determine the effects of social integration versus isolation on women compared to men. Sociality is so fundamental and persistent a characteristic of human and most other primates, it would be surprising not to find that it is influenced and reinforced by numerous biological factors.

One final cautionary note about genetic effects. Properly used, genetics refers very narrowly to DNA differences among individuals that are inherited from generation to generation. It does *not* refer to the vast majority of DNA that is the same for all of us, or to many DNA events that are *not* inherited, such as mutations in DNA in cells other than the sex cells. An organism's phenotype, from behavior to personality to physical appearance, depends on the way its genotype has been expressed in environments that may vary considerably. Environmental change can trigger changes in one's phenotype, just as one's cumulative life history can, so that along with genetic legacy, one's history is encoded in the wiring of the nervous system (Gallagher 1996, 124), not merely in the conscious memories of the past.

We return now to the sequential ordering of predictors of adult social responsibility. In doing so, we first give attention to the effects of early family life and personality traits on religiosity and generativity. Following that we analyze the determinants of normative obligations (obligations to family and close friends, civic obligations, and a general scale on altruism). The last step in our sequential analysis focuses on socially responsible behavior in the domains of family and community. At each stage, we bring forward significant predictors from previous steps in the analysis so that we can test whether there are *direct* or *indirect* effects of the early determinants in the model on actual behavioral indices of social responsibility.

EFFECTS OF EARLY FAMILY AND PERSONALITY ON CURRENT RELIGIOSITY AND GENERATIVITY

In chapter 3 we found that generativity is the most important intervening variable between the demographic variables of age, sex, and education and the several dimensions of social responsibility in the domains of family and community. Now we explore what lies behind these findings as we pose the question of whether early family characteristics make their own contributions to the level of generativity and religiosity reported in adulthood. Because we have already found that religiosity increases in linear fashion with age whereas generativity peaks in midlife, we use an open age code in the multivariate analysis of religiosity, but a dummy age variable for the analysis of generativity, differentiating between middle-aged respondents and the combination of young and old respondents.

Table 7.13 shows two sets of regression equations each for religiosity and generativity: Model 1 is limited to early family variables and respondents' age, sex, and education. Model 2 expands the predictor variables to include personality traits, so we can test whether early family characteristics have *direct* or *indirect* effects on adult religiosity and generativity. If family of origin characteristics have only *indirect* effects, their significance will be minimal when personality traits are introduced in model 2, but if their effects are *direct,* their significance will remain in the model 2 equations.

One primary result of this analysis is readily seen by comparing the coefficients in the model 1 and model 2 equations: the general tendency is for a retention of significance for the effects of early family characteristics on adult religiosity and generativity. In no case does any early family variable lose statistical significance in model 2 compared to model 1. Parental generativity, affection, religious salience, and chore assignment and time use supervision all have direct effects on the level of religiosity and generativity of adult respondents. Adding personality traits increases the overall amount of explained variance modestly for religiosity, with an increase from an R^2 of .237 to .250, and more significantly for generativity, from an R^2 of .107 to .256. Other major findings are as follows:

1. The level of cross-generational transmission of religiosity is strik-

TABLE 7.13 Regressions of Religiosity and Generativity on Family of Origin Characteristics (Model 1) and Family of Origin plus Personality Traits (Model 2) (beta coefficients)

	Religiosity		Generativity	
Variable	Model 1	Model 2	Model 1	Model 2
Parents' premarital characteristics				
Averaged educational attainment	−.087***	−.086***	.030	.033
Religiosity	.352***	.350***	.022	.012
Generativity	.005	−.018	.113***	.049*
Early family life				
Sibship size	.029	.023	.047*	.043*
Parental affection	.107***	.097***	.103***	.054**
Chores/time-use rules	.080***	.077***	.142***	.088***
Demographic characteristics of respondent				
Sex[a]	.159***	.126***	.059**	.011
Educational attainment	−.005	.007	.197***	.176***
Age[b]	.060***	.058**	.072***	.050**
Personality traits of respondent				
Communion	—	.126***	—	.250***
Agency	—	−.025	—	.252***
Conscientiousness	—	−.020	—	.071***
R^2	.237***	.250***	.107***	.256***
N	2,653	2,636	2,652	2,652

[a] 1 = male; 2 = female.
[b] Because generativity has a curvilinear relationship to age, a dummy variable was created for the generativity equation, in which 1 = middle aged (40–59) and 0 = young (25–39) or old (60–74).
*$p < .05$. **$p < .01$. ***$p < .001$.

ing. In model 2, as in model 1, the religious emphasis of parents in early family life is the strongest predictor of current religiosity, as assessed by the size of the standardized beta coefficients.

2. Personality traits are the strongest predictors of respondents' generativity, especially the contributions of agency and communion, slightly less so for that of conscientiousness, thus confirming our prediction that generativity draws on the qualities of a warm and caring personality (indexed by the communion scale) *and* those of a motivated and driven one (captured by the agency scale). Parental modeling of generativity is highly predictive of adult generativity of respondents in model 1, but much reduced in its contribution once personality traits are entered in model 2. In light of our finding in the previous section that communion has a significant heredity component, it may also be the case that the measure of parental modeling of generativity con-

tains a comparable genetic component. There is undoubtedly a socialization factor involved here as well: if parents are generally helpful, friendly, and sociable toward people outside the family, the probability is strong that their children will be exposed to many family, friends, and kin and as a result will early on acquire social skills plus an interest and ability to be helpful toward other people.

3. In previous bivariate analysis, we found that religiosity increases with age, whereas generativity peaks in midlife; the same age effects are shown in multivariate analysis. Net of all other predictors shown, these age effects remain strong and significant.

4. Parental affection and parental emphasis on chores and time use are independent significant predictors of both religiosity and generativity, with or without personality variables in the equations.

5. Women report higher religiosity than men, net of all other predictors of religiosity, and this holds true even when personality measures are taken into account (i.e., the standardized beta coefficient on sex of respondent drops only from .159 to .126, significant at the .001 level, between the two models). By contrast, women score higher than men on generativity only in the model 1 equation. The sex difference in generativity in bivariate analysis is due to women's personality tendency to greater helpfulness and warmth toward others that is caught by the communion scale.

6. Educational attainment plays a different role in predicting religiosity than it does in generativity. Respondents from families with less-educated parents are more religious than those from well-educated families, with no added net effect of their own educational attainment. By contrast, the more education respondents have achieved on their own, the more their generativity is enhanced. Higher education adds to an individual's knowledge base in many subtle and tangible ways that contribute to a sense that one has a lot to offer others as an adult by way of teaching skills, modeling behavior, and providing counseling and advice. Higher education is also a gateway to human service occupations and professions that in turn contribute to an increasing mastery of skills to pass along to others by midlife.

7. Growing up in a large family is more conducive to generativity than growing up in a small family. As noted previously, larger groups require more delegation of tasks, with children from large families routinely contributing to domestic maintenance, which may predispose them to being of help and service to others generally, qualities caught by the generativity scale.

Effects of Early Family, Personality, and Values on Normative Obligations

Following our model of an expanding circle of predictors of adult social responsibility, the next step in the sequential analysis consists of multivariate analyses of the predictors of our three major normative obligation scales—obligations to family and close friends, civic obligations, and altruism. The best-fitting equations predicting variance in these three obligation scales are shown in table 7.14, the highlights of which are summarized as follows:

1. With only a few exceptions, there are no longer direct effects of early family variables; they have been largely absorbed by the inclusion

TABLE 7.14 Regression of Normative Obligations on Respondent Family of Origin Characteristics, Personality Traits and Values, and Demographic Characteristics (beta coefficients)

	Normative Obligation Scales		
Variable	Family	Civic	Altruism
Family of origin characteristics			
Parents' premarital characteristics			
Religiosity	−.012	−.018	−.038
Generativity	.092***	.034	.060**
Averaged educational characteristics	−.023	.026	−.018
Early family life			
Sibship size	−.014	−.019	.024
Parental affection	.067**	.017	.042*
Chores/time-use rules	−.002	.052**	.019
Personality traits and values			
Communion	.164***	.116***	.138***
Agency	−.016	.053**	.018
Religiosity	.041*	.082***	.098***
Generativity	.134***	.138***	.148***
Demographic characteristics			
Married/cohabiting[a]	.061***	.067***	−.004
Number of children reared/rearing	.015	−.073***	−.005
Sex[b]	.123***	.001	.078***
Age[c]	−.135***	.253***	.102***
Educational attainment	−.022	.100***	.061**
R^2	.139***	.156***	.131***
N	2,636	2,636	2,636

[a] 1 = yes; 0 = no.
[b] 1 = male; 2 = female.
[c] 1 = middle-aged; 2 = young or old.
*$p < .05$. **$p < .01$. ***$p < .001$.

of personality traits and values in predicting variation in normative obligations. For example, the effect of growing up in a family that emphasizes the importance of religion has no direct effect on normative obligations, its influence having been absorbed by current religiosity. By contrast, parental generativity and affection remain significant contributors to two of the three normative obligation scales—family obligations and altruism. Once again, this finding is consistent with the possibility that parents' generativity and affection have a component of inherited tendencies toward close attachment to primary group members and to service to others even when at some expense to themselves (the substantive emphasis of the items in the altruism scale). If despite the time-pressured quality of the childrearing phase of life, parents are seen as generous and helpful toward people *outside the family,* children grow up with numerous examples of parents extending themselves to others despite their own work and family responsibilities, thus blurring the boundary between primary family attachments and other people; such exposure may pave the way for a broad predisposition to altruism as defined by our scale—for example, a willingness to contribute time and money to social causes or to collect contributions for heart or cancer research if asked to do so.

2. The communion scale contributes an increment to felt obligation on all three normative obligation scales, whereas agency is significant only to civic obligations. Exercising civic obligations involves *active* engagement in the community, as indexed by voting, serving on a jury, or testifying in court. Adults low in agency may feel uncomfortable in public settings that require an active role in interaction with strangers and casual acquaintances.

3. Despite the inclusion of many sex-linked variables in these equations, sex of respondent remains a significant predictor of normative obligations: women feel more strongly obligated than men to family and close friends and to contributing to the community at some expense to themselves, but the sexes do not differ in level of civic obligations. Age and education also remain significant predictors: young people and those with less education score higher on family obligations, older and better-educated adults score higher on civic obligations and altruism.

Testing the Developmental Model in Contributions to Family and Community

We have now reached the final step in the developmental trajectory model: a test of the extent to which the ground we have covered explains variation in the contributions respondents were making to the two domains of family and community. MIDUS contained six types of variables that are indices of behavioral responsibility to others. Three fall in the family domain: the amount of time devoted to advising and comforting family members, the amount of financial assistance given to nonresident family members, and the amount of time spent in actual hands-on caregiving to nonresident family members. The other three variables fall in the community domain: time devoted to volunteer work, financial contributions made to organizations, causes, or charities, and number of meetings of religious groups, unions or other professional groups, sports or social groups, or any other groups (excluding any required by employers) attended in the course of a month. Hands-on caregiving may be more a function of the need for such help by members of the family and requires living close enough to attend to such needs, which makes it too specialized a measure for our purposes in this analysis. Hence we concentrate on two measures for each of the domains: in the family domain, the time devoted to providing advice or comfort to family members (labeled family support), and the amount of money given to family members; in the community domain, the amount of time spent in volunteer work and the amount of money given to organizations, causes, or charities. Note that only one of these four measures, volunteer work, involves behavior restricted to local residence. Financial aid can be handled by mailing a check to a distant parent or grown child or to an organization or charity, whether local or national. Social and emotional support of a family member can be given by phone or occasional visits; it is not restricted to close proximity of residences.

A few additional words concerning the prevalence of the four behaviors are also appropriate. (See chapter 3 for greater detail.) The most prevalent behavior is providing social support to family members: 96% of the MIDUS respondents report giving *some* support to a family member, ranging from a low of only 84% by old lesser-educated men and a high of 100% by young better-educated women. Financial aid to family members, by contrast, is reported by only 50% of our respondents, the lowest proportion by young better-educated men (37%), the highest by old better-educated men (67%). Social support is twice as prevalent as financial assistance in the family domain.

Just the reverse profile holds for contributions in the community domain: 43% report doing *some* volunteer work, but 71% report making *some* financial contributions to organizations or charities. On volunteer work, the lowest proportion doing some volunteer work is 26% by young lesser-educated men, the highest proportion (55%) by old better-educated women. On financial contributions to organizations or charities, the lowest proportion is by young lesser-educated men (55%), the highest (83%) by old better-educated men. As seen by these figures, men tend to give money more often than women, and women give of their time more than men do. In other analysis (data not shown here) the single instance in which we do *not* find sex differences in social responsibility is in comparing mainline Protestants with Christian fundamentalists. Like the profile shown throughout this chapter, among mainline Protestants, women give more time to both community and family members than men do. Among fundamentalists, by contrast, men are just as likely as women to contribute family support time and volunteer service in the community, a pattern sustained with statistical controls on education and total income. This interesting behavioral pattern is consistent with the teachings of Christian fundamentalist churches that encourage men to be active family members dedicated to service and to the spreading of the gospel to others in their communities (Willmer, Schmidt, and Smith 1998).

There are also differences between the family and community domains in the relationship between giving of time and giving of money: there is a significant correlation between doing volunteer work and contributing financially to organizations or causes ($r = .24$), but in the family domain there is only an insignificant correlation of .05 between giving social support and giving money to family members. The emphasis in our analysis is only on the *giving* of support, not the *receiving* of social support, but it should be borne in mind that those who *give* also *get* in the family domain: the correlation between the two measures of social support is a very high .84. In data analysis not reported here, we found that the profile of predictors of *giving* social support also occurs for *getting* social support from family members. One last point worth noting: there is only a very minor tendency for those who give social support in the family domain to also be active in volunteer work ($r = .07$), but financial assistance is somewhat more likely to characterize both the private domain of family and the public domain of organizations ($r = .18$), the major reason being that giving money is strongly dependent of one's income resources.

The key questions in the analysis to follow are whether and the extent to which early family and personality traits retain any direct effect on socially responsible *behavior* in the domains of family and commu-

TABLE 7.15 Regressions of Time and Money Given in the Family Domain and the Community Domain on Respondent Early Family Characteristics, Personality Traits and Values, Normative Obligations, and Demographic Characteristics (beta coefficients)

	Family Domain		Community Domain	
Variable	Hours per month of support given to family members	$ per month given to family members	Hours per month of volunteer work	$ per month given to causes/ organizations
Family of origin characteristics				
Generativity	.007	−.001	.005	−.017
Parental affection	.003	.039	.019	−.032
Chores/time-use rules	.002	.005	.024	−.014
Sibship size	.013	−.023	.012	.006
Personality traits and values				
Communion	.024	−.001	−.027	−.034
Agency	.033	.015	.030	.004
Religiosity	−.036	.002	.093***	.283***
Generativity	.069***	.068**	.150***	.086***
Normative obligations[a]	.053**	.084***	.059**	.047**
Demographic characteristics				
Married/cohabiting[b]	.171***	−.005	.044*	.111***
Number of children reared/rearing	.092***	.110***	.050**	.022
Sex[c]	.140***	−.070***	.048**	−.088***
Age[d]	−.231***	.075***	−.006	.073***
Educational attainment	−.114***	.081***	.125***	.210***
R^2	.125***	.045***	.077***	.170***
N	2,724	2,721	2,724	2,721

[a] For the family domain, the family obligation scale is entered into the equation; for the community domain, the civic obligation scale is entered.
[b] 1 = yes; 0 = no.
[c] 1 = male; 2 = female.
[d] 1 = middle-aged; 0 = young or old.
$*p < .05.$ $**p < .01.$ $***p < .001.$

nity, or whether their influence is totally absorbed by the intermediary variables of values, norms, and the demographic characteristics of respondents. Table 7.15 provides the four regression equations on time and money contributions in the two domains of life. The most striking point to note in all four equations is that *none* of the family of origin variables and neither of the two personality traits (agency and communion) have any *direct* effects on the four dependent variables involved.

Their influence is totally absorbed by the more proximate variables of values, normative obligations, and demographic characteristics. Other major findings are as follows:

1. High contributions of time in both the family and community domains are given by married women who score high on generativity and normative obligations specific to the relevant domain (family norms and family support time or civic obligations and volunteer time) and who have reared (or are currently rearing) a number of children.

2. The major differences in predictors of time given to family compared to time given to volunteer service are these: in family domain, high supporters are young adults with limited education; by contrast, in the community domain it is better-educated adults and those with high scores on religiosity who engage in significantly more volunteer work than those with lesser education or lower scores on religiosity.

3. Financial contributions show a profile in both the family and community domains similar to time commitments in the effect of religiosity, generativity, and normative obligations. The major differences in financial aid compared to social support are sex, age, and education: in the family domain, men and older adults take the lead in giving money, women and younger adults in giving time to family members; in the community domain, it is the well educated who predominate in *both* volunteer work and financial contributions.

The fact that being married and having a large family are significant predictors of time contributions suggests that an enlargement of other indicators of *social embeddedness* will increase the amount of variance in the time estimates we can explain: this includes frequency of contact with family, kin, and friends and attendance at religious services, all of which involve primary groups and social interaction in the context of which social and emotional support can be expressed. In addition, we add three factors that represent potential *constraints* on helping behavior: the total hours respondents spend on the jobs they held, the hours devoted to domestic chores at home, and since poor health might limit helping behavior, current health status. The results appear in table 7.16.

The addition of the new social embeddedness and constraint variables increases the R^2s in the equations in table 7.16 compared to those in table 7.15: in family domain, from .125 to .145, and in the community domain, from .077 to .110. The inclusion of contact frequency with family, religious service attendance, and domestic chores—all sex-linked variables—reduces the significance level of respondent's sex from a coefficient of .140 (significant at the .001 level) in table 7.15 to

TABLE 7.16 Regressions of Time Devoted to Family and Friends and Volunteer Work on Values, Social Embeddedness, and Constraints on Helping Behavior (beta coefficients)

Variable	Family and Friends (Hours per month of social-emotional support)	Volunteer Work (Hours per month of volunteer work)
Values		
Generativity	.074***	.141***
Religiosity	.026	−.018
Normative obligations[a]	.056**	.069**
Social embeddedness		
Married/cohabiting[b]	.001	.013
Number of children reared/rearing	.072**	.074**
Frequent contact with family/kin	.084***	−.017
Frequent contact with friends	.027	.101***
Frequent religious service attendance	−.092**	.155***
Potential constraints on helping		
Health status[c]	−.023	−.013
Total hours employed per week	.020	−.075**
Total hours of domestic chores per week	.200***	.041
Demographic characteristics		
Sex[d]	.048*	−.010
Age[e]	−.231***	−.046
Educational attainment	−.094***	.118***
R^2	.145***	.110***
N	2,886	2,886

[a] Family norms scale in family and friends equation, civic obligations scale in volunteer work equation.
[b] 1 = yes; 0 = no.
[c] Scale range = 1–10 (poor to excellent).
[d] 1 = male; 2 = female.
[e] 1 = middle-aged; 0 = young or old.
*$p < .05$. **$p < .01$. ***$p < .001$.

only .048 (significant at the .05 level) in table 7.16; age and education remain essentially the same, with young adults and the less well educated putting in more hours in family support and the better educated doing more volunteer work. Several other findings have special interest because they relate in very different ways to time committed to family compared to community:

1. High frequency of social interaction with family increases time devoted to social-emotional support, but in the community domain, frequency of contact with friends and religious service attendance are the predictors of time devoted to volunteer service. For some adults,

interaction with friends can stimulate becoming involved in community affairs, and providing volunteer service may in turn be a route to enlarging one's friendship circle. In a similar way church attendance can stimulate volunteer service, as Robert Wuthnow's research has shown, and involvement as a volunteer, especially in religious groups, may enhance religious attendance (Wuthnow 1991, 1994).

2. The profile of constraint variables shows that the more hours adults spend on the job significantly reduces volunteer time. By contrast, the more hours spent on domestic chores, the *more*, not *less*, *time* is spent listening to and providing support to family and friends. Since hours on the job is controlled in these equations, time spent at home doing domestic chores means greater accessibility by phone and casual visits from both family members and friends. Health status had no effect.

One last empirical question remains: Are there different clusters of variables that predict one type of volunteer work from other types of service? The MIDUS instrument requested separate time estimates for volunteer work of four types: health-related volunteer work, school- or youth-oriented work, work for political organizations and causes, and any other type of service for an organization or charity. We regressed the same set of predictor variables shown in table 7.16 on each of these four types of volunteer work. Table 7.17 does not produce the full detail of coefficients and their significance for the four equations; rather, we rank the predictor variables by the size of their standardized beta coefficients and describe them in terms of the direction of their effects. This procedure simplifies comparisons across the four types of volunteer service.

High generativity is the only predictor variable that is significant in all four types of volunteer service. Frequent religious service attendance is a significant predictor of all but political volunteer work, a finding consistent with a *U.S. News and World Report* survey on volunteerism that reported 56% of adult volunteers said it was important to them that their services have a "spiritual basis" (Gerson 1997). Both political volunteer work and the residual "other" category clearly recruit participants from among the well-educated members of the community who score high on civic obligations. Age shows an interesting profile familiar to anyone who has visited hospitals or voted at election time: in both contexts, one quickly becomes aware that the volunteers are largely older adults and, in health facilities, largely women. In sharp contrast, the volunteers one encounters at a PTA meeting or youth

TABLE 7.17 Significant Predictors of Time Devoted to Volunteer Work, by Type of Organization or Cause, Ranked by Size of Standardized Beta Coefficients

Hospital or Other HEALTH-Related Volunteer Work	School or Other YOUTH-Related Volunteer Work	Volunteer Work for POLITICAL Organizations or Causes	Volunteer Work for Any OTHER Organization, Cause, or Charity
*** Older adults	*** Younger adults	** High generativity	*** Frequent contact with friends
** Women	*** Large family	** High civic obligations	*** Frequent religious service attendance
** High generativity	*** Frequent religious service attendance	* Older adults	*** Well educated
* Frequent religious service attendance	*** High generativity	* Well educated	*** High generativity
	** High domestic chores		*** Shorter work week
	** Less well educated		* High civic obligations

Note: Variables in the four equations that were not significant in any type of volunteer service: marital status, frequency of contact with family members, and current health status.

$* p < .05.$ $** p < .01.$ $*** p < .001.$

group are apt to be young adults, both men and women, particularly if they have a large family, and among women, if they devote a relatively large amount of time to home care.

CONCLUSION

We have covered considerable ground (and many pages!) in the analysis of the developmental trajectory of adult social responsibility. We provide an overview of our major findings in figure 7.4, which charts the significant *direct* effects between variables associated with one or another stage of development. This figure highlights only the major substantive variables in the developmental model, excluding any status, family structure, or demographic variables, which are summarized and discussed below. Had the design of MIDUS been limited to concurrent variables, we would have demonstrated that high levels of religiosity, generativity, and family and civic obligations are the primary determinants of the time committed to social support and financial assistance to family members and of the amount of volunteer service and financial contributions to organizations, causes, and charities.

The major contribution of retrospective measures on the family of origin is the provision of considerable *depth* to the developmental model by showing what lies behind and contributes to the concurrent ratings. As highlighted in figure 7.4, there are qualities associated with early family life that contribute to the developmental trajectory of adults who show high levels of social responsibility, including qualities respondents' parents brought to their marriage: high educational attainment, religious commitment, and the capacity for sociability and generosity to others (kin, neighbors, friends). These background characteristics of the parents are conducive to increased capacity to show love for and build trust in their children, to assign some responsibility for domestic chores to their youngsters, to supervise their use of time, and to set standards for their performance at school as at home. Families of origin with these qualities pave the way for the children to enter adulthood with compassionate concern for others, agreeable and nurturant personalities, and self-confidence sufficient to be active and assertive in dealing with the social worlds they participate in and provide service to.

From the demographic characteristics of the MIDUS respondents, we have also shown both status and life course predictors of numerous variables that entered the developmental model. Adults who have had fewer years of schooling tend to limit their contributions to others to

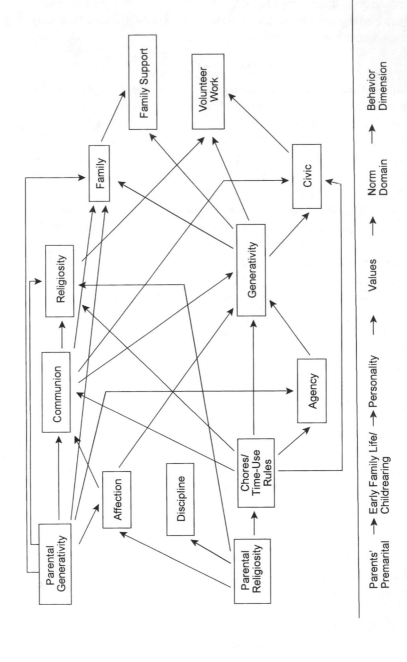

FIGURE 7.4. Developmental trajectory of predictors of adult social responsibility, extracted from tables 7.7, 7.8, 7.9, 7.11, 7.13, 7.14, and 7.15. Only predictor variables with direct effects significant at $p \le .01$ or $p \le .001$ are shown.

Parents' → Early Family Life/ → Personality → Values → Norm → Behavior
Premarital   Childrearing   Domain   Dimension

the primary worlds of family, friends, parish, and neighborhood, whereas better-educated adults move in an expanded circle of social contacts that involves inducements to community level participation, reflecting the deeper knowledge of the world and of the obligations of citizenship acquired during their college years. It is also highly likely that the occupations college graduates enter are themselves conducive to concern for the community and to active participation in community organizations. Indeed, numerous corporations and nonprofit organizations require some degree of community participation as part of the job requirements for managers and professional staff. In addition, many better-educated adults work in occupations in which the content of their jobs is more directly experienced as a contribution to society, such as teaching, nursing, social work, and numerous types of human service work in private and governmental social agencies. Paid work that is defined by adults themselves as their major contribution to society is well illustrated in the chapters of this volume by Kathy Newman and Anne Colby.

Sex of respondent has been a major variable at all stages of the developmental analysis. We have suggested that both genetic and social factors are intricately involved in sex differences. On genetic grounds, we noted the large heredity component of personality traits, and interestingly, the lack of any significant correlation between *opposite* sex fraternal twins compared to *same*-sex fraternal twins on the two scales that most sharply differentiate men from women—agency and communion. Even in the final multivariate regression analyses that included many sex-linked variables, respondent's sex remained a significant predictor. The only exceptions to this pattern are Christian fundamentalists, among whom men contribute as much time to social support of family members and community volunteer work as women do.

A systems approach to developmental analysis assumes complex gene-environment interactions, which in this instance suggests that within the range of sex-linked genetic factors, there may still be strong social pressures for women to contribute in different ways than men in both the family and the community. There is room in this perspective for *compulsory altruism* on the part of women who are often subjected to community and family pressure to contribute to caregiving even when that is actually against the grain of their own preferences. If a parent with both a grown son and a grown daughter is terminally ill and requires hands-on caregiving, it is typically the daughter who is expected to provide such care rather than the son; elderly adults who

303

have a son but no daughters often rely as much or more on their daughter-in-law as on their son.

Men's roles in a community, Carol Heimer suggests, are often *opportunities* to enhance their own social status, whereas women's roles are more often *fates* that preclude individual choice and require specific women to occupy them (Heimer 1996). Men may experience the same social pressure that women do, but it is more likely to be pressure to make financial contributions than to serve as volunteers; recruiters often assume that men's roles as primary breadwinners preclude their serving as volunteers. Then too, many men feel less inclined to serve as an ordinary volunteer because they view such work as relatively low in status; by contrast, they are more likely to respond positively if recruited to serve in some significant capacity as an officer of an organization or as a head of a charitable drive. We set forth many examples of the differences in the responsibilities men and women carry in several chapters in this volume, particularly in chapter 8 on the impact of family problems on social responsibility and in chapter 11 on the effects of work and family on community service.

We have also argued that there are tendencies rooted in our genetic legacy that contribute to adult social responsibility: as a species, humans have evolved to be social and cooperative creatures, more than other primates because our large brains require postponement of much brain and organ development to the vulnerable months of early infancy, which in turn calls for a high order of parental investment in rearing the young on the part of both men and women. In the course of this evolution, we became equipped with emotions that predispose us to feel guilt when we are not cooperative and trustworthy and to be quick to identify those who are *not* trustworthy. (See Ridley 1996 for a detailed exploration of this position on the origins of virtue and cooperation.) The same social predisposition leads us to be concerned that we earn good reputations in the eyes not only of those intimately related to us, but of those we encounter in the workplace and in the larger community as well. This was undoubtedly more readily achieved during the countless millennia during which humans lived in relatively small groups, rarely in excess of 150 individuals. Today the expanded circle of cooperation extending beyond the family is more often found in small communities where everybody knows their neighbors. However, even in today's congested metropolitan areas, it is very likely that we behave in more civil and kindly ways in our residential suburban communities than in the anonymous world of the central city. Matt

Ridley (1996) suggests that no one would drive wildly or make obscene gestures to other drivers on the familiar streets of their suburban neighborhood the way that many do on a highway or on the crowded downtown streets of a large city.

From an evolutionary perspective, the general contours of the developmental trajectory we have shown in this chapter come as no surprise. What this perspective alerts us to is the possibility that we have posed the wrong question. We should not ask what causes socially responsible behavior, but what prevents the flowering of such behavior. If most of our evolution took place in small groups in which cooperative behavior was adaptive, then the question becomes what dampens or damages this innate predisposition of human beings to be cooperative, sociable, compassionate beings? It is doubtful that cross-sectional surveys, even one like MIDUS that included retrospective questions about early family life, are up to the task of answering such a question empirically; the answer may require analysis at a macro-level of societal and historical trends rather than in the life histories of individuals. Had we included measures in MIDUS that tapped antisocial behavior (e.g., arrest history, life-threatening risk taking, unkindly or cruel acts), our interpretation of the survey results would still limit us to individual life histories and therefore would not be adequate to answer macro-level questions such as the one posed above.

Before pursuing this question further, let me be frank to admit that even posing such a question has come hard to someone like myself who was trained in the traditions of sociological survey research, perhaps uncritically assuming that there was not much that a clever survey analyst could not design for and investigate empirically. But a macro-societal level of interpretation is not readily possible with representative samples of a national population. Furthermore, like most social scientists, I have long been of a secular liberal persuasion that tends to exclude any great array of measures on religious beliefs. It was this background that left me unprepared to find how significant religiosity turned out to be in the analysis of the MIDUS data. Indeed I came close to not including even one measure on religiosity in the design of the MIDUS module on the family of origin, because there was no suggestion in my readings on child development that religious and spiritual values might be important precursors of adult social responsibility. Yet now I must be open to the view espoused by William Damon, editor-in-chief of the four-volume *Handbook of Child Psychology* (1998), that the MIDUS findings on the importance of religion in the family of origin would be "replicated many times over if social scientists were not so leery of including the benighted notion of religiosity as a variable in their research with children" (Damon 1995, 82). Indeed, in one of the rare landmark studies of children's adaptation to difficult circumstances, religiosity was the *only* nonnegative quality that protected children from risk (Garmezy 1983); all the other protective factors were the "absence" of something—for example, drug use, hormonal imbalance, or parental conflict. It may be as true of research on adults as of that on children that religious bodies are neglected; as Garry Wills puts it, "it seems careless for scholars to keep misplacing such a large body of people" (Wills 1990, 15)

Our finding that religious values held by adults are significantly related to their normative obligation levels and actual behavior in caregiving, social support, and community service provides further evidence of the role played by religiosity in encouraging adult social responsibility. To those with deep religious commitments, our findings may provide empirical confirmation of the social value of their belief in the goodness and dignity of all human beings as God's creatures, a tradition that carries with it an obligation to love, respect, and serve other human beings. Indeed, many contemporary religious scholars (e.g., Browning 1995) believe that religious traditions not only support a natural moral order that grows out of basic affective ties of humans to their family members but also emphasize the importance of service to others that transcends the family and involves the expanding circle of social networks within which we live out our lives.

To those of a secular persuasion, it is difficult to believe that religion is the only possible source of a belief system that honors the dignity of human persons or provides the only basis in terms of which to value generosity, compassion, and an obligation to serve our fellow creatures. Indeed, our Western liberal theories have their origins in the reaction to the terror unleashed in Europe by the religious wars that followed in the wake of the Protestant Reformation. The founding fathers were as concerned for avoiding religious factionalism as for assuring freedom of religious expression. The major three democratic values underlying the American Constitution—freedom, equality, and mutual respect— have their roots in both liberal theory and religious beliefs. But instead of a state religion, what developed in the early days of the American republic was a civic religion and a civic piety, often invoked by language directly from Protestant Christianity, though couched vaguely by reference to "providence" rather than to "Jesus Christ our Lord." Ronald

Thiemann makes the point that "the peculiar version of civil religion that grew up in American soil was a form of nonchristological theism that relates the history and destiny of the nation to divine providence," as revealed in the national emphasis on our "manifest destiny" that for so long underlay the self-righteous foreign policy of the United States (Thiemann 1996, 31).

The complex role that religion plays even in our day can be seen in recent East European history. On the one hand, in East Germany, Czechoslovakia, Hungary, and Poland, the churches provided a safe haven within which people could think and act in ways not sanctioned by their Communist governments; the churches were in effect "cells of resistance to the totalitarian regimes" (Thiemann 1996, 153–54). On the other hand, after the collapse of Communism in these East European countries, the Christian churches contributed to the rise of anti-Semitism and anti-Islamic sentiments in the emerging ethnic republics. It is not yet clear to what extent this scapegoating and xenophobia is a result of the inevitable insecurity attending the transition from total dependence on the state to what is for them unprecedented demands for personal economic responsibility, a pattern familiar in our own history as evidenced by the anti-immigrant sentiment that accompanied shrinking job opportunities after World War I, and again in more recent years.

This is in no sense to denigrate the vast array of good works that religious groups continue to engage in, involving hundreds of thousands of individuals dedicated to helping others in need and thereby fulfilling themselves through human service consistent with their understanding of what their religion requires of them. Church membership and attendance among mainline Protestants and Catholics have plummeted since their peaks in 1959, but Christian fundamentalism has spread enormously over the past several decades, not only through formal churches but through a vast network of what are now called *parachurches,* supplementary institutions in the religious domain similar to the paramedical and paralegal supplements to the professions of medicine and law. The presence of four criteria define a parachurch: organized as a nonprofit; espousal of a Christian mission statement; independence of traditional church structures; and fulfillment of one or more specific ministries or services, for example, camps, foreign missions, social services, relief efforts, media, publishing, or private schools (Willmer, Schmidt, and Smith 1998). Scholars who have studied the parachurch movement argue that for centuries Christians were comfortable with an understanding that God works in this world only through the traditional church and its numerous denominations, but for the past half-century parachurches have become necessary to meet the challenges of a secularizing postmodern age and do so by moving into the many channels of society. As Wesley Willmer puts it: "No church is able to provide all the resources needed to sustain a Christian in this postmodern age" (Willmer, Schmidt, and Smith 1998, 9).

Numerous indicators of parachurch growth include the distribution by Gideons International of some 38 million Bibles in 70 languages to 158 countries and the Billy Graham crusades that have reached 100 million people in person, 2 billion on television. Included among parachurches are the 19,000 church-affiliated schools and the 8000 to 9000 Christian bookstores in the United States. Many parachurch organizations are large, national, and international such as Youth for Christ or World Vision International. That church attendance has declined is no barometer of a loss of interest in worship, since Christian Broadcasting radio stations and TV channels permit participation, if from a distance, in a worship service before getting on with one's Sunday morning golf game or work in the garden. Some estimates suggest that almost *half* of the money given to religious bodies in the United States goes to such parachurch organizations rather than to the traditional churches or denominations (Barrett 1997).

Parachurch growth is not just a contemporary phenomenon. The Civic Engagement Project at Harvard University has amassed a large set of archival data tracing the emergence, development, and duration of thousands of voluntary associations and organizations from 1790 to the present time, and analyses now being published report a large proportion of such associations involved religious commitments (Skocpol 1992; Skocpol and Fiorina 1999). Nor were such organizations in the past merely local or totally independent of government, as some contemporary conservatives have claimed (Olasky 1992). Those that lasted for any length of time tended to become three-tier organizations at the local, state, and national levels, often working closely with public agencies and legislatures at the state and national level. The same close working relationship between government and religiously based charitable organizations is characteristic of the national scene today. Unfortunately one of the prices paid by religiously affiliated charities that apply for public funds has often been to shed themselves of precisely the religious aura and program content that motivated their development in the first place because of, for example, federal requirements that no religious services be conducted on their premises or that they not limit their staff of paid employees and volunteers to those of a particular religious persuasion.

These are impressive achievements by the array of religious organizations and churches even in the most advanced superpower in the world at the turn of the twenty-first century. But the growing edge represented by Christian fundamentalism is premised on four central beliefs difficult for secularists, liberals, and moderate conservatives to accept in light of scientific knowledge: (1) biblical literalism, or *inerrancy*—that is, the idea that every word in the Bible is the voice of God; (2) personal transformation through being reborn—"except a man be born again, he cannot see the Kingdom of God"; (3) evangelical commitment—that is, an obligation to try to convert others to the faith; and (4) apocalypticism, a belief in an "end time," including evil and destruction attending the premillennium as a stage on the way to a postmillennial era that believers assume will show an enlargement of the human to embrace the divine (Strozier 1994). Only one in four Americans are Christian fundamentalists, but national polls continue to report that four in five Americans believe Jesus is the son of God, that they will appear before God on judgment day, and that God works miracles (Gallup and Castelli 1989). Far fewer—40%—believe in biblical literalism.

Christian fundamentalism in the twentieth century, and in particular as it has grown in the United States, is far more nostalgically oriented than are developments in mainstream liberal Judeo-Christian theology. As far back as the Enlightenment, many liberal theologians sought to accommodate theism with a more rationalist view of the material world and did so by moving away from a view of God as a literal person and toward a conception of God as a transcendent substance or spirit present everywhere in the universe. Such a depersonalization of God has continued steadily into the modern era, moving in a direction foreseen by Baruch Spinoza in the seventeenth century—"Deus sive natura"—God and nature are interchangeable. This view, so sharply in opposition to the views of contemporary fundamentalists, suggests even more profound sectarian differences in the domain of religion than exists between liberals and conservatives in the political domain: a "crazy quilt" religious map indeed, as Martin Marty describes the complexity of religion in America (Carroll, Johnson, and Marty 1979).

Christian fundamentalism apart, the major religions have given up ground to science over the centuries since the Enlightenment. Most

American Catholics no longer accept papal infallibility, and their sexual and social attitudes and behavior no longer differ markedly from mainline Protestants, with comparable rates of premarital sex, cohabitation, abortion, and divorce. Indeed, William D'Antonio (1999) has shown that young Catholics today are more prochoice in abortion attitudes than young Protestants are, and three-quarters of young Catholics believe the Pope deserves respect but that individuals should follow their own conscience even if it disagrees with papal teaching. In our national survey, Catholics were just as likely as mainline Protestants or Jews to *agree* that "single parents can rear children just as well as married adults" and that "women can have full and happy lives without marrying" and to *disagree* with the view that "to grow up emotionally healthy, children need to be raised in an intact family with both parents." Only fundamentalists took the more traditional view on such issues in our survey.

A recent book by Stephen Jay Gould, *Rocks of Ages* (1999), claims that there is no need for any acute separation between the magisteria of religion and science, but his argument is based on the assumption that "facts" and "theories" of natural life are solely in the domain of science, while religion is restricted to a search for the "meanings" and "goals" of human lives. To do so on Gould's terms, however, would require that religion be stripped of all traditional meanings, that Christians abandon the genesis story and their beliefs in Jesus as the son of God, the virgin birth, the resurrection, and an afterlife in heaven. But the empirical sciences have already undercut most transcendentalist beliefs and continue to do so at a quickened pace in recent years. As E. O. Wilson puts this point, "the spirits our ancestors knew intimately first fled the rocks and trees, then the distant mountains. Now they are in the stars, where their final extinction is possible" (Wilson 1998, 264). As modern men and women increasingly view our earthly planetary habitat as a tiny "pale blue dot" (Sagan 1994) in a swirling mass of billions of galaxies, in what dimension of time and space can a heaven figure in such a vision?

Though sharing the same background in science, Stephen Gould sees no possibility of a religious answer to such a question, but Edward Wilson does mark the way to one. Wilson argues that we cannot live without a sacred narrative. Humans will refuse to yield to the despair of animal mortality; we need a sense of a larger purpose in one form or other, however intellectualized. But let his words speak for themselves:

If the sacred narrative cannot be in the form of a religious cosmology, it will be taken from the material history of the universe and the human species. That trend is in no way debasing. The true evolutionary epic, retold as poetry, is as intrinsically ennobling as any religious epic. Material reality discovered by science already possesses more content and grandeur than all religious cosmologies combined. The continuity of the human line has been traced through a period of deep history a thousand times older than that conceived by the Western religions. Its study has brought new revelations of great moral importance. It has made us realize that *Homo sapiens* is far more than a congeries of tribes and races. We are a single gene pool from which individuals are drawn in each generation and into which they are dissolved the next generation, forever united as a species by heritage and a common future. Such are the conceptions, based on fact, from which new intimations of immortality can be drawn and a new mythos evolved (Wilson 1998, 265).

Implicit in this perspective is the expectation that an eventual resolution of the competition between science and religion will be not merely the secularization of the human epic and of religion itself, but the development of a sacred ethos and poetry that honor the human story and human interdependence with all other earthbound creatures.

Neither Stephen Gould nor Edward Wilson seem aware of changes already taking place within theological circles in recent years. In both Protestant and Catholic theology, there has been a strong current of new ideas about the Christian life, perhaps best illustrated by changes in the image of God from that of hierarchal lawgiver and judge to a conception of God as spirit, present everywhere like one's own breathe inside oneself, and the wind external to oneself, a nonmaterial reality both outside and within us. In theological terms, God as spirit evokes both transcendence and nearness or immanence. In this view, a Christian life is not about pleasing a finger-shaking and judgmental God or being good for the sake of heaven later, but about entering a relationship in the present, an opening of the heart to a God that is already here.

In my limited reading of this trend in the theological literature, perhaps best illustrated by the work of Marcus Borg (1994, 1997), "creation" itself looks very different: it is not something that happened once and for all in the past, "in the beginning" as told in Genesis, but an ongoing process, a theological concept fully consistent with evolutionary theory in biology. Also consistent with evolutionary theory is the premise that human beings are fundamentally social creatures, equipped with emotions to feel and show generosity and altruism toward each other. In this view, generosity and acts of giving help to others is not some human invention that shapes and determines our nature. It is our nature to be generous and sociable, an innate predisposition that societies either permit to flourish or attempt to curb in favor of self-serving competition.

Sin also undergoes a fundamental change once the image of God changes from the finger-shaking judge, king, or lord to an image of God as nurturant spirit, friend, or lover: rather than seeking forgiveness or asking for material goods of some kind, prayer and meditation involves basking in a warm relationship and experiencing grace. Consequently, sin becomes not the infraction of rules or commandments, but the absence of compassion in our interaction with others.

I infer from the changes taking place in theology that there is already a head start toward a rapprochement between religion and science within religious circles. This trend is not restricted to theological seminaries. Pressure from the laity for more participation in church decision making is consistent with these changed images, as indexed by the attitudes of young Catholics, the majority of whom support the ordination of women and a greater role for the laity in the selection of priests for their parishes (D'Antonio 1999). Indeed, Marcus Borg argues that the emergence of feminist theology, well illustrated by Elizabeth Johnson's book *She Who Is: The Mystery of God in Feminist Theological Discourse* (1992), is the single most important development in theology in his lifetime. As Borg puts it, "how can women be in the image of God if God cannot be imaged in female form?" A telling personal anecdote reveals much about the roots of his own revised image of God from patriarchal to a nurturant figure. Borg's wife is an Episcopal priest, and he watched her in her role distributing the bread of the Eucharist one Sunday morning: "Among the people kneeling at the altar rail was a four-year-old girl, looking up expectantly at my wife's face as she bent down to give her a piece of bread. My wife has a beautiful face and a wonderful smile. As I watched the little girl, I suddenly wondered if my wife's face was filling her visual screen and being imprinted in her mind as an image of God, much as the face of the male pastor from my childhood had been imprinted in mine. And I was struck by the difference: an image of God as a male authority figure shaking his finger at us versus an image of God as a beautiful loving woman bending down to feed us." (Borg 1997, 71). Concern for relationships, intimacy, and closeness marks not only feminist theology, but work by women scholars in numerous fields—Carol Gilligan (1982) and Jean Baker Miller (1986) in psychology, Nel Noddings (1984, 1989) in moral philosophy, and Carol Heimer and Lisa Staffen (1998) in sociology are prime examples.

There is yet another important point to note: most of the Protestants in the MIDUS sample belong to mainline denominations. We know nothing of what their particular churches are like, who their clergy are, or what the sermons that they have listened to over the years contain. But the sheer overall finding of our analysis that shows how significant religiosity and church attendance is for the extent to which they have been caring adults in their families and participants in community efforts to help others alerts us to the possibility that they have an internal image of God and a religious belief that may be much closer than we can know to the image of God reflected in the work of theologians like Marcus Borg. Church-going Americans are sometimes faulted for not knowing very much about biblical stories, but such knowledge may not be very significant in their religious experiences: they may redefine sacred rituals, prayers, and hymns with meanings special to them, relying on the rituals only as aids to opening the heart, experiencing grace, feeling at peace with themselves and others in their congregations and beyond.

Of far greater concern is the very limited knowledge Americans have of science, in particular the biological and neurosciences and modern evolutionary theory in these fields. We remain as a culture too ill-informed about science, still "Paleolithic thrill seekers preferring *Jurassic Park* to the Jurassic Era, and UFOs to astrophysics" (Wilson 1998, 268) One can hardly predict the emergence and acceptance of a new sacred ethos and new poetry celebrating the mystery and wonder of the universe and of the place of human beings in their biosphere in the absence of an adequate understanding of science. But here, I believe, is the road to travel so that at some future time in the twenty-first century when another MIDUS study is launched, our descendants may draw inspiration and commitment as responsible adults from our own evolutionary past and view their highest priority to be leaving our pale blue dot of an earth in greater health and beauty than they found it in their youth.

References

Alwin, D. F. 1990. Historical changes in parental orientations to children. In *Sociological studies of childhood,* ed. N. Mandell and S. Cahill, 3:65–86. Greenwich, CT: JAI.

———. 1996. Parental socialization in historical perspective. In *The parental imperative in midlife,* ed. C. Ryff and M. Seltzer, 105–67. Chicago: University of Chicago Press.

Alwin, D. F., and A. Thornton. 1984. Family origins and the schooling process: Early versus late influence of parental characteristics. *American Sociological Review* 49: 784–802.

Baltes, P. B., U. Lindenberger, and U. M. Staudinger. 1998. Life-span theory in developmental psychology. In *Theoretical models of human development,* ed. R. M. Lerner, 1029–44. Vol. 1 of *Handbook of child psychology,* ed. W. Damon. New York: John Wiley and Sons.

Barrett, D. 1997. Annual statistical table on global mission: 1996. *International Bulletin of Missionary Research* 18:23–24.

Baumeister, R. F., and M. R. Leary. 1995. The need to belong: Desire for interpersonal attachments as a fundamental human motivation. *Psychological Bulletin* 117:497–529.

Bem, S. L. 1981. *Bem sex role inventory.* Palo Alto, CA: Consulting Psychologists Press.

Blake, J. 1989. *Family size and achievement.* Los Angeles: University of California Press.

Blau, P. M., and O. D. Duncan. 1967. *The American occupational structure.* New York: John Wiley.

Borg, M. 1994. *Meeting Jesus again for the first time.* San Francisco: Harper.

———. 1997. *The God we never knew: Beyond dogmatic religion to a more authentic contemporary faith.* San Francisco: Harper.

Bowlby, J. 1969. *Attachment.* Vol. 1 of *Attachment and loss.* New York: Basic Books.

———. 1973. *Separation anxiety and anger.* Vol. 2 of *Attachment and loss.* New York: Basic Books.

Bradburn, N. M., L. J. Rips, and S. K. Shevell. 1987. Answering autobiographical questions: The impact of memory and inference on surveys. *Science* 236: 157–61.

Brandtstädter, J. 1998. Action perspectives on human development. In *Theoretical models of human development,* ed. R. M. Lerner, 807–63. Vol. 1 of *Handbook of child psychology,* ed. W. Damon. New York: John Wiley and Sons.

Browning, D. S. 1995. Altruism, civic virtue, and religion. In *Seedbeds of virtue: Sources of competence, character, and citizenship in American society,* ed. M. A. Glendon and D. Blankenhorn, 105–29. Lanham, MD: Madison Books.

Bumpass, L. L., and J. A. Sweet. 1989. Children's experience in single-parent families: Implications of cohabitation and marital transitions. *Family Planning Perspective* 21:256–60.

Bushman, B. J., and R. F. Baumeister. 1998. Threatened egotism, narcissism, self-esteem, and direct and displaced aggression: Does self-love or self-hate lead to violence? *Journal of Personality and Social Psychology* 75:219–29.

Carmichael, M. S., R. Humbert, J. Dixen, G. Palmisano, W. Greenleaf, and J. M. Davidson. 1987. Plasma oxytocin increases in the human sexual response. *Journal of Clinical Endocrinological Metabolism* 64:27–31.

Carroll, J. W., D. W. Johnson, and M. E. Marty. 1979. *Religion in America: 1950 to the present.* San Francisco: Harper San Francisco.

Caspi, A., G. H. Elder, and D. J. Bem. 1987. Moving against the world: Life-course patterns of explosive children. *Developmental Psychology* 23:308–13.

Clausen, J., and S. Clausen. 1973. The effects of family size on parents and children. In *Psychological perspectives on population,* ed. J. F. Fawcett, 185–208. New York: Basic Books.

Cleary, P. D. 1997. Subjective and objective measures of health: Which is better when? *Journal of Health Service Research Policy* 2:3–4.

Colby, A., and W. Damon. 1992. *Some do care: Contemporary lives of moral commitment.* New York: Free Press.

Costa, P. T., and R. R. McCrae. 1994. Set like plaster? Evidence for the stability of adult personality. In *Can personality change?* ed. T. F. Heatherton and J. L. Weinberger, 21–30. Washington, DC: American Psychological Association Press.

Csikszentmihalyi, M. 1997. *Finding flow: The psychology of engagement with everyday life.* New York: Basic Books.

Dabbs, J. M., and D. deLaRue. 1991. Salivary testosterone measurements among women: Relative magnitude of circadian and menstrual cycles. *Hormone Research* 35:182–84.

Damon, W. 1995. *Greater expectations: Overcoming the culture of indulgence in America's homes and schools.* New York: Free Press.

———, ed. 1998. *Handbook of child psychology.* New York: John Wiley and Sons.

D'Antonio, W. V. 1999. Conscience and commitment: Young adult Catholics in the United States today. *Conscience* 20:2–7.

Duncan, O. D., D. L. Featherman, and B. Duncan. 1972. *Socioeconomic background and achievement.* New York: Seminar Press.

Easterlin, R. A. 1980. *Birth and fortune.* New York: Basic Books.

Eaves, L. J., H. J. Eysenck, and N. G. Martin. 1989. *Genes, culture, and personality: An empirical approach.* San Diego, CA: Academic Press.

Eisenberg, N. 1992. *The caring child.* Cambridge: Harvard University Press.

Espenshade, J., G. Kamenske, and B. A. Turchi. 1983. Family size and economic welfare. *Family Planning Perspectives* 15:289–394.

Falconer, D. S. 1981. *Introduction to quantitative genetics.* 2d ed. London: Longman.

Featherman, D. L. 1980. Retrospective longitudinal research: Longitudinal data elicited within cross-sectional designs. *Journal of Economics and Business* 32:158–68.

Featherman, D. L., and R. M. Hauser. 1978. *Opportunity and Change.* New York: Academic Press.

Fox, C. A., and G. S. Knaggs. 1969. Milk-ejection activity (oxytocin) in peripheral venous blood in man during lactation and in association with coitus. *Journal of Endocrinology* 45:145–46.

Franz, C. E., D. C. McClelland, and J. Weinberger. 1991. Childhood antecedents of conventional social accomplishment in midlife adults: A 36-year prospective study. *Journal of Personality and Social Psychology* 60:586–95.

Freud, S. 1930. *Civilization and its discontents.* Trans. J. Riviere. London: Hogarth Press.

Furstenberg, F., Jr., and A. Cherlin. 1991. *Divided Families.* Cambridge: Harvard University Press.

Gallagher, W. 1996. *Just the way you are: How heredity and experience create the individual.* New York: Random House.

Gallup, G., and J. Castelli. 1989. *The people's religion: American faith in the 90's.* New York: MacMillan.

Garfinkel, I., and S. McLanahan. 1986. *Single mothers and their children: A new American dilemma.* Washington, DC: Urban Institute.

Garmezy, N. 1983. Stressors of childhood. In *Stress, coping, and development in children,* ed. N. Garmezy and M. Rutter, 43–84. New York: McGraw Hill.

Gerson, M. J. 1997. Do do-gooders do much good? *U.S. News and World Report,* 28 April, 34.

Gilligan, C. 1982. *In a different voice: Psychological theory and women's development.* Cambridge: Harvard University Press.

Glendon, M. A., and D. Blankenhorn, eds. 1995. *Seedbeds of virtue: Sources of competence, character, and citizenship in American society.* Lanham, MD: Madison Books.

Goldberg, L. R. 1993. The development of markers for the big five factor structure. *Psychological Assessment* 4:26–42.

Gottlieb, G. 1991. The experiential canalization of behavioral development. *Developmental Psychology* 27:4–13.

Gould, S. J. 1999. *Rocks of ages: Science and religion in the fullness of life.* New York: Ballantine.

Harris, J. A., J. P. Rushton, E. Hampson, and D. N. Jackson. 1996. Salivary testosterone and self-report aggressive and pro-social personality characteristics in men and women. *Aggressive Behavior* 22:321–31.

Harris, J. R. 1998. *The nurture assumption: Why children turn out the way they do.* New York: Free Press.

Heath, A. C., M. C. Neale, R. C. Kessler, L. J. Eaves, and K. S. Kendler. 1992. Evidence for genetic influences on personality from self-reports and informant ratings. *Journal of Personality and Social Psychology* 63:85–96.

Heer, D. M. 1985. Effects of sibling number on child outcome. In *Annual Review of Sociology,* ed. R. H. Turner and J. F. Short Jr., 27–47. Palo Alto, CA: Annual Reviews.

Heimer, C. A. 1996. Gender inequalities in the distribution of responsibility. In *Social differentiation and social inequality,* ed. J. N. Baron, D. B. Grusky, and D. J. Treiman, 241–73. Boulder, CO: Westview Press.

Heimer, C. A., and L. A. Staffen. 1998. *For the sake of the children: The social organization of responsibility in the hospital and home.* Chicago: University of Chicago Press.

Henry, B., T. E. Moffitt, A. Caspi, J. Langley, and P. A. Silva. 1995. On the "remembrance of things past": A longitudinal evaluation of the retrospective method. *Psychological Assessment* 6: 92–101.

Hetherington, E. M., D. Reiss, and R. Plomin. 1994. *The separate social worlds of siblings: The impact of nonshared environment on development.* Hillsdale, NJ: Erlbaum.

Insel, T. R. 1992. Oxytocin—a neuropeptide for affiliation: Evidence from behavioral receptor autoradiographic and comparative studies. *Psychoneuroendocrinology* 17:3–35.

Jackson, D. N. 1974. *Personality research form manual.* 2d ed. Port Huron, MI: Research Psychologists Press.

John, O. P. 1990. The big five factor taxonomy: Dimensions of personality in the natural language and in questionnaires. In *Handbook of personality theory and research,* ed. L. A. Pervin. New York: Guilford.

Johnson, E. 1992. *She who is: The mystery of God in feminist theological discourse.* New York: Crossroad.

Johnson, R. C., F. M. Ahern, and R. E. Coles. 1980. Secular change in degree of assortative mating for ability. *Behavior Genetics* 10:1–8.

Kaplan, G. A., and T. Camacho. 1983. Perceived health and mortality: A nine-year follow-up of the human population laboratory cohort. *American Journal of Epidemiology* 117:292–304.

Lecky, W. E. H. [1886] 1955. *History of European morals from Augustus to Charlemagne,* New York: Braziller.

Lerner, R. M. 1998. Theories of human development: Contemporary perspectives. In *Theoretical models of human development,* ed. R. M. Lerner, 1–24. Vol.1 of *Handbook of child development,* ed. W. Damon. New York: John Wiley and Sons.

Lytton, H., and D. M. Romney. 1991. Parents' differential socialization of boys and girls: A meta analysis. *Psychological Bulletin* 109:267–96.

Maccoby, E. E. 1998. *The two sexes: Growing up apart, coming together.* Cambridge, MA: Belknap Press.

Maccoby, E. E., and C. N. Jacklin. 1987. Gender segregation in childhood. In *Advances in child behavior and development,* ed. H. Reese. New York: Academic Press.

Mare, R. D., and M. D. Chen. 1986. Further evidence on sibship size and educational stratification. *American Sociological Review* 51:403–12.

Marshall, W. A., and J. M. Tanner. 1986. Puberty. In *Human growth,* 2d ed., ed. F. Falkner and J. M. Tanner, 2:171–209. New York: Plenum Press.

Mauger, P. A., and D. R. Adkinson. 1980. *Interpersonal behavior survey (IBS) manual.* Los Angeles: Western Psychological Services.

McAdams, D. P., and E. de St. Aubin. 1998. Epilogue: Emerging themes and future directions. In *Generativity and adult development: Psychosocial perspectives on caring for and contributing to the next generation,* ed. D. P. McAdams and E. de St. Aubin, 483–92. Washington, DC: American Psychological Association Press.

McAdams, D. P., H. M. Hart, and S. Maruna. 1998. The anatomy of Generativity. In *Generativity and adult development: Psychosocial perspectives on caring for and contributing to the next generation,* ed. D. P. McAdams and E. de St. Aubin, 7–43. Washington, DC: American Psychological Association Press.

McLanahan, S., and G. Sandefur. 1994. *Growing up with a single parent: What hurts, what helps.* Cambridge: Harvard University Press.

Miller, J. B. 1986. *Toward a new psychology of women.* Boston: Beacon Press.

Modell, J. 1997. Family niche and intellectual bent. *Science* 275 (31 January):624–25.

Mossey, J. M., and E. Shapiro. 1982. Self-rated health: A predictor of mortality among the elderly. *American Journal of Public Health* 72:800–808.

Murphy, M. R., J. R. Seckl, S. Burton, S. A. Checkley, and S. L. Lightman. 1987. Changes in oxytocin and vasopressin secretion during sexual activity in men. *Journal of Clinical Endocrinological Metabolism* 65:738–41.

Newton, N. 1973. Interrelationships between sexual responsiveness, birth, and breast feeding. In *Contemporary sexual behavior,* ed. J. Zubin and J. Money, 77–98. Baltimore, MD: Johns Hopkins University Press.

Noddings, N. 1984. *Caring: A feminine approach to ethics and moral education.* Berkeley, CA: University of California Press

———. 1989. *Women and evil.* Berkeley, CA: University of California Press.

Olasky, M. 1992. *The tragedy of American compassion.* Wheaton, IL: Crossway Books.

Oliner, S. P., and P. M. Oliner. 1988. *The altruistic personality: Rescuers of Jews in Nazi Europe.* New York: Free Press.

Panksepp, J. 1992. Oxytocin effects on emotional processes: Separation, distress, social bonding, and relationships to psychiatric disorders. *Annals New York Academy of Sciences* 652:243–52.

Plomin, R. 1990. *Nature and nurture: An introduction to human behavioral genetics.* Pacific Groves, CA: Brooks/Cole.

Plomin, R., and S. A. Petrill. 1997. Genetics and intelligence: What's new? *Intelligence* 24:53–77.

Ridley, M. 1996. *The origins of virtue: Human instincts and the evolution of cooperation.* New York: Viking.

Robbins, L. C. 1963. The accuracy of parental recall of aspects of child development and of child rearing practices. *Journal of Abnormal and Social Psychology* 66:261–70.

Robins, L. N., S. P. Schoenberg, S. J. Holmes, K. S. Ratcliffe, A. Benham, and J. Works. 1985. Early home environment and retrospective recall: A test for concordance between siblings with and without psychiatric disorders. *American Journal of Orthopsychiatry* 55:27–41.

Rosenham, D. L. 1970. The natural socialization of altruistic autonomy. In *Altruism and helping behavior,* ed. J. Macaulay and L. Berkowitz, 262–74. New York: Academic Press.

Rossi, A. S., and P. H. Rossi. 1990. *Of human bonding: Parent-child relations across the life course.* Hawthorne, NY: Aldine de Gruyter.

Rowe, D. C. 1994. *The limits of family influence: Genes, experience, and behavior.* New York: Guilford Press.

———. 1997. A place at the policy table? Behavior genetics and estimates of family environmental effects on IQ. *Intelligence* 24:133–58.

Rushton, J. P., D. W. Fulker, M. C. Neale, D. K. B. Nias, and H. J. Eysenck. 1986. Altruism and aggression: The heritability of individual differences. *Journal of Personality and Social Psychology* 50:1192–98.

Sagan, C. 1994. *Pale blue dot.* New York: Random House.

Scarr, S. 1992. Developmental theories for the 1990s: Development and individual differences. *Child Development* 63:1–19.

———. 1993. Biological and cultural diversity: The legacy of Darwin for development. *Child Development* 64:1333–53. Quoted in D. C. Rowe, A place at the policy table? Behavior genetics and estimates of family environmental effects on IQ. *Intelligence* 24:155.

Scarr, S., and K. McCartney. 1983. How people make their own environments: A theory of genotype → environment effects. *Child Development* 54: 424–35.

Sears, R. R., E. E. Maccoby, and H. Levin. 1957. *Patterns of child-rearing.* Evanston, IL: Row, Peterson.

Sewell, W. H., R. M. Hauser, and D. L. Featherman, eds. 1976. *Schooling and achievement in American society.* New York: Academic Press.

Singer, P. 1981. *The expanding circle: Ethics and sociobiology.* New York: Farrar, Straus, and Giroux.

Skinner, B. F. 1953. *Science and human behavior.* New York: MacMillan.

Skocpol. T. 1992. *Protecting soldiers and mothers: The political origins of social policy in the United States.* Cambridge: Belknap Press of Harvard University Press.

Skocpol, T., and M. P. Fiorina. 1999. Making sense of the civic engagement debate. In *Civic engagement in American democracy,* ed. T. Skocpol and M. P. Fiorina. Washington, DC: Brookings Institution Press.

Snarey, J., and P. Y. Clark. 1998. A generative drama: Scenes from a father-son relationship. In *Generativity and adult development: How and why we care for the next generation,* ed. D. P. McAdams and E. de St. Aubin, 45–74. Washington, DC: American Psychological Association Press.

Spence, J. T., and R. L. Helmreich. 1978. *Masculinity and femininity: Their psychological dimensions, correlates, and antecedents.* Austin: University of Texas Press.

Strelau, J., and A. Angleitner, eds. 1991. *Explorations in temperament: International perspectives on theory and measurement.* New York: Plenum Press.

Strozier, C. B. 1994. *Apocalypse: On the psychology of fundamentalism in America.* Boston: Beacon Press.

Sulloway, F. J. 1996. *Born to rebel: Birth order, family dynamics, and creative lives.* New York: Pantheon.

Tanner, J. M. 1962. *Growth at adolescence.* Springfield, IL: Thomas.

Thiemann, R. 1996. *Religion in public life: A dilemma for democracy.* Washington, DC: Georgetown University Press.

Thomson, E., S. McLanahan, and R. B. Curtin. 1987. Family structure, gender, and parental socialization. *Journal of Marriage and the Family* 54:368–78.

Trapnell, P. D., and J. S. Wiggins. 1990. Extension of the interpersonal adjective scales to include the big five dimensions of personality. *Journal of Personality and Social Psychology* 59:781–90.

Waller, N. G., B. A. Kojetin, T. J. Bouchard Jr., D. T. Lykken, and A. Tellegen. 1990. Genetic and environmental influences on religious interests, attitudes, and values: A study of twins reared apart and together. *Psychological Science* 1:138–42.

Watson, J. B. 1930. *Behaviorism.* New York: Norton.

Whiting, B. B., and J. W. M. Whiting. 1975. *Children in six cultures: A psychocultural analysis.* Cambridge: Harvard University Press.

Whiting, J. W. M., and B. B. Whiting. 1973. Altruistic and egoistic behavior in six cultures. In *Cultural illness and health,* ed. L. Nader and T. Maretzki. Washington, DC: American Anthropological Association.

Willmer, W. K., and J. D. Schmidt, with M. Smith. 1998. *The prospering parachurch: Enlarging the boundaries of God's kingdom.* San Francisco: Jossey-Bass.

Wills, G. 1990. *Under God: Religion and American politics.* New York: Simon and Schuster.

319

Wilson, E. O. 1998. *Consilience: The unity of knowledge.* New York: Alfred Knopf.

Wilson, J. Q. 1995. Liberalism, modernism, and the good life. In *Seedbeds of virtue: Sources of competence, character, and citizenship in American society,* ed. M. A. Glendon and D. Blankenhorn, 17–34. Lanham, MD: Madison Books.

Wolf, A. 1995. *Sexual attraction and childhood associations: A Chinese brief for Edward Westermarck.* Stanford, CA: Stanford University Press.

Wolfe, A. 1998. *One nation, after all: What middle-class Americans really think about God, country, family, racism, welfare, immigration, homosexuality, work, the right, the left, and each other.* New York: Viking.

Wolkind, S., and E. Coleman. 1983. Adult psychiatric disorder and childhood experiences: The validity of retrospective data. *British Journal of Psychiatry* 143:188–91.

Wuthnow, R. 1991. *Acts of compassion: Caring for others and helping ourselves.* Princeton, NJ: Princeton University Press.

———. 1994. *Sharing the Journey.* New York: Free Press.

Wright, L. 1998. *Twins: And what they tell us about who we are.* New York: John Wiley.

Yarrow, M. R., J. D. Campbell, and R. Burton. 1970. Recollections of childhood: A study of the retrospective method. *Monographs of the Society of Research in Child Development,* ser. 138, vol. 35, no. 5.

Zuckerman, M. 1994. Impulsive unsocialized sensation seeking: The biological foundations of a basic dimension of personality. In *Temperament: Individual differences at the interface of biology and behavior,* ed. J. E. Bates and T. D. Wachs, 219–55. Washington, DC: American Psychological Association Press.

EIGHT

The Impact of Family Problems on Social Responsibility

Alice S. Rossi

INTRODUCTION

The underlying assumption of the analysis reported in this chapter is that adults do not move through life as either solitary individuals or members of small isolated nuclear families, but are instead embedded in the larger social context of extended families. A three-generation lineage is the typical generational depth at all stages of the life course. A further assumption is that individuals are affected not merely by events that touch on their own health and well-being, but also by what happens in the lives of their significant others. In specific terms, we first explore the prevalence of problems in the lives of parents, children, and spouses of MIDUS respondents and how the multiple problems of such family members affect the help and support respondents give to them. Second, we investigate whether providing such support and help to kin precludes or stimulates participation in volunteer work in the larger community. A third purpose links this chapter to the preceding one on the developmental trajectory from early family life that best predicts adult social responsibility to family and community: a test of whether the quality of the relationship with parents in early life has an impact on the extent to which adults rise to the needs of their parents many years later.

But first we address the changing composition of the larger kin network across the life course, with special attention to the changes occurring during the middle years as a consequence of the unfolding dynamics of generational succession.

THE DYNAMICS OF GENERATIONAL SUCCESSION

A widely held image of midlife is that of a "sandwich generation" (Bureau of the Census 1996) composed of adults caught between increasingly fragile elderly parents on the one hand and ongoing responsibilities toward their children on the other (e.g., Briar and Kaplan 1990; Brody 1990; Uhlenberg 1993). The implication of such a view is that middle-aged adults today carry a much heavier set of burdens than previous generations of middle-aged adults did. One can readily visualize a midlife scenario of role conflict for a middle-aged woman who works full-time to support her children's education, while at the same time her mother is in need of significant caregiving due to declining health. To meet her mother's need she considers withdrawing from the workforce or reducing the hours she works, but to do so would restrict her ability to support her children through the prolonged schooling they require. Guilty feelings attend either choice.

But how prevalent is such a burdened middle generation? Some demographic realism seems in order (Soldo 1996). Parental mortality is a very infrequent event for adults under forty years of age: in the MIDUS survey, 92% of adults in their thirties report that one or both of their parents are still alive, as are 81% of the parents of adults in their forties. One asks such adults "How are your parents?" Of the adults in their fifties, the proportion with at least one living parent has dropped to 55%; hence it becomes more appropriate to ask "Are your parents still alive?" (Hagestad 1996, 215). Generational succession is a relentless process and by the latter half of midlife, it is more realistic to assume that the older generation has been lost (one's parents) and a new generation added (one's grandchildren).

Nor is it demographically realistic to assume that adults in their fifties are typically coping with both very elderly parents and young children. The average age of the youngest child of adults in their forties is fifteen years, but for those in their fifties it is twenty-five. Putting together the trend in parental mortality with the ages of the children of adults in midlife underlines the relatively low prevalence of even a *potentially* burdened middle generation. If we restrict attention to the presence of at least one child under thirteen years of age to capture the years of most intense childrearing, the proportion of midlife respondents who also have *at least one living parent* undergoes a dramatic reduction: a *third* of adults in their forties but only 7% of adults in their fifties have both one living parent and one child under thirteen. Far from being an added burden of responsibility, young adult children may actually be of help to adults in their fifties who are caring for an elderly parent (Hagestad 1986).[1]

Because men on average marry later than women do and have wives younger than themselves, there is a significant difference in midlife between men and women who still have young children: among our respondents in their forties, for example, 40% of the men but only 20% of the women have a child under twelve years of age. Since women are far more likely to be the kinkeepers and caregivers than men are, even men in their forties with young children and parents in need of assistance are less likely than their sisters to extend help to the older generation (Finch and Groves 1982; Lewis and Meredith 1988; Rosenthal 1985; Soldo 1996).

But thus far we have only defined the outer demographic limits. Not all parents in old age are ill or require hands-on care. The elderly in the United States today are in a better position financially and have greater access to state-funded medical care, private health insurance, or both than any previous cohort of elderly in human history. Even confining attention to MIDUS respondents who have a living parent and at least one preadolescent child, only seventy-three adults in their forties and twenty-one adults in their fifties report having a parent with a "chronic disease or disability." This represents only 10% of all respondents in their forties and a very small 3% of those in their fifties. Furthermore, having a chronic disease does not necessarily mean the elderly parent is in need of caregiving from adult children, only that there is a *potential* need for such caregiving. Note too that midlife adults today are the baby-boom cohort and have more siblings to share responsibility with than either their parents had (because the Depression restricted family size), or their children have (because baby-boomers have produced very small families).[2]

The fact that there is only a slim empirical base for supporting the image of a burdened middle generation does not mean there is no heartache attached to coping with parents' terminal illnesses and death, nor does it suggest that midlife adults are not coping with numerous problems in the lives of close relatives. The sharp drop from 55% of adults in their fifties who have at least one living parent to only 21% of adults in their sixties implies that significant numbers of adults experience a parent's death during their forties and early fifties. Clearly some of these midlifers will have been involved in hands-on caregiving, and almost all will have experienced grief in connection with the loss of a key person in their lives. No one ever becomes an "ex-child," just as no one is ever an "ex-parent." Even in the years beyond our parents' deaths, most of us carry an internalized image of our parents, and this image often provides a standard against which we judge ourselves favorably or unfavorably; and rightly or wrongly, as parents ourselves our psychological well-being is intricately related to how well or poorly our adult children are doing (Ryff and Seltzer 1996). While the children of most middle-aged adults are no longer primarily dependent on their parents, their lives may well be "off track" due to unemployment or marital breakdown (Smith 1983). Job or marital failure often precipitates a return to the parental nest, which disrupts expectations concerning the timetable of life events in children's lives that can be a source of stress and worry to their middle-aged parents.

The dynamics of change in longevity in this century have also had an important psychological and social impact on the nature of the relationship between parents and children: parents and children now have from forty to sixty years of "shared lives" as co-adults (Hagestad 1996; Rossi and Rossi 1990). As the child's dependency on parents ebbs, the relationship shifts to one of greater equality, although many parents play a significant role as what David Gutmann calls "emeritus parents" for their fully mature adult children (Gutmann 1987), serving as a backup source of help when it is needed. Further along in the life course, middle-aged children begin to show "filial maturity," that is, a readiness to accept some dependence by their aging parents (Blenkner 1965).[3] This shift in the balance of dependency may be a particularly difficult one for Americans to make due to our cultural emphasis on autonomy, a difficulty facing not only the elderly but the middle-aged children as well. In a historical perspective, however, this transition to parental dependency may be far easier in our time due to the long intervening years as peer-like co-adults; no longer is there an abrupt transition as in the past when many young children were confronted by the sudden health crises and deaths of their middle-aged parents.

Adult children and their parents are in frequent contact and very much involved in many aspects of each other's lives. In the MIDUS sample, *two-thirds* report some kind of contact with one or more members of their families (parents, siblings, or children no longer living at home) at least *several times a week;* 15% report contact *several times a day;* a mere 7% report contact only *once a month or less.* Despite social and geographic mobility, American families are far from isolated nuclear units. A more apt characterization of contemporary families is as a "bundle of interwoven lives" (Hagestad 1996; Pruchno, Blow, and Smyder 1984).

A good index to the changed nature of the parent-child relationship as a result of the long years they spend as co-adults is the high degree to which the help exchanged between the generations is *reciprocal:* if you *give,* you also *get!* Sociological studies of reciprocity have a long history (e.g., Gouldner 1960), recently illustrated by the study of normative obligations to kin compared to that for friends and neighbors

(Rossi and Rossi 1990). The degree of relatedness in terms of shared genes provides the latent principle underlying the level of felt obligation between people: the highest level of obligation holds for parents and children, followed in descending order of obligation by grandparents, grandchildren, and siblings; aunts, uncles, nieces and nephews; first cousins; friends and neighbors. The least obligation of all is to ex-spouses, especially if the former spouse remarried. This same study also shows that actual behavior in terms of both social contact and helping patterns is consistent with this ordering of normative obligations by degree of biological relatedness.

The high degree of reciprocity that is a mark of close kin relationships is illustrated in table 8.1, which reports the correlation between the number of hours devoted to *giving* social-emotional support to close kin—spouses, parents, and children—and *getting* social-emotional support from the same significant others. Support is empirically defined as the hours per month respondents estimate they spend giving such informal support as "comforting, listening to problems, or giving advice." Note that this does not require face-to-face interaction. Telephone lines are abuzz with intimate conversations between family members across many miles as well as across town. The highest degree of reciprocity, as measured by the size of these correlation coefficients, is between husbands and wives, and this does not vary across the life course from young adulthood to old age. Such reciprocity is a significant characteristic of the parent-child relationship as well: a correlation of .73 in reciprocity between respondents and their parents, .57 between respondents and their children. The higher correlation for parents than for children reflects the fact that a large proportion of respondents' children are still very young (30% of their children are under

TABLE 8.1 Reciprocity of Caregiving between Family Members, Total and by Age of Respondent

| | Total | Age of Respondent | | |
		25–39	40–59	60–74
A. Respondent and spouse/partner	.88	.89	.86	.88
B. Respondent and child(ren)	.57	.47	.66	.72
C. Respondent and parent(s)	.73	.71	.78	.54

Note: Pearson correlation coefficients between hours per month of social-emotional support given and received. Base Ns = respondents who (A) are married or cohabiting; (B) have at least one child; and (C) have at least one living parent.

twelve years of age); preschool- and school-age children are simply not yet able to reciprocate the social-emotional support they receive from their parents. This is reflected in the finding that the lowest degree of reciprocity between children and parents is among respondents in their late twenties and thirties $r = .47$), compared to the correlation for respondents in midlife $r = .66$), most of whose children range in age from adolescence to young adulthood. In parallel fashion, reciprocity between respondents and their parents is at a nadir among the oldest respondents: not only are there very few living parents of respondents who are over sixty years of age themselves, but the remaining old-old parents, well over eighty years of age, are not as capable of reciprocating the time and attention their children provide to them. At the extremes of old age, parents have undergone a critical transition from reciprocity to dependence, important in order to compensate for age-related losses and to free up psychological energy for use in other domains of life that permit reward and gratification (Baltes 1996). Hence, overall, reciprocity in time devoted to emotional support goes *up* with the age of children, *down* with the age of parents.[4]

High correlations in social support between the generations does not mean the same *degree* of support is received as is given. A high correlation can be found whether parents generally give *a great deal more time* or the *same amount of time* to counseling their children as children return to them. In point of fact, our MIDUS data shows that on average, parents give *twice* as much time to providing social support to their children as they receive from their children. This is partially a function of age: respondents under forty years of age, whose children are quite young, report almost twice as much time (forty hours per month) devoted to support of their children as middle-aged adults do (twenty-two hours per month).

The long stretch of years today's parents and children enjoy as co-adults may explain the reciprocal exchange in counseling and advising each other, but this does not extend to the exchange of money between the generations. Compared to the high correlations shown in table 8.1 on social support, the correlations between giving and receiving *financial assistance* hover around .05 in all age groups. The flow of money tends to be one-directional: for the most part, money flows from the old to the young, from parents to children and grandchildren.[5] MIDUS data are consistent with data from the Health and Retirement Study (Soldo and Hill 1995) and a national probability sample of Canadian

TABLE 8.2 Average Amount of Time and Money Given and Received
per Month between Respondents and Their Children
or Grandchildren

	Mean	SD	N^a
Hours of social-emotional support per month			
Respondent as donor	25	29	2,282
Respondent as recipient	13	21	1,660
Amount of financial assistance per month ($)			
Respondent as donor	165	236	1,020
Respondent as recipient	18	30	179

[a]N = respondents who have at least one child and who give or get *any* support or money.

adults (Rosenthal, Martin-Matthews, and Matthews 1996): both studies report a very low incidence of financial transfers to older parents.
Table 8.2 shows the extent of this imbalance in dollar terms: as donors,
respondents report giving an average of $165 a month to children or
grandchildren, compared to the very small average of $18 they received
from one or more of their descendants. These averages are restricted to
those who give or receive *any* money; hence the base *N*s shown also
reflect the general tendency for money to flow from older to younger
kin, a ratio of almost six to one between serving as *donors* to children
or grandchildren and being the *recipients* of financial aid. Financial help
reaches a peak among middle-aged adults (a mean dollar contribution
to children or grandchildren of $176); its nadir is money from children
reported by elderly adults ($17). Note too the enormous extent of vari-
ation in both the time and money estimates reported by respondents,
for example, a standard deviation of $236 in the case of money given
to children or grandchildren, far in excess of the mean of $165. Time
estimates show a similar though less extreme pattern of variation in the
number of hours a month devoted to social support.

Though the concept of midlife family "burdens" is tempered by the
findings reported above, it remains important and interesting to ask
how extensive and of what kind are the problems being experienced by
close family members. Physical health is not the only potential problem
elderly parents may be experiencing; they may, for example, have ongoing personality problems, loneliness associated with widowhood, or
financial or emotional stress associated with retirement. Children may
be having difficulty getting or keeping a job or a relationship with a sig-

nificant other, carrying heavy debts, or coping with alcoholism or substance abuse. We turn now to the prevalence and types of problems in the lives of close family members.

The Prevalence of Problems in Lives of Family Members

Table 8.3 sets the stage for this analysis, showing the prevalence of problems over the course of the past year in the lives of the parents, spouses or partners, and children of respondents. Respondents were asked whether or not each of these three types of close relatives had one or more of ten specified and varied problems: health problems (chronic disease or disability, frequent illnesses); emotional or alcohol/substance abuse problems; difficulty getting along with people generally or specifically with a marital partner; job or school problems (getting or keeping a job or poor job performance for employed family members, or problems at school like failing grades for younger family members);

TABLE 8.3 The Prevalence and Type of Recent Problems in the Lives of Parents, Spouses/Partners, and Children of Respondents (percentage)

Problem	Parent(s)	Spouse/Partner	Child(ren)
A. Summary score			
No problems	46.3	49.0	43.6
1–2 problems	36.4	35.3	34.0
3–10 problems	17.3	16.7	22.4
B. Type of problem			
Physical/mental health			
Chronic disease/disability	27.8	11.5	7.3
Frequent illnesses	34.6	19.9	24.9
Emotional problems	27.0	37.4	24.4
Alcohol/substance problems	6.5	6.0	6.8
Interpersonal			
Marital/partner relationship	8.8	16.8	18.5
Difficulty getting along	8.7	7.6	9.6
School/job performance	2.3	7.7	21.5
Getting/keeping a job	2.8	7.0	12.7
Financial problems	16.9	21.0	27.3
Legal problems	3.2	7.0	10.2
N	1,389	1,585	1,579

Note: Respondents answered yes or no to each of the specific problems, hence percentages in panel B of the table exceed 100%. Summary scores (range = 0–10) are the number of problems reported for each of three categories of specified kin.

financial problems (low income or heavy debts); or legal problems (e.g., law suits, police charges, traffic violations). Overall, slightly more than *half* of parents, marital partners, and at least one child are reported to have at least *one* problem. Multiple problems are most prevalent in the lives of respondents' children, 22% of whom are reported to have *three or more* problems.

The nature of the problems reported differs between those experienced by parents and those by spouse and children. As one might expect, chronic disease and frequent illnesses are the most often cited problems for parents; emotional problems predominate in reporting on spouses or partners. The most frequently reported problems of children involve personal finances or work or school roles (either trouble keeping a job or difficulty in job or school performance). That one in four respondents report their children have financial problems may reflect the fact that most such children were young adults confronting a tighter job market in the late 1980s and early 1990s, and as in any era, household and family formation entails expenses close to or in excess of current earnings of adults in their twenties and early thirties. Nicholas Zill and Christine Nord (1994) report that the real wages of young workers declined in the decade of the early 1980s to the early 1990s, by 9% for men, 4% for women.

There are surprisingly high correlations in problem prevalence for all pairs among the three categories of close family members. Significant correlations in problem prevalence might be expected for blood kin on both genetic and shared environment grounds, for example, between spouses' and children's problems ($r = .26$, significant at the .001 level), which in all but a very few cases involve biological parents and their biological children. The correlation is just as high between respondents' parents and their children's problems (.29, significant at the .001 level). What is surprising is that the correlation is even higher between the number of problems reported for respondents' parents and their spouses or partners (.34, significant at the .001 level), family members who do not share any genes. We can only infer some degree of assortative mating such that spouses and parents have some similar attributes, supplemented perhaps by relatively small social class differences between proximate generations in a family.

Closer inspection of the correlations by specific type of problem provides an interpretive clue: the correlations are highest in all three dyadic relationships for physical health, emotional problems, and difficulty getting along with people. For example, the pair correlations on "frequent illnesses" vary only in a narrow range from .27 (parents and children) to .34 (spouses and children). The correlations on emotional problems differ hardly at all, .30 between spouses and children as well as between parents and children. Genetic tendencies toward poor or excellent health may play a role in the case of spouses and children, or even parents and children, but this is clearly not the case for affinal relationships like parents and respondents' spouses, yet here the correlations are as high as for blood kin (.31 for frequent illnesses, .29 for emotional problems).

The connecting link common to all three types of dyadic relationships is, of course, the respondents themselves. One can hypothesize that parents with emotional problems as elderly adults might have had similar problems as young adults, and consequently, stress in their relationship to their children (i.e., our respondents when they were growing up). Such a background could trigger personality problems in respondents' earlier lives such that they too experienced social-emotional problems reflected in their choice of marital partner and the quality of the childrearing they in turn were capable of. Some hint of such intergenerational transmission is provided by several relevant findings: For one, there is a significant correlation between respondents' scores on neuroticism and the number of problems in the lives of their parents ($r = .19$, significant at the .001 level) and their spouses ($r = .16$, also significant at the .001 level). So too, there are significant correlations between respondents' reporting they had a serious bout of depression during the past year and multiple problems of their parents (.18, significant at the .001 level) and their spouses (.22, significant at the .001 level). While one could well expect that adults whose parents or spouses have multiple problems could *become* depressed as a consequence of such problems, this is less sustainable where elevated neuroticism is concerned, which tends to be a long-standing, not an episodic, personal trait: twin studies show that 40–50% of the variation on neuroticism in a population can be explained by heredity. The genetic proclivity to neuroticism is therefore a likely *precursor* to the onset of a depressive episode (Gallagher 1996).

We put such speculation to an empirical test in table 8.4. Respondents rated their parents' health when they were about sixteen years of age, just as they rated the quality of their relationship with their parents when they were growing up (i.e., the parental affection scales analyzed in chapter 7). If the intergenerational transmission model is at work in the life histories of our respondents, then it should follow that multiple

TABLE 8.4 Regression of Current Parental Problems Score
on Past Health of Parents and Early Parental Affection Scales
(beta coefficients)

Variable	Current Parental Problems
Mother	
health when respondent at age 16	−.162***
affection scale	−.123***
educational attainment	−.019
R^2	.050***
N	1,343
Father	
health when respondent at age 16	−.138***
affection scale	−.088**
educational attainment	−.020
R^2	.036***
N	1,210

**p < .01.   ***p < .001.

problems in the lives of parents today have their roots in earlier poor health and less than optimal childrearing competence. Therefore in table 8.4 we regress *current* parental problems on their *past* health and the parental affection scales. Since physical and mental health are class-related, educational attainment of parents is included as a control in both equations. Independent of parents' educational attainment (negative but not statistically significant), poor health in the past of either mothers or fathers and low levels of affection in the relationship with either parent when respondents were growing up are significant predictors of multiple problems in the lives of parents today. We infer that the parental affection scales tap underlying characteristics of the parents; an inability to show affection toward their children or to make room in their lives for the emotional needs of their youngsters by being available when the children need them is not limited to relationships to children but indicative of a personality predisposition to poor relational skills affecting all social relationships that persists over the decades after children have left the household.

In designing the inventory of major potential problems, we made every effort to cover a wide range of life domains (physical and mental health, work or school problems, interpersonal problems in intimate relationships, legal problems, alcohol or substance abuse, etc.). The aim was to make the problem types applicable to all three types of significant others and to all phases of the life course. This has obvious limitations, particularly for respondents with very young children, because we made no attempt to inquire about problems particular to early childhood (e.g., bedwetting, eating problems, deviant behavior in school or around the neighborhood). Young children clearly do not have legal, financial, or marital problems, though the item on problems at work was expanded to cover problems in school or failing grades. The fact that respondents have only one spouse but potentially two living parents and from one to twelve children further complicates the analysis task. To simplify the format of this complex set of questions, we asked respondents to indicate whether or not *"either parent"* or *"any of your children"* experienced each of the problems on the inventory. This makes comparison of multiple problems across the categories subject to potential misinterpretation. However, we find that there is no significant correlation between the number of problems cited for children and family size $r = .01$), nor did having only one versus both parents alive correlate with the number of parental problems reported by respondents. Hence it is of interest to chart the life course profile of multiple problems by each of the three categories of kin, as shown in figure 8.1. Note that the life course in question is defined in terms of the age of respondents; hence both parents and children differ in age accordingly. Adults in their thirties are largely reporting on preschool- and school-age children and parents in their fifties; by contrast, most respondents in their fifties have grown children and if their parents are still alive, they are likely to be in their seventies or older.

Figure 8.1 illuminates an interesting profile of problem prevalence across the life course: multiple problems in the lives of respondents' spouses peak in early midlife and then decline from late midlife through early old age. Multiple parental problems show no significant change in prevalence across the life course. The most striking pattern shown in figure 8.1 is the sharp upward climb in multiple problems experienced by respondents' children, reaching a peak of 38% with multiple problems when respondents are in their sixties, when the majority of their adult children are in their early thirties. The middle years are often seen as a relatively stable phase of life, but they are years during which there is great change in the lives of those closest and dearest to midlifers. Note in figure 8.1 that adults under forty years of age report more problems involving parents and spouses than children, but as adults move into their forties and fifties the profile changes dramatically: by late midlife parents have died or have fewer problems and marriages have stabilized or partners have been changed, but by late

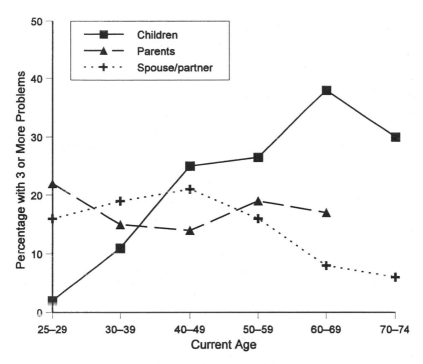

FIGURE 8.1. Current problems in lives of child(ren), parent(s), and spouse/partner, by age of respondent (percentage). See the text for the specific ten problems reported for parents, spouses/partners, and children. Base *N*s are respondents with at least one child, or one living parent, or married/cohabitating. There are too few cases of living parents among the oldest respondents (twelve cases). The only significant difference by age is for children's problems ($p \le .001$).

midlife respondents' children have moved into adulthood and are experiencing a wide array of problems in their lives, some carried forward from their youth, others newly acquired as they establish families and secure their place in the economy. It may be true, as Gullette (1997) claims, that when women speak frankly, they say that life was more complicated when the nest is full than when it is empty, but the physical presence of children in the home is not required for parents to be worried about their health, happiness, and security.

Having found significant predictors of current parental problems rooted in the early years of childrearing and relatively high correlations between problems reported for spouses and children, an appropriate next step is to test the extent to which spouse problems are implicated

TABLE 8.5 Regression of Children's Problems Score
on Spouse/Partner's Problems Score, and Neuroticism, Age, Sex,
and Education of Respondent (beta coefficients)

Variable	Children's Problem Score
Spouse/partner's problem score	.218***
Respondent characteristics	
Neuroticism	.092**
Age	.271***
Sex[a]	.076**
Educational attainment	−.010
R^2	.121***
N	1,353

[a] 0 = male; 1 = female.
** $p < .01$. *** $p < .001$.

in children's problems, net of an array of respondents' own characteristics. In table 8.5 we regress children's problems on spouses' problems, along with respondents' age, sex, educational attainment, and the extent to which they characterize themselves as neurotic. The neuroticism scale serves as a proxy for respondents who themselves have problems in interpersonal skills that are rooted in the quality of their early family life.[6] Sex of respondent is added because women report more problems in the lives of their children than men do ($\chi^2 = 25.2$, significant at the .01 level), reflecting the likelihood that women have more intimate interaction with children than fathers typically have (Rosenthal 1985; Rossi and Rossi 1990). Age of respondent is an indirect measure of children's age, relevant in light of the sharp upturn in multiple problems shown in figure 8.1. Table 8.5 shows that both age and multiple spouse problems strongly and significantly predict multiple problems in the lives of respondents' children; sex of respondent adds a modest increment, but the problem score of children is not significantly related to educational attainment of their parents. Of special interest is that respondents' neuroticism contributes a significant net effect on multiple problems of their children. All told the results of tables 8.4 and 8.5 suggest a continuing thread of poor relational abilities across three generations, a result consistent with the fact that there are genetic components to the predisposition to neuroticism (Plomin 1994).[7]

We turn now to the effect of problems in the lives of parents and children on the pattern of social-emotional support and financial assistance between the generations.

The Impact of Family Problems on Help Exchange between Parents and Children

In analyzing the extent to which family problems affect the help given to parents and children, we select variables that are significantly predictive of the prevalence of problems in the lives of parents and children in order to test for direct and indirect effects on the level of help provided. Problem scores themselves express the presence of potential *need* for help from others. Whether that need is met depends on many factors: the emotional quality of the relationship, personality, and the time and money resources parents and children can draw upon. MIDUS data are not adequate to a full test because we have no direct measures of the personality, education, or financial resources of respondents' children, nor of the financial resources of respondents' parents except as they are reflected in the types of problems parents were reported to have. Hence we concentrate on help *given by* respondents to their parents and children and rely on characteristics of the respondents as predictors. Since income is a more finite resource and time a more flexible one, we expect far smaller R^2s in multivariate predictions of financial help than of social-emotional support.

We include in this analysis a measure of the closeness of the parent-child relationship, the neuroticism scale, sex and age of the respondent, and the two socioeconomic status markers of educational attainment and total household income. Table 8.6 shows the results for the flow of help to *parents*, table 8.7 the flow of help to respondents' *children*.

Looking first at the results shown in table 8.6 on help to parents, the key findings are as follows: The quality of affection respondents enjoyed in their relationship to their parents early in life, which we found to significantly predict the prevalence of parental problems (table 8.4), also has *direct* effects on the *time* respondents now devote to supporting their parents, net of the level of problems parents are experiencing. The more affectionate the relationship has been and the more problems parents are currently facing, the greater the time given to providing advice and comfort to parents. This is particularly the case for women, who devote significantly more time providing support to parents than men do, net of problem level or the emotional quality of the relationship in the past. Income per se is not significantly related to either time or money contributions to parents, but less well educated respondents give significantly *more* support than better-educated adults do, a pattern consistent with all our analyses of the sociodemographic correlates

TABLE 8.6 Regressions of Time and Money Given to Parents on Quality of Early Relations with Mothers, Number of Current Parental Problems, and Selected Respondent Characteristics (beta coefficients)

Variable	Time (hours of support given to parents per month)	Money (amount given to parents per month)
Maternal affection in childhood	.098***	.035
Number of parental problems	.076**	.104***
Neuroticism	.031	−.088**
Educational attainment	−.116***	.004
Total household income	−.019	−.021
Sex[a]	.169***	−.038
Age	−.025	−.037
R^2	.060***	.020***
N	1,257[b]	1,257

Note: To assure inclusion of 197 respondents who did not have a biological father or other surrogate father while they were growing up, and hence no measure of paternal affection, we use the maternal affection scale rather than the combined parental affection scale in these equations.

[a] 0 = male; 1 = female.
[b] Respondents with at least one living parent.
** $p < .01$.   *** $p < .001$.

of socially responsible behavior in the family domain (see chapter 3). Though not statistically significant, those with relatively low family income contribute more financial help to parents than high-income respondents do. But as we have seen, the overall financial help given to parents is minimal compared to the money contributed to children, reflecting the far better economic condition of today's elderly compared to today's young adults. When analysis is restricted to parents and children who have *financial problems* (rather than their total problem scores), we find that money problems significantly predict financial help to both parents and children. Respondents' own total income plays no role in financial help to parents, but income is a major predictor of financial help to children (betas of .001 in the equation on parents, .189, significant at the .001 level, in equations on children). The fact that a much greater amount of money is given to children than to parents may itself explain why the donor's income is less a factor in financial aid to parents than to children.

We have no ready explanation for why neuroticism predicts less financial aid to parents, unless neurotic respondents retain some resent-

TABLE 8.7 Regressions of Time and Money Given to Children on Quality of Parent-Child Relationship, Number of Current Child Problems, and Selected Respondent Characteristics (beta coefficients)

Variable	Time (hours of support given to children per month)	Money (amount given to children per month)
Global rating of relationship to children[a]	.131***	.022
Number of child problems	.005	.104***
Neuroticism	.041*	.030
Educational attainment	−.029	.029
Total household income	−.039*	.203***
Sex[b]	.110***	−.023
Age	−.332***	.105***
R^2	.149***	.072***
N	2,335[c]	2,335

[a]Range = 0–10 (worst possible to best possible) for overall relationship of respondents to their children "these days."

[b]0 = male; 1 = female.

[c]Respondents with at least one child.

*$p < .05$.   ***$p < .001$.

ment toward their parents as being partially responsible for their own predisposition. The point remains that parental problems are the only highly significant predictors of financial assistance to parents. Age plays no significant role in providing either type of assistance.

Turning to the predictors of help to children (table 8.7), a rather different profile appears. Note that we have no measure of the quality of respondents' relationships to their children in the past; the global rating concerns the *current* relationships with children. Time given to advising and comforting children is significantly greater from mothers than from fathers, and from younger rather than older respondents, reflecting the fact that it is younger children who require a good deal of advice and emotional support. The childrearing phase of parenting implies availability and concern for children regardless of whether the children are experiencing problems in their lives or not. As children mature and they encounter serious problems, the financial help parents extend increases with the number of problems the children have. This reflects the kinds of problems included in our inventory, that is, difficulty getting or keeping a job, low income, or having heavy debts. These are problems for which financial help is appropriate, hence household income is a strong predictor of support when children have many problems (.203, significant at the .001 level), but not when parents do (−.021, not significant).

That the neuroticism scale is a significant *positive* predictor of support time given to children is one of the rare instances of a positive correlate of this scale, suggesting that parents who are nervous, worrying types are more attuned to and involved in their children's lives. When regressions were run on the support time respondents report *receiving* from their children, we find an even stronger positive coefficient on neuroticism, suggesting the pressure to provide reciprocal help may enmesh neurotic parents and their children in particularly intense and frequent contact with and support of each other (data not shown). How effective such support is under such conditions, we cannot tell from our data.

These findings demonstrate that most adults do not live in isolation but are embedded in a three-generation kindred, deeply affected by events and problems in the lives of significant others. This conception challenges the view of American culture as preeminently focused on autonomy. The high frequency of social contact with parents, siblings, adult children, and grandchildren and the high degree of reciprocity we noted in social-emotional support attest to the high degree of *interdependence* among close kin, and at a macro-societal level, interdependent generations provide stability and continuity to the social fabric.

For many, the multigenerational family is the *only* ongoing domain of life within which social responsibility and concern for the welfare of others are acted out. As we have noted, this is particularly the case for less well educated working-class adults in the United States. In the section to follow, we investigate whether the involvement in family members' problems serves as a *barrier* to or a *facilitator* of participation in the larger community.

THE EFFECT OF FAMILY PROBLEMS AND SUPPORT TIME ON COMMUNITY VOLUNTEER SERVICE

Time is a precious commodity in an industrial or fast-paced information age. Social science journals and the mass media are replete with articles about the time constraints of adults today as they attempt to deal with the often conflicting demands of family and work (Crosby 1987, 1991; Eckenrode and Gore 1990; Voydanoff 1984). The focus of such analysis has been primarily on women, presumably because the majority are no longer homemakers but co-breadwinners.[8] The work-family conflict is assumed to have been minimal in the decades when men were the primary breadwinners because their wives did almost all of the domestic chores and childrearing. Whether this was actually the case or not, we do not know. I suspect that it was not deemed manly for men to admit to conflict or to any preference for more time with their families, as younger men today are more willing to do. Why multiple roles are often deemed to be problematic and the source of stress for women but not for men is an interesting question. Terms like being "caught in the middle" or "the conflict between work and family" have a pejorative ambience conveying a negative view of multiple roles. Recent research has begun to question this by pointing out that multiple roles may complement or even strengthen each other (Baruch and Barnett 1986). Indeed, Stull, Bowman, and Smerglia (1993) report that the number of roles daughters of elderly parents occupy is unrelated to their levels of stress, with the single exception of employed daughters reporting more physical fatigue. As will be shown in chapter 11, many young *men*, not just women, report job-related stress that results in negative effects on their home life.

In this section, we explore the implications of heavy investment in family affairs for moving outside the family domain to participate in the larger community as volunteers. Do multiple problems of close kin and the resulting hours of counseling and comforting *preclude* such service in the community? Or does such involvement *stimulate* an interest in specific kinds of volunteer work? One often hears of women moving into hospital volunteer work following prolonged hospitalization of a parent or child, or becoming active in anti-smoking campaigns following the death of a spouse from lung cancer, or in leukemia drives after a child has been diagnosed with the disease. Are these exceptions? Does time devoted to family support on top of a full-time job preclude volunteer service even if the motivation to do so is present?

We explore this question in the multivariate analysis reported in table 8.8. Our major dependent variable is the total hours of volunteer work of any kind that respondents report they engage in on a monthly basis. Education is a critical control because with each higher level of schooling, there is a sharp increase in the level of felt civic obligations and participation in community organizations generally, as shown in chapter 3. Weekly hours of employment is also a significant predictor, because such employment may be a major barrier to engaging in volunteer service. Of key interest is whether respondents who report multiple problems and a good deal of support time to parents or children

TABLE 8.8 Regressions of Total Monthly Hours of Volunteer Work on Problems and Support Time to Parent(s), Spouse/Partner, and Child(ren) (beta coefficients)

Variable	Hours of Volunteer Time Affected by Problems of and Support Time to		
	A. Parent(s)	B. Spouse/partner	C. Child(ren)
Number of current problems	−.003	−.032	.001
Hours of support	−.017	.037	.080***
Educational attainment	.137***	.143***	.166***
Hours of work per week	−.089**	−.085***	−.071***
Sex[a]	.061*	.010	.037*
R^2	.030***	.027***	.036***
N	1,378	1,571	2,492

Note: Problem and support variables are tailored to each of the three family member types: number of parent problems and hours of support to parents in equation A; number of spouse problems and hours of support to spouse in equation B; and number of child problems and hours of support to children in equation C.

[a]0 = male; 1 = female.

$^*p < .05.$ $^{**}p < .01.$ $^{***}p < .001.$

are *more* or *less* likely to devote time to volunteer work. Either eventuality could be predicted: concern for health problems of parents or school or job problems of children might stimulate participation in any number of community organizations. By contrast, the sheer time pressure of work and support might restrict such community service, particularly for women because they do much more kinkeeping and caregiving than men do in the family domain.

As expected, the time devoted to volunteer work *increases* with higher educational attainment but *decreases* as a function of hours spent at work. The sheer presence or absence of problems in the lives of close kin has no significant effect on volunteer service, and support time affects volunteer service only in the case of children and does so in a *positive* way: the more time adults spend counseling and advising their own children, the more time they devote to volunteer service in the community. By itself this finding is difficult to interpret, though it is consistent with research that shows the transition to parenthood is often the pathway through which adults become involved with neighborhood and community issues—for example, recreation facilities, neighborhood safety, school curricula (O'Donnell 1983).

We get one handle on interpreting this finding by analyzing the role

TABLE 8.9 Regressions of Total Monthly Hours of Volunteer Time, by Type of Volunteer Service, on Problem Scores and Hours of Support Given to Children and Parents (beta coefficients)

| | Type of Volunteer Service (hours per month) | | | |
Variable	Youth-Related	Health-Related	Political Organizations/ Causes	All Other Volunteer Work
Children				
Hours of support to children	.142***	−.005	.009	.003
Number of child problems	−.013	.007	.009	.006
Sex[a]	.034	.068***	.008	−.012
R^2	.030***	.010**	.007*	.025***
N	2,492	2,492	2,492	2,492
Parents				
Hours of support to parents	−.022	.002	.036	−.018
Number of Parent problems	.029	.032	−.001	.007
Sex[a]	.056*	.069*	−.029	.015
R^2	.009*	.011*	.007	.030***
N	1,378	1,378	1,378	1,378

Note: All eight equations include controls on respondents' education and hours worked per week.

[a]0 = male; 1 = female.

*p < .05.   **p < .01.   ***p < .001.

of support time to children and parents by the *type* of volunteer service involved. The summary score of *all* volunteer service was used in table 8.8. In table 8.9, we specify volunteer service by four category types: youth- or school-related, hospital- or health-related, political organizations or causes, or all other types of volunteer work. The major finding of interest in these regression results is that support time to children is the only significant predictor of *any* type of volunteer service, and this is explicitly to youth-related volunteer work (β = .142, significant at the .001 level). Against expectation, support time to parents or multiple problems in parents' lives does not predict any health-related community service. Last, it is specifically youth- and health-related volunteer work that women are more active in than men.

One last bit of analysis adds further to the interpretation of the effect of support time to children on volunteer service. In table 8.10 we show the results of multivariate analysis within age groups to test whether

TABLE 8.10 Regressions of Total Hours per Month to All Volunteer
Work and of Hours per Month to School- or Youth-Related
Volunteer Work, by Age of Respondent

| | Age of Respondent | | |
Type of Volunteer Work	25–39	40–59	60–74
Total hours of ALL volunteer work per month	.079*	.078**	.104***
Total hours of SCHOOL/YOUTH-related volunteer work	.399***	.295***	.189***

Note: Shown are only the standardized beta coefficients of support time to children. All six equations include controls for number of children's problems, educational attainment, hours worked per week, and sex of respondents.

the linkage between support time to children and youth-related volunteer work is a pattern only among young and middle-aged adults who have children still in school or college. Shown in the table are only the standardized beta coefficients of the major predictor variable of interest, support time to children, by age of respondent in two sets of equations: the total time given to *all* volunteer work per month and the total time given specifically to school- and youth-related work. As the pattern clearly shows, it *is* the case that support time to children has the greatest role in predicting youth-related volunteer service among young respondents ($\beta = .399$, significant at the .001 level), but note two other major features of these results: support time to children remains significant though at a less powerful level among both middle-aged and elderly adults as well. Even among respondents between sixty and seventy-four years of age, support time to their now mature adult children continues to show a spillover effect to youth-related volunteer work, and as shown on the total amount of *all* kinds of volunteer service, support time to children has the most significant effect among the *oldest* respondents. Consequently, involvement with one's own children for the years after they have become independent adults on their own is clearly one pathway that attracts and keeps parents invested in the larger world of community service. In an analysis of data from the 1992 National Household Education Survey (consisting of parents of children in grades three through twelve), Nicholas Zill reports that parents who score high on involvement in their children's schools have children who are more involved in extracurricular activities, suggesting a family lifestyle of diverse interests shared between the generations not only in the family domain but involving both parents and children in the larger community (Zill and Nord 1994). Echoes of this early pattern may be reflected in our findings, even among elderly respondents.

One general important implication of this last finding is that there is no single developmental trajectory that leads to significant socially responsible involvement in the community. Some adults may become concerned for others through personal tragedy (for example, a child's death from cancer leading to action for all children suffering from the disease), through a burglary or an assault on a child in a neighborhood stimulating efforts to form neighborhood watch groups, or, as we have shown, through the more widespread experience of continuing in an active helpful parental role when children are grown that stimulates concern for all children and youth.[9]

CONCLUSION

The major findings reported in this chapter are as follows:

1. At least half of the MIDUS respondents report one or more problems currently confronting their spouse/partner, parents, or children. Multiple problems (three or more of the ten specified) are most common for children, increasing with age to a peak of 38% of elderly respondents who report three or more problems in their children's lives.

2. The major problem confronting respondents' parents concerns their physical health (chronic disease, disability, frequent illnesses). The major problems reported for spouses are emotional and financial problems, and for children, financial, emotional, and role-performance problems.

3. There is some continuity across the generations for both health and poor relational skills: low parental affection and poor health of parents during respondents' childhood predicted heightened prevalence of current parental problems. So too, respondents whose spouses had multiple problems reported more problems among their children. Respondents' own high scores on neuroticism are related to low affection from parents in early life, a reduction in support time to parents today, and predict multiple problems for their children.

4. Social-emotional support is highly reciprocal between the generations: those who *give* support also *get* support, although parents generally devote twice the time to support of their children as children provide to their parents. Financial help, by contrast, tends to flow from older to younger generations, but with a great deal of variation in the amount of

money contributed to children. The more problems children have and the higher parents' income, the more money children receive.

5. Multiple problems in the lives of close kin has no effect on volunteer service in the community, and support time to children actually *increases* volunteer time, both overall and in particular to youth-related volunteer service. This effect of support time to children is *not*, however, limited to respondents with young children; it applies as well to elderly parents who may persist in such community involvement as grandchildren arrive on the scene, or merely because they have become familiar figures to call upon in youth-related service organizations in their community.

All told, our analysis supports the image of American families as interdependent and multigenerational, with considerable social interaction and helping behavior between the generations, an emotional and behavioral social network that contributes to the social cohesion of society without being turned inward to the family domain alone. Rather, the trajectory that follows the transition to parenthood in early adulthood is enlarged later in the life course by continued concern and assistance to adult children and grandchildren, as well as involvement at a community level in volunteer service, in particular but not exclusively to youth-related volunteer work.

NOTES

1. Using data from NSFH-II, Beth Soldo shows that "with the mean age of childbearing hovering around twenty-six years since 1960, very little of the generational overlap occurs at a point when both the elderly parents and offspring of middle-aged adults are likely to need care" (Soldo 1996, S271). Furthermore, the point at which elderly parents or in-laws are at greatest risk for frailty is typically after age seventy-five, by which time midlife adults may be more likely to be conflicted between care and involvement with grandchildren and their parents than between care for their own children and their parents.

2. Deborah Gold (1987, 1989, 1996) has studied sibling relationships in old age and, through retrospective interviewing, has sketched the quality of their relationship to each other and to their parents over the life course.

3. Margret Baltes (1996) claims that only by invoking dependency and support can the elderly free up resources for use in other domains involving personal efficacy and growth.

4. Table 8.1 provides an example of findings that give an analyst confidence in a data set: note the fact that our *oldest* respondents report the same degree of reciprocity in relations with *children* (.72) as our *youngest* respondents report for relations with *parents* (.71), identical pairs in terms of cohort membership, though in the first instance respondents report in their roles as parents, in the second instance in their roles as children.

5. The survey questions on social support are not limited to respondents' children but to "children or grandchildren," and in the case of money, the question refers not merely to respondents' own contributions but to money from "you or your family living with you." Respondents were also asked to count the dollar value of "any food, clothing, or other goods" in making their estimate of the amount of money they contributed. Such data are therefore only very crude estimates of help exchange between the generations.

6. As shown in chapter 7, low levels of affection from parents in childhood and adolescence are predictors of contemporary neuroticism of respondents as adults. Being moody, nervous, worrying types may well contribute to their children's interpersonal difficulties as tapped by several types of problems in the children's problem score: trouble in their marital or significant-other relationship, trouble getting along generally with other people, having emotional problems, even falling short in school or job performance or difficulty in keeping a job.

7. It used to be assumed that if a personality trait has a genetic component, it should be most clearly shown early in life and subsequently tempered by social influences in late adolescence and adulthood. Once researchers realized, however, that older adult identical twins are more alike than younger identical twins on many temperamental traits, theory in behavioral genetics shifted to the view that young adults actively seek out "niches" in society congenial to their temperament (Rowe 1991; Scarr and McCartney 1983).

8. Not all researchers adhere to the role conflict view in dealing with work and family issues. Faye Crosby, for example, argues that focusing on conflict between roles is a diversionary tactic that deflects attention from the real problems *within* roles: sex discrimination at work, sex-role expectations concerning division of labor at home, and a cultural assumption of rugged individualism in which nuclear families are supposed to be self-sufficient (Crosby 1991).

9. Analogously, Paul Baltes invokes the concept of *equifinality* in his overview of ontogenesis, that is, the same developmental outcome can be reached by different means and combination of means, for example, many different paths may be followed to reach the same level of psychological well-being (Baltes, Lindenberger, and Staudinger 1997).

References

Baltes, M. M. 1996. *The many faces of dependency in old age.* New York: Cambridge University Press.

Baltes, P. B., U. Lindenberger, and U. M. Staudinger. 1997. Life-span theory in developmental psychology. In *Theoretical models of human development,* ed. R. M. Lerner, 1029–44. Vol. 1 of *Handbook on child psychology,* ed. W. Damon. New York: John Wiley and Sons.

Baruch, G. K., and R. C. Barnett. 1986. Role quality, multiple role involvement, and psychological well-being in midlife women. *Journal of Personality and Social Psychology* 51:578–85.

Blenkner, M. 1965. Social work and family relationships in later life, with some thoughts on filial maturity. In *Social structure and the family,* ed. G. F. Streib, 46–59. Englewood Cliffs, NJ: Prentice-Hall.

Briar, K. H., and C. Kaplan. 1990. *The family caregiving crisis.* Silver Spring, MD: National Association of Social Workers.

Brody, E. M. 1990. *Women in the middle: Their parent-care years.* New York: Springer.

Crosby, F. J. 1991. *Juggling: The unexpected advantages of balancing career and home for women and their families.* New York: Free Press.

Crosby, F. J., ed. 1987. *Spouse, parent, worker: On gender and multiple roles.* New Haven, CT: Yale University Press.

Eckenrode, J., and S. Gore, eds. 1990. *Stress between work and family.* New York: Plenum Press.

Finch, J., and D. Groves, eds. 1982. *A labour of love.* New York: Routledge.

Gallagher, W. 1996. *Just the way you are: How heredity and experience create the individual.* New York: Random House.

Gold, D. T. 1987. Siblings in old age: Something special. *Canadian Journal on Aging* 6:199–215.

———. 1989. Generational solidarity: Conceptual antecedents and consequences. *American Behavioral Scientist* 33:26–43.

———. 1996. Continuities and discontinuities in sibling relationships across the life span. In *Adulthood and aging,* ed. V. L. Bengtson, 228–43. New York: Springer.

Gouldner, A. W. 1960. The norm of reciprocity. *American Sociological Review* 25: 161–78.

Gullette, M. M. 1997. *Declining to decline: Cultural combat and the politics of midlife.* Charlottesville: University Press of Virginia.

Gutmann, D. 1987. *Reclaimed powers: Towards a new psychology of men and women in later life.* New York: Basic Books.

Hagestad, G. O. 1986. Dimensions of time and the family. *American Behavioral Scientist* 29:679–94.

Hagestad, G. O. 1996. On-time, off-time, out of time? Reflections on continuity and discontinuity from an illness process. In *Adulthood and aging: Research on continuities and discontinuities,* ed. V. L. Bengtson, 204–22. New York: Springer.

Lewis, J., and B. Meredith. 1988. *Daughters who care.* London: Routledge.

O'Donnell, L. 1983. The social world of parents. *Marriage and Family Review* 5:9–36.

Plomin, R. 1994. *Genes and experience: The developmental interplay between nature and nurture.* Newbury Park, CA: Sage.

Pruchno, R. A., F. C. Blow, and M. A. Smyder. 1984. Life events and interdependent lives. *Human Development* 27:31–41.

Rosenthal, C. J. 1985. Kinkeeping in the familial division of labor. *Journal of Marriage and the Family* 47: 965–74.

Rosenthal, C. J., A. Martin-Matthews, and S. H. Matthews. 1996. Caught in the middle? Occupancy in multiple roles and help to parents in a national probability sample of Canadian adults. *Journal of Gerontology* 51B:S274–83.

Rossi, A. S., and P. H. Rossi. 1990. *Of human bonding: Parent-child relations across the life course.* New York: Aldine de Gruyter.

Rowe, D. C. 1991. *The limits of family influence: Genes, experience, and behavior.* New York: Guilford Press.

Ryff, C., and M. M. Seltzer, eds. 1996. *The parental experience in midlife.* Chicago: University of Chicago Press.

Scarr, S., and K. McCartney. 1983. How people make their own environments: A theory of genotype → environment effects. *Child Development* 54: 424–35.

Smith, L. 1983. The kin-keeping roles of middle generation women in middle and later adulthood. Master's thesis, Pennsylvania State University, State College. Quoted in G. O. Hagestad, On-time, off-time, out of time? Reflections on continuity and discontinuity from an illness process, in *Adulthood and aging: Research on continuities and discontinuities,* ed. V. L. Bengtson (New York: Springer, 1996), 204–22.

Soldo, B. J. 1996. Cross pressures on middle-aged adults: A broader view. *Journal of Gerontology* 51B:S271–73.

Soldo, B. J., and M. S. Hill. 1995. Family structure and transfer measures in the Health and Retirement Study: Background and overview. *Journal of Human Resources* 30 (special issue):S138–57.

Stull, D. E., K. Bowman, and V. Smerglia. 1993. Women in the middle: A myth in the making? *Family Relations* 43:319–24.

Uhlenberg, P. 1993. Demographic change and kin relationships in later life. In *Annual Review of Gerontology and Geriatrics: 13,* ed. G. L. Maddox and M. P. Lawton. New York: Springer.

U.S. Bureau of the Census. 1996. *65+ in the United States.* Current Population Reports, Special Studies, no. P23-190. Washington, DC: Government Printing Office.

Voydanoff, P., ed. 1984. *Work and family: Changing roles of men and women.* Palo Alto, CA: Mayfield.

Zill, N., and C. W. Nord. 1994. *Running in place: How American families are faring in a changing economy and an individualist society.* Washington, DC: Child Trends.

NINE

Themes and Variations in American Understandings of Responsibility

Hazel Rose Markus, Carol D. Ryff, Alana L. Conner,

Eden K. Pudberry, and Katherine L. Barnett

In the dichotomy often drawn between rights and responsibilities, rights are basic, inalienable, natural, and self-definitional. American legal and political culture promotes and protects these rights, and Americans are adept at enumerating the rights they already have and at claiming new rights for themselves (Glendon 1991; Meyer 1990). In the individualist culture that animates many middle-class contexts, talking about individual rights, as well as about the individual who has those rights (by expressing opinions, abilities, and attributes), comes quite easily to most Americans.

Responsibility, on the other hand, is a more nebulous concept for Americans (Wertsch and Penuel 1996). While there seems to be an understanding of responsibility as the price one pays for individual rights, the idea of responsibility as anything more than the undesirable side of a necessary trade-off is seldom publicly or officially elaborated. The social representation (Moscovici 1998) of responsibility—the web of values, ideas, and practices that enables orientation and communication within a community—is weak, muted, and sometimes incoherent, especially in comparison to the social representation of individual rights. Responsibility in most common senses of the word involves others and connections to others. At the same time, however, Americans "know" that God helps those who help themselves, and so responsibility can pose a dilemma for individualistic, self-reliant, autonomous Americans. This dilemma may become accentuated for Americans at midlife, when lives have become increasingly intertwined and interdependent with the lives of others.

OVERVIEW

The focus of this chapter is a careful study of just how Americans at midlife talk about responsibility. We will argue that some ideas about responsibility are shared by all Americans, but that educational level, because it is associated with different ways of being a self and being connected to others, shapes the form and content of these understandings of responsibility in important ways. We will also address the concerns of cultural critics and social scientists who fear that Americans are becoming more isolated and less socially responsible in comparison with people of other nations or with themselves in the past. We will contend that the eighty-three Americans (a subsample of the MIDUS) who participated in our Everyday Well-Being Study are indeed quite responsible, albeit in ways that reflect their culture-specific notions of the self, of others, and of the relationship between the two.

MIDUS participants during the course of the questionnaire were asked to consider each of a series of thirty-one personal attributes (e.g., sympathetic, intelligent, responsible) and to determine how much each attribute described them. At least 70% of all respondents, regardless of gender or educational level, said that "responsible" described them "a lot" (point four on a four-point scale). From many perspectives, including their own, this level of self-proclaimed responsibility could be seen as surprising. Americans are repeatedly telling each other in newspaper columns, magazine articles, and town meetings across the country that they are not as responsible as they used to be, or as they should be, and that civic participation and social conscience are waning (Newman, chapter 5, this volume; Putnam 1995).

In this chapter we take both a broad and an in-depth look at what our subsample of MIDUS respondents may have had in mind when they characterized themselves as responsible. We began our study by asking the respondents for specific examples of being responsible. A qualitative analysis of the responses from this lengthy face-to-face interview suggests that while there is an American consensus on the necessity of being responsible, there are also strikingly different understandings of what responsibility is, what its consequences and antecedents are, and very importantly, who the person is who has responsibility, acts responsibly, or is responsible. In a subsequent analysis we chart when and how themes of social responsibility arise in respondents' discourses about why their lives have gone well and about their hopes for the future. We find that the lives of these respondents are pervaded by the socially responsible intentions and actions of themselves and others.

Responsibility, American Style

What does "responsibility" mean in the American context? As we asked our respondents about responsibility, we asked ourselves whether there is a common or everyday understanding of responsibility in America. According to many analysts, the official American cultural goal—the right and moral way to be—is to be an autonomous, "free" entity who exercises her or his natural rights. One only needs to turn on network television or to open the pages of mainstream magazines or newspapers to find an unequivocal message about the right way to be: "be free," "be independent," "be unique," "individualize," "go your own way," "chart your own course," "think different," "break the rules," "be free from convention," and "be a driver, not a passenger, on the road of life." Whether referring to cosmetics, alcohol, a car, or insurance, the message is the same. In the classroom and in the workforce, people are urged to know themselves, to develop themselves, to express themselves. While American parents used to emphasize the values of discipline and obedience, they now emphasize the importance of independence and autonomy (Alwin 1989), and schools no longer claim a responsibility to inculcate notions of citizenship, civic responsibility, or respect for others. It has become a matter of individual parental discretion whether or to what extent a child receives some socialization with respect to responsibility.

Americans seem to know that it is important to pay attention to themselves and their rights and to maintain a good attitude toward themselves. Yet responsibility implicates others, and here the American imperative is less clear. While relationships with others are as important for Americans as they are for people everywhere, the nature of those relationships, whether with individuals or with institutions, is contested territory in the United States.

Although there are American communities where the way to think and talk about responsibilities is spelled out, overall the American dialogue on the whens, whys, and hows of responsibility is not particularly well developed (Bellah et al. 1985; Wertsch and Penuel 1996). It is instructive that while Americans are intensely concerned about not treading on the rights of others, the ways in which people should pay attention to others, connect to others, or respond to their expectations, needs, or predicaments are decidedly less emphasized in public policies and practices. Such matters are most often left to individual discretion and are not a matter of public discourse (Miller, Bersoff, and Harwood 1990). Moreover, tending and bending to the needs and demands of another is often cast as compromising one's own autonomy and independence and, very significantly, can be seen as an intrusion on the development and expression of the recipient's autonomous, intricately rendered self. As a result, "being responsible" can be a delicate matter;

at times it may be experienced as opposing the pursuit of the culturally appropriate, autonomous self. Responsibility to others may also be viewed as harmful to its recipients, construed as fostering their dependence and hampering their independence.

Responsibility as Protecting Individual Rights

A highly individualist perspective on responsibility has been directly incorporated into psychological theorizing about responsibility. According to Kohlberg (1981), an understanding of responsibility as protecting individual rights and avoiding the infliction of harm on others is the very basis of morality. From Kohlberg's perspective, responsibility in the sense of honoring interpersonal obligations and responding to the needs of others is a matter of personal choice and of social convention. In response to Kohlberg, Gilligan (1982) argues that moral truth is diverse, and that a concern for caring and social obligation (a concern that she suggests is particularly characteristic of women) should not be regarded as a moral weakness, but as a strength that recognizes social embeddedness and views responsibility to others as natural. Miller and Bersoff (1992) suggest, however, that even Gilligan's powerful critique of Kohlberg remains firmly within the individualist paradigm, due to its emphasis on conflicts between responsibility to the self and responsibility to others.

Miller (1994) contends that independence and salience of responsibility to the self and one's own rights is European-American in origin and decidedly less prominent in the discourse about responsibility in other parts of the world. One of the more striking demonstrations of the primacy and importance of rights-based responsibility among Americans comes from a comparative study of the moral reasoning of Americans and Hindu Indians. Miller and Bersoff's (1992) study of both children and adults show that Americans subordinate interpersonal responsibilities to concerns of justice and view interpersonal responsibilities as matters that should be left to the individual's personal choice. Conversely, Hindu Indians view interpersonal responsibilities as decidedly more important than the preservation of individual rights, and therefore subject to social regulation.

Theorists of responsibility seem to suggest that in American cultural contexts, a concern for others or a sense of social duty or interpersonal obligation will typically be secondary to a concern for one's own needs and rights. For some people, in some situations, a responsibility to others may be elevated so that it becomes as important as a concern for one's own needs, but it rarely becomes *more* important. Many observers of the American scene claim that the current American perspective on responsibility, which focuses more on the individual than on the other, is in fact the basis for the lack of social cohesiveness and the growing sense of isolation among Americans. In their ground-breaking account of responsibility, Bellah and associates (1985) even suggest that this hyper-awareness of individual rights has led to an atrophying of the very language with which Americans discuss social responsibility. As a result, the interpersonal responsiveness that is actually quite widespread in the American context goes under-reported, making American lives "sound more isolated and arbitrary than . . . they actually are" (21).

Responsibility, Education, and Agency

Until quite recently (this volume contains several exceptions) the most detailed theoretical and empirical analyses of responsibility have focused on the middle class and on respondents with at least some college education. It is not surprising then that responsibility seems bound up with self-definition, with responsibility to the self, with protecting one's own rights, and with avoiding dependence on others or the influence of others. A variety of recent studies document a clear relationship between education and indicators of an agentic, independent self, and also between education and well-being (House et al. 1994; Herzog et al.1998; Mirowsky 1995; Ryff and Singer 1998; Ryff et al. forthcoming; Ross and Wu 1995). For example, Heise (1990) argues that performing a role that is relatively esteemed or powerful, like those requiring or associated with a college education, will contribute to a sense of self-efficacy. Related studies comparing different social classes have noted a similar relationship, such that increased socioeconomic status is associated with increased individualism (Argyle 1994; Marshall 1997). Feagin (1972), for example, found that educated respondents are more likely to endorse individualistic explanations of poverty. Triandis and colleagues (Triandis 1995) also suggest that individualism increases with education. The ways of life typically associated with completing a college education are likely to result in the self of the American cultural imperative—an autonomous, free (from the undue influence of others), in-control self. Responsibility for such a self will be more "self-centered," and cast more in terms of "taking responsibility" or "having responsibilities" that have to be managed so they do not impinge upon the separated self.

353

The MIDUS data show striking demographic differences between high school–educated respondents (high school graduates without higher education) and college-educated respondents (those who have a bachelor's degree or higher graduate degrees) who have similar levels of psychological well-being. Compared to the college-educated respondents, high school–educated respondents earn less money, have spouses who earn less money, are more likely to be divorced, have more children, have less educated parents, have more total family abuse, and are much less healthy—reporting worse physical health, more chronic conditions, more symptoms (especially back pain), more smoking, more weight problems, and less exercise. In other words, the high school–educated respondents live in a world with more economic hardship and situational limitations than do the college-educated respondents. These differences lead us to believe that responsibility for those with a high school education will be understood and practiced in ways that seem more responsive to the needs or requirements of others and to the contingencies of the situation. Moreover, responsibility is less likely to be understood and expressed in terms of the actions of an agentic self, but experienced instead as accommodating to the expectations of others.

SAMPLE AND METHODS

Our Everyday Well-Being Study focused on structured, in-depth personal interviews with a subsample of eighty-three individuals who participated in the MIDUS national survey: twenty-one men with a bachelor's degree or higher; twenty-one women with a bachelor's degree or higher; twenty men with a high school degree; and twenty-one women with a high school degree. Our selection criteria reflected the objectives of focusing on the middle years of adulthood (ages forty to fifty-nine), educational differences, and gender differences. In addition, because we were interested in probing the experience of well-being, we selected our respondents from among those in the top two tertiles of overall well-being (as measured by Ryff's six dimensions of positive psychological functioning; Ryff and Keyes 1995) for the two educational groups. Each educational group consisted of equal numbers of respondents from the first and second tertile. Three trained and experienced interviewers conducted the interviews at either respondents' homes or a nearby location of their choice. The subsample includes residents from twenty-one states, representing a wide diversity of geographic regions in the continental United States.

The participation rate for our study was 86.5%, which is quite high considering that all of our respondents had already completed the MIDUS telephone survey and self-administered questionnaire, as well as the Harvard Study of Daily Experiences. To assess the similarities and differences between our subsample and the larger MIDUS sample, we compared our college-educated and high school–educated respondents with MIDUS respondents of the same educational levels, age group, and psychological well-being ($n = 497$). We found that our interview respondents were comparable to the MIDUS subsample with regard to work status, marital status, early life and family background (e.g., parental work status, quality of relationships with parents), physical and mental health (e.g., subjective health, chronic conditions, positive and negative affect), psychological traits, quality of life indicators (e.g., satisfaction with spouse/partner, children, religiosity) and social responsibility (e.g., primary and public obligations, generative concern and giving). For limited variables (e.g., personal and household income, and satisfaction with finances, work, and life overall), our interview subsample rated slightly higher than the MIDUS respondents, whereas for other variables (e.g., heart problems, amount of weekly exercise, number of prescription medications), MIDUS respondents rated slightly higher than our interview respondents.

We conducted in-depth, open-ended interviews (approximately two hours each) with respondents to ascertain, in their own words, what *being well* meant to them. Prior to the interview we mailed respondents a short (four-page) self-administered questionnaire that contained Ryff's psychological well-being items and twelve personality items. We began the actual interviews by inquiring about any major life changes in the past two years (approximately the amount of time that had passed since they had responded to the MIDUS questionnaires). We then asked subjects to give examples to explain why they answered structured questions about well-being or personality descriptors in the manner that they had. Some of these questions pertained directly to responsibility issues. We asked respondents to explain why they chose a certain quantitative response to the question "I am good at managing the responsibilities of life." We also asked respondents to provide real-life examples to help clarify the degree to which they rated themselves as "responsible." We then explored the meaning of well-being and positive life events across several dimensions of time (past, present, future) and life domains (family, work, home, community). Our initial review of protocols revealed that two particular questions prompted considerable discussion of issues and concerns directly relevant to social responsibility: "Thinking back over your life, what are some of the reasons why your life has gone well?" and "What are your hopes for the future?" However, it is important to note that the four questions we use in the current analysis constitute less than 15% of the entire interview protocol, which covered questions regarding what *being well* meant to respondents and asked about respondents' work and home lives, family events, and their daily lives in general.

We trained three research assistants in qualitative interviewing techniques for this study (two at Stanford University and one at the University of Wisconsin, Madison). The interviewers from Stanford concentrated their efforts on the West Coast, the Southwest, and parts of the Northeast, whereas the interviewer from Madison covered the Midwest, some of the East Coast, and parts of the South. All interviews followed a strict protocol, and two of the sections included probes. The first probe was "tell me why you said that" and the second probe asked respondents for an example that supported the answer they had given. Interviewers used additional probes only to elicit varied examples or to bring the focus of the interview back to the question at hand.

All interviews were tape recorded and later transcribed and reviewed for accuracy. Multiple members of the research team read and re-read a representative subsample of transcript excerpts to develop inductive coding schemes that remained true to the concepts and words subjects presented. After several iterations, we agreed upon a set of codes and then created a database from the transcripts using a qualitative software package (QSR NUD*IST). The researchers at Stanford and Madison analyzed the data on a question-by-question basis and, where appropriate, grouped questions together. They began the analysis by applying the inductive codes to all the data and combining or eliminating categories that did not produce high enough frequencies.

In this chapter, we first elaborate the proportion of respondents (high school educated vs. college educated) who answered in each of our primary categories. We then probe more deeply into the meanings of these responses by examining subcategories within the primary coding categories as well as the actual text of the responses. The overarching aim is to summarize the findings, both quantitatively (e.g., how many persons answered in a particular category) and qualitatively (e.g., what were the kinds of answers given by high school– and college-educated individuals in particular categories). This combination of percentages and actual words illustrates how social responsibility can take on different meanings and forms depending on one's education.

RESULTS: THEMES AND VARIATIONS IN AMERICAN UNDERSTANDINGS OF RESPONSIBILITY
"What Does Responsibility Mean to Me?"

Two interview questions made possible a direct exploration of respondents' understandings and ideas about responsibility. Both of these probes asked respondents to explain answers they gave earlier on the Everyday Well-Being Study questionnaire. For the first question, respondents were reminded of the extent to which they had agreed with the statement "I am good at managing the responsibilities of life" and then were asked why they had given those answers. The second responsibility probe was similar in format: respondents were reminded of their answers to the item asking how much the word "responsibility" describes them and then were asked to give examples supporting the answers they had given. By giving respondents the opportunity to discuss these limited-choice survey items in their own words, we were able to chart the wide array of meanings and practices that middle-aged Americans associate with the terms "responsible" and "responsibility." Because these two probes evoked similar themes, we analyzed responses to both simultaneously.

When charting ways of being responsible, we sought to reflect the language, styles, and concepts used by the respondents. Their responses suggested eight seemingly distinct ways of being responsible: (1) Meeting Obligations; (2) Attending to the Needs of Others; (3) Being Dependable to Others; (4) Adjusting to Circumstances; (5) Juggling and Balancing; (6) Taking Initiative; (7) Doing What I Don't Want to Do; and (8) Taking Care of Myself.

The types of responses coded under each way of being responsible and the percentages of respondents who mentioned each category appear in table 9.1.[1] We computed the percentages presented in this table in the following manner: if respondents mentioned a category one or more times in the course of answering the two probes, they received a one for that category. If they did not mention the category, they received a zero. We then summed the ones and zeroes for each category across all respondents and divided by the total number of respondents ($N = 83$).

As table 9.1 shows, the majority of respondents endorsed Meeting Obligations, Attending to the Needs of Others, and Being Dependable

TABLE 9.1 Ways of Being Responsible

Meaning of Responsibility	Phrases Coded	Endorsers (%)
Meeting Obligations	I live up to my responsibilities I do what I'm supposed to do I do what I need to do I fulfill my day-to-day duties I take care of things I get things done	86.75
Attending to the Needs of Others	I help when asked If others need help, then I help I take care of others	60.24
Being Dependable to Others	People can count on me I don't let others down I do what I say I'm going to do I am on time	50.60
Adjusting to Circumstances	I go with the flow I do what I can I try my best	27.71
Juggling and Balancing	I juggle many different tasks I balance the needs of others with my own needs I keep all the balls in the air	28.92
Taking Initiative	I seek out new responsibilities I take control of the situation I do more than is expected	19.28
Doing What I Don't Want to Do	I will fulfill an obligation, even if it involves a task that I dislike	15.66
Taking Care of Myself	I take time out for myself I keep my health up	20.48

to Others as ways to be responsible. We will characterize this triad below under the subheading "The Common Notion of Responsibility." Endorsement of the five remaining categories of responsibility, however, differed significantly between the high school–educated and college-educated subgroups. Accordingly, we will describe those categories endorsed by a significantly higher proportion of high school–educated respondents than college-educated respondents under "High School–Educated Responsibility," and we will describe those categories endorsed by a significantly higher proportion of college-educated respondents than high school–educated respondents under "College-Educated Responsibility."

Although we have divided the ways of being responsible into high school–educated responsibility and college-educated responsibility, both education groups were represented with some frequency in all of the categories of responsibility. It appears, however, that responsibility is construed differently by the two educational groups, reflecting diversity in their understandings of the self, the social world, and the relationship between the two.

The Common Notion of Responsibility

As mentioned above, responses that could be categorized as Meeting Obligations, Attending to the Needs of Others, or Being Dependable to Others were generated by the highest percentages of respondents across educational groups (87%, 60%, and 51%, respectively). Responses that enumerated things that one "takes care of," such as obligations for which one is responsible, requirements or duties that one meets, or tasks that one gets done were coded as Meeting Obligations. Attending to the Needs of Others encompasses those responses which explicitly mentioned meeting the material or psychological needs of others, that is, giving care. The others being attended to could either be people in general or specific others, such as co-workers or loved ones. Mentions of role-related responsibilities, such as being "a father to my two children" or "a responsible teacher" were also subsumed under this category. Finally, communicating that others can rely on, can count on, or are not let down by a respondent were coded in the third most popular category, Being Dependable to Others.

Figure 9.1 shows the percentages of high school–educated ($n = 41$) and college-educated ($n = 42$) respondents endorsing each category. High school–educated and college-educated respondents equally generated responses of Meeting Obligations and Attending to the Needs of Others. This was not the case for Being Dependable to Others, which was endorsed by significantly more high school–educated respondents than college-educated respondents. Because of this difference between educational levels, Being Dependable to Others will be discussed at greater length under the subheading "High School–Educated Responsibility."

Men and women equally invoked the three categories that make up the common notion of responsibility. The lack of gender differences for Meeting Obligations and Attending to the Needs of Others is somewhat surprising because these two categories map roughly onto responsibility as "taking care" of things (a man's prerogative) and as "giving care" to others (a woman's sphere), respectively (Tronto 1993). Given our

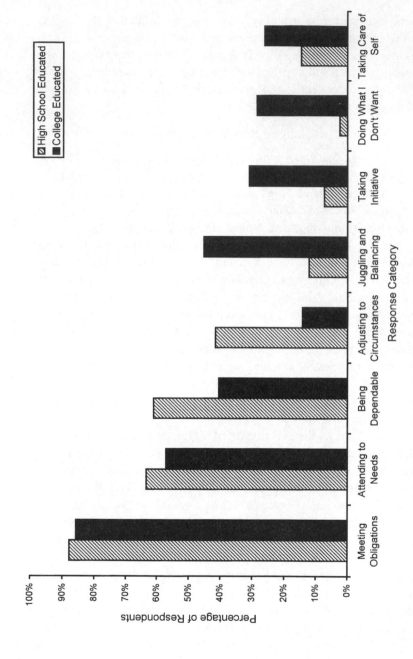

FIGURE 9.1. Mentions of categories of responsibility, by education level.

categories, we predicted that more men than women would mention Meeting Obligations and that more women than men would generate examples of Attending to the Needs of Others. While we did not find these differences, a closer analysis of the category Attending to the Needs of Others, in which the attention mentioned was further classified as either "material care" or "psychological/'being there' care," revealed that slightly more men talked about giving material care than did women (27% of men vs. 14% of women). Because giving material care may be considered as "taking care of" instead of "giving care," this gender difference is in keeping with those already noted in research on responsibility. However, equal numbers of men and women produced examples of giving psychological care (44% of men vs. 47% of women), a subcategory which more closely resonates with Tronto's idea of caregiving and for which we predicted a greater number of mentions from women. A possible explanation for the gender similarities in mentions of Meeting Obligations and Attending to the Needs of Others and its subcategories may be that men and women at midlife are facing more similar challenges and goals than are the younger men and women among whom gender differences are often found.

Although there were no gender differences in Meeting Obligations and Attending to the Needs of Others, the greater frequency of mentions of Meeting Obligations is consonant with previous research showing the relative lack of emphasis on Attending to the Needs of Others within the mainstream American culture. Yet the fact that the entire respondent population mentioned Attending to the Needs of Others second most frequently out of the eight categories indicates that other-focused responsibility is indeed very much on the minds of some of these respondents. However, instead of the social causes and civic responsibilities often assumed to constitute the domain of social responsibility, family and employment (e.g., clients and co-workers) were usually the recipients of these respondents' attention (mentioned by 71% of respondents and 58% of respondents, respectively). This observation echoes the growing sentiment that Americans may be socially responsible in their own individualistic and culturally mandated way— that is, by taking care of themselves, their jobs, and their own families.

An emphasis on taking care of local concerns, that is, taking care of the self and one's own, may be the core of American-style social responsibility in that these are the first and most commonly produced explanations of responsibility. As with the New York minority group members in Newman's study (see chapter 5, this volume), our respondents sometimes construed being socially responsible as not being socially destructive. Rather than as proactively contributing to and expanding the social good, social responsibility in the current American perspective may be understood as not bothering others, as not contributing to social ills, or as not requiring help from other people or organizations—that is, social responsibility as independence or self-reliance. The relatively few mentions of social or charitable organizations as domains for which this sample of respondents feels responsible hints that Newman's characterization of minority groups may also accurately describe most Americans at midlife.

In summary, the frequency with which respondents mentioned Meeting Obligations, Attending to the Needs of Others, and Being Dependable to Others suggests that these categories form the backbone of American-style responsibility. The finding that more respondents mentioned Meeting Obligations than Attending to the Needs of Others or Being Dependable to Others as ways of being responsible reflects the greater concern among Americans for a contractual sense of responsibility than for more interpersonal concerns. However, the large number of respondents equating responsibility with Attending to the Needs of Others or Being Dependable to Others indicates that Americans are indeed socially oriented, although the "others" implicated in their explanations tend to reside in local worlds (the family or the workplace).

High School–Educated Responsibility

In addition to subscribing to the core American notion of responsibility, high school–educated respondents sketched a sense of responsibility that highlights adjustment, effort, and a focus on others that is markedly different from the college-educated notion of responsibility depicted below. These differing senses of responsibility are evidenced by high school–educated respondents' significantly greater emphasis on Being Dependable to Others (61% of high school–educated vs. 40% of college-educated respondents) and Adjusting to Circumstances (41% vs. 14%).

As the labels for these two categories imply, the high school–educated respondents' sense of responsibility is defined with respect to other people and features of the shared world. For example, statements coded in the category Being Dependable to Others had to mention or imply other people. In the case of explicit mentions of others, respondents most often communicated that others "can rely on," "can count on," or "aren't let down by" them. As one high school–educated woman put it, "People know they can count on me. That's being responsible, in my book." Likewise, a high school–educated man responded, "I have an employer that depends on me [and] friends that trust me."

Another type of response in this category that implies others most often took the form of "I do what I say I am going to do." Formulated exclusively by high school–educated respondents, this variant of response was included under Being Dependable to Others because it was very frequently accompanied by the sentiments "and if I cannot, I let others know" and "I don't let others down." As one high school–educated woman asserted, "If I say I'm gonna do something, I do it, unless something just prohibits it. Definitely then I would come and explain what had happened. I believe that you're as good as your word." Similarly, a high school–educated man stated, " 'Responsible,' to me, means doing what you say you're going to do and not letting people down."

Being responsible, for high school–educated respondents, is not only contingent on the judgments of others, but is also constrained by situations and respondents' perceived limitations in affecting those situations. Many explanations given by high school–educated respondents when discussing responsibility reveal a sense of the need to adjust or adapt to one's circumstances. Responses of this type convey an acceptance of situations, accompanied by attempts to adapt the self to them. Responses coded in this category include mentions of "coping," "dealing," "adapting," "surviving," and "making do." A high school–educated man summarized the spirit of this category best: "Life is a big responsibility. And it's not going to always go . . . the way that we want it to go. So there's just sometimes where you've got to go with the flow."

Also coded as Adjusting to Circumstances were comments to the effect of "I try," "I try my best," and "I do (did) my best." Although such explanations convey pushing oneself or striving, such comments were considered as indicative of adjusting to the given situation because they communicate that efforts were made, but that they were constrained by personal abilities or immutable features of the external world. Furthermore, respondents' answers often combined the ideas of enduring situations and doing one's best. For example, a high school–educated woman commenting on her familial responsibilities offered, "There's certain family members I'd just as soon not see again. But . . . we run into them all the time, and there's nothing you can do about it. But I try." Emphasizing his efforts while revealing a sense of his own limitations, a high school–educated man stated, "I'm not the most responsible person, but at the same time, I make a lot of effort to be that."

College-Educated Responsibility

In contrast to the accommodating, effort-focused, socially situated style of responsibility portrayed by the high school–educated respondents, college-educated respondents depicted a sense of responsibility that was more proactive, achievement-oriented, and self-focused. In addition to Meeting Obligations, Attending to the Needs of Others, and Being Dependable to Others, college-educated respondents' sense of responsibility included Juggling and Balancing, Taking Initiative, Doing What I Don't Want to Do, and Taking Care of Myself. As figure 9.1 shows, these four additional ways of being responsible were ranked third, fifth, sixth, and seventh in percentage of college-educated respondents mentioning them. In comparison to 12% of high school–educated respondents, 45% of college-educated respondents mentioned Juggling and Balancing responsibilities as a way of being responsible. Similarly, significantly more college-educated than high school–educated respondents mentioned Taking Initiative (31% vs. 7%) and Doing What I Don't Want to Do (29% vs. 2%). Likewise, Taking Care of Myself was mentioned by substantially more college-educated respondents (26%) than high school–educated respondents (15%), although this difference did not reach significance at the .05 level.

Juggling and Balancing proved to be the dominant metaphors that college-educated respondents used to discuss responsibility. Via these metaphors, responsibilities become depersonalized and objectified commodities that can be selected, manipulated, controlled, "fudged," or even dropped altogether. Work, family, social life, and "self-time" then become "balls in the air" that must be kept aloft, and the task of the responsible college-educated person becomes to "lay things down just perfectly so all the pieces fit." In keeping with the idea of controlling responsibilities, mentions of prioritizing, planning, list-making, organizing, or otherwise "taming" responsibilities were also included in this category. One college-educated woman gave a typical example of this way of being responsible: "I am good at juggling multiple tasks. I have a family life that demands that, I have a personal life that demands that, and I have a professional life that demands that."

This category is not just the sentiment of working mothers; college-educated men also more frequently summoned the metaphor of Juggling and Balancing responsibilities than did high school–educated respondents: "Life should be a balance, you know, of work, of fun, of commitments." However, among college-educated respondents, significantly more women than men mentioned Juggling and Balancing in the course of their interviews (57% vs. 28%). This interaction of gender with education may reflect both the greater number of domains for which college-educated women are responsible as well as the type of self required by the work and community roles that they occupy. While high school–educated women doubtlessly encounter the same array of responsibilities as homemakers, caregivers, workers, and community members, college-educated women often face greater expectations in each of these domains, by virtue of the increased status, skills, and resources that their education imparts. As the number of responsibilities and the time and attention that they demand increase for college-educated women, so may the premium they place on organization and planning. Moreover, in assuming higher-status work and community roles that have traditionally been occupied by college-educated men, college-educated women may also be adopting the ways of being often associated with their predecessors—namely, an independent, autonomous, and proactive approach to the world. Thus this heightened emphasis on Juggling and Balancing by college-educated women may reflect both their interaction in historically male workplaces and the panoply of domains to which they are accountable.

Similar to Juggling and Balancing, the category Taking Initiative communicates the idea of having control over one's responsibilities. Instead of subscribing to the high school–educated respondents' idea of social responsibility as adjusting themselves to circumstances, college-educated respondents equated being responsible with adjusting circumstances to themselves, that is, with affecting situations according to their own needs, desires, and abilities. Responses in this category took two forms. The first sense of Taking Initiative involves seeking out new responsibilities, taking on extra responsibilities, exceeding expectations, and taking control of outcomes. As a college-educated man expressed this idea, "I seek out responsibility, and I believe in an individual being responsible for his or her own actions." A college-educated woman echoed this controlled, self-focused sense of responsibility with, "I tend to take a little more responsibility than maybe what's expected of me. When I want to do something, I want to do it right."

This woman's emphasis on "doing things right"—as opposed to the high school–educated way of being responsible, "doing my best"—hints at a second manifestation of the category Taking Initiative. In this formulation of the category, respondents list good outcomes or their current contentment as evidence of having been responsible. Thus being responsible is not merely a matter of exerting effort, but of achieving and succeeding. For example, a college-educated man reasoned, "Things have turned out reasonably successful for me. . . . I sort of believe that if you have some successes, you've had to manage in certain ways to achieve that success." Discussing the responsibility associated with building a house of her own, a college-educated woman stated, "I have to say, I did a great job."

The experience of control over responsibilities by college-educated respondents also seems to heighten their awareness of those responsibilities that they would prefer not to have. This is reflected in their significantly greater tendency to explain that they are responsible because they are Doing What I Don't Want to Do. When defining responsibilities as undesirable impositions, these respondents seem to be suggesting that what one has to do is inherently antithetical to what one wants to do. The college-educated woman quoted above cinched this opposition between "extrinsic" and "intrinsic" motivators—between "have to" and "want to"—with her claim, "when I want to do something, I want to do it right, not because I'm supposed to, but because that makes me feel good." In this distinction, responsibilities are typically designated as have-to's that conflict with want-to's. Thus responsibilities that are "things I don't want to do" are experienced as encroaching or impinging upon the self instead of as integral or desirable to the self. A college-educated woman captured the essence of this category with, "There are things that I have to take care of, and that doesn't necessarily mean that it's all going to be for my gratification. It's not all going to be because I'm going to get something out of it." Speaking about his church duties, a college-educated man echoed this sentiment with, "I take on the responsibility and I complete it, which is the reason for instance why I have stuck with being treasurer at church and with this other committee that I'm on that I'd really rather not be spending all my time at right now."

The idea of responsibilities as objects in the world that are juggled, balanced, sought, mastered, external, and often unwanted presumes the existence of a self that juggles, balances, takes initiative, and knows its preferences. As alluded to by their relatively higher endorsement of Taking Care of Myself, college-educated respondents seem to have reified this elaborated, independent self as another obligation. A result of this reification is their frequent lament of failing to take care of the self.

As a college-educated woman related, "And typically what gets lost for me is . . . a sense of responsibility to myself, which would be, you know, take a weekend off and just go sit under a tree."

Moreover, respondents often viewed Taking Care of Myself as a necessary precursor to, and yet competing with, fulfilling obligations to others. For example, college-educated respondents often expressed that attending to others hinges on first taking care of the self: "Be good to myself, responsible to myself . . . realize that I have to, you know, go to the gym and, you know, keep my health up, and get my down time. . . . Otherwise [I] build up a lot of passive-aggressive resentment." The need to take care of the self in order to take care of others, as expressed by many college-educated respondents, contrasts with the high school–educated respondents' references to others as the source of their own sense of being responsible. Thus for college-educated respondents, the experience of responsibility seems to be more self-situated, while for high school–educated respondents, the experience of responsibility may be more socially derived and maintained.

Contrasting High School–Educated and College-Educated Selves

We have argued that the meanings and understandings of responsibility outlined so far are differentially distributed across educational strata because of differences in the primary and extended social worlds of these respondents, and thus in the selves that are developed and maintained to link individuals to their relevant communities and societies. Based on findings from the national data set, we know that respondents with a high school education, compared to respondents with a college education, are likely to participate in communities where there are more people confronting serious illness, unemployment, and a variety of complex financial and family problems either of their own or of the significant others in their lives. Moreover, these respondents have fewer resources of every type with which to confront these difficulties.

It is reasonable then that the everyday lived experiences of the high school–educated respondents afford and foster the greater awareness of social embeddedness that characterizes their explanations of responsibility. In many working-class contexts, it is essential to be attuned to and responsive to the needs and requirements of others—such needs and requirements structure everyday life. Agency may be experienced as adjusting to these contingencies and obligations—"catching the ball when it's thrown." The immediate pressures associated with lives in these contexts may well preclude the opportunity to focus on and care for one's self and thus also preclude a sense of responsibility to do so. Moreover, the structure of networks and communities with fewer financial resources is likely to foster reciprocity and interdependence among people. If people do not help or respond to others when required to do so, they are unlikely to get help when they need it.

In contrast, respondents with a college education live lives in which they confront more "individualized" problems and stresses that need to be "controlled" and "managed" and in which immediate hands-on support from other people is less likely to be required and is also not as useful. The college educated are then relatively more "free" to focus on themselves and their responsibilities to their own individual needs and requirements. Moreover, as a consequence of the more extended social world of those with a college education, they are likely to encounter a more diverse set of expectations and requirements from others—expectations that call on them to take initiative and control, which fosters a proactive sense of agency.

The self then is the primary locus of sociocultural influence and will reflect the patterns of interpersonal relationships and the ways in which people habitually relate to each other in their relevant social worlds. Some ways of being responsible imply a sense of self that is fully interdependent with the encompassing social world, while other ways define the self as separate from and even in opposition to the social world and the responsibilities it entails. Attending to the Needs of Others and Being Dependable to Others are examples of the former, while Juggling and Balancing, Doing What I Don't Want to Do, and Taking Care of Myself are examples of the latter. Adjusting to Circumstances suggests a self that exercises agency by adapting to the external world, while Taking Initiative suggests a self that exercises agency by influencing the external world. Given the differences between high school–educated and college-educated respondents in their mentions of these different ways of being responsible, we may infer that the high school–educated respondents and college-educated respondents have somewhat different senses of self.

To provide better snapshots of these two kinds of self, we calculated the relative emphases placed on different ways of being responsible within each educational group. Using the categorical coding described above, we summed the total number of coded statements for high school–educated respondents ($n = 119$) and college-educated respondents ($n = 138$). There was no significant difference in number of coded statements between education groups. Within each education group, we then summed the number of coded statements for each category and divided them by the total number of coded statements for the group. Figure 9.2 represents the resulting percentages.

For high school–educated respondents, the ways of being responsible that make up the common notion of responsibility—that is, Meeting Obligations, Attending to the Needs of Others, and Being Dependable to Others—account for 73% of their codable responses to the two probes. In contrast, the same combination of responses accounts for only 56% of the college-educated respondents' answers. This comparison suggests that while the majority of respondents across educational levels adhere to the common notion of responsibility, high school–educated respondents place a greater emphasis on these core ideas than do college-educated respondents.

By adding Adjusting to Circumstances to the common notion of responsibility, we can account for almost 90% of high school–educated respondents' answers to the two direct questions about their responsibility. Yet the same combination of reasons only explains 60% of the college-educated respondents' answers. The remaining 40% fell into the more self-focused categories of Juggling and Balancing, Taking Initiative, Doing What I Don't Want to Do, and Taking Care of Myself. Comparing the charts for the two groups, it is these four segments of the pie that differ the most between educational levels, constituting a much larger proportion of the pie for college-educated respondents than for high school–educated respondents. Accordingly, the more other-focused ways of being responsible are less prominent for the college-educated respondents.

These comparisons of the relative emphases on the different ways of being responsible within each educational group echo the findings from the group comparisons discussed above. High school–educated respondents' relatively greater emphasis on the common notion of responsibility is largely due to their greater emphasis on Being Dependable to Others (high school educated: 21%; college educated: 12%), suggesting that these respondents' experiences of being responsible are more dependent on the trust, dependence, and reliance of others. From this we may infer that for high school–educated respondents, the self is experienced as more interdependent with specific others than is the case for college-educated respondents. High school–educated respondents also placed greater relative emphasis on Attending to the Needs of Others (high school educated: 22%; college educated: 17%), providing further evidence that being responsible is more other-focused for

High School–Educated Respondents

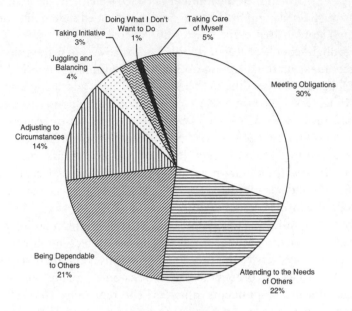

College-Educated Respondents

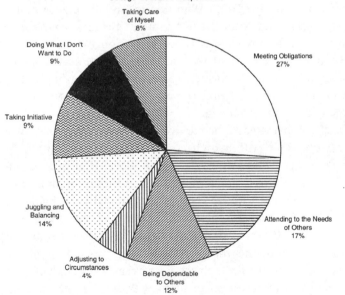

FIGURE 9.2. Relative emphases on categories of responsibility, by education level.

them than it is for college-educated respondents. Finally, their greater relative emphasis on Adjusting to Circumstances (high school educated: 14%; college educated: 4%) suggests that the more interdependent high school–educated respondents are more intent on tailoring themselves to a world of which they are an integral part, instead of manipulating a world from which they are independent.

College-educated respondents, on the other hand, seem to have a more defined, more separated sense of self that not only requires their responsiveness, but is sometimes in conflict with the requirements of others or at odds with the contingencies of the shared world. As their greater relative emphasis on the metaphor of Juggling and Balancing would suggest (high school educated: 4%; college educated: 14%), college-educated respondents may view the self as separated from its obligations and responsibilities. Not only is this self separated, but its preferences and desires are also more highly elaborated, as shown through their more frequent endorsement of Doing What I Don't Want to Do as a way of being responsible (high school educated: 1%; college educated: 9%). Finally, this more individuated, autonomous self may also express its preferences, traits, and abilities by Taking Initiative—that is, by selecting and excelling at those responsibilities that best reflect one's "true" self (high school educated: 3%; college educated: 9%). In this manner, the external world in which one participates is chosen, controlled, and even changed according to the needs and desires of the self.

Self-Focused versus Other-Focused Answers

To explore further the emerging trend for college-educated respondents to portray a self that is more elaborated, separate, and autonomous than high school–educated respondents do, we coded every sentence of the answers explaining the statements "I am responsible" and "I am good at managing the responsibilities of life" according to whether the emphasis of the sentence was on the self or on other people. There were no significant differences among the gender and education subgroups in the number of sentences spoken. These self/other coding categories (Mention of Self, Mention of Others, Focus on Self, Focus on Others) were designed to determine (1) who (the self, the other, or both) was mentioned in each sentence of a respondent's answer and (2) who was the main focus of each sentence.

Sentences were coded in the Mentions of Self category when the respondent explicitly mentioned the self by using the words "me," "myself," or "I" (e.g., as when a college-educated woman said, "I guess, because I think like that, I'm list maker, and, you know, following through on the tasks, and that kind of thing"). This category included the words "you," "we," and mentions of the generic person ("everybody," "people," etc.) when they were appropriate substitutes for the words "I" or "me" (i.e., when they implied that the self was included in their meaning).

Sentences were coded in the Mentions of Others category when the respondent explicitly mentioned other people in the sentence. This category included both specified others such as children, relatives, friends, and co-workers as well as unspecified others labeled "people," "others," etc. (e.g., as when a high school–educated man answered, "And if I were not responsible, if I made a mistake, I could be responsible for hurting someone"). Mentions of roles that implied relations with others were also counted (e.g., parent).

Sentences were coded in the Focus on Self category when the self was the subject of the sentence or the main focus of the content was the self. Respondents often portrayed the self as a proactive agent influencing the external world. They may have mentioned other people, but others were not the primary focus of the sentence. For example, a college-educated man expressed this kind of self-focus with his statement, "I believe that, uh, I have a strong personality, and I am a person who accepts responsibility—in fact seeks it out."

Sentences were coded in the Focus on Others category when other people were the subject of the sentence or the main focus of the content was on other people. The respondent may have mentioned himself or herself , but he or she was not the primary focus of the sentence. Respondents often portrayed themselves as playing a reactive role in response to external circumstances, as when a high school–educated man explained, "I have a sense of responsibility towards my family and my community."

In general, the majority of sentences for the total population only mentioned the self ("The older I got, the more responsibilities I got"), and a few sentences mentioned only the other ("She was always the strong one"). Many sentences like the following mentioned both the self and the other: "When someone's asked me to do something, I've done it to the best of my ability." Some sentences mentioned others, but focused on the self: "I was independent for years before I married my husband." Other sentences mentioned the self, but focused on others: "If somebody tells me they're going to be somewhere and they want to meet me, I'll be there." A few sentences like the following focused equally on the self and the other: "Not a day goes by that my daughter and I don't talk; either she calls me or I call her."

All of the self/other coding categories contained at least one sentence from each of the subgroups created by educational level and gender. We divided each respondent's sentences mentioning or focusing on the self by his or her sentences mentioning or focusing on others. The ratios presented below are the means for each subgroup.

Men mentioned the self 1.89 times more often than they mentioned others, while women mentioned the self 1.28 times more often than they mentioned others. This finding is in accordance with a variety of findings that suggest that women are more interconnected with others than men are (Cross and Madson 1997).

A more striking difference occurs when we compare the sentence ratios of Focus on Self to Focus on Others between education subgroups. College-educated respondents focused on the self 3.85 times more often than they focused on others, while high school–educated respondents focused on the self only 1.79 times more often than they focused on others (figure 9.3). A college-educated woman focusing on the self gave the following response: "Because I am very responsible, even when it's something I really don't like to do, and there are quite a few things like that." In contrast, a high school–educated man focusing on others said, "For my family and . . . if somebody's counting on me for something, I try not to let him down, you know."

Furthermore, when we compared the ratios of self/other mentions with self/other focused sentences (figure 9.3), we found that even though both college-educated and high school–educated respondents mention the self and others in similar ratios, the focuses of these sentences differ. In other words, even though college-educated respondents mentioned the self or others just as many times as high school–educated respondents, the college-educated respondents focused more on themselves, even when they mentioned others. For example, the following response from a college-educated man mentions others but focuses on the self: "Well, I mean, I'm responsible in that, if when, when people bring work in to have it done, I mean, I get it done. I get it back to them." In contrast, the following response from a high school–educated man mentions others and focuses on others: "Responsibilities that I have have to do with her [wife] . . . make sure she's happy and

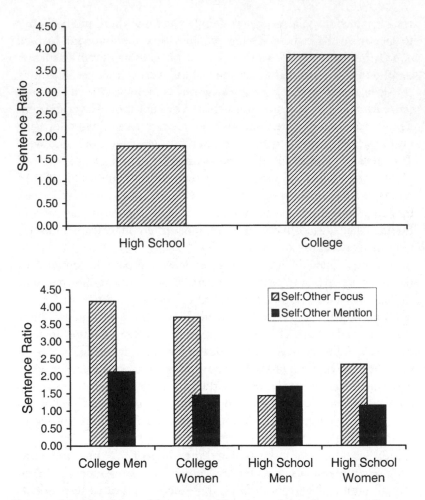

FIGURE 9.3. Mentions of focus on self versus others when providing examples and explanations of responsibility. The top chart shows the ratio of self-focused to other-focused sentences. The bottom chart shows the ratios of self-mentioned to other-mentioned sentences and corresponding ratios of self-focused to other-focused sentences.

pleased." This difference in focus occurs most strongly among men. High school–educated men were more likely to focus on others when others were mentioned in a sentence than any other subgroup.

In summary, college-educated respondents did mention others in their answers just as often as high school–educated respondents, but the college-educated respondents' language and phrasing reveal a focus on a self that is separate from others. The following statement from a college-educated man exemplifies this self-focus in mentions of others: "I went away to college, seven hundred miles from my family and everyone I knew. That made me responsible." As this response illustrates, the college-educated, independent and proactive selves might be due in part to the geographic move away from families of origin and into the diffuse social world of the university.

Responses from the high school–educated, on the other hand, reveal a self which is embedded in a network of other people. Responsibilities are framed and explained from the perspective of other people. A high school–educated woman provides a clear example: "My pastor even says when somebody says something to him, you just give it to [respondent], she'll take care of it, she knows what to do." This interconnected sense of self might also contribute to the high school–educated respondents' readiness to adjust to circumstances. For example, if they are subject to multiple demands from close kin, they might adopt a more reactive style of acting in the world.

"Why Has My Life Gone Well?"

Mentions of responsibility also occurred in responses to open-ended questions that did not directly ask about responsibility. The question "Thinking back over your life, what are some of the reasons your life has gone well?" generated extensive commentary from respondents about the socially responsible behavior of others that they regarded as part of the explanation for their own well-being. That is, our sample participants accounted for why their own lives had turned out well by pointing to the responsible, caring, giving actions of significant others, such as parents. These responses underscore an important connection between the giving and receiving ends of social responsibility and, thereby, convey possible socialization avenues through which individuals come to be responsive to the needs of others (i.e., by having been the recipients of such efforts from others).

Overall, our respondents provided a wide variety of reasons to account for why their lives had gone well, such as their early family life, their current family life, or their hard work, education, or faith. Organized from a social responsibility perspective, their answers generated eight primary categories, five of which speak directly to issues of responsibility: generativity (e.g., being helped or encouraged by others, especially at work, or mentoring others), early family (e.g., having nurturing, supportive parents), current family (e.g., having wonderful children, a loving spouse), caring (e.g., caring about and for others), and support (e.g., from friends, social networks, co-workers). For some of these answers (e.g., those in the categories of generativity, early family, and support), the respondents were speaking of themselves as recipients of others' social responsibility. For others (e.g., those in the caring category), their comments described themselves as doing for others. Other typical answers to why life had gone well dealt with themes of work (e.g., working hard, following a work ethic), agency (e.g., pursuing goals, having control), and religion/spirituality (e.g., having faith in God). These answers may be indirectly linked to social responsibility (i.e., by working hard, pursuing goals, or practicing my faith, I may contribute positively to the lives of others). Alternatively, answers in the work and agency categories may reflect strongly individualistic themes in accounting for why life has gone well. Finally, two kinds of responses for why life has gone well (pertaining to luck or openness to experience) revealed little connection to the theme of social responsibility and, as such, were not included in the analyses summarized below.

Figure 9.4 reveals the proportion of persons (by educational level) who answered in the eight primary response categories. References to early family were made by most respondents across both groups, although significantly more college-educated than high school–educated respondents answered in this category. Second highest, in terms of proportion of respondents, were answers pertaining to current family, where there was minimal difference by educational standing. Significantly more college-educated respondents spoke of their own agency in explaining why their lives had gone well, thereby underscoring their more individualistic, proactive ways of framing life success; significantly more high school–educated respondents spoke of religion/spirituality. Similarly, significantly more college-educated respondents spoke of support from friends and others, while more high school–educated respondents referred to their own hard work. High school–educated respondents were also more likely to emphasize caring than college-educated respondents, and both groups gave comparable emphasis to generativity. Men and women revealed generally similar patterns (i.e., what category was first, second, third, etc. in proportion of respondents), although within each category, men responded with greater frequency than women.

Figure 9.5 further differentiates the types of answers obtained when respondents spoke about aspects of their early family in explaining why their lives had gone well. The pie charts summarize the frequency

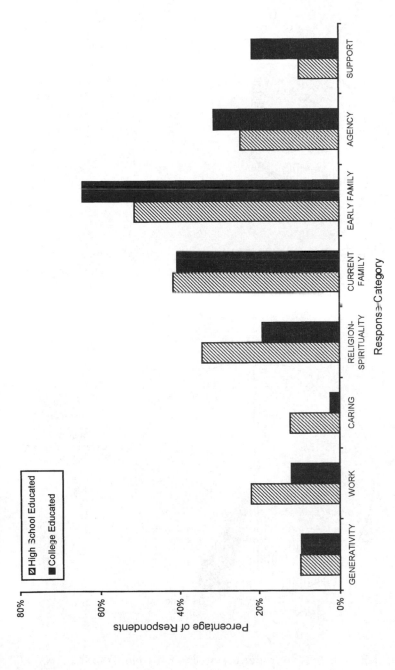

FIGURE 9.4. Social responsibility categories of responses to the question "Why has your life gone well?" Note that 11.9% of the college educated and 2.4% of the high school educated did not mention any social responsibility category.

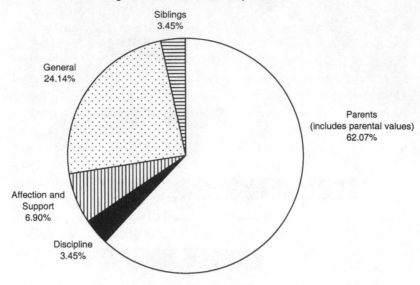

High School–Educated Respondents

Siblings
3.45%

General
24.14%

Parents
(includes parental values)
62.07%

Affection and
Support
6.90%

Discipline
3.45%

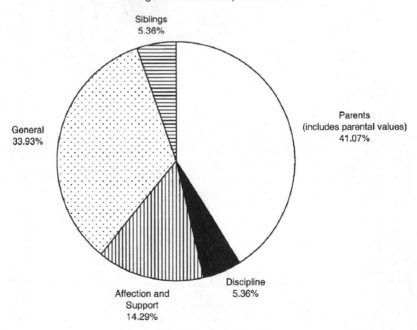

College-Educated Respondents

Siblings
5.36%

General
33.93%

Parents
(includes parental values)
41.07%

Affection and
Support
14.29%

Discipline
5.36%

FIGURE 9.5. "Why has your life gone well?": Early family influences. For high school–educated respondents, $n = 41$, total number of mentions = 29. For college-educated respondents, $n = 42$, total number of mentions = 56.

of mentions about parents (including specific mentions of mother, father, and parental values), discipline, affection/support (includes affection and support of parents, grandparents, and other family members), siblings, and general early family influences (e.g., a good foundation, a wonderful family). Note that because each respondent could answer in more than one category, these charts do not show percentages of respondents (as in the bar graphs), but frequencies of mentions of particular categories. Educational level, again, reveals more noticeable differences than gender does. For example, nearly two-thirds of comments from high school–educated respondents cited parents in explaining why their lives had turned out well, compared to only about 40% of the comments of college-educated respondents, a significant difference. College-educated individuals, however, made significantly more specific mentions of the affection/support of their parents than did high school–educated respondents.

Apart from these percentage differences, differences in how respondents spoke about these early family influences were evident. Illustrative comments when respondents spoke about parental values and parental support are summarized in table 9.2. We selected these answers from among the larger pool of responses because they show overlap in certain values, such as honesty and hard work, for both educational groups, as well as distinctive differences in values. For example, these high school–educated respondents referred to being taught "right from wrong," while the college-educated respondents emphasized being taught the importance of education and volunteering. In speaking about parental support, these selected responses exhibit more college-educated respondent commentary about being loved and having opportunities than do the responses from the high school educated. However, both groups frequently mentioned supportive parents.

Figure 9.6 elaborates the subcategories of answers coded under the primary category of agency: being self-made, exercising control/responsibility, pursuing goals, and being resilient. Both educational groups (and both genders) revealed generally similar patterns of emphasis, although college-educated respondents spoke more frequently of pursuing goals than did high school–educated respondents, and the latter, in turn, spoke more frequently about their resilience in the face of life's adversities than did those with college degrees. The resilience category reveals the same emphasis on reacting to external circumstances that is central to the category Adjusting to Circumstances noted in the earlier depiction of high school–educated responsibility.

Table 9.2 Early Family Influences

"WHY HAS YOUR LIFE GONE WELL?"

HIGH SCHOOL–EDUCATED RESPONDENTS

Parental Values: (female) *Well, the way I was raised, the things my parents taught me—I guess right from wrong, basically.* • (female) *I think it was the love and some of the values that she tried to teach me. . . . To do it the right way the first time, and you won't have to go back to it. I never forget that. And I've always told my girls that, "If you do it right the first time, you won't have to go back and do it again." And she also taught me: "If you tell one lie, you'll have to tell another one to support that lie, and before you know it, you done tell so many lies that you're bogged down until you don't know what the truth is yourself." So she always told me, "Be truthful and the truth will always win."* • (male) *I think he was extremely honest, an extremely hard worker, and taught me that whatever I was going to make, I would have to do it on my own.* • (male) *They taught me right from wrong. And I just knew what was right and what was wrong, and just as far as I go up from there, as far as going from the ground up. And in all of those areas.*

Affection/Support: (male) *My parents were fairly strict, not overly, but made sure we knew right from wrong. And they encouraged us to do a lot of different things, to try a lot of different things.*

COLLEGE-EDUCATED RESPONDENTS

Parental Values: (female) *Honesty and trustworthiness, religion, hard work—they're just hard workers. Just basic kinds of moral-type values.* • (female) *They gave us a strong sense of values. Education was very important. Sharing and giving back something was always important. Strong sense of family.* • (male) *My father worked in a factory all of his life. He taught me to always do your best in whatever you do. I've tried to adhere to that. I've tried to pass that on to my kids.* • (male) *My parents demonstrated to me that hard work was necessary and worthwhile. That volunteering in certain things was the right thing to do because I got a lot of satisfaction from that kind of stuff, although it's a pain in the neck sometimes, too. But I feel good about me when I've done something, and I know that's why (wife) does it, and why she's at the soup kitchen this afternoon.*

Affection/Support: (female) *Well, I think because I feel like my parents love me, and I had a happy childhood, and opportunities to learn things, go to school, and was supported in worthwhile things that I wanted to do.* • (male) *I had parents that were extremely supportive. In terms of my talent and my abilities in where I wanted to go and what I wanted to do with my life, they understood it partially because they're both artistic. . . . And I'm their pride and joy, and they love me to death, and we have a great relationship, and a lot of mutual respect, and they were always encouraging me.*

High School–Educated Respondents

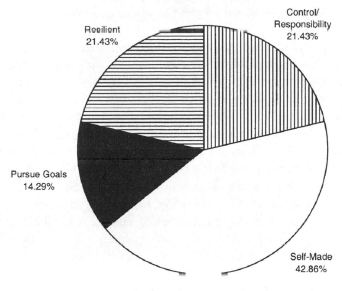

College-Educated Respondents

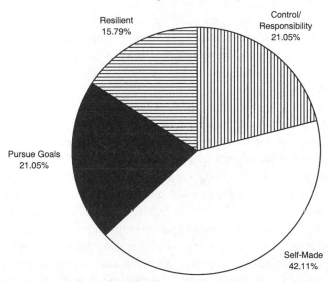

FIGURE 9.6. "Why has your life gone well?": Agency. For high school–educated respondents, $n = 41$, total number of mentions $= 14$. For college-educated respondents, $n = 42$, total number of mentions $= 19$.

Similarly, the theme of pursuing goals is similar in tone to the proactive, achievement-oriented Juggling and Balancing conception of social responsibility found among college-educated individuals.

The quantitative contrasts are again embellished by examination of differences in the actual words coded into these categories. Rather than provide an exhaustive summary of all comments, we chose responses that reveal both similarities (at the level of abstract categories) and differences (at the level of specific illustrations) between educational groups. Table 9.3 provides select responses for high school–educated and college-educated men and women across the subcategories of agency. Both genders and both educational groups spoke about pursuing goals, having a sense of control/responsibility (e.g., "I've always accepted responsibility for making my own way through life"; "I'm the kind of person who says I'm going to take control of my life") and being self-made ("taking initiative," "making it happen"), but these were described with different examples according to educational level (i.e., college-educated respondents spoke of working to get a college education or to finish nursing school, whereas high school–educated respondents spoke of these qualities with regard to efforts to quit smoking, make a down payment on a house, or have another child). All respondents, but especially high school–educated respondents, emphasized similar themes of hanging tough, not buckling under, and surviving obstacles (coded as resilient responses) in explaining why their lives have gone well.

In summary, our analyses of spontaneously generated answers to why life has gone well revealed numerous patterns. Overall, men answered with greater frequency in all categories than did women, although the general pattern of responses was similar by gender. With regard to education, the college-educated respondents gave greater emphasis to early family, agency, and support, while the high school–educated respondents gave greater emphasis to religion/spirituality, work, and caring. The emphasis on agency among college-educated respondents extends the more proactive, individualistic themes found among college-educated respondents in the prior analyses of questions that asked directly about responsibility. In addition, the other-oriented responses regarding caring given more often by the high school–educated respondents reveal an emphasis on the self giving to others. In contrast, the responses regarding support given more often by college-educated respondents reveal a need for others to be giving to the self. This college-educated self-focus versus the high school–educated

TABLE 9.3 Agency Responses

"WHY HAS YOUR LIFE GONE WELL?"

HIGH SCHOOL–EDUCATED RESPONDENTS

Control/Responsibility. (female) *I thought, if I worked hard enough and got money for a down payment on a house and got out of the apartment—that's when I wanted to have another (child); that's when I was beginning to see that I could, didn't have to drift with things; I could take charge of things.*

Self-Made: (male) *I don't know, whenever I've made up my mind to do something, really made up my mind to do it, I could do it. I wanted to quit smoking. I made up my mind to quit smoking. I was smoking two and a half packs a day, and I just made up my mind that that was it. It took me six months on a smoking program. . . . I was smoking two and a half packs, I cut it down to a pack. And I did that because that was a unit that I could work with. And so then when I made up my mind that I was quitting altogether, I was then smoking a pack a day. And I just stopped smoking. I haven't had a cigarette since.*

Pursue Goals: (female) *You have goals and you work for them. . . . I had to work at night and go to school in the daytime. I worked till midnight every night and went to school all day to achieve what I wanted. But you know if you want somethin', and you work hard, then you know, you know, you're gonna get it, sooner or later.*

Resilient: (male) *Yeah, probably the self-confidence, endurance, you know, not giving up. Just hang in there, hang tough. Things are going to get around to here real eventu-ally. ● (female) I've worked hard—physically, mentally. I have ● been a lot of hard times, but we've come through them all. . . . So all of those things just taught me more and more about what was important. It's how you survive the obstacles, and probably with truth for knowing that I've done pretty well with it is just that—at least I did go find the help and sought and sought and sought till somebody gave me some answers and helped me, even though it took four years of total frustration.*

COLLEGE-EDUCATED RESPONDENTS

Control: Responsibility: (male) *But probably the main reason I think is I've always accepted responsibility for making my own way through life, not look for excuses, or things like that.*

Self-Made: (male) *I don't sit back and wait for things to happen. You know, I'm very motivated and engageable. So I'm always thinking about "What do I want to do now?" and "What do I want to do next?" . . . [S]o I'd have to say one of the reasons why my life has gone well is because . . . I'm not leaning against a tree somewhere watching things, just waiting for something to happen to me. You know, I'm actively pursuing, and I'm researching and looking and figuring out, and uh, and enjoying that process. . . . I think that's another reason why my life goes where it does, because I push it along.*

Pursue Goals: (male) *Well, one of the reasons is I set up my goals, and I, uh, followed my goals. In other words, it's like early in the game, I set a goal: "Okay, I'm gonna get a college education." I knew exactly what college I was gonna go, and I could. I knew exactly what degree I was gonna get and everything, and that was my first goal. Also, a goal at that time was start investing, which I did. So the goals I have set, you know, that the reason that, I guess I'm fairly well off.* ● (female) *Because I was goal-oriented from an early age. . . . I was blessed with ability to do whatever it was I wanted to do.*

Resilient: (female) *I will take some credit for things going well because I think I'm a, a fairly strong person, and I think when there are things that are tough for some peo-ple, maybe would, would buckle under or not be able to move forward, I, I think I'm stronger than some in that way.*

other-focus is similar to the results of the self/other coding mentioned earlier.

The unpacking of subcategories from the major categories revealed largely similar gender profiles, but markedly different profiles between educational levels. High school–educated respondents made more frequent mentions of their parents (including parental values), while college-educated respondents spoke more frequently about the affection and support from parents and other family members. Both groups emphasized values of honesty and hard work that had come from parents, but discipline was a more prominent topic among high school–educated respondents. Finally, not only did the frequency of responses within the agency category reveal different patterns by education (college-educated respondents generated responses about pursuing goals, and high school–educated respondents generated responses with resilience themes), but actual text, again in preliminary fashion, also illustrated distinct life challenges and pursuits for the high school educated versus college educated, among whom different types of agency are enacted.

Despite the prominence of the agentic, self-oriented responses among college-educated respondents, we underscore the notable emphasis they gave to acknowledging their parents and early home life in accounting for why their lives had gone well. Conceivably, their own midlife experiences as parents, where focus on the "other" is required, may prompt among them a new appreciation of the love, discipline, and resources provided by their own parents.

"What Are My Hopes for the Future?"

Themes of social responsibility were also evident in our respondents' answers to questions about their hopes for the future. Figure 9.7 reveals the proportion of college-educated versus high school–educated respondents who answered in the five primary response categories: own generativity, family and work, behavior and attitudes, religion/spirituality, and health. The most frequently occurring answer type involved family and work, which included references to various aspects of family life, work, and education. Significantly more college-educated than high school–educated respondents (as well as more women than men) answered in this category. The second most prominent answer among all subgroups was health (especially remaining healthy). Again, more college-educated than high school–educated respondents and more women than men generated this category and de-

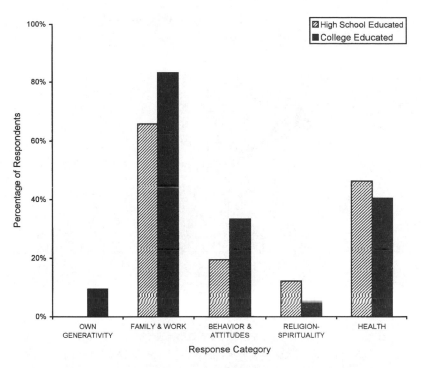

FIGURE 9.7. Social responsibility categories of responses to the question "What are your hopes for the future?" Note that 4.76% of the college educated and 9.76% of the high school educated did not mention any social responsibility category.

scribed their future hopes according to health topics. The third most frequently occurring response referred to prosocial behaviors and attitudes (e.g., concern about caring for the aging population; hopes for cures for major diseases; particular volunteer activities). More college-educated than high school–educated respondents referred to their future hopes in such terms. More high school–educated than college-educated respondents (and also more women than men) spoke about religion/spirituality (e.g., expressions of faith or religious practices such as praying or going to church) in describing their future hopes. References to their own generativity (e.g., helping future generations through efforts that revolve around teaching) were provided only by college-educated women.

Figure 9.8 differentiates the various types of answers obtained when respondents spoke about family and work in describing their hopes for

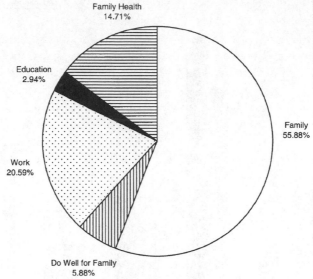

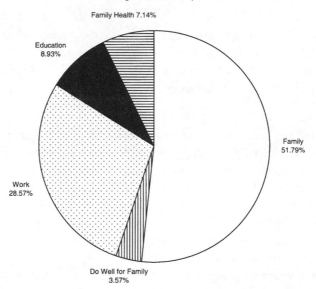

FIGURE 9.8. "What are your hopes for the future?": Family and work. For high school–educated respondents, $n = 41$, total number of mentions = 34. For college-educated respondents, $n = 42$, total number of mentions = 56.

the future. The most frequently mentioned subcategory for both educational groups was family. High school–educated respondents gave comparatively greater emphasis to speaking about family health, while college-educated respondents gave greater emphasis to speaking about their work and education. Women gave more emphasis to family, while men gave greater emphasis to work (data not shown). Illustrative answers (by educational subgroups) for some of these subcategories appear in table 9.4. Both educational groups spoke in detail about family, but they spoke about different things. High school–educated respondents spoke of wanting their children to find a good partner and of wanting grandchildren. College-educated respondents spoke about their children's education and careers. With regard to their own personal future hopes about work or education, high school–educated respondents spoke of wanting work to wind down or of wanting to continue learning for a specific activity (dog judging), while college-educated respondents spoke of getting another book published, establishing a new line of business (a court reporting firm), or learning new surgical techniques. These specifics about respondents' future hopes thus reflected differences in actual work lives and pursuits linked with occupations, which are in turn linked with different levels of educational attainment.

Figure 9.9 summarizes the distributions of subcategories within the main category of behaviors and attitudes when respondents spoke about their hopes for the future. College-educated respondents spoke most about making a contribution, having social concerns (such as having systems in place in society to handle the aging population, improved family values, and less prejudice) and being engaged in volunteerism. High school–educated respondents emphasized altruistic hopes (such as cures for diseases in the world and hopes that the whole world would be at peace) along with social concerns, and making a contribution, but did not mention volunteerism. Additionally, men gave greater emphasis to making a contribution, and women to social concerns and volunteerism. The fact that only college-educated respondents mentioned volunteerism while only high school–educated respondents mentioned altruistic hopes reflects their different ways of being an agent in the world. In the case of wanting to address societal concerns, college-educated people directly act on the cause by volunteering while high school–educated people indirectly act on the cause by expressing altruistic hopes.

Table 9.5 provides illustrative answers for our educational sub-

TABLE 9.4 Family and Work

"WHAT ARE YOUR HOPES FOR THE FUTURE?"

HIGH SCHOOL–EDUCATED RESPONDENTS

Family: (female) *To have grandkids, take care of them. See my son do well. But my son's just starting, so I would really, I'm looking forward to him getting a good job, and finding a nice girl, and having whatever kids if he wants kids. But that's—he's my life. Yeah, after my husband, he's my life. And that's what I'm looking forward to. After that everything else is fine.* • (male) *Hopes for my future are probably more targeted toward my kids and being happy, and finding someone that they can share their life with, like my wife and I have.*

Work: (female) *I really would like to put in about fifteen more years working, and I'm hoping that I really will have enough money or enough something, equity in my house or something.* • (male) *I'd like to enjoy the trips more, that's all. My business, I don't want the business necessarily to grow. I want it to grow enough to sustain itself, but not to, I don't need—If I make eighty chairs this year, I'll be very happy to make eighty chairs next year. I don't need to make eighty-five.*

Education: (female) *I would like to continue advancing with my career with dog judging. I have two groups. I'm applying now, working on the third group, which is a constant learning process. You have to take tests and do a lot of research and studyin' to each breed to apply, so it's a lot of work. I'd like to continue doing that.*

COLLEGE-EDUCATED RESPONDENTS

Family: (female) *You know, most of my hopes about the future, my thoughts turn to my children and what they're gonna do with their lives. Uh, I don't have any great hopes for starting a new career or things like that, but my hopes are tied up in the choices my kids are gonna make about which education they're gonna get. Are they going to be happy in their careers? Are they gonna marry? I've got a couple of kids who are older, who are not married, and so there's kind of a concern there. Will they marry? And if they don't, will they be happy? And I look forward to grandchildren. That's kind of an unknown area, but I think that's something that I'm looking forward to.* • (male) *Hopes for the future are to, to make sure my children get off to a good start when they get out of high school. That they're able to make some decisions about where they want to go with their education and not be prevented from doing it. And those areas of support, either financial support, or, um, sometimes it's just transportation, or whatever I can do in those areas to really make sure they get off on the right foot, they feel comfortable, and positive about their learning experience in college.*

Work: (female) *Well, I hope to graduate from court reporting school. And I would like actually to, what I would like to do is freelance, which, freelance reporters kind of make their own hours, schedule their own appointments. Uh, my eventual goal is to have my own court reporting firm, but I'm gonna get out and kind of work for awhile and kind of learn the ropes of that and, how to put it all together, and then that's really my plan as far as personally, I mean, for myself.* • (male) *Well, in the immediate future, I hope to get the second book published and uh, see what happens from that. I intend to keep studying and doing research, 'cause it's what I really enjoy doing. I just hope to be able to do it as long as I can.*

Education: (female) *I'm taking particular medical classes in surgical techniques, tropical medicine—things that will prepare me to even be better in what I like to do. And by this summer I should have a bed and breakfast. Other concrete hopes are I might do midwifery, which is a two-year, but mostly in-house. I wouldn't have to travel to Kentucky; I would do it through the local midwives, because I basically have a lot of the credentials already.* • (male) *I think by working towards this certification with these night classes that I'm taking—that'll certainly prepare me to go out and find another job if I need to.*

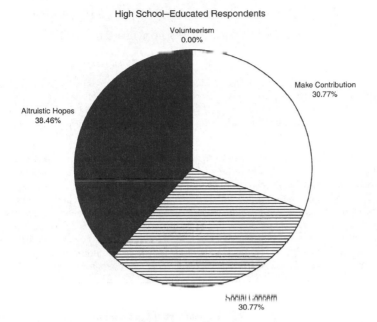

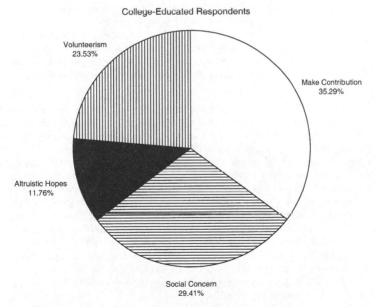

FIGURE 9.9. "What are your hopes for the future?": Socially responsible behaviors and attitudes. For high school–educated respondents, $n = 41$, total number of mentions = 13. For college-educated respondents, $n = 42$, total number of mentions = 17.

TABLE 9.5 Socially Responsible Behaviors and Attitudes

"WHAT ARE YOUR HOPES FOR THE FUTURE?"

HIGH SCHOOL–EDUCATED RESPONDENTS

Make Contribution: (male) *I ask the Lord, use me use, me in any way he see fit. Use me. Use me till you use me up. Whether it's preaching your word, whether it's singing your word, whether it's helping people. Whatever it is, use me. And that's for the future.* • (female) *Be a person that's willing to go that extra mile to help somebody in need.*

Social Concern: (male) *As far as my hopes for society, I guess you would say, or the world, I just would really like to see a lot of people change their attitudes. It seems like today a lot of people just don't care about themselves or anybody else. I think I'd like to see everybody just be a little more caring and think about other people's feelings a little more. I think the world would be a lot better place to live in all over if people just did that.* • (female) *As far as the, uh, world is concerned, I wish that, I would hope that they would come to their senses and come back to the Lord. I would hope that we would get a president and some men that were leaders of our country that would be true Christians. I firmly believe our country is going directly to hell.*

COLLEGE-EDUCATED RESPONDENTS

Make Contribution: (male) *It's been good, and if I can continue this kind of life and eventually, since I do not have any heirs, I would like to make sure that whatever I do accumulate goes to somewhere where it can be used beneficially for the most people.* • (female) *Yeah I like trips, but, I don't see those things as having any kind of meaning, or being any kind of contribution to the world, whereas by staying working, I think you can continue to impact, have some kind of driving force within your life that keeps you going, keeps you alive, and not dying in an intellectually or emotional fashion.*

Social Concern: (male) *Well, I hope that man goes on and explores the stars. I think it's important that humanity continues. We've explored all of this planet, and I think that we're surviving on a very, very fragile place. I think if humanity is going to survive this next millennium, we're going to need to spread ourselves to the universe, otherwise I don't think we'll survive. I hope that we're able to protect and take care of this planet of ours, but I don't know if we will. . . . I also hope that because the world is shrinking—due to travel and communications and all of that—that we will get beyond our differences. One of the most frustrating things in my life is seeing the fear and the hate between races and religions and countries. . . . I just hope that the consciousness of humanity will be raised to the point where we just all nurture each other.* • (female) *I would hope that people would, in general, realize the consequences of the choices they make, and how much impact that has on their lives and others. I really feel like correct choices with your interpersonal relationships and trying to do your best there could have the biggest impact on making changes in the world for the better. People can have a more stable and happier family life. I definitely believe that making the change with individuals, the individual lives, is much more important than big social or government programs. I think changes need to come in individual lives.*

groups. High school–educated respondents spoke of having the "Lord use me" or going "that extra mile to help somebody" in elaborating their version of making a contribution, while college-educated respondents emphasized making beneficial use of what they had accumulated (presumably wealth) and also "continuing to have impact." With regard to social concerns, high school–educated individuals spoke of people needing to be "more caring" and the need to "come back to the Lord." The college-educated version of social concerns addressed the need to "spread ourselves out into the universe" so as to "survive the next millennium" and to make "correct choices" with regard to interpersonal relationships. Such answers suggest additional educational differences in how social concerns are perceived and pursued, although further quantitative summaries are needed to gauge the extent of such differences.

In summary, when describing their hopes for the future, we found that more high school–educated than college-educated respondents emphasized family and work. Within this category, those with less education spoke more frequently about family health, perhaps reflecting education-based inequalities in health and healthcare resources (see chapter 3). In addition, high school–educated respondents spoke more often about wanting their children to "find a good partner" in life. Such findings converge with the greater "other" orientation found among high school–educated respondents in our prior self/other analyses. College-educated respondents spoke more often about work or education goals for their children as well as their own occupational pursuits, thereby underscoring their proactive desires to have a wide sphere of influence. Both groups demonstrated themes of socially responsible behaviors and attitudes in articulating future hopes, but among the college-educated this was linked with volunteerism, "having impact," or making beneficial use of their resources. That is, the college-educated conception of a socially responsible future assumes the possession of time, resources, and energy, and being well-positioned to proactively make the world a better place. For high school–educated respondents, a socially responsible future is tied more to religious sentiments (having the "Lord use me," needing to "come back to the Lord") and helping or caring for others (altruistic hopes). Religion and spirituality thus emerged as more prominent among high school–educated responses, not only for why their lives had gone well, but also as a theme in their hopes for the future. Such religious beliefs may be part of dealing with adversity (linked with the prior high school–educated emphasis on resilience and finding the strength to persevere) as well as central to how an uncertain future is to be negotiated (e.g., being a vessel of the Lord).

A theme underlying these educational differences in hopes for the future is that the more expansive social worlds of the college educated lead them to think of their communities or even of global issues, whereas the high school–educated respondents focus on the proximal social worlds of work and family, along with their religious connections.

CONCLUSION

In this chapter we explored responsibility in two ways: via direct questions about responsibility and indirect probes coded for mentions of social responsibility. The direct route involved asking respondents to tell us *why* they described themselves as more or less responsible. These items allowed respondents to discuss responsibility in their own words, offering insight into the variety of meanings that may be assigned to "responsibility." In answers to the indirect probes, "Why has your life gone well?" and "What are your hopes for the future?" the centrality of social responsibility concerns was striking. In addition, this set of questions provided us with multiple avenues into the notion of responsibility over time. In other words, we were able to find out the ways in which respondents consider themselves to be responsible in everyday life, how other people's past socially responsible actions have enabled respondents' lives to go well, and the ways in which respondents hope to be socially responsible in the future. These findings enable us to identify the agreements about responsibility among midlife Americans, as well as to illuminate gender and educational differences in these notions. In addition, our results allow us to sketch the complexities of social responsibility in late-twentieth-century American life.

Educational differences provided insight into the different ways in which people are responsible, conceive of the self, and perceive the self in relation to others. As analyses of the direct probes demonstrate, college-educated respondents presented more elaborated conceptions of the self, as reflected in their greater emphasis on self-focused responsibility categories. Further, these self-focused ways of being responsible (e.g., Doing What I Don't Want to Do, Juggling and Balancing, Taking Care of Myself) suggest a sense of self that is autonomous, separated from, and sometimes in opposition to, other people. In contrast, high school–educated respondents placed less emphasis on these self-focused categories and greater emphasis on the common notion of responsibility and on more socially situated ways of being responsible (e.g., Being Dependable to Others).

We found further evidence for educational differences, both in the conception of the self and in the relationship between the self and others, in the coding for self-focused and other-focused sentences. While both high school–educated and college-educated respondents mentioned other people in their answers, high school–educated respondents focused on the self significantly less than did college-educated respondents. Additionally, in response to the indirect probe asking why one's life had gone well, high school–educated respondents' more frequent mentions of caring for others (i.e., *others* are the recipients of care) contrasts with college-educated respondents' heightened emphasis on receiving support (i.e., the *self* is the recipient of care).

Differences in high school–educated and college-educated conceptions of the self and the social surround were also revealed by the types of agency that respondents at each educational level described. Across direct and indirect probes, the way of interacting with the world espoused by high school–educated respondents portrayed a sense of self as embedded in, adapting to, and constrained by external situations, while college-educated respondents' way of interacting with the world implied a sense of self as independent of, acting on, and controlling external situations. This difference is reflected in the finding that more high school–educated respondents than college-educated respondents invoked Adjusting to Circumstances in their answers to the direct probes. In contrast, college-educated respondents placed greater emphasis on Taking Initiative as a way of being responsible.

In addition, responses to the indirect probes coded as agency from high school–educated respondents tended to reflect the idea of resilience (e.g., surviving obstacles, hanging tough), whereas college-educated respondents more often exhibited agency through actively pursuing goals (e.g. set goals from an early age, "blessed with an ability to do whatever I wanted to do"). Similar differences emerged within the category socially responsible behaviors and attitudes: more college-educated respondents spoke of volunteerism—suggesting that better-educated people feel empowered and able to effect change—while high school–educated people more frequently mentioned altruistic hopes—indicating less of a sense of one's own personal, tangible influence on the world.

A final contrast between high school–educated and college-educated respondents is reflected in the examples and particular details they used in their narratives. For instance, coding of the family subcategory, within the category of family and work, revealed that high school–educated respondents spoke more about concern for their children's future health and choice of spouse. In contrast, college-educated respondents' concerns for their children focused more on educational and career goals. Similarly, college-educated respondents spoke of work aspirations, such as publishing another book, whereas high school–educated respondents spoke of putting in just enough time to retire comfortably. These differences in content reflect the realities of life for those occupying different social classes.

Though gender was one component of our selection criteria, gender differences were not pronounced in our analyses for this chapter. Regarding the direct probes, the only category which revealed gender differences was Juggling and Balancing responsibilities; more than twice as many college-educated women as college-educated men mentioned this category (57% vs. 28%). This finding may reflect the "second shift" that more college-educated women than men experience; several studies suggest that women maintain primary responsibility for domestic chores and upkeep (e.g., Hochschild 1989).

In addition, the self/other sentence coding revealed that men mentioned the self more often than they mentioned others with much greater frequency than women did. This finding supports the commonly held notion that women are more interconnected with others than men are. It should be noted, however, that high school–educated men were more likely to *focus* on others when others were mentioned in a sentence than any other subgroup. This second finding seems to reflect the overarching influence of educational level on a socially embedded sense of self.

The indirect questions about why one's life has gone well and what one's hopes are for the future revealed few but intriguing gender differences. Nearly twice as many men as women endorsed the category of work (22% vs. 11.9%). This may reflect the fact that work outside of the home plays a more central role for these midlife men than for the women. Nearly all the men were working outside the home for pay at the time of the MIDUS survey, and they had nearly three times more earnings than their spouses, on average. In contrast, only 50% of the high school–educated women were working for pay. Though 90% of college-educated women were working for pay, their earnings were about half of their husband's earnings, on average (see chapter 11, this volume). When talking about hopes for the future, women spoke more frequently about their families. Specifically, of the respondents who endorsed the category of family, 45.2% of the women (vs. 9.8% of the men) mentioned grandchildren. Thus the analysis of indirect probes reveals typical gender differences regarding separate spheres of influence for men and women: work and family, respectively.

Though we have highlighted the above gender differences, on the whole, our analyses did not reveal extensive differences between men and women. In some ways this trend is consistent with prior studies showing few differences in reported well-being of adult males and females (Ryff and Singer 1998). The one exception to this pattern is women's consistently higher profiles on positive relations with others. The fact that we preselected our respondents to be in the top two tertiles of well-being (see "Sample and Methods") may also account, in part, for the absence of strong gender differences.

Because we collected the data for the analyses in this chapter during our study of well-being at midlife, it is appropriate to mention connections between well-being and social responsibility. Our sample, chosen because they demonstrated high levels of psychological well-being, articulated varied examples of responsibility in many domains suggesting a link between well-being and responsibility. Evidence of this link is found in respondents' answers to our inquiry about why their lives have gone well: respondents frequently pointed to other people's socially responsible attitudes and actions. In addition, our respondents articulated their hopes for the future in terms of social responsibility, suggesting that being socially responsible may be one aspect of having a good life. Clearly, being responsible to one's self and others has potential psychological benefits that have not yet been explored, proffering an area for future research in the social sciences.

These qualitative data provide a rare opportunity to investigate meaning in a variety of ways. First, unpacking survey questions allows us to understand the layered meanings behind similar answers. Thus, when many respondents say that "responsible" describes them a lot, our analysis provides insight into what the word "responsible" means to different people. Second, open-ended questions allow researchers to explore meaning from the respondent's point of view, rather than creating a viewpoint with which respondents are only able to either agree or disagree. A clear example of this is the category names which were generated from respondents' replies, such as the categories Juggling and Balancing for the direct probes, or religion/spirituality for the indirect ones.

Analysis of qualitative data enables us to look at meaning from several perspectives, including the content of responses as well as the meaning behind the content, which we gathered from close examination of language use. We pursued this type of analysis by the coding of self-focused versus other-focused responses, but further analyses could be conducted by examining word usage through word counts, etc. Furthermore, despite our small sample size ($N = 83$), our results are quite consistent with the educational differences shown in the MIDUS analysis of social responsibility in chapter 3. Since our study was an offshoot of a larger, quantitative-based research endeavor, it demonstrates the unique complementarity between qualitative and quantitative data, which can deepen current understanding of social phenomena and inform directions for future research and theories.

Our qualitative data also implicate differing social worlds for the high school– versus the college-educated respondents. For the former, the focus is narrower (primarily family) and involves fewer distant institutions (e.g., community organizations), whereas the focus of the latter involves a wider sphere of influence and participation. The content of these primary social worlds may differ as well. Among the high school–educated respondents, proximal familial environments likely involve more confrontations with illness, unemployment, and financial constraints, which may prompt greater reciprocity between the self and significant others. In contrast, those in upper socioeconomic strata may confront fewer such challenges and therefore rely less on reciprocity. Qualitative inquiries provide valuable tools for probing the content of surrounding social worlds as well as the beliefs and behaviors of the individuals within those worlds.

In concluding this chapter, we return to where we began. The tension between individual rights and obligations to others has made the area of social responsibility contested terrain in the highly individualized context of mainstream America. While Americans sense the importance of creating and maintaining community, American culture has only a skeletal blueprint of the path to these ideals. In competition with this pale collective representation of the socially responsible citizen is the highly crystallized, well-learned representation of the individual as self-reliant, independent, and self-sufficient. As a result of this cultural notion of the good person, the way to be a socially responsible citizen is often translated as taking care of the self so that no one else will have to. Similarly, a second translation of the way to be socially responsible is to allow others to become self-reliant, independent, and self-sufficient individuals.

Our results, coupled with the dramatic social changes that have occurred during the latter half of the twentieth century, suggest the need to rethink our concepts of social responsibility so that they better reflect current society. An earlier American context was the two-parent family with a solitary breadwinner, intergenerational socioeconomic advancement, and less geographic mobility. Currently there are more women participating in the workforce (Oppenheimer 1996), more single-parent households, and a higher divorce rate than ever before (Bumpass 1990). Added to these social shifts are the rapid technological changes that have occurred in the past decade—more personal computers than ever before, the World Wide Web, and the myriad forms of communication (e-mail, fax, the Internet, cellular phones, etc.). These many changes are so recent and multitudinous that social scientists have only begun to assess the impact that they have on our lives.

While some might argue that these changes have eroded the moral fiber of American society, our results indicate otherwise. Our systematic probe via quantitative and qualitative methods reveals a great deal of social responsibility in contemporary American life, which includes being attentive to others as well as to one's self. Rather than seeing the component of self-care as in opposition to caring for others, such self-care may be what enables individuals to care for others (Hahn 1991). In a world where people juggle competing demands of work, childcare, and familial and social obligations, it is increasingly important to take care of one's self so that one can continue to care for others. Furthermore, our respondents conveyed the multifaceted nature of social responsibility: it is taking care of your offspring financially and emotionally; it is working; it is caring for society through prosocial actions and beliefs; it is meeting obligations, being dependable, attending to needs of others and taking care of one's self. Explicating how these avenues of social responsibility contribute to the well-being of individuals and of society is a key challenge for the future.

NOTES

1. For each of the eight categories, the number of high school– and college-educated respondents mentioning that category were compared, using the chi-

square (χ^2) statistic (df = 1, N = 83). Men's and women's mentions of each category were compared in this way. When a difference between educational levels or sexes is described as "significant," the p-value of χ^2 is less than .05.

References

Alwin, D. F. 1989. Changes in qualities valued in children in the United States, 1964 to 1984. *Social Science Research* 18:195–236.

Argyle, M. 1994. *The social psychology of social class.* New York: Routledge.

Bellah, R. N., R. Madsen, W. M. Sullivan, A. Swidler, and S. M. Tipton. 1985. *Habits of the heart: Individualism and commitment in American life.* New York: Harper Row.

Bumpass, L. L. 1990. What's happening to the family? Interactions between demographic and institutional change. *Demography* 27:483–98.

Cross, S. E., and L. Madson. 1997. Models of the self: Self-construals and gender. *Psychological Bulletin* 122:5–37.

Feagin, J. R. 1972. Poverty: We still believe that God helps those who help themselves. *Psychology Today* 6:101–29.

Gilligan, K. C. 1982. *In a different voice: Psychological theory and women's development.* Cambridge: Harvard University Press.

Glendon, M. A. 1991. *Rights talk: The impoverishment of political discourse.* New York: Free Press.

Hahn, T. N. 1991. *Peace is every step.* New York: Bantam.

Heise, D. R. 1990. Careers, career trajectories, and the self. In *Self-directedness: Cause and effects through the life course,* ed. J. Rodin, C. Schooler, and K. W. Schaie, 59–84. Hillsdale, NY: Erlbaum.

Herzog, A. R., M. M. Franks, H. R. Markus, and D. Holmberg. 1998. Activities and well-being in older age: Effects of self concept and educational attainment. *Psychology and Aging* 13:179–85.

Hochschild, A. R. 1989. *The second shift: Working parents and the revolution at home.* New York: Viking.

House, J. S., J. M. Lepkowski, A. M. Kinney, R. P. Mero, R. C. Kessler, and A. R. Herzog. 1994. The social stratification of aging and health. *Journal of Health and Behavior* 35:213–34.

Kohlberg, L. 1981. *The philosophy of moral development: Moral stages and the idea of justice.* Vol.1 of *Essays on Moral Development.* San Francisco: Harper and Row.

Marshall, R. 1997. Variances in levels of individualism across two cultures and three social classes. *Journal of Cross-Cultural Psychology* 28:490–95.

Meyer, J. W. 1990. Individualism: Social experience and cultural formulation. In *Self-directedness: Cause and effects throughout the life course,* ed. J. Rodin, C. Schooler, and K. W. Schaie, 51–58. Hillsdale, NY: Erlbaum.

Miller, J. G. 1994. Cultural diversity in the morality of caring: Individually oriented versus duty-based interpersonal moral codes. *Cross-Cultural Research* 28:3–39.

Miller, J. G., and D. M. Bersoff. 1992. Culture and moral judgement: How are conflicts between justice and interpersonal responsibilities resolved? *Journal of Personality and Social Psychology* 62:541–54.

Miller, J. G., D. M. Bersoff, and R. Harwood. 1990. Perceptions of social responsibilities in India and the United States: Moral imperatives or personal decisions? *Journal of Personality and Social Psychology* 58:33–47.

Mirowsky, J. 1995. Age and the sense of control. *Social Psychology Quarterly* 58:31–43.

Moscovici, S. 1998. The history and actuality of social representations. In *The Psychology of the Social,* ed. U. Flick, 3–69. Cambridge: Cambridge University Press.

Oppenheimer, V. K. 1996. Women's rising employment and the future of family in the industrial societies. *Population and Development Review* 20:293–342.

Putnam, R. 1995. Bowling alone: America's declining social capital. *Journal of Democracy* 6:65–78.

Ross, C. E., and C. U. Wu. 1995. The links between education and health. *American Sociological Review* 60:719–45.

Ryff, C., and C. Keyes. 1995. The structure of psychological well-being revisited. *Journal of Personality and Social Psychology* 69:719–27.

Ryff, C. D., W. J. Magee, K. C. Kling, and E. N. Wing. 1999. Forging macro-micro linkages in the study of psychological well-being. In *Linking the self and society in the study of aging processes,* ed. C. D. Ryff and V. W. Marshall, 247–78. New York: Springer.

Ryff, C. D., and B. Singer. 1998. The contours of positive human health. *Psychological Inquiry* 9:1–28.

Triandis, H. C. 1995. *Individualism and collectivism.* Boulder: Westview Press.

Tronto, J. 1993. *Moral boundaries: A political argument for an ethic of care.* New York: Routledge.

Wertsch, J. V., and W. R. Penuel. 1996. The individual-society antinomy revisited: Productive tensions in theories of human development, communication, and education. In *The handbook of education and human development: New models of learning, teaching, and schooling,* ed. D. Olson and N. Torrence, 415–33. Cambridge, MA: Blackwell.

IV   SOCIAL RESPONSIBILITY AND WORK

TEN

The Association between Chronic Medical Conditions and Work Impairment

Ronald C. Kessler, Kristin D. Mickelson, Catherine Barber,

and Philip Wang

The MIDUS survey design focuses on three broad classes of outcomes: health, well-being, and social responsibility. We hypothesized that some aspects of these outcomes would be positively associated. This chapter reports the results of analyses that investigate the hypothesized positive association between chronic medical conditions (one aspect of ill health) and work impairment (one aspect of diminished social responsibility).

The impact of chronic medical conditions on work performance has become a topic of considerable interest to health policy analysts in recent years (Murray and Lopez 1996). The incidence of chronic conditions in the general population is increasing as the age structure of society shifts upward (Fox 1989). This growing prevalence and the proliferation of costly therapies compromise our ability to provide medical treatment to people who suffer from chronic conditions (Burner, Waldo, and McKusick 1992). Healthcare administrators confront the practical problems of allocating scarce treatment resources and the ethical issues of letting availability and affordability affect medical treatment decisions. Concerned providers and policy-makers need and are seeking rational and humane triage rules.

The growing use of cost-effectiveness and cost-benefit analyses as tools for medical decision making is a result of the search for reasonable and acceptable treatment guidelines (Weinstein and Fineberg 1980). These approaches estimate ratios of the costs of health resources consumed by particular therapies to the benefits of treating each condition either in dollar terms (cost-benefit analysis) or in broader terms of quality of life outcomes (cost-effectiveness analysis). By using these ra-

Preparation of this chapter was supported, in part, by a Research Scientist Award from the National Institute of Mental Health, the John D. and Catherine T. MacArthur Foundation Initiative on Depression and Workplace Performance, and an unrestricted educational grant from Wyeth-Ayerst Pharmaceuticals. The authors appreciate helpful comments from Paul Cleary and Richard Frank on a previous version of this chapter.

tios to make intervention determinations for individuals and resource allocations across conditions, healthcare administrators, providers, and policy-makers confer the maximum aggregate health benefit to the entire population (Hillner and Smith 1991; Pauker and Pauker 1987).

Cost-effectiveness studies regarding the benefits of treating versus not treating medical conditions are heavily dependent on the quality and availability of information. Many dimensions, such as well-being, quality of life, and societal burden, must be considered both from the perspective of the ill person and from the perspectives of family, friends, and others whose lives are affected by the illness. Because of difficulties in interpreting and valuing these outcomes, considerable uncertainty exists about the implications of current information on cost-effectiveness. Despite this uncertainty, the available evidence clearly shows irrationalities in the allocation of healthcare resources.

One of the most unfortunate of these irrationalities is the underutilization of inexpensive early detection and intervention programs. Preventive measures available for many illnesses avoid both direct and indirect costs (Breslow 1990). The disproportionate allocation of healthcare resources across conditions and therapies illustrates another irrationality. For example, the resources devoted in the United States to fatal disorders and to acute conditions are much greater in relation to their comparative prevalence and effects on functioning than the resources devoted to nonfatal disorders and chronic conditions (Hoffman, Rice, and Sung 1996; Verbrugge and Patrick 1995). Also problematic is the differential allocation of treatment resources to mental disorders versus physical disorders. Empirical studies show clearly that mental disorders affect functioning about as much as or more than most physical disorders (Hays et al. 1995; Ormel et al. 1998), but U.S. health insurance plans traditionally impose special barriers to mental health treatment, such as considerably higher co-payments and caps on number of visits (Frank and McGuire 1994).

The healthcare community must move beyond making broad conclusions about existing irrationalities and make practical decisions about particular therapies for particular conditions. Future research needs to focus on the direct costs of treating medical conditions versus the indirect costs of not treating these conditions and versus the cost-saving effects of restoring lost functional capacities by means of these treatments. Cost-effectiveness comparisons available to date are largely indirect because most studies focus on only a single condition at a time (Farnham 1994; Stang, Von Korff, and Galer 1996) or on only a small set of conditions at a time (Tarlov et al. 1989; Verbrugge and Patrick 1995). This report takes a first step toward expanding this comparative picture by presenting nationally representative data on a wide range of chronic conditions.

Work impairment is not the only important factor to consider in a comprehensive comparative analysis of the costs of illness, but it has generated considerable interest recently because it can be operationalized and monetized fairly easily and it represents a cost both to employees and to employers. Initial study results estimating the effects of specific illnesses on work performance reveal enormous implications for the economy. For example, depression is the mental disorder thought to have the largest effect on work disability (Conti and Burton 1994; Kouzis and Eaton 1994). A recent analysis estimated that depression alone leads to an annual loss of $17 billion due to work absenteeism in the United States (Greenberg et al. 1993). With costs as great as this, can society afford not to treat disorders that not only are highly prevalent and highly impairing, but that also are responsive to treatment? Given the preceding example, the indirect cost reductions from improved workplace performance likely would substantially outweigh the costs of treatment for at least some chronic conditions. Treatment of these conditions becomes an investment opportunity for employers, rather than a cost of doing business.

Employers clearly are aware that certain health programs are cost-effective in increasing worker performance, as worksite-sponsored initiatives for flu vaccination and substance abuse treatment demonstrate. Many health policy researchers believe that aggressive outreach and treatment would be cost-effective for a much larger set of conditions. Accurate information on the indirect costs of medical disorders and on the direct costs of prevention could substantiate this hypothesis and also would inform the health insurance debate, have an impact on workplace intervention programs, and help direct future cost-benefit research. Considerable interest already exists for conducting comparative studies that would examine the relative effects of many different chronic conditions on workplace functioning. The current chapter presents the first nationally representative study of this sort.

METHODS
Measures

The data analyzed in this chapter result from MIDUS questions regarding the twelve-month prevalence of twenty-nine chronic medical conditions or clusters of conditions and the thirty-day prevalence of work-loss days and work-cutback days. Respondents selected from a standard checklist of conditions preceded by the question "In the past twelve months, have you experienced or been treated for any of the following?" Twenty-seven of the twenty-nine items on the list are physical disorders (e.g., tuberculosis, hay fever); the other two refer more generally to substance disorders ("alcohol or drug problems") and mental disorders ("anxiety, depression, or some other emotional disorder").

A separate section of the interview expanded these last two items using the World Health Organization Composite International Diagnostic Interview Short-Form, or CIDI-SF (Kessler et al. 1998), screening scales for the DSM-III-R (American Psychiatric Association 1987) disorders of alcohol dependence, drug dependence, major depression (MD), generalized anxiety disorder (GAD), and panic attacks (PA). Respondents were classified as having alcohol or drug dependence if they screened positive for these items on the CIDI-SF. If they did not screen positive for alcohol or drug dependence, but did endorse the checklist item "alcohol or drug problems," they were classified as having some "other substance disorder." Respondents were classified as having MD, GAD, or PA based on the CIDI-SF. If they did not screen positive for MD, GAD, or PA, but did endorse the checklist item about mental disorders, they were classified as having some "other emotional disorder."

This augmentation of the original checklist resulted in a total of thirty-four items, twenty-seven physical and seven mental. We reduced this list to twenty-nine for purposes of analysis by collapsing tuberculosis (TB) and "other lung problems" into the "other lung problems" category and by collapsing stroke with hypertension into one category of "hypertension/stroke" due to the small number of respondents reporting strokes. We combined "lupus or other autoimmune disorders" and "multiple sclerosis, epilepsy, or other neurological disorders" into an "autoimmune/neurological disorders" category because few respondents fell into the original categories. We deleted "AIDS or HIV infection" and "other substance disorder" entirely because only a handful of people endorsed these choices.

The questions on thirty-day prevalence of work-loss days and work-cutback days asked each respondent how many days out of the past thirty he or she was "totally unable to work or carry out your normal household work activities because of your physical health or mental health" and how many additional days out of thirty he or she was able to work, but had to "cut back on work or how much you got done because of your physical health or mental health." We combined the information on work-loss and work-cutback days into a summary measure of work "impairment" days. This report defines work "impairment" days as a weighted sum of work-loss days and work-cutback days with each work-cutback day counted as a half day. This weighting scheme is based on results from a national phone survey pilot for MIDUS in which respondents estimated that they were about half as productive on reported work-cutback days as on normal work days.

Analysis Procedures

We examined the aggregate distribution of work-loss days and work-cutback days in the total sample as a function of number and type of chronic conditions. Using a series of regression equations, we then determined whether some conditions are more powerful than others in predicting work impairment. We also checked for any significant interactions among conditions. Finally, we used a series of moderated regression equations to estimate the relative effects of different conditions on work performance as a function of age, sex, education, and occupational status.

All results are based on weighted data that adjust for differential probabilities of selection within households and for differences between the sample distribution and census population distribution on a range of sociodemographic variables. Statistical significance was evaluated using .05-level two-sided tests. These tests did not take into consideration the design effects introduced by weighting because simulations using jackknife repeated replications (Kish and Frankel 1974) have found that inflation of standard errors in design-based estimation for most univariate and bivariate estimates are too small to affect significance tests of the sort reported in this chapter.

RESULTS
Prevalence of Work-Loss Days and Work-Cutback Days

As shown in table 10.1, approximately one-sixth of MIDUS respondents (16.0%) reported at least one work-loss day in the previous thirty days, and a somewhat larger number (18.8%) reported at least one work-cutback day. The monthly averages for number of work-loss days among those with any work loss and for number of cutback days among those with any cutback are 6.7 and 5.9, respectively. Over one-fourth of respondents (28.0%) reported at least one work loss or work-cutback day, with a monthly average of 5.8 impairment days among

TABLE 10.1 Prevalence and Frequency of Work Loss, Work Cutback, and Work Impairment

		Frequency	
	Prevalence[a]	Mean[b]	Average per Capita[c]
A. Total sample			
Work-loss days	16.0 (0.6)	6.7 (0.3)	1.1 (0.1)
Work-cutback days	18.8 (0.6)	5.9 (0.2)	1.1 (0.1)
Work-impairment days	28.0 (0.7)	5.8 (0.2)	1.6 (0.1)
B. Employed			
Work-loss days	13.9 (0.9)	4.2 (0.4)	0.6 (0.1)
Work-cutback days	16.5 (0.8)	4.7 (0.3)	0.8 (0.1)
Work-impairment days	24.6 (0.7)	3.8 (0.3)	0.9 (0.1)
C. Retired			
Work-loss days	11.9 (2.2)	8.4 (1.3)	1.0 (0.2)
Work-cutback days	19.7 (2.0)	8.9 (0.9)	1.8 (0.3)
Work-impairment days	26.2 (1.6)	7.0 (0.8)	1.8 (0.3)
D. Homemaker			
Work-loss days	21.3 (3.6)	6.8 (1.2)	1.5 (0.3)
Work-cutback days	30.0 (3.3)	5.1 (0.7)	1.5 (0.3)
Work-impairment days	43.3 (2.9)	5.0 (0.7)	2.2 (0.4)
E. Other employment status			
Work-loss days	36.0 (1.3)	14.8 (0.6)	5.3 (0.3)
Work-cutback days	26.7 (1.2)	10.2 (0.4)	2.7 (0.2)
Work-impairment days	44.9 (1.3)	14.9 (0.5)	6.8 (0.3)

Note: "Work-impairment days" are defined as a weighted sum of work-loss days plus 50% of work-cutback days. For example, a person with three work-loss days and four work-cutback days has five work-impairment days, since 3 + (.5 × 4) = 5. Respondents reporting at least one day of either work loss or work cutback are also counted as having at least a partial work-impairment day. Numbers in parentheses in the body of the table indicate standard error.

[a] The percentage of respondents in each specified category who reported at least one work-loss or work-cutback day during the preceding thirty days.

[b] The mean number of days of the indicated type accumulated during the preceding thirty days by respondents who reported at least one work-loss or work-cutback day during that time.

[c] The mean number of days of the indicated type accumulated during the preceding thirty days by all respondents in the specified category, including those who reported no work impairment.

those with at least one day of either sort. The estimated average per capita number of work-impairment days in the total sample ages twenty-five to seventy-four is 1.6 per month. This is equivalent to an annualized national estimate of over three billion work-impairment days in the age range of the sample.

The remainder of table 10.1 presents comparable results broken down by employment status. The highest average per capita number of work-impairment days (6.8 per month) occurs among respondents in the "other" employment status category, which consists largely of the disabled or people looking for work. The lowest average per capita number of work-impairment days (0.9 per month) occurs among employed people. It is noteworthy that work impairment is not markedly more likely among the "other" employment status respondents (44.9%) than among homemakers (43.4%), but that the average monthly frequency of impairment is much higher among the "others" (14.9 days) than among homemakers (5.0 days). Presumably this is because many people with long-term disabilities fall into the "other" category.

Bivariate Associations of Conditions and Work Impairment

The summary results in table 10.2 show associations of number and prevalence of chronic conditions with probability of any work-impairment days, average frequency of impairment, and average per capita number of impairment days accumulated during a thirty-day

TABLE 10.2 Bivariate Associations between Number of Chronic Conditions and Work Impairment

Number of Conditions	Prevalence of Conditions	Prevalence of Impairment[a]	Mean Number of Impairment Days[b]	Average per Capita Number of Impairment Days[c]
0	21.9 (0.6)	13.6 (1.0)	2.6 (0.4)	0.3 (0.1)
1	19.9 (0.6)	19.1 (1.4)	3.4 (0.4)	0.7 (0.1)
2	16.1 (0.6)	23.4 (1.6)	5.2 (0.6)	1.2 (0.2)
3	13.1 (0.5)	30.0 (2.1)	4.4 (0.6)	1.3 (0.2)
4–5	16.1 (0.6)	39.5 (2.0)	6.4 (0.6)	2.6 (0.4)
6+	13.0 (0.5)	55.1 (2.3)	8.7 (0.6)	4.8 (0.4)
		$\chi^2_5 = 273.1$	$F_{5,832} = 13.0$	$F_{5,3026} = 56.0$
		$p < .001$	$p < .001$	$p < .001$

Note: "Work-impairment days" are defined as a weighted sum of work-loss days plus 50% of work-cutback days. For example, a person with three work-loss days and four work-cutback days has five work-impairment days, since $3 + (.5 \times 4) = 5$. Numbers in parentheses in the body of the table indicate standard error.

[a] The percentage of respondents who reported at least one work-loss or work-cutback day during the preceding thirty days.

[b] The mean number of days accumulated during the preceding thirty days by respondents who reported at least one work-loss or work-cutback day during that time.

[c] The mean number of days accumulated during the preceding thirty days by all respondents, including those who reported no work impairment.

period. A clear dose-response relationship exists between number of conditions and probability of any work impairment, from a low of 13.6% for respondents with no conditions to a high of 55.1% for those with six or more conditions. A dose-response relationship also exists between number of conditions and average monthly frequency of work impairment, from a low of 2.6 days for respondents with no conditions to a high of 8.7 days for those with six or more conditions. Overall average per capita impairment frequency ranges from a low of 0.3 days per person per month for respondents with no conditions to a high of 4.8 days per person per month for those with six or more conditions.

More detailed results regarding prevalence and frequency of work impairments associated with each of the twenty-nine chronic conditions derived from MIDUS appear in table 10.3. Physical and mental disorders are listed separately in order of prevalence. Condition-specific probabilities of any work impairment range from a low of 33.8% for foot problems to a high of 61.3% for generalized anxiety disorder (GAD). Four of the five most commonly reported chronic conditions are mental disorders. In addition to GAD, these are drug dependence (60.8%), panic attacks (56.4%), and major depression (51.9%).

TABLE 10.3 Condition-Specific Prevalence of Work Impairment

Chronic Condition	Prevalence of Condition	Prevalence of Impairment[a]	Mean Number of Impairment Days[b]	Average per Capita Number of Impairment Days[c]
Physical				
Stomach problems[d]	20.4 (0.6)	42.9 (1.9)	7.3 (0.5)	3.1 (0.2)
Back problems[e]	20.3 (0.6)	39.7 (1.8)	8.0 (0.5)	3.2 (0.2)
Arthritis[f]	19.4 (0.6)	38.8 (1.8)	8.3 (0.6)	3.2 (0.3)
Hypertension/stroke[g]	18.2 (0.6)	34.6 (1.8)	9.0 (0.6)	3.1 (0.3)
Hay fever	15.7 (0.6)	39.6 (2.0)	5.1 (0.5)	2.0 (0.2)
Bladder problems[h]	13.5 (0.5)	41.9 (2.2)	7.9 (0.6)	3.3 (0.3)
Sleep problems[i]	12.8 (0.5)	50.6 (2.3)	9.8 (0.7)	5.0 (0.4)
Asthma[j]	12.6 (0.5)	44.7 (2.3)	7.7 (0.6)	3.5 (0.3)
Foot problems[k]	11.6 (0.5)	33.8 (2.3)	7.4 (0.4)	2.5 (0.3)
Piles or hemorrhoids	11.4 (0.5)	34.0 (2.4)	7.8 (0.8)	2.7 (0.3)
Migraine headaches	11.2 (0.5)	49.9 (2.6)	7.2 (0.6)	3.6 (0.4)
Skin problems[l]	10.5 (0.5)	44.5 (2.4)	5.7 (0.5)	2.6 (0.3)
Teeth problems[m]	10.3 (0.5)	35.3 (2.5)	8.0 (0.7)	2.8 (0.3)
Gum problems[n]	8.3 (0.4)	37.1 (2.9)	7.3 (0.8)	2.7 (0.4)
Constipation[o]	6.9 (0.4)	46.0 (3.4)	8.0 (0.8)	3.7 (0.5)
Diabetes[p]	5.6 (0.4)	40.2 (3.5)	7.6 (1.1)	3.1 (0.5)

TABLE 10.3 *continued*

Chronic Condition	Prevalence of Condition	Prevalence of Impairment[a]	Mean Number of Impairment Days[b]	Average per Capita Number of Impairment Days[c]
Ulcer	4.4 (0.3)	52.7 (4.1)	10.9 (1.1)	5.8 (0.7)
Thyroid disease	4.3 (0.3)	35.5 (3.8)	5.6 (0.9)	2.0 (0.4)
Other lung problems[q]	3.7 (0.3)	49.1 (4.2)	11.0 (1.1)	5.4 (0.7)
Hernia[r]	3.2 (0.3)	44.8 (4.8)	11.3 (1.5)	5.1 (0.8)
Autoimmune/neurological disorders[s]	2.6 (0.2)	51.6 (4.8)	9.7 (1.0)	5.0 (0.7)
Gall bladder	2.6 (0.2)	44.8 (5.4)	9.5 (1.4)	4.3 (0.8)
Varicose veins[t]	1.5 (0.2)	40.7 (7.3)	13.2 (2.0)	5.4 (1.2)
Mental				
Major depression[u]	14.1 (0.5)	51.9 (2.0)	8.3 (0.5)	4.3 (0.3)
Other emotional disorder[v]	9.6 (0.5)	39.7 (2.6)	4.9 (0.5)	2.0 (0.2)
Panic attacks[u]	6.8 (0.4)	56.4 (2.9)	9.5 (0.7)	5.3 (0.5)
Alcohol dependence[u]	4.3 (0.3)	37.1 (3.7)	4.3 (0.8)	1.6 (0.3)
Generalized anxiety disorders[u]	3.3 (0.3)	61.3 (4.4)	9.8 (1.0)	6.0 (0.8)
Drug dependence[u]	2.0 (0.2)	60.8 (5.9)	8.1 (1.2)	4.9 (0.8)

Note: "Work-impairment days" are defined as a weighted sum of work-loss days plus 50% of work-cutback days. For example, a person with three work-loss days and four work-cutback days has five work-impairment days, since $3 + (.5 \times 4) = 5$. Numbers in parentheses in the body of the table indicate standard error.

[a] The percentage of respondents in each specified category who reported at least one work-loss or work-cutback day during the preceding thirty days.

[b] The mean number of days accumulated during the preceding thirty days by respondents who reported at least one work-loss or work-cutback day during that time.

[c] The mean number of days accumulated during the preceding thirty days by all respondents in the specified category, including those who reported no work impairment.

[d] "Recurring stomach trouble, indigestion, or diarrhea."

[e] "Sciatica, lumbago, or recurring backache."

[f] "Arthritis, rheumatism, or other bone or joint diseases."

[g] "High blood pressure or hypertension" or "stroke."

[h] "Urinary or bladder problems."

[i] "Chronic sleeping problems."

[j] "Asthma, bronchitis, or emphysema."

[k] "Persistent foot trouble (e.g., bunions, ingrown toenails)."

[l] "Persistent skin trouble (e.g., eczema)."

[m] "Persistent trouble with your teeth."

[n] "Persistent trouble with your gums or mouth."

[o] "Being constipated all or most of the time."

[p] "Diabetes or high blood sugar."

[q] "Tuberculosis" or "other lung problems."

[r] "Hernia or rupture."

[s] "Lupus or other autoimmune disorder" or "multiple sclerosis, epilepsy, or other neurological disorder."

[t] "Trouble with varicose veins requiring medical treatment."

[u] Screened positive for this DSM-III-R diagnosis in the CIDI-SF.

[v] Endorsed the MIDUS item "anxiety, depression, or some other emotional disorder," but did not screen positive for MD, GAD, or PA on the CIDI-SF.

The only physical disorder in the top five is ulcer (52.7%). Average monthly frequency of work impairment for people with specific conditions range from a low of 4.3 days for alcohol dependence to a high of 13.2 days for varicose veins. The other conditions with highest average impairment frequency are hernia (11.3), other lung problems (11.0), ulcer (10.9), GAD (9.8), and sleep problems (9.8). The conditions with the highest per capita number of impairment days, taking into consideration both probability of impairment and average frequency of impairment, are GAD (6.0 impairment days), ulcer (5.8), varicose veins (5.4), other lung problems (5.4), and panic attacks (5.3).

Multivariate Associations of Conditions and Work Impairment

The results in table 10.4 show that both probability of work impairment and average frequency of impairment significantly vary with age and employment status. Young adults are more likely than older adults to have any work impairment, but the average frequency of their impairments is less than that of older adults. Employed people are significantly less likely than homemakers, the retired, and those in the "other" employment category (those looking for work, the disabled, and students) to have any work impairment. The respondents from the "other" category, without employment, have a dramatically higher average frequency of impairment than those with employment, reflecting the fact that "other" includes respondents who are disabled. Women are significantly more likely than men to have any work impairment, but their average frequency of impairment is marginally less than that of men. Although probability of work impairment did not vary by level of educational attainment, education is significantly related to average frequency of impairment such that those with a high school education or less have greater average frequency of impairment than those with at least a college education.

We began our multivariate analysis of condition-specific effects on per capita impairment by estimating a multiple regression equation that controlled for all the sociodemographic influences. The equation also included separate dummy variables for each of the twenty-nine conditions in table 10.3 in order to adjust for the fact that some people suffer from more than one condition. Results (not shown) found that only fifteen of the twenty-nine conditions were either statistically significant or substantively meaningful predictors of per capita work impairment. Results of a reduced model that included these fifteen predictors plus sociodemographic controls appear in table 10.5. This

TABLE 10.4 Regressions of any Work Impairment and
Mean Number of Impairment Days on
Sociodemographic Predictor Variables

Variable	Prevalence of Impairment Days[a]		Mean Number of Impairment Days[b]	
	OR	(95% CI)	b	(SE)
Sex				
Female	2.1*	(1.7–2.5)	−1.0	(0.5)
Male	1.0	(—)	0.0	(—)
Age				
25–35	1.8*	(1.4–2.3)	−1.6*	(0.8)
36–54	1.5*	(1.2–1.9)	−0.7	(0.7)
55–74	1.0	(—)	0.0	(—)
Education				
0–12	0.8	(0.7–1.0)	2.4*	(0.6)
13–15	1.0	(0.8–1.2)	1.2	(0.7)
16	1.0		0.0	(—)
Employment				
Employed	1.0	(—)	0.0	(—)
Retired	1.7*	(1.2–2.3)	1.6	(0.9)
Homemaker	1.9*	(1.5–2.6)	0.8	(0.8)
Other	2.4*	(1.8–3.1)	10.5*	(0.8)
	$\chi^2_8 = 160.3$		$F_{8,829} = 31.3$	
	$p < .001$		$p < .001$	

Note: "Work-impairment days" are defined as a weighted sum of work-loss days plus 50% of work-cutback days. For example, a person with three work-loss days and four work-cutback days has five work-impairment days, since $3 + (.5 \times 4) = 5$.

[a] The percentage of respondents in each specified category who reported at least one work-loss or work-cutback day during the preceding thirty days. The coefficients and confidence intervals were estimated using logistic regression (OR = odds ratio; 95% CI = 95% confidence interval of the OR).

[b] The mean number of days of the indicated type accumulated during the preceding month by respondents who reported at least one work-loss or work-cutback day during that time. The coefficients and standard errors were estimated using linear regression (b = nonstandardized regression coefficient; SE = standard error of the regression coefficient).

* Significant at the .05 level, two-sided test.

reduced set of conditions includes eleven physical disorders and four mental disorders, with net condition-specific effects on per capita impairment ranging from a low of 0.4 for migraine and back problems to a high of 1.8 for panic attacks.

Conditions are presented in table 10.5 in order of their per capita

TABLE 10.5 Regression of per Capita Number of
Impairment Days on a Reduced Set of Chronic
Conditions

Chronic Condition	b	(SE)	β
Panic attacks	1.8*	(0.3)	0.09
Ulcer	1.7*	(0.4)	0.07
Sleep problems	1.6*	(0.3)	0.11
Autoimmune/neurological disorders	1.5*	(0.5)	0.05
Major depression	1.4*	(0.2)	0.10
Generalized anxiety disorder	1.4*	(0.5)	0.05
Drug dependence	1.2*	(0.6)	0.03
Hernia	1.3*	(0.5)	0.04
Other lung problems	1.2*	(0.4)	0.04
Bladder problems	0.9*	(0.2)	0.06
Hypertension/stroke	0.8*	(0.2)	0.06
Asthma	0.7*	(0.2)	0.05
Arthritis	0.7*	(0.2)	0.06
Migraine headaches	0.4	(0.3)	0.03
Back problems	0.4*	(0.2)	0.04
	$F_{15,3008} = 34.8$		
	$p < .001$		

Note: See notes to table 10.1 for definitions of the outcome. The coefficients and standard errors were estimated using linear regression, controlling for the sociodemographic predictors in table 10.4 (b = nonstandardized regression coefficient; SE = standard error of the nonstandardized regression coefficient; β = standardized regression coefficient).

* Significant at the 0.05 level, two-sided test.

effects. The standardized coefficients presented in the last column of the table take into consideration both this variation in per capita effects and variation in the prevalence of the conditions. The conditions with the highest standardized coefficients are sleep problems, major depression, and panic attacks. The first two of these three have high prevalence in comparison to the other conditions (12.8% for sleep problems and 14.1% for major depression) in conjunction with comparatively large nonstandardized regression coefficients (third highest rank for sleep problems and fifth highest rank for major depression). Panic attacks, in comparison, are considerably less prevalent (6.8%), but have the highest nonstandardized regression coefficient of any condition considered in the table. Each of these three conditions uniquely explains approximately one percent of the variance in overall per capita work impairment (i.e., the square of each of their standardized regression coefficients is close to .01).

Next we tested the significance of between-condition variation in average per capita effects on impairment. We rejected the hypothesis that this variation is due entirely to chance ($F_{14,3008} = 2.8$). We also tested the significance of comorbidities among the conditions in predicting per capita impairment. Aggregate measures of having exactly two, exactly three, or four or more conditions were associated with significant explained variation in impairment over and above the variance explained by an additive model ($F_{3,3005} = 14.8$). The regression coefficients associated with these aggregate measures of comorbidity were all negative, which means that the impairment associated with comorbidity is less than the sum of the impairments associated with the component conditions.

Finally, we tested whether the effects of conditions on per capita work impairments vary as a function of sociodemographic variables. Statistically significant variations of this sort were found by sex ($F_{18,2987} = 1.7$), age ($F_{16,1303} = 2.2$), education ($F_{36,2969} = 1.8$), and employment status ($F_{53,2952} = 1.8$). Summary results appear in tables 10.6 and 10.7. Significant variations were found for twelve of the fifteen conditions, the largest number of which occurred for employment status (eight conditions) and the smallest for sex (three) and education (two). The general trend for conditions with significant variation was for effects to be lowest for respondents in the age range of twenty-five to thirty-five (lung, migraine, and bladder), higher for women (drug dependence, panic, and lung) than men, and higher for homemakers (autoimmune/neurological, ulcer, hypertension/stroke, migraine) than employed people. No consistent pattern in the conditions with significant variation exists by level of educational attainment. However, there is a clear pattern in the overall set of coefficients for the average effects to be higher among respondents with the lowest level of educational attainment than it is among those with higher levels of education.

In order to compare rank orderings of average effects across the subsamples in tables 10.6 and 10.7, we focused on the five conditions in each of the twelve subsamples with the highest average effects. The most consistently elevated effects are associated with mental rather than physical illnesses: major depression (a high ranking in eight of the twelve subsamples), panic (eight), and drug problems (seven). Other conditions with consistently high effects include sleep problems (seven) and ulcer (seven). Among employed people, four of the five most impairing conditions are mental disorders.

TABLE 10.6 Regression of per Capita Number of Impairment Days on a Reduced Set of Chronic Conditions, by Sex and Age

	Sex				Age					
	Female		Male		25–35		36–54		55–74	
	b	(SE)	b	(SE)	b	(SE)	b	(SE)	b	(SE)
Chronic condition										
Panic attacks	2.6*[a]	(0.5)	1.0	(0.6)	2.3*	(0.7)	1.6*[a]	(0.5)	4.0*	(0.8)
Ulcer	1.9*	(0.6)	2.0*	(0.6)	2.0*	(0.8)	2.8*	(0.6)	1.3*	(0.7)
Sleep problems	1.8*	(0.4)	2.5*	(0.4)	1.1	(0.6)	2.8*	(0.5)	2.0*	(0.5)
Autoimmune/neurological disorders	1.8*	(0.7)	2.0*	(0.8)	6.2*[a]	(1.2)	0.7	(0.7)	1.1	(1.0)
Major depression	1.9*	(0.4)	2.1*	(0.4)	1.7*	(0.5)	2.5*	(0.4)	1.1	(0.6)
Generalized anxiety disorder	1.5*	(0.6)	3.2*	(0.8)	1.6*	(0.9)	1.4*	(0.6)	5.2*	(1.5)
Drug dependence	2.7*	(1.1)	1.0	(0.7)	2.5*	(0.8)	0.7[a]	(0.9)	7.5	(3.9)
Hernia	1.1	(0.7)	1.9*	(0.6)	−0.7	(1.3)	1.9	(0.7)	1.7*	(0.7)
Other lung problems	2.3*[a]	(0.7)	0.3	(0.6)	0.0[a]	(0.9)	0.5[a]	(0.7)	2.8*	(0.8)

	b	(SE)	b	(SE)	b	(SE)	b	(SE)	b	(SE)
Bladder problems	1.3*	(0.4)	1.5*	(0.4)	0.5a	(0.5)	1.4*	(0.4)	2.1*	(0.5)
Hypertension/stroke	1.8*a	(0.4)	0.5	(0.3)	0.5	(0.6)	1.6*	(0.4)	1.4*	(0.4)
Asthma	1.2*	(0.4)	1.2*	(0.4)	0.8	(0.5)	1.0*	(0.4)	2.1*	(0.5)
Arthritis	1.7*	(0.4)	0.8*	(0.4)	0.9	(0.7)	1.9*	(0.4)	1.1*	(0.5)
Migraine headaches	0.9*	(0.4)	1.3*	(0.5)	0.2a	(0.5)	1.1*	(0.4)	1.9*	(0.7)
Back problems	0.8*	(0.4)	1.5*	(0.3)	0.8	(0.5)	1.6*	(0.4)	0.6	(0.5)
Number of conditions										
2	−1.8*	(0.4)	−1.8*	(0.4)	−1.3*	(0.6)	−2.1*	(0.4)	−1.7*	(0.6)
3	−2.3*	(0.6)	−1.8*	(0.6)	−1.9*	(0.8)	−2.5*	(0.6)	−1.9*	(0.8)
4+	−2.7*	(0.9)	−2.0*	(1.0)	−0.8	(1.3)	−2.8*	(1.0)	−3.7*	(1.3)
	$F_{18,1535} = 17.4$		$F_{18,1445} = 16.0$		$F_{18,682} = 9.2$		$F_{18,1342} = 18.5$		$F_{18,906} = 8.4$	
	$p < .001$		$p < .001$		$p < .001$		$p < .001$		$p < .001$	

Note: "Work-impairment days" are defined as a weighted sum of work-loss days plus 50% of work-cutback days. For example, a person with three work-loss days and four work-cutback days has five work-impairment days, since $3 + .5 \times 4) = 5$. The per capita number of days is defined as the mean number of work-impairment days accumulated during the preceding thirty days by all respondents in the specified category, including those who reported no work impairment in the prior thirty days. The coefficients and standard errors were estimated using linear regression, controlling for the sociodemographic predictors in table 10.4 (b = nonstandardized regression coefficient; SE = standard error of the nonstandardized regression coefficient).

a Indicates that the slope for the particular category is significantly different than the norm category (i.e., male and age 55–74).

* Significant at the .05 level, two-sided test.

TABLE 10.7 Regression of per Capita Number of Impairment Days on a Reduced Set of Chronic Conditions, by Education and Employment

| | Education | | | | | | Employment | | | | | | | |
| | 0–12 | | 13–15 | | 16+ | | Employed | | Retired | | Homemaker | | Other | |
	b	(SE)	b	(SE)	b	(SE)	b	(SE)	b	(SE)	b	(SE)	b	(SE)
Chronic condition														
Panic attacks	2.5*	(0.6)	1.9*	(0.6)	1.9*	(0.5)	1.7*	(0.3)	8.8*a	(1.6)	0.2	(1.2)	2.6	(2.1)
Ulcer	1.9*	(0.6)	2.3*	(0.7)	1.1	(0.7)	1.7*	(0.4)	1.5	(1.1)	4.0*	(1.6)	1.0	(2.3)
Sleep problems	2.6*a	(0.5)	2.1*	(0.5)	0.5	(0.4)	0.9*	(0.3)	2.1*	(0.8)	-0.4	(1.3)	8.9*a	(1.7)
Autoimmune/ neurological disorders	-0.4a	(0.9)	4.2*	(0.8)	4.0*	(0.7)	2.3*	(0.5)	1.1	(1.4)	5.7*	(2.6)	0.9	(2.9)
Major depression	2.4*	(0.5)	1.3*	(0.5)	1.6*	(0.4)	1.8*	(0.2)	-0.1a	(1.0)	1.1	(1.2)	2.5	(1.6)
Generalized anxiety disorder	1.7*	(0.9)	1.7*	(0.8)	2.3*	(0.8)	1.9*	(0.4)	-2.6	(3.1)	4.1	(2.2)	-2.2a	(2.7)
Drug dependence	2.8*	(1.2)	1.1	(0.8)	2.5*	(0.8)	2.2*	(0.5)	—	(—)b	4.3	(2.7)	-1.8	(3.5)
Hernia	1.6*	(0.7)	1.8	(1.1)	1.2	(0.7)	1.1*	(0.5)	1.8	(1.0)	2.2	(1.8)	-2.4a	(2.7)

	b	SE	b	SE	b	SE	b	SE	b	SE	b	SE	b	SE
Other lung problems	1.8*	(0.7)	0.6	(0.8)	1.3	(0.7)	0.7	(0.4)	1.2	(1.3)	−0.7	(1.6)	1.8	(2.6)
Bladder problems	1.6*	(0.4)	1.0*	(0.5)	0.6	(0.4)	0.8*	(0.2)	1.5*	(0.7)	1.8	(1.1)	0.5	(1.8)
Hypertension/stroke	1.1*	(0.4)	2.2*	(0.4)	1.1*	(0.4)	0.7*	(0.2)	0.8	(0.6)	3.0*a	(0.9)	1.6	(1.5)
Asthma	1.6*	(0.5)	0.9*	(0.5)	0.6	(0.4)	1.2*	(0.2)	0.6	(0.9)	1.2	(1.2)	−0.4	(1.9)
Arthritis	1.6*	(0.4)	1.5*	(0.5)	0.2	(0.4)	0.9*	(0.2)	−0.1	(0.7)	1.1	(1.2)	5.4*	(1.8)
Migraine headaches	0.8	(0.5)	1.2*	(0.5)	0.7	(0.4)	0.3*	(0.2)	2.0a	(1.1)	2.3*	(1.3)	2.0	(1.8)
Back problems	0.7	(0.4)	2.0*	(0.4)	0.8*	(0.3)	1.1*	(0.2)	0.4	(0.8)	0.5	(1.1)	0.5	(1.6)
Number of conditions														
2	−1.8*	(0.5)	−2.6*a	(0.5)	−1.0*	(0.4)	−1.2*	(0.3)	−1.2	(0.9)	−1.4	(1.2)	−1.3	(2.0)
3	−1.9*	(0.7)	−3.7*a	(0.7)	0.1	(0.6)	−1.8*	(0.4)	0.1	(1.3)	−2.5	(1.7)	−1.2	(2.5)
4+	3.1*	(1.1)	−2.6*	(1.2)	0.1	(1.0)	−1.7*	(0.6)	−2.4	(2.0)	−2.8	(2.3)	1.9	(3.9)
	$F_{18,1163} = 12.6$		$F_{18,920} = 12.9$		$F_{18,872} = 13.4$		$F_{18,279} = 23.3$		$F_{17,388} = 4.3$		$F_{18,170} = 3.5$		$F_{18,240} = 7.0$	
	$p < .001$		$p < .001$		$p < .001$		$p < .001$		$p < .001$		$p < .001$		$p < .001$	

Note: "Work-impairment days" are defined as a weighted sum of work-loss days plus 50% of work-cutback days. For example, a person with three work-loss days and four work-cutback days has five work-impairment days, since $3 + .5 \times 4) = 5$. The per capita number of days is defined as the mean number of work-impairment days accumulated during the preceding thirty days by all respondents in the specified category, including those who reported no work impairment. The coefficients and standard errors were estimated using linear regression, controlling for the sociodemographic predictors in table 10.4 (b = nonstandardized regression coefficient; SE = standard error of the nonstandardized regression coefficient).

[a] Indicates that the slope for the particular category is significantly different than the norm category (i.e, male and age 55–74).

[b] None of the respondents reported this condition with these sociodemographic predictors.

*Significant at the .05 level, two-sided test.

DISCUSSION
Limitations

Three limitations are important to note. First, the comparatively low response rate of the MIDUS survey mandates caution in generalizing the findings. Second, errors in respondent retrospective self-reports about work impairments could lead to additional bias in estimates. In particular, some respondents with mental disorders may have overestimated their impairments; there is evidence that some types of mental disorders lead to distorted and pessimistic perceptions about personal self-worth (Coyne and Gotlib 1983). This might help explain the finding that the reported work impairments due to mental disorders are generally higher than those due to physical disorders. Third, the use of respondent self-reports to classify medical conditions could introduce error due to recall bias, a misunderstanding of the true nature of the disorder, or an unwillingness to report stigmatizing conditions. Because mental disorders are among the most stigmatizing of medical conditions, we attempted through the design of the instrument to mitigate the impact of respondents' unwillingness to report them by augmenting the conditions checklist with symptom screening scales. This is admittedly only a partial solution.

Consistency of Results with Previous Research

Within the context of these limitations and to the extent that comparative data exists, the MIDUS results are quite similar to those found in previous surveys. The MIDUS estimate of 1.8 days of total work limitation (work loss plus work cutback) per month per capita is close to the estimated 1.6 days in the most recently published data from the CDC Behavioral Risk Factor Surveillance System, or BRFSS (CDC 1998). The MIDUS estimate of 1.1 days of work loss per month per capita is equivalent to approximately 4 million lost productivity years in the population as a whole. This projection is close to the 4.5 million lost productivity years estimated in the most recently published data from the U.S. National Health Interview Survey, or NHIS (Hoffman, Rice, and Sung 1996). Finally, the finding that 78.1% of MIDUS respondents reported one or more chronic conditions is very close to the estimate of 77.8% in another recent national survey (Eisenberg et al. 1998).

The MIDUS finding that chronic conditions are associated with substantial work impairment is also consistent with previous research (Verbrugge and Patrick 1995). Regrettably few prior studies examine the rank ordering of condition-specific work impairments. The most relevant data on these relationships come from a recent eight-state investigation of univariate condition-specific thirty-day activity limitations that was a component of the BRFSS (CDC 1998). Two of the five conditions associated with the greatest impairments in that survey are comparable to two of the top five most often associated with work impairment in MIDUS, as reported in the last column in table 10.3: "Depression, anxiety, or some other emotional problems" make up the most impairing set of conditions in the BRFSS survey. This is consistent with the top ranking of GAD in the MIDUS data as well as with the fact that panic is among the top five MIDUS conditions in terms of work impairment and with the finding in tables 10.6 and 10.7 that mental disorders are associated with consistently high impairment across MIDUS subsamples. "Lung or breathing problems" are the fourth most impairing set of conditions in the BRFSS survey. This is consistent with the ranking of lung problems in the top five most impairing MIDUS conditions. There is no agreement, however, on the other conditions in the top five of the two surveys. The other top-ranked BRFSS conditions are high blood pressure and stroke (which are combined into a category of "hypertension/stroke" in MIDUS) and back problems (comparable to the MIDUS category of "sciatica, lumbago, or recurring backaches"). None of these was found to be associated with comparatively high impairment in the MIDUS data, nor were the other top MIDUS conditions (ulcer and varicose veins) found to be among those with the highest impairments in the BRFSS data.

The MIDUS study's documentation of lower average effects of some conditions among younger adults than among older adults is consistent with the finding of Verbrugge and Patrick (1995). Conversely, the MIDUS study finding that a number of conditions are associated with a higher rate of any impairment among women than men is not. Verbrugge and Patrick's failure to find meaningful variation in condition-specific impairment by sex (other than for ischemic heart disease) may be attributable to the smaller number of chronic conditions examined in that study (seven) compared to the MIDUS study (twenty-nine). We found no previous research that investigated variation in condition-specific impairments by level of educational attainment or employment status.

Implications

The enormous magnitude of the work impairments associated with illness in general, and with chronic conditions in particular, must be considered in the current debate on universal health insurance. The present cost of lost productivity due to chronic conditions should be calculated and measured against the cost of aggressive outreach and treatment, which could reduce or eliminate some currently under-treated conditions. The resultant cost savings in increased work may substantially outweigh the increased costs of treatment (Berndt et al. 1997) and therefore should be factored into calculations of the total cost of expanding health insurance coverage.

The MIDUS finding that work-cutback days are as common as work-loss days is consistent with data from other recent surveys (Kessler and Frank 1997). This is important from an employer cost per-spective for at least two reasons. First, most previous research on the workplace costs of specific illnesses ignores cutback days (Greenberg et al. 1993) and therefore substantially underestimates productivity loss due to illness. Second, work-cutback days often represent hidden costs that are extremely difficult for employers to control, unlike work-loss days that are visible and manageable by caps on paid sickness leave and by disability insurance. For employers, this intangibility means cutback days actually pose greater risks than work-loss days.

The clear evidence that mental disorders are among the most im-pairing conditions, especially for people in the labor force, is especially important and is also consistent with previous empirical studies (CDC 1998; Hays et al. 1995; Ormel et al. 1998) and with the clinical experts' ranking of the comparative effects of disorders in the World Health Or-ganization's Global Burden of Disease Study (Murray and Lopez 1996). Epidemiological evidence shows that work impairments associated with mental disorders no longer exist among people with remitted mental disorders (Kessler and Frank 1997). This indirect suggestion that successful treatment of the disorders removes these impairments makes these findings noteworthy. The small amount of existing experi-mental research in this area supports this tentative conclusion. Clinical trials for mental disorders, which most often deal with depression, have documented significant effects of treatment on increased work perfor-mance (Mintz et al. 1992).

These results suggest that mental disorders represent an especially attractive target for aggressive intervention and treatment in the workplace. Two additional observations support this conclusion. First, mental disorders are highly prevalent. Comprehensive epidemiological surveys estimate that as many as one in every four adults in the United States meets criteria for at least one mental disorder in a given year (Kessler et al. 1994). Second, unlike the proportions for a number of other chronic conditions, only a small minority of people with mental disorders obtain treatment (Kessler et al. 1999). This means that aggressive outreach efforts to detect and treat people with attended mental disorders not only could have a very high benefit-cost ratio but also could greatly reduce the total indirect costs of illness associated with reduced workplace performance. Additionally, the current low rate of treatment means that these employees most likely would continue indefinitely to work at impaired levels without employer intervention in the potential treatment.

Quality assurance standards are less developed for the treatment of mental disorders than for many other chronic conditions. A substantial proportion of the people who obtain treatment for mental disorders are treated inappropriately (Katz et al. 1998; Wells et al. 1994). While high rates of inappropriate treatment also can be found for some physical disorders (Kogan et al. 1994; Mainous, Hueston, and Clark 1996; Meijler et al. 1997), mental disorders present unique difficulties because precise standards for the evaluation of psychotherapy do not exist.

These concerns highlight the need for improved quality assurance protocols for the implementation of mental disorder workplace outreach and treatment programs. A number of model quality assurance systems are already in use in the United States to monitor overall quality of medical care (Felt-Link and St. Peter 1997; Jencks 1995; National Committee for Quality Assurance 1997), but most include fairly superficial evaluations for mental healthcare (National Committee for Quality Assurance 1997). Focused systems to monitor quality of care for specific commonly treated mental disorders must be developed. A number of such systems already exist for specific physical conditions and medical procedures (e.g., Chassin, Hannan, and DeBuono 1996; Schneider and Epstein 1996). There is good evidence that some of these systems led to improvements in quality of care (e.g., Hannan et al. 1994; Korn et al. 1997), and the same likely would be true of systems developed to treat mental disorders.

REFERENCES

American Psychiatric Association. 1987. *Diagnostic and statistical manual of mental disorders.* 3d ed. (revised). Washington, DC: American Psychiatric Association.

Berndt, E. R., S. N. Finkelstein, P. E. Greenberg, A. Keith, and H. Bailit. 1997. *Illness and productivity: Objective workplace evidence.* Working Paper 42-97, MIT Program on the Pharmaceutical Industry, Cambridge, MA.

Breslow, L. 1990. A health promotion primer for the 1990s. *Health Affairs* 9:6–21.

Burner, S. T., D. R. Waldo, and D. R. McKusick. 1992. National health expenditures projections through 2030. *Health Care Financing Review* 14:1–29.

Centers for Disease Control and Prevention. 1998. Health-related quality of life and activity limitation—eight states, 1995. *Morbidity and Mortality Weekly Reports* 47:134–39.

Chassin, M. R., E. L. Hannan, and B. A. DeBuono. 1996. Benefits and hazards of reporting medical outcomes publicly. *New England Journal of Medicine* 334: 394–98.

Conti, D. J., and W. N. Burton. 1994. The economic impact of depression in a workplace. *Journal of Occupational Medicine* 36:983–88.

Coyne, J. C., and I. H. Gotlib. 1983. The role of cognition in depression: A critical appraisal. *Psychological Bulletin* 94:472–505.

Eisenberg, D. M., R. B. Davis, S. Ettner, S. Appel, S. Wilkey, M. Van Rompay, and R. C. Kessler. 1998. Trends in alternative medicine use in the United States 1990–1997: Results of a follow-up national survey. *Journal of the American Medical Association* 280:1569–75.

Farnham, P. G. 1994. Defining and measuring the costs of the HIV epidemic to business firms. *Public Health Reports* 109:311–18.

Felt-Link, S., and R. St. Peter. 1997. Quality assurance for Medicaid managed care. *Health Affairs* 16:248–52.

Fox, D. M. 1989. Health policy and changing epidemiology in the United States: Chronic disease in the twentieth century. In *Unnatural causes: The three leading killer diseases in America,* ed. R. Maulitz, 11–31. New Brunswick: Rutgers University Press.

Frank, R. G., and T. G. McGuire. 1994. Health reform and financing of mental health services: Distributional issues. In *Mental health, U.S., 1994,* ed. R. W. Manderscheid and M. A. Sonnenscheim, 8–20. Washington, DC: Government Printing Office.

Greenberg, P. E., L. E. Stiglin, S. N. Finkelstein, and E. R. Berndt. 1993. The economic burden of depression in 1990. *Journal of Clinical Psychiatry* 54:405–18.

Hannan, E. L., H. Kilburn, Jr., M. Racz, E. Shields, and M. R. Chassin. 1994. Improving the outcomes of coronary artery bypass surgery in New York state. *Journal of the American Medical Association* 271:761–66.

Hays, R. D., K. B. Wells, C. D. Sherbourne, W. Rogeras, and K. Spritzer. 1995. Functioning and well-being outcomes of patients with depression compared with chronic general medical illnesses. *Archives of General Psychiatry* 52:11–19.

Hillner, B. E., and T. J. Smith. 1991. Efficacy and cost-effectiveness of adjuvant chemotherapy in women with node-negative breast cancer. *New England Journal of Medicine* 324:160–68.

Hoffman, C., D. Rice, and H. Y. Sung. 1996. Persons with chronic conditions: Their prevalence and costs. *Journal of the American Medical Association* 276:1473–79.

Jencks, S. 1995. Changing health care practices in Medicare's health care quality improvement program. *Journal on Quality Improvement* 21:343–47.

Katz, S. J., R. C. Kessler, E. Lin, and K. B. Wells. 1998. Medication management of depression in the United States and Ontario. *Journal of General Internal Medicine* 13:77–85.

Kessler, R. C., G. Andrews, D. Mroczek, B. Ustun, and H.-U. Wittchen. 1998. The World Health Organization Composite International Diagnostic Interview Short Form (CIDI-SF). *International Journal of Methods in Psychiatric Research* 7:171–85.

Kessler, R. C., and R. G. Frank. 1997. The impact of psychiatric disorders on work loss days. *Psychological Medicine* 27:861–73.

Kessler, R. C., K. A. McGonagle, S. Zhao, C. B. Nelson, M. Hughes, S. Eshleman, H.-U. Wittchen, and K. S. Kendler. 1994. Lifetime and 12-month prevalence of DSM-III-R psychiatric disorders in the United States: Results from the National Comorbidity Survey. *Archives of General Psychiatry* 51:8–19.

Kessler, R. C., S. Zhao, S. J. Katz, A. C. Kouzis, R. G. Frank, M. Edlund, and P. Leaf. 1999. Past year use of outpatient services for psychiatric problems in the National Comorbidity Survey. *American Journal of Psychiatry* 156:115–23.

Kish, L., and M. R. Frankel. 1974. Inference from complex samples. *Journal of the Royal Statistical Society* 36:1–37.

Kogan, M. D., G. R. Alexander, M. Kotelchuck, D. A. Nagey, and B. W. Jack. 1994. Comparing mothers' reports on the content of prenatal care received with recommended national guidelines for care. *Public Health Reports* 109:637–46.

Korn, J. E., A. Casey-Paal, D. Lazovich, J. Ball, and J. S. Slater. 1997. Impact of the Mammography Quality Standards Act on access in Minnesota. *Public Health Reports* 112:142–45.

Kouzis, A. C., and W. W. Eaton. 1994. Emotional disability days: Prevalence and predictors. *American Journal of Public Health* 84:1304–7.

Mainous, A.G., III, W. J. Hueston, and J. R. Clark. 1996. Antibiotics and upper respiratory infection: Do some folks think there is a cure for the common cold? *Journal of Family Practice* 42:357–61.

Meijler, A. P., H. Rigter, S. J. Berstein, J. K. Scholma, J. McDonnell, A. Breeman, J. B. Kosecoff, and R. H. Brook. 1997. The appropriateness of intention to treat decisions for invasive therapy in coronary artery disease in the Netherlands. *Heart* 77:219–24.

Mintz, J., L. I. Mintz, M. J. Arruda, and S. S. Hwang. 1992. Treatments of depression and the functional capacity to work. *Archives of General Psychiatry* 49:761–68.

Murray, C. J. L., and A. D. Lopez. 1996. *The global burden of disease: A comprehensive assessment of mortality and disability from diseases, injuries, and risk factors in 1990 and projected to 2020.* Cambridge, MA: Harvard University Press.

National Committee for Quality Assurance. 1997. *HEDIS 3.0: Narrative: What's in it and why it matters.* Washington, DC: National Committee for Quality Assurance.

Ormel, J., G. I. Kempen, D. J. Deeg, E. I. Brilman, E. van Sonderen, and J. Relyveld. 1998. Functioning, well-being, and health perception in late middle-aged and older people: Comparing the effects of depressive symptoms and chronic medical conditions. *Journal of the American Geriatrics Society* 46:39–48.

Pauker, S. P., and S. G. Pauker. 1987. The amniocentesis decision: Ten years of decision analytic experience. *Birth Defects* 23:151–69.

Schneider, E., and A. Epstein. 1996. Influence of cardiac-surgery performance reports on referral practices and access to care: A survey of cardiovascular specialists. *New England Journal of Medicine* 335:251–56.

Stang, P., M. Von Korff, and B. S. Galer. 1996. Reduced labor force participation among primary care patients with headache. *Journal of General Intern Medicine* 13:296–302.

Tarlov, A. R., J. E. Ware, Jr., S. Greenfield, E. C. Nelson, E. Perrin, and M. Zubkoff. 1989. Medical outcomes study. *Journal of the American Medical Association* 262: 925–30.

Verbrugge, L. M., and D. L. Patrick. 1995. Seven chronic conditions: Their impact on U.S. adults' activity levels and use of medical services. *American Journal of Public Health* 85:173–82.

Weinstein, M. C., and Fineberg H. V. 1980. *Clinical decision analysis.* Philadelphia: W. B. Saunders.

Wells, K. B., W. Katon, B. Rogers, and P. Camp. 1994. Use of minor tranquilizers and antidepressant medications by depressed outpatients: Results from the medical outcomes study. *American Journal of Psychiatry* 151:694–700.

ELEVEN

The Interplay between Work and Family and Its Impact on Community Service

Alice S. Rossi

INTRODUCTION

Age, sex, and social class represent hierarchies within which our lives are embedded, determining what we do to earn a living, what paycheck we bring home, where we live, and even what we do in our leisure hours. For most adults, daily life revolves around jobs, homes, family, and friends. For all our vaulted claims to personal freedom and individualism, Americans are not primarily unencumbered selves pursuing life goals according to their own self-interests. This has long been a fundamental premise in sociological theory, but it has become a lively issue in moral philosophy as well and is at the heart of recent communitarian challenges to rights-based liberalism (Blustein 1991; MacIntyre 1984; Sandel 1982). The goals we seek, and the probability of our reaching them, are circumscribed by sex and race and by religious and ethnic background, birth cohort, and location on the ever-changing trajectory of age. This holds true even in broad historical and geographical terms: Natalie Davis and Arlette Farge (1993) tell us that their study of Europeans from the sixteenth through the eighteenth centuries reveals that "daily life unfolded within the frame of enduring gender and social hierarchies." Anthropologists studying societies extremely different from those in the developed nations in the West have drawn the same conclusion. One of the shocks adolescents experience when they finally become independent adults is the realization that they have exchanged one set of restrictions—those imposed on them by parents and schools, for another—those imposed by employers, spouses, and the responsibilities that attend childbearing and rearing.

This chapter focuses on the jobs held by adults in our national survey. Because jobs and wages are strongly influenced by sex and education, we give these two characteristics consistent attention throughout the analysis. Because our interest is in the life course, we also give special attention to age. Topics covered include objective characteristics of jobs in terms of demands on time and energy, the stress level respondents attribute to the nature of their work, the extent to which the work they do is a source of pride and respect from others, their overall satisfaction with their work situation, and the returns they bring home in the form of pay. We examine variation in how jobs affect home life and, finally, how the combination of job and family characteristics affect community service, as indexed by the time respondents spend in volunteer work and the money they contribute to organizations and charities.

To set the stage for this analysis, we briefly discuss several social and economic changes that have been taking place in the larger society in recent years that have serious implications for the lives of adults, young and old, men and women, trends that provide interpretive clues for the results of our analysis.

Economic Trends

There have been both bright and dismal reports concerning the American economy over the last decade. In 1998 the Clinton administration reported the lowest unemployment rate in thirty years and the creation of millions of new jobs, but there are less sanguine indicators as well: the continuing, and in fact increasing, inequality in wage distribution; a record level of consumer debts and personal bankruptcies; a mushrooming of high incomes among the very rich, with 1% of Americans now holding 35% of the nation's wealth; and, despite the low unemployment rate, the fact that there were almost two million more children living in poverty in the late 1990s (14.5 million) than in 1989 (12.6 million) (Reich 1998).

Another recent economic trend concerns the stock market. We no longer hear the phrase "playing the market"; stock purchases are now described in purely optimistic terms as "investments." Incredibly, among registered voters in 1997, shareholders outnumbered those not in the market 53% to 43%, according to an October 1997 NBC News/ *Wall Street Journal* poll, and it has been reported that in 1998 the share of wealth Americans had in stock holdings hit a fifty-year high, exceeding the value of their homes for the first time in three decades (Wyatt 1998). As Jacob Weinberg suggests (1998), there is now a mass culture of investing, the first to exist anywhere in the world. This trend must have been in James Atlas's mind when he proposed a contemporary equivalent of an old Jewish joke: "What's the difference between a garment worker and a poet? A generation. Maybe that joke should be retooled for our entrepreneurial age: What's the difference between a poet and a venture capitalist?" (Atlas 1998, 34).

It is an open question, however, how this radical change will affect society, particularly because a rising market exacerbates social inequality. In the short run, there clearly are benefits from stock investments, which have been generating gains of about 18% a year since 1982, far in excess of safer investments in money-market accounts and certificates of deposit, which have earnings of only about 5%, even less if you subtract a 2% inflation increase. The problem is that investors do not adequately view their stock purchases as a form of gambling, but assume a continuation of high gains well into the future. Most such investors do not see themselves as occupying the top of a hierarchy of gambling, with those less well off gambling in casinos, and the poor gambling in lotteries. More serious still is the possibility that the lure of the stock market encourages speculative gains in lieu of savings or earned income, and hence undercuts the traditional virtues of industry and thrift. It is sadly ironic that the poorest members of society, welfare mothers, are being subjected to shorter periods of public support and encouraged to take jobs that by and large pay very poorly, while those at the top of the class hierarchy are enjoying speculative gains for which they did nothing but gamble to obtain. Because they are members of a particularly fortunate birth cohort, today's elderly fare far better economically than the young and middle aged, and far better than the elderly of only a few decades ago, thanks to the increased value of their homes and a steady flow of income from pensions, stocks, and social security.

Social Trends

Over the course of the past several decades, there have been slow but steady changes taking place in the relations between men and women. Opportunities have opened in the economy for women, while they have diminished for many men, particularly those with low or outmoded skills or those affected by downsizing who often have had to take new jobs with much lower wages. There have been widespread discussions, often stimulated by feminist scholars and activists, concerning the inequities in the division of labor between husbands and wives, a particularly sore point now that the majority of married women are employed yet still handle a majority of the domestic chores (e.g., Hochschild 1989). Men are urged to become more involved in infant and child care as the plight of women juggling family and work responsibilities is spotlighted. Far less attention is given to the pressures men experience on their jobs and on the homefront as women increasingly expect, and more men themselves desire, more equitable sharing in chores and childcare responsibilities (Coltrane 1996; Crosby 1987, 1991; Eckenrode and Gore 1990; Parcel and Menaghan 1994). The overwhelming majority of our MIDUS respondents believe men and women should share equally in domestic chores and childrearing, but the actual division of labor they report still shows the traditional pattern of women performing a far larger proportion of such chores than their partners do. Little wonder, then, that Reed Larson and Maryse Richards found a decided sex difference in the emotional well-being of dual-earning married couples when they return home from work: husbands' moods improve while the moods of women, who often face household chores and the end-of-day scrappiness of their children, worsen, thus suggesting opposite cycles of emotional well-being in the daily lives of men and women (Larson and Richards 1994).

There are many intriguing but unsettled questions concerning the implementation of this new ideology of sex roles. One very broad thesis dominates our perspective as we examine the interplay between work and family: the ongoing sex stratification of the workplace represents a barrier to equitable roles for men and women in their homes and family life. Men's jobs are valued far more than the jobs women have traditionally held, and as a result there are still very few couples who earn comparable salaries, even if they have similar levels of education and job experience and are close enough in age to be at similar stages of their careers. As we will report below, among the dual-earning couples in the MIDUS sample, only 10% have similar earnings; 37% of husbands earn $21,000 or more than their wives earn; only 5% of wives earn that much more than their husbands, a ratio of more than 7:1. Differences in pay matter; no matter how committed a couple is to sharing home responsibilities equitably, rational decisions may dictate that the partner earning the most, whose job is therefore of greatest economic importance to the family, may be excused from carrying a fair share of homefront burdens.

It is also possible for a changing sex role ideology to effect a change in social stigma: thirty years ago, women who worked while having young children at home were often targets for social criticism; today, women who remain at home at this early stage of family life are more apt to experience social stigma than are working mothers. Clearly when

AFDC was implemented decades ago, it was on the belief that mothers of young children should remain at home; today, welfare reform is premised on the notion that children do not need exclusive maternal care and young mothers should return to the workforce as soon as possible after the birth of a child. We shall look closely at our data for clues to the stresses and pleasures attending changes such as these, particularly among young adults who have felt the impact of such value changes most keenly.

Our first topic is respondents' judgment of the adequacy of their income in meeting their needs or those of their families living with them. This is particularly interesting because it highlights the fact that a surprisingly large proportion of our sample of adults are feeling financial strain despite the high employment rate of recent years. Those who are hurting the *most* are our youngest respondents, whereas those feeling the *least* financial strain are older adults over sixty years of age, a profile consistent with some of the points made above.

Actual Earnings Level and Subjective Assessment of Its Adequacy

Table 11.1 sets the stage for this initial analysis, showing the proportion of adults who feel their income is not sufficient to meet their needs. Inspection of these results shows highly significant differences as a function of age, sex, and marital status. In all eight possible comparisons, the elderly are *least* apt to feel their incomes are insufficient to meet their needs, a dramatic example of the far more secure circumstances confronting today's elderly compared to that which their grandparents and great-grandparents faced. In ten of the twelve comparisons, those who are *not* married feel greater financial duress than the married do. Here too one suspects this is a new pattern in our time, reflecting the fact that married women are far more likely to be working and contributing to household income, apparently sufficiently so that despite the greater likelihood that they have children to feed and clothe, they and their husbands are experiencing less income inadequacy than are adults who are not living with a partner. More to be expected is the fact that unmarried *women* are far more likely to feel financial pressure than are unmarried *men*. This is particularly the case among less well educated adults at all three stages of life. Many such women are single parents, which undoubtedly adds to their financial strain. Note, however, that it is among young, less-educated men that marital status makes the greatest difference (44% of the unmarried vs. 32% of the

TABLE 11.1 Percentage of Respondents Who Report They Do Not
Have Enough Money to Meet Their Needs, by Age, Sex,
Education, and Marital Status

	Young (25–39)	Middle Aged (40–59)	Old (60–74)
Men			
High school or less			
Not married	43.6	33.3	18.8
	(39)	(57)	(32)
Married	31.9	30.4	18.8
	(116)	(181)	(96)
More than high school			
Not married	29.5	26.6	24.1
	(112)	(109)	(29)
Married	30.0	21.6	7.9
	(217)	(324)	(126)
Women			
High school or less			
Not married	53.7	60.0	33.8
	(67)	(95)	(80)
Married	44.0	26.0	16.0
	(116)	(181)	(94)
More than high school			
Not married	45.4	36.8	24.4
	(119)	(182)	(78)
Married	30.0	27.4	18.4
	(203)	(63)	(76)

Note: The question read, "In general, would you say you (and your family living with you) have *more money* than you need, *just enough* for your needs, or *not enough* to meet your needs?" The majority of the sample report they have "just enough" (55%); only 15% report "more than they need"; twice as many (30%) report "not enough" money. There is enormous variation in the percentage reporting "not enough" by all four demographic variables; the extremes are represented by older, married, well-educated men (8%) and young, unmarried, less well educated women (54%).

married men report not having enough money to meet their needs). It is likely that many of these men have poor prospects of marriage due to low wages or an erratic employment history.

Note, finally, the very wide range in this subjective sense of income inadequacy when taking into consideration age, education, and marital status. In both sexes, the contrast is very sharp: from only 8% among married, well-educated men in the oldest age group to 44% among the young, less well educated, unmarried men; among women the same sharp contrast holds, though at a higher level of stress— 24% versus 54%.

There is of course an objective reality underlying these subjective

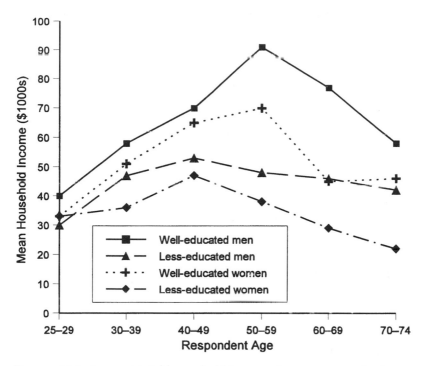

FIGURE 11.1. Average total household income, by age, sex, and education.

judgments, which can be seen by inspecting the differences in actual income by the same sociodemographic variables. To depict the life course trajectory of earnings more finely, figure 11.1 shows six categories of age, from under thirty to seventy or older. This figure compares the *total household income* among less- and well-educated men and women. Among the better educated, income peaks in their fifties, for the less well educated, in their forties, a longstanding pattern that has differentiated middle- from working-class adults for many decades: those who go on to higher education begin their careers at older ages, but their education eventually pays off with significantly higher wages later in life. Also, within each level of educational attainment, women report smaller household incomes than men, and once more the sex difference, like the educational difference, increases with age. Education and sex differences are minimal among young adults in their late twenties, maximal among those in their fifties and sixties.

If we restrict attention to *personal earnings* rather than total household income and compare men and women by marital status, as shown

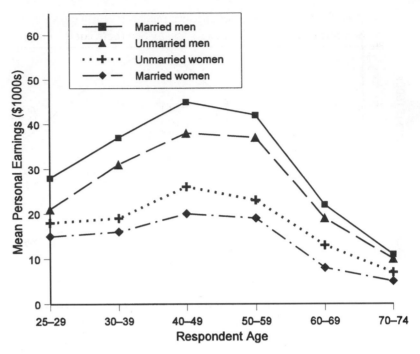

FIGURE 11.2. Average personal earnings, by age, sex, and marital status.

in figure 11.2, the same curvilinear age profile occurs, though more so among men than among women. Figure 11.2 also shows a reversal by marital status within the two sexes: Among men, those who are married earn more than the unmarried at all stages of life. Among women the reverse holds: unmarried women report higher earnings than married women. Married men carry more family responsibility, and many feel pressure to work harder by taking on more than one job. Then too, adequate resources continue to be a factor in mate selection, often leaving men with lesser drive and hence lower income out of the marriage market. By contrast, many well-educated women with ambition choose not to marry. Consequently it is men at the *lowest* level of skill and education and women at the *highest* level of skill and education who tend to remain unmarried or to experience marital breakups.

Multivariate analysis permits us to see the relative contribution of each of the four sociodemographic factors to the subjective judgment that earnings are inadequate to meet either personal or family needs, or both. In addition, we add the number of children to the analysis, since

TABLE 11.2 Regression of Income Inadequacy Judgment on Sociodemographic Characteristics, by Sex (beta coefficients)

Variable	Men	Women
Age	−.198***	−.212***
Total household income	−.293***	−.277***
Educational attainment	−.084***	−.091**
Number of children	.073**	.115***
Married/cohabiting[a]	.039	−.085***
R^2	.150***	.157***
N	1,436	1,519

Note: For income inadequacy judgment, high = not enough money, low = more money than needed.

[a]1 = yes; 0 = no.

**$p < .01$, ***$p < .001$.

obviously this plays a role in such judgments. Table 11.2 shows the re-sults of a regression analysis of income inadequacy judgments as a function of the five predictor variables. All five show significant net ef-fects on income judgment calls: those who report not having enough money to meet their needs are younger, low income, less well educated adults with one or more children. Marital status, as one might surmise from table 11.1, is significant for women: unmarried women, net of age, income, presence of children, or educational attainment, are feel-ing financial duress to a much greater extent than are married women. The reverse is true for men, although statistically not significantly so.

The results to this point underline the fact that sex and social class represent social hierarchies built into the structure of the economy. It is not only that marriage continues to be a route to stronger, more secure financial situations for women, but even within marriage, an imbalance in earnings leaves men in more favorable circumstances because their incomes remain significantly higher than those of their wives. Figure 11.3 provides the evidence, in the distribution of income differences between husbands and wives among dual-earning couples alluded to in the introduction above. Some may take comfort from the fact that a full 18% of wives earn five thousand dollars or more in excess of what their husbands earn, but the longstanding overall pattern remains. A full 61% of husbands earn much more than their wives; a good 37% earn over twenty thousand dollars more.

In light of the fact that it is young adults who are feeling much greater financial stress than are the elderly, one might anticipate that

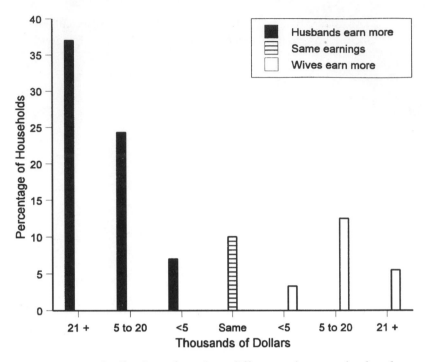

FIGURE 11.3. Distribution of earnings differences between husbands and wives among dual-earning couples.

they would also report greater commitment to their jobs, working harder than others who do their kind of work or taking every opportunity to work overtime even if it meant cancelling social plans. But this is surprisingly not the case, as we will see in looking at the same structural parameters in relation to our measure of work obligation. As shown in chapter 7, normative obligations are significantly related to the quality of life experiences in the families in which our respondents grew up, providing the rationale for the next step in our analysis.

NORMATIVE OBLIGATIONS TO WORK

Were norms fully consistent with motivation and behavior, one might predict that young adults who report that their incomes are inadequate to their needs would feel much greater obligation to their job duties than older adults do, would go out of their way to do well in their jobs, and would work hard even under unpleasant circumstances or despite a lack of respect for those who supervise them. As mentioned

TABLE 11.3 Mean Ratings on Work Obligation Scale, by Age, Sex, and Education (beta coefficients)

	Young (25–39)	Middle Aged (40–59)	Old (60–74)
Men			
High school or less	22.3	23.0	23.9
More than high school	20.7	22.8	23.4
Women			
High school or less	22.6	23.5	23.4
More than high school	22.2	23.6	23.9

Note: The work obligation scale is a three-item scale of ratings on degree of obligation felt, from 0 ("no obligation") to 10 ("very great obligation"), to do more than most people would on their kind of job, to work hard even if they didn't like or respect their supervisors, and to cancel plans to visit with friends if asked (but not required) to work overtime. The work obligation scale (range 0–30) is significantly related to age (f = 20.9, significant at the .001 level), modestly to gender (f = 6.3, significant at the .01 level): older adults have higher ratings than younger adults, and women, higher than men. Education is not significant. Note that the subgroup with the *lowest* rating on work obligation is, surprisingly, young, better-educated men.

previously and shown now in detail in table 11.3, this is not the case: uniformly among both men and women, and at both levels of educational attainment, our oldest respondents show higher levels of obligation to work than the young adult respondents do. In chapter 3 we showed that a similar pattern holds for civic obligations and altruism, but there we suggested that this age profile is due to family life stage and a resurgence of religious beliefs in the later years: as family obligations are fulfilled, attention shifts in midlife to the welfare of others and a broader participation in civic life. The pattern shown for work obligations is not consistent with this interpretation. It seems more likely that young adults are confronting new circumstances that dampen the degree of work obligation from what their parents felt at comparable ages: many younger adults today are seeking a better balance in life between the pressure and pleasure of work on the one hand and family life and leisure on the other (Coltrane 1996; Gerson 1993). Despite the prevalence of social expectations that dictate women should seek their place in the economy, many young women are in the labor force out of necessity, in order to attain and maintain the standard of living they desire. Many young men may also desire a better balanced life, with family commitments undercutting their dedication to go beyond the call of duty in job performance. Note that the subgroup with the very *lowest* work obligation rating is young, well-educated men (mean = 20.7).

There may also be another source of historic change that affects the age relationship to work obligations: changes in parental childrearing practices. Duane Alwin has documented this trend in numerous studies, showing that over the past several decades, parental socialization values have changed in the direction of stressing more flexibility and independence in rearing children, with less emphasis on conformity and obedience (Alwin 1984, 1990, 1991, 1996). It is possible that our younger MIDUS respondents are showing the effect of their parents' emphasis on independence and autonomy, with the unintended consequence that they have not acquired the values and habits underlying work obligations to the degree of earlier cohorts whose parents emphasized conformity and submission to authority and the work ethic.

Our MIDUS module on the characteristics of the family of origin has no extensive battery of items on parental socialization values, but two measures are relevant here: the general religious ambience of the home when respondents were growing up, and the chores and rules they were subjected to, that is, whether they were given regular chores to do and the extent to which their parents had rules about how they spent their time. We have already shown, in chapter 3, that there is a strong net effect of parental religious values on those held by the respondents themselves and that there is an increase in religiosity over the life course. Hence in exploring the age difference in work obligation, we incorporate these two attributes of the family of origin along with age in a multivariate analysis of work obligation (table 11.4). We also include one personality scale of greatest relevance to normative obligations—agency—on the premise that it takes some degree of self-confidence and assertiveness to outperform co-workers and to work hard despite harboring unfriendly feelings toward supervisors, items in the work obligation scale.

These four predictor variables are not powerful determinants of work obligation for either men or women, as indexed by the modest R^2s shown in table 11.4. There is evidence, however, that both personal agency and an early experience of parental supervision and of participation in home maintenance (via regular chores) do play a role in contributing to work obligation. But age itself, independent of such predictors, continues to be positively associated at a significant level with work obligation levels. Despite the fact that men and women do not differ in their reports of how religious their families of origin were, this background variable predicts only men's work obligation level. We have no ready explanation for why this may be the case; our best guess is that men grow up taking for granted that employment will be a fea-

TABLE 11.4 Regression of Work Obligation Scale on Family of Origin Characteristics, Agency Personality Scale, and Age, by Sex

Variable	Men	Women
Family characteristics		
Religion important in family of origin[a]	.067**	−.008
Chores/time-use rules scale[b]	.053*	.082**
Respondent characteristics		
Agency personality scale[c]	.155***	.116***
Age	.124***	.111***
R^2	.055***	.035***
N	1,414	1,480

[a] High = very important; low = not important.

[b] The chores/time-use rules scale is based on two items rating extent to which respondents had regular chores to do and were subject to rules on how they spent their time while they were growing up. Scale range is from 2 ("no rules or chores") to 8 ("a lot of rules and chores"); mean = 5.9, SD = 1.4, alpha = .65.

[c] The agency personality scale, described in detail in chapter 7, is based on self-ratings on the extent respondents consider themselves to be dominant, assertive, self-confident, forceful, and outspoken. Scale range is 5–20; mean = 13.7, SD = 3.2, alpha = .79.

$*p < .05.$ $**p < .01.$ $***p < .001.$

ture of their adult lives, whereas more women anticipate employment on conditional terms as a function of family economic needs and ages of children.

The question of why young adults report more income inadequacy but lower work obligation remains largely unanswered to this stage of the analysis. We turn next to how adults feel subjectively about what they do on their jobs compared with what they do in their homes as a source for deriving pride from what they do and respect from others in reaction to their roles in these two major life domains.

PRIDE AND RESPECT DERIVED FROM WORK ON THE JOB AND IN THE HOME

Two parallel items concerning the two domains of home and work are the measures used in this analysis: we label them "job pride" and "home pride" for simplicity's sake, though both scales include items on respect gained from others as well. We will first inspect the sociodemographic characteristics of the two scales (age, sex, and education), then test whether either or both scales contribute to overall satisfaction with current life situations, and then explore more deeply what aspects of current jobs or what circumstances at home are significant factors in determining whether adults derive pride and respect from these two domains of life.

Demographic Correlates of Job and Home Pride

Attitudes toward home maintenance have a long history of being associated with chores and drudgery. One readily thinks of domestic chores as cleaning away dirt, a monotonous repetitive job with few intrinsic rewards; far more rarely is it associated with a high order of skills in organization and management or with fine cooking and its aesthetic presentation, despite the lure of women's magazines or TV shows on cooking and home decoration. On all sides we are inundated with advertisements for home appliances and cleaning products that will reduce the time required to maintain a shiny clean home. Some feminist scholars go so far as to claim a male-female dualism that encompasses the cultural oppositions of reason and emotion, purity and impurity, cleanliness and dirt. Phyllis Palmer points out that *white* clothing was required in suffrage marches in the 1910s and in Equal Rights Amendment rallies in the 1970s because "white is visually dramatic, but as the bride's color, it also conveys messages of virginity, nonsexuality, physical purity, and fragility" (Palmer 1989, 150).

By contrast to unpaid work in the home, paid work is socially valued work, and it comes as no surprise that in rating the extent to which pride and respect are garnered from the work done at home and on the job, both men and women show higher ratings on job pride than they do on home pride. In table 11.5, this is true for all twelve possible comparisons. Note, however, that this contrast is *most* sharp among well-educated young and middle-aged women, whose home pride ratings are an average of 5.7 and 5.9, respectively, whereas the average job pride rating is 6.7 among the well-educated young women and 7.1 among their middle-aged counterparts. Once again, however, we find that older respondents of both sexes and both levels of educational attainment have higher ratings on both scales than do younger adults.

Pride and respect derived from the two domains are significantly and positively correlated ($r = .27$, significant at the .001 level), suggesting some common element shared by both measures. Preliminary analysis (not reported here) found one measure of this common element, a subscale of Carol Ryff's measures of psychological well-being (Ryff 1989,1992): *self-acceptance,* which taps respondents' feelings about themselves in terms of liking most parts of their personality and feeling pleased with how things are turning out in their lives. While

TABLE 11.5 Pride and Respect Derived from Work at Home and on the Job, by Age, Sex, and Education

	Young (25–39)	Middle Aged (40–59)	Old (60–74)
Home pride[a]			
Men			
High school or less	6.4	6.7	6.9
	(153)	(237)	(122)
More than high school	6.2	6.4	6.6
	(328)	(432)	(155)
Women			
High school or less	6.0	6.2	6.7
	(181)	(272)	(167)
More than high school	5.7	5.9	6.5
	(322)	(407)	(147)
Job pride[b]			
Men			
High school or less	6.5	7.1	7.2
	(136)	(185)	(52)
More than high school	6.7	6.9	7.1
	(300)	(379)	(57)
Women			
High school or less	6.4	6.8	6.9
	(118)	(187)	(38)
More than high school	6.7	7.1	7.4
	(257)	(336)	(59)

[a] Two-item scale based on rating the extent to which respondents take pride in the work they do at home and the respect others show for the work they do at home. Alpha = .81; score range, from 2 ("not at all") to 8 ("a lot"). Analysis shows all three variables are statistically significant: mean rating of men = 6.5, of women = 6.1, anova f = 41.4, significant at the .01 level; on education, low-educated mean rating = 6.4, high = 6.2, anova f = 20.4, significant at the .001 level; on age, mean rating of young = 6.0, middle aged = 6.3, old = 6.7, anova f = 29.4, significant at the .001 level.
[b] Two-item scale based on rating the extent to which respondents take pride in the work they do on their jobs and the respect others show for the work they do on their jobs. Alpha = .79; score range from 2 ("not at all") to 8 ("a lot"). Base Ns for job pride mean ratings are employed adults. Only age is statistically significant, i.e., older respondents report more pride and respect from their jobs than younger respondents do.

conceding that self-acceptance may be a *result* as well as a *determinant* of the pride and respect scales, it is nonetheless worth testing whether the pride scales remain independent and significant as predictors of overall life satisfaction. The results of this test are shown in table 11.6. As the table shows, self-acceptance is indeed a powerful determinant of how satisfied respondents are about their lives in general. But it is also the case that both job pride and home pride contribute significantly to the life satisfaction ratings and do so for both men and women. Educa-

TABLE 11.6 Regression of Overall Life Satisfaction on Job Pride, Home Pride, and Self-Acceptance, by Sex, among Employed Respondents (beta coefficients)

Variable	Men	Women
Job pride	.114***	.117***
Home pride	.146***	.194***
Self-acceptance scale	.452***	.409***
Age	.111***	.059
Educational attainment	−.014	−.048
R^2	.332***	.303***
N	1,098	978

Note: Overall life satisfaction is a single-item rating in response to the question "Using a scale from 0 to 10 where 0 means "the worst possible life overall" and 10 means "the best possible life overall," how would you rate your life overall these days?" Self-acceptance is a three-item modified version of Ryff's psychological well-being subscale of self-acceptance: self-ratings on liking most parts of their personality, pleased with how things have turned out so far in their lives, and not disappointed about achievements in life. The scale is modest in reliability (alpha = .58), mean = 16.5, SD = 3.5, on a 3–21 scale range.

*** $p < .001$.

tion is negatively related to life satisfaction, but not significantly so net of the self-acceptance and pride scales. Older men are significantly more satisfied than are young men, but age does not differentiate women.

Determinants of Job and Home Pride

Job Pride

What job characteristics are likely to explain variation in the extent to which adults take pride in their work and garner respect from others? Clearly the rewards obtained from work are tapped by the size of paychecks, so one prediction is that personal earnings may explain some part of such variation. Putting in very long hours on the job plus the time it takes to travel to work may predispose adults to greater satisfaction with their jobs for a variety of reasons, for example, as a rationalization for the toll taken by long hours of work or as a proxy for deep commitment to one's work role. Conversely, the variation may exist simply because part-time jobs involve lesser skills and hence less intrinsic gratification. Qualities of the work day may also affect whether the job triggers pride or not, and we therefore include a job stress scale in exploring the determinants of job pride. The open question is whether these job characteristics are powerful enough as determinants

TABLE 11.7 Regression of Job Pride Scale on Job Characteristics,
Personality, and Norms among Employed Respondents
(beta coefficients)

Variable	
Job characteristics	
Respondent's earnings	.080**
Job stress scale[a]	−.046*
Hours at work plus commute per week	.018
Personality and normative obligation	
Self-acceptance scale	.251***
Work obligation scale	.188***
Sociodemographic characteristics	
Sex[b]	.034
Age	.112***
Educational attainment	−.009
R^2	.144***
N	1,843

[a] Three-item scale on frequency with which respondents experience too many demands on them, a lot of interruptions, and not having enough time to get everything done during their work days. Alpha = .67, score range 3–15, mean = 8.9.
[b] male = 1; female = 2.
*$p < .05$. **$p < .01$. ***$p < .001$.

to override the influence of personality, work obligation, and the sociodemographic characteristics of sex, age, and education. Table 11.7 shows the results of this multivariate analysis.

Inspection of the table quickly indicates the primacy of high self-acceptance, high work obligation, and age as predictors of job pride: adults who feel good about themselves, have a strong sense of commitment to work, and are older show the highest degree of pride in their work. In terms of job characteristics, the results suggest that time on the job plays no role whereas higher earnings predispose to high pride, qualified by a reduction in pride if the jobs involve pressure (too many demands), distraction (a lot of interruptions) and lack of closure (feeling at day's end that there was not enough time to finish the tasks of the day). Neither sex nor education contribute significantly. It is of particular interest that age continues to contribute a significant increment to pride in one's work, despite the presence in the regression equation of many age-related variables, in particular personal earnings and work obligation. It may be that younger adults have not yet reached their preferred position in the economy, as more older adults have. It is also possible, however, that young adults are under far more pressure in the attempt to juggle work and family responsibilities, undercutting the degree to which they feel pride in their work. We will return to this issue in the next section.

Home Pride

A very different cluster of characteristics is invoked in explaining variation in the extent to which adults take pride in home maintenance. A preliminary analysis suggests that a major source of such pride concerns how home chores are handled—the sheer amount of time devoted to domestic chores, whether the chores are divided fairly and equitably in combination with more general qualities of the relationship with spouses or significant partners. Table 11.8 shows the results of our multivariate analysis that includes such major predictor variables, plus

TABLE 11.8 Regression of Home Pride Scale on Marital Team Scale, Personality, and Characteristics of Domestic Division of Labor among Married or Cohabiting Adults (beta coefficients)

Variable	
Self-acceptance scale	.218***
Household and marital characteristics	
Marital team scale[a]	.197***
Division of domestic labor[b]	.101***
Respondent's weekly hours on domestic chores	.068**
Division of labor fairness rating[c]	.090***
Homeowner[d]	−.039
Socio-demographic characteristics	
Sex[e]	−.213***
Age	.100***
Educational attainment	−.167***
R^2	.188***
N	1,994

[a] Four-item scale measuring the extent to which respondents and spouses/partners consult each other, plan and make decisions together, feel better talking things over with partner. Alpha = .88, scale range 4–28, mean = 24.6.

[b] High = respondent does a lot more than partner; low = respondent does a lot less.

[c] High = very fair; low = very unfair.

[d] Own = 1; rent = 0. Homeowners score higher than renters on the home pride scale ($f = 40.8^{***}$) and do more domestic chores (owners, 13.6 hrs; renters, 11.4 hrs; $f = 10.4^{***}$), hence with domestic chores in the equation, homeowning has no significant net effect on home pride.

[e] Male = 1; female = 2.

*$p < .05$.   **$p < .01$.   ***$p < .001$.

the well-being measure of self-acceptance and the three primary socio-demographic variables of age, sex, and education.

Unlike job pride, which showed only age to be significant among the sociodemographic characteristics, the multivariate home pride analysis indicates that all three such variables remain significant predictors, over and above the interesting new characteristics of household management and marital characteristics: being older, male, and less well educated predisposes to deriving greater pride from home care. Adults who score high on the home pride scale tend to be those whose marital relationship reflects a fair and equitable style as team members who consult with each other, make plans together, and find conversations with each other to be a source of subjective good feelings. Of equal interest is the finding that those who do the largest *proportion* of home chores, contribute the most *time* to them, and consider their division of labor to be fair to them are most apt to score high on home pride. We had hypothesized that homeowners would score higher on pride than renters, which they do, but this distinction is not an independent predictor; homeowners contribute more time to caring for their homes, which is the stronger of these two variables in predicting level of home pride.

It is of particular interest that men derive more pride from what they do at home than do women, perhaps reflecting the changes wrought in recent decades in sex role expectations: younger women today are far less likely to take pride in home care than were women in the past, and as we saw in table 11.5, this is particularly the case for well-educated women. Younger men are now expected to play a larger role in home care than in the past and may derive more respect for doing so than men did in the past. Many of today's elderly men would not have been seen even wheeling a baby carriage in public places or caught with an apron on in their younger years, whereas many young men today are rewarded with public and private acclaim when they are vocally and visibly active in the care of the homefront. Other analyses we have conducted with MIDUS data found that men work longer hours and take more time getting to and from work than do women, and women take on more domestic chores than their partners do, but if one adds up all the hours spent on the job, the commute, and doing domestic chores, there is little residual sex difference, with married women exceeding married men in such time allocations by less than two hours a week (Rossi, 1996).

Further clues to the place of jobs in the life experience of contemporary adults can be found in respondents' judgments about how their jobs affect their home life, the next step in our analysis.

Negative Effects of Jobs on Home Life

Though we can conceptually distinguish work from family as two distinct and different domains of life, in reality the two domains have strong effects on each other. A common concept invoked in sociological analyses of this interaction is "spillover," the extent to which jobs affect home life and home life affects jobs (Eckenrode and Gore 1990). In the design of MIDUS we measured these spillover effects in both directions (from job to home and from home to job) and with separate measures on positive and negative effects. In the analysis to follow, we concentrate on the scale that measures the negative effects of jobs on home life. (We refer to "home life" rather than "family life" to assure that those who live alone as single, divorced, or widowed adults could report as readily as married or cohabiting adults to the items in our battery.)

We initiate the analysis with the same three sociodemographic characteristics used throughout—sex, age, and education. Table 11.9 provides this rudimentary profile. It is immediately clear from these results that age is by far the most significant predictor of this negative spillover effect from work to home life: it is young adults who report the highest mean scores on this scale, and the very subgroup that we found earlier

TABLE 11.9 Mean Ratings on Negative Effects of Job on Home Life Scale, by Age, Sex, and Education, among Employed Respondents

	Young (25–39)	Middle Aged (40–59)	Old (60–74)
Men			
High school or less	10.5	10.3	7.9
	(135)	(185)	(55)
More than high school	11.1	10.9	8.6
	(300)	(378)	(57)
Women			
High school or less	10.6	10.1	7.6
	(120)	(188)	(40)
More than high school	10.6	10.8	9.6
	(255)	(338)	(60)

Note: Home life scale is a four-item scale of ratings on job making respondents irritable at home, tired at home, distracted by job problems at home, or reducing their efforts given to home activities. Alpha = .83, scale range from 4 (no negative effects of job on home life) to 20 (high negative effects).

to have the lowest level of work obligation—well-educated younger men—here shows the highest level of negative effects. Jobs that require advanced training at higher skill levels are more apt to leave one tired and irritable at day's end, and these jobs make it more difficult for one to disengage from work while at home (as tapped by the item determining whether job problems distract one while at home). In five of six comparisons, women exceed men in these reports, perhaps reflecting the fact that women's jobs tend to involve less self-pacing and flexibility. That age plays so strong a role suggests it is a proxy for stage of family life: one assumes (and we will test below, whether it is the case) that the presence of young children captures some of the variance in these negative job effects and explains why the young, women, and the better educated experience greater negative spillover from work to home life.

We bring together a variety of measures of greatest relevance to explain what determines the negative effects of work on home life: Job stress is a top candidate because it measures the extent to which work involves many demands and interruptions and tasks that never seem to reach closure, all of which can contribute to irritability and fatigue at home. Sheer time required for the job plus the commute may encroach upon the time needed or desired for home activities. A separate measure consists of ratings on the extent to which respondents feel their jobs have negative effects on their physical and mental/emotional health. For couples with children, it is reasonable to assume that irregular hours of employment are disruptive to family schedules, hence we include a dichotomous code that differentiates between those who work only during the daytime versus those who are on a rotating day-night shift schedule or only work during evening or nighttime hours. Personal earnings is included because variation in income is very great, and it is reasonable to assume that the top-paying jobs have greater potential to increase pressure at work and to reduce the time available for home-centered activities. The presence of children who require supervision and training is potentially a chief factor in explaining why younger adults report more negative job effects than do older adults.

Table 11.10 shows that three major job characteristics have strong and independent negative effects on home life and do so at comparable levels for both men and women: Jobs that involve high levels of daily stress and negative effects on health and require long hours on the job and the commute are critical determinants for negative impact of work on home life. The presence of young children at home contributes even

TABLE 11.10 Regression of Negative Effects of Job on Home Life Scale
on Job Characteristics and Presence of Young Children, by Sex
(beta coefficients)

Variable	Men	Women
Job stress scale	.405***	.361***
Effects of job on physical/mental health[a]	.256***	.333***
Hours at work plus commute per week	.146***	.139***
Daytime work only[b]	−.053*	−.040
Personal earnings	.070**	.024
One or more children under thirteen years	.055*	.067**
R^2	.381***	.395***
N	(959)	(875)

[a] Two-item scale rating the effect of job on physical health and on mental/emotional health. Alpha = .77, scale range from 2 ("very positive") to 10 ("very negative").
[b] 1 = yes; 0 = no. Women are more likely than men to work only during the daytime (71.5% vs. 62.8%; χ^2 = 18.3**), and working evenings or nights has more negative effects on home life than working only during the day (26.3% vs. 19.4% high negative effects; χ^2 = 24.6**).
*$p < .05$. **$p < .01$. ***$p < .001$.

further, over and above the characteristics of the jobs held. High personal earnings increase such negative effects for both men and women, though significantly so only for men: high-paying professional and managerial jobs, more often held by men than women, are likely to involve greater responsibilities, more people to supervise and evaluate, and greater difficulty in avoiding bringing home tension, fatigue, and distraction from work. Any job that requires evening or nighttime hours at work imposes an additional source of stress at home, cutting into family time and relaxation and making difficult the coordination of family social schedules.

OVERALL SATISFACTION WITH WORK SITUATION

We turn now to one final analysis of the work domain: an overall rating of the degree of satisfaction adults derive from their work situation. We phrased the question for this overall single-item rating so as to embrace any kind of work MIDUS respondents were doing: not merely paid work, but unpaid as well; and not only jobs, but also work done at home. This permits us to explore how employment status affects such subjective overall judgments, in particular among older adults, many of whom are retired, and among younger women, many of whom are homemakers. Table 11.11 allows us to see how employ-

TABLE 11.11 Mean Ratings of Satisfaction with Work Situation, by Age, Sex, Education, and Employment Status

	Employed			Not Employed		
	25–39	40–59	60–74	25–39	40–59	60–74
Men						
High school or less	7.2	7.3	8.2	4.4	4.1	7.2
	(143)	(201)	(47)	(14)	(34)	(67)
More than high school	7.1	7.4	8.3	4.2	5.7	8.1
	(308)	(383)	(53)	(21)	(47)	(83)
Women						
High school or less	7.2	7.3	8.2	6.3	6.5	6.9
	(124)	(185)	(43)	(55)	(81)	(106)
More than high school	7.3	7.5	7.8	7.0	6.8	7.7
	(260)	(344)	(60)	(61)	(65)	(82)

Note: Satisfaction with work situation scale is a single-item rating from 0 ("worst possible") to 10 ("best possible") work situation. The question was phrased to cover all kinds of work situations ("whether part-time or full-time, paid or unpaid, at home or at a job.") Anova analysis shows only age is statistically significant ($f = 14.6$, significant at the .001 level), i.e., older respondents report higher satisfaction than younger respondents. Note in particular, however, the very low ratings given by young adult men who are *not* employed, whether low or high education.

ment status differs within the subgroups structured by age, sex, and education and to pinpoint the most interesting subgroups from this comparative perspective.

What immediately stands out in these results is the very great importance of sheer employment among younger and middle-aged men. For all but the non-employed in these subgroups of men, ratings are above the mid-point on the 0–10 rating scale; but non-employed young and middle-aged men, at either educational attainment level, show the lowest ratings of satisfaction with their work situation. The satisfaction level of men in these circumstances reflects the broader societal expectation that adult men *should* be working for pay, an expectation clearly internalized by the men themselves. By contrast, younger women who are not employed show only modestly lower ratings of their work situation (as homemakers) compared to their employed counterparts. Somewhat surprising is the finding that among non-employed women, it is those who have not gone beyond high school who show far lower ratings of satisfaction than the employed women do, and this is true in all three age groups. Despite feminist rhetoric that would suggest otherwise, better-educated women at home are almost as satisfied with their circumstances as their employed sisters are.

The profile shown for older adults reflects a similar pattern: it is less well educated men and women for whom not working involves a sharp reduction in satisfaction ratings (7.2 for less-educated men vs. 8.2 for well-educated men; 6.9 for less-educated women vs. 8.2 for well-educated women). We suspect it is the general income level at which adults are living that underlies these effects of educational attainment and employment status: most of the better-educated women homemakers have husbands of equal or better education than themselves, hence they have more options for how to spend their time and can enjoy a lifestyle with greater amenities and opportunities for service and pleasure than women homemakers in lower socioeconomic circumstances can. This same factor applies to older men as well: those who have had more education have enjoyed higher earnings, hence there is a less negative impact of retirement upon their lifestyles.

We narrow our attention in table 11.12 to adults who are employed, and we explore the relative contribution of the various characteristics of jobs that we used in the course of earlier analyses—negative effects of jobs on health and home life; derivation of pride and respect from jobs; earnings; and work obligation—for their effects on overall satisfaction ratings of work situations.

On the down side, jobs that have negative effects on either health or home life reduce the satisfaction derived from the work situation. On the up side, the more pride and respect adults derive from their jobs, the more they earn, and the greater their commitment to work gener-

TABLE 11.12 Regression of Work Situation Satisfaction Rating on Job Effects on Health and Home Life, Earnings, and Work Obligation Scale, among Employed Respondents (beta coefficients)

Variable	
Effect of job on physical/mental health[a]	−.279***
Negative effects of job on home life[b]	−.200***
Job pride scale	.231***
Personal earnings	.132***
Work obligation scale	.054**
Sex[c]	.040*
R^2	.298***
N	2,078

[a] High = very negative; low = very positive.
[b] High = very negative; low = not at all negative.
[c] Male = 1; female = 2.
*$p < .05$.   **$p < .01$.   ***$p < .001$.

ally, the higher the overall satisfaction reported by adults. No surprise here, except to note that each of these variables makes an independent contribution to work satisfaction, net of all others, and does so to a highly significant degree.

There is also a slight increment of higher satisfaction reported by women compared to men, over and above all the job-related variables in the equation. We probe more deeply into how employment status affects the work situation ratings of women in table 11.13, which reports the results of a multivariate analysis done separately for employed and non-employed women and which brings together a variety of measures about circumstances in their family and home settings. Heading the list of predictor variables is the quality of the marital relationship, in this instance the same scale we used previously that deals with the extent to which the couple works as a team, consulting each other, talking things through, and so forth. The results for women whose lives are centered at home rather than split between home and the workplace show how important marital teamwork is, which has the highest beta coefficient in the equation for homemaking women; by contrast, employed women's ratings of overall work situation are most strongly affected by self-acceptance (i.e., whether they feel good about themselves

TABLE 11.13 Regression of Work Situation Satisfaction Ratings on Family Characteristics and Personal Resources among Married Women, by Employment Status (beta coefficients)

Variable	Not Employed	Employed
Family characteristics		
Marital team scale	.212***	.126**
Home stress scale[a]	−.124*	−.145***
Number of children under thirteen	.096	.110**
Home pride scale	.100*	−.018
Hours on domestic chores	.130*	−.027
Personal resources		
Educational attainment	.059	−.026
Self-acceptance scale	.154**	.249***
Age	.164**	.054
R^2	.199***	.130***
N	292	609

[a] Four-item scale on frequency respondents report their home situation involves too many demands, not enough time to get everything done, lots of interruptions, and no control over the amount of time to spend on tasks. Alpha = .69, mean = 10.0 on 4–20 scale range, SD = 2.8.

$*p < .05.$ $**p < .01.$ $***p < .001.$

and how their lives are working out), followed by whether their home settings are low in friction and stress.

Of particular interest is the contrast between homemaking and employed women on the home pride scale and the time investment they make in domestic maintenance: these variables have no effect on the ratings employed women give, though they are negative in sign, that is, employed women who put in a lot of time doing chores and who take pride in their homes report less satisfaction with their work situation (in a job setting), whereas among homemaking women, a high degree of pride in their home duties and longer hours devoted to such care significantly increase the satisfaction they derive from their work setting (their homes). Having children under thirteen at home does not *reduce* work satisfaction for either group of women; rather the data show a *positive* effect of having young children on work satisfaction for women at home as well as for employed women. In the latter case, work may be gratifying as a means for contributing to the support of such children, as a respite from young children's activities, and as a source of adult stimulation and interaction.

This brings to a close our analysis of adult experience in the workplace and the interplay between jobs and family or home life. We turn, for the last step in our overall analysis, to the question of how job and family characteristics affect the extent to which adults contribute to the larger community, by means of giving time and money to community organizations, causes, and charities.

THE IMPACT OF JOB AND FAMILY CHARACTERISTICS ON COMMUNITY SERVICE

In planning this analysis we drew upon results shown in chapter 3 on the sociodemographic pattern most closely associated with the various domains and dimensions of social responsibility. In the community domain, we reported a marked difference between men and women: women are more likely to serve as volunteer workers to fulfill their obligations to the community, while men are more likely to contribute financially to community organizations. Since we have also seen sex differences in numerous threads of analysis in the preceding sections of this chapter, we conduct this final multivariate analysis separately for women and men within the two dimensions of community service, time and money.

Preliminary analysis showed, surprisingly, that the amount of time spent on the job plus commuting has no significant relationship to volunteer time, nor do any job effects on home life. Hence we limit the job characteristics in this analysis to overall satisfaction with work situation and whether the job entails any impairment of physical or emotional health. In light of the finding reported in chapter 3 that having children is an important inducement to volunteer work, we include family size as a predictor variable along with amount of time devoted to domestic maintenance, though our prediction that time spent on home chores would reduce the time available for volunteer service was not confirmed. As reported below, investment of time in home care carries quite a different meaning than we had assumed. We include both education and income in the analysis because we have already found they play quite different roles in time compared to money investment in the community. We also include frequency of religious service attendance because, as Robert Wuthnow has reported (1994) and as we confirmed in chapter 3, active involvement in a religious institution often provides a pathway from a general biblical command to love and serve others to commitment to broader public welfare concerns. Some degree of personal agency is also required for adults to actively and voluntarily seek out settings in which they can contribute to the public good. Finally, we presume civic obligation to be a powerful predisposing stimulus to individual action in helping others.

Many of the results shown in table 11.14 merely confirm prior findings or support the direction of effect we predicted: Of the two resource variables, education is the major predictor of hands-on volunteer time, whereas household income serves that role for financial contributions. Frequent religious service attendance is a powerful predictor of contributing both time and money for men and women. Being assertive, outspoken, and self-confident (qualities in the agency personality scale) clearly contributes to competence in moving into the larger world of community organizations as a volunteer, whereas even the most shy and introspective adult can contribute money.

Beyond these confirmations of our predictions, however, there are some surprising results shown in table 11.14, and they relate in interesting but contrasting ways to sex differences. For married employed women, time devoted to volunteer work actually increases if they do not find satisfaction in their work situation. This suggests that work dissatisfaction stimulates women to seek gratification elsewhere, through volunteer service, so long as their jobs do not have serious negative effects on their physical and mental health. And the more time women invest in caring for their homes, the *greater* is the time they

Table 11.14 Regressions of Time and Money Contributions to Community Organizations/Charities/Causes, by Sex, among Employed Married or Cohabiting Adults (beta coefficients)

Variable	Time (hours per month of volunteer work)		Money (amount per month to organizations/ charities/causes)	
	Men	Women	Men	Women
Normative obligations				
Civic obligation scale	.106**	.081*	.024	.059
Job characteristics				
Work satisfaction rating	.015	−.130**	.014	−.029
Negative effect of job on physical/mental health	−.001	−.086*	−.037	−.035
Family characteristics				
Weekly hours on chores	.067*	.132***	−.046	.008
Number of children	.096**	.058	.119***	.034
Personal characteristics				
Agency personality scale	.094**	.085*	.006	.034
Frequency of religious service attendance	.169***	.099**	.410***	.290***
Resources				
Educational attainment	.101**	.212***	.161***	.045
Total household income	−.026	−.036	.225***	.295***
R^2	.093***	.099***	.332***	.196***
N	853	614	853	614

*$p < .05$. **$p < .01$. ***$p < .001$.

contribute to volunteer work, an interesting support for Alan Wolfe's argument (1989) that civic virtue is a matter of generalizing family and neighborhood affections to include the wider community. In our MIDUS finding, we infer that time invested in domestic maintenance may function as an index of commitment to the personal care and pleasure of others at home, which is then generalized to include concern for the welfare of more distant members of the community. Many leaders in the world of voluntary organizations have expressed concern that women's movement into the labor force reduces their availability for filling the ranks of volunteers. Our evidence qualifies this; it is not the time spent on the job but the pleasure or pain associated with work that may affect volunteer service. Employed women who do not find gratification in their jobs may seek involvement in voluntary associations, where their presence is welcomed and their service is gratefully acknowledged perhaps more now than ever in the past precisely because the pool of women available to work as volunteers has shrunk.

A rather different set of life circumstances seems to be at work in men's commitment to volunteer service. Having children encourages men to contribute both time and money to community organizations. So too, the more frequently men attend religious services and the more time they contribute to maintaining their homes, the greater their investment in community service. This suggests that when adult men become fathers, continue in or rejoin religious congregations, and move in the direction of sharing responsibility with their wives in home upkeep, they become more oriented to the public good and the welfare of others in a larger sense as well. This profile is strikingly similar to that which we found in a Boston area–based study of parent-child relations across the life course (Rossi and Rossi 1990), in which parenthood was more strongly associated with high scores on expressivity in men than in women. Whether married or not, or mothers or not, women's social roles and choice of occupations provide outlets for expressive behavior, which is less common for men. By contrast, men are more likely to become expressive and nurturant when they become fathers, which in turn predisposes them to community service. There are larger political and policy implications to these findings, which we shall discuss in the following, concluding section of this chapter.

CONCLUSION

We began this chapter by emphasizing the structural constraints imposed by age, sex, and education, and the significant ways in which recent social and economic changes are challenging such traditional hierarchies. Despite the profound changes that have accompanied political and legal efforts to move more quickly toward an egalitarian society, it remains the case that economic inequalities continue largely unabated. This is dramatically evident from the demographic profile of household incomes, personal earnings, and subjective assessments of financial duress reported by our MIDUS respondents. We find that earnings are structured by age, sex, marital status, and educational attainment: Women's earnings in the aggregate are moving closer to men's wages (though a sizable gap still exists), but in the context of marriage, it remains overwhelmingly the case that husbands typically earn thousands of dollars more than their wives do. The relation between economic resources and marital status is reciprocal, however, in that low-earning males have fewer marriage opportunities and increasing numbers of women need not depend on marriage for economic survival.

Economic reality also imposes constraints on the extent to which men and women, however ideologically committed to an egalitarian partnership in marriage, can manage their daily lives in accord with their beliefs. Differences in pay may necessarily affect couples' decisions about the division of childcare and home maintenance responsibilities. Despite the research showing that men rank fatherhood as more important than paid work (e.g., Gerson 1993; Lamb and Sagi 1983; Pleck 1983), work role requirements make it extremely difficult for young adult men to practice what they espouse. Our analysis shows that it is younger, well-educated men, especially those with high earnings, who report the highest mean scores on the negative effect of jobs on their home life. To the extent that holding down a high-paying job makes a man successful, it is his success that subjects him to work that involves longer hours, tension, often a considerable amount of work-related travel, and a level of responsibility that makes it very difficult not to bring home job-related problems and worries, thus reducing the likelihood that he can fully participate, without distractions, as an equal in childrearing and home care.

Other of our findings illustrate the impact of changing sex role expectations: Women derive more pride and respect from their jobs than they do from their work at home; men report more pride in their work at home than women do. Being a woman homemaker has become devalued in contemporary society, whereas men can anticipate social praise from their wives and neighbors and often from their work colleagues if they take on more responsibility for child care and home maintenance than was usual for men of a previous generation. This author experienced a dramatic example of this in the 1970s when her husband answered a doorbell, vacuum cleaner in hand. The caller was a woman graduate student, who lost no time informing her peers that the male Professor Rossi not only espoused a belief in sex equality but acted upon it as well!

On the other hand, not being employed continues to carry far greater social stigma for a man than for a woman: as we saw, men in their twenties through their forties who were not employed at the time of our survey rated their situation far more unfavorably than women their age who were not employed. Among young and middle-aged women who are well educated, homemakers appear as satisfied with their circumstances as employed women. This is not so, however, for women with no more than a high school diploma, among whom those employed are significantly better satisfied than those at home. We also infer a very different effect of having young children at home on men compared to women. For men with young children, jobs impose a greater negative effect on their home life. For women, having young children at home increases the satisfaction of both employed and homemaking women with their respective work situations. In all these examples of our findings, there is evidence of the significant influences of economic pressures and job requirements that are barriers to further social change in the roles of men and women in their private family lives. A more positive note is struck by our finding that having young children stimulates a significant increase in time devoted to volunteer work for both men and women. We will return to the significance of this finding at a later point in this discussion of findings.

Among our most intriguing, but at the same time puzzling and difficult to interpret, findings are age differences, often stronger than differences in sex, education, or marital status. Young adults report the highest levels of financial duress and the highest negative effects of jobs on family life. Older respondents, by comparison, report the lowest income inadequacy and the highest scores on pride and respect derived from home and job, both of which are highly predictive of overall life satisfaction. Yet despite their job-related stress and financial duress, it is also young adults who scored the lowest on our work obligation scale. A cross-sectional survey is a snapshot, frozen in time, resulting in data from which it is typically difficult to differentiate change rooted in normal developmental processes from change reflecting cohort characteristics and historical factors. Consistent with the historic change in childrearing techniques from high stress on conformity and obedience toward a more permissive approach that encourages independence and autonomy in children, we found that older respondents, whose parents routinely assigned them domestic chores and held consistent standards concerning how they used their time, were as adults highly committed to work obligations, whereas younger adults reported the lowest levels of work obligation. It should be noted that permissive childrearing that encourages self-reliance and autonomy on the part of children is an ideology congenial to busy parents desirous of active lives of their own away from parenting. The eventual impact on the children, however, may be an undercutting of their subsequent motivation, drive, and ability to postpone gratification, all qualities typically required for job success in modern economies.

The counterpart to this cohort interpretation of low work obligation among young adults is the generally more satisfactory economic situation of today's elderly. Our survey results impress us anew with the prescience of demographers like Samuel Preston (1984) and Richard Easterlin (1980), who more than a decade ago were among the first social scientists to describe the fundamental change that had begun to take place in the socioeconomic status of the elderly compared to the plight of young children over the preceding several decades. In the 1930s it was the plight of the elderly that researchers defined as problematic; today it is the plight of children that concerns us, and on the basis of our analysis, such concern should include young adults. Not only are our elders living longer, but they have more secure benefits in social security and federally funded health care than any preceding cohort of elderly in Western history has had. Although our survey did not include the very old (the age cut-off being seventy-four) and did not include any young adults below twenty-five years of age, we were nonetheless impressed to find the persistent significance of age differences in this survey.

This is not to say that all the age differences we noted are grounded in cohort differences. Clearly a family life stage is implicated as well. We noted that incomes peak for adults in their fifties if they are well educated, in their forties if they have lower levels of educational attainment. But economic pressures associated with childbearing and early childrearing occur much earlier—for the less well educated, in their twenties, for the better educated, in their thirties. The flatness of real wages in recent decades has left many young adults with a lesser probability of enjoying any significant increase in wages over time, despite imminent increases in need. This sets the stage for low rates of procreation, higher rates of employment among married women, and shorter periods of maternity leave after a birth.

There is one final issue of considerable importance that our findings highlight: becoming a father and taking more responsibility for home maintenance stimulates men to extend themselves to the larger community. We suspect that just as growing up in a home that assigns domestic chores to children and supervises how they spend their time stimulates higher levels of work obligation in adulthood, so too the increasingly significant role that men are playing in domestic management and child care has important consequences for society. We have found the most illuminating perspective in terms of which to appreciate the broader societal significance of men's increased commitment to family roles to be that of Joan Tronto. In her important book, *Moral Boundaries* (1993), Tronto distinguishes between several meanings of "caring". *caring about, taking care of,* and *caregiving.* Society has traditionally held that a man's key responsibility is to work at his job in order to "take care of his family." By contrast, a woman's role should be centered on *giving care,* not *taking care of.* We have seen this sex difference in numerous chapters in this volume: women give more social and emotional support to family and friends, interact more with kin and friends, provide more hands-on caregiving, and do more volunteer work than men do; men are more likely to make financial contributions to younger family members and community organizations than women are.

Tronto argues that we should not necessarily think of money contributions as caregiving; financial support is more a matter of "taking care of" than it is of "caregiving" because money does not in itself satisfy human needs, it only provides the resources by which such needs can be met. Feminist scholars have long noted that there is a great deal of work involved in converting a paycheck into a satisfaction of human needs; as Tronto points out, to equate providing money with satisfying needs is to undervalue caregiving in our society.

When caregiving is undervalued, it becomes relegated to the least well off members of society. Throughout history, care work has typically been the charge of slaves, servants, and women. In occupational terms, jobs that require giving care directly are devalued and offer low pay: cleaning hotels, offices, and homes; providing childcare; maintaining buildings. These jobs are disproportionately held by the relatively powerless members of society—women, blacks, and Hispanics. By contrast, "caring about" and "taking care of" are the duties of the powerful and are typically associated with masculinity. Doctors "take care of" patients, but nurses and aides "give care." The hierarchy of prestige therefore follows cultural values that have long dominated Western society: public accomplishment, rationality, and autonomy are defined as worthy qualities, whereas caregiving has been devalued to such an extent that it is viewed as the opposite—private rather than public, interdependent rather than independent, emotional rather than rational. When caring is thought of as a disposition rather than as a practice, as an individual attribute rather than an aspect of social structure, Tronto suggests, it is an easy step to defining care work as "naturally" appropriate for women and those of lower status in society, leaving higher status men to indulge in "caring about" such larger issues as the International Monetary Fund and in "taking care of" needy kin or the poor in their community by writing a check. Tronto proposes a redefinition for this latter type of caring: "privileged irresponsibility" (Tronto 1993, 121). Finally, if care work is to be viewed in the context of human interdependence, as a society we should be upgrading, not downgrading, those who do care work of the "caregiving" variety.

Even a moment's reflection suggests there is a long, difficult road ahead before any such development can occur. It calls for a *downgrading* of the rewards that accrue to those whose labors do not contribute significantly to human welfare and an *upgrading* of the pay and prestige accorded to those in occupations that do contribute significantly. But large social changes are often achieved through incremental changes hardly recognized for their potential contribution to societal goals of greater equity and fairness. It is our belief that encouraging children to take active roles in home chores is one such incremental change. By setting a table, doing laundry, or shopping for others in the family, children can develop an appreciation for and commitment to contributing to others, a first step toward a broader conception of service and responsibility. Men who are now struggling to achieve a genuine partnership with their wives in home and family life, from participation during childbirth through infant care and child supervision, as well as sharing repetitive domestic chores, are no longer merely "taking care of" their family by the money they bring home; they are actively engaged in "giving care" to their young. By so doing, they are learning, often for the first time, to express the intense feelings of love and tenderness that an infant or young child evokes and to master the hundreds of skills needed to run a household well and beautifully, not merely efficiently. Scott Coltrane's recent book, *Family Man* (1996), provides insightful descriptions of men attempting precisely such role changes. So we take our finding that despite their busy lives, it is not merely women, but young adult fathers who are contributing more hours to volunteer work as a hopeful omen of a slow but very important transition to a more equitable and interdependent society.

REFERENCES

Alwin, D. F. 1984. Trends in parental socialization values: Detroit 1958 to 1983. *American Journal of Sociology* 90:359–83.
————. 1990. Historical changes in parental orientations to children. In *Sociological studies of childhood*, ed. N. Mandell and S. Cahill, 3:65–86. Greenwich, CT: JAI.

————. 1991. Changes in family roles and gender differences in parental socialization values. In *Sociological studies of childhood,* ed. N. Cahill and S. Cahill, 4:201–24. Greenwich, CT: JAI.

————. 1996. Parental socialization in historical perspective. In *The parental imperative in midlife,* ed. C. Ryff and M. Seltzer, 105–67. Chicago: University of Chicago Press.

Atlas, J. 1998. The whistle of money. *New Yorker,* 2 February, 34–37.

Blustein, J. 1991. *Care and commitment: Taking the personal point of view.* New York: Oxford University Press.

Coltrane, S. 1996. *Family man: Fatherhood, housework, and gender equity.* New York: Oxford University Press.

Crosby, F. J. 1991. *Juggling: The unexpected advantages of balancing career and home for women and their families.* New York: Free Press.

————, ed. 1987. *Spouse, parent, worker: On gender and multiple roles.* New Haven, CT: Yale University Press.

Davis, N., and A. Farge, eds. 1993. *A history of women in the West.* Cambridge: Harvard University Press.

Easterlin, R. 1980. *Birth and fortune: The impact of numbers on personal welfare.* New York: Basic Books.

Eckenrode, J., and S. Gore, eds. 1990. *Stress between work and family.* New York: Plenum Press.

Gerson, K. 1993. *No man's land: Men's changing commitments to family and work.* New York: Basic Books.

Hochschild, A. 1989. *Second shift: Working parents and the revolution at home.* New York: Viking.

Lamb, M., and A. Sagi, eds. 1983. *Fatherhood and family policy.* Hillsdale, NJ: Erlbaum.

Larson, R., and M. Richards, 1994. *Divergent realities: The emotional lives of mothers, fathers, and adolescents.* New York: Basic Books.

MacIntyre, A. 1984. *After virtue.* Notre Dame, IN: University of Notre Dame Press.

Palmer, P. 1989. *Domesticity and dirt.* Philadelphia: Temple University Press.

Pleck, J. 1983. Husbands' paid work and family roles. In *Research in the interweave of social roles,* ed. H. Lopata and J. Pleck, 3:251–333. Greenwich, CT: JAI Press.

Preston, S. H. 1984. Children and the elderly: Divergent paths for America's dependents. *Demography* 21:435–57.

Reich, R. B. 1998. When naptime is over. *New York Times Magazine,* 15 January, 32–34.

Rossi, A. S. 1996. How Americans spend their time: Time allocations to job, family, home, and community. Unpublished paper read as the Burgess Award Lecture at the annual meeting of the National Council on Family Relations, November, Kansas City.

Rossi, A. S., and P. H. Rossi. 1990. *Of human bonding: Parent-child relations across the life course.* New York: Aldine de Gruyter.

Ryff, C. D. 1989. Happiness is everything, or is it? Explorations in the meaning of psychological well-being. *Journal of Personality and Social Psychology* 57:1069–81.

Ryff, C. D., and M. J. Essex. 1992. Psychological well-being in adulthood and old age: Descriptive markers and explanatory processes. In *Annual Review of Gerontology and Geriatrics,* ed. K. W. Schaie, 11:144–71. New York: Springer.

Sandel, M. 1982. *Liberalism and the limits of justice.* Cambridge: Cambridge University Press.

Tronto, J. 1993. *Moral boundaries: A political argument for an ethic of care.* New York: Routledge.

Weinberg, J. 1998. United shareholders of America. *New York Times Magazine,* 25 January, 29–32.

Wolfe, A. 1989. *Whose keeper? Social science and moral obligations.* Berkeley: University of California Press.

Wuthnow, R. 1994. *Sharing the journey: Support groups and America's new quest for community.* New York: Free Press.

Wyatt, E. 1998. Share of wealth in stock holdings hits 50-year high. *New York Times,* 11 February, sec. A.

TWELVE

Social Responsibility and Paid Work in Contemporary American Life

Anne Colby, Lorrie Sippola, and Erin Phelps

INTRODUCTION

Late-twentieth-century scholarly discourse, especially in the social sciences, has focused a great deal of attention on community or civic engagement, social responsibility, and moral commitment. Concern over these issues has been fueled by a perception—widely discussed by the mass media as well as among many circles of scholars—that the social fabric of modern society is fraying due to a decline in the allegiance of individuals to social and religious institutions, cultural traditions, their families and workplaces, political parties, voluntary neighborhood associations, and civic life itself.

Accordingly, social scientists and social critics have been asking a number of questions following from this perception, such as: What is left of community in our society? To whom, if anyone, do people feel responsible, other than to themselves? What is the nature and strength of the feelings of social responsibility that still exist in the modern world; what are the boundaries and limits of such feelings; and how do they play out in people's daily lives? In what ways do people today balance obligations toward others with more narrowly defined personal concerns?

Many contemporary social scientists and social critics (e.g., Bellah et al. 1985; Etzioni 1993; Gardner 1991; Mansbridge 1990; Wilson 1993; and Wuthnow 1991) have written about the urgent need to move beyond the prevailing worldview that is morally relativistic and that assumes the necessary preeminence of self-interest and individual preference in explanations of human behavior. They argue that without some shared standards for what is acceptable behavior, with only morally arbitrary preferences for guidance, a kind of moral void develops in which there is no basis for any enduring commitment beyond the self. In large part, the outcry on this issue is motivated by a concern about the unmitigated individualism of contemporary American culture and the negative implications of this individualism for the society. As John Gardner has said, "We shall have to rehabilitate the idea of commitments beyond the self. This reverses a century of fruitless search for happiness in an ever more insatiable shattering of limits so that the self might soar free and unrestrained" (Gardner 1991, 10).

In *Habits of the Heart*, Robert Bellah and his co-authors made the case that American individualism, which has been a central part of our national identity since the nation's inception, is no longer balanced, as it once was, by traditions that emphasize moral commitment and socially responsible citizenship. They document the prevalence of several forms of radical individualism in present-day Americans' lives and the wide split between people's public and private concerns. They point out that "this is a society in which the individual can only rarely understand himself and his activities as interrelated in morally meaningful ways with those of other, different Americans." Bellah and his associates argue that, in order to counter this dangerous trend, we must work to reformulate within the current context traditions that see the individual in relation to a larger whole and reconstitute communities that allow us to connect our aspirations for ourselves with the aspirations of that larger whole and see our own efforts as being, in part, contributions to a common good.

Although *Habits of the Heart* makes a convincing case for the dominance of radical individualism in American culture, the book also documents a range of positions on this issue, with some people exhibiting "second languages" of social commitment along with their first language of individualism. The authors contrast the perspective of radical individualism with other, more balanced and socially connected perspectives that could point the way toward a more humane, just, and cohesive society.

In order to explore one end of this range of social commitment, the first author of the present chapter, along with William Damon, conducted a study of people ("moral exemplars") who had devoted themselves very intensively to the common good for decades of their lives. In their report of this study (Colby and Damon 1992), the researchers describe a developmental process involving the transformation of goals through social influence, which represents the progressive deepening of the moral exemplars' commitment to others' welfare. The study also identifies a number of qualities that are common to the very diverse group of people who participated in the study. These include *certainty*, which refers to the exemplars' exceptional clarity about what they believe is right and about their own personal responsibility to act on those beliefs; *positivity*, which refers to the exemplars' positive approach to life, enjoyment of their work, and optimism; and *unity of self and moral goals,* which refers to the central place of the exemplars' moral goals in their conceptions of their own identity and the integration of their personal and moral goals. This final characteristic is one that Bellah and his co-authors also note in the people who most clearly exhibited "second languages" of social connection and commitment: "Such 'natural citizens' of a community such as Suffolk experience little conflict between their self-interest and the community's public interest precisely because a long-term involvement in the community has led them to define their very identity in terms of it. Insofar as one defines oneself as a 'natural citizen' of the town, to harm the town would be to harm oneself" (Bellah et al. 1985, 175).

Despite the differing lenses that sociological and psychological analyses bring to any question, a number of common themes have emerged across these programs of research. Bellah et al. 1985, Colby and Damon 1992, and other related studies such as McAdams et al. 1997 and Wuthnow 1991 show how, even in a society marked by a great degree of individualism and materialism, many people manage to find communities that support their connections with others; and many people organize large portions of their lives around a sense of responsibility to such communities. Moreover, when this occurs, the individual's perspective on life is marked by strong feelings of certainty, positivity, and a belief in the unity of personal and moral goals. Of course, this does not occur for all people. Many participate only rarely in experiences that reflect a sense of community; and many do very little in their daily lives that suggests a strong sense of social responsibility. We need to know more about the social conditions that promote community and social responsibility as well as the personal qualities that support individuals' commitment to these essential pillars of social life.

A QUALITATIVE STUDY OF SOCIAL RESPONSIBILITY AT MIDLIFE

The study reported here attempts to map out the various patterns of social responsibility exhibited in the lives of a representative group of middle-aged American women and men. By social responsibility, we mean action taken for the benefit of others or for the welfare of society more generally. We begin with the assumption that there are a number of ways of being socially responsible, that one must understand the individual's social responsibility within his or her context and opportunities, and that the broad boundaries of social responsibility can encompass family, community, society more broadly, paid work, volunteer work, personal assistance, and financial contributions to individuals and institutions. The study describes how people understand social responsibility in various domains of their lives and investigates the relation of social responsibility to people's central life goals and their sense of meaning in their lives. In this chapter, we will discuss some preliminary findings about social responsibility in the domain of paid work.

This study draws from semistructured interviews with a MIDUS subsample of ninety-four people. Participants were selected from areas within a fifty-mile radius of five cities chosen to cover the major geographic regions of the United States: Atlanta, Boston, Chicago, Phoenix, and San Francisco.

The subsample differs from the full MIDUS sample in a few ways, but is representative of the larger group on the great majority of variables we have compared. Although the MIDUS sample was selected to cover the age range from twenty-five through seventy-four, we limited the subsample to a narrower age range (thirty-four through sixty-five) because the sample size was to be so much smaller and because we were especially interested in the midlife period. For this reason, we evaluated the representativeness of our subsample by comparing it against subjects aged thirty-four to sixty-five from an age-restricted MIDUS sample. The two samples differed in educational attainment, with our subsample being more highly educated. Forty-three percent of our subsample had a bachelor's degree or more, whereas only 21% of the MIDUS sample did. Only 30% of the subsample had twelve or fewer years of education, as compared with 55% of the MIDUS sample. This education difference was not intentional and may have been due to the selection effect of our requesting a lengthy personal interview. Members of our subsample were significantly higher in openness to experience and lower in perceived life constraints than members of the MIDUS sample were. These differences may have derived from the education difference, since both of these variables are related to education. As indicated in table 12.1, the subsample did not differ significantly from the full sample in gender, race, religious affiliation, religiosity, church attendance, proportion currently working, proportion working full time, household income, personal income, occupational prestige, physical health, life satisfaction, scores on the Loyola Generativity Scale, hours spent in volunteer work, hours spent helping family members or helping others outside the family, or MIDUS social responsibility scales.

TABLE 12.1 Comparison of Social Responsibility Study Respondents
with MIDUS National Probability Sample

	Interview ($n = 94$)	MIDUS Sample ($N = 3485$)	Test Statistic[a]
Education (%)			
Twelve or fewer years	30	55	23.32*** (χ^2)
Some college	27	34	
Bachelor's degree or more	43	21	
Perceived constraints (1–7)	2.45	2.76	5.071* (F)
Personal mastery (1–7)	6.01	5.81	3.252$^+$ (F)
Openness to experience (1–4)	3.14	3.03	4.312* (F)
Conscientiousness (1–4)	3.32	3.22	3.312$^+$ (F)

Note: Only statistically significant comparisons are shown in the table. The following variables were tested for differences between the social responsibility study respondents and the national probability sample. Demographic variables: gender, age, race, education, religion, church attendance. Work variables: whether currently working, working full time, experiencing ongoing stress at work, occupational status (Duncan's Socioeconomic Index), how rewarding job is, perceived inequality at work. Financial variables: current financial status, how well-off growing up, personal income, household family obligation scale, family time scale, family financial help, work obligation scale, civic obligation scale, civic time scale, civic financial contributions, altruism scale. Health, mental health, and personality variables: physical health, generativity, perceived constraints, personal mastery, agency, agreeableness, openness to experience, neuroticism, conscientiousness, extroversion.

[a]F-tests were used to test differences between means; χ^2-tests were used to test for categorical differences. The test used is shown in parentheses.

$^+p < .10.$ $^*p < .05.$ $^{**}p < .01.$ $^{***}p < .001.$

In lengthy, open-ended interviews (two to three hours each), we asked participants to talk about their life histories and what they do for their families, friends, and communities; about their paid work and volunteer work; their political engagement; and their financial contributions to charities and directly to other people. The interviews were tape recorded and transcribed.

The Meaning of Paid Work

Although some authors (Armon 1993; Boyte and Kari 1996a, 1996b; Kohn 1977; Sullivan 1995) have written about work as the expression of people's values, including moral values, the more prevalent view of paid work at the present time is that work is primarily an economic endeavor, that Americans are overly focused on the pursuit of material goals, and that this search for material success is in opposition to community service, family life, spirituality, and self-realization. In *The Overworked American* (1991), for example, Juliet Schor writes about the long hours many people work, the consumerism which is one driving force behind this overwork, and the destructive consequences of this pattern for families and communities.

In *Poor Richard's Principle* (1996), Robert Wuthnow presents a more nuanced and perhaps more accurate view of the moral and social significance of work. He argues that traditionally the American Dream has provided a moral framework, encouraging people to work hard and to expect rewards for their work but also centrally concerned with family, community, and religion. According to Wuthnow, this conception of the American Dream had begun to change by the end of the nineteenth century, so that "work and money [have become] more intimately linked with each other but farther removed from those conceptions of the human spirit that had once constrained them. . . . [Now] economistic thinking dominates discussions of work and money, while questions of moral commitment, character, and human values seem more difficult to relate to economic behavior" (Wuthnow 1996, 5). According to Wuthnow, the American Dream has lost its moral meaning, and we no longer have any moral basis for keeping our work commitments within bounds, curbing our wants, abiding by rigorous ethical standards at work, or taking more time for ourselves. Like many other contemporary authors, he points to the ill effects of overwork, including health problems, stress, and inadequate attention to family and community. But unlike most contemporary observers, he sees the problem in moral terms: "If we are to grasp the origins of our discontent with the material life, we must look beyond the current language of stress and overwork and seek to rediscover the moral ambivalence toward economic pursuits that lies deep within our own tradition" (Wuthnow 1996, 59).

Wuthnow recognizes that work is not devoid of values or entirely separate from the rest of our lives. His own data show that Americans are deeply committed to their work and find it meaningful and fulfilling. On the other hand, he makes the case that these moral values are seldom fully integrated into our thinking about our work commitments; rather they are compartmentalized as a "work self" separate from many of our other values. He concludes that we must rediscover the moral values that place positive limitations on our economic striving. He urges us to limit our work for the sake of higher dimensions of human existence, not just because we are too tired, stressed, or lacking in ambition.

We understand Wuthnow to be claiming that the imbalance between work and other important human pursuits is problematic in two
ways: first, that people's work is not adequately integrated with their
deepest values, especially their moral values; and second, that many important human values and goals are being sacrificed to the demands of
work, driven largely by pressure from employers and the weakening of
moral limits on the pursuit of professional and material success. Although Wuthnow acknowledges the moral aspects of work and the fact
that people seek personal meaning and fulfillment through work, his
proposed solution to the problematic imbalance between work and the
rest of life focuses almost exclusively on a need to constrain work rather
than a need to support, enhance, and develop the moral value of work.
Thus, for the most part, he treats work as primarily an "economic commitment" which increasingly conflicts with other needs and therefore
has to be kept within bounds. In this, he joins others who have called
for Americans to reconsider the place of work in their lives.

Without wishing to dispute the validity or importance of Wuthnow's position, which is an original and compelling variant of the case
for balance that others have made, we believe that a full solution to
these problems involves increasing the meaningfulness of work as well
as keeping work in the proper balance with the rest of life. We need to
bring a moral framework not only to the justifications for limiting
work, as Wuthnow argues, but also to the shaping of the work itself.
This paper will, therefore, attend to the first of the two problems Wuthnow has laid out—the integration of moral meaning with paid work.
In doing so, we will look at how people understand the personal meaning of their work and the relation of that meaning to their other values
and goals.

Pride in Performance

In response to our questions about whether and how their work is
personally meaningful to them, the great majority of study participants
said that their work *is* meaningful (79% of the seventy participants for
whom this item could be coded). They have many different ways of defining that meaning. In order to describe the terms in which study participants talked about the meaning of their work and related issues, we
coded the interview material for a number of themes. These include a
wide range of ideas such as the importance of work as contributing to
the economic maintenance of one's family, the job as allowing one to

have a positive impact on the organization, work as self-expression, alienation from or criticism of the institutional setting of work, and references to burn-out.

A graduate student independently coded twenty cases in order to establish inter-rater reliability. Overall agreement on all codes within the interviews was 77%. Agreement across the sample on specific items ranged from 75% to 100%.

In discussing the personal meaning of their work, two-thirds of the sample said that the meaning of their work derives at least in part from their desire to do a good job, their pride in accomplishment, conscientiousness or dependability, and the like. A very typical response was, for example, "The biggest reward of working is the self-satisfaction of knowing that I did a good job, that I did the best that I could possibly do."

A woman with a very troubled background talks about her satisfaction with her job as a supermarket manager this way:

> I take a lot of pride in what I do. I'm more of a perfectionist, so I like things to run smoothly. I like to keep things organized. I enjoy what I do. I enjoy the challenge of being in charge. I don't like to be a follower; I'm more of a leader, and I'm comfortable in that situation . . . [b]ecause it gives me a feeling of accomplishment, a feeling of success. . . . I enjoy the pace. I think it's very, very stressful, and I think you have to be able to take a high level of stress to be in the retail business today. But it's very challenging work, and it does give you a feeling—especially when everything just sort of fits together and everybody works well together, and people respect you because you stand up for your principles—it gives you a feeling of accomplishment." (case 46488)

The fact that so many people talk about their own sense of accomplishment as a major factor in the personal meaning of their work is consistent with other studies (e.g., Wuthnow 1996), which also report that people often mention how important it is to them to do a good job, taking pride in quality work. Wuthnow sees this pride in performance as an element of work motivation that employers can use to bind workers to work that is not intrinsically meaningful. The participants in his study describe their performance not as a matter of achieving some goals they have set for themselves in life, but in narrowly specialized terms.[1] "Performance thus becomes an end in itself rather than being part of the quest for beauty, truth, or goodness" (Wuthnow 1996, 115).

Wuthnow's analysis is consistent with our own interview data in that many people who refer to their pride in doing a good job do not connect the issue of competence to (or indeed refer in any way to) any broader social or moral value of their work or any way in which their work contributes to the welfare of others. That is, a concern for excellence is often (though not always) an end in itself rather than a means to more socially or morally defined goals. But Wuthnow's account fails to recognize the deeper significance of the satisfaction derived from doing a job well. Developmental psychologists (e.g., Clausen 1993; White 1959) have identified competence motivation as a fundamental human striving and an engine of development from infancy onward.

Translating to the workplace this idea of a basic motivation toward competence, mastery, or a feeling of efficacy, we would argue that if people are going to invest themselves in their work over long periods of time and face the challenges entailed in learning new skills, they cannot rely solely on extrinsic rewards or even the ultimate goals of the work; they also need to care about doing a good job, about their own competence, efficacy, and striving for excellence.

Themes of Social Responsibility and Personal Reward

Aside from the issue of competence, the participants in our study cited many other ways in which their work is fulfilling and meaningful to them. Our primary interest is in assessing the extent to which people see their work as connected with their moral concerns, or their desire to contribute to the welfare of specific others or to the community or society. For this reason, we divided the things that people said gave meaning to their work into two categories: social responsibility themes and personal themes. Slightly more than *half* of the people in the study described the meaning of their work at least in part in terms of what the work contributes to particular others or to society. For the rest, the meaning has more to do with their own enjoyment, personal satisfaction, and self-expression without reference to its social value.

The seven social responsibility themes (table 12.2) concern the ways that one's paid work contributes to the welfare of organizations, the society more broadly, or other individuals. They include mention of the direct contributions the work makes to a community or society, efforts to improve conditions for others in the workplace, teaching and men-

471

TABLE 12.2 Social Responsibility Themes

Themes	Percentage of Participants
1. Work is important or meaningful because of what it contributes to society or the community; the mission/purpose of the work is important (in terms of contributing to society or the community).	35.1
2. Social responsibility is expressed not through the primary responsibilities of the job but through ancillary activities such as union work, efforts to promote justice in the workplace, activities that involve doing good for people at work, and the like.	7.4
3. Work is important/meaningful because it involves helping others, compassion for people.	27.7
4. Work is important/meaningful because of or satisfaction is gained from teaching or mentoring more junior employees, colleagues, students, and so on.	16.0
5. The job allows one to have a positive impact on the organization, make a difference to the organization, etc. Enjoyment of leadership role as a way to make a difference.	11.7
6. Work is important because it allows one to pass on the work ethic to one's own children or to be a role model for young people. Work allows one to pass on ambition to one's children, giving the message that you can do something if you try hard enough.	7.4
7. Work is important because it allows one to be a breadwinner, to provide for one's family.	4.3

toring, making a positive impact on the organization, serving as a role model, and providing economic support for one's family. The nine personal themes (table 12.3) concern various rewards of work, such as self-expression and creativity, personal growth, challenge, enjoyable relationships, or financial gain, which do not relate directly to the ways that work could contribute to others' welfare.

Tables 12.2 and 12.3 list the percentage of people in the sample who expressed each theme. As indicated in table 12.2, the most frequently mentioned social responsibility theme (35%) is theme 1, which refers to the contribution the individual's work makes to the community or society. The second most commonly cited social responsibility theme is theme 3: work is meaningful because it involves helping others, compassion for people. Frequently mentioned personal themes include references to work as fun or interesting, enjoyment of working with other people, personal growth through work, and appreciation from one's "clients."

TABLE 12.3 Personal Themes

Themes	Percentage of Participants
1. Satisfaction of appreciation from people served. Satisfaction of developing relationships with people served.	31.9
2. Personal growth through work—it changes you. Work shows you something positive about yourself. Part of identity to be reliable; work gives one a sense of purpose.	31.9
3. Satisfaction from solving problems at work, sorting out puzzles, etc. Challenge a positive thing about work.	24.5
4. Work as self-expression. Seeks or has creativity in work.	11.7
5. Job itself an education, learned a lot on the job, work as a learning experience. Had meaningful mentor-like experience—someone he/she really learned from.	16.0
6. Satisfaction from the fact that this job is respected, satisfaction from recognition and respect.	20.2
7. Enjoyment of work, job described as fun or interesting.	40.4
8. Enjoyment of being with people. Supportive supervisor and/or co-workers. Teamwork, importance of working well with others.	34.0
9. Work involves trying to achieve financial/material success.	10.6

Although people differed in the number of social responsibility and personal themes they used, we did not conceive of the number of themes used as an indicator of the salience or importance of social responsibility or personal satisfaction in their work. Some people focused on one theme in a very thoroughgoing way that seemed to infuse their attitude to their work with significant intensity. In other cases, individuals made brief reference to several themes yet appeared to be no more strongly oriented toward social responsibility in the way they approached their work than those who referred to one theme. Because of the subjective nature of this judgment, we did not try to assess the intensity of individuals' orientations to social responsibility in their work. For this reason, we have classified people as using *no* social responsibility themes or using *one or more*. Inter-rater reliability for this dichotomous classification is 95%. (This represents agreement on nineteen of the twenty reliability cases.) As indicated in table 12.4, 55% of the sample discussed the meaning of their work at least in part in terms of what the work contributes to others. All but one of these also used one or more personal themes. Eight people (8.5%) used neither social responsibility nor personal themes. The remaining 36% used personal themes but no social responsibility themes. That is, almost everyone who used

TABLE 12.4 Comparison of Interviewed Respondents with and without Social Responsibility (SR) Themes

	With SR Themes (n = 52)	Without SR Themes (n = 42)	Test Statistic[a]
Gender (%)			5.81* (χ^2)
Male	67	33	
Female	42	58	
Race (%)			8.46* (χ^2)
White	50	50	
Black	100	0	
Other	83	17	
Type of work (%)			11.04** (χ^2)
Executive, administrative, managerial	72	28	
Technical, clerical, sales	33	67	
Household and protective services	58	42	
Manufacturing, construction, agriculture	40	60	
Nonprofit (%)	81	19	9.42** (χ^2)
Job is personally meaningful (%)	73	27	13.43*** (χ^2)
Job relates to self (%)	83	52	7.91** (χ^2)
Occupational status (SEI)	46.1	37.3	12.88*** (F)
How rewarding job is (1–4)	3.4	3.0	8.64** (F)
Perceived inequality at work (1–4)	2.9	3.3	8.34** (F)
Pride in job (1–4)	3.6	3.1	6.44** (F)
Number of hours worked per week	43.6	37.4	4.14* (F)
Net worth			5.50+ (χ^2)
Money still left over	63	37	
Still owe more	33	67	
Break even	25	75	
Rate overall life (0–10)	8.1	7.1	12.92*** (F)
Psychological well-being (1–7)	6.0	5.2	23.34*** (F)
Generativity (1–4)	3.0	2.5	17.93*** (F)
Perceived constraints (1–7)	2.2	2.8	6.65* (F)
Personal mastery (1–7)	6.2	5.8	3.24+ (F)
Openness to experience (1–4)	3.3	3.0	6.53* (F)

Note: Only statistically significant comparisons are shown in the table. The following variables were tested for differences between those who used and did not use social responsibility themes. Demographic variables: gender, age, race, education, religion, church attendance, religiosity, number of children. Social responsibility variables: amount contributed to others, family obligation scale, family time scale, family financial help, work obligation scale, civic obligation scale, civic time scale, civic financial contributions, percentage of household income to charitable contributions, altruism scale, and a combined scale of community social responsibility. Work variables: whether currently working, working full time, experiencing ongoing stress at work, type of work, profit or nonprofit organization, whether job is personally meaningful, whether job relates to self, occupational status (Duncan's Socioeconomic Index), how rewarding job is, perceived inequality at work, effects of job on mental health, pride in job, hours worked per week. Financial variables: current financial status, how well-off growing up, personal income, household income, how difficult to pay bills, net worth. Health, mental health, and personality variables: physical health, rating of overall life, control over life, life satisfaction, social well-being, psychological well-being, generativity, perceived constraints, personal mastery, agency, agreeableness, openness to experience, neuroticism, conscientiousness, extroversion.

[a]F-tests were used to test differences between means; χ^2-tests were used to test for categorical differences. The test used is shown in parentheses.

+p < .10.   *p < .05.   **p < .01.   ***p < .001.

social responsibility themes also used personal themes, but many of those who used personal themes did not use social responsibility themes

The following examples illustrate the two different orientations toward work expressed by those who use social responsibility themes (often along with personal themes) and those who use only personal themes. Mr. Andrew Wiley, a college graduate, is commissioner of public works for a city government. He expresses social responsibility themes 1 and 5, as well as several personal themes, when he talks about the meaning that his work has for him. He says:

> I love my job. In my job, the most important conviction I have is that there is a trust that I have to uphold with the public, and I am committed to maintaining that trust and credibility with the public. I feel that the worst thing I could possibly do is damage that sense of trust or credibility. Without my credibility, I have nothing. . . .
> . . . I get to do things that make a difference in this community. I also get to do some projects that are environmental in nature. I'm working on a program to clean up the bathing water quality and the shellfish beds in Quincy Bay, which is important to me because I care about the environment. I was born here. This is my city, and I can see every day something that we did that made a difference, that made something better, and it's important to me to be able to see tangible results from what I do. (case 47408)

Jack Hedges, a man with some postsecondary education but no college degree, is the assistant director of a Boys and Girls Club. He is so dedicated to his work that he goes in on his free days if there is unfinished work to do. He talks about how much he loves working with young people and what he is trying to accomplish with them:

> Work is very important to me. If you work with children, you don't last with kids for twenty years and not love kids. . . . The way it works with me is every one of those kids that walk into my building, I consider one of my kids, and I will protect them. I will stick up for them, as long as they're in the right, and I will go out of my way to help them. . . . We have a facility that has a gym and a games room, an art room, a computer room, and things like that.

But kids don't just come down for the building. They come down for the people that work there. I've had instances where kids confided in me about things that have taken place in their lives that they wouldn't tell their parents or friends. I've had instances of neglect by parents. . . . When I first started, I felt that I should be able to reach every single kid. But that's why you have different staff people, because if they can't relate to one staff person, maybe they can relate to another.

When asked what is most important about his work, he replies:

Hopefully sending kids down the right path. What I get out of it is the personal satisfaction of watching them grow up into mature young adults. I have kids that come back to visit, and we reminisce, kids that come back and help out. And you end up over a period of time developing relationships with certain kids. There's an impact on their life, and they'll come down to me when they're adults to talk to me about it. The reward is teaching a kid a new skill or something. . . . If you show a kid how to do something, and just that gleam when they look at you like, "Oh, look what I did." And now they have that confidence so they can take it to the next step. (case 47477)

Jenny Bridges, also with some college but no degree, is a police officer at a tough housing project in Chicago. She talks about some of the things she has done for the residents of this extremely desolate area:

I extend myself quite a bit for people through my job. I spent three years trying to help this one girl and her kids. . . . I got her out of Cabrini [the housing project]. She was a witness in a murder case; I was there for her, took her shopping every week. . . . One thing I accept about life is you can't do for people and expect immediate or actual feedback from that person. Because if you want to project . . . who you are in goodness and acceptance of other people, you just do. Once you're on a positive level . . . putting forth positive energy . . . which I do . . . it does come back to me. Police do such fabulous things for people that you can't even imagine. . . . Nobody ever writes about it. People are hungry. . . . [T]hey want to be acknowledged . . . to acknowledge they're alive. . . . Police do that for people. . . . We give people recognition. There's a lot of humanness in police work. (case 45006)

These and other cases that express social responsibility themes contrast with cases in which contributing to others is not evident in the way the respondents talk about their work. People who talk about their work in terms of personal themes without using social responsibility themes may be just as satisfied with their work and just as committed to it, but they think about its meaning in very different terms. Helen Preston, who has a college degree, talks about the satisfaction she gets from her work as a buyer for clothing stores this way:

It's afforded me things that I never dreamed of. I've been to Hong Kong and Italy, and all the mileage that I do for business, I get dividends on frequent flyer programs. So I fly for free to Greece or England or Florida on vacation. I've been to Montana, California, Colorado, New Orleans, all with the mileage that I've accumulated from the business travel. And then I go to New York every week on business. So it's been really exciting. I love what I do. It's not like work. I would do it for free if I was so altruistic. I love the challenge because we sit across from another person, and they may have ten thousand jeans that they want to sell. The challenge is for me to buy them as cheaply as possible so that I can offer them out at a great price to the customers, and the other person's challenge is to get me to pay as much as he can. So it's a lot of psychology, a lot of acting.

I always dreamed of having a job that I really loved so much that I didn't feel as if I was going to work in the morning. For 99% of the time, that's how it is. My career is everything to me. You hear conversations about how men identify themselves personally with who and what they are on the job, and if a guy loses his job, he almost loses his self-identity or his confidence, and I truly feel that way about this. I feel like this is who I am, what I do. (case 47407)

Nat Hilgard, who has a master's degree, talks about the satisfaction he gets from his work as a computer designer in terms of the challenge, what he has learned from the work, the financial rewards, and the respect of his co-workers:

> I was always in a position to be at the leading edge of technology . . . [a]nd I always felt that I did exceptionally well in that particular discipline [i.e., computer design]. . . . The products that I designed and worked on oftentimes would wind up being a product that was sold worldwide, and that makes you feel pretty good, when you know you designed something way down in the bowels of a major system that's used by the biggest companies in the world, the U.S. government, and these research institutions. . . . Just starting with the idea that doing something and learning something is better than sitting around and doing nothing and drawing unemployment, and that has been my take on life. . . . The work was challenging. It was not a routine kind of thing because you were always designing something. You know, the technology changed so fast, and you had to change with it to keep up with it. It was always a challenge to invent the new mousetrap. There was always another way to do something better and faster. Oh, first and foremost, after . . . never having enough money to buy anything, I was financially, you know—my salary was a reward. Beyond that, the rewards of, say, respect from your peers was a reward of sorts. But I would think that *most of the rewards were things you could take to the bank* [emphasis added]. . . . I grew up in a life where you didn't have things. (case 46587)

Social Responsibility in Work and Related Measures

The fact that some but not all of the study participants talked about their work in terms of what it contributes to others raises a number of questions about why this is so. The first question is whether social responsibility in paid work as defined in terms of our themes is related to other measures of social responsibility in this or other domains. One obvious candidate is the Loyola Generativity Scale, which was included in the MIDUS survey instrument. This scale includes items such as "Others would say that you have made unique contributions to society," "You feel that other people need you," and "You like to teach things to people." Generativity (Erikson 1963) involves commitment to the well-being of the next generation and activities that aim to contribute a positive legacy that will outlive the self. These concerns are very close to our conception of social responsibility. This interpretation is supported by the fact that the study participants who used social responsibility themes had a significantly higher mean score on the generativity scale than did participants who used only personal themes ($\chi^2 = 22.04$; $p < .0001$). (See table 12.4.) We believe that this strong empirical relationship reflects the fact that to a large extent the two indicators are measuring the same thing.

People who used at least one social responsibility theme also have significantly higher scores on the MIDUS civic obligation and altruism scales, combined into a measure of community social responsibility. The items on these scales include statements such as "How much obligation would you feel to . . . serve on a jury"; ". . . keep fully informed about national news and public issues"; ". . . testify in court"; ". . . vote"; and ". . . pay more for health care so that everyone had access to health care." (See table 3.1 for more information.) Both these scales and our social responsibility themes deal with the individual's concern for the common good and thus also appear to be measuring overlapping constructs. We interpret the findings on these scales and the generativity scale as providing validation for the social responsibility themes.

Somewhat surprisingly, at least at first blush, those who used at least one social responsibility theme did not score significantly higher on the MIDUS work obligation scale. The explanation for this becomes apparent when we examine the three items on this scale, which ask people to rate how much obligation they would feel to "do more than most people would on your kind of job"; "work hard even if you didn't like or respect your employer or supervisor"; and "cancel plans to visit friends if you were asked but not required to work overtime." Clearly, this scale defines social responsibility in work more in terms of what we would call conscientiousness than in terms of the extent to which their work contributes to the welfare of others.[2]

Also, perhaps somewhat surprisingly as well, the use of social responsibility themes was not related to the spirituality or religiosity scales that were included in the MIDUS battery. These scales include items such as "How important is religion in your life?" and "How important is it for you to send your children for religious or spiritual services or instruction?" Although others (Rossi, chapter 7, this volume; Wuthnow 1991) have found religious involvement to be related to volunteering and other forms of service, this relationship of religiosity and social responsibility does not appear to carry over to the interpretations people give for the meaning their paid work has for them.

Except for its relationship with the generativity, civic obligation, and altruism scales, social responsibility in work appears to be quite separate from social responsibility in other domains. We do not consider social responsibility in the work area to be an indicator of a generalized tendency to be socially responsible across domains. For example, many of the individuals in our sample who did not use social responsibility themes in regard to their paid work talked at length about their volunteer work or the kinds of things they did routinely to help extended family and friends. This may be particularly true of people whose jobs are not easy to construe as making important social contributions. This is consistent with Newman's observation in chapter 5 that the low-income black and Latino families in her sample considered their jobs as parents, supervising their children and keeping them out of trouble, as their major contribution to society. So too, Rossi (chapter 3) reports that less well educated, lower paid MIDUS respondents do little volunteer work and contribute little money to charities but do more than better-educated adults in providing social-emotional support and hands-on caregiving to family and friends.

In line with the impressionistic sense from our interviews that social responsibility in paid work is not an indicator of overall social responsibility, people in our sample who mentioned one or more social responsibility themes in regard to paid work did not score significantly higher on the family obligation scale and scored lower, though not significantly lower, in number of hours spent helping family members. Nor did they volunteer significantly more hours in civic activities (see table 12.4). As we said in the introduction to this chapter, we began the study with the assumption that there a number of different ways of being socially responsible, and we did not expect that individuals' profiles would be flat across the different domains of life. Table 3.2 shows that internal to MIDUS as well, correlations between domains and dimensions are modest at best.

Social Responsibility in Relation to Demographic Variables

In trying to determine why some people see their work as contributing to others' welfare, we began by examining the demographic variables age, race, gender, and education, finding that race and gender show significant associations with social responsibility group, while age and education do not (see table 12.4). It is perhaps not surprising that age is not related to social responsibility group, since we intentionally chose a sample within a restricted age range such that everyone in the sample was in the midlife period when the data were collected. We were more surprised that social responsibility is not significantly associated with education, since education has often been found to be related to various aspects of civic responsibility such as voting. In fact, the data do show a trend in this direction with higher proportions of individuals in each education group (no college, some college, bachelor's degree or more) using at least one social responsibility theme. The trend is not significant, however.

Race is significantly related to the use of social responsibility themes, with blacks most likely to use these themes (100% of the eight respondents), whites least likely (50% of the seventy-nine respondents), and "other" minorities in between (83% of the seven respondents). We must be cautious in interpreting these findings, given the small number of nonwhite participants in the sample. However, the findings are consistent with other reports that blacks tend to be less individualistic and more concerned about the welfare of the group than white Americans are.

Gender is also significantly related to the use of social responsibility themes, with more men than women using at least one social responsibility theme. This gender difference is accounted for by differences on two of the seven social responsibility themes: theme 1 (work is meaningful because of what it contributes to society, etc.) and theme 6 (work is important because it allows one to be a role model for young people, etc.). There were no significant gender differences in the use of any of the other five themes, in spite of the fact that some of them seem to fit gender stereotypes, for example, caring for others in the workplace, helping others and being compassionate toward them, and being the family breadwinner. Theme 6 was mentioned by only 7% of the sample, so it is difficult to know how meaningful the gender difference on this item is. Theme 1, on the other hand, is the most frequently cited social responsibility theme, so it is clearly the most important source of the overall gender difference in the social responsibility group. We believe that the most plausible interpretation of the apparent gender difference on this item is a confounding of gender with type of occupation. Professionals were the most likely to use social responsibility theme 1, as were individuals with higher scores on the Duncan Socioeconomic Index (SEI). As in the society as a whole, the men in our sample were more likely to be professionals and men had higher SEI scores than women did. In addition, perhaps due to the differences in their job status, men were more likely than women to say that their jobs were closely related to their sense of self.

Relation of Social Responsibility to Job Type

If we are to understand why some people talk about their work in terms of its social contributions and some do not, we must consider the possibility that it is the nature of the job that determines how people describe their work: Will nurses talk about helping people, public officials about what they contribute to society, and people in business about making money? In order to address this question on a general level, we coded participants' occupations according to the main categories of the 1980 Census of Population Classified Index of Industries and Occupations. We then grouped these into four categories of work: (1) executive, administrative, and managerial occupations; (2) technical support, administrative support (clerical), and sales occupations; (3) service and private household occupations; and (4) agricultural, manufacturing, and construction occupations.

As indicated in table 12.4, job category is significantly related to the use of social responsibility themes, with executive, administrative, and managerial (professional) workers most likely to use at least one social responsibility theme (72% of individuals in these occupations used at least one social responsibility theme). Service workers had the next highest proportion using at least one social responsibility theme (58%), followed by 40% of agricultural, manufacturing, and construction workers. Clerical and sales workers were least likely to use social responsibility themes (33%). Consistent with these categorical data, we also found that occupational status (as defined by the SEI) was significantly higher in the group that used at least one social responsibility theme (see table 12.4).

In addition to looking at the census categories, we also divided study participants according to whether they worked in nonprofit or for-profit settings. The profit/nonprofit dimension is also significant, with workers in the nonprofit sector being significantly more likely to talk about their work in terms of social responsibility themes (81% vs. 46%). It is noteworthy that all of the professional and service workers employed by nonprofits described their work in terms of what it contributes to others.

For most professions, contributing to society or helping others is an explicit part of the occupation's self-definition and professional ethic.

In his book *Work and Integrity,* William Sullivan points out that the very idea of professionalism historically has included a "broader, more socially responsible sense of calling" (Sullivan 1995, xvi). Sullivan makes the case, however, that few professions have lived up to this ideal and argues that "professional life can and needs to be restructured in ways that suffuse technical competence with civic awareness and purpose" (xix). Our data are at least modestly encouraging on this score, since *three-quarters* of the executive, administrative, and managerial workers bring at least some concern for social responsibility to their work. Thus, the moral and social concerns that characterize the professions' self-definitions do tend to show up in the way these people talk about the meaning of their work. This does not mean, of course, that even these individuals are as fully oriented toward "civic purpose" as they might be, and we must also note that 28% of the individuals in these occupations show no indication that such concerns are salient to the personal meaning of their work.

A similar argument can be made in regard to the profit/nonprofit dimension. Nonprofit organizations are by definition pursuing missions that benefit the community or society and are no doubt more likely than for-profit organizations to be suffused with ideologies that reflect these goals. It is, therefore, not surprising that employees of nonprofits are more likely to discuss the meaning of their work with reference to social responsibility.

Although the occupational differences in the proportion of people describing the meaning of their work in terms of the social responsibility themes are of considerable magnitude, it is also important to note that there is a great deal of overlap in the categories. Just as more than a *quarter* of professionals do *not* talk about their work in terms of what it contributes to others, so too, we see that a *third* of clerical and support workers do. We also see substantial overlap in regard to the profit/nonprofit dimension. We believe this indicates that any job can be experienced as contributing to others' welfare or not and that the nature of the job itself is not the sole determinant of whether or not this occurs.

If we organize actual job titles into two lists, the jobs of the participants who do and do not use any social responsibility themes, we can see the same pattern—that people in some kinds of jobs are extremely likely to use social responsibility themes, but that most jobs can be construed in terms of either set of themes. The one general occupational category with enough cases to be meaningful that appears only on the social responsibility list is health care (physician, physician's assistant, nurse, veterinarian, pharmacist, nursing home aide, home healthcare aide). In these healthcare occupations it seems that the themes of helping others or serving the public are so intimately tied to the nature of the job and the normative way of talking about it that just about everyone in these fields will talk about their work at least to some degree in these terms.

A radiologist talks about the importance that his work holds for him this way:

> The reason it's important is because I make a difference. . . . I am involved directly with helping to save the lives of other people. There's nothing more important on the planet. Policemen, firemen, people who do this kind of job . . . really you cannot reward them enough . . . teachers . . . these are just a few of the many jobs in this country—in the world—that make a difference. And I think I have one of them. I enjoy going to work because I interrelate with people. And the challenge is that I usually interrelate with people who are under duress. So the challenge is . . . how do I make them, for a brief minute, forget that they're in here for diagnostic purposes? (case 45315)

This kind of satisfaction is expressed not only by those at the upper end of the occupational prestige scale, but also by nonprofessionals such as Cathy Matin, a patient services representative. Cathy works for about twenty doctors, checking in patients, answering basic questions for them, rescheduling appointments, scheduling referral appointments with specialists, and the like. In talking about the meaning of her work, she says:

> I feel I'm helping these people, even though when they come in they may be angry and screaming, but they're sick, but I'm performing a service for people. . . . I deal with people that have cancer, they have AIDS, they are going through the scare of operations. . . . There are so many people out there that are saying, "I need, I need, I need." . . . But I'm seeing less and less people out there [who are helping them]—and I know they're out there and I know there's a lot of them, but you just don't hear about them. There needs to be just as many people that can help the

people that say "I need." We're all put here for a reason, and I guess that one part of me being here is to go out and be among people and do whatever I can do [to] make things easier for them. . . . People need to get back to where they're caring for others as well as themselves. . . . I just feel that I need to be out there. It's my way; I guess it's my one contribution to whatever it is we're supposed to be contributing to." (case 46576)

Almost all of the teachers and former teachers in the sample were similarly likely to cite concerns for others or the common good in talking about the meaning their work has for them. Other categories, such as firefighter or police officer, appear to share the same tendency to be described in these terms, but there were so few cases of each of these occupations that generalizing about them does not seem warranted. Likewise, those in some jobs, such as bookkeeping, cited only personal themes, but there were too few cases of each to draw any firm conclusions from this, especially since none of the study participants in the clerical and support category worked in a nonprofit setting.

As we would expect from the overlap in the occupational category analyses, most kinds of jobs could be described either in terms of social responsibility or in terms of personal themes only. Sometimes the opportunities to contribute to the welfare of others through one's work involve activities outside one's immediate job description, as in the case of this laborer in a soda can factory. The job itself provides little satisfaction, but Jim Richards has found a number of ways to contribute to things he believes in that do create meaning for him at work. Asked about the meaning of his work, Jim says: "It's not a particularly rewarding, you know, job. It's a, you know, make four million cans a day, day in and day out. It's not rewarding for me personally, no" (case 46321).

Jim's interview is coded as expressing social responsibility theme 2 because of several other activities he participates in at work. He is the elected financial officer for the Steel Workers Union, having run for office because he thought the union was wasting the money of the members: "They kind of got me mad, the spending . . . when they take money out of your check, hey, where's it going? What are they doing? So I took an active part and got elected." Jim is also in charge of employee participation at work. People come to him with special projects, and he pushes them through, or if "one of the guys dies at work, and his widow gets short-changed from the company, I go after the company and make sure they get what they're owed." He also started a recycling program at the plant:

> Before I got there, they would throw everything into a landfill, and I started a program for them and recycled all their wood and paper products, and then got—I got an award from the city and the company for the football fields of landfill I saved or whatever—and the trees and that sort of thing. And then Earth Day I designed a can and brought in a hundred first graders from my son's school and had a tour of the plant and gave them a big Earth Day celebration. Showed them how to recycle various things in their home. You know, so those parts, you know, that I have done personally to derive some satisfaction out of the job. Some of the personal projects that I help people with at work are rewarding. (case 46321)

Similarly, Murray Santini, who runs a carpet cleaning franchise, finds ways to serve others through his work:

> In my business I have a policy. I have a group, they're sort of the inner circle, and they're about thirty-five people now. These are people who are financially having problems. Eddie called me at 7:30 this morning after I got home at 3:30, and Gina, Gina's husband has been injured two or three times, she needs work done at her house. I will probably do $150 worth of work for a lunch and twenty bucks. And I do that for about thirty-five people. There's no way she's gonna get the work done. No way. And I'm never gonna make any money doing this, but, Gina, she's OK. Then I have a group of elderly people that, because I have the kind of equipment I have, if they ever have a basement flood or they ever have a catastrophe, I'll take care of it. Now, if they have three thousand dollars' worth of insurance and a five-hundred-dollar deductible, I waive the deductible. I'll do six, eight, ten thousand dollars worth of work for three thousand dollars just to make sure they're OK. These were people who were in the area, who were around my children when they grew up. They were always nice to my children, so, they don't have to worry. So, I will

go in and clean all their carpet, clean all their curtains. I will take care of them for nothing. Then there are some people who just are the unluckiest people in the world. And I have three. And they make me feel pretty lucky. Even though I don't have very much, they are worse—whoa, they are really bad. I did for one lady over a period of three years I did about five thousand dollars worth of work for nothing. And she was in deep doo-doo; she still is. She's sixty-three years old and she's trying, she's going off onto a new venture. If it works, she'll have retirement money, but if it doesn't . . . I've never met anyone that had this much bad luck. . . . I know they know how to manipulate me, I know that, and I am such a sucker for it. And I know that if I didn't do it, no one would do it and they would probably be in worse shape, so I do it. (case 46936)

These examples illustrate some of the ways that people can find meaning in a diverse array of jobs through the contributions they make to other people and to the society.

The Case of Teachers

Although it is possible to approach any occupation with a positive sense of what that work contributes to others and the world, some occupations are especially likely to be experienced this way. In addition to health care, teaching is another profession that seems naturally to call forth a concern for contributing to others' welfare. Teaching can be a quintessentially generative profession, and we have already noted the close conceptual and empirical relationship between generativity and social responsibility (see also MacDermid et al. 1998).

Although not all teachers are highly generative, teaching is closely linked with generativity, and several items on the Loyola Generativity Scale refer to it directly (e.g., "I try to pass along knowledge I have gained from experience"; "I enjoy teaching things to others"). In a study of people who exhibit high generativity, McAdams and associates (1997) began by selecting teachers who had been recognized for excellence and volunteers who had made significant contributions to their communities. When McAdams and his colleagues compared these highly generative individuals to a group lower in generativity, they found that the highly generative adults were more likely to reconstruct the past and anticipate the future as variations on a prototypical commitment story, which includes, among other things, a stable commitment to prosocial goals and what the authors call "redemption sequences," which are affective sequences in the narratives in which bad scenes (those involving sadness, fear, shame, anger, and so on) are transformed into good outcomes. McAdams and associates describe a number of parallels between the moral exemplars described in *Some Do Care* and the highly generative people in their study, including the similarity of these optimistic redemption stories to what we have called "positivity" and the similarity of the generative individuals' "steadfast commitment" to what we have called "moral certainty."

McAdams and associates do not consider theirs to be a study of the teaching profession per se and are careful to point out that not all teachers, not even all successful teachers, are high in generativity. Theirs was a sample selected to be high in generativity. The positivity and steadfastness of these highly successful and generative teachers contrast with the high levels of distress, depressive symptomatology, and attrition from the profession reported by some studies of more representative groups of teachers. A number of studies (Hammen and deMayo 1982; Schonfeld 1992; and Finlay-Jones 1986) indicate that veteran teachers had much higher levels of distress and depression and lower levels of job satisfaction than norms from community samples or national samples of American workers. In a longitudinal study which assessed seniors at teacher training institutions and followed them in their first years as teachers, assessing both their pre-teaching symptomatology and their job conditions, Schonfeld (1992) found that teachers who worked in the most adverse school environments showed far more depressive symptoms than those who worked in the better schools, although there were no pre-employment differences in depression between these groups. It seems clear that adverse school conditions, especially chronic rather than episodic stresses, have detrimental effects on mental health, and more benign work environments are related to increased mental health. The effect of school conditions on symptoms is quite sizable when other risk factors are controlled. Although it is not possible to tell from these studies, in light of McAdams's study and our own work on moral exemplars, we wonder whether teachers who are especially generative and who find ways to maintain their strong desire to nurture their students' growth fare better under difficult circumstances than less fully committed individuals do.

Our sample of ninety-four participants included twelve teachers or former teachers. Of these twelve, three who were teachers very briefly and then went on to do other things used exclusively personal themes in talking about their work. The remaining nine people all used at least one social responsibility theme. For some of these, the social responsibility themes were very central to their discussions of their work and constituted a central focus of meaning for their lives. A teacher who later became a principal said, "A close friend convinced me that I could really make a difference with kids and teachers and make an impact on education, that I could lead a high school to be a place where kids are welcomed and dealt with fairly and allow them to reach their potential as human beings. My family often came second, I have to admit" (case 46823).

Another teacher, Dan Rustin, talks about his work as having saved him from a life of drug and alcohol abuse. He is now drug-free and teaches at an alternative public school for kids who have been expelled from other schools. He also runs an after-school program for high school students who are trying to make up credits they lack so they can graduate.

> The work is very important personally. . . . I feel like I'm doing something not everybody can do, so I have the challenge of that. I've got the kind of job, and the type of kids that I work with, that people will look at me, "God, I don't know how you do it, how do you do it." Everybody asks, "How can you deal with those kids?" So I have, I get a lot a respect from my peers. . . . I'm working with the kids that are most at risk in the district.
>
> I feel very strongly that a lot of it has to do with my background in recovering from alcohol and drug addiction . . . [to] be able to separate behavior from a kid. Because a kid punches a teacher in the mouth doesn't make the kid a bad kid. He just did something bad, you know, he made a bad decision. . . . I'm forever believing in these kids, and forever trusting them. . . . I want to help them at least take care of some of their academic requirements, and then if they ever get straightened around, there's got to be some exhilaration straightening out their life. I like that . . . the rush of helping a kid. . . . I'm contributing in our society. . . . I'm helping people that society doesn't want to help. They're tired of them, . . . they're tired of the crime they're

doing, they're tired of the gangs, they're tired of the drugs that they're selling, and the drugs that they're using. We're talking about human lives, and I've done it for long enough, so that I've had people, you know, kids come back and they say, if it hadn't been for you, Mr. Rustin, I would have died. . . . [I]t's a powerful influence . . . on a young person's life. (case 46373)

Quality of Life

As indicated in table 12.4, the people who used social responsibility themes in describing their work rated their lives as better overall than those who used only personal themes, reported significantly higher psychological well-being, said their jobs were more rewarding, and experienced a lower degree of life constraints. This is consistent with McAdams and associates' finding that highly generative individuals show an optimistic pattern in their life narratives (which they call redemption sequences) and our finding (Colby and Damon 1992) that people who are deeply committed to the common good have a strikingly positive approach to life. Of course, we cannot draw causal conclusions based on these data, but the impression is strong that those who see their work as contributing in important ways to others have a greater sense of meaning or purpose in life, and this leads to greater satisfaction with their work and their life more generally. As Boyte and Kari have written, "Infusing work with public dimensions—recognizing the larger potential meaning and impact of what one does as a teacher or nurses' aide, as a county extension agent or computer programmer, or as a college professor—can turn an unsatisfying 'job' into much more significant 'work.' The old story of the two bricklayers who were asked what they were doing conveys this sense. One said, 'Building a wall.' The other said, 'Building a cathedral'" (Boyte and Kari 1996a, B3). Unlike life satisfaction, physical health and satisfaction with one's financial situation were not related to the use of social responsibility themes.

Personal Rewards of Work

In addition to providing opportunities to contribute to others' welfare, people's work can also serve their personal goals of sociability, personal development, creativity, challenge, learning, and the respect and recognition of others. When Wuthnow and others talk of the need to limit work commitments, they place these personal values, as well as the moral values of concern for others, in opposition to paid work, conceived primarily as an economic pursuit. Wuthnow recognizes that many people, especially Americans, say that they work for self-fulfillment, but he also says that "economic commitments seem increasingly to get in the way of other needs that cry out from the depth of our souls: the need to cultivate intimate relationships with our families, the desire to be part of a caring community, the quest for spirituality and truth, and, perhaps most of all, the longing to know ourselves better and to grow as persons" (Wuthnow 1996, 7).

Although we do not at all wish to claim that the work domain can fully meet all of the human needs to which Wuthnow and others are calling attention, many people *do* successfully pursue these goals within the realm of work. The personal themes that participants in our study cite as significant aspects of their work experience represent many of these goals or needs. Almost everyone in our sample talked about one or more of these issues as central to the meaning of their work, whether they also referred to the social responsibility themes or not.

It is noteworthy that only 15% of the participants talked about trying to achieve financial or material success through their work, although many more acknowledged that they needed to work in order to support themselves. Many study participants said that they were willing to trade career achievement and financial success for more time with their families or for less stressful, less demanding jobs. It was quite common for respondents to refer to having passed up opportunities for promotion because of a wish to avoid taking on too much responsibility. In the group as a whole (a relatively well-educated group), we were struck by how few people seemed "driven" or very ambitious. In fact, we wondered whether more willingness to take on greater challenges and more responsible positions might not be a good thing for some of the people in the study. It was not unusual for people to talk of their regrets about not having pushed a bit harder to achieve more in their careers. As Wuthnow has reported, our interviews also indicate that people are likely to refer to their desire to minimize stress and overwork as reasons to limit their professional commitments rather than making the case on moral grounds. On the other hand, family obligations were also cited fairly frequently as a reason for limiting work commitments. This is the one way in which a moral obligation was used to justify limiting one's ambitions in the work area.

The various kinds of satisfaction in work that we have classified as personal themes represent important human goals or values that people pursue in many domains of life. Paid work can both contribute to and conflict with the pursuit of these goals. Fully satisfying work will no doubt include many of these, along with opportunities to contribute to others' welfare. In addition, some people may contribute to the world in very important ways by pursuing some of the goals we have called personal themes rather than through direct intentions to benefit society. Many great artists, for example, would describe their work in terms of creativity and self-expression rather than in terms of contributing to the world. Likewise, many well-intentioned people, pursuing what they believe to be socially responsible goals through their work, may unintentionally do more harm than good. Overall, however, intentions do matter. In the long run, if most people approach their work *only* in terms of the personal satisfaction they can derive from it rather than what good it does for others and the world, we will see a deepening of the isolation, individualism, and self-absorption that have so concerned the social commentators we quoted at the beginning of this chapter.

In *Habits of the Heart,* Robert Bellah and his co-authors talk about two main ways that the individualism of contemporary American life is typically expressed. They call these *utilitarian individualism* and *expressive individualism.* By *utilitarian individualism* they mean "a form of individualism that takes as given certain basic human appetites and fears and sees human life as an effort by individuals to maximize their self-interest relative to these given ends. . . . Utilitarian individualism has an affinity to a basically economic understanding of human existence" (Bellah et al. 1985, 336). According to Bellah and associates, *expressive individualism* "holds that each person has a unique core of feeling and intuition that should unfold or be expressed if individuality is to be realized . . . [and] enables the individual to think of commitments—from marriage and work to political and religious involvement—as enhancements of the sense of individual well-being rather than as moral imperatives. . . . The expressive culture, now deeply allied with the utilitarian, reveals its difference from earlier patterns by its readiness to treat normative commitments as so many alternative strategies of self-fulfillment" (Bellah et al. 1985, 47–48, 334, 330).

A close look at the list of personal themes reveals that many of these themes could be construed as manifestations of instrumental or expressive individualism, particularly in the absence of social responsibility themes. Brenda Jackson, a social worker who expresses a number of personal themes but no social responsibility themes, describes the meaning of her work this way:

> [Is the work you do important to you personally?] Maybe not as important as it used to be, because I've realized that in the professions that I've had it's been more service-oriented, and I—and if anyone would ever say to me, "Thank you for helping me," or "You're helping those people," I hate the word help. I don't want to think like Ms. Goodie Two Shoes coming along. So maybe first when I started out it might have been to get approval, and helping—maybe it was to help people, but now I feel like, now I just like people. I like people and I just find it like an adventure every day. I like my job now, but I may not stay in it. I don't know what I'll do. I may just do something totally opposite (laughs). Not help people! (case 46885)

This interview material illustrates what Bellah and his co-authors have called expressive individualism. The justification Brenda makes for her work is not expressed in terms of what it contributes to others, but in terms of the personal satisfaction it affords her. Her account is somewhat difficult to follow, probably because her own thinking on these issues is confused, but she seems to hint at authenticity as a more important criterion for life choices than moral concern. In the end this orientation leaves her without a strong sense of commitment or direction in her work. In other parts of her interview, Brenda also exhibits the kind of "therapeutic orientation" and moral relativism that Bellah and associates describe as integral to expressive individualism. When asked whether she has ever felt a conflict between what she wants to do and what she sees as morally right, she responds: "See, my problem is I had Gestalt training, and we throw 'should' out the window, so everything has to be 'want.'" Brenda has contributed to society by raising two sons as a single parent and helping to care for her ailing parents as well as through the help that she gives her clients on an individual level. Even so, the orientation of expressive individualism that frames her thinking is limited, failing to provide a basis for thoughtful civic engagement or guidance on difficult moral questions. Thus, it is not surprising that she says elsewhere in the interview that she knows and cares nothing at all about politics. As Bellah and his co-authors have argued, a well-functioning democracy requires social bonds and commitments to institutions and the common good that go beyond a concern with self-expression, personal growth, authenticity, and autonomy.

Conflicts between Work and Personal Goals

As we mentioned earlier in this chapter, one of the most notable features of the highly dedicated people that we wrote about in *Some Do Care* was the relationship between their personal goals and their moral goals, which were so fully integrated that the people found their most intense personal satisfaction in helping others. Thus, they rarely experienced conflicts between what they wanted to do and what they felt it was right to do, and they talked at length about the great joy they experienced in their work. In line with this, in our sample, those who describe their jobs in terms of social responsibility themes have a higher mean score on job satisfaction on the MIDUS rating than those who talk only about the personal themes. However, we did not often see the kind of inner harmony and thoroughgoing positivity in the present study that we saw in the moral exemplars study.

Despite their higher reported job satisfaction, many people who used social responsibility themes also talked about internal conflict, distress about their work, frustrations they faced, and their feelings of being burned out. This was true for the individuals who used only personal themes as well. At least at this level of commitment, seeing one's job as contributing to others does not lead to *greater* frustrations, but neither does it fully protect people from distress and burn-out. Even those who spoke eloquently about how much they felt they were able to contribute through their work also talked about the negative side as well. They spoke not only or even primarily of overwork, but of the barriers to accomplishing their goals due to the characteristics of their clients/constituents or the organizations for which they work. Many felt they had no chance of changing the conditions in their workplace.

Earlier we quoted Jenny Bridges, a police officer who spoke about what she had been able to do for the residents of an extremely low-income neighborhood in Chicago. She talks of believing deeply in what she is doing and the satisfaction that she gets from her work, but she also talks about frustrations with the people she is trying to help, the police department bureaucracy itself, the draining nature of the work she does, and the resulting burn-out she feels.

> [One of the girls I was helping] was a witness in a murder case, I was there for her, took her shopping every week. . . .

[But] when people like that become dependent on you, . . . they don't even make an effort anymore. I tried to make that moral voyage onto that territory and it didn't do any good. . . . Some people you can't save. [This kind of work] drains you. . . . What I don't feel good about is that I . . . schedule too much, I am too short of time for myself. . . . You're not completely in control of your life. . . . [The police department is] like your mother and your father. . . .[T]hey control . . . change or adjust your hours. . . . I sacrifice . . . the ability to be with friends or be with my family. . . . [I]t controls my life completely.

The hardest part is dealing with the department. . . . The police department itself, and the superiors . . . the bosses. . . . I just accept. . . . My uncle told me . . . keep your mouth shut and do what they tell you to do, . . . so I . . . keep my mouth shut and do what they tell me to do.

I did a lot of good police work. And now I'm burnt out and I don't want to do anything. . . . [But] I'd like to be a gang officer as long as I can. . . . I want to . . . work until I can retire.

Asked if she would continue to work if she won the lottery, she says that she "would probably not work. I'd build a gazebo, get a Jacuzzi" (case 45006).

Others in this sample express feelings similar to those of Jenny Bridges. For example, the radiologist who talked about how meaningful his work is, whom we quoted earlier, goes on to say that he hopes to change fields or retire early. When asked how his work relates to his sense of who he is, he responds:

It's a big part of my life. . . . It gives me a sense of self-worth. . . . I do feel I make a difference. I don't just go to work and collect a paycheck. I make a big difference. . . . There are very few down times, if any. . . . [I think to myself,] "Gee, I guess I could have had my arm amputated today,". . . and all of a sudden things come right back into perspective. . . . It keeps me in touch . . . whenever I've started to feel a little bit disappointed about something, I immediately snap back. . . . I can just look at my job. . . . I'm very fortunate that I can tap any source to keep the negative from coming in. . . . So there's no question about it: it's a major part of developing both my character and my fiber, my being.

Given this attitude, it is rather surprising, though not unusual in our sample, to hear him say the following when asked about his goals:

> My goals would have to be not to continue very much longer at this rate. I have to chop way back, and eventually, if I don't deviate from the field, retire from it. If I don't retire from the field, I'm going to have to deviate from it, actually, I suppose. Burn-out. It's just too long. . . . I don't want to get to a point where, like so many other guys just going through the motions and taking their checks and going home. I don't ever want to reach that point. Because I am fulfilled by what I do. . . . I think I should be doing other things. It's time . . . not very much longer. (case 45315)

These two examples are quite typical of many people in this sample who seem to care very much about their work and what it allows them to contribute to others but who also experience conflicts between their work and their personal life goals. Many say that they may turn away from the work in the long run or would do so if their finances would permit it. It is not clear whether the prevalence of this feeling is due to increasingly problematic and stressful working conditions or to an almost inevitable ennui that many people experience after long service in the same job and workplace.

This attitude contrasts dramatically with the moral exemplars we wrote about in *Some Do Care*, who said that nothing could stop them from continuing the work to which they had dedicated their lives. For example, Charleszetta Waddles is a black woman with an eighth-grade education who has for decades run a mission in inner-city Detroit, offering food, clothing, and other services to the poor. When asked about her plans for the future, she says, "You can go away twenty years and come back, and if I'm living you know you're going to find me doing the same thing. . . . I didn't promise that I would do it contingent upon what kind of building, what kind of clothes I could wear, what kind of money I had; just as long as I can find something I can do, I'll do it. So no matter where I'm going, people can at least know to pinpoint me in what category I'm in. Without even asking anybody, 'I know wherever she is, if she's alive and well, she's a missionary'" (Colby and Damon

1992, 218). We attribute this wholehearted persistence to the fact that for these exceptionally dedicated people their moral commitments and goals are at the center of their sense of who they are, and to the fact that their moral and personal goals are so well integrated that they rarely conflict. This is a qualitatively different kind of commitment than we see in the current sample, even among most of those who construe their work in terms of what it contributes to others.

References to the stresses and difficulties of their work and to feeling burned out were also common among the teachers in our sample, even though almost all of them talked about the social significance of their work and its personal meaning for them. All of the teachers and former teachers except two, one of whom taught at the college level, talked about having become discouraged or burned out by disciplinary problems, lack of cooperation from parents, and lack of support from the school administration. (We have excluded two former teachers for whom there was little information about their previous jobs.) Jay Brennan echoed the sentiments of many others when he said:

> When you have good days, you drive home and you say, "You know, this is awesome." When you know that the lesson that day struck home, when you've made the kids laugh and you know you've made a connection. Those are good days. But I have reached that stage in my career where I have to be brutally honest and say that I'm a little fried. I consider myself to be a very dedicated teacher, a very good teacher. But the kids we deal with now are a whole lot different than the kids that I started teaching twenty-five years ago. Society has changed, the kids have changed, families have changed, and it's a daily struggle in some cases. Is it important to me? Yeah . . . it is. It's important to me mostly in that I have become a real pessimist about the future of mankind, because I see year in and year out, I see the families getting more screwed up. And on one hand, that's a challenge. I mean, it's a massive challenge, but what we do is important to me. I think that every teacher out there, every good teacher, every hard-working teacher, ought to be canonized and elevated to sainthood, because we are, as far as I'm concerned, we are on the front lines, and we're losing the battle, I'm afraid.
>
> [What do you get out of your work?] Ulcers. [What is

hard about your job as a teacher?] [That] . . . education is not important to [the kids]. Education is not important to parents. [It's hard when teachers in schools] . . . become the whipping boy for [parents]. . . . Kids that come from homes that are so screwed up: substance abuse and sexual abuse . . . single parents. . . . We run the gamut of kids that it's lucky they're in school at all. And when they're in school, sometimes what is going on in their lives prevent them from learning. Some of the kids just . . . don't want to be there. We have budget cuts. It's . . . a real thankless job. We very much liken what we do . . . to . . . post-traumatic stress syndrome or battle fatigue . . . where you just go in and butt your head against the wall day after day. . . . [Y]ou get out of the car in the morning, and it's war.

Bronson says he is pessimistic about "the future of mankind" but also says:

. . . [P]art of it is that never-ending faith . . . that you're going to have a better day than you had yesterday. At the end of the [school] year . . . I hope to be able to say that I have reached as many kids as possible. I want to be able to say I've done the very best job that I can. And I think I can say that. I'm a better teacher now at age forty-seven . . . than I was when I was twenty-five. And in a lot of different ways, I certainly know more than I did then, but . . . I'm a mellower person than I was then, and I just think I'm more . . . dedicated to the job than I was a long time ago. (case 46692)

This mix of dedication, sense of purpose, frustration, and anguish represents in stark form both the positive and negative potentials of work that engages seriously with some of society's challenges and seeks to find personal meaning through social responsibility. The teaching field is one of many professions with tremendous potential for satisfaction from the contributions that it makes to individuals and to the society more generally. But it is also subject to great stresses and frustrations from multiple sources. In recent years, some approaches to school reform have attempted to address the issues these teachers raise by finding ways for parents, teachers, and school administrations to work together toward common goals. It may be that the experiences of school reformers can provide lessons not only for the improvement of education but also for other occupations in which people need more support for their efforts to be socially responsible in their work. Ultimately, the ideal goal would be to provide the scaffolding required to move at least some people to the level of internal harmony and stamina that allows them to gain joy from working even in very difficult circumstances, as we saw in the "moral exemplars" we studied.

CONCLUSION

Work can and should be a domain of life in which people can be caring, socially responsible, experience personal growth, and develop a sense of community. Work should not be seen as mutually exclusive with these goals, a zero-sum game. Of course, work has to be kept within reasonable time limits and cannot be the only means to these ends. But the reality of contemporary life is that people do spend a lot of time working and will no doubt continue to do so. As Alice Rossi writes in chapter 3, "Most people in most societies today, as in the past, contribute to their communities and nations through their primary ties to children, parents, siblings, and friends, and through the work they do to earn their way in life." If social responsibility consists entirely of volunteer work, community involvement, and political participation, time limits will prevent most people from being socially responsible except to a very modest extent. These domains are surely very important areas in which people contribute to others and to their communities, but paid work can also contribute to others and the society rather than being a barrier to a socially responsible life. Boyte and Kari (1996a) argue that in recent decades work has lost much of its civic overtone and that with changes in the meaning of work came transformations in notions of citizenship. As this happened, the concept of engaged citizenship became equated with volunteerism, what one did "after work." In their view, we have lost the sense that our common work builds the nation, and we need to return to this perspective. "We come to understand that this land *is* our land, when we see that we help to build it" (Boyte and Kari 1996a, B3).

Although we agree with Boyte and Kari (1996a, 1996b), Bellah and his co-authors (1985), and Sullivan (1995) that the potential for individuals' work to serve the public good is far from realized, we also see many people struggling to incorporate this perspective into their work. Now we need to find ways to build on and sustain people's desire to find meaning in their work, to experience competence, to contribute something important to society, to express compassion and care for others, and to experience a sense of community and common purpose. At this point, many workplaces present barriers to this, and many jobs include debilitating stresses for which people need support, as we have seen in the cases of the police officer, the doctor, and the teachers. We need to find ways to clear away those barriers and provide the necessary support so that people's moral engagement with their work can grow rather than burn out. If we do this, paid work can more fully realize its potential as an enduring "commitment beyond the self" rather than be a force for increasing social fragmentation and narrow self-interest.

NOTES

1. Wuthnow conducted two hundred in-depth interviews with respondents from central city, suburban, and ex-urban areas in or around New York, Philadelphia, Trenton, Boston, Chicago, Minneapolis, Portland, San Francisco, Los Angeles, Houston, and Atlanta. The sample included about equal numbers of men and women and younger and older people. African Americans, Asian Americans, and Hispanics were included in numbers approximately equal to the proportions in the U.S. population. One hundred fifty of the participants were working men and women, twenty-five were unemployed, and twenty-five were recent immigrants.

2. In chapter 11, Rossi interprets this scale as measuring the felt obligation to work, to do well in one's job, and to work hard even under unpleasant circumstances, an interpretation that is consistent with our concept of conscientiousness. Rossi reports that among both men and women, and at both high and low levels of educational attainment, her oldest respondents show higher levels of obligation to work than young adults do. According to Rossi, young adults may be confronting new circumstances that dampen the degree of work obligation from that which their parents felt at comparable ages. We cannot assess age differences on this dimension in our sample, since we sampled a narrower age range than the MIDUS sample did, but we speculate that the frequency of the references to conscientiousness in regard to work might be due in part to the fact that all of the participants in our study were at least thirty-five years old.

REFERENCES

Armon, C. 1993. Developmental conceptions of good work: A longitudinal study. In *Development in the Workplace*, ed. J. Demick and P. M. Miller, 21–34. Hillsdale: Erlbaum.

Bellah, R., R. Madsen, W. Sullivan, A. Swidler, and S. Tipton. 1985. *Habits of the heart: Individualism and commitment in American life.* New York: Harper and Row.

Boyte, H., and N. Kari. 1996a. Renewing democracy through public-spirited work. *Chronicle of Higher Education*, 5 July, B3.

————. 1996b. *Building America: The democratic promise of public work.* Philadelphia: Temple University Press.

Clausen, J. A. 1993. *American lives: Looking back at the children of the great depression.* New York: Free Press.

Colby, A., and W. Damon. 1992. *Some do care.* New York: Free Press.

Erikson, E. H. 1963. *Childhood and society.* 2d ed. New York: Norton.

——. 1993. *The spirit of community.* New York: Crown.

Finlay-Jones, R. 1986. Factors in the teaching environment associated with severe psychological distress among school teachers. *Australian and New Zealand Journal of Psychiatry* 20:304–13.

Gardner, J. 1991. *Building community.* Washington, DC: Independent Sector.

Hammen, C., and R. deMayo. 1982. Cognitive correlates of teacher stress and depressive symptoms: Implications for attributional models of depression. *Journal of Abnormal Psychology* 91:96–101.

Kohn, M. 1977. *Class and conformity.* 2d ed. Chicago: University of Chicago Press.

MacDermid, S. M., C. E. Franz, and L. A. De Reus. 1998. Adult character: Agency, communion, insight, and the expression of generativity in midlife adults. In *Competence and character through life,* ed. A. Colby, J. James, and B. Hart, 205–29. Chicago: University of Chicago Press.

Mansbridge, J., ed. 1990. *Beyond self-interest.* Chicago: University of Chicago Press.

McAdams, D. P., A. Diamond, E. de St. Aubin, and E. Mansfield. 1997. Stories of commitment: The psychosocial construction of generative lives. *Journal of Personality and Social Psychology* 72, no. 3:678–94.

Schonfeld, I. S. 1992. A longitudinal study of occupational stressors and depressive symptoms in first-year female teachers. *Teaching and Teacher Education* 8, no. 2:151–58.

Schor, J. 1991. *The overworked American: The unexpected decline of leisure.* New York: Basic Books.

Sullivan, W. M. 1995. *Work and integrity: The crisis and promise of professionalism in America.* New York: Harper Collins.

White, R. W. 1959. Motivation reconsidered: The concept of competence. *Psychological Review* 66, no. 5:297–333.

Wilson, J. Q. 1993. *The moral sense.* New York: Free Press.

Wuthnow, R. 1991. *Acts of compassion.* Princeton: Princeton University Press.

——. 1996. *Poor Richard's principle: Recovering the American dream through the moral dimension of work, business, and money.* Princeton: Princeton University Press.

V Summary

THIRTEEN

Analysis Highlights and Overall Assessment
Alice S. Rossi

INTRODUCTION

In this concluding chapter, we first present an overview of our major findings on social responsibility with an emphasis on common themes that run across our analyses of the main MIDUS data set and the data from several spin-off studies (in-depth interviews with selected respondents from the MIDUS sample). Second, we conduct an assessment of the design and analyses of the module on social responsibility in the core national survey, with special attention to the measures we wish, in retrospect, that we had incorporated in that design and to the analysis topics that remain to be pursued using the MIDUS data set.

MAJOR FINDINGS

The single most important general finding common to the numerous analyses we report in this volume is the multifaceted nature of the broad construct of *social responsibility*. Had we approached the design of our study of this dimension of life in a manner that was in keeping with the recent and widespread claims of Americans' diminished civic and political participation, we would have limited our measures to political and community involvement. To have done so, however, would not have been consistent with the research network's theoretical commitment to viewing human lives as integrated wholes. This perspective obligated us to a view of adult development that embraces physical and mental health, psychological well-being, and social role performance—the three criteria for assessing how well adults are doing in their lives. In our analysis of social roles, we included those roles most central to what occupies adults day in and day out: their roles in the family domain as spouses, parents, and adult children, and in the work domain as employed and domestic workers. Given all we know about the time limitations and psychological pressures on adults coping with obligations at home and in the workplace, it did not seem reasonable to focus narrowly on adults' roles as citizens and community members. In fact, in light of the enormous time commitments adults make to their families and their jobs, we were surprised to find as high a level of volunteer involvement in organizations and charitable causes as we did.

Our concern for social stratification required that we give attention to the different social worlds in which less-educated working- and lower-middle-class adults live and work as compared to the social worlds in which highly educated professional and managerial adults live and work. Life begins for all of us in the small worlds of our families, expands to embrace neighbors and peers during our school years, and expands further during our transition to adulthood. For better-educated adults, this last transition often involves migrating away from hometowns to distant cities and embracing a network of work colleagues, new friends, and upon marriage, new relatives. Those for whom a high school degree is the last one attained are far more likely to obtain jobs in the same general area if not the same town they grew up in. In my own extended family in New York City, all but two people over three generations have lived out their lives in either Brooklyn, Queens, or nearby towns on Long Island. From among nine aunts and uncles, a dozen cousins, and two siblings, only one uncle and I are college graduates, and only we two moved away from New York and have spent our adult years in several major cities in the Midwest and the Northeast. Many of my undergraduate students at the University of Massachusetts were similarly the first of three or four generations of Irish and Italian Americans to attend college. Most of their grandparents, aunts and uncles, and cousins live in the Boston area and its suburbs. Awareness of the complex extended families in which many working-class adults are embedded and the physically taxing or psychologically stressful circumstances under which so many labor at work further reinforced the network's decision to conceptualize social responsibility in a multidomain manner, to embrace family and work along with community and civic participation in the design of the MIDUS module on social responsibility.

Looking across the numerous measures we developed to tap the contributions of either time or money in the domains of family and community illustrates that there are many discrete paths for the manifestation of social responsibility. As shown in table 3.1, there are many significant positive correlations across these measures, but none exceed an r of $+.24$ (the correlation between the amount of volunteer work provided and the financial contributions made to charities or organizations). Most correlations hover around $+.10$: the level of civic obligation correlates with doing volunteer work at only $+.13$; providing social support to family members and providing hands-on caregiving show a correlation of only +.05.

Clearly there are numerous non-overlapping ways in which adults show social responsibility, but our multivariate analyses reveal underlying patterns. Consistently across several chapters in this volume, we have shown the extent to which three primary sociodemographic variables—education, sex, and age—structure the domains and dimensions of social responsibility. For adults who have no more than a high school education, it is the proximal world of kin, co-workers, and friends that predominate, with high levels of hands-on caregiving, social-emotional support, and when needed, financial aid. Such altruistic behavior is premised on expected reciprocity: one helps others in need on the expectation that one will receive help in turn should the need arise. Such need is more likely among the lower social strata of society. Diane Hughes (chapter 6) and Katherine Newman (chapter 5) suggest that for the working poor they studied in New York City, the outer limits of their world beyond family are defined by race or ethnicity, not by social class or the nation at large. In fact, the working poor subjects in Hughes's analysis are willing to be helpful to known poor neighbors like themselves, yet retain a notion of the "undeserving poor" for those in their neighborhoods who have been on welfare for prolonged periods of time or show signs of social deviance. For themselves, the New York respondents consider being responsible parents as their major contribution to society. By comparison, adults who have higher educational attainment move in more expanded social worlds and carry more responsibility to the community level through volunteer work, involvement in organizations, and financial contributions to numerous social and political causes and charities.

Sex is the second major axis that structures social responsibility. In a pattern persistent in numerous chapters, women do more caregiving than men do. Their caregiving is of a hands-on variety such as household chores, child care, or transportation, as well as of a social-emotional support variety such as providing advice or just listening to a troubled family member or friend. Men are more likely than women to provide financial assistance, either to family members or to organizations, churches, or charities. This is not an either-or pattern; both men and women extend both social and financial help to others. The point is merely that women tend to do more of one type of help giving, men another. Such findings are in keeping with Joan Tronto's distinction between "giving care"—typical of women, servants, and other adults low in power and autonomy, and "taking care of"—typical of men and high-status persons in positions of power and prestige (Tronto 1993). The single instance in which level of social support is not differentiated between men and women, net of all other related factors, is among adults with fundamentalist religious beliefs: fundamentalist men engage in family help of the caregiving and social-emotional support variety just as much as fundamentalist women do.

Of particular concern and interest to the research network is variation in behavior and belief over the life course, in particular the question of whether there are characteristics unique to the middle years. For this reason, age is a focus of almost all our analyses of MIDUS data and data from the spin-off studies. In this volume, we report several striking life course profiles. In our analysis of normative obligations, we found that family and work obligation levels decrease with age, whereas civic and altruistic obligation levels increase with age, both in a linear fashion. We suggest that the middle years are a watershed period of life during which the relative levels of obligation undergo a change, from giving priority to family to increasing focus on obligation to the larger community.

Both frequency of religious service attendance and strength of religious beliefs increase with age, a pattern that holds net of the salience of religion in the respondents' families of origin. This finding strengthens the interpretation that this is a maturational pattern rather than an age cohort difference. By contrast, we found that scores on the generativity scale peak in the middle years, a profile that holds when controlled for the extent to which parents of respondents were generative models (i.e., were helpful and friendly to people outside the family). The accumulation of experience over the earlier adult years is undoubtedly important before adults feel in a position to mentor, teach, or advise others—the core meaning of generativity. However, we believe that the decline of generativity among our oldest respondents may be a cultural issue. In societies which accord status and respect to the elderly, generativity may remain high or even increase in old age. Hazel Markus and Carol Ryff (chapter 9) report one finding in their qualitative interviews of middle-aged adults that may also be relevant here. The comments of less-educated subjects asked about their hopes for the future suggest an acute awareness of waning strength and aspirations. They hoped for continued good health and an ability to cope with the demands of their jobs despite declining strength and energy. By contrast, highly educated midlife subjects spoke of ongoing or new goals—

another book to be written, a new direction in their work, increased competence and success in dog judging. A sense of one's ability to mentor and advise others, core elements of high generativity, is apparent in contrasting hopes of less-educated compared to well-educated respondents, a finding consistent with our report that education is even more strongly related to generativity than age per se (see table 7.12). William Fleeson reports in chapter 2 that the overall self-ratings on contributing to the welfare of others declined among the less well off respondents in old age, but that among the wealthiest respondents, scores continued to increase into old age. This finding bolsters our suggestion that the midlife peak and subsequent decline of generativity applies to the *majority* of the MIDUS respondents, but that the status and reputation associated with higher education and income make for predictable exceptions.

In many analysis areas, we found a cumulative effect of all three sociodemographic variables upon our social responsibility measures, perhaps most vividly illustrated by the variance in the percentage of adults engaged in volunteer work. Numerous other surveys summarized in chapter 1 merely report a national figure for adults reporting engagement in volunteer service, typically in the vicinity of 45%. In chapter 3, we show the great range in the percentage reporting volunteer service in the previous year when age, sex, and education are taken into account: less-educated young men make up the *lowest* percentage of volunteers (27%); well-educated older women make up the *highest* percentage (57%).

Beyond such demographic correlates of current measures of caring and doing for others, our analyses of the MIDUS data also explore an array of factors that contribute to one or another indicator of social responsibility. Among the most important are these:

1. The *amount* of time adults commit to volunteer work is significantly affected by the extent of their social embeddedness; that is, the larger their families, the more frequent their contact with friends, and the more frequent their attendance at religious services, the greater the number of hours they contribute to volunteer service. Independent of such indicators of social embeddedness, high scores on generativity and civic obligations, a shorter work week, and higher levels of educational attainment make independent contributions to the amount of time devoted to volunteer work (see table 7.15).

2. The *type* of volunteer service adults engage in varies by several characteristics: *Health-related* volunteer service (e.g., in a health center

or hospital) attracts older women who report a high frequency of religious service attendance and score high on generativity. One encounters such women volunteers in almost any hospital in the United States. *Youth-related* volunteer service (e.g., in schools or community youth programs) attracts younger, married adults with large families who report frequent religious service attendance and score high on generativity. Those who are less well educated and who devote a large amount of time to home maintenance are also more prone to volunteer time in youth-oriented activities in the community. The image of a skilled worker dividing his leisure hours between car repair or carpentry work in the home and coaching a Little League baseball team come to mind here. *Political* volunteer work, by contrast, attracts older, well-educated adults with high scores on both generativity and civic obligations. In New England, one sees such adults in the flesh at town meetings.

3. The *timing* of volunteer service differs as a function of age. As David Almeida reports in chapter 4, older adults volunteer on weekdays, whereas younger adults are more likely to volunteer on weekends. In light of the high rate of employment among married women today, recruiting women to serve as volunteers is clearly more apt to be successful if the volunteer work can be done on a Saturday than if only on a weekday.

4. Across all the analyses we report in this volume, of both the MIDUS sample and the spin-off studies, family and work are the primary domains in terms of which adults define and behaviorally manifest social responsibility. Analysis of respondents' family of origin in chapter 7 further emphasizes the importance of the family domain as the seedbed for adult social responsibility: adults who show high scores on social-emotional support time given to family and friends in their adult lives tend to come from families in which parents showed high levels of affection blended with high levels of discipline (in the sense of imposing rules on respondents when they were children by supervising their use of time and by assigning chores to them on a regular basis), in addition to acting as generativity models by being particularly helpful and friendly to people outside the family.

Consistent with this profile is Markus and Ryff's report (in chapter 9) that the majority of their middle-aged subjects, when asked what explains how well their lives have gone, spoke of their parents as models or as the source of the values they had brought with them into their own adult lives. One might have expected that in answering such a question at least the better-educated adults would speak less of their early family life and their parents and more about their own competence and achievements, taking personal credit for how well their lives have gone, but this was not the case. One should note that the men and women Markus and Ryff interviewed were drawn from the top two tertiles of Ryff's combined scale on psychological well-being. A high level of well-being in adulthood may reflect a healthy good start in life thanks to parents who combined great affection and discipline in rearing their children. This authoritative style of childrearing may well be conducive to grown children acknowledging their indebtedness to parents rather than taking exclusive credit for their doing very well in life.

It came as a surprise that in their qualitative exploration of what "responsibility" meant to midlife adults, Markus and Ryff did not find any references to civic obligations or community interests. Their analysis identifies three major elements common to respondents' interpretation of "responsibility": meeting obligations, attending to the needs of others, and being dependable to others. But the examples of the people they felt obligated to and helped or who depended on them were all members of their families, their friends, or their co-workers. Respondents made no reference to larger organizational involvement, political participation, or identification with the nation or common welfare. Only in a few cases, and those were confined to well-educated subjects, did Markus and Ryff report concern for issues beyond the personal world of family and work. This was in response to a question on respondents' "hopes for the future." Though high school graduates' responses referred largely to their proximal personal social world, some college graduates referred to hopes for finding cures to diseases, to better care for the aged, or to helping future generations in some way, not typically by any contribution of their own, but by unspecified political or professional experts.

5. High involvement in home care and having a number of young children do not detract from but *add* to married adults' time contributions to volunteer work. Children draw parents into greater involvement in their parishes, schools, and local agencies, if only out of concern for their children's development and safety. In particular, the combination of putting in a lot of time on domestic chores, having several children, and regularly attending religious services precipitates higher levels of volunteer work. Domestic work may increase social contact and friendship with neighbors and, like frequent religious ser-

vice attendance, serve as a proxy for a higher level of commitment to being of service and help to others. These findings are reported in chapter 11.

6. Scales that measure the pride and respect respondents report they experience in the work they do on their jobs and the work they do at home show some interesting and, at first, surprising results. Men report higher pride from what they do at home than from what they do on their jobs, but women show the reverse pattern: more pride from their jobs than from work they do at home. Men's participation in domestic maintenance is a departure from tradition, whereas holding down a job is simply what one expects of all adult men. For many women, the reverse holds: traditional expectations assume women's presence and competence in domestic duties so they may get little positive praise from others about their work at home and more for the work they do on their jobs. Let a neighbor or friend see how competent a man is in the kitchen and he is highly likely to be praised to the hilt.

7. Having young children (under thirteen years of age) in the home also affects men and women differently. Men report that their jobs have *negative* effects on their home lives if they are fathers of young children, but women report more *positive* effects of their jobs on their home lives if they have young children. This pattern is at least partially due to the greater stress, time, and responsibility that men carry at work than is the case for most employed women. The relevant discussion in recent years has been exclusively about the special difficulty employed mothers have in juggling work and family responsibilities (e.g., Crosby 1991), but younger men today are also experiencing such pressure. As a result of the coincidence of heightened global competition and changing sex role expectations, men are working harder, for longer hours, and with less job security, while at the same time, desiring a more balanced life that permits more time for their wives, children, and home care. Sue Shellenbarger, who writes the column "Work and Family" for the *Wall Street Journal,* has been charting the development of family-friendly workplaces for the past several years. She recently reported a growing tendency among *younger* CEOs to be open to such changes in their firms, drawing on their own personal experiences in juggling work and family responsibilities (Shellenbarger 1999).

Our analysis of normative obligations to work also shows that it is younger, well-educated men who are particularly inclined to have *lower* obligations to work than any other sociodemographic subgroup in the sample, the same group of men who put in the longest hours, travel the most, and report more negative spillover of job effects on their home lives.

A national probability sample like MIDUS includes very few if any multimillionaire corporate executives, so our group of young, well-educated, highly paid men are more likely to be middle managers in private firms, professionals in nonprofit organizations, or self-employed small businessmen. Any discontent they show may at this juncture in time be limited to their private lives, not yet spurring any action of a directly political nature. Clearly there has been little public protest on the issue of growing income inequality in the United States, despite the facts that the ratio of executive pay to factory-worker pay has jumped from 42 to 1 in 1980 to 419 to 1 in 1998 (Schlesinger 1999) and CEO salaries and stock options have gone up even in corporations laying off thousands of workers. Isabel Sawhill, an economist at the Brookings Institution, suggests that one reason for this lack of protest about this growing inequality is that so many American workers have retained their faith in being upwardly mobile. A recent survey conducted by KPMG LLP, a professional services firm, found that 77% of college students expect to become millionaires in their lifetimes (Schlesinger 1999, 1)! The gambling craze that has driven so many Americans to casinos, lotteries, and stock purchases may be feeding such unrealistic expectations about future social mobility. Countless hard-working, middle-class, dual-earning couples probably do not realize the extent to which the rash of new multimillionaire families in America costs *them* a good deal of money. Any community with numerous newly rich young families will experience sharp increases in the cost of housing, private schools, and services of all kinds: "the richer rich ratchet up prices for everyone else," as Cornell University economist Robert Frank put it recently (quoted in Schlesinger 1999). The potential tragedy is that while the very rich could absorb dramatic losses if the market turned severely bearish, disastrously heavy burdens would be experienced by the 90% of stockholders who are not rich at all.

It is in this context of growing inequality that some of the findings in Diane Hughes's analysis of poor minorities in New York City (chapter 6) are of special interest. Hughes notes that among respondents in her study, unlike among the larger MIDUS sample, neither altruism nor civic obligations show any increase in the middle years. Nor did her respondents show any attenuation of family obligations in the middle years, perhaps reflecting the need to maintain a steady flow of social and economic support to extended kin throughout life, often involving taking on primary responsibility even in the rearing of grandchildren. Hughes suggests that this profile may be due to racial and ethnic minorities' disengagement from mainstream social institutions that do not serve their group's interests; their loyalties are restricted to their own ethnic communities. Katherine Newman (chapter 5) reports similar findings of a restriction of the social world of Dominican, Puerto Rican, and black New Yorkers to a narrow range; they are locals, not cosmopolitans.

Interestingly, Diane Hughes found that *foreign-born* Latino respondents showed higher altruism and higher civic obligations than their native-born counterparts, though her data did not permit her to determine if this was because more recent immigrants to New York still hold on to the American dream, whereas the native born have given up on that dream, or if the foreign-born men and women simply feel better off, even in their rundown New York neighborhoods, than they did in the Dominican Republic or Puerto Rico.

Robert Wuthnow has explored quite a different aspect of American work life, the moral significance of work (Wuthnow 1996). He assumes the American Dream as it developed in our history has provided a moral framework that encourages people to work hard and expect rewards from their work, but to remain centrally focused on family, community, and religion. This conception has gradually changed as money has become more important, lifestyles more materialistic, and work removed from concerns for the human spirit and matters of social meaning and self-worth. Consequently economistic thinking dominates discussion of work and money, while questions of moral commitment, character, and human values seem more difficult to relate to economic behavior. Wuthnow suggests that Americans now tend to submit to the pressure to spend their money on consumer goods and therefore do not limit their involvement in their jobs (Wuthnow 1996, 9). He urges us to rediscover the moral values and the higher dimensions of human existence that beg for a curbing of economic striving.

On the other hand, Anne Colby's explorations of how adults view their work in terms of social responsibility (chapter 12) suggest that many adults in quite ordinary jobs actually do take such factors into consideration: they find reward in just doing a good job, in going out of their way to be helpful to co-workers, taking pride in what they do regardless of the skills the jobs entail. Not all workers aim for the fast lane: many aspire to and work in occupations that do not pay particularly well (e.g., nurses, social workers, teachers); others work for nonprofit organizations that pay less than a for-profit corporation doing similar work; others have highly routine jobs in mechanized factories but find gratification in efforts to unionize the firm, citing such activities as their greatest contributions to the common good. Many jobs that are dissatisfying or devoid of any social worth prompt women workers to find fulfillment in volunteer service, as reported in chapter 11. Colby also makes the interesting point that different people can define the same job in very different terms, as illustrated by two stonemasons, one of whom says he is building a wall while the other says that he is building a cathedral!

To this point the focus of this chapter has been on what we accomplished in our analysis, but there are also many things we could not do because of the limitations of the data we gathered and the inadequacy of our original problem formulation. There are also topics that have not yet been analyzed with the data at hand.

DESIGN AND ANALYSIS ASSESSMENT

There are two major gaps in the design of MIDUS that placed serious limitations on the analyses we could undertake: one gap is simply the price one pays in collaborative research projects that require compromise and negotiation with colleagues' competing interests; the other gap consists of omissions only realized in retrospect.

In keeping with the program goals of the health division of the MacArthur Foundation, which supported the network, the major focus of our research was premised on a wellness model, not a disease model. We wanted to know what explained success in midlife in terms of our three major outcome criteria: being in good health, having high levels of psychological well-being, and showing reasonably high degrees of social responsibility as family members, workers, and citizens. It is probably fair to say the MacArthur program all told has contributed to the movement in psychology away from a focus on societal ills and toward a focus on what works, as evidenced by the recent shift from studies of physical and mental disease to studies of bodily health and well-being (Ruark 1999). This does not mean that we gave no attention to illness. MIDUS is replete with health histories, symptom inventories, and questions on alcohol consumption and drug usage. But it does mean that we asked numerous questions about what respondents were doing to maintain good health, such as engaging in moderate or vigorous exercise, putting effort into remaining healthy, or having control over the state of their health. We also incorporated into the instrument shortened versions of measures of mental disease—depression, anxiety, and panic disorders—the negative counterparts to our positive indicators of psychological well-being (scales on positive relations with others, autonomy, self-acceptance, purpose in life, environmental mastery, and personal growth).

But in the domain of social responsibility, we have no negative measures. We can differentiate between respondents who are low versus high on normative obligations, but we have no measures of antisocial behavior. We can measure the extent of social embeddedness of adults, but we have no measures of acute alienation or anomie. Similarly, we made no effort even in the pilot surveys to test the extent to which telephone interviews or self-administered questionnaires could obtain reliable data on such matters as gambling, tax evasion, calling in sick in order to attend, say, a ball game or horse race, stealing from employers, violating traffic rules, betraying friends, and so forth.

In the early stages of designing MIDUS, we considered including items that would indicate respondents' positions on a variety of controversial social and political issues and, for the baby-boom midlifers who would be in our sample, some measures of their activities in their youth, such as participation in the civil rights movement, the women's rights movement, antiwar protests, or debates about environmental issues. Under the pressures of negotiating for space in the MIDUS surveys, there was greater support for obtaining details on volunteer service and estimates of financial contributions to family members and civic organizations and charities than there was for pursuing information about respondents' current or past political activities and sympathies.

With the benefit of hindsight, I now wish we had included much more detail on the kinds of groups and organizations respondents were involved with and their motivation for doing so. MIDUS was designed during 1993 and 1994 and fielded in 1995. During the planning years, I was not particularly steeped in the literature on civil society or changes in American associational membership that has become better known over the past several years. This is only too apparent in that a full half of the references cited in chapter 1 are to publications since 1996, a third to just 1998 and the first eight months of 1999. It would have been enormously useful to our analysis of social responsibility in the community domain had we included items similar to the attitude and value questions used in previous research, items on, for example, confidence in various social institutions mirrored on the GSS surveys in the 1980s and 1990s (shown in figure 1.1), political participation, party affiliation, voting record in presidential and local elections, and so forth.

Another gap in our data concerns the childrearing practices of the respondents themselves. We developed reasonably good short measures on the affection and discipline respondents experienced in their families of origin, but it would have been enormously interesting to have identical measures on their own childrearing practices. After all, our youngest respondents were adolescents in the 1980s, the oldest during the 1930s. Comparable measures on respondents' own childrearing practices would have provided an overlap of the decades involved as well as data on the practices of young parents today. Such data provided a rich analysis in a previous study of mine on parent-child relations in the Boston area, in which identical measures were obtained on the parent-child relationship, as viewed by respondents, for their families of origin and their families of procreation. These measures were supplemented by interviews including similar measures obtained from small samples of respondents' own parents and grown children (Rossi and Rossi 1990). It would have been a rare opportunity to have had comparable data from a national survey, particularly one as rich as MIDUS with measures on health, well-being, and social responsibility to bring into the analysis of family relationships. This topic had low priority, however, and was left untapped in the final MIDUS instruments.

I also now wish we had had the foresight to provide a great deal more depth to our exploration of religious beliefs and practices. MIDUS included only a single item on the importance of religion in the early family life of our respondents, and for their current profile, a single item on religious service attendance, another on church-related group meetings, and a short battery of items on religious beliefs. I am embarrassed to reveal that only at this writing did I remember one interesting question that we had at the very end of the self-administered questionnaire, "When you have decisions to make in your daily life, how often do you ask yourself what your religious or spiritual beliefs suggest you should do?" Marginals on this question show that 31% of our respondents said they "often" engage in this practice, 29% "sometimes," 20% "rarely," and only 21% "never," a very nice distribution for an analysis that could provide a window on the process whereby adults keep their eyes on moral and transcendent values rather than fleeting existential matters.

This neglected item is not alone among the measures included in MIDUS that might be used to enrich and expand the ground covered in this volume. None of the authors, myself included, gave any attention to the potential significance of regional differences, type of employer or occupation, or social mobility between generations, yet our instrument contains measures on all such variables. The one possible consolation is the realization that our data sets are now public access files. We hope that future researchers will explore them further as well as conduct research with new surveys, either by returning to the MIDUS respondents or by creating new surveys that use some of our existing measures supplemented by the types of measures we did not have the time or foresight to include in our instruments.

REFERENCES

Crosby, F. J. 1991. *Juggling: The unexpected advantages of balancing career and home for women and their families.* New York: Free Press.

Rossi, A. S., and P. H. Rossi. 1990. Of human bonding: Parent-child relations across the life course. New York: Aldine de Gruyter.

Ruark, J. K. 1999. Redefining the good life: A new focus in the social sciences. *Chronicle of Higher Education,* 12 February, A13–15.

Schlesinger, J. M. 1999. Wealth gap grows; why does it matter? *Wall Street Journal,* 13 September, sec. A.

Shellenbarger, S. 1999. Family-friendly CEOs are changing cultures at more workplaces. *Wall Street Journal,* 15 September, sec. B.

Tronto, J. C. 1993. *Moral boundaries: A political argument for an ethic of care.* New York: Routledge.

Wuthnow, R. 1996. *Poor Richard's principle: Recovering the American dream through the moral dimension of work.* Princeton, NJ: Princeton University Press.

Methodology of the National Survey of Midlife Development in the United States (MIDUS)

FIELD PROCEDURES

The National Survey of Midlife Development in the United States (MIDUS) is based on a nationally representative random-digit-dialing (RDD) sample of noninstitutionalized, English-speaking adults, aged twenty-five to seventy-four, selected from working telephone banks in the coterminous United States. Field procedures lasted approximately one year, with all data collected during 1995. Households were selected in random replicates, one-fourth of which were predesignated for participation in a refusal conversion study. Initial contact persons were informed that the survey was being carried out through Harvard Medical School and was designed to study health and well-being during the middle years of life. They were told that participation would entail completing a telephone interview and two mailed questionnaires and that a check for twenty dollars would be enclosed in the mailing.

After the study was explained to the contact person, a listing was generated of people in the household who were between twenty-five and seventy-four and a potential respondent was selected at random from among those in this listing. Oversampling of older people and of men was achieved at this stage by varying the probability of selection of the potential respondent as a function of age and sex. This meant that a probability sample of randomly selected respondents in certain age-sex subsamples were purposefully not interviewed, leading to an oversample in other strata. No other person in the household was selected if the randomly selected respondent was purposefully not interviewed, or did not agree to the interview, or did not complete the interview.

Once it was determined that the randomly selected respondent should be included in the survey, an attempt was made to talk with this person and recruit him or her to be a participant. A brochure about the study was mailed to those potential respondents who asked to have more information before deciding whether to participate, and then they were recontacted to make an appointment for the telephone interview. Senior study staff were available to respondents who asked to have information not contained in the brochure before deciding whether to participate.

Once a potential respondent decided to participate, we carried out a telephone interview that lasted an average of thirty minutes. We then mailed two questionnaires to the respondent, which we estimate to have taken an average of two hours to complete. The mailing included a boxed pen along with the check for twenty dollars. A reminder post-card was mailed to each respondent three days after the initial mailing of the questionnaires. A second copy of the questionnaires, with a cover letter urging the respondent to participate, was mailed two weeks later to each respondent who had not returned his or her questionnaires by that time. Two weeks after that, a reminder telephone call was made to each respondent who still had not returned his or her questionnaires. In these final calls, those who were among the subsample of replicates predesignated for participation in the refusal conversion study were offered an additional incentive of one hundred dollars to complete and return the questionnaires.

The Response Rate

We cannot compute an exact overall response rate for the MIDUS because we only wanted to interview about half of the people we contacted, and it is only these who should be included in the denominator when computing the response rate. We have no way of knowing how many of the refusers would have been selected for interview, which means that we cannot compute the denominator exactly. However, it is possible to make an estimate of the number of people in the denominator we wanted to interview and, based on this, an estimate of the response rate. Our estimate, the calculation of which is described below, is that 70.0% of the predesignated respondents we wanted to interview completed the telephone interview. When combined with the fact that 86.8% of those who completed the telephone interview also completed the main questionnaires, the estimated overall response rate is 60.8% ($.700 \times .868$).

The total sample disposition (table A.1) shows that 3,323 respondents completed the telephone interview before the refusal conversion. Of those in the refusal conversion study, 162 completed the telephone interview (see table A.2 for the disposition of the refusal conversion subsample). Each of these 162 carries a weight of 4 to adjust for the fact that only one-fourth of households were predesignated for refusal con-

TABLE A.1 MIDUS Sample Disposition in the National RDD prior to Refusal Conversion

	Total Sample	Subsample 1 (predesignated for refusal conversion study)	Subsample 2
A. Potential respondent screening completed			
Eligible for participation			
Telephone interview completed			
Interview usable	3,323	881	2,442
Interview unusable	2	0	2
	3,325	881	2,444
Telephone interview not completed			
Not started	111	18	93
Started but not completed	20	9	11
	131	27	104
Telephone interview refused			
Before start of interview	932	238	694
After start of interview	76	24	52
	1,008	262	746
Total eligible	4,464	1,170	3,294
Ineligible for participation			
No one aged 25–74 in household	988	240	748
Inappropriate due to weighting procedure[a]	2,473	540	1,933
Language problem	71	23	48
Circumstantial problem	104	27	77
Total ineligible	3,636	830	2,806
B. Potential respondent screening not completed			
Language problem	362	80	282
Circumstantial problem	154	46	108
Screening interview not completed	66	2	64
Screening interview refused	2,087	582	1,505
No contact after maximum number of calls	1,246	327	919
Non-household number	2,743	632	2,111
Non-working number	5,242	1,331	3,911
Total numbers dialed	20,000	5,000	15,000

[a] In order to include a significant proportion of older respondents, we purposefully did not interview a percentage of the randomly selected younger adults.

TABLE A.2 MIDUS Refusal Conversion Subsample Disposition

A. Potential respondent screening completed	
Telephone interview completed	162
Short-form questionnaire completed	14
Telephone interview refused	
Before start of interview	174
After start of interview	15
	189
Ineligible for participation	
No one aged 25–74 in household	23
Inappropriate due to weighting procedure	50
Language problem	0
Circumstantial problem	6
	79

B. Potential respondent screening not completed	
Language problem	2
Circumstantial problem	9
Screening interview refused	383
Non-household number	6
Total initial refusers[a]	884

[a] Total equals 238 (telephone interview refused before start of interview) + 24 (telephone interview refused after start of interview) + 582 (screening interview refused).

version. The weighted numerator of the response rate for the telephone interview, then, is 3,971 (3,323 plus 4 × 162).

The denominator of the telephone response rate is the total number of people we wanted to interview. As noted above, we cannot be certain of this number because it must include the unknown number of those we would have wanted to interview from among those who were not screened. We determined the eligibility rate of the people for whom screening was completed (prior to refusal conversion) to be 56.3%: 4,464 eligible ÷ (4,464 eligible + 3,636 ineligible − 71 with language problems − 104 with circumstantial problems). Note that we subtracted those with language and circumstantial problems from the denominator based on the conservative assumption that the respondents with such problems were detected during screening. If we assume the same eligibility rate for the 2,157 people not screened (66 who did not keep their screening appointments + 2,087 who refused a screening appointment), we can estimate that there were 1,212 eligible people in that group. So out of 5,676 (1,212 + 4,464) eligible, there was the weighted equivalent of 3,971, or a 70.0% response rate.

Once the telephone interviews were completed, we developed a weight to adjust the profile of telephone respondents to be representative of the population. We applied this weight to the telephone respondents and then computed the weighted percentage of these people who also returned the self-administered questionnaires. This conditional response rate is 86.8%.

The overall response rate, 60.8%, is then computed by multiplying the telephone response rate (.700) by the conditional self-administered questionnaire response rate (.868).

SAMPLE WEIGHTS

We increased the representativeness of the sample using a series of weights that adjusted for differences in probability of selection and differential nonresponse. We developed a total of six weights and used the product of these weights to create a final summary weight for analysis of the MIDUS data.

Typically, MIDMAC analyses of the MIDUS data are made with weighted and also unweighted data; when outcomes differ, the analyst reports this fact and attempts to interpret the bias. Conventions by various social science disciplines differ in the preference for unweighted or weighted data. MIDMAC's convention is to present both when results warrant.

A detailed description of the procedure we used to create these weights is entitled *Weighting the MIDUS Data* and can be found on the MIDMAC Web site: http://midmac.med.harvard.edu.

COMPARISON OF MIDUS DATA WITH CURRENT POPULATION SURVEY DATA

The results in table A.3 show the distribution of the unweighted and weighted MIDUS data on the poststratification variables compared to the nationally representative data in the October 1995 Current Population Survey (CPS). The weighted MIDUS data generally are more similar to the population than the unweighted data are. The most dramatic difference is found in education: 47.8% of the population have more than twelve years of education compared to 60.8% in the unweighted MIDUS data. To a degree this difference may reflect the fact that the two lengthy self-administered questionnaires require a relatively high degree of literacy. This cannot be the whole story, however, because one would expect a greater difference at the low end of educational attainment than there is. We cannot know for sure why so large a propor-

TABLE A.3 Comparison of MIDUS and Current Population
Survey Data

Variable	CPS (October 1995)	MIDUS Unweighted	MIDUS Weighted
Region			
Northeast	20.6	18.0	18.7
Midwest	23.7	27.4	25.1
South	34.1	35.2	37.7
West	21.6	19.5	18.4
City size			
Major metropolitan area	74.7	76.7	76.9
Non–major metropolitan area	25.3	23.3	23.1
Sex			
Male	48.3	48.5	43.5
Female	51.7	51.5	56.5
Race			
White	84.8	87.3	84.1
Black	11.2	6.1	10.8
Other	4.0	6.5	5.1
Age			
25–34	27.6	20.8	26.0
35–44	27.0	24.2	27.8
45–54	19.2	24.0	19.1
55–64	13.9	19.9	15.2
65–74	12.2	11.1	11.8
Education			
Less than twelve years	15.8	10.0	13.2
Twelve years	36.4	29.3	38.3
More than twelve years	47.8	60.8	48.5
Marital status			
Married	67.5	64.0	68.1
Not married	32.5	36.0	31.9

tion of respondents in MIDUS had some degree of higher education, but it seems reasonable to suggest that the better-educated adults were more highly motivated to participate because they believe in the importance of research of this nature and expected to find participation in the study of interest to them. The weighted MIDUS data were corrected to 48.5% to account for this over-representation of the better educated. The correction is not perfect because we were trying to balance the competing threats of bias (which we tried to correct by weighting) and inefficiency (which is increased by high variance in the weights).

One might ask if the weighting adjusts for the fact that the 10% of people in the MIDUS sample who have less than twelve years of education may not be representative of the 15.8% of the population with this amount of education. The answer is no. The weighting does, however, adjust for the possibility that the less-educated people in the sample differ from those in the population on the weighting variables we used. We do not know if this is better than nothing, but our intuition is that it is better to make the sample as representative as possible on the variables we were able to use.

David M. Almeida received his Ph.D. in developmental psychology from the University of Victoria and is currently associate professor in the Division of Family Studies and Human Development at the University of Arizona in Tucson. The topics of his recent publications include sources of gender differences in psychological distress and emotional transmission in the daily lives of families. His current research interest focuses on environmental and genetic components of daily stress processes during adulthood.

Catherine Barber received her master's degree in public administration from the Kennedy School of Government at Harvard University. She is currently project director of the Workplace Depression Study at Harvard Medical School. Her background is in designing and implementing population-based public health surveillance systems, with a particular interest in weapon injury surveillance. Her publications have appeared in *Public Health Reports,* the *American Journal of Preventive Medicine,* the *Journal of Public Health,* and *Morbidity and Mortality Weekly Report.*

Katherine L. Barnett will receive a master's degree in psychology from Stanford University in 2001. She graduated Phi Beta Kappa from Stanford University with departmental honors in the undergraduate program in human biology. Her senior honors thesis explored a cultural psychological approach to understanding the time perspective of the New Zealand Maori, and as an undergraduate she also researched the effectiveness of Stanford's Health Improvement Program and analyzed Antarctic weather patterns for the National Oceanographic and Atmospheric Association in Boulder, Colorado. Her recent research entails the collection and quantitative analysis of face-to-face interviews for the Everyday Well-Being Study.

Anne Colby received her Ph.D. in psychology from Columbia University and is currently Senior Scholar at the Carnegie Foundation for the Advancement of Teaching at Menlo Park, California. Her previous appointment was as director of the Henry A. Murray Research Center of Radcliffe College from 1980 to 1998. She is the principal author of two books, *The Measurement of Moral Judgment* and *Some Do Care: Contemporary Lives of Moral Commitment,* as well as a monograph, *A Longitudinal Study of Moral Judgment.* She co-edited *Ethnography and Human Development: Context and Meaning in Human Inquiry* and *Competence and Character through Life.* Her current research interests concern social responsibility in midlife, higher education and the development of moral and civic responsibility, and education for the professions.

Alana L. Conner is a doctoral student in social psychology at Stanford University. Her research explores cultural variability in stereotyping, prejudice, and intergroup conflict in Japan and the U.S.

William Fleeson received his Ph.D. in psychology from the University of Michigan in Ann Arbor and is currently an assistant professor in the Department of Psychology at Wake Forest University in Winston-Salem, North Carolina. His research interests include personality, adult development, and psychological well-being.

John J. Havens received his training in mathematics, economics, and physics at Yale University and his graduate training in economics at the Massachusetts Institute of Technology. He is currently a senior research associate and associate director of the Social Welfare Research Institute at Boston College. His current research interest is the study of philanthropy in connection with which he has directed the Boston Area Diary Study, gathering and analyzing information on giving, volunteering, and caring.

Diane Hughes received her Ph.D. in community and developmental psychology from the University of Michigan and is currently an associate professor in the Department of Psychology at New York University (Community program). Her recent publications focus on the influences of occupational stress on families; ethnic minority families; race-related socialization; and culturally anchored research methods. She is also co-author of *Community Psychology: A Quarter-Century of Theory, Research, and Action in Social and Historical Contexts.*

Ronald C. Kessler received his Ph.D. in sociology from New York University and is currently professor of health care policy at the Harvard Medical School. He is the recipient of a Research Scientist Award and a MERIT Award from the National Institute of Mental Health. His research deals with the psychosocial determinants and consequences of mental illness. He is the principal investigator of the National Comorbidity Survey, which investigates the psychosocial risk factors for and consequences of psychiatric morbidity and comorbidity. He is also the director of the World Health Organization's International Consortium in Psychiatric Epidemiology, a cross-national collaborative group founded to foster comparative studies of psychological disorders throughout the world. Other current projects include investigation of gene-environment interactions for common psychiatric disorders among twins, assortative mating for psychiatric disorders in married couples, adjustment to specific life events in separate longitudinal samples of job losers and widows, and the workplace costs of psychiatric disorders.

Hazel Rose Markus received her Ph.D. in psychology from the University of Michigan and is currently a professor of psychology and co-director of the Research Institute for Comparative Studies in Race and Ethnicity at Stanford University.

She previously has held positions as a research scientist at the Institute for Social Research and a faculty member in the Department of Psychology at the University of Michigan. She has served on the editorial boards of numerous journals and study sections at the National Institute of Mental Health and the National Science Foundation. She is a fellow of the APS and the APA and was elected to the American Academy of Arts and Sciences in 1994. She was recently named the Davis-Brack Professor in the Behavioral Sciences at Stanford University. Her research has focused on the role of the self in regulating behavior. The topics of her published work are self-schemas, possible selves, the influence of the self on the perception of others, and the constructive role of the self in adult development. Her most recent research is in the area of cultural psychology and explores the mutual constitution between psychological structures and processes and sociocultural practices and institutions.

Daniel A. McDonald received his Ph.D. from the Division of Family Studies and Human Development at the University of Arizona in Tucson, where he is currently a research associate. He has published a chapter on temporal rhythms of parent-offspring tensions and his current research concerns the daily ecology of fathering.

Kristin D. Mickelson received her Ph.D. in social psychology from Carnegie Mellon University and completed postdoctoral fellowships at the University of Michigan and Harvard University. She is currently an assistant professor of psychology at Kent State University. Her recent publications have focused on three areas: the relation of stress to social support and mental health in various populations (e.g., parents of children with special needs, the elderly, the poor, and homeless women); the correlates and patterns of adult attachment in a nationally representative sample; and coping as a communal process. Her current research examines differential vulnerability to life events by socioeconomic status and whether social support may serve as an explanatory mechanism.

Katherine S. Newman received her Ph.D. in anthropology from the University of California at Berkeley. She is currently the Malcolm Wiener Professor of Urban Studies in the Kennedy School of Government, Harvard University. Her most recent book is *No Shame in My Game: The Working Poor in the Inner City*. She is currently working on a book about growing old in the inner city, while completing several research projects on the long-term career pathways of minority youths entering the labor market in minimum wage jobs.

Erin Phelps received her Ed.D. in developmental psychology from the Harvard Graduate School of Education in human development. She is co-author of the *Inventory of Longitudinal Studies in the Social Sciences* and has authored numerous research articles in the areas of child cognitive and social development. Her current research focuses on identifying the reasons why women students turn away from science and mathematics majors. In addition, she is a methodologist with special interest in developing models for studying change over time at multiple levels of social organization.

Eden K. Pudberry received her master of science degree in sociology from the University of Wisconsin at Madison. She is currently a project director at the University of Wisconsin Survey Center. Her major research interests are in the sociology of work, and mental and physical health.

Alice S. Rossi received her Ph.D. in sociology from Columbia University and is currently professor emerita of sociology at the University of Massachusetts at Amherst. She has published widely on family and kinship, sex and gender, feminist politics, sexuality, and human development. Her most recent books are *Of Human Bonding: Parent-Child Relations across the Life Course* (co-authored with her husband, Peter H. Rossi) and *Sexuality across the Life Course,* an edited volume of commissioned papers. Her current major research interests are social responsibility, and the reproductive phase of women's lives from menarche through menopause.

Carol D. Ryff received her Ph.D. in psychology from Pennsylvania State University and is currently professor of psychology and director of the Institute on Aging at the University of Wisconsin at Madison. Her research interests have been the sociodemographic, experiential, and psychosocial influences on psychological well-being. She has co-edited two books in recent years: *The Parental Experience in Midlife* (with Marsha M. Seltzer) and *The Self and Society in Aging Processes* (with V. W. Marshall). Her current research interests are age, gender, and social class differences in well-being; biopsychosocial understanding of healthy aging, with emphasis on resilience vis-à-vis adversity; and the integration of quantitative and qualitative methods in understanding positive human health.

Paul G. Schervish received his Ph.D. in sociology from the University of Wisconsin at Madison and is currently professor of sociology and director of the Social Welfare Research Institute at Boston College. His research interests include philanthropy, the sociology of money, and the sociology of religion. He is completing work on a book, *The Modern Medicis: Strategies of Philanthropy among the Wealthy.*

Lorrie Sippola received her Ph.D. in psychology from Concordia University in Montreal and is currently an assistant professor of psychology at the University of Saskatchewan. She has recently published on loneliness in developmental perspective, and the developmental significance of heterosocial relations in adolescence. Her current research interests are in interpersonal relationships and adolescent development, with an emphasis on the transition into heterosocial relationships.

Philip Wang received his Ph.D. in public health from the Harvard School of Public Health and his M.D. from the Harvard Medical School. He is currently an instructor in medicine and health care policy at the Harvard Medical School and Brigham and Women's Hospital. His recent journal articles focus on pharmaco-epidemiology of psychotropic medications. His current research interests are pharmaco-epidemiology and mental health services.

in-person contacts, importance of, 30–31

Institute of American Values, 12

institutional memberships, change in size, 100–101

intelligence: genetic component, 234, 270–271, 279–289; and self-esteem, 19

internationalism, 37–38

International Labor Organization, 24

international markets, 37–38

International Monetary Fund, 36

Internet: and individualism, 100; need for connectedness, 33; virtual communities, 33, 100

interpersonal problems, *328*

investment culture, 428–429

ischemic heart disease, 421

isolation, effects of, 288

Italy: environmental groups, 47; north/south differences, 33–34; private associations, 47

Jackson, Brenda, 492–493

Japan: marriage attitudes in, 98; menarcheal age changes, 238

job influences, 427

job instability, 3

job pride, 105, 471; and age, 443; demographic correlates, 440–441, 512; determinants, 442–444; and life satisfaction, 439–440; work motivation, 470. *See also* job satisfaction; work

job problems, *328*

jobs: impact on community service, 452–455; occupational changes, 27; part-time, 442

job satisfaction: among teachers, 488; personal rewards, 490–494; and social responsibility themes, 490; and volunteer activities, 54

job security, 27

job type, and social responsibility, 482–487

Johnson, Elizabeth, *She Who Is: The Mystery of God in Feminist Theological Discourse,* 312

juggling and balancing, 357, *358,* 364

kin networks, 182, 214–215

kinship norms, 236–237

Kiwanis, 45

KPMG LLP, 513

labor: societal necessity, 10; women in, 12

labor market, changes in, 3, 4

labor unions, 7, 25

Latinos/Latinas: altruism, 514; child-rearing, 161–162; civic obligations, 514; pensions, 161; volunteers, 161

League of Women Voters, 45

legal problems, *328*

leisure, and work, 51

liberalism, challenges to, 427

life: anomie of, 34; satisfaction with, 375–384

life-after-death beliefs, 125

life expectancy, changes in, 27–28

life span, changes in social responsibility, 75. *See also* midlife

Lippman, Walter, 5

loneliness, physiological effects, 30–31

The Lonely Crowd (Riesman), 45

longevity: and parent/child relationships, 323; sexual gap, 30

longitudinal studies, and retrospective recall, 240–249

long-term care, 11

Loose Connections (Wuthnow), 50

The Lost City (Ehrenhalt), 34

lotteries, state, 21

Loyola Generativity Scale, 116, 478

lung problems, *411,* 412, 421

MacArthur Foundation, health program goals, 515

MADD, 46

Malcolm X, 169

male-female relationship, 10

males, early mortality of, 14

managerial occupations, social responsibility themes, 482, 483

Mandel, Irene, 170

Manpower Inc., 15

marital counseling, 12